# Psychological Theories of Motivation

SECOND EDITION

# Psychological Theories of Motivation

**SECOND EDITION**

Hal R. Arkes
John P. Garske
Ohio University

Brooks/Cole Publishing Company
*Monterey, California*

Brooks/Cole Publishing Company
A Division of Wadsworth, Inc.

Printed in the United States of America

10 9 8 7 6 5 4

**Library of Congress Cataloging in Publication Data**

Arkes, Hal R., 1945–
 Psychological theories of motivation.

 Bibliography: p.
 Includes index.
 1. Motivation (Psychology)   I. Garske, John P.,
1945–      II. Title.
BF503.A74      1981      153.8      81–10057
ISBN 0–8185–0465–X      AACR2

*Subject Editor:* C. Deborah Laughton
*Manuscript Editor:* Marilu Uland
*Production Editor:* Fiorella Ljunggren
*Interior and Cover Design:* Victoria A. Van Deventer
*Illustrations:* Alan Arellano
*Typesetting:* Computer Typesetting Services, Glendale, California

*Chapter-opening photographs:* pp. 1, 11, and 311, © Kira Godbe; p. 61, © The Bettmann
Archive, Inc.; pp. 107, 137, 196, 226, 251, and 373, © Victoria A. Van Deventer; p. 172, © Stan
Rice; p. 289, © Jim Pinckney.

# Preface

This second edition of our text contains the two major distinguishing features of the first edition and several new characteristics. From the first edition we have maintained the coverage of both experimental and clinical approaches to motivation. We believe that this breadth of coverage is necessary to provide a complete introduction to theories of motivation. We also have maintained our use of a wide variety of everyday examples and applications, because most students will comprehend any theory more fully if it can be easily related to their personal experience.

The new aspects of this second edition include a chapter on social learning theory and its treatment of such topics as aggression and pornography, new sections on equity theory and opponent-process theory, and discussions of the application of motivational theory to work, economics, television, and several other areas.

Our wide coverage should make this book appropriate not only as a text for courses in motivation but also as a sourcebook for students of personality and social psychology.

In writing this book, we have received help from a number of reviewers, whom we'd like to thank for their constructive suggestions: Richard Buckham, of Dordt College; John Hampton, of Oklahoma State University; Carl Scott, of the University of Houston; Joseph Sgro, of Virginia Polytechnic Institute; Barry Smith, of the University of Maryland; Richard Teevan, of the State University of New York at Albany; Robert Theodore, of the University of Wyoming; Frank Webbe, of the Florida Institute of Technology; and Gerald Svendsen, of Ohio University. We'd also like to express our appreciation to C. Deborah Laughton, Fiorella Ljunggren, and Marilu Uland of Brooks/Cole for their assistance and support.

*Hal R. Arkes*
*John P. Garske*

# Contents

CHAPTER **1**

# Introduction
# and Prospectus

*A man always has two reasons for doing any-
thing—a good reason and the real reason.*

*J. P. Morgan*

Much of the time we do not question our reasons for acting as we do.
At times, however, our actions or those of other people are so puzzling
that we do stop and ask ourselves what motivated the behavior.

Some time ago, for example, one of the authors was standing in a
slow-moving checkout line at a local supermarket. (Somehow he always chooses the slowest line.) At the end of the adjacent line was one
of his graduate students, and her line moved so fast that she reached
the cashier before the author's line had moved an inch. The graduate
student graciously shouted out, "Hal, come on over to this line. There's
nobody else here." The author turned down the offer! "No, thanks,
Cathy. I'll stay here." What could have motivated this seemingly non-
sensical behavior?

As another example, a movie actress a few years ago shot and killed
a famous skier. There was no doubt that she shot him, but there was a
huge controversy about her motivation for doing so. If the act was in-
tentional (murder), the punishment would be more severe than if the
act was accidental (involuntary manslaughter).

In analyzing the first example, we can try to use common sense and
layman's theories of human behavior. Such theories might include sensible postulates such as "People seek pleasure and avoid pain." This
postulate fails to explain the author's behavior, however, as does common sense. It doesn't help us understand why anyone (especially a psychologist) would prefer to suffer in a slow-moving line. The maxims
"Haste makes waste" and "He who hesitates is lost" are in direct contradiction and therefore they, too, give us no help in explaining behavior. In short, there's a homily to explain or predict nearly every
possible human behavior. That's why such homilies aren't very helpful
and why psychologists prefer theories that are more scientifically derived. These psychological theories are usually based on research,
which provides a foundation of knowledge to draw upon as we attempt
to analyze behavior—even peculiar behavior such as volunteering to
suffer.

In the second example, the controversy over the actress's motivation,
unlike the shooting, arose from the fact that motivations, unlike behav-

ior, cannot be observed. This is one of the factors that have made the study of motivation so difficult. Indeed, it has caused some psychologists to suggest that the whole concept of motivation should be discarded. These psychologists believe that, if motivation cannot be observed, it has no place in the scientific study of human behavior. Other psychologists, however, argue that motivation is too important a part of human behavior to be ignored, regardless of how difficult it may be to study.

It has been suggested recently, for example, that pornography increases the likelihood that men will commit violence against women. If a violent act does occur and if the man has viewed pornography, can we conclude that the pornography motivated the behavior? Can we ever be sure? Because motivation can only be inferred and never observed, the question is a difficult one.

A related problem for those who study motivation is the fact that people often are unaware of their own motivations. Consider the fact that every year millions of people struggle to lose weight or quit smoking. When you look at the situation in a coldly logical way, these behaviors are completely under the control of the individual and therefore should be easy to accomplish. Yet people who insist that they are very highly motivated to diet or to smoke less find it excruciatingly difficult to do so. Are they perhaps unmotivated or do they have contradictory motivations of which they're unaware? Some theorists, such as Freud, have insisted that we are unaware of many of our motivations. Other theorists have suggested that we vastly underestimate the power of external influences on our behavior; as a result, we search in vain within ourselves for causes that may in fact be external. Thus, analysis of our motivations is a challenging task.

## Definitions of motivation

By *motivation* we mean those processes that influence the arousal, strength, or direction of behavior. For example, showing an attractive toy to a child can *arouse* approach behaviors. Depriving yourself of food for a long time results in an increase in the *strength* of your tendency to approach food. The *direction* of your behavior can be influenced by the relative attractiveness of two potential courses of action.

Although our definition of motivation adequately characterizes the topic, it may also be helpful to point out how motivation differs from learning. Learning is the process by which a relatively permanent change in behavior occurs as a result of experience. Thus learning, like motivation, influences the direction of behavior. However, as the definition of *learning* suggests, the study of learning emphasizes events in the organism's past (experience) that influence present behavior. The study of motivation emphasizes contemporaneous influences on present behavior (for example, hunger as an influence on eating). Also, learning is relatively permanent, whereas motivation is not. A person is sometimes hungry, sometimes full.

We have intentionally defined *motivation* quite broadly in order to cover the large variety of topics contained within the field of motivation. But just because the field *is* so diverse, there are, in fact, many acceptable definitions. Littman (1958), when faced with the task of devising a truly comprehensive definition, only half facetiously offered the following definition.

> Motivation refers to processes or conditions which may be physiological or psychological, innate or acquired, internal or external to the organism which determine or describe how, or in respect of what, behavior is initiated, maintained, guided, selected, or terminated; it also refers to end states which such behavior frequently achieves or is designed to achieve whether they are conditions of the organism or environment; it also refers to the behavior engaged in, or aspects of that behavior, in respect of its organization, occurrence, continuation, reorganization, or termination with regard to past or present or future organic or environmental conditions; further, it refers to the fact that an individual will learn or remember or forget certain material, as well as the rate or manner in which these processes occur and the ease or difficulty with which they are altered, as well as to some of the processes or conditions which are responsible for this behavior; similarly, it determines how and what perceptual and judgmental activities and outcomes will occur, as well as some of the conditions and determinants of such activities and outcomes; similarly, it also refers to the fact of and the determinants of the occurrence and fate of affective process; finally, it describes and accounts for various individual differences which appear in respect of the various behaviors, processes, conditions, and outcomes referred to above. Motivation refers to any one or more of the above behaviors, conditions, processes, or outcomes in any combinations [pp. 136–137].[1]

As Littman suggests, in order to include everything motivational in nature, a definition has to include everything in nature. As you will discover in this book, theories of motivation have included the physiological and psychological, the innate and acquired, and the internal and external determinants of behavior. Littman's definition is not such a parody; the field of motivation is broad indeed.

We study motivation to understand *why* people behave in certain ways. In short, we seek the determinants of behavior. A primary reason for the vastness of the field of motivation is the fact that behavior can be determined by influences at several different levels. First, some behaviors have physiological determinants. Hunger motivation has a strong physiological component, but we would not expect to learn

---

[1]From "Motives, History, and Causes," by Professor Richard A. Littman. In Marshall R. Jones (Ed.), *Nebraska Symposium on Motivation.* © 1958 by University of Nebraska Press. This and all other quotations from this source are reprinted by permission.

much about one's persistence at a task, for example, by studying the person's physiology. Instead, we would look at a second class of determinants, contemporary influences. These would include the social situation involved and the character of the task to be performed. A third group of determinants might be the person's past experiences. What happened to the person when prior difficult tasks were attempted? Finally, personality factors would certainly play a major role in a person's appraisal of a challenging task.

Determinism, as Young (1961) points out, has many different levels. Since motivation deals with the determinants of behavior, motivation is necessarily a multifaceted area of study. For this reason, motivational theorists include physiologists (Chapter 2), personality theorists (Chapters 3 and 4), learning theorists (Chapter 5), social psychologists (Chapters 7, 8, 9, 10, and 11), and even a smattering of child psychologists, economists, musicians, and architects (Chapter 6)!

Because the domain of motivation is so broad, recent theories have tended to focus on the explanation of particular types of behavior. This specialization has developed because psychologists have realized that a theorist who investigates the motivating properties of money, for example, cannot use the same analysis in explaining the motives for loving one's children. Littman (1958), after abandoning his global definition of *motivation,* also comes to the conclusion that the specialization of motivation theories is necessary, given the immense breadth of the field.

> *There are many different kinds of motivational phenomena.* It is simply not the case that the analysis of one kind of motivational phenomenon provides us with the analysis of all, or even a substantial portion, of other motivational concepts. Motivation is not a unitary phenomenon in the sense that all motivational things have the same properties and enter into the same laws in the same ways [p. 163].

In a sense, it is disappointing that one grand motivational scheme that encompasses all behavior has not been found and probably never will be. The hope of finding "the one true theory" offers a sense of security to students and psychologists much like Linus's blanket. The history of science, however, has amply demonstrated that few collections of phenomena can be explained simply and adequately by a single viewpoint. The psychology of motivation is an illustration *par excellence* of this truism.

With this understanding, let us proceed to discuss briefly the theories to be covered.

## Prospectus

The plan of this book derives from our conceptualization of motivation as a complex, multifaceted phenomenon. Most textbook authors take one of two tracks. Some disagree with our view and choose to define *motivation* narrowly, Hence, their coverage tends to be a detailed exposition of a single theory or a closeknit group of theories. Others agree in principle that motivation has many facets and they cover a wide range of viewpoints. However, as is apparent from their organization and discussion, they strongly advocate one position. Consequently, their presentation of other theories is less comprehensive, sometimes glaringly restricted. The purpose seems to be not a discussion of the competing positions but rather a use of them as cannon fodder. The less favored theories are systematically destroyed, and from their ashes arises the "best" theory.

We have not entirely transcended our biases and opinions, as you will see. However, we have tried to keep our judgments in check and to represent fairly the divergent theories we have selected. We have attempted to be comprehensive and representative in each chapter so that the flavor and intent of each theory can be discerned. The wisdom and shortcomings of each theory will be revealed by the theory itself.

## Criteria for inclusion of theories

In making our selections, we considered it essential that a comprehensive survey of motivational theories meet two criteria. The first criterion was that it include some theories of great historical importance and some of great contemporary importance. Consequently, we have selected some theories that were monumental in their day but have since waned in influence and some that are currently drawing attention. The rationale for including older theories is that, besides giving birth to newer ones, they have contributed uniquely and meaningfully to the psychology of motivation. Although these theories no longer dominate the field, research involving their concepts persists. The second criterion was that the survey include theories that address motivation from each of two distinctive traditions in psychology, the experimental and the clinical. Most previous books have lopsidedly advocated one view at the expense of the other.

The experimental approach has been identified with the *scientific* investigation of motivation. This approach requires that every proposal of a construct or a process be testable under the controlled conditions of the psychological laboratory. Hence, experimentalists are insistent upon formulating operational definitions for their motivational constructs and processes. (An operational definition is one that specifies a set of operations by which one can detect the construct or process. For example, in physics, an operational definition of *length* would describe a method of measuring.) All concepts established by operational definitions are meaningful in the sense that they can ultimately be reduced to observable phenomena. Consequently, such definitions permit the formulation of hypotheses that can be supported or not supported by experimental investigation.

As an example, consider the hypothesis that the cessation of cigarette smoking among habitual smokers results in an increase in the amount they eat. We might test this hypothesis by first collecting a large group of smokers, each of whom eats the same amount of food and smokes the same number of cigarettes each day. Next, we would deprive half of the people of all cigarettes for a month. This group is called the *experimental group*. The other half of the subjects, the *control group*, would be allowed to smoke the usual number of cigarettes each day. During the subsequent month, the amount of food each subject ate would be carefully measured. In this way we could assess whether those who were deprived of cigarettes ate more during the month than those who were not deprived. Note that both measurements—amount eaten and amount smoked—are easy to make. There are no constructs, such as "ego strength," that are difficult to assess objectively.

The advantage of this experimental method is that it allows us to draw conclusions with confidence. The disadvantage is that in order to perform the experiment it is usually necessary to disrupt the person's everyday activities in some way. Thus, an artificial, contrived situation may be created. Conclusions based on behavior exhibited in such situations may be invalid, since such behavior may not closely approximate behavior in natural situations. Many people other than psychologists recognize the unnaturalness of experimental situations. The authors once wrote, for example, to a famous newspaper columnist who had written an essay on pornography. He wrote us a very strong letter, saying in essence that psychologists are idiots for trying to measure sexual arousal by objectively assessing blood pressure and other physiological measures while showing the subjects pornography. He did not believe that covering the subjects with physiological recording devices would give accurate information about the typical human response to pornography because the situation was not natural. Many people share the columnist's viewpoint.

In contrast to the experimental approach, however, is the clinical approach, which has been identified with the *naturalistic* investigation of motivation. Unlike experimental theories, clinical theories are based on observations of motivated behavior *as it occurs* outside the psychological laboratory. Such observations have been undertaken largely in conjunction with the study of personality and psychotherapy. Since natural conditions are more complex and uncontrolled than laboratory conditions, however, the motivational constructs and processes derived from this method of investigation are less precise and more global than those derived from experimental analyses. Hypotheses are difficult to formulate and test systematically in natural situations.

The advantages of the experimental approach are the disadvantages of the clinical approach, and vice versa. Experimental theories have received varying degrees of scientific support for their constructs and processes. Accordingly, there exists some confidence among researchers that these theories are valid—that is, that they contain reasonable information about how motivation operates. The drawback of the experimental approach is a by-product of this strength. In order to make experimental theories of motivation fit for scientific investigation, theorists must define their constructs and processes narrowly and examine them under highly specific laboratory conditions. Thus, the major disadvantage of experimental approaches is the problem of generalizing from specific laboratory situations to real-life situations. Better generalizations can often be made from clinical theories than from experimental theories, because a greater variety of situations and of people have been studied naturalistically. Clinical constructs and processes are rooted in concepts of personality, and as such are broad and complex. Thus, they are useful in telling us why certain people are motivated to behave in certain ways; one theory we will discuss later, for example, describes most human motivation in terms of the influence of a hierarchy of psychological needs. The drawback of clinical theories is that they do not lend themselves to objective validation. In summary, experimental theories tend to have greater testability and narrower applicability, and clinical theories tend to have broader applicability and less testability.

This second criterion for selecting theories will also be a basis for evaluating the theories as we present them: we shall present scientific research—or discuss the dearth of it—for each theory. We place a premium on scientific support for theoretical constructs and processes. Hence, we will judge the quality and relevance of the research on this basis throughout our discussion. This approach naturally leads us to deal most critically with the research methods of the clinical theories.

## Overview of the chapters

Chapter 2 discusses the biological bases of human motivation, with particular emphasis on hunger, thirst, sex, sleep, and stress. The chapter also includes a discussion of instinct, since some theorists believe that instincts such as territoriality and aggression, which influence animal behavior, also operate in humans. Although the use of instinct as an explanation of human behavior has diminished greatly during the last 50 years, the topic is still important in several areas of behavior. Chapter 2 does not attempt to present a particular theory; rather, it lays the foundation for subsequent chapters.

Chapter 3 covers Freud's psychoanalytic theory of motivation. The psychoanalytic theory of human behavior is perhaps the most comprehensive one devised, and at its core is a complicated theory of motivation. The theory is based on the prominence of two instinctual sources of motivation: sex and aggression.

Chapter 4 deals with the humanistic motivation theories of Rogers and Maslow. These theorists emphasize an instinctlike concept of motivation that is generally called "self-actualization." The basic tenet of this perspective is that we are motivated toward psychological growth and enhancement in order to fulfill our potential as human beings. The chapter also discusses the application of these theories to work situations.

Hull's theory of learning and motivation, which is of great historical importance, is reviewed in Chapter 5. Hull believed that all behavior was ultimately motivated by primary innate drives, such as hunger, thirst, and sex. He was strongly influenced by a few physiologists whose findings helped to mold the motivational premises of Hullian theory. Upon these physiological assumptions, Hull constructed a massive theory using stimulus-response principles of learning.

Neo-Hullians, such as Berlyne, were influential in the formulation of optimal level theory, discussed in Chapter 6. Optimal level theory postulates that each person has an optimal level of stimulation, which he or she is motivated to maintain. This optimal amount of stimulation differs from person to person, but the existence of an optimal level is common to all members of the species. Thus, the optimal level is to some extent an innate characteristic.

The social learning theories of Rotter and Bandura, reviewed in Chapter 7, are geared primarily to complex human learning and motivation in a social environment. These theories differ from traditional learning theories such as Hull's in that they emphasize the role of cognitive mediating variables, such as expectancy, attention, and symbolic coding. The learner is conceptualized as an active processor of information. The concept of reinforcement is reworked and broadened to reflect the impact of cognition, and the concepts of drive and tension reduction are dropped in favor of cognitive variables. Research on aggression, including the effects of television and pornography, is also reviewed from this social learning perspective.

Lewin's "field theory," the subject of Chapter 8, represents an interesting transitional conception between innate and learned motivation. Lewin's scheme certainly encompasses the primary biological drives, but Lewin emphasized what he called "quasi-needs," motivations that are not based on biological deprivation. For example, the intentions to finish a task and to achieve a goal are important motivational topics in Lewinian theory.

Closely related to Lewinian theory is the theory of achievement motivation, discussed in Chapter 9. This formulation deals strictly with achievement situations and thus is more limited in scope and greater in predictive precision than Lewinian theory. More than Lewinian theory, the theory of achievement motivation emphasizes the importance and measurement of individual differences in assessing an organism's interaction with its environment. The theory of achievement motivation is even further divorced from the biologically based theories than is Lewinian theory, because it makes no mention of inborn tendencies. Achievement motivation is entirely learned.

Chapter 10 discusses consistency theories, which also are entirely noninstinctual. Consistency theories deal with one's motivation to maintain concordance among all one's thoughts and actions. Special emphasis will be given to the best-known consistency theories, cognitive dissonance theory and equity theory.

Chapter 11 deals with attribution theory. Unlike all the prior formulations, attribution theory focuses not on the causes of behavior but on how people *perceive* the causes of behavior, both their own and that of others. The cause to which one attributes behavior has important consequences for one's subsequent motivation. For example, if a man attributes his miserable failure to his low ability, he will not bother to try hard next time. If he attributes his failure to low effort, he may try extremely hard next time.

Chapter 12 offers an analysis of a specific example from the point of view of each of the theories. Also, we present comparisons of many of the theories and discuss some basic issues in motivation. Finally, we stress the importance of motivational considerations in the analysis of behavior and discuss several basic issues in motivation.

Thus, Chapters 3, 4, 5, and 8 describe theories that are essentially historical milestones; Chapters 6, 9, 10, and 11 deal with more contemporary theories. The theories in Chapters 3 and 4 are clinical; those in Chapters 5, 6, 10, and 11 are experimental; and those in Chapters 7, 8, and 9 show both influences. All the chapters are independent and can generally be read without reference to one another, but their order of appearance is based on two considerations: (1) theories substantially influencing others (that is, having historical importance) are presented first; (2) theories utilizing narrow, highly specific concepts of motivation, such as drive and instinct, are presented before those utilizing broader, more general concepts of motivation, such as cognitive dissonance and causal attribution.

Before we begin our examination of these theories, however, it is necessary to explain the foundation of motivation, the biological substrate responsible for such basic motivations as hunger. It is this important topic to which we turn first.

# CHAPTER 2

# Instinct and the Biological Bases of Motivation

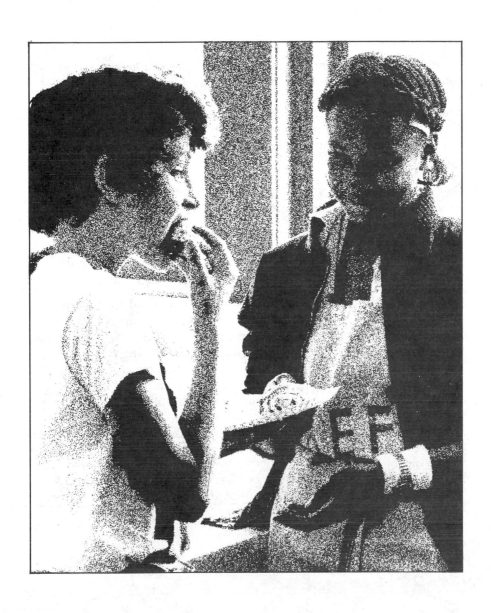

*It is superfluous to point out the analogies be-
tween the social behavior patterns of many
animals, particularly wild geese, and those of
man. All the truisms in our proverbs seem to
apply equally to geese.*[1]

*Konrad Lorenz*

Some theorists believe that all sources of motivation are innate; all
theorists would agree that at least some sources are. Humans may be
taught how to eat with a fork or how to eat oysters, but they are not
taught how to be hungry: hunger is an unlearned source of motivation.
Early in the 20th century, some theorists postulated that much of
human behavior was instinctual. They maintained that most behavior
was unlearned, innate, and characteristic of the entire species. Although such "explanations" of human behavior have fallen into dis-
favor, all theorists believe that inherited physiological mechanisms play
an important role in motivation. This chapter will first review the role
of instinct in motivational theory and then elaborate on some physiological bases of motivation.

## The role of instinct in motivational theory

Beach (1955) has pointed out that instinct was used by theorists as
early as the ancient Greek philosophers to explain some aspects of behavior. Christian theologians fostered the use of instinct as an explanatory device by attributing animal behavior to it. Having postulated the
existence of a soul in humans, theologians thought that individuals
would need to discriminate right from wrong and good from evil in
order to gain salvation of the soul. Such discriminations demanded
sound reasoning ability. Since lower animals had neither a soul nor the
chance for salvation, they did not need any reasoning powers. All their
activities were therefore said to be caused solely by instinct.
   The dichotomy between instinct in lower animals and reasoning in
Man was vigorously challenged by Darwin's theory of evolution. A
crucial tenet of Darwin's theory is that those organisms best suited to

[1]From *On Aggression*, by Konrad Lorenz. New York: Harcourt Brace Jovanovich,
1966.

their environments will be able to survive and reproduce. Darwin postulated that through survival of the fittest the phylogenetic chain had finally reached its most highly evolved member—Man. One of the most important implications of this theory was that those sources of motivation present in Man's relatives should also be present to some extent in Man. The sources most evident in lower animals were instincts. Consequently, in the late 19th and early 20th centuries, many psychologists believed that instincts were the unobservable motivational forces responsible for much of human behavior. Because the theory of evolution posited continuity between Man and lower animals (through lines of descent from a common ancestor), its adherents assumed that all species had both instincts and reason, in varying quantities.

The use of instincts to explain behavior grew rapidly. McDougall was one of the strongest advocates of the position that much of human behavior was instinctive: "The human mind has certain innate or inherited tendencies which are the essential springs or motive powers of all thought and action, whether individual or collective, and are the bases from which the character and will of individuals and of nations are gradually developed under the guidance of the intellectual faculties" (1908, p. 20). McDougall included gregariousness, pugnacity, acquisition, construction, and reproduction as some of the more important human instincts.

The use of instincts to explain behavior soon mushroomed to a ridiculous degree. Atkinson (1964, p. 17) reports that by 1924 over 14,000 instincts were used to "explain" virtually all of behavior. In other words, if behavior X occurred, instinct X was postulated to account for behavior X. And what was the evidence that instinct X existed? Behavior X, of course. "Explaining" a behavior by creating an instinct constitutes a circular argument. Beach (1955) has pointed out that "the degree of assurance with which instincts are attributed to a given species is inversely related to the extent to which that species has been studied, particularly from the developmental point of view" (p. 405). After the 1920s, in a reaction against indiscriminate use of the term *instinct,* the term became much less prevalent.

In two areas of theory, however, instinct still plays a major role. The first area includes psychoanalytic theory and the fulfillment theories proposed by Maslow and Rogers, all of which postulate that Man has innate, instinctive urges that strongly influence behavior. A full explanation of these theories will be deferred until Chapters 3 and 4.

The second area is ethology—the study of animal behavior. Some ethologists (such as Lorenz and Tinbergen) believe that certain instincts of lower animals are direct progenitors of particular human behaviors. For this reason, we shall briefly present the ethological concept of instinct here.

### Ethological analysis of instinct

Instinct is "an inherited, specific, stereotyped pattern of behavior" (Cofer & Appley, 1964, p. 60). Most theorists hold that the most important defining characteristics of an instinctive behavior are that the behavior be unlearned and species-specific. For example, if every spider of a given species built webs of precisely the same pattern, and if that behavior occurred even in spiders that had never seen webs of other members of their species, then the web-building behavior would be considered instinctive.

Three concepts are central to the ethological discussion of instinct. The first is *reaction-specific energy.* Each instinct is assumed to have associated with it a reservoir of energy that is available only for the performance of that particular instinctive act. Because the energy is bound to only one act, it is called reaction-specific.

The second concept, the *innate releasing mechanism,* refers to the triggering of the instinct by some very specific environmental stimulus, called a *sign stimulus* (the third concept). Tinbergen (1951, 1952) has documented the innate releasing mechanism in his research on the stickleback fish. During the mating period, the male stickleback establishes a territory and defends it against all other male sticklebacks. The instinctive defense behavior is released by the red color on the undersides of the other males. Pelkwijk and Tinbergen (1937) constructed several models of male sticklebacks, using varying degrees of realism, and displayed them to real male sticklebacks. The experimenters found that only those stimuli with red undersides elicited attack. Very poor imitations of sticklebacks elicited fighting if their undersides were red, and very good imitations did not elicit fighting if their undersides were not red. Evidently, then, the red ventral surface is the sign stimulus to which the innate releasing mechanism responds. The reaction-specific energy motivates the instinctive behavior of fighting other male sticklebacks.

The relation between the sign stimulus and the innate releasing mechanism, however, is not as straightforward as this example might suggest. If the animal has not been able to perform the instinctive activity—because appropriate environmental stimuli are lacking, for example—the reaction-specific energy accumulates. As this occurs, the adequacy a stimulus must have in order to trigger the innate releasing mechanism tends to diminish. The male stickleback, deprived for a long time of any opportunity to defend his claim, might attack a stimulus that isn't quite red. If enough energy accumulates, the threshold for activation of the innate releasing mechanism can decrease so far that eventually the instinctive activity may occur when nothing resembling the sign stimulus is present. Such behavior is called *vacuum activity.* (Some ethologists (Armstrong, 1950; Thorpe, 1948) believe that true vacuum activity is not probable. They suggest that something in the environment bears some resemblance to the sign stimulus, thus triggering the innate releasing mechanism.) Vacuum activity bears similarity to the Freudian concept of displacement, the process of rechanneling energy from one goal object to another. An employee who wants to take aggressive action against his supervisor but doesn't want to lose his job may vent his hostility on his wife instead. In other words, when reaction-specific energy (in the ethological model) or libido (in the Freudian model) accumulates to a high degree, release may occur in stimulus situations that are somewhat inappropriate. Tinbergen (1952) also describes displacement activity (not to be confused with the Freudian concept of displacement) as an abnormal instinctive response that occurs when the reaction-specific energy for one behavior is blocked or is in conflict with another drive. This blockage results in a behavior not entirely appropriate for the existing stimulus situation. For example, Tinbergen (p. 12) describes a case in which an experimenter tapped a male stickleback with a model of a male stickleback. The male at first fled, but as his fear waned, the male prepared to attack the model. As this aggressive instinct began to overtake his instinct to flee—that is, as these opposite instincts became equal in strength—the animal began sanddigging behavior. This displacement behavior allowed some outlet for the two instinctive drives that were in conflict.

Both vacuum and displacement activities weaken the close relation originally postulated between a sign stimulus and its associated innate releasing mechanism.

## Extrapolation to humans

Ethologists' concern with instincts in lower animals has, quite expectedly, led to speculations that such instincts may also be present in Man. Ardrey (1966), Lorenz (1966), and Tinbergen (1951) are ethologists who have claimed that certain important human behaviors are instincts similar (if not identical) to those found in lower animals. Ardrey, for example, emphasizes the similarity between animal and human territoriality. As Edney (1974) points out, *territoriality* has no unanimously agreed-upon definition; however, many definitions mention something akin to "space-associated intolerance" (Eibl-Eibesfeldt, 1970, p. 309), in which an organism defends a geographic territory against outsiders. The instinct (if indeed it is an instinct) of territoriality serves a very important purpose in lower animals. It spreads the animals of a given species over the area where food is available, thus maximizing the number that can survive and reproduce. In fact, Carpenter (1958) lists 32 ways territoriality benefits the species. Ardrey maintains that the territoriality instinct persists in human behavior, as when elevator passengers rearrange their positions, always maximizing interpersonal distance, every time other passengers get off. Ardrey and Lorenz both believe that Man's aggression in the name of national integrity is also a manifestation of this instinct.

Lorenz's famous book *On Aggression* (1966) popularized his belief that our species has inherited the aggressive instinct necessary for our ancestors' survival. Lorenz points out that many animals developed inhibitors to limit aggression. For example, if a baboon adopts a submissive posture, an attacking baboon will cease his aggression. Since Man has no potent natural (bodily) weapons, we have developed no natural inhibitors. Now that we have developed thermonuclear devices, our lack of inhibitors on aggression creates a grave peril. Lorenz suggests substitute means of releasing instinctive aggression (for example, sports) in order to make less likely its manifestation for destructive ends.

Continuity between animal instinct and human instinct is difficult to prove. Unfortunately, ethologists arguing for such continuity have more often than not relied merely on interesting analogies and charming anecdotes. Similarities between animal and human behavior may not be grounds for the close relation posited by ethologists such as Lorenz. (Note his quote at the very beginning of this chapter.) The ethological viewpoint has been heartily criticized by Skinner (1966): "Contingencies which shape the organization of a large company or governmental administration show little in common with the phylogenic contingencies responsible for the hierarchy in the poultry yard. Some forms of human society may resemble the anthill or beehive, but not because they exemplify the same behavioral process" (p. 1212). Edney (1974), in fact, lists eight fundamental ways in which territoriality differs in Man and in lower animals. For example, Edney refutes Ardrey's statement that territoriality is an "imperative" by pointing out that many people have chosen communal, aterritorial modes of life. Further, a person, unlike a lower animal, maintains a large number of separate territories. Edney concludes that the phenomenon of human territoriality is in an embryonic stage of investigation and cannot now be said to be a manifestation of an instinct, much less an instinct identical to that found in lower animals.

## Criticisms of the ethological analysis of behavior

From the early part of this century, when the word *instinct* was used so freely, to more recent years, when its use has been restrained, critics of instinct theories have never been hard to locate. Beach (1955) and Skinner (1966), among many others, have criticized the use of the term *instinct*. Beach suspects that use of the term may actually have retarded empirical research, because attributing behavior to a phylogenetic origin precludes much experimental manipulation. (See also Kuo, 1922.) Skinner believes that the term has been used to obscure (and excuse) the fact that the variables controlling certain behaviors have not been clearly identified: instinct has been a null explanation, an explanation of last resort.

Other criticisms of appealing to instinct to explain behavior concern methodology. Cofer and Appley (1964, p. 98) summarize criticisms of the isolation studies that provided support for the instinct position. In those studies an animal was reared in total isolation from other members of its species. Typically the correct performance of instinctive behavior occurred. Supporters of the instinct explanation inferred that since the animal could not have learned the behavior by imitation or any other means of peer or parental influence, the behavior must have been innate. Lehrman (1953, 1956) and Schneirla (1956, cited in Cofer & Appley, 1964; 1957) criticize these isolation studies on several grounds. First, the animal is not truly isolated. It is able to perceive one member of its species—namely, itself—and is thus able to obtain tactual, olfactory, visual, and other cues. It may acquire during isolation such things as the ability to recognize members of its species through use of any of these cues. Second, the prenatal environment may influence subsequent behavior during isolation. The fact that a behavior takes place during isolation does not mean its occurrence is entirely due to genetics. Schneirla states that the isolation study may only show which behaviors can be manifested under an unusual early environment, not which behaviors are necessarily totally genetic in origin.

Other experiments subvert the claim that certain complex behaviors are solely instinctual in origin. Harlow (1965) has shown that in adult monkeys normal species-specific sexual activity depends on early peer interaction, even though the prepubescent monkey is incapable of explicit sexual activity. Kuo (1930) has shown that species-specific behavior such as a cat's response to a rodent is greatly dependent on early experience.

Perhaps the most direct criticisms concern instincts for which the appropriate sign stimuli were presumed to have been identified. For example, Figure 2-1 shows a model that when moved to the right elicits flight in some species of birds, but when moved to the left does not. Tinbergen (1948) maintained that the model resembles a bird of prey when moved to the right, thereby frightening birds that are preyed upon by hawks; it serves as the sign stimulus for an instinctive flight reaction. When moved to the left, the model resembles a long-necked goose, provoking no alarm. However, Ginsburg (1952, cited in Schneirla, 1957, and Cofer & Appley, 1964) suggests a noninstinctual explanation. When the model moves to the right, the broad part of the silhouette intrudes into the visual field first. This is more startling than when the thin part intrudes first, as happens when the model moves to

**Figure 2-1.** When this stimulus is moved to the right, it elicits flight in some species of birds, but when moved to the left, it does not. *(From "Social Releasers and the Experimental Method Required for Their Study," by N. Tinbergen,* Wilson Bulletin, *1948, 60, 6-52. Reprinted by permission of the Wilson Ornithological Society.)*

the left. Thus what appeared to Tinbergen as an instinctive flight reaction to a specific sign stimulus may be nothing more than a startle reaction. The existence of such different interpretations of the same experiment illustrates some of the pitfalls of ethological research. Behavior occurs in a complex environmental setting, and it is hard to tell which aspect (or aspects) of the setting is the stimulus.

Whether an "innate" behavior has any learned components is difficult to ascertain unless the developmental history of the animal is carefully documented. The discussion of whether a given behavior is innate or learned has come to be known as the nature/nurture controversy. Although the controversy began as an "either/or" battle, recent work has suggested that neither the influence of nature nor the influence of nurturance can be manifested without the other. For example, Harnly (1941) showed that the shape of a particular insect's wings depends both on genetic makeup and on the temperature during development. As Whalen (1971) points out, the genetic endowment of an animal is manifested within an environment. Since each factor influences the expression of the other, no behavior can be said to be due entirely to only one of the two factors. Those supporting this interactionist viewpoint find the nature/nurture controversy obsolete and the ethologists' insistence on the primacy of instincts objectionable.

## Imprinting

The most heavily researched topic in psychological ethology is imprinting. Imprinting is a kind of learning that occurs during a particular interval (called the *critical period*) early in an animal's life and that is difficult to alter thereafter. The phenomenon is easiest to observe in birds. Shortly after hatching, a young bird develops an attachment to its mother and will thereafter follow her around; we say that the hatchling has imprinted on her. If some moving object is substituted for the mother and presented during the critical period, the bird becomes attached to that object instead, even if the object is a wooden decoy, a person, a football, or a gym shoe. Lorenz (1952) believes that imprinting is innate but that the tendency to imprint on a *particular* stimulus (the mother) is not. In nature, since the most prominent stimulus present shortly after hatching is usually the mother, imprinting on the mother does almost invariably take place.

In the typical imprinting experiment, a young bird—say, a duckling—hatches in the experimental apparatus, a large, circular runway around which a mechanical decoy can be slowly moved. Imprinting of the duckling on the decoy is accomplished by moving the decoy around the runway, usually as it emits a tape-recorded sound of a human trying to imitate a duck. The imprinting procedure ceases when the duckling has followed the decoy a certain distance around the runway. To test whether imprinting has indeed occurred, the duckling is later placed in the runway between the original decoy and a new one. Various lures are frequently used to make the new decoy attractive: it may emit the tape-recorded sound of a real mother duck; it may look like a female duck whereas the original looks like a male. Nevertheless, the duckling usually approaches the decoy on which it initially imprinted.

Hess (1959) claims that the characteristic which most clearly distinguishes imprinting from typical forms of learning is that imprinting takes place most strongly during a critical period. If a mallard duckling is briefly exposed to its mother (or—as is more frequent in experiments—a mother substitute) anytime between approximately 13 and 16 hours after hatching, imprinting will be stronger than if such exposure occurs at any other time. Hess (1959) provides evidence that there are two reasons the critical period in mallards (and some other species) is 13 to 16 hours of age. First, the duckling's locomotor ability is very poor before that time, so that physical following of the mother is impossible—and Hess has shown that strong imprinting requires that the duckling follow the model. (In fact, Hess believes that the more effort such following requires, the stronger will be the imprinting.) Second, the mallard develops fear of strange objects at about 16 hours of age, and this fear discourages following of the model. As Figure 2-2 shows, these two factors combine to produce the critical period for imprinting.

A second feature that Hess believes distinguishes imprinting from other learning is the effect of punishment. If the young animal is punished for following the imprinting object, imprinting is strengthened! Hess believes this effect contradicts normal learning principles.

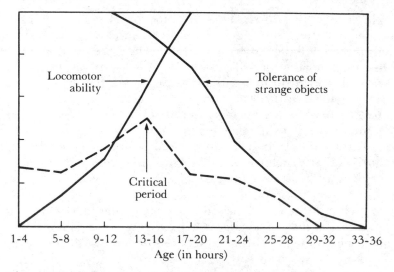

**Figure 2-2.** Interaction of developing locomotor ability and developing fear of strange objects explains the occurrence of the critical period at 13 to 16 hours of age for particular species of birds. *(Reprinted from "The Relationship between Imprinting and Motivation," by E. H. Hess. In* Nebraska Symposium on Motivation, *1959, by Marshall R. Jones (Ed.). By permission of the University of Nebraska Press.* © *1959, University of Nebraska Press.)*

(In Chapter 5, however, we will see that this is not necessarily a contradiction after all.)

Ethologists view imprinting as a case of instinctive activity, albeit a special case. The imprinting stimulus is a sign stimulus that releases instinctive activity-approach behavior in the young (Hess, 1959).

Just as other instincts were extrapolated to humans by Lorenz, Ardrey, and others, some theorists have suggested that imprinting occurs in humans. Bowlby (1969) believes that the human infant indeed imprints on the mother, presumably during a critical period. Harlow, Gluck, and Suomi (1972) strongly disagree. The issue remains unresolved.

### Reformulations of imprinting

Opponents of instinct theory disagree with the contention of Hess and Lorenz that imprinting is an instinctive activity. A large number of theorists believe that imprinting is an instance of learning. Dimond (1970), Salzen (1970), and Bateson (1966, 1971) believe that the young bird develops an attachment for its primary caretaker through mere exposure to her. No reinforcement is necessary. After this learning takes place, the offspring will approach only this source of stimulation. Other animals, being discrepant from the original imprinting stimulus, elicit withdrawal reactions.

More recently, H. Hoffman and Ratner (1973) have suggested a provocative reinforcement explanation of imprinting. They propose that the perception of a moving object is innately reinforcing to the very young bird. (As they point out, there is only weak evidence that perception of the motion of the imprinting object is innately reinforcing. Therefore, they do not wish to suggest that no other aspect of the object may be innately reinforcing to some extent.) This stimulation elicits affiliative behavior. Hoffman and Ratner explain imprinting according to stimulus-response theory (see Chapter 5): the motion of the imprinting object is an unconditioned stimulus; affiliation is an unconditioned response; through classical conditioning, other characteristics of the imprinting object acquire the power to elicit affiliative behavior. Since the initial stimulus and response are unconditioned, however, Hoffman and Ratner's theory may still be considered a form of instinct theory: the eliciting property of the moving object is postulated to be innate.

Hoffman and Ratner agree with Hess and Lorenz that the young bird quickly develops a fear of novel objects and that it is this fear that makes imprinting so difficult beyond the critical period. In fact, the ethologists think imprinting may be impossible after the critical period. Recall that this point supports the ethologists' contention that imprinting differs from learning. However, Bateson (1969) summarizes evidence that, although imprinting is more difficult after the critical period, it can occur. For this reason Bateson thinks that the term *critical period* is misleading, since it implies that imprinting can take place only at that time. Ratner and Hoffman (1974) try to reconcile the ethologists and Bateson by noting an important methodological difference. In Lorenz's naturalistic settings, older birds fled from the imprinting stimulus when it was presented. Hence no imprinting occurred. Consequently Lorenz concluded that imprinting can occur only during the critical period. In laboratory settings, such as those cited by Bateson, the animal cannot escape. It remains exposed to the imprinting stimulus despite any escape tendencies the animal may have. Its fearfulness in response to novel stimulation, posited both by Hoffman and Ratner and by Hess, diminishes as it becomes habituated to the imprinting stimulus. Thus imprinting can occur in older birds in the laboratory.

Hoffman and Ratner (1973) also show that their reinforcement model of imprinting can explain why punishment strengthens imprinting. Any stimulation that causes discomfort to the animal makes the innately reinforcing properties of the imprinting stimulus even stronger by contrast. Imprinting is thereby strengthened.

In summary, Hoffman and Ratner (1973) say that normal learning principles can fully explain imprinting. Further, they present evidence against ethologists' assertion that two features—the critical period and the strengthening effect of aversive stimulation—distinguish imprinting from other types of learning.

## Sociobiology and motivation

Theories of evolution have had an immense impact on our understanding of biological diversity and selection. It seems axiomatic to say that those members of a species who reproduce most successfully and leave the greatest number of offspring that reproduce are those that are best suited for their environment. As a result of natural selection, then, future generations of the species resemble the most successful ancestors more closely than the less successful ones.

Although theories of evolution have dealt largely with the hereditability of physical characteristics, sociobiology pertains to the application of evolutionary principles to the social behavior of animals (Barash, 1977; Wilson, 1975). According to sociobiologists, *social behaviors* that result in superior adaptation to one's environment may be passed on to one's offspring just as superior physical traits are.

That a behavior can have a strong genetic determinant has been known for years. For example, Dilger (1962) has described the behavior of two species of African parrots. Among one species the nest-building materials are carried in the mouth; members of the other species transport such construction materials in their rump feathers. Hybrids resulting from the mating of one member of each species are inept in carrying their nest-building materials. These offspring attempt a feeble combination of their parents' techniques but are woefully incompetent. As a result they are not likely to build adequate nests and raise offspring of their own. First, this example shows that behavior can be very strongly controlled by heredity. Second, it shows that certain behaviors, such as inadequate nest building, can cause extinction of a species just as disadvantageous physical characteristics can.

This example, however, does not tell us how sociobiology relates to motivation. We move a step closer to the implications of sociobiology for motivation with an example from Barash (1977): Why do we like sweet foods? Why don't bitter foods taste good? These questions are not as silly as they sound. Sweetness and bitterness are not inherent in the foods. These are sensations that originate within the sensory system of the organism. There was probably some reason why humans who found sugary foods pleasurable survived while humans who found sugary foods distasteful did not. Barash points out that our primate ancestors ate a great deal of fruit, and fruit is much more nutritious when it is ripe and contains large quantities of sugar. Primates who liked the taste of unripened fruit would have had a less nutritious diet and would have been less likely to produce generations of offspring. Those who disliked unripe fruit but liked the taste of sugar would have been at an advantage. Thus, these latter primates are more likely to have been our ancestors. That is why we are positively motivated toward sweetness and negatively motivated toward bitterness, according to Barash.

This example shows a strong evolutionary influence on our taste preference, but still we have not quite reached the level of social motivation—motivation involved in interactions with other members of the species. We escalate in a final example from Barash (1977). Suppose a hungry coyote approaches a prairie-dog "town." A prairie dog who sees the coyote will utter a loud yelp. This noise has two effects. First, it warns the other prairie dogs, who quickly scramble into their burrows. Second, it brings the attention of the coyote squarely upon the animal making the noise. This second factor would lead us to expect that prairie dogs who take the role of noisy sentry would be likely to be eaten and therefore would produce fewer offspring than their comrades hiding in the burrows. This in turn would lead us to expect that whatever genetic component resulted in loud yelps when a predator approached would certainly be eliminated during the course of evolution. However, this altruistic behavior of warning others has not been eliminated. Sociobiologists suggest that by warning those around it, the prairie dog is saving the lives of its relatives who carry many of the same genes the sentry carries. Thus, the proclivity to yelp when seeing a predator is preserved in the genes of the large number of relatives who are saved. The sociobiologist thus posits an evolutionary basis for altruistic behavior.

The application of sociobiology to human motivation is controversial and speculative. As sociobiologists would predict, humans are more likely to be altruistic to close relatives. Consider the prairie-dog example again. If the altruistic prairie dog were saving the lives of those who had no genes in common with his, his altruistic genes would be digested by the coyote and no altruistic genes would be saved. Altruism would become extinct. Therefore altruism will persist only if directed toward those with genetic similarity to the original altruistic organism. The tendency of humans to be more altruistic to relatives than to strangers is consistent with this. The problem for the sociobiologist is that there may be nonbiological reasons why we are likely to be more altruistic to those to whom we are closely related. Our relatives are more familiar to us than strangers are. We have warm emotional attachments to some of our close relatives, and we have received important, powerful rewards from at least some of those relatives. Although the application of sociobiology to human motivation is thus still somewhat conjectural, the approach does represent a new and very provocative application of instincts to human behavior.

### Summary and conclusions: Instinct

No psychologist doubts that there are some innate influences on motivational processes. Even Hoffman and Ratner's reinforcement theory of imprinting, which minimizes the role of innate factors in motivation, still assumes that perception of motion is *innately* reinforcing to the young animal. Ethologists and instinct theorists differ from other theorists in believing that behavior such as territorial defense by the male stickleback is motivated by inherited factors; the others believe that heredity merely provides a substrate, which is greatly elaborated by learned factors. The question is not whether a behavior is motivated by innate or learned factors. Instead, there are two questions: "How?" and "How much?" The reason that there remains a controversy over "how much" of motivation is inherited is that at present it is not known "how" genetic information is manifested in behavior. We do not know the mechanism by which the slight overproduction of a hormone (presumably caused genetically) affects human behavior or the mechanism by which the stickleback's genetic code influences its territorial defense. Because we have not traced the causal route between most behaviors and the genetic influences on them, we cannot be sure to what extent a behavior is motivated by innate factors.

A major reason for the difficulty of learning the connection between genes and behavior is that each behavior is probably influenced by several genes. Blood type or eye color may be determined by one gene, but territorial behavior probably is not. Locating the gene-to-behavior causal route is therefore immensely complicated. Some investigators do not think the inability to specify this route need detract from the genetic analysis of motivation: "Failure to achieve a complete explanation for gene action has not prevented genetics from moving forward on the basis of statistical rather than mechanistic associations between genes and traits. In a parallel fashion psychology has made great progress in relating behavior to previous experience without much success in explaining learning in physiological terms" (Fuller & Thompson, 1960, p. 3). Nevertheless, the inability to specify precisely how genes influence the motivation for a given behavior makes some psychologists wary of accepting explanations based on instinct.

## *Physiological bases of motivation*

The extent of genetic and physiological influences on some behaviors has been a matter of spirited debate, but there is another class of behaviors whose physiological determinants are unquestionably important. In this section we shall explore the physiological substrates of several types of fundamental motivations. We begin with hunger, the motivation that has attracted the most research.

## Hunger

Rosenzweig (1962) has documented the history of the investigation of the physiological basis of hunger. Investigators as early as Plato and Aristotle speculated on the cause of hunger sensations, but it was Galen (138–201) who made systematic investigations of the problem. After creating lesions in various areas of the brain and transecting nerves, Galen concluded that the sensation of hunger originated in the stomach, which, through its rich supply of sensory nerves, was able to convey information to the brain. Galen's was the first of what are called *local* theories of hunger. Such theories postulate that hunger is detected in only one place in the body, outside the central nervous system—namely, in the stomach.

Over 1600 years later, Albrecht von Haller, a physiologist, suggested a local theory more detailed than that of Galen. Haller said that hunger arose when the tender folds of the stomach rubbed against each other. Since the stomach was so sensitive, this rubbing produced the discomfort we call hunger. This discomfort could be relieved by eating.

In the mid-19th century, an army surgeon, William Beaumont, suggested still another local theory of hunger. Beaumont was able to learn a great deal about hunger and gastric activity thanks to a Canadian hunter, Alexis St. Martin. St. Martin suffered a severe gunshot wound at Fort Mackinac, where Beaumont was stationed. The wound never completely healed; as a result, a small hole in the abdominal wall allowed Beaumont to monitor St. Martin's gastric activity under various experimental conditions.[2] From his investigations Beaumont concluded that hunger resulted from distension of the glands that secrete gastric juices. When a person had not eaten for some time, the gastric juices were not released. Instead they built up in the glands, causing discomfort (hunger), which was relieved when food entered the stomach.

The final local theory to be mentioned, and probably the best known, is that of Walter Cannon. In the early part of this century, Cannon suggested that stomach contractions caused the sensation of hunger. Cannon came to this conclusion in part because of the results of a famous experiment. Cannon's assistant, Washburn, surely one of the unsung heroes of science, swallowed a balloon attached to a long air hose that protruded from his mouth. Cannon attached a pump to the air hose and inflated the balloon inside Washburn's stomach. The hose was then connected to a pressure gauge. Whenever Washburn's stomach contracted, it squeezed the balloon, thus forcing air through the hose so that the contraction registered on the gauge. Meanwhile, the

---

[2]St. Martin was a rough, independent frontiersman who strongly resented being a guinea pig for Beaumont's experiments. Their rather strained relationship makes for interesting reading (Myer, 1912).

beleaguered Washburn was supposed to push a telegraph key whenever he felt hungry. Cannon found that Washburn's reports of hunger
coincided with his stomach contractions. Cannon concluded (Cannon
& Washburn, 1912) that the physiological event (stomach contraction)
caused the psychological event (sensation of hunger).

Although local theories of hunger have enjoyed great longevity and
popularity, both attributes are undeserved. Two crucial experiments
indicate that local theories cannot by themselves account for the physiological basis of hunger. First, experimenters have severed the vagus
nerve, by which stomach sensations are transmitted to the brain. Under
this circumstance animals still gave the normal response to insulin injection—that is, eating (M. I. Grossman, Cummins, & Ivy, 1947; C. T.
Morgan & Morgan, 1940). The eating could not have been caused by
increased gastric activity, since such activity could not have been
monitored by the brain. Second, persons whose stomachs have been
surgically removed still report hunger (Wangensteen & Carlson,
1931). Obviously then, local theories of hunger are incomplete.

In contrast to these theories are *general* theories of hunger, which
posit hunger detectors distributed over a large portion of the body.
Dumas (1803) believed that the lymphatic system somehow sensed
hunger. Since this system courses throughout the body, Dumas's theory
is classified as a general one. Probably the most general theory of hunger, however, was that of Roux (1897), who believed that hunger was
sensed by each cell in the body when its own nutritional needs were not
being met. Neither of these theories provided the local theories with
much competition for popularity.

The third class of theories, *central* theories, holds that hunger is mediated by changes somewhere in the brain. Schiff (1867) believed that
centers in the brain stem detected changes in blood composition as the
body removed nutrients from the blood. Activation of these centers resulted in hunger. Early in this century, however, clues began to appear
that lent support to a different central theory.

In 1904 a physician, J. Erdheim, reported that humans who had
suffered hypothalamic damage grew obese. Other investigators had believed that the pituitary gland controlled hunger and eating behavior,
but Erdheim's report appeared plausible, since the pituitary lies just
beneath the hypothalamus. Perhaps symptoms attributed to pituitary
damage were really caused by damage to the adjacent hypothalamus.

The hypothalamus itself (see Figure 2-3) is a small region of the
brain that is connected to the pituitary gland both by neural circuits
and by a portal system that carries secretions from the hypothalamus to
the pituitary. Little was known about the function of the hypothalamus
when Erdheim reported its relation to obesity. During the next few
decades, several other experimenters agreed that the hypothalamus
somehow controlled hunger. However, not until 1940 did Hether-

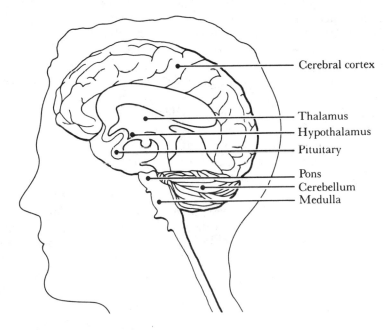

**Figure 2-3.** The location of the hypothalamus in relation to other major brain structures.

ington and Ranson conclusively identify the ventromedial hypothalamus as the main area of the hypothalamus concerned in hunger regulation.[3] In a large number of species, damage to this area resulted in extreme obesity. This obese condition later was termed *hyperphagia,* which literally means "overeating." Rats with lesions in their ventromedial hypothalamus eat gross amounts, finally attaining a body weight two or three times normal. Then they eat enough to maintain this very high weight. Theorists speculated that the ventromedial hypothalamus was a "satiation center." When this area was damaged, the animal no longer had the means to detect satiation, and therefore it overate.

In 1951 Anand and Brobeck discovered that the lateral hypothalamus seemed to function in a manner exactly opposite to the ventromedial area.[4] Damage to the lateral areas stopped an animal's eating. The animal would starve to death even if it was sitting on a pile of food. This area was called the *excitatory area,* or "feeding center." Leibowitz (1970) has presented evidence that the lateral and ventromedial centers are interconnected in such a way that through their

[3]*Ventral* means "toward the front of the body" (literally, "toward the belly"). *Medial* means "toward the middle." Hence the ventromedial hypothalamus is the front, central portion of the hypothalamus.
[4]*Lateral* means "toward the sides."

influence on each other they regulate an animal's hunger motivation precisely. (Stellar, 1954, was the first to suggest that the ventromedial satiation center and the lateral excitatory center regulate hunger through mutual inhibition.)

The question remained, however, exactly how this regulation takes place. A likely way for the hypothalamic centers to control hunger would be to somehow monitor nutrients in the blood. Should nutrients become scarce, hunger would be aroused. Investigators began tampering with the amount of blood sugar (glucose) to determine whether it affected hypothalamic activity and hunger. Soon it was suggested that the hypothalamic centers were monitoring not the absolute amount of glucose but instead the difference in glucose level between arterial blood and venous blood. Arteries carry blood and its nutrients to capillaries, where the nutrients are exchanged for waste products. Veins carry this blood back to the heart. When there is much more glucose in arterial blood than in venous blood, that means the arterial blood must still contain nutrients available for cell use. When the glucose levels in arterial and venous blood are the same, the nutritional reservoir must be empty; it is at such times that hunger occurs.

There is increasing evidence to support the *glucostatic hypothesis*—the hypothesis that hunger is largely controlled by hypothalamic monitoring of glucose levels, probably the difference between arterial and venous glucose levels. For example, Anand, Dua, and Singh (1961) have shown that altering blood-sugar levels affects electrical activity in the excitatory and inhibitory areas in the hypothalamus.

Although the glucostatic hypothesis has received considerable support, it appears that hypothalamic monitoring of arterial/venous glucose differences is responsible only for short-term hunger motivation. In other words, should the "glucostat" indicate a need for nutrition, hunger occurs. The body's long-term nutritional needs, however, are met by using stored fat, not stored glucose. Therefore, monitoring of fatty acids in the blood has been suggested as a means of regulating long-term needs. That the hypothalamus monitors fats is known as the *lipostatic hypothesis* (Kennedy, 1952–1953). J. Mayer (1955), who proposed the glucostatic hypothesis, believes that the two hypotheses are perfectly compatible, one explaining the body's response to short-term needs (daily hunger motivation), the other, its response to long-term needs (regulation of gross body weight).

**Alternate theories.** The glucostatic hypothesis has unquestionably been the most influential theory of hunger motivation. If this book had been written in the early 1970s, we would not even have mentioned any alternatives. In the last decade, however, a number of pieces of evidence have arisen which suggest that the monitoring of glucose by the ventromedial or lateral hypothalamic centers may not be the total explanation for hunger. First, a number of investigators have found that infusing glucose into the ventromedial hypothalamus does not reduce food intake (for example, Panksepp & Nance, 1972). Second, damage to brain areas outside the hypothalamus has profound effects on level of food intake (S. P. Grossman & Grossman, 1973). Third, some investigators (see Novin, 1976) have found evidence that glucoreceptors may exist in the gastrointestinal tract. None of these findings are consistent with our present understanding of the glucostatic hypothesis.

Because of these troublesome findings, alternate theories of hunger have begun to emerge. Stricker and Zigmond (1976) have suggested that lesions in the lateral hypothalamus do not affect hunger motivation per se. Such lesions merely lower the animal's general arousal level so very far that normal nutritional needs are not enough to goad the animal to eat. S. P. Grossman (1966) hypothesized that ventromedial lesions merely cause increased sensitivity to hedonic properties such as taste. Indeed, as we shall elaborate later, hyperphagic rats will eat immense amounts of palatable food but will ignore slightly less delicious foods. This suggests that hedonic properties are crucial to hyperphagic rats.

Perhaps the most promising alternative to the hypothalamic-glucostat hypothesis is one advocated by Russek (1971) and Friedman and Stricker (1976). These theorists note that the liver is prominently involved in the breakdown and delivery of metabolic fuels to the rest of the body. Therefore, these theorists suggest, the liver in its normal functioning would be ideally suited to provide information to the brain regarding metabolic needs. According to this viewpoint, then, the triggering mechanism for hunger is located in the liver.

Several pieces of evidence seem to support this theory and to cast doubt on the theory that posits a glucostat in the hypothalamus. First, the brain is not subject to large fluctuations in "fuel" supply. It is to the very best interests of the organism that brain functioning be staunchly defended; therefore, even during fasting the flow of nutrients to the brain is not substantially reduced. As a result, a glucostat located in the hypothalamus would not receive accurate information concerning the nutritional needs of the body. Because the liver, however, is involved in the breakdown of both newly ingested food and previously stored fat, it would be a much more likely place to monitor the body's total nutritional needs. Second, rats with depleted glucose levels can be induced to stop eating after they are provided with nutrients other than glucose. The implication of this fact is that a glucostat cannot be the sole determinant of hunger. If rats will stop eating even though they are low in glucose, we are led to conclude that the total nutritional situation, not just the glucose level, must be considered in assessing hunger motivation. As previously stated, the liver is the organ involved in the orchestration of nutrient metabolism and delivery. Research showing that infusions of glucose into the liver affect the firing of hypothalamic cells (M. Schmitt, 1973) further strengthens the hypothesis that the liver may be the trigger for hunger motivation.

Numerous other theories have also been formulated recently (Novin, Wyrwicka, & Bray, 1976; Powley, 1977), but their usefulness has not yet been established. The reader should be aware, however, that the time-honored explanations of hunger are being seriously challenged.

**Rats and humans.**   Since most research on hypothalamic control of hunger has been done with subhuman animals, psychologists and physiologists were unsure how far this research was applicable to human motivation. Some provocative research by Schachter (1971), Nisbett (1972), and others now indicates that the animal research may be quite applicable indeed.

Schachter began his research program by noting that, unlike normal-weight people, obese people do not regulate their eating behavior according to their internal physiological needs. In one experiment, Schachter, Goldman, and Gordon (1968) asked obese and normal-weight subjects to sample five types of crackers, ostensibly in order to rate the taste characteristics of the crackers. Half of each subject group had missed the meal prior to the experiment; half had not. Schachter et al. simply recorded the number of crackers the subjects ate. Table 2-1 contains the results. Subjects of normal weight ate quite logically.

**TABLE 2-1.** Mean number of crackers eaten as a function of body weight and stomach fullness

|  | Full stomach | Empty stomach |
|---|---|---|
| Normal subjects | 15.32 | 21.89 |
| Obese subjects | 18.65 | 17.89 |

Adapted from "Effects of Fear, Food Deprivation, and Obesity on Eating," by S. Schachter, R. Goldman, and A. Gordon, *Journal of Personality and Social Psychology*, 1968, *10*, 91–97. Copyright 1968 by the American Psychological Association. Reprinted by permission.

Those who had missed the prior meal were hungry. They therefore ate more than those who hadn't skipped a meal. Obese subjects ate the same amount regardless of their internal states. It thus appeared that nonobese people, on the one hand, were more sensitive to their *internal* states than obese people were. Subsequent work by Schachter and others indicated that obese people, on the other hand, were more sensitive to *external* (environmental) cues than normal people were. For example, Decke (1971, reported in Schachter, 1971) provided obese and normal subjects the opportunity to drink a vanilla milk shake, but the milk shakes offered to half the subjects had been laced with bitter quinine. The number of ounces consumed is presented in Table 2-2.

**TABLE 2-2.** Mean ounces of milk shake consumed as a function of body weight and taste

|  | Good taste | Bad taste |
| --- | --- | --- |
| Normal subjects | 10.6 | 6.4 |
| Obese subjects | 13.9 | 2.6 |

Based on data from "Effects of Taste on the Eating Behavior of Normal and Obese Humans," by E. Decke, cited in "Some Extraordinary Facts About Obese Humans and Rats," by S. Schachter, *American Psychologist*, 1971, *26*, 129–144. Copyright 1971 by the American Psychological Association. Reprinted by permission.

Decke's data support the hypothesis that obese subjects are much more sensitive to external cues. Taste, the external cue in this study, influenced the eating behavior of obese subjects almost three times as much as it influenced the behavior of normals.

Schachter has noted that rats with lesions of the ventromedial hypothalamus act much as the obese subjects in Decke's study do. Hyperphagic rats will eat a mountain of regular food but will not touch food that is even slightly stale or distasteful.

Having concluded that both obese humans and hyperphagic rats are finicky eaters, Schachter sought to determine whether obese humans are highly emotional, as are hyperphagic rats. Schachter (1971, p. 134) has summarized the behavior of hyperphagic rats as "hyperexcitable, easily startled, overemotional, and generally bitchy to handle." Rodin (1970) performed a study in which a tape was played while obese and normal subjects did proofreading or monitoring tasks that demanded their close attention. Some tape recordings dealt with neutral topics; others dealt with such emotional issues as a thermonuclear holocaust. The task performance of obese subjects deteriorated much more than that of normal subjects during the arousing tapes. Thus, obese humans, like hyperphagic rats, seem to be quite emotional.

Schachter also found that obese humans, again like hyperphagic rats, will not expend much effort to obtain food. He gave some subjects the opportunity to snack on almonds in the shell; others, almonds already shelled. Obese and normal subjects behaved quite differently (see Table 2-3). About half the normal subjects ate the nuts, whether the nuts had to be shelled or not. However, obese subjects ate the nuts only if little effort was required to obtain them; if they had to shell the nuts, they weren't interested.[5]

---

[5]Nisbett (1972) believes this result has nothing to do with willingness to expend effort. Instead, he hypothesizes that obese people, being emotional, react very negatively to the frustration and delay encountered as they struggle to open the shells.

A very similar experiment was done by Costanzo and Woody (1979). Since a great deal of evidence has shown that overweight children usually maintain their obesity into adulthood, Costanzo and Woody examined children 9 to 11 years of age to see whether the same nut-eating

**TABLE 2-3.** Number of persons eating nuts as a function of body weight and condition of nuts

|  | Nuts in shell | Nuts already shelled |
|---|---|---|
| Normal subjects | | |
| Eating | 10 | 11 |
| Not eating | 10 | 9 |
| Obese subjects | | |
| Eating | 1 | 19 |
| Not eating | 19 | 1 |

Adapted from "Some Extraordinary Facts about Obese Humans and Rats," by S. Schachter, *American Psychologist*, 1971, *26*, 129–144. Copyright 1971 by the American Psychological Association. Reprinted by permission.

result would occur in that age range. Table 2-4 contains the results. Obese youngsters eat seven times as many nuts when the shells are off. To the normal weight youngsters, the presence of the shell makes little difference. Like hyperphagic rats, overweight adults and children are greatly influenced by such external factors as the amount of effort needed to obtain food.

**TABLE 2-4.** Nut consumption (in grams) as a function of body weight and condition of nuts

|  | Normal | Obese |
|---|---|---|
| Shells off | 18.97 | 43.50 |
| Shells on | 11.07 | 6.29 |

Adapted from "Externality as a Function of Obesity in Children: Pervasive Style or Eating-Specific Attribute," by P. R. Costanzo and E. Z. Woody. In *Journal of Personality and Social Psychology*, 1979, *37*, 2286–2296. Copyright 1979 by the American Psychological Association. Reprinted by permission.

Schachter lists many more similarities between obese humans and hyperphagic rats. Although he is unwilling to say that some types of obesity in humans are due to malfunction of the ventromedial hypothalamus, the implication is certainly there. Schachter summarizes his findings by concluding that the eating behavior of normal rats and humans is governed by internal factors (presumably regulated by the hypothalamus) and the eating behavior of obese rats and humans is governed more by external factors.

Nisbett (1972) also believes that some types of obesity in humans may be due to hypothalamic misregulation. Nisbett's hypothesis is quite simple: the hypothalamus acts as a "ponderostat." (Nisbett coined this term from the Latin *ponderis,* "weight"; a ponderostat is a mechanism that monitors changes in weight.) The hypothalamus, then, causes the animal to be hungry whenever the animal's weight falls below a certain level. Obese people have their ponderostats set at an abnormally high level. Therefore they are almost always hungry, since they are constantly "trying" to attain the high weight-setting dictated by their hypothalamic ponderostats. Nisbett presents a large amount of evidence that obese people behave much like hungry, nonobese people on a variety of emotional, sexual, physiological, and behavioral measures. This is to be expected if obese people are constantly below their ponderostat settings, just as hungry, nonobese people are temporarily below their ponderostat settings. Nisbett agrees with Schachter that both the obese person and the hyperphagic rat are overweight because of hypothalamic misregulation. In the former, misregulation is due to an abnormally high ponderostat setting; in the latter, the ponderostat has been surgically demolished.

**Specific hungers.** To this point in our discussion of hunger, we have presented research dealing with motivation toward food *in general.* However, a large amount of recent research has dealt with the question of motivation toward particular foods—foods that contain nutrients crucial to our survival. What motivates us toward these specific foods?

This question has baffled psychologists and physiologists since the early part of this century, when it was shown that lower animals (Evvard, 1916) and human infants (Davis, 1928) would select a proper diet from a cafeteria of choices. How can a 10-month-old infant know what's good for her? Equally enigmatic are the anecdotal cases of children with calcium deficiency who nibble on calcium-rich chalk during school. Does chalk taste good to such children?

One line of research designed to answer these questions has examined motivation toward sodium-rich foods following deprivation of that critical substance. Since the mechanism responsible for "sodium-hunger" appears to be different from the mechanism responsible for other specific hungers, we will treat the sodium case separately.

Richter (1942) showed that animals deprived of sodium will display a marked preference for sodium-rich foods over sodium-deficient foods. Since sodium deprivation will eventually be fatal, the sodium preference exhibited by the animals was obviously highly adaptive. Kalat and Rozin (1971) and other investigators have suggested that sodium-deprived animals are *innately* attracted to the taste of sodium. A study by Krieckhaus (1970) provides some evidence. Rats that had never experienced any sodium deficiency were deprived of water and placed in a T-maze. In one arm of the maze was water; in the other was a sodium solution. Half of the animals were trained to choose water; the others to choose the sodium solution. Following this training, all of the animals were made sodium-deficient and then placed back in the maze with no liquid available. Krieckhaus found that the animals previously trained on the sodium solution continued to run to that arm longer than the water-trained animals ran to the other arm. We would expect this result if sodium deprivation automatically increased preference for sodium solutions. Note that, since the animals had never been sodium-deprived before the experiment, there had been no prior opportunity for them to learn that sodium alleviates the symptoms of sodium deficiency. Thus the study supports the view that sodium preference in sodium-deprived animals is innate.

A different mechanism is thought to be responsible for specific hungers other than sodium. For example, Harris, Clay, Hargreaves, and Ward (1933) showed that, if thiamine-deficient rats are given a thiamine-rich food for several days and then exposed to several different foods, the rats will prefer the thiamine-rich diet. This result occurs not only with thiamine but also with many other crucial nutrients, even though none of the nutrients has a distinctive taste of its own. How do the animals learn to eat these foods to alleviate their deficiencies?

A clue to the solution of this mystery appeared in the 1960s, thanks to the research of Garcia and his colleagues. In one study (Garcia, Ervin, Yorke, & Koelling, 1967), thiamine-deficient rats were allowed to drink saccharine-flavored water and were then given thiamine injections 30 minutes later. Garcia found that such animals drastically increased their subsequent drinking of the saccharine-flavored water. The beneficial effects of thiamine apparently reinforced drinking of the saccharine solution. This study showed that for a special group of behaviors the reward (thiamine) need not follow immediately after the rewarded behavior (saccharine-solution drinking) for the association between them to be formed. This was an important finding for two reasons. First, it had previously been thought that learning would occur only when the reward closely followed the behavior. Second, the study showed that, although the benefits of thiamine might not be felt for quite some time, these benefits could still result in an increase in the intake of the food that had preceded the beneficial effects.

Subsequent work by Garcia (Garcia, Hawkins, & Rusiniak, 1974; Green & Garcia, 1971) uncovered the principle that pertained not only to "thiamine-hunger" but also to hunger for many other specific nutrients. First, rats who are made very ill by x-rays or by a poison will avoid whatever harmless food they ate before they became ill. This explains "bait shyness": Sheep farmers often put out some poisoned rabbit meat in the hopes of killing the coyotes who terrorize the flock; unfortunately for the farmer, those coyotes who survive the poison will never again go near other poisoned rabbit bait. As Garcia showed, animals will subsequently avoid whatever food was eaten before the onset of a sickness. Second, Garcia found that animals will show increased intake of a food that precedes the onset of recuperation from illness! In one study (Green & Garcia, 1971) some rats were given grape juice before illness and milk before recuperation. Subsequently the rats avoided grape juice and increased their milk intake. Other rats were given milk before illness and grape juice before recuperation. These rats later preferred grape juice and avoided milk.

The relation of the Garcia et al. studies to thiamine-hunger and other specific hungers is straightforward. If some food containing the missing nutrient is eaten, recuperation will occur. Animals learn to associate the taste of that food with recuperation, even though the recuperation does not begin instantly. This results in an increase in the intake of the "medicinal" food, thereby eliminating the deficiency. Apparently, chalk does taste good to calcium-deficient children.

## Smoking

Cigarette smoking is a highly motivated behavior among heavy smokers—so much so that such people collectively spend millions of dollars each year on various products and programs designed to help them stop performing this highly motivated activity. Yet the large majority of such "quitters" resume smoking within one year. Schachter (1977) and his colleagues have recently suggested that one of the main principles of hunger motivation may also apply to smoking behavior. Recall that Schachter proposed that normal-weight people attend to internal hunger cues and obese people attend predominantly to external cues. Schachter now suggests that heavy smokers are addicted to nicotine and therefore rather carefully regulate the amount of this chemical in their system. To do this they must attend to internal cues that tell them how much nicotine is already in their system and how much more, if any, is needed. On the other hand, light smokers attend to external cues, as do obese people. They smoke for reasons other than maintaining a homeostatic level. Therefore, external cues, such as the visibility of a pack of cigarettes, should influence these people.

These principles are illustrated in a clever study by Herman (1974). Light smokers and heavy smokers participated in a manual task that prevented any cigarette smoking for a half hour. Then one-third of the members of each group were offered a high-nicotine cigarette, one-third were offered a low-nicotine cigarette, and one-third were given no cigarette. In this way the experimenter was able to vary the amount of nicotine in the subjects by preloading them with a cigarette of known nicotine content. After the manual task and the preload cigarette, each group was again divided. Half of the subjects relaxed where a high-intensity lamp illuminated some nearby cigarettes (high salience) while the other half of the subjects relaxed where the nearby cigarettes were not illuminated (low salience). Herman measured how long each subject waited before grabbing one of the nearby cigarettes. The data are presented in Table 2-5. The light smokers were influenced more by the external cue of salience than they were by the amount of nicotine in their system. The heavy smokers, however, were much more sensitive to the internal cue of nicotine preload than they were to the external cue of salience.

The sensitivity of heavy smokers to internal cues helps to explain several other facts concerning cigarette smoking among such people. For example, heavy smokers increase their smoking behavior during stressful situations. The reason for this increase is that stress causes the urine to become more acidic, and high-acidity urine absorbs more nicotine than low-acidity urine. Thus, heavy smokers excrete more nicotine from their system in stressful situations than they do in nonstressful situations. Because heavy smokers carefully regulate the amount of nicotine in their system, they must increase their smoking in stressful situations to restore the amount of nicotine they are losing through excretion. As Schachter points out, at least part of the mind of a smoker is in the bladder.

### Thirst

The search for the physiological bases of thirst motivation has followed much the same path as the search for those of hunger motivation. Again, three types of theories have been proposed—local, general, and central.

Albrecht von Haller (1803) proposed a local theory of thirst, which complemented his local theory of hunger: thirst was caused by dryness in the tongue and alimentary canal. In 1918 Cannon also proposed a local theory of thirst. When the body's supply of water dwindled, salivation would be reduced, resulting in a dry throat. This unpleasant condition could be relieved by drinking.

**TABLE 2-5.** Pause before lighting up the first cigarette (measured in minutes)

| | Light smokers | | Heavy smokers | |
|---|---|---|---|---|
| Preload | Low salience | High salience | Low salience | High salience |
| None | 11.0 | 1.9 | 0.5 | 1.1 |
| Low nicotine | 15.0 | 5.3 | 7.4 | 9.0 |
| High nicotine | 18.8 | 8.0 | 9.8 | 9.2 |

Adapted from "External and Internal Cues as Determinants of the Smoking Behavior of Light and Heavy Smokers," by C. P. Herman. In *Journal of Personality and Social Psychology*, 1974, *30*, 664–672. Copyright 1974 by the American Psychological Association. Reprinted by permission.

As with hunger, local theories of thirst were discredited. For example, Bellows and Van Wagenen (1939) severed the nerves of the mouth region in dogs. The animals could no longer detect any dryness in the mouth, but they exhibited normal drinking behavior. Furthermore, when a dog's esophagus is severed and the upper segment diverted outside the body, so that water swallowed does not enter the stomach, the animal will drink enormous amounts. This unsuccessful attempt to replenish the body's water supply continues long after the throat area has been thoroughly moistened (Bellows, 1939).

While local theories of thirst have been rejected as total explanations of thirst motivation, this does not mean that a dry mouth cannot motivate drinking. The discomfort of a dry throat can be eliminated by moisture, but the majority of the body's water-regulatory processes are not triggered by dryness in the mouth region. For this reason, drinking motivated solely by a dry mouth is often termed "nonregulatory."

Dumas (1803) proposed a general theory of thirst similar to his theory of hunger: the lack of water in the blood irritates the entire vascular system, and drinking alleviates the discomfort. A. Mayer (1900) hypothesized that the osmotic pressure of the blood regulated thirst. If the blood was more dilute than the fluid in the body's cells, then, by osmosis, water would pass from the blood into the cells. If the cells contained fluid more dilute than the blood, water would pass from the cells into the blood. Wettendorff (1901, cited in Rosenzweig, 1962) hypothesized that it was the osmotic pressure of the fluid surrounding body cells, not the blood, that was critical. Both Mayer and Wettendorff maintained that information about changes in osmotic pressure, detected by receptors throughout the body, was somehow relayed to the brain.

As happened with hunger, the central theory of thirst became dominant following advances in brain-surgery technique. Bailey and Bremer (1921) demonstrated that hypothalamic lesions cause extraordinary amounts of drinking. As work on the physiology of thirst continued, it became apparent that the body's primary means of regulating water intake and outflow is secretion of the antidiuretic hormone (ADH), which is synthesized in the hypothalamus. The hormone then travels to the pituitary, enters the bloodstream, and finally circulates through the body, eventually reaching the kidneys (Bargmann & Scharrer, 1951). ADH then inhibits water loss from the body by causing the kidneys to reabsorb water from the urine before excretion.

Verney (1947) detected some cells in a dog's hypothalamus that provided a clue as to how hypothalamic ADH secretion is triggered, and his central theory was somewhat similar to A. Mayer's general theory (1900). The Verney theory states that certain cells in the hypothalamus, called *osmoreceptors*, are particularly sensitive to dehydration. As these cells lose water, their shriveling causes them to fire, just as light

causes rods and cones in the eye to fire. The firing of these osmoreceptors results in the release of ADH, which in turn retards water loss
(Ishikawa, Koizumi, & Brooks, 1966). Simultaneously, the hypothalamus conveys information to the cortex, which initiates drinking behavior.

This elegant research performed by Verney was done in the
mid-1940s. Subsequent work, however, has shown that, although Verney's theory is partially correct, the regulation of thirst in humans is
substantially more complex than he originally hypothesized.

Two systems actually regulate thirst motivation. The first is the osmoregulatory system, which is composed of osmoreceptors in the anterior hypothalamus and in the posterior hypothalamus.[6] Activation of
the osmoreceptors in the anterior area results in release of ADH,
which in turn results in water conservation (Andersson, Olsson, &
Warner, 1967), as explained before. However, activation of this anterior area does not cause an increase in drinking; that activity is regulated by the posterior region. Activation of the posterior area, however,
results in an increase in drinking but has no effect on the secretion of
ADH. Thus, the osmoregulatory system divides its "responsibilities":
one part conserves fluids already in the system; the other part regulates
acquisition of more fluid.

The second system controlling thirst motivation is that of volume
regulation. Extreme thirst results when sufficient blood volume has
been lost, even if the concentration of the blood does not change. The
body's volume regulatory system, like its osmoregulatory system, has
two parts. First, when blood loss occurs, renin is released from the
kidneys. Renin reacts with angiotensinogen in the blood to form angiotensin II, which has several functions. These include preserving the
body's sodium; promoting the secretion of ADH, which preserves the
body's water; and stimulating drinking behavior, which replaces lost
fluid. Second, receptors in the heart and large veins detect changes in
blood volume and then initiate blood-pressure modification and ADH
secretion (Stricker, 1973).

In summary, the regulation of thirst appears to be more complex
than the regulation of hunger. The fact that changes in either blood
concentration or blood volume can initiate thirst and the fact that a
large number of hormones play crucial roles in the system make thirst
regulation an intricate process.

## Sleep

Since the average person spends nearly one-third of his or her life
asleep, the motivation to sleep must obviously be a powerful instinct. In

---

[6]The exact location of this second region is still a matter of debate (Almli & Weiss,
1974; Blass & Epstein, 1971; Simpson & Routtenberg, 1973). The osmoreceptors in
the anterior region, however, are located in the supraoptic nuclei.

trying to identify the physiological basis of this instinct, sleep researchers in the modern era began with investigation of the *reticular formation,* a diffuse structure that extends from the medulla up to the thalamus (see Figure 2-3). Pathways from the reticular formation extend upward into the cortex. Moruzzi and Magoun (1949) discovered that the system largely responsible for alertness lies within the reticular formation. Through its fibers extending into the cortex, the *ascending reticular activating system* centered in the reticular formation can regulate the alertness of many regions of the cortex. Lesions in this system produce a comatose state, and activation of this area in a sleeping animal produces instant alertness. Although the hypothalamus in the last 20 years also has been strongly implicated in the control of alertness (Feldman & Waller, 1962), the reticular formation is still considered to play an important role in this function.

The major technique used by researchers to index alertness is the electroencephalogram (EEG). Electrodes placed on the scalp and forehead are used to monitor electrical activity in the brain. (Figure 2-4 shows EEG recordings made during various states of human wakefulness and sleep.) During wakefulness the EEG "brain waves" are short, choppy, and fast, and many waves occur in a given period of time. As the person becomes drowsy and lapses into sleep, however, the waves get taller and much slower. At approximately 90-minute intervals during sleep, a person experiences a stage called "active sleep," or "REM sleep." (REM stands for rapid eye movement.) During this stage of sleep, the eyes move rapidly under the closed eyelids, and the brain waves appear very much like those occurring during wakefulness. Perhaps the most intriguing facet of REM sleep is that those awakened during such periods are more likely to report dreaming than those awakened during "quiet sleep," or "slow wave sleep" (SWS). Some early theorists thought that people were motivated to sleep because it was necessary to dream. They suggested that a period of fantasy was needed for normal mental functioning. This idea was encouraged by the "rebound effect": If a person is deprived of REM sleep one night by being awakened every time the EEG speeds up, then that person will spend an abnormally large amount of time in REM sleep the following night. However, the motive-to-dream explanation has fallen on hard times. Under limited-sleep regimens, the amount of SWS remains constant but the amount of REM sleep declines (Greenberg, 1966). Horne (1976) showed that the priority for SWS rebound is greater than that for REM rebound following total sleep deprivation. Also, REM sleep has been found in an enormous number of warm-blooded animals. Does a pig have a "need" to dream? In short, there is little support for the notion that people need sleep because they need to dream.

The more scientific theories concerning sleep include an influential one by Jouvet (1967), which has not, however, met with total accep-

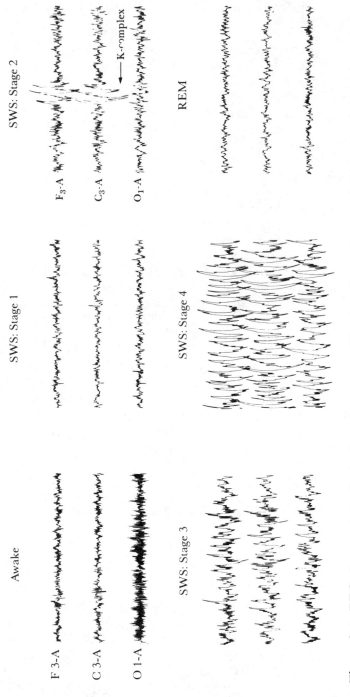

**Figure 2-4.** EEG characteristics for various sleep stages. The three lines of the tracings show electrical activity from frontal, central, and occipital regions of the cortex. (From "Are Stages of Sleep Related to Waking Behavior?" by L. C. Johnson. In American Scientist, 1973, 61, 326–338. Reprinted by permission, American Scientist, journal of Sigma Xi, The Scientific Research Society of North America.)

tance (Wyatt, 1972). Jouvet proposed that the raphe nuclei in the pons release serotonin, which in turn affects the reticular formation. The resulting decrease in the activity of the reticular formation brings on SWS.

**Purpose of sleep.**    Hunger and thirst are two motives whose presence leads to behaviors crucial for survival. Without food or water, no animal could survive; the overwhelming motivating properties of hunger and thirst are therefore highly adaptive. The motivation to sleep can also be overwhelming. After being awake for 16 to 18 hours, continued wakefulness becomes highly aversive. Yet physiologists and psychologists are hard pressed to discover why sleep has evolved in such a large number of animals. We are therefore very highly motivated to participate daily in a behavior that has no apparent benefit other than the relief of the symptoms that cause it.

A common belief is that sleep allows the body to rest and recuperate from the day's strenuous behavior. However, Horne and Porter (1976) have shown that no increase in SWS occurs when a person has engaged in more exercise than usual. (No one suggests that REM sleep is a recuperative period, because many bodily indices are highly elevated during REM sleep.)

Other researchers point out that more growth hormone is released during sleep, but Quabbe (1977) points out that this occurs only in certain primates, whereas sleep occurs in all primates, as well as many other animals. Also, Horne (1979) maintains that there is negligible support for the contention that the growth hormone is released to restore body tissue or to synthesize protein.

The theories that posit bodily recuperation during sleep are called *body-restitution hypotheses,* and support for them is very weak. Body restitution could be accomplished quite well by short rest periods; an 8-hour period of unconsciousness would seem to be unnecessary.

A second viewpoint is called the *brain-restitution hypothesis.* Advocates of this viewpoint can cite evidence that memory consolidation in the brain may occur during sleep, particularly during REM sleep (Fishbein & Gutwein, 1977), although the evidence is new and therefore rather fragmentary (Albert, 1975). Related evidence comes from Laborit (1972), who found increased synthesis of important central-nervous-system proteins during sleep. It can be said that the brain-restitution hypothesis is faring much better than the body-restitution hypothesis, but the evidence is not conclusive.

The third hypothesis is the most unusual. Put forth by Meddis (1977), Snyder and Washburn (1966), and Webb (1971), this proposal may be called the *evolutionary hypothesis:* Animals typically have one portion of the day/night cycle during which they are more vulnerable. The vision of many animals, for example, is very acute during either night or day but poor during the other period. Should these animals be wandering about during the period of poor vision, they would be unable to locate food and, worse yet, unable to see predators. Thus, it is maladaptive for animals to waste calories in looking for food during the period of poor vision or to provide calories for their predators by roaming about during this vulnerable period. Animals who exhibited such foolhardy behaviors have been eradicated; animals who became immobilized during their vulnerable period have survived. These latter animals are the ones from whom we have evolved. Therefore, we have inherited their biological "clocks." We feel an overwhelming urge to sleep during our more vulnerable portion of the day/night cycle.

A startling corollary of the evolutionary hypothesis, however, is the idea that sleep is totally obsolete for humans! Indeed, there are humans who get almost no sleep and are in perfect mental and physical health (Meddis, 1977). Not sleeping has no drawbacks and many advantages for these people. For animals, however, it is just the reverse: not sleeping has many drawbacks and no advantages.

Several other facts appear consistent with the evolutionary hypothesis. For example, the young members of a species typically sleep much more than the mature members. Since the young are particularly helpless, especially in higher animals, their immobilization for long periods of time frees the caretaker for food gathering and other crucial behaviors. Some species of birds, for example, fly to polar regions during their nesting periods. The longer daylight hours there provide them the opportunity to gather food for the immature young. Thus, the evolutionary hypothesis suggests that sleep is very adaptive for nonhuman animals and that it probably once was adaptive for humans. Now that we have artificial light, however, sleep has become an outmoded behavior we must perform daily. It remains a powerful motivating force— our eyes feel sore, our eyelids become heavy, and our limbs feel leaden—although the reason for it has disappeared.

## Sex

Speculation about human sexual motivation has generated several theories, little knowledge, and a lot of poetry. Several factors make this particular motivation difficult to research.

First, ethical concerns prevent many types of experimentation. Second, a great deal of evidence suggests qualitative differences between human sexual motivation and sexual motivation of lower animals. Thus, generalization from experiments done with lower animals is not always advisable. Third, as Beach (1956) points out, sexual motivation differs in several ways from other motivations, again limiting the extent to which motivational findings in other areas can be applied to human sexual motivation. For example, no animal can survive without food and water, but an individual (not the species) can survive without sex. For another example, eating or drinking restores the body and replaces nutrients, but sexual activity causes a loss of energy.

As might be expected, local theories were among the first proposed to account for the physiological basis of sexual motivation. Tarchanoff (1887) and Nissen (1929) believed that uncomfortable tensions in the genital area motivated sexual release. The tensions were caused by uncomfortably distended vesicles, for example. However, these local theories were discredited in much the same way as local theories of hunger and thirst. Severing of nerves to the genital area or even castration does not necessarily abolish sexual arousal (Money, 1961). Therefore, local theories of sexual motivation must be incomplete, although this certainly does not mean genital sensations play no role in sexual motivation.

Like hunger and thirst, sexual motivation has been traced to the influence of the hypothalamus. The gonadotropic center in the hypothalamus regulates the secretion by the anterior pituitary of gonadotropic hormones. These hormones enter the bloodstream and affect the gonads (ovaries or testes). The gonads then secrete gonadal hormones—estrogen and progesterone by the ovaries; testosterone, or androgen, by the testes. These hormones are crucial to the occurrence of primary sexual behavior, particularly in nonhuman species.

**Hormonal influences in the female.**   In all mammals except humans, females will copulate only during the hormonally induced state called "estrus," which occurs around the time of ovulation. (The highest apes are a partial exception in that females are somewhat willing to copulate at other times.) The female's hypothalamus secretes follicle-stimulating hormone (FSH), which causes one of the follicles in her ovary to grow and an egg to mature inside it. As the follicle grows, it produces estrogen. Eventually the follicle ruptures, releasing the egg ready for fertilization. The ruptured follicle produces progesterone, which, in conjunction with the estrogen, radically influences the female's behavior. The female who would resist sexual advances by a potential mate at other times will, during estrus, become extremely receptive to such advances: she adopts precopulatory behaviors and copulatory postures, which facilitate impregnation. An anestrous female can be made estrous by injection of estrogen, or in some species, estrogen and progesterone. Thus, hormones are absolutely critical for the performance of sexual activity in almost all female mammals.

The major exception to this rule is the human female, whose sexual receptivity does not vary markedly during the menstrual cycle, as the receptivity of lower mammals does during the estrous cycle. Udry and Morris (1968) did find, however, that in two samples of American women, intercourse was more likely to occur near ovulation than at any other time during the menstrual cycle. Nonetheless, abundant evidence exists that sexual arousal and behavior in human females can take place in the absence of the usual levels of estrogen and progesterone. Two examples of this evidence should suffice. First, W. H. Masters and Johnson (1966) document the fact that postmenopausal women, whose hormonal levels are greatly reduced, usually do not report a decrease in sexual motivation. Second, Ford and Beach (1951, p. 224) document the story of a woman who had both ovaries removed. In the years following the operation, her typical pattern of sexual activity involved an hour and a half of coitus, during which she had five or six orgasms. The important point illustrated by these examples is that satisfactory sexual activity can occur in the human female in the absence of ovaries and their hormones. Removal of the ovaries in lower mammals, however, abolishes all sexual activity. Ford and Beach emphasize that the sexual behavior of animals higher in the phylogenetic scale is progressively less subject to hormonal control, and the fact that estrogen administered to human females has no discernible effect on sexual motivation is evidence for this assertion.

One hormone, however—androgen—does appear to influence female sexual motivation. The testes of the male and the adrenal glands of both sexes produce androgen. Waxenberg, Drellich, and Sutherland (1959) report that, although removal of the ovaries has no effect on female sexual motivation, removal of the ovaries and the adrenals strongly reduces it. Money (1961) mentions several studies showing that androgen increases genital sensitivity and sexual motivation in the human female. From these facts Money concludes that in humans "the sex drive appears from the hormonal point of view to be neither male nor female, but undifferentiated—an urge for the warmth and sensation of close body contact and genital proximity" (p. 246). We shall return to this important conclusion later in the chapter.

**Hormonal influences in the male.**   Sexual behavior of male mammals, like that of females, depends progressively less on hormonal influences as the phylogenetic scale is ascended. Removal of the testes in lower mammals substantially reduces sexual behavior, although the reduction may not occur immediately, but the later in life castration takes place, the less severe will be its effects on sexual behavior. Castration in the human male, however, has quite variable effects. Some men report no diminution in sexual motivation or behavior for decades after the castration; others do report a diminution.

Administration of androgen to castrated lower mammalian males completely restores sexual behavior, just as administration of estrogen to analogous females restores their behavior. Androgen given to human males with low androgen levels does increase sexual behavior in general, and impairment of male sexual motivation due to castration can be remedied by administration of androgen. Males who are hormonally normal, however, show no effects when additional androgen is administered (Heller & Maddock, 1947). Money (1961) states that androgen injections can influence sexual behavior if the male is deficient in androgen; if no deficiency exists, the hormone will be without effect. In other words, "Once an optimal level of circulating hormone has been reached, the control of sexual desire is strictly nonhormonal" (p. 241). Evidence shows, for example, that sexually more aggressive people do not have a greater hormone level than sexually less aggressive people, and homosexuals do not have a different hormonal constellation than heterosexuals (Money, 1975). Administration of androgen to male homosexuals does not promote heterosexuality; it either has no effect or intensifies the homosexual behavior. This supports Money's contention that "the sex drive appears from the hormonal point of view to be neither male nor female, but undifferentiated" (1961, p. 246).

Ford and Beach (1951) discuss at some length the topic of hormonal effects on sex drive. They concur with Money that hormones may intensify a drive but not determine the target toward which the sexual behavior is directed. Hence, there is no reason to expect a homosexual to become heterosexual after hormones are administered. As we shall discuss later in the chapter, experience, habit, and other nonhormonal factors play an enormous role in human sexual behavior. Hormones do not dominate human sexual behavior to the same extent as they do the sexual behavior of lower animals.

**Hormones and sexual differentiation.**   We have just seen that androgen is influential in regulating the sex drive of both males and females. Since adrenal glands in both sexes produce androgen, the differences between male and female sexual behavior may depend partially on differences in neural structure, rather than on differences in postpubertal hormonal composition. Yet even neural organization has been shown to depend on hormones—specifically, the hormones present while the fetus is developing. For example, some girls born to mothers receiving androgen therapy during pregnancy have masculine external genitals (Wilkins, Jones, Holman, & Stempfel, 1958). Phoenix, Goy, Gerall, and Young (1959) injected androgen into pregnant guinea pigs. Offspring with the female chromosome pattern had male genitalia. The gonads were then removed from these animals so that their response to gonadal hormones of both sexes, undistorted by any influence from their own gonadal hormones, could be assessed. These animals displayed little female sexual behavior when injected with estrogen and progesterone, but they did display male sexual behavior when given androgen. So even though hormones can only activate behavior whose direction is already fixed in the adult, they can govern the type of neural circuitry being formed in the developing embryo. If enough androgen is present during gestation, chromosomally female offspring will show male sexual behavior when given androgen.

Milner (1970) points out that these studies leave open the possibility that both female and male neural circuits are present in both sexes. The presence of a high level of androgen while the fetus is developing makes the male circuits easier to fire; the absence of it makes the female circuits easier to fire. A study by Roberts, Steinberg, and Means (1967), showing that female opossums could demonstrate male sexual behavior during electrical brain stimulation, lends credence to the possibility that both circuits are available.

We have seen that sex hormones have at least two functions for sexual behavior. First, in adults, they can activate behavior: androgen can increase sexual behavior in either sex. Second, in fetuses, they affect neural circuitry: prenatal exposure to androgen determines whether an individual, at maturity, will react to androgen by exhibiting male sexual behavior. Thus, hormones play a primary role in sexual behavior.

**Neural involvement in sexual behavior.**    Neural involvement is also critical in sexual behavior, especially in humans. Many aspects of human sexual behavior are mediated by the spinal cord. Evidence that the brain is not involved in some aspects of sexual activity includes the fact that men whose spinal cords are severed from the brain are nevertheless capable of erections and emissions (Ford & Beach, 1951), and stimulation of the genitals of such men results in involuntary pelvic thrusts. Because the cord is cut, there can be no involvement of the cortex in this sexual activity.

Such findings show that the spinal cord can control these sexual activities. It is true, nevertheless, that the cerebral cortex plays an increasingly important role in the regulation of sexual activity as the phylogenetic scale is ascended. Cortical involvement replaces the hormonal control that is almost total in lower species but which is somewhat relaxed in higher mammals, particularly humans. Complete removal of the cortex does not abolish normal mating behavior in the male rabbit, for example, but it does so in male rats, cats, dogs, and other higher animals. It also appears that male sexual behavior may be more dependent on cortical control than female behavior, since decorticate female rats, cats, and dogs can mate but decorticate males cannot (Beach, 1958). Most theorists believe that the reason for this is that in most mammals the male takes a more active role during mating than the female. Since destruction of the cortex causes great sensorimotor deficits, the sexual behavior of the male would be more affected by such deficits than would the behavior of the female (S. P. Grossman, 1967, p. 473).

The species with the largest cortex and the most cortical involvement in sexual behavior is our own. Consequently, sexual behavior is much less stereotyped in the human species than in any other. Ford and Beach (1951) summarize this point:

> It is to be expected . . . that a high degree of cortical development will be associated with more variable behavior and with more easily modified inherited behavioral tendencies. Because all complex human behavior is heavily dependent upon cortical processes it is automatically open to modification through the influences of previous experience. This explains why in human beings more than in any other species, sexuality is structured and patterned by learning [p. 255].

**Learning and early experience.**    Because higher primates are less bound by hormonal influences, the roles of learning and early experience are quite substantial. Harlow (1965) has shown, for example, that young male and female rhesus monkeys have substantially different play patterns. The males exhibit infantile sexual responses more often than the females. When another monkey approaches, males much more frequently perform a threat response, females a withdrawal response. This withdrawal response includes orienting the head away from the approaching monkey. Females also are more likely to exhibit rigidity—stiffening of the posture—when another monkey approaches. Finally, males are more likely to participate in "rough and tumble" play than females. It is Harlow's opinion that these sex differences are necessary for the development of normal heterosexual behavior in adult monkeys. For example, the infantile sexual responses performed by young monkeys include pelvic thrusts by the males directed toward virtually any body part of a playmate of either sex. The playmate may be in any posture. With age, however, as the behavior of young males and females continues to differentiate, the female is more likely to perform a withdrawal or rigidity response, thus exposing the proper area to the male's pelvic thrusts. Thus, the immature behavior of the monkeys, although more playful than procreative in nature, does begin to resemble adult heterosexual behavior.

Several experiments have shown that monkeys raised in isolation are sexually inept at maturity (Harlow, 1965; W. A. Mason, 1960; Nissen, 1954). Being deprived of contact with mothers and peers makes rhesus monkeys incapable of adequate sexual relations (and affective relations of any kind). Zingg (1940) has noted that human males raised in isolation or near-isolation also are uninterested in sexual activity. However, both Harlow and Zingg report that monkeys and humans raised in isolation appear excited when in the presence of a member of the opposite sex. Early social experience, then, seems crucial to adult sexual behavior, although it may not be crucial to sexual arousal.

**Culture.**    A second important influence on adult sexual behavior is culture. Cultural differences in sexual behavior are enormous: differences in types of sexual stimulation, tolerance of homosexual behavior, circumstances for sexual behavior, characteristics of preferred sexual partners, and so on. For example, Ford and Beach (1951) point out that grooming or delousing one's potential sexual partner is considered very sexually arousing in some cultures. Many cultures consider kissing to be sexually stimulating, whereas others consider it repugnant. The members of some societies consider aggression before and during coitus to be highly arousing, and others consider sexual foreplay disgusting. A thorough reading of Ford and Beach's *Patterns of Sexual Behavior* (1951), in which the varied sexual practices of 190 societies are reviewed, will convince anyone that most human sexual behavior is learned, not innate.

**Pornography.**    A third possible influence on human sexual behavior is discussed in the following quotation:

> Pornography is intended to arouse the sexual appetite—one of the most volatile appetites of human nature. Once that appetite is aroused, it will seek satisfaction—and the satisfaction sought—without proper moral restraints—is often reflected in the social statistics [on increases in illegitimacy and venereal disease] [Keating, 1970, p. 617].

The author of this passage was a member of the Commission on Obscenity and Pornography, which was created by President Johnson and maintained by President Nixon. Obviously, Keating believes pornography motivates sexual behavior. What is the evidence on this controversial subject?

The Commission's research examined both physiological responses and overt behavioral responses to erotic stimuli. Two studies showed that a majority of males and females responded to erotic films with physiological arousal. Which erotic stimuli were most arousing differed between the two sexes and between individuals (Mann, Sidman, & Starr, 1970; Mosher, 1970). Recent research (W. A. Fisher & Byrne, 1978) confirms another of the Commission's findings: males and females were approximately equally responsive to scenes depicting heterosexual activity.

These findings are less than surprising. N. E. Miller (1948), Estes (Estes & Skinner, 1941), and others have been investigating for many years the effects of stimuli associated with primary reinforcers. In general, such a stimulus acquires some of the properties of the primary reinforcer (see Chapter 5). If intercourse is considered a primary reinforcer, then watching others engage in intercourse should be arousing, albeit less arousing than actually engaging in intercourse.

The Commission's findings about the effects of erotic stimuli on sexual behavior were also expected. Basically, viewing erotic films and slides caused a temporary increase in frequency of masturbation among those with established masturbatory patterns and in frequency of coitus among those who had sexual partners available. Such increases in frequency of behavior dissipated after 48 hours. New patterns of sexual activity or modifications of existing sexual activity rarely resulted. By far the greatest change in the behavior of married couples was that they felt more open in discussing sexuality (Commission on Obscenity, 1970, Part 3, Chapter 2, Section C).

In summary, erotica were arousing to a substantial proportion of the population, and they caused a transitory increase in frequency of the sexual behavior within an individual's established pattern. Their effect, then, resembles the effect of androgen; they increase arousal and sexual activity in those deficient in it but do not change the nature of the sexual activity typical of the individual.

One more possible effect of pornography has often been discussed: some people have suggested that the viewing of pornography increases the likelihood that the viewer will engage in violence against women. We will treat this topic in detail in Chapter 7, where we discuss aggression.

**Summary of sexual motivation.** Since rejecting local theories of sexual motivation, investigators have identified three major influences on the sexual motivation of higher animals. First, hormones play a major role. In immature or hormone-deficient animals, administration of estrogen (and occasionally progesterone) to females and androgen to males results in adult sexual behavior. Hormones can also induce sexual behavior in castrates and anestrous animals. In humans, however, hormonal control is less complete than in lower animals; thus, castration does not abolish all sexual motivation or activity. Androgen therapy in humans does, however, promote sexual motivation in both males and females who have low natural hormonal levels.

Second, cortical involvement in sexual activity is particularly critical in higher animals, especially males. Decorticate female rats, cats, and dogs can mate; male rats, cats, and dogs cannot.

Third, the increase in cortical involvement in the sexual behavior of higher animals is accompanied by an increase in the roles of learning and experience. In rhesus monkeys, for example, early social experience is critical to the development of normal adult sexual behavior. In humans, the importance of learning is reflected in the extraordinary variety of sexual practices among various cultures.

Several important questions about human sexual motivation remain to be answered. First, precisely how much of the motivation is innate?

Harlow's work on primates indicates that sex differences in infant play behaviors are innate and that these behaviors are probably important for adequate adult sexual activity. Arousal in response to a member of the opposite sex may also be innate. Exactly how much of human sexual activity is innate, however, is as yet undetermined.

Second, what is responsible for fluctuations in human sexual desire? Money (1961) states, "It is most likely that, once an optimal level of circulating hormone has been reached, the control of sexual desire is strictly nonhormonal. Fluctuations of sexual desire might then be explained as dependent on factors like cognitional stimulation and the time interval since the last sexual release" (p. 241). Stating that the "interval since the last sexual release" governs sexual behavior begs the question. No hormone has been discovered that builds up during sexual abstinence. No related tissue damage has been discovered.

In the next chapter we shall see that Freud postulated a sexual instinctual drive, which was always present but which varied in magnitude. Freud, however, posited no physiological basis for this ever-present urge; that was not critical to his theory. What physiological mechanism, if any, *is* responsible for satiation is as yet unknown.

## Stress

In 1957, Richter made an unusual discovery. He placed rats in a container filled with water, and within only 20 minutes a large proportion of the animals stopped swimming and died. The surprising feature of the study was that the deaths were caused neither by drowning nor by exhaustion; the animals died from stress. This was an important finding, reminiscent of accounts of certain concentration camp prisoners who appeared to lose the motivation to live. In their immensely stressful situation, many inmates gave up and died. Obviously, stress has an important influence on motivation.

In humans there are important physiological and psychological reactions to stressful stimuli. First, the stimulus must be perceived as stressful. This interpretive step in the stress response is most important, and we shall return to it when we discuss the psychological facets of the stress reaction. Given, however, that the event is indeed perceived as stressful, a constellation of neural and hormonal responses then occurs. (See Table 2-6 for a summary of the main hormonal responses to stress.) The first of these responses is immediate. The nerve fibers leading from the sympathetic nervous system to the adrenal medulla are activated, causing the adrenal medulla to secrete epinephrine and norepinephrine (also called adrenalin and noradrenalin). These chemicals galvanize the body for the stressful situation by dilating the pupils and increasing heart rate and blood pressure.

A second response to stress is somewhat less immediate than the epinephrine/norepinephrine response. In this response, the hypothalamus

**TABLE 2-6.** The major hormonal responses to stress

| Chemical | Main effects | Release time |
|---|---|---|
| Epinephrine | Reticular arousal<br>Increased heart output<br>Mobilization of blood glucose | Immediate |
| Norepinephrine | Reticular arousal | Immediate |
| ACTH | Glucose utilization<br>Stimulation of adrenal cortex | 10 seconds |
| Corticoids | Protein and carbohydrate metabolism | 15–60 minutes |

secretes hormones that cause the adjacent anterior pituitary gland to secrete another hormone, ACTH (adrenocorticotropic hormone). ACTH in turn causes the cortex of the adrenal gland to produce corticoids. These chemicals serve the essential function of converting proteins and fats to glucose so that the body will have an extra reservoir of energy available for dealing with the stressful situation.

Although it has long been known that hormones have critical physiological effects, it has been shown only relatively recently that they also may influence psychological processes such as learning. For example, King (1969) and Levine and Brush (1967) have found significant relations between the amount of certain adrenal hormones present in the bloodstream and the performance of animals who are learning to avoid noxious stimuli. DiGuisto, Cairncross, and King (1971) conclude that high ACTH and high corticoid levels prolong fear-motivated responding. These effects of the hormones, of course, are immensely adaptive in that they would help keep the animal away from the stressor.

Selye (1956), in fact, has described the body's response to stress as a general adaptation syndrome, which Selye divides into three stages. During the first stage, an "alarm reaction" takes place, and the entire constellation of hormonal responses occurs during the first part of this reaction. If the stress persists, signs characteristic of prolonged stress occur: an enlarged adrenal gland and stomach ulceration. If the stress continues still further, the second stage is entered, the "state of resistance." During this period the body reaches the point of maximal resistance to the stress. For example, the cortex of the adrenal gland accumulates the large reserve of hormones needed to cope with the stress. Certain body processes already may have been modified because of the long-term stressful environment. Selye (1956), for example, describes an experiment in which rats who had spent five weeks in a refrigerator at near-freezing temperature were then placed in an even colder temperature. These rats fared the colder temperature much better than did rats who had previously been housed at normal temperature. The refrigerator rats had developed chronic constriction of the blood vessels near the skin, which increased their resistance to the cold.

Such modifications are characteristic of the stage of resistance and enhance the organism's ability to cope with a long-term stressor. However, if the stress continues even further, the "stage of exhaustion"
begins. Resistance to stress deteriorates during this stage. The body
responds with a second hormonal reaction, but any stress that causes
the body to enter this final stage is usually fatal. The second hormonal
wave may even hasten deterioration in that the body cannot easily tolerate the greatly elevated hormonal levels.

Walter Cannon (1942) described several types of "voodoo death"
that later theorists have suggested may illustrate Selye's stress analysis.
For example, Cannon described an aboriginal man who had incurred
the wrath of the tribe's "medicine man." Upon being cursed by the
powerful medicine man, the unfortunate victim showed intense fear
and trembling. Then, in a state of terror, he went off by himself, lay
down, and awaited imminent death. The prolonged period of extreme
stress experienced by the victim eventually resulted in death. The curse
thus became a self-fulfilling prophecy. Such stress deaths illustrate the
immensely powerful role played by our cognitive interpretations of potentially stressful stimuli.

Richard Lazarus has researched the effects of various cognitions on
the impact of stressful stimuli. In one of the studies, Speisman,
Lazarus, Mordkoff, and Davison (1964) presented subjects with a
gruesome film illustrating a puberty rite of Australian aborigines, depicting genital surgery being performed with crude instruments. A different soundtrack for the film was provided for each of three groups of
viewers. One group heard the narrator emphasize the pain and trauma
of the surgery. A second group heard the narrator deny that any real
harm was being done to the boys; instead, the operation was characterized as harmless and as a ceremony that the adolescent boys eagerly
awaited. A final group heard a narrator intellectualize the incident in
an emotionally detached manner, much as an anthropologist might describe it scientifically. The researchers, using self-report and autonomic
measures, found that the trauma soundtrack increased stress compared
to the level found in a control group of subjects, whereas the denial and
intellectualization groups showed reduced stress levels compared to the
control group. The researchers also found that the occupations of the
subjects influenced the stress reactions: those subjects who were students showed less stress reduction in response to the intellectualization
soundtrack than in response to the denial soundtrack. Those subjects
who were airline executives, however, showed more stress reduction in
response to the intellectualization and less in response to denial. Both
the characteristics of the soundtrack and the characteristics of the person, then, influenced the perceived stressfulness of the film.

The relation between a person's appraisal of the stressfulness of a
stimulus and the person's physiological response to the stimulus has

recently received a substantial amount of research. In such research, a convenient physiological index of stress is one of the corticoids, 17-hydroxycorticosteroid (mercifully abbreviated "17-OHCS"). C. T. Wolff, Friedman, Hofer, and Mason (1964), for example, in examining the coping strategies of parents of children dying of cancer, found that those parents using denial as a coping strategy had the lowest levels of 17-OHCS. This result indicates that such coping strategies are at least temporarily effective in minimizing stress.

Researchers have found, too, that a number of psychological factors can greatly influence the physiological stress response. In an elegant series of studies, J. Weiss (1977) has shown the importance of conflict in causing stomach ulceration. Rats in one group were trained to turn a wheel in order to avoid a series of shocks to the tail, the shocks, of course, being stressful events. Then the situation was altered so that wheel-turning *resulted* in a brief shock, although continuing to turn the wheel would cancel the series of shocks. The animals in this "conflict" group were thus put in the unenviable position of having to perform a behavior guaranteed to result in one shock. A second group of animals received precisely the same shocks as the first group, but these shocks could not be controlled by the animals. Thus, there was no conflict for this control group. Weiss found that the conflict animals developed stomach ulcerations that were twice as severe as those of the control animals, even though the magnitude of the shocks was the same for both groups. Weiss also found, in subsequent research, that predictably occurring aversive stimulation causes far less ulceration than aversive stimulation that occurs unpredictably. Perhaps his most remarkable finding, however, was that rats who are shocked simultaneously in the same cage will attack each other vigorously. These animals showed far less ulceration than did animals given the identical shocks without the opportunity for aggression.

Psychological factors such as predictability of the stressful event and the opportunity for aggression following the stressful event are in fact so powerful that they can completely negate the normal physiological response to stress. Miller and Mason (reported in J. W. Mason, Maher, Hartley, Mougey, Perlow, & Jones, 1976) deprived monkeys of food for three days—surely a stressful event. One group of animals was deprived of food after the animals were given two or more weeks to adapt to their surroundings. These animals were housed in private booths and were given nonnutritive pellets to reduce the discomfort of an empty gastrointestinal tract. Another group was deprived of food while being housed in a typical laboratory, where much activity occurred around the animals. Figure 2-5 shows the level of 17-OHCS in the urine of these two groups. The "busy lab" group showed a large hormonal stress reaction to the fasting. (These animals did not exhibit decorous behavior, either; they protested strongly when food was deliv-

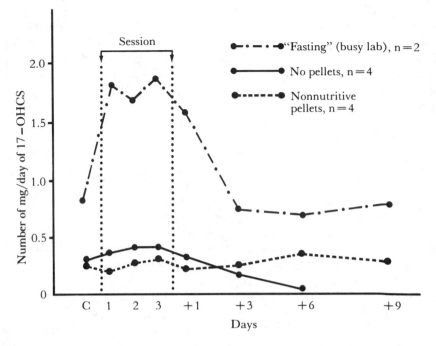

**Figure 2-5.** Urinary 17-OHCS responses to fasting in the monkey under three different experimental conditions. *(From "Selectivity of Corticosteroid and Catecholamine Responses to Various Natural Stimuli," by J. W. Mason, J. T. Maher, L. H. Hartley, E. Mougey, M. J. Perlow, and L. G. Jones. In G. Serban (Ed.), Psychopathology of Human Adaptation. Copyright 1976 by Plenum Publishing Corporation. Reprinted by permission.)*

ered to their nonfasting neighbors.) The animals fasting in a more serene environment showed no elevation of 17-OHCS levels whatsoever.

That these studies have relevance for psychosomatic medicine is clear. Because psychological factors have such a powerful influence on physiological responses, researchers have been investigating whether many common diseases might be caused, or at least influenced, by psychological factors. Perhaps the most systematic investigation has concerned the "Type A" or "coronary-prone behavior pattern." Type A people are competitive, aggressive, and hurried. Both interview and questionnaire assessment techniques have been used to identify Type A people. In one study, more than 3000 men employed by ten California companies were given medical examinations over an 8-year period. Those who exhibited Type A behavior early in that period showed a much higher incidence of cardiovascular disease later in the period. It is not surprising to learn that Type A persons have elevated neurohormonal stress responses (Friedman, Byers, Diamant, & Rosenman,

1975). The moral of this story is clear: the physiological response to stress and the psychological response to stress are highly interrelated.

## *Electrical stimulation of the brain*

In 1954, Olds and Milner discovered that animals would press a bar in order to receive a brief pulse of electrical stimulation in certain parts of the brain. Because it appeared that psychologists had at last discovered the "reward system" underlying such natural drives as hunger, thirst, and sex, this rather simple "self-stimulation" experiment set off a vast research program. The motivation to give oneself electrical stimulation of the brain (ESB) is clearly not a natural drive, yet animals would bar-press at furious rates for 15 to 20 hours in order to keep receiving the stimulation. Theorists interested in motivation and reward quickly began investigating this phenomenon, both to help them better understand the natural drives and to map the brain locations that might be part of the newly discovered "reward system."

At about the same time that Olds and Milner made their discovery, Delgado, Roberts, and Miller (1954) reported that ESB could also be a negative reinforcer. Subsequent studies (for example, Delgado, 1955) showed that animals receiving ESB in particular brain locations would bar-press in order to turn *off* the stimulation. It was unlikely that the stimulation was causing pain, since the brain itself is insensitive to pain. Also, animals would bar-press to turn off stimulation to the hippocampus, which is not believed to be a part of any sensory pathway involved in the transmission of pain. Therefore, investigators were tempted to consider such parts of the brain to be responsible for negative reinforcement.

A few patterns emerged as investigators began mapping which areas were positively reinforcing when stimulated and which were negatively reinforcing. For one, when some sites were stimulated for "free"—that is, when the animal didn't have to do anything in order to receive ESB—such stimulation resulted in the performance of consummatory behaviors or species-specific behaviors. Animals would eat, drink, ejaculate, gnaw, groom, or preen whenever the current was turned on. Research by Flynn and his associates (for example, Bandler & Flynn, 1974) has shown that aggression can be elicited by ESB in cats, and Karli, Vergnes, and Didiergeorges (1969) have demonstrated that hypothalamic stimulation can elicit a predatory response in the Norway rat.

Another pattern that quickly became apparent was that the positive and negative ESB sites seemed to be concentrated in the *limbic system*. This system contains the hypothalamus, the anterior thalamus, and the lowermost portions of the cerebral hemispheres (those portions of the hemispheres that form a border around the central core of the brain).

The limbic system had been implicated in the physiology of motivation and emotion long before ESB research began. Papez (1937) had surmised that the limbic system must be crucial in emotional experience, since the lower animals and humans he studied who suffered damage to this area experienced bizarre emotional disturbances. And rabies, which destroys the limbic system, causes extremely emotional behavior in its victims. Consequently it was not surprising when research revealed that both the positive and the negative sites for ESB were concentrated in the limbic system.

Since ESB was purported to activate the physiological substrates of motivation, researchers began studying the relation between ESB and conventional types of motivation. The relation can be curtly summarized as unclear. Some electrode sites, using particular levels of current, elicit more self-stimulation when the animal is food-deprived than when it is not (Brady, Boren, Conrad, & Sidman, 1957). For other electrode sites, food deprivation does not influence bar-pressing rates for ESB, but androgen level does (Olds, 1958). Since the result of such investigations depends on the precise location of the electrode, sweeping generalizations about the relative reinforcing power of ESB and other rewards are risky.

ESB and rewards such as food or water have been found to differ in a number of ways. First, conventional rewards, but not ESB, are easily able to maintain responding on partial-reinforcement schedules that deliver very infrequent rewards (Sidman, Brady, Boren, Conrad, & Schulman, 1955). Second, a neutral stimulus, when paired with a conventional reward, acquires some of the reward's reinforcing power. It does not always do so when ESB is the reward (Mogenson, 1965). Third, animals that have been trained to bar-press for conventional rewards will start to bar-press as soon as they are placed in the Skinner box at the beginning of a new experimental session. But occasionally animals previously given ESB for bar-pressing will not begin to bar-press until they are given one "free" pulse of ESB. Then they press enthusiastically (Milner, 1970, p. 390).

More recent research has shown that some of these reputed differences between ESB and conventional rewards may be artifactual (Gibson, Reid, Sakai, & Porter, 1965; Pliskoff, Wright, & Hawkins, 1965). Gibson et al. pointed out that bar-pressing for ESB results in immediate reward, whereas performing a learned response for a conventional reward usually involves a delay between the end of the response and the delivery of the reward. When this delay is eliminated, the effects of ESB reward and conventional reward appear identical.

There have been several rather perplexing results in ESB research. For example, Roberts (1958) showed that ESB at a single electrode site can have both rewarding and punishing properties. Animals will work to turn on such stimulation, and then will perform a response to turn it off. Roberts hypothesized that the initial burst of ESB may be intensely rewarding, but if the duration or intensity of the stimulation is too great, ESB becomes aversive. This hypothesis is supported by a great deal of non-ESB research, showing that moderate amounts of stimulation elicit approach behavior and intense amounts elicit withdrawal (Schneirla, 1959).

Probably the most puzzling aspects of ESB are summarized by Valenstein, Cox, and Kakolewski (1970). They point out that ESB at a given electrode site can elicit different behaviors in different situations. If a rat is given ESB at a particular site when in the presence of food, the ESB causes eating. However, if the food is removed and water is placed in the cage, ESB causes drinking. Valenstein et al. report, in fact, that few hypothalamic electrode sites elicited only one behavior. This finding calls into question the conclusion that a particular region of the hypothalamus regulates one drive exclusively.

Valenstein et al. also document some important differences between natural states of motivation and those that seem to be elicited by ESB. For example, when one type of food is removed from the cage of a hungry rat and another type is put in its place, the rat will begin eating the new food. An animal eating in response to ESB, however, will not readily switch from one type of food to another. Can it be said, then, that ESB causes hunger? Similarly, animals drinking in response to ESB will not switch their drinking behavior to a new container. Valenstein, Kakolewski, and Cox (1968) report that animals drinking in response to ESB will often continue to lap at a water container after all the water is gone. This behavior suggests that the response of drinking, rather than the ingestion of water, was being activated by ESB.

Valenstein et al. (1970) have proposed a theory of hypothalamic ESB that emphasizes the role of the response. These investigators believe that hypothalamic ESB does not create hunger or thirst, thereby causing the animal to eat or drink. Instead, ESB activates well-established, species-specific response patterns. Thus the ESB excites some prepotent, dominant responses whose neurological organization is innate. It activates a response of grooming, eating, preening, drinking, without actually affecting the motivation underlying the response. This hypothesis has not met with universal agreement (Bergquist, 1972); nevertheless, it does provide a parsimonious explanation of a large number of findings.

Two other experiments provide evidence that ESB triggers prepotent responses, not motivation. Kim and Umbach (1972, cited in Valenstein, 1973, p. 90) describe research in which the amygdaloid nuclei of aggressive and nonaggressive patients were stimulated. Such stimulation resulted in violence only in the aggressive patients, for whom aggression was a prepotent response. Even stronger evidence that natural motivation and the effects of ESB differ comes from a study by A.

Phillips, Cox, Kakolewski, & Valenstein (1969). A rat was placed in a box and was given ESB whenever it moved to one end of that box. The stimulation stopped whenever the rat moved to the other end. The rat quickly learned to run back and forth in the box, giving itself bursts of ESB. (Studies have shown that long-duration ESB may not be as pleasurable as short bursts. Thus, the rat kept running back and forth, turning the ESB on and off.) In a related experiment, food pellets were placed at the "on" end of the box for one rat. This rat picked up a pellet when the stimulation came on, carried it to the other end of the box, and dropped it there as soon as the ESB terminated. After several such trips, it appeared that this rodent was exhibiting food-hoarding behavior. However, when rat pups were substituted for food pellets, the pups were carried to the other end of the box, too. Retrieval of the young is a common maternal behavior of rats. Does ESB at this one electrode site therefore cause maternal motivation at some times and food-hoarding motivation at other times? It is more likely that ESB at this site causes a response, carrying behavior, and not the equivalent of a natural motivational state.

The ESB-research area remains unsettled and controversial. To the extent that ESB mimics natural motivational phenomena, investigation of it may provide valuable insights. If ESB is merely an electrical assault whose effects are quite different from those of natural physiological events, however, then ESB may not be a helpful tool for discovering the physiological substrates of motivation. Much more research is needed.

## Summary

This chapter has dealt with the instinctual and physiological bases of motivation. The use of instinct as an explanation of behavior flourished early in this century, and its overuse led to its decline later in the century. Those critical of the appeal to instinct as a determinant of behavior have ridiculed its limited explanatory power and its antiempirical stature. Nevertheless, the concept of instinct persists in a few areas in motivational literature. Ethologists, for example, insist that much animal behavior and even some human behavior is instinctive, and the influence of heredity on a wide range of social behaviors has been suggested by sociobiologists. Although extrapolation from nonhuman to human behavior has been overzealous at times, even the most ardent environmentalists agree that certain motivations are truly innate. Where nativists and environmentalists disagree is on the *extent* to which human behavior is motivated by instinct. This argument, however, has waned as investigators have determined that heredity and environment interact: some genetic characteristics are manifested to varying degrees in different environments.

Efforts to identify the physiological bases of hunger, thirst, and sex have had similar histories. For all three motivations, local theories have given way to central theories in which the hypothalamus is crucial. Some evidence, for example, suggests that hypothalamic misregulation may be responsible for obesity in some humans, although very recent research has cast some doubt on the traditional hypothalamic explanations of hunger motivation. Instead, the liver has been implicated as the "trigger" that provides the hypothalamus with information about the body's nutritional needs. The puzzling phenomena of specific hungers, however, have been clarified in recent years. It appears that one-trial, long-term conditioning results when a substance is ingested prior to sickness or recuperation; the substance becomes associated with the illness or recovery. Thus, the substance will be avoided (in the case of illness) or ingested (in the case of recovery) when encountered again.

Some of the same factors that influence eating behavior appear to influence smoking behavior as well. Specifically, addicted smokers, like normal-weight persons, attend predominantly to internal cues; nonaddicted smokers, like overweight persons, are influenced by external factors.

Thirst motivation, which involves intricate patterns of hormonal influences, is controlled by two systems, the osmoregulatory and the volume-regulatory systems. The former system is triggered by the dehydration of certain cells in the hypothalamus. The latter system is sensitive to blood loss. Both systems are characterized by a complex pattern of hormonal responses.

The motivation to sleep has perplexed psychologists for a number of years, since sleep has no obvious benefits other than relieving the symptoms that cause it. Two of the most likely explanations that have been offered are the brain-restitution hypothesis and the evolutionary hypothesis. The former merely posits that sleep is necessary so that the brain can perform such recuperative functions as memory consolidation and synthesis of central-nervous-system proteins. The latter states that humans are endowed with the genes that forced our evolutionary ancestors to sleep approximately one-third of their lives, despite the fact that the reasons for sleep—such as increased vulnerability because of poor night vision—are obsolete.

The physiological basis of the motivation for human sexual behavior has been difficult to study, partly because of the ethical concerns in such research. Although hormones have been shown to exercise strict control over the sexual behavior of lower animals, their influence greatly decreases as the phylogenetic scale is ascended. Instead, learning and experience play increasingly important roles in human sexual behavior.

Stress can be an important influence both on human motivation and on emotion. The reaction to stress includes a constellation of hormonal responses that influence physiological and psychological functioning. One's psychological interpretation of a potentially stressful stimulus can have a profound effect on that stimulus's impact. The implications of this for psychosomatic medicine are being vigorously pursued.

Most theorists believe that there are substantial differences between "natural" motivated behaviors and behaviors occurring as a result of electrical stimulation of the brain. Although early research appeared to indicate that physiological reward and punishment systems were present at discrete brain locations, more recent theory has rejected this simplistic view. No longer are investigators confident that one particular brain location is a part of one particular behavioral system, and some researchers believe that ESB does not activate normal motivational systems at all.

The reader should be aware that not all motivational theorists consider the study of the physiological bases of motivation to be necessary. In fact, the most famous instinct theorist, Sigmund Freud, postulated innate urges, mostly sexual in nature, and never felt compelled to elaborate on the physiological substrates of, for example, sexuality or anxiety. It is his extremely important theory that we turn to next.

CHAPTER **3**

# The Psychoanalytic
# Theory of Motivation

*There are two tragedies in life. One is not to get your heart's desire. The other is to get it.*

*George Bernard Shaw*

Psychoanalysis was created and largely constructed by Sigmund Freud. The psychoanalytic theory of behavior and behavior change looms massive in the history of psychology. It is rivaled in scope and explanatory significance perhaps only by behaviorism. In his psychoanalytic writings, which fill 24 volumes, Freud set forth a most comprehensive theory that addresses, directly or indirectly, all the central issues of human motivation, thought, and action. Although it is mainly a theory of personality and psychopathology, its implications are by no means restricted to abnormal psychology. Freud and his followers thought that psychoanalytic constructs such as psychic determinism, unconscious processes, repression and psychological defense, and psychosexual development were relevant for understanding all behavior. From this broad theoretical foundation, psychoanalysis strives to explain both the fundamentals and the subtleties of human motivation. The theoretical constructs developed by Freud for this purpose seriously jolted the previously unquestioned beliefs about human behavior that had been firmly established in the highly rationalistic traditions of Western civilization. As we shall see, the theory remains unique and controversial.

Psychoanalysis has generated frequent misunderstanding and misinterpretation. These problems seem to have arisen because (1) the theory is unique and complex and (2) its data have been collected by a nonexperimental method of investigation. These features have set psychoanalysis apart from the mainstream of theories of motivation.

What has been called "the psychoanalytic theory" is not one but many theories and models that are only informally linked together. Freud's writings are a record of psychological and philosophical discovery, not an attempt to build a scientifically sound theory. Freud sought explanations for psychological phenomena of lasting interest, such as memory, attention, perception, thought, and motivation. He tried to deal with difficult philosophical issues regarding the nature of consciousness and the function of religion, analyzed culture and its institutions, mapped the course of human development, pioneered modern concepts of psychopathology and psychotherapy, and even proposed a model of how the mind works. Despite his intellectual vigor, however, he was indifferent to the painstaking standards of systematic theorizing. The result was that Freud amassed many complicated concepts that, although compelling, did not mesh together in a coherent way. Moreover, most of his concepts were not defined in concrete, operational terms that permitted experimental investigation, and even many of the definitions he provided were changed in the course of his writings. This ambiguity has made the experimental testing of Freudian hypotheses a formidable task and has allowed both proponents and critics to select aspects of the theory that support their viewpoints. The rich complexity of the theory is thereby both its advantage and its disadvantage compared with more specific motivational theories.

The method by which psychoanalytic data were collected also has helped make the theory unique and controversial. Although Freud based his ideas on intensive observations, he did not use the experimental method, which is the primary means of verifying psychological knowledge. Rather than placing subjects in a laboratory under controlled conditions and testing a specific hypothesis, Freud recorded freely the associations, memories, dreams, and emotions of his patients as they lay on his historic couch. Over time his methods led to an expansion of his concepts, rather than making them narrower and more precise. This clinical perspective—the perspective of detailed observation in naturalistic settings—sets psychoanalytic theory apart from experimentally derived theories of motivation. Both the clinical and the experimental perspectives have their pros and cons. It must be acknowledged, however, that the experimental method is the preferred mode for approaching psychological truth. The issues to be resolved are whether psychoanalytic constructs are formulated concretely enough to be subject to experimental investigation and, if so, whether they can withstand the critical test of experimentation.

## Background and formative influences

Psychoanalytic theory, by virtue of its content, was and remains a unique, even revolutionary, model of human behavior. Yet its structure and its pitfalls arise directly from the impact of 19th century science and medicine on Freud's thinking.

Freud was born in the small town of Freiberg, Moravia (in Czechoslovakia), in 1856 and died in London in 1939.[1] For all but a few years of his life he lived in Vienna. During Freud's life span, that cosmopolitan European city was at the crossroads of burgeoning intellectual and scientific developments. The fertile intellectual climate and his personal and professional experiences had a great impact on the development of psychoanalytic theory. Because these were times of conflict and

[1]Unless a source is cited, factual information in this section is taken from E. Jones (1953).

controversy in intellectual quarters and in Freud's personal life, many opposing forces affected Freud's theorizing. For some conflicting influences, he sought compromise; for others, he attempted no reconciliation and incorporated them into his theory independently. The outcome was a theory with many assumptions, some of them contradictory.

## Intellectual currents: *Naturphilosophie* and physicalism

Freud, who was attracted to the study of human problems, was influenced in his decision to enter medical school by a transition in the current of belief (Boring, 1950) in the intellectual circles of Western Europe. Scholars were shifting their attention from *Naturphilosophie*—speculative inquiry based on metaphysical theories with philosophical and romantic underpinnings—to more scientific modes of interpretation emphasizing physical, not philosophical, analysis of natural phenomena (Holt, 1963). Advocates of *Naturphilosophie* viewed the universe as a vast organism consisting of interlaced activities and forces and organized according to basic conflicts believed to be timeless opposites. The mind and hence human psychology were manifestations of these universal conflicts (Bernfeld, 1944). In stark contrast to the rich and far-reaching—yet highly speculative—approach of *Naturphilosophie* was the mode of inquiry of the increasingly popular scientific philosophy of physicalism. For the physicalists, the elements of nature to be studied were discrete and definable, and the method of investigation was the controlled experiment. The physicalist perspective held that only physical and chemical forces were active in an organism and that such notions as "basic conflicts" were irrelevant (Bernfeld, 1944). Displacing *Naturphilosophie* as the dominant scholarly view, physicalism gained steadily in prestige among the universities of Germany and Austria. Among the central figures in the movement were the physiologists Hermann Helmholtz, who founded the so-called Helmholtz school of medicine on physicalist principles, and his protégé Ernst Brücke, under whom Freud trained in medical school.

The physicalist belief was influential in leading Freud to choose medicine as his career. But Freud viewed himself more as a researcher than as a physician: his ultimate goal was to help mankind, not just his patients. At first, Freud's physicalism directed him toward medicine and Brücke's physiology laboratory. Subsequently, it became a guiding force that led Freud first to creative investigations in histology and neurology and later to his pioneering work in psychiatry upon which psychoanalytic theory was built. *Naturphilosophie* inspired two elements of Freud's view of human nature: that people were in conflict with their environments, others, and themselves and that their behavior had meaning and purpose. Physicalism provided Freud with the scientific principles for conducting his investigations. The two movements—one philosophical, the other scientific—left Freud with a worldview that was humanitarian and concerned with individuals' emotions and at the same time founded on the principles of 19th century science. This personal viewpoint eventually gave rise to the psychoanalytic theory: The philosophical perspective defined the subject matter—the motivation of human thought and action. The scientific perspective dictated an empirical method of inquiry and provided the explanatory concepts in the theory, such as force and energy. The joint influence of *Naturphilosophie* and physicalism made psychoanalytic theory a blend of separable, essentially different components, rather than a uniform whole.

Two formative professional experiences provided Freud with his basic theoretical concepts and data. The first was his work as a research assistant in the physiology laboratory of Ernst Brücke, while in medical school. The second was his work as a clinician studying hysteria and its treatment by hypnosis, mainly with Josef Breuer, a practicing physician.

### Research in neurology

While at the University of Vienna, Freud's primary role model was the eminent physiologist and neuroanatomist Brücke. With Helmholtz and others, Brücke had once endorsed the scientific principle that epitomized physicalism: "No other forces than common physical-chemical ones are active within the organism" (E. Jones, 1953, p. 40). Freud worked in Brücke's laboratory for several years, performing many investigations of the nervous system and earning himself a minor reputation in the scientific community. In Brücke's laboratory he absorbed the physicalist doctrine. Freud's scientific studies, however, were not experiments in the sense that they stressed control and prediction. Rather, his method was based on rigorous, painstaking observation.

Experiences with Brücke and other scientists during this period gave Freud several physicalist notions about how the nervous system functioned. Holt (1965, 1966, 1967) has noted that Freud acquired during his early work three neurological assumptions that are reflected in his psychological theorizing. As we shall see, these assumptions greatly influenced Freud's theory of motivation.

The first assumption was that of the constancy principle, which assumed that the nervous system functioned, through discharge, to keep itself free from tension. By this process, the nervous system maintained a constant equilibrium. This assumption was important in Freud's development of the psychological concept of the pleasure principle, in which reduction of tension was the basis of pleasure.

The second assumption, which derived from the first, was contained in Freud's passive-reflex model of neural functioning. This model asserted that the nervous system had an innate tendency to discharge any tension it received, whether from inside or outside the organism. The nature of neural functioning was thus assumed to consist of reactions against both internal and external stimuli. The parallel in Freud's psychological theory is the idea that internal instincts (drives) and the external demands of reality produce painful stimulation that the person *must* protect himself or herself against. Hence the need for psychological defenses.

The third neurological assumption derives from the physicalist idea of energy and can be termed the closed energy model. This assumption had two parts: first, the magnitude of an effect on the nervous system was directly proportional to the amount of stimulation received; second, increases in stimulation were painful, and decreases (discharges) were pleasurable. This third neurological assumption was important in defining Freud's psychological operation of libido, or sexual energy, which Freud believed was the primary source of human motivation. He theorized that sexual stimulation from thought or action increased the activity of sexual energy. Proceeding on physicalist notions about the conservation of energy, Freud further assumed that the personality, like the nervous system, was a closed system. It had a fixed amount of libido, which if used for one purpose could not be used for another. Freud considered this distribution of sexual energy a determinant of behavior.

In adopting these assumptions in his early work, Freud remained consistent with the neurological ideas that were prevalent in the late 19th century, hence gaining scientific belief for his budding psychological ideas. But later, when he turned away from neurological research, the neurological assumptions still provided structure for his scientific thinking. The development of psychoanalytic theory was thus shaped by these notions, which the development of physiology and neuroanatomy in the 20th century has proved invalid (Breger, 1969). Consequently, the outcome of Freud's early scientific experiences was that psychoanalysis has never been purely psychology, and its neurological components have been burdened with dated physicalist notions that make them difficult to deal with.

## Clinical work in hypnosis

The second formative influence on Freud's theory, his clinical work in hypnosis, began just six months before he set up his private practice in neurology. Freud went to Paris in 1885 to study with Jean Charcot, an internationally known neurologist who had been experimenting with hypnosis as a treatment for hysteria—a psychological disorder in which there was loss of a sensory function (such as touch) or a motor function (such as walking) with no discernible physiological cause. Charcot theorized that hysterical symptoms were caused by an "impression" on the nervous system and that this impression was the direct result of some traumatic experience. In essence, Charcot argued that a painful idea—the memory of a psychological trauma—was at the root of hysteria. Charcot demonstrated that hysterical symptoms could be either induced or removed by direct suggestion under hypnosis. Charcot's ideas were a radical departure from physicalist doctrine: the causes of hysterical symptoms were not "common physical-chemical ones" but appeared to be psychological. Freud's observations of hysteria rekindled his philosophical concerns about the bases of human thought and action. Subsequently, he would no longer be interested just in the functioning of the brain but also in that of the mind.

In the 15 years that followed Freud's work with Charcot, during which Freud was to make his most creative discoveries and derive the fundamental concepts of psychoanalysis (Stewart, 1967), the major influence on his work was his association with Josef Breuer, a prominent Viennese physician. After years of professional collaboration, Breuer and Freud coauthored a book, *Studies on Hysteria* (1895). The basis of the book was the celebrated case of "Anna O.," a 21-year-old woman who had been suffering from a "museum" of hysterical symptoms, including visual distortions, loss of speech, headaches, and most notably the contracture and anesthesia of her right arm. Breuer had treated her years earlier using a hypnotic technique in which he took her back in time and directed her to recall the onset of her symptoms. It seemed that each symptom had originated on an occasion when Anna was unable to express an emotion she was experiencing. Breuer termed this emotional blockage "strangulated affect." He observed that when Anna, under hypnosis, relived the events surrounding the onset of a symptom, she experienced the emotion that had been bottled up since the original occasion. To his surprise, with each hypnotic recall, her symptoms improved dramatically. Anna herself named this process "the talking cure." Breuer and Freud called the expression of the previously blocked emotion *catharsis* and the cognitive reexperiencing of the past *abreaction*. These terms are usually used interchangeably to refer to the process of emotional release through the reliving of a traumatic psychological event. These observations of emotional blockage and release formed the foundation of present-day psychotherapy.

A central feature of hysteria that was present in Anna's case and others reported by Breuer and Freud was a tendency to "split consciousness." In this state, significant, emotion-laden ideas had a great impact on the patient's psychological functioning, without his or her awareness or control. Breuer and Freud offered different reasons for splitting of consciousness. Consistent Breuer took the physicalist perspective that the phenomenon resulted from a physiologically determined "hypnoid state," the propensity for which was inherited. Freud's view was radically different and clearly psychological. He theorized that the strangulation of emotion and the resulting dissociation of it from consciousness were due to a traumatic sexual experience in adolescence or early adulthood that was psychologically unacceptable to the patient. Thus Freud saw hysterical symptoms not as accompaniments of a genetically-determined hypnoid state but as purposeful behaviors that were symbolically related to traumatic sexual experiences. He used the term *defense hysteria* to describe the defensive, self-protective function of the symptoms in keeping the trauma from entering consciousness.

In two ways, Freud's analysis of hysteria was an important step in the development of his theory. First, it signaled a shift in his thinking from investigating the *causes* of behavior, on a physiological level and in terms of physicalist concepts, to exploring the *motivations* for behavior, on a psychological level. Although his motivational construct was vague, Freud was hypothesizing that a *thought* associated with an alleged sexual trauma had *motivated* the patient to *unconsciously* dissociate the emotion from experience and develop hysterical symptoms. Second, Freud's analysis emphasized not only the underlying motivating force but also a counterforce—the defense. Freud was hypothesizing here that psychologically every action has a reaction. Most important in this notion is the function of the reaction. He saw the defensive components of hysterical symptoms as purposeful. The strangulation of affect and splitting of consciousness lessened the hysteric's conscious anguish.

From these beginnings, Freud's concepts of motivation and defense underwent revision and reformulation time and again. Eventually, he hypothesized "unconscious instinctual drives" as the bases of human motivation and devised a complex theory of repression and defense to account for the consequences of these motivating forces. As his theory evolved, its structure and content bore the mark of the intellectual traditions and professional experiences that had been influential in his early work. As a result, psychoanalytic theory has two distinct perspectives that were inseparable for Freud (G. S. Klein, 1969). The first is a clinical perspective, which is expressed in belief in the purposeful meaning of behavior and the inevitability of psychological conflict. It stems from the *Naturphilosophie* tradition and Freud's clinical work with hypnosis. The second is a metapsychological perspective. The term *metapsychology* referred to the realm "beyond psychology" in which physicalistic principles and concepts are applied to understanding the conscious and unconscious operations of the mind. To understand the psychoanalytic theory of motivation, one must be aware of these two levels; the theory is expressed in metapsychological language, but its content derives from clinical observations and implications.

## The six psychoanalytic hypotheses

Because a number of different intellectual and professional influences affected the development of psychoanalytic theory, the theory can be viewed as consisting of six points of view regarding human behavior: topographic, dynamic, economic, genetic, structural, and adaptive.[2] Each can be seen as a separate theory that attempts to explain the functioning and organization of the personality from a certain perspective. Yet none is independent of the other hypotheses. None alone provides a comprehensive explanation of behavior. For psychoanalytic theory to be adequately represented, it is necessary for all six viewpoints to be addressed. Psychoanalytic theory is much more than the popular conception of it in terms of id, ego, and superego. Because a comprehensive discussion of psychoanalytic theory would be well beyond the scope of a single chapter, we shall briefly sketch the six hypotheses and then turn to a detailed treatment of the motivational constructs. Our discussion should provide the necessary overview of the theory and an introduction to the different ways in which Freud explained the causes and motivations of human behavior.

## The topographic hypothesis: Unconscious processes

The basic assumption of the topographic hypothesis is that unconscious psychological processes exist and that they are the most significant sources of motivation. Hence, *topographic* here refers to Freud's division of thinking and experience into conscious and unconscious components. In positing an unconscious, Freud was not breaking new ground. Philosophers and psychologists had long addressed themselves to the phenomena. Freud's contribution lay in the emphasis he gave to the unconscious construct and in his systematic theorizing. He broke with tradition in viewing the unconscious as *more important* than conscious experience for the understanding of psychological events.

Two aspects of Freud's concept of the unconscious are critical to his motivational theory. The first is a topographic model of the functioning of the mind (known as the "mental apparatus"), in which Freud attempted to map the layers of consciousness and specify their interrelationships. The second is the operation of censorship, which kept certain ideas unconscious—a concept that became the cornerstone of psychoanalytic theory.

In developing his topographic model in Chapter 7 of *The Interpretation of Dreams* (1900), Freud theorized that there existed three separate systems that bore quasispatial relationships to one another: the conscious (Cs), the preconscious (Pcs), and the unconscious (Ucs). The model is depicted in Figure 3-1.

The Cs was defined as a "sense organ" for understanding the world and one's experiences. It had two functions for the individual: (1) to bring sensory input (sights, sounds, and so forth) into awareness and

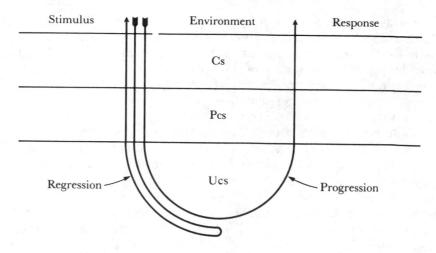

**Figure 3-1.** Topographic model of the mind. *(Adapted from Freud, 1900.)*

(2) to produce recognition of pleasant and unpleasant experiences. The Cs was thus relegated to a minor role in motivation. Its function was restricted to deploying attention; it yielded awareness but not impetus.

The ultimate determinants of behavior instead resided in the Ucs. The primary sources of motivation were unconscious instinctual drives, which became associated with thoughts and memories. They were the exclusive properties of the Ucs. Conscious ideas were linked together in a logical fashion, but unconscious ideas were timeless—not subject to memory decay—and they were free to undergo transformations in which they became illogical, condensed, or displaced. They could also coexist with their opposites. These unconscious, drive-related thoughts were persistent and forceful, pushing for satisfaction through action or fantasy. Freud called the illogical, drive-laden style of cognition of the Ucs primary-process thinking and the logical, drive-free style of cognition of the Cs secondary-process thinking. It is difficult to give an example of primary-process thinking, since it is by definition unconscious. However, a slip of the tongue or the recall of a dream, although conscious, each have primary-process components. Dreams, for example, may be seemingly meaningless, filled with puzzling symbols, childhood memories, and illogical events. Examples of secondary-process thinking are numerous, as they dominate conscious experience. Solving the *New York Times* crossword puzzle, driving a car, and taking a photograph all involve secondary-process thinking.

The Pcs was conceived of as an intermediary system: unconscious thoughts passed through the Pcs in striving to become conscious. It was under partial conscious control, and it exercised a censorship function by blocking thoughts and actions that were initiated by the Ucs. The censorship could be primary, occurring between Ucs and Pcs, or secondary, occurring between Pcs and Cs. The well-known Oedipal conflict provides an example of primary censorship. Simply stated, the Oedipal conflict occurs because a male child unconsciously strives for the love of his mother and simultaneously wishes to kill his father, the chief competitor for the mother's love. The Pcs blocks this unconscious thought from consciousness through primary censorship. In this instance, the censorship serves the apparent function of controlling and regulating sexual and aggressive thought so that it does not create conscious conflict for the individual or lead to sexual and aggressive actions.

Although both Pcs and Ucs involve idea formation that takes place outside awareness, the two systems are qualitatively different. Ordinary information that slips from the Cs and is later recovered, such as a street address or a telephone number, is believed to be temporarily stored in the Pcs. Ideas that derive from the Ucs are distinctive in that they have primary-process characteristics and are unlikely to reach the Cs in their original form; they are blocked, diverted, or altered as they pass through the Pcs. The effect of this censorship by the Pcs is to produce drive derivatives, ideas and actions that are symbolically related to unconscious drives. Examples of drive derivatives from the censorship of the Oedipal conflict might be a boy's playful fighting or competitiveness with his father or his wish to be cuddled and held by his mother. Each is hypothesized to derive from an unconscious idea— the Oedipal conflict—that has been altered so that it leads to an acceptable conscious experience.

In describing functioning within the topographic system, Freud relies on the reflex arc, a pattern widely applied in the physicalist neurology of the late 19th century. The first function, progression (see Figure 3-1), faithfully depicts the movement of a thought through the mental apparatus from stimulus to response in the same way as a bodily reflex occurs—for example, as a puff of air (stimulus) in the eye causes the eye to blink (response). The important feature of the reflex-arc model is that stimulation is believed to have an impact on the Ucs by arousing ideas and memories that press for gratification through a motor response.

Freud also introduced a second topographic function, regression, which appears to be alien to the reflex-arc model. Regression is movement through the mental apparatus in a reversed direction. Presumably, through this assumption of reversed direction Freud was attempting to present the idea that thoughts originating in the Ucs are frequently experienced as sensory stimuli—for example, they may take the form of auditory or visual hallucinations. Regression, however, is not restricted to abnormal states: it also underlies normal processes such as dreaming and fantasy.

Whether progression or regression occurs depends on the stimulus. Although every stimulus passes through Cs, Pcs, and Ucs, a stimulus not associated with an unconscious instinctual drive will not evoke ideas that might be censored, and progression will occur. For example, if you are walking across campus on an autumn day and a leaf flutters down in front of you, you probably will just watch its flight. The stimulus (leaf) causes a progression through the mind to a motoric response (watching). If, however, stimulation is associated with an instinctual drive, censorship is likely. Regression will then occur. Let us illustrate this by referring to the sexual instinctual drive, which we shall discuss in detail later. Suppose that a woman student becomes aroused by an attractive male nude model who is posing for her photography class. Freud would say that in this instance the stimulus (nude) becomes associated with an instinctual drive (sexuality), and runs into censorship (because of the conflict, anxiety, and guilt that Freud assumed were associated with sexual activity in this context), producing drive derivatives. Under such conditions, the topographic function of regression becomes operative. Sexual satisfaction is attained through an imagined, or fantasied, sexual experience. This substitute satisfaction is a wish fulfillment. The regression function is an early form of a cornerstone of the psychoanalytic theory of motivation—that ideas associated with unconscious instinctual drives give rise to thoughts and actions that are altered by censorship to produce drive derivatives.

Progression and regression might occur simultaneously following a certain stimulus. For example, a boy watching a boxing match on television (stimulus) with his father might have unconscious Oedipal fantasies of competitiveness aroused and start playing fisticuffs with him (response) under the guise of acting like a boxer. At the same time, the boy may daydream of defeating his father in the boxing ring. The daydream fantasy results from regression; the fisticuffs result from progression. In both instances, the unconscious has played a significant role by enriching the effects of the initial stimulus.

The topographic model of mental functioning is generally considered the least distinctive of the psychoanalytic hypotheses, mainly because it forms a significant aspect of the other hypotheses and so is not clearly separable from them (Gill, 1963; D. Rapaport & Gill, 1967). Despite the criticisms of Freud's three-layered scheme of mental functioning, the concept of dynamic unconscious processes that provide the foundations for human motivation is an enduring principle basic to Freudian thought (Brenner, 1955). Paradoxically, the topographic hypothesis is the least distinctive just because it is so central to the other hypotheses. It is not merely a part of psychoanalytic theory; it is the fiber of it.

## The dynamic hypothesis: Intrapsychic conflict

The basic assumption of the dynamic hypothesis is that conflict exists between psychological forces and counterforces. These two kinds of forces are Freud's primary motivational constructs. The psychological forces are the fundamental sources of motivation; they initiate action and thought aimed at the achievement of a goal. The counterforces have aims that conflict with those of the motivating forces, and they therefore oppose expression of the forces. The counterforces do not initiate behavior independently; they only *react* to thought and action deriving from the motivating forces. This dynamic conflict is termed "intrapsychic" because it is postulated *within* the individual (on an unconscious level).

The dynamic hypothesis had its origin in Freud's early work with Breuer on hypnosis. Freud interpreted the "strangulated affect" present in hysteria as a defense against bringing painful memories into consciousness. The concept of defense suggested an unconscious, dynamic conflict between opposing forces in the mind. Freud could observe the action of the counterforce (the defense), but the nature of the motivating force was unclear and had to be inferred. Freud engaged in a series of clinical investigations of this underlying force (for example, 1894, 1896), in which he speculated about the causes of the conflict. He attributed the conflict to various actual experiences in patients' histories: a traumatic sexual experience in adolescence or early adulthood, inhibited sexual behavior (such as coitus interruptus), or sexual seduction by the parent before the patient's puberty (the "seduction theory"). He later discarded this last explanation, childhood seduction, in favor of the explanation that a fantasied, rather than actual, experience had caused the conflict. Freud reasoned that since it was improbable that Viennese fathers were seducing their daughters as frequently as his female patients had reported (and dismaying if they were!), the patients' sexual traumas must have occurred only in their minds. This conclusion led to the controversial theory of infantile sexuality and the formulation of the motivating force in hysteria as the sexual instinctual drive (Freud, 1905a). This instinctual force was believed to produce sexual fantasies or ideas that, like a traumatic experience, led to conflict and defense.

Instinctual drives thenceforth were the basic sources of motivation in psychoanalytic theory. Instinctual drives were defined as the demands that the body places on the psychic apparatus (Freud, 1915a). As such, the principal psychoanalytic concept of motivation was given a clear physical source. Its heritage was obviously the physicalist tradition of physiology and biology. However, Freud did not hypothesize that instinctual drives affected behavior in an automatic, reflexlike manner, as 19th century physiologists would have held. Rather, motivation had a cognitive component. The instinctual drives produced a psychical representation, or mental image, of the object. A series of such drive-related ideas formed a forceful train of thought that motivated activity. A drive derivative was a fantasy or behavior that served to express the instinctual drive in a disguised manner.

Freud hypothesized two classes of instinctual drives. For many years, he recognized only the sexual instinctual drive. Later in his writings, Freud (1920) set forth the controversial concept of the death instinct, part of which was the aggressive instinctual drive. The psychical representations that unconsciously motivated thought and action were thus sexual and aggressive.

Freud characterized the instinctual drives of sex and aggression as having "primacy"; that is, he viewed them as so strong that, when aroused, they press for direct expression and immediate gratification. However, those results rarely occur, because of opposition put forth by the counterforces. The counterforces produce what in the topographic model is called "censorship." In early childhood, external opposition to expression and gratification of the instinctual drives is encountered in restrictions and threats by the family and society. Repeated encounters result in internalization of the prohibitions against instinctual-drive expression, and the child's eventual perception of such expressions as negative leads to anxiety and guilt. These internalized prohibitions become counterforces that restrain and regulate the instinctual drives. Impulses to gratify sexual and aggressive drives activate the defenses because of the anxiety and guilt associated with overt sexual and aggressive behavior. The result of this intrapsychic conflict is neither complete expression nor complete restraint, but a compromise formation between the forces and counterforces. Neurotic symptoms, dreams, slips of the tongue, artistic creation, and other phenomena can all be seen as dynamic outcomes of the drive/defense conflict. The frequency and quality of the compromise formations are determined by the characteristics of the instinctual drives and the defenses against them.

The dynamic hypothesis is central to the psychoanalytic theory of motivation and makes it distinctive among theories of motivation. Behavior is not viewed as arising directly from some motivational source. Rather, the dynamic viewpoint postulates intervening intrapsychic events, in the following sequence:

$$\text{instinctual drives} \rightarrow \text{psychical representations} \rightarrow \text{conflict with defenses} \rightarrow \text{compromise formations}$$

The path from arousal of motivation (instinctual drives) to some behavioral outcome (compromise formation) is thus composed of several steps. The instinctual drives provide only the initial impetus; the internalized sources of regulation (defenses) control the drives and contribute significantly to the outcome. The presence of intrapsychic conflict has an important corollary called psychic determinism (Brenner, 1955). Psychic determinism describes the complicated motivational process by stating that any behavior is determined by the interaction of unconscious psychological forces and counterforces that preceded it. Therefore, all behavior, whether trivial or significant, is viewed as "dynamically" motivated. The motivation arises not from a single source but from a process of unconscious intrapsychic conflict.

### The economic hypothesis: Psychic energy

In the economic hypothesis, *economic* refers to the amount and distribution of psychic energy within the three layers of the mind. The basic assumptions of the economic hypothesis are that psychic energy exists and that it has quantitative effects on behavior. The antecedents of the economic hypothesis were principles deriving from the physicalist perspective and Freud's early work with Brücke, and the discredited neurological assumptions present throughout psychoanalytic theory are most apparent in this viewpoint. Brücke's principle of the conservation of physical energy underlies Freud's (1900) theorization that psychic energy has quantity and displaceability. The individual has a fixed, presumably biologically determined amount of psychic energy for psychological activities. The total quantity is constant, but it can be distributed within the mental apparatus in various ways. The distribution of energy determines the nature and outcome of intrapsychic conflict. If much energy resides in drive-related thoughts, they are more likely to attain their goals and become conscious. To keep these psychical representations under control and unconscious, there must be additional energy residing in the defenses. Intrapsychic conflict is therefore energy consuming: it appropriates large quantities of energy from other psychological activities. For example, theoretically one who is undergoing prolonged, intense intrapsychic conflict is unable to be creative or to love another person, since these activities require psychic energy.

The relative strengths in the dynamic viewpoint of the motivational constructs of instinctual drive and defense are understood in terms of the economic concept of psychic energy. The use of psychic energy in a drive-related idea, such as the mental image of a person, is called *cathexis*. For example, Dave might be said to have a strong cathexis toward Karen, his lover; that is, he uses a large amount of psychic energy in thinking about Karen. In terms of the economic hypothesis, this would mean that Dave's sexual energy (libido) is directed toward Karen. He sees her as an object for gratification, and his motivation toward sexual contact with her is greatly increased. Increased cathexis, or the direction of psychic energy into a drive-related idea, strengthens the motivational force toward action. The strength of the defenses aimed at blocking direct expression of drive-related ideas also is described in terms of deployment of psychic energy; the distribution of energy in the defenses is called *countercathexis* (Freud, 1915b). In economic terms, then, intrapsychic conflict is conflict between cathexis and countercathexis.

The principle of tension reduction, which is central to the psychoanalytic theory of motivation, derives from this economic hypothesis.

The presence of an instinctual drive is believed to produce a state of excitation, or tension. Since the influence of the drive is assumed to be continuous, the tension is constantly present. Changes in the intensity of the tension are caused by increases and decreases in the amount of psychic energy invested in the drive. Accumulation of psychic energy (cathexis) without gratification increases tension and creates a state of "unpleasure" (analogous to pain; no English word is an exact translation of the German). Reduction of tension by expressing the instinctual drive through fantasy or action produces a state of pleasure. The reduction of unpleasure is called the pleasure principle. Freud conceived of the psychological state of tension as a state of imbalance that created forces to restore balance. Here he was using a mechanism borrowed directly from physicalism. The concept of the pleasure principle implies that an individual is motivated to achieve a tension-free state of pleasure. However, *pleasure* is defined not as some positive or ecstatic feeling in the absolute sense but rather as the absence or lessening of tension through gratification of the motivating instinctual drive. For example, a sexual fantasy is pleasurable in that it reduces the unpleasurable tension caused by the intensity of the sexual instinctual drive.

Psychic energy is obviously a hypothetical construct; it cannot be directly measured or even observed. Consequently, the economic hypothesis is the most abstract and most problematic of the psychoanalytic hypotheses. Contemporary theorists (for example, Breger, 1969; Peterfreund, 1971) maintain that the economic concepts can be discarded without damaging the psychoanalytic theory of motivation. They argue that Freud's motivational constructs are less ambiguous without the energy metaphor. Although the mistaken neurological assumptions that Freud acquired in Brücke's laboratory are most apparent in the economic hypothesis, this hypothesis remains valuable for explanatory reasons.

The strengths of motivational forces and counterforces, and the changes in their strengths, are described in terms of quantities and distributions of psychic energy. Differences among individuals are thereby described according to the economic viewpoint in terms of two factors: (1) the total quantity of psychic energy (determined biologically), and (2) the distribution of that psychic energy, which determines the relative strengths of instinctual drives and defenses.

## The genetic hypothesis: Psychosexual development

The basic assumption of the genetic hypothesis is that the influences of past experiences, especially in childhood, persist throughout a person's psychological development. The term *genetic* is used here in a psychological—not a biological—sense, to refer to significant experiences in development. The idea that the past influences the present is a truism and of course was not new with Freud. However, this developmental concept is made distinctively psychoanalytic by the *way* in which early psychological events affected subsequent behaviors according to Freud. The genetic hypothesis evolved over several years, during which Freud pondered over what motivational force might underlie his patients' hysterical symptoms. This effort culminated in his most revolutionary and controversial publication, *Three Essays on the Theory of Sexuality* (1905a). From his dissatisfaction with the "seduction theory" of hysteria, he concluded that his patients' reports of childhood seduction by their parents derived from their sexual fantasies, not from actual occurrences. From this perspective, Freud developed a theory of infantile sexuality: he hypothesized that the sexual instinctual drive and its associated form of psychic energy, libido, were present as the dominant sources of motivation in early childhood. Moreover, he contended that the sexual drive sought expression and gratification through action and thought associated with a different part of the body during each of several phases in the child's development. During each phase, the tension caused by accumulation of libido, or sexual energy, was experienced in a particular erogenous zone of the body. As the economic hypothesis predicts, reduction of tension in that erogenous zone produced pleasure. The manifestation of the sexual drive in a particular zone defined a stage of psychosexual development. The sequence of shifts of libido through the successive zones was biologically determined and universal—it occurred in all children.

The stages of psychosexual development are too commonly known to warrant detailed discussion. Brief mention should suffice. Freud formulated three stages in early childhood: the *oral* stage (birth to 1½ years), during which sucking and biting provide tension reduction and pleasure; the *anal* stage (1½ to 3 years), during which the retention and expulsion of feces provide outlets for libido; and the *phallic* stage (3 to 7 years), during which sexual pleasure is derived from the genitals through masturbation and through indirect gratifications, such as the showing of one's genitals or seeing of another's. A central aspect of indirect satisfaction during the phallic stage is the presence of sexual fantasies, chief of which occurs in the Oedipus complex, in which the child's burgeoning sexual interest is directed toward the other-sex parent as an object of gratification; this interest is accompanied inevitably by feelings of hostility and rivalry toward the same-sex parent. The phallic stage is followed developmentally by the *latency period* (7 to 12 years), during which the sexual instinctual drive is relatively inactive before reemerging with increased intensity at puberty. Puberty signals the onset of the *genital* stage, during which mature sexual thoughts and actions toward appropriate others constitute the primary sources of pleasure.

The importance of the psychosexual theory resides in the emphasis that it places on developmental events as central determinants of adult behavior. Two aspects of the theory are relevant in this regard. The first is the concept of partial instinctual drives. Although the theory says that libido shifts from zone to zone in the succession of stages, the functions of these stages do not halt once they are passed. Elements of oral, anal, and phallic sexuality are present in the action of the sexual drive throughout life. These stage-specific motivational sources are called partial instinctual drives. They can, depending on the individual's psychosexual experiences, either enrich adult personality or induce problems through character disturbance or neurosis. For example, excessive smoking, eating, and alcohol consumption in adulthood may represent oral gratifications of partial instinctual drives that were dominant for tension reduction and pleasure during the oral stage.

The second critical aspect of the theory involves the concepts of fixation and regression. In fixation, as the result of a conflict in development, the central characteristics of one stage are excessively maintained throughout subsequent stages. Fixations arise for two reasons: first and more commonly, excessive frustration of pleasure seeking from an erogenous zone causes the individual to persist in seeking pleasure from that zone during the later stages; second and less commonly, excessive gratification causes the individual to cling to the pleasure of that erogenous zone and be reluctant to pass to another stage. Two examples of excessive frustration would be long, irregular intervals between feedings and harsh weaning during the oral stage. An example of excessive gratification would be excessively permissive toilet training during the anal stage. Regression, which is characteristic of persons who have fixations, is a return to behavior typical of the stage at which the fixation occurred. It usually appears during times of stress and anxiety, presumably as a distorted attempt to reduce tension. For example, during a stressful period of negotiations with a labor union, a business executive fixated in the anal stage may regress into manifesting behavior that was more typical of that stage of psychosexual development than of adulthood. Such regressions might be direct (he might be plagued by constipation or diarrhea) or symbolic (he might become excessively stingy or frugal, or he might become inappropriately generous or charitable). The operations of fixation and regression in the anal stage are depicted in Figure 3-2.

In the genetic hypothesis, partial instinctual drives, fixation, and regression are critical determinants of adolescent and adult motivation. They are components of the personality that determine the object and type of motivated behavior. Through them, earlier events in psychosexual development influence (1) the targets (persons or things) toward which motivational drives are directed in thought and action and (2) the types of defenses that regulate the expression of the motivational drives.

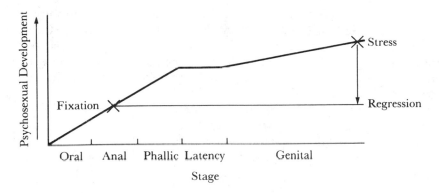

**Figure 3-2.** Fixation and regression in the anal stage.

Since its inception, the genetic viewpoint has been the most contro-versial aspect of psychoanalytic theory. The theory of infantile sexu-ality and psychosexual development caused irreconcilable theoretical differences between Freud and many of his colleagues, notably Breuer, and continues to be the least accepted aspect of psychoanalytic theory. In the face of mounting criticism, Freud clung to his genetic formula-tions. In doing so, he seemed to be concerned with a theory that offered a means by which adult behavior could be predicted from childhood experience (Jung, 1963). The goal of prediction was clearly scientific; the model for prediction was flawed. But this shortfall is not uniquely characteristic of Freud. Prediction of adult behavior on the basis of childhood experiences still cannot be done well by contemporary devel-opmental psychologists. Even with its obvious problems of validity, however, the genetic perspective is important for understanding moti-vation in that it emphasizes that any explanation for a given motivated behavior must take into account the developmental psychology of the individual. It adds a temporal dimension to motivation: a behavior is determined not only by factors in the present, such as the arousal of an instinctual drive, but also by factors in the past.

### The structural hypothesis: Id, ego, and superego

In the structural hypothesis, *structural* refers to the hypothesized parts of the personality: the id, the ego, and the superego. The basic assump-tion of the structural hypothesis is that psychological functioning can be explained in terms of the characteristics of and interrelations among distinct structures within the personality. Freud (1900) developed his first structural model as part of his topographic explanation of mental functioning, in which he viewed the Cs, Pcs, and Ucs as separate but interrelated parts of the mind. The details of that model, however, are not essential elements in what is now called the structural hypothesis. Rather, the structural-hypothesis viewpoint has become synonymous with Freud's well-known division of the mental apparatus into id, ego, and superego (1923, 1933, 1940). Since this structural model was developed late in Freud's career and was clearly aimed at a systematic understanding of behavior within the psychoanalytic framework, it is the most definitive and comprehensive of the six hypotheses, incorporating many elements of those discussed previously.

Since the structural hypothesis is commonly known, we shall give only a brief presentation, emphasizing the aspects of the model that are relevant for motivation. Throughout, the reader should be aware that id, ego, and superego are *not* concrete entities that can be located and observed. Rather, they are abstractions—metaphors that represent functions of the personality.

The id is the primary source of motivation in the mental apparatus. It is the reservoir of instinctual drives and psychic energy, and the functions of the instinctual drives and psychic energy are ascribed to the id. The unconscious instinctual impulses become associated with ideas and push for admission into consciousness and immediate gratification. These unconscious drive-related ideas have primacy and create a state of psychic tension that must be reduced by discharge through operations dictated by the pleasure principle; the ideas are characterized by primary-process thinking, which, it will be recalled, is illogical and forceful. The id provides psychic energy for the whole mental apparatus. The functions of the id are totally unconscious and are not directly affected by information from the outside world; the demands of reality are imposed on the id by the ego and superego. Over time, the influence of the ego and superego causes maturation in the id's functioning, so that the instinctual drives become less demanding motivators of behavior.

The ego has as its central function the control and integration of the determinants of behavior. It deals with the pressures imposed upon it by the id, the superego, and external reality (the environment). Freud described the relation between the ego and these determinants of behavior using the metaphor of "a horse with three harsh masters." Accordingly, the ego carries out an "executive function" in which the impinging demands must be simultaneously taken into account in any thought or action. The ego thus negotiates a compromise. For such a mammoth task, the ego utilizes memory, cognition, and perception. These operations, called ego functions, are characterized as secondary-process thinking. In stark contrast to the functions of the id, those of the ego are logical and responsive to the requirements of external reality. The ego's functions are determined not by the pleasure principle, as are the id's, but by the reality principle; the ego delays or displaces gratification of an instinctual drive until an appropriate goal can be found. The ego's chief weapon for controlling id impulses is a defense called repression. By means of repression, primary-process ideas are "warded off," or forced from consciousness. Other defenses derive from repression and produce the same end (that is, warding off) through different means. (These will be discussed later.) Besides the defenses, the ego functions are rational, realistic operations that take place on the conscious and preconscious levels. The ego is theorized to have developed with the id from an "undifferentiated matrix" of psychic energy a few weeks after birth and to maintain an unconscious, irrational component.

The superego has two main functions, which have their bases in the two subdivisions of the superego, the conscience and the ego ideal. The conscience is the repository wherein the moral standards of the culture, mediated by the family, are internalized. It thus defines as right and wrong those actions and thoughts that are rewarded and punished. It sets the boundaries for morally acceptable behavior. The ego-ideal is a set of goals toward which the individual strives. These goals are seen as appropriate for the culture and approved of by the parents. Violating the standards of the conscience by thinking or acting in a "wrong" way or those of the ego-ideal by not striving for the internalized goals results in feelings of guilt. Like instinctual drives, feelings of guilt can produce discomfort. Hence, they constitute potent sources of motivation. The content and feelings of the superego have conscious, preconscious, and unconscious components. The unconscious superego is related to the id, and it produces impulse-laden, irrational guilt feelings. The superego has genetic origins in the phallic stage, during which it develops from the ego as the Oedipus complex is resolved.

The structural model is depicted in Figure 3-3. Note first the clear emphasis derived from the topographic hypothesis; the ego and superego have conscious, preconscious, and unconscious components, and the id is entirely unconscious. Note also the expansion of the dynamic hypothesis. The basic intrapsychic conflict between drives and defenses is depicted structurally as id versus ego. Because the ego has a pivotal position in the structural scheme, two other sources of conflict with the ego are also apparent: the superego and external reality. When the ego selects a course of thought or action, that thought or action—that is, the ego function—has been multiply determined by the id, superego, and external reality.

The structural hypothesis is the most significant of the psychoanalytic viewpoints for two reasons. First, it has the broadest explanatory power for human motivation, thought, and action. Described from the structural point of view, behavior is motivated by a driving internal force (from the id) in conflict with defense (from the ego). The model's importance for the explanation of motivation, however, resides in its emphasis on noninstinctual determinants of motivation: internalized values, goals, and expectancies (in the superego) and considerations (by the ego) based on environmental input (external reality) significantly

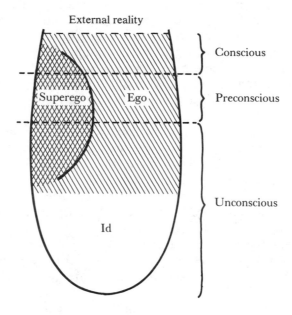

**Figure 3-3.** The structural model of the mind. *(Adapted from "New Introductory Lectures on Psychoanalysis," by S. Freud. In Volume XXII of* The Standard Edition of the Complete Psychological Works of Sigmund Freud, *revised and edited by James Strachey. Reprinted by permission of Sigmund Freud Copyrights Ltd., The Institute of Psycho-Analysis, and The Hogarth Press Ltd. Also in* The Complete Introductory Lectures on Psychoanalysis, *by Sigmund Freud. Translated and edited by James Strachey. Copyright © 1966 by W. W. Norton & Company, Inc. Copyright © 1965, 1964, 1963, by James Strachey. Copyright 1933 by Sigmund Freud. Copyright renewed 1961 by W. J. H. Sprott. Copyright 1920, 1935 by Edward L. Bernays. Reprinted by permission.)*

influence the course of action and thought. The psychoanalytic concept of overdetermination is used to explain this state of affairs, in which any behavior can be viewed as being caused by two or more factors— id, ego, superego, and external reality—in prolonged interaction. Second, the structural hypothesis is important because it is the only point of view in which Freud gives emphasis to the ego, and in doing so develops the foundations of ego psychology, in which characteristics of the ego (strength, defenses, development) are viewed as the central elements for understanding behavior. From these origins, ego psychology became the central movement of contemporary psychoanalysis. The original theory's preoccupation with motivational forces (the instinctual drives) was supplemented by investigations of the counterforces and other influences originating in the ego, based largely on the work of Hartmann (1939/1958, 1950) and D. Rapaport and Gill (1967). Ego psychology has offered substantial theoretical alternatives to the economic hypothesis (Breger, 1969) and the genetic hypothesis (Loevinger, 1966, 1969).

### The adaptive hypothesis: Environmental influences

The basic assumption of the adaptive hypothesis is that any psychoanalytic explanation of behavior must take into account the individual's relations with the environment. This viewpoint is seldom included with the five psychoanalytic hypotheses discussed above, as it is present only in Freud's later writings (for example, 1923) and derives largely from psychoanalytic ego psychology (Erikson, 1950; Hartmann, 1939/1958). It was explicitly formulated by Rapaport and Gill (1967). The adaptive hypothesis is the most distinctive theoretical perspective, sharing little with the topographic, dynamic, economic, and genetic theories; in the structural model, it is implicit in the interactions between the ego and external reality.

Throughout psychoanalytic theory the environment is generally seen as having two primary effects on the individual: either it acts as a source of pain, frustrating drives, creating trauma, and so on, or it acts as a source of pleasure, providing objects for the gratification of drives. In both cases, its impact on behavior is secondary to that of intrapsychic factors. The adaptive hypothesis does not limit its view of external reality to this polarity but instead emphasizes the inevitability of environmental influences to which the individual must continually adapt. Adaptation is not seen as a one-sided state of affairs in which the individual must passively knuckle under to the demands of the environment. Rather, growth and change occur in both the individual and the environment through their interaction. The individual shapes the environment, which then becomes more harmonious with the individual's needs.

The main contribution of the adaptive viewpoint resides in this emphasis on mutual person/environment interaction as a factor in motivation and behavior. This principle includes the structural notion of conflict between ego and external reality but extends its implications to take into account nonconflictual interaction. The adaptive hypothesis is important in that it counters a frequent criticism of psychoanalytic theory—that it has an intrapsychic bias and accordingly views behavior as arising purely from conflicts within the individual, with little if any external influence, as if the individual were a closed system of forces and energies. The adaptive hypothesis, on the contrary, attributes considerable influence to the environment. The environment is thus given equal status with the instinctual drives as an important motivational variable.

## Conclusions: The six hypotheses

The various aspects of the six psychoanalytic hypotheses that are particularly pertinent to motivation are presented in Table 3-1. Some obvious trends run through the hypotheses. All of them, except the adaptive, suggest that motivation arises from a force related to the concept of instinctual drive. This force operates unconsciously, becoming associated with ideas and pressing unceasingly for conscious expression and gratification. Because direct expression of the instinctual force is incompatible with the functions and norms of society, sources of regulation and restraint are developed. The result of the motive/regulation conflict is that behavior does not arise directly from the source of motivation but, rather, follows a circuitous path: the behavior (or other outcome) is defined jointly by the strength and characteristics of the motive and by the restraint. The structural hypothesis suggests that other, nonmotivational sources (guilt and reality) have an impact on the outcome.

In the following section, we shall examine in greater detail these central motivational constructs—instinctual drive and defense—and related aspects of psychoanalytic theory.

## *Motivational constructs*

The motivational constructs embedded in the fundamental psychoanalytic hypotheses have two important components. First and more obvious, they are expressed in the terminology of the metapsychological theory, in which the abstract principles and concepts of 19th century physicalism were applied to the phenomenon of motivation. Second and less obvious, the metapsychological concepts were attempts at ex-

**TABLE 3-1.** Motivational constructs in the six psychoanalytic hypotheses

| *Hypothesis* | *Source of motivation* | *Source of restraint* | *Nonmotivational influences* | *Outcome* |
|---|---|---|---|---|
| Topographic | Unconscious | The preconscious censor | — | Regression to sensory mode—e.g., dreams, hallucinations |
| Dynamic | Instinctual drives | Defenses | — | Compromise formations |
| Economic | Cathexes | Countercathexes | — | Maldistribution of psychic energy |
| Genetic | Libido | Excessive frustration (or excessive gratification) | Environment | Fixation |
| Structural | The id | The ego | Environment; superego | Compromise; over-determined behavior |
| Adaptive | — | — | Environment | Adaptation |

plaining Freud's actual clinical observations of his patients. The clinical observations acted as the guide for his metapsychological theory of motivation: the observations demanded explanations, and as the observations changed or were enriched, the theoretical explanations also required alteration or embellishment. The result was that the motivational constructs, like the whole theory of psychoanalysis, were not static—as, indeed, the existence of six points of view implies. The fitting of theory to clinical data propelled the psychoanalytic theory of motivation through at least four versions (Holzman, 1970).

The first version derived from Freud's early clinical work, in which he searched for the causes of defenses in his hysterical patients. From the ashes of his "seduction theory," Freud reasoned that sexual fantasies, rather than actual experiences, were at the root of hysterical symptoms and that from these fantasies arose "endogenous" stimuli (stimuli in the body), which he termed "sexual instinctual drive" (1905a). He explained the operations of this motivational force by means of psychic energy, libido. Freud also gave instinctual status to the defenses—the forces that opposed the sexual instinctual drive—by designating them *ego drives,* or *self-preservative drives.* These drives included attitudes, tendencies toward mastery and competence, and aspirations. In this early version, the ego drives were given minimal importance in motivation, being only passively reactive to the sexual instinctual drive and unable to curtail through conscious volition its urgent motivating force.

This distinction between instinctual forces and self-preservative counterforces was weakened in the second version of Freud's motivation theory, in which self-interest was explained as having a sexual component. Freud (1914a) theorized that extreme self-love, in which one aggrandizes and becomes preoccupied with oneself, might be a normal phase in psychological development that can recur in adulthood during physical illness or in the course of neurotic syndromes that include physical symptoms. Freud termed this excessive self-interest *narcissism.* Applying economic and quantitative considerations, he further reasoned that libido was withdrawn from others and directed toward the self. There was thus an inverse relation between the amounts of the two types of libido: narcissistic libido, which is invested in the self (self-cathexis), and object libido, which is invested in others (object cathexis). This version weakened the first theory by replacing different sexual and self-preservative energies with a single energy source, libido; libido was thus seen as the exclusive source of energy.

Freud developed the third version of his motivation theory to account for behaviors that had aggressive components and were inadequately explained by the construct of sexual instinctual drive. From clinical observations of destructiveness, competitiveness and rivalry in childhood, sadistic and masochistic behavior, the omnipresent strivings for dominance, control, and power, and self-protective behavior, Freud (1917) hypothesized an aggressive instinctual drive. His motivation theory thus became a dual theory of instinctual drives. The hypothesis of an aggressive drive broadened the base of explanation, but also created problems; the relation of that drive to the sexual drive was not clear. They were sometimes related harmoniously, at other times antagonistically. They were sometimes aroused simultaneously, at other times independently. Freud's tentative—and insufficient—solution was to construe the aggressive instinctual drive as a self-preservative drive, implying that its goals and operations were unlike those of the sexual instinctual drive.

The fourth and final version of Freud's motivation theory accompanied his formulation of the structural hypothesis (Freud, 1923). Again, several clinical observations were instrumental in moving him to revise his motivational model. These were the persistent self-abasement and misery of depressed persons, the suffering and pain that others who were not depressed managed to get themselves into, and the reliving by war veterans of their traumatic military experiences in fantasies and dreams. These observations led Freud to conclude that the aggressive instinctual drive was not exclusively self-preservative and, by implication, not independent of sexuality, which also was not self-preservative. On the contrary, the aggressive instinctual drive could impose pain, punishment, and even death, not only on others but also on the self. Accordingly, Freud hypothesized psychic structures to represent these qualitative differences between instinctual and self-preservative drives: motivation in the form of psychic energy emanated from the id, the repository of sexual and aggressive instinctual drives; control functions were attributed to the ego, the repository of self-preservative drives. In the process of developing his structural theory of motivation, Freud (1920) put forth some of his most speculative ideas about instinctual drives. These ideas appeared more philosophical than psychological. To explain the different effects of sex and aggression, he modified some of his basic physicalist notions about psychological functioning. He continued to define the operations of the sexual instinctual drive in terms of the pleasure principle—that is, the accumulation of libido created tension, the reduction of which was pleasurable. However, clinical observations of patients' aggression against themselves implied that the operations of the aggressive instinctual drive could be explained only by going "beyond the pleasure principle." Freud hypothesized that the principle that governed aggression was a search for pleasure through a return to early states of psychological adaptation, the earliest of which was preanimate. The goal of the aggressive motive was thus a return to death! Freud described the principle regulating sexuality as *anabolism,* involving growth and synthesis, and that regulating aggression as *catabolism,* involving disintegration and tearing down. Later he termed the instinctual drives of sex and aggression "life instincts" (Eros) and "death instincts"(Thanatos), respectively.

Throughout Freud's revisions of his motivation theory, the most enduring construct was that of instinctual drive. The major problems were caused by his dual theory of sex and aggression: the sexual instinctual drive is well integrated into psychoanalytic theory, as the foregoing discussion of the psychoanalytic hypotheses documents; the aggressive instinctual drive is not. The aggressive instinctual drive is most troublesome from the economic and genetic viewpoints, since sexual energy is hypothesized to be the central form of psychic energy and there is no parallel form of aggressive energy. Freud grappled unsuccessfully with this theoretical dilemma. Schafer (1968) has proposed a solution that differentiates sex and aggression according to their qualitative features and suggests a single, quantitative source of psychic energy, which fuels all motivations.

Although the construct of instinctual drive persisted through revisions of the theory, the construct of defense underwent considerable elaboration, so that the ego processes of defense, control, and regulation became central determinants of motivated activity. Thus, instinctual drive and defense became the fundamental constructs of the psychoanalytic theory of motivation.

### Instinctual drives

Freud defined *instinctual drive* "as a concept on the frontier between the mental and somatic, as the psychical representative of the stimuli originating from within the organism and reaching the mind, as a measure of the demand made upon the mind for work in consequence of its connection with the body" (1915a, pp. 121–122).[3] This definition is obviously vague and global—perhaps purposely so, for it is surprisingly more psychological than physiological. The emotionally charged idea (the "psychical representative") that motivates behavior does have internal, somatic origins, but the motivational processes are not said to be somatic (physical) conditions, such as a surplus or deficit of hormones, a change at a neural level, or an imbalance in physiological equilibrium. The concept of instinctual drive implies mind/body unity, rather than dualism. The physical source (internal stimulus) activates behavior through a forceful mental representation. Two assumptions in this definition distinguish it from other notions of instinct and drive: (1)

[3]From "Instincts and Their Vicissitudes," by S. Freud. In Volume XIV of *The Standard Edition of the Complete Psychological Works of Sigmund Freud*, revised and edited by James Strachey. Reprinted by permission of Sigmund Freud Copyrights Ltd., The Institute of Psycho-Analysis, and The Hogarth Press Ltd. Also in Volume XIV of *The Collected Papers of Sigmund Freud*, edited by Ernest Jones, M.D., Basic Books, Inc., Publishers, New York, 1959. This and all other quotations from this source are reprinted by permission of the publishers.

the principles and laws of psychological functioning can and must be studied on a behavioral level without reference to physiological processes; (2) the relation between behavior and physiological processes must be left open until the understanding of *both* is sufficiently advanced, unless psychological explanation is to be prematurely reduced to physical terms (D. Rapaport, 1960).

Instinctual drive therefore is a motivational construct whose goals and implications are interestingly psychological yet whose source is described in physiological terms. It is clearly a hybrid concept fostered by Freud's physicalistic and clinical background. Attributing a constant, unyielding motivational influence to the instinctual drive makes it more akin to the ethological concept of instinct than to the behavioral concept of drive, which is assumed to wax and wane as a function of situational stimuli. The assumption of unconscious, drive-related ideas as the primary determinants of behavior differentiates the psychoanalytic concept of instinctual drive from both instinct and drive.

Freud (1915a) elaborated on his definition of instinctual drives by describing four characteristics of them: pressure, aim, object, and source.

**Pressure.**   "By the pressure of an instinct[4] we understand its motor factor, the amount of force or the measure of the demand for work which it represents. The characteristic of exercising pressure is common to all instincts; it is in fact their very essence" (Freud, 1915a, p. 122). The pressure of an instinctual drive, then, is its force and energy. That a drive has pressure is central to the economic hypothesis. The force of the instinctual drive is usually stopped short of motor action and is hence transformed, or displaced, into fantasies, dreams, or other substitutes. Implied in this definition is the assumption of primacy, the persistent, forceful demand of motivation that characterizes psychoanalytic theory.

**Aim.**   "The aim of an instinct is in every instance satisfaction, which can only be obtained by removing the state of stimulation" (Freud, 1915a, p. 122). Thus, the aim of an instinctual drive is expressed through the pleasure principle; the accumulation of psychic energy creates tension, and tension reduction through discharge is pleasurable. From the economic viewpoint, the aim determines the functions of the personality that regulate the expenditure and distribution of energy.

**Object.**   "The object of an instinct is the thing in regard to which or through which the instinct is able to achieve its aim. It is what is

[4]Strachey's translation, like most British translations, interprets Freud's term *Instinkt* as "instinct." The customary American rendering, made popular by D. Rapaport, is "instinctual drive." The two terms are synonymous.

most variable about an instinct and is not originally connected with it, but becomes assigned to it only in consequence of being peculiarly fitted to make satisfaction possible. The object is not necessarily something extraneous: it may equally well be a part of the subject's own body. It may be changed any number of times in the course of the vicissitudes which the instinct undergoes during its existence; and highly important parts are played by this displacement of instinct" (Freud, 1915a, pp. 122–123). This is perhaps the most curious characteristic of the instinctual drive; its force and energy are defined by the object of its discharge. Freud states that, although the object is selected because it is "peculiarly fitted" to provide pleasure through tension reduction, the choice of object is not innately determined. Hence, there is not a single object of the instinctual drive but instead a group of reasonable objects that are capable of providing satisfaction. Accordingly, the instinctual drives have a quality called *plasticity* (G. S. Klein, 1969), which is their capability for changing direction as a function of the availability of an object. Through the concept of displacement, objects are theorized to change during the course of psychosexual development and as a result of qualitative changes in the environment. The view implies that "learning" has an impact on object selection. However, the means by which the coordination between an instinctual drive and its object is learned or relearned have not yet been specified by psychoanalytic theory (D. Rapaport, 1960).

**Source.**    "By the source of an instinct is meant that somatic process which occurs in an organ or part of the body and whose stimulus is represented in mental life by an instinct. We do not know whether this process is invariably of a chemical nature or whether it may also correspond to the release of other, e.g. mechanical, forces. The study of the sources of instincts lies outside the scope of psychology ... [and] ... is not invariably necessary for purposes of psychological investigation" (Freud, 1915a, p. 123). As in his definitions of instinctual drive, Freud is assuming that there is a physical source of instinct. Yet, the physical source of instinct is not important in understanding how it functions psychologically as a motive. It is important to note in this regard that in his genetic hypothesis Freud was not explaining the oral, anal, and phallic zones as sources of instinctual drive during the psychosexual stages of childhood. Rather, they were "points of application" of libido through which the sexual instinctual drive became manifest (D. Rapaport, 1960).[5]

[5]Starting from the psychoanalytic theory of instinctual drive, D. Rapaport (1960) has formulated a definition of motivation that consolidates Freud's writings on instinctual drive and frees them of their cumbersome physicalist terminology. He proposes that motives are *appetitive internal forces* that are characterized by four variable qualities: peremptoriness, cyclic character, selectiveness, and displaceability. *Peremptoriness* refers to the mandatory character of motivated behavior; unlike voluntary behavior, which one can "take or leave," motivated behavior must be undertaken. *Cyclic*

The instinctual drives are manifested in two ways. First, they can directly initiate some motor action that would produce discharge, such as an overt sexual or aggressive behavior. However, defensive regulation would demand an alternate means of expression. Second, instinctual drives can be expressed indirectly by means of instinctual-drive representations. These representations have two elements: idea and affect (Freud, 1915b). The idea is a mental image (a fantasy) that has been cathected (that is, a mental image in which a quantity of psychic energy has been invested). Thus, the formation of ideas involves instinctual drive. Affects (emotions) directly related to the idea become detached from it and find expression as feelings. Ideas and affects serve the joint function of being psychological representations of the instinctual drives and of acting as points of release for tension caused by the accumulation of psychic energy.

## Repression and defense

Our discussion of the six fundamental hypotheses revealed that a trend is present throughout psychoanalytic theory: the backbone of the theory is the principle that the motive force of the instinctual drives invariably comes into contact with counterforces established for restraint and regulation, and the motivated behavior is determined by the interaction of these and other factors. The dynamic viewpoint, for example, depicts this intrapsychic conflict as one between instinctual drives and defenses. *Defense* is a generic term that denotes any of the various processes of regulation. Throughout most of his writings Freud used the terms *defense* and *repression* synonymously, and his important statements on the defensive process evolve from his many papers on repression. Only late in the development of his theory (for example, Freud, 1926) did Freud view repression as one defense among others—reaction formation, projection, and so forth. And even then it was clear that repression was the fundamental concept of instinctual-drive regulation and that the other defenses were only derivations (Madison, 1961). The concept of repression thus has two meanings—a general process of instinctual control and a particular mechanism of defense. The former meaning is the focus here.

**Repression.** In describing the essentials of the mechanism of repression, Freud said that "repression is not a defensive mechanism which is present from the very beginning [of life] and . . . it cannot

---

*character* refers to the rise and fall of motivation: peremptoriness increases and attenuates. *Selectiveness* refers to the inevitability of an object or goal for the motive force; the target may vary as a function of the behavioral context but is always present. *Displaceability* refers to the process of substituting alternate goals and objects for those that are unattainable; it implies a series of options for motivated behavior. Every motive has each of these qualities to some degree; thus instinctual drive is conceptualized as peremptory, cyclical, selective, and displaceable.

arise until a sharp cleavage has occurred between conscious and unconscious mental activity. . . . *The essence of repression lies simply in turning something away, and keeping it at a distance, from the conscious"* (1915b, p. 147).[6] This description of repression illustrates several important features. First, repression is not an innate biological process; it is acquired through experience. Second, the experiences that give rise to repression involve a conflict between unconscious and conscious thinking in that the unconscious poses a threat to the conscious. Third, the repressive process tries to resolve the conflict by preventing the threatening unconscious idea from coming into conscious awareness. By implication, this "turning away" and "keeping from" consciousness of some unconscious idea may be accomplished by any mental activity, not just by the motivated forgetting, or amnesia, that is meant by the term *repression* in its narrow sense.

Freud, then, used *repression* to mean any counterforce that "warded off" threatening unconscious ideas from conscious recognition. All repressive processes, however, consisted of three definite, interrelated stages. Freud called the first stage "primal repression":

> We have reason to assume that there is a *primal repression*, a first phase of repression, which consists in the psychical [ideational] representative of the instinct being denied entrance into the conscious. With this a *fixation* is established; the representative in question persists unaltered from then onwards and the instinct remains attached to it [1915b, p. 148].

Elsewhere (1911), Freud made it clear that this form of repression was confined to childhood, occurring in the pregenital psychosexual stages (oral, anal, and phallic) before the development of the superego at age 5 or 6. The instinctual-drive representations, or fantasies, that become primally repressed are those that induce an intolerable "traumatic anxiety," experienced as a feeling of overwhelming helplessness. The intensity of the traumatic anxiety requires immediate action (through repression) to ward off the fantasies causing it. These fantasies involve the frustration of basic physical needs, separation from the mother, Oedipal conflicts, and so forth. Primal repression of a psychical representation is permanent; only derivatives can ever reach consciousness, and these in turn must be repressed in Freud's next stage, repression proper:

> The second stage of repression, *repression proper,* affects mental derivatives of the repressed representative, or such trains of thought as, origi-

⁶From "Repression," by S. Freud. In Volume XIV of *The Standard Edition of the Complete Psychological Works of Sigmund Freud,* revised and edited by James Strachey. Reprinted by permission of Sigmund Freud Copyrights Ltd., The Institute of Psycho-Analysis, and The Hogarth Press Ltd. Also in Volume IV of *The Collected Papers of Sigmund Freud,* edited by Ernest Jones, M.D., Basic Books, Inc., Publishers, New York, 1959. This and all other quotations from this source are reprinted by permission of the publishers.

nating elsewhere, have come into associative connection with it. On account of this association, these ideas experience the same fate as what was primally repressed. Repression proper, therefore, is actually an after-pressure. Moreover, it is a mistake to emphasize only the repulsion which operates from the direction of the conscious upon what is to be repressed; quite as important is the attraction exercised by what was primally repressed upon everything with which it can establish a connection. Probably the trend toward repression would fail in its purpose if these two forces did not cooperate, if there were not something previously repressed ready to receive what is repelled by the conscious [1915b, p. 148].

Repression proper is the process of repressing, in adulthood, a derivative of a fantasy that the person primally repressed in childhood. The central feature of repression proper is that it is an "after-pressure"—it is causally related to the primally repressed ideas of the previous stage. Without primal repression, repression proper could not occur. There is thus a temporal connection between repressions that span many years. Repression proper is triggered by "signal anxiety," an anticipatory response that warns the adult of imminent threat. This threat results from the fear that unconscious childhood fantasies of traumas might recur if one engages in sexual or aggressive thoughts or actions that are associated with primally repressed ideas (Freud, 1926). This notion of association is important because it identifies the means by which innocent, drive-free behavior can become connected with drive-related thoughts and subsequently be repressed.

The final stage of repression Freud calls "return of the repressed":

The third phase, and the most important as regards pathological phenomena, is that of failure of repression, of *irruption*, or *return of the repressed*. This irruption takes its start from the point of fixation, and it implies a regression of the libidinal development to that point [1911, p. 66].

The failure of repression thus brings about a return of the repressed idea to conscious experience. However, previously repressed ideas *never* return to consciousness unaltered. Instead they must undergo some distortion or transformation, the mark of the defensive process. What is expressed in the return of the repressed is therefore a "compromise formation" of the instinctual-drive representations and repression; it is a product of the intrapsychic motivational conflict.

The "irruption" of previously repressed ideas is central to the psychoanalytic theory of neurotic-symptom formation and psychopathology. Abnormal behaviors are influenced by the return of the repressed in two ways: first, by providing compromise formations in the form of symptoms of psychopathology; second, by affecting the type of defense (projection, isolation, and so forth) that an individual uses (unsuccessfully) to ward off the unconscious idea (Freud, 1896). However, repressive failure is by no means restricted to abnormal processes. It is common in such normal processes as artistic appreciation (Ehrenzweig, 1965) and creation (Ehrenzweig, 1967; Kris, 1952), imagination, and even humor and wit (Freud, 1915b).

The occurrence of irruptions requires that the instinctual drive be stronger than the repressive force; seen from the economic viewpoint, therefore, irruption is determined by the distribution of psychic energy. A redistribution of psychic energy that results in an irruption can occur in three ways: (1) by an increase in instinctual activity as a result of associated environmental stimuli—for example, seeing an explicitly sexual movie or witnessing death and carnage in an auto accident; (2) by an absolute increase in psychic energy, such as that which occurs at puberty; and (3) by a weakening of repression and defense—for example, through the influence of large doses of drugs or alcohol, excessive physical fatigue, or neural deterioration or damage.

Repressive failure caused by an environmental association can be illustrated clinically by reference to a former patient of one of the authors. The presenting problem of Michael, a student, was the rapid onset of uncontrollable sexual and aggressive fantasies and hallucinations following his return to college after a visit home. He was panicked by the quality and insistence of the ideas, and both he and his friends believed he was "going crazy." The remarkable aspect of Michael's case was that, by all available information, he had never before had experiences that in any way resembled his present disturbance. If anything, he had been a model of mental health: he was an outstanding student, had many friends and interests, came from a loving, accepting family, and appeared to have been free of chronic anxiety or depression. He was treated by means of psychopharmacological medication, short-term hospitalization, and psychotherapy, and in about ten days he seemed to be completely recovered. Yet he could not identify what had caused his psychological distress. More information was uncovered accidentally in a follow-up interview with his parents about a month later. They mentioned that nothing unusual had happened on his visit home except that he had inadvertently walked into their bedroom while they were having intercourse! Theoretically, this episode was associated with Oedipal fantasies, primally repressed in early childhood, regarding his attraction to his mother and consequent fear of his father. The stimulus of observing parental intercourse provided a causal connection with the repressed idea, and increasing the strength of the idea so that it became stronger than the repression. This produced the irruption of ideas and hallucinations that were, symbolically, compromises of drive and defense.

One critical aspect of repression is that, since the instinctual-drive representations are unconscious, their control and regulation by repression and defense also occur without conscious awareness or volition.

Freud reserved the term *repression* for the unconscious defensive process directed against unconscious drive-related ideas. A conscious warding off of unpleasant thoughts or emotions, sometimes called *suppression* (Breuer & Freud, 1895), is not repression in the psychoanalytic sense and is not related to the instinctual drives.

The psychoanalytic theory of repression has five features that differentiate the concept of repression from other phenomena that appear similar. First, the unconscious instinctual drives are the only bases for repression. Second, repression has a temporal dimension in that ideas must first be primally repressed in early childhood for repression proper in adulthood to occur. Third, repression proper is discriminative and selective; it always entails the expulsion from consciousness of only those ideas that are derived from or have become associated with the contents of primal repression. Fourth, the idea previously repressed returns (in disguised form) when there is defensive failure. Accordingly, repression is not synonymous with memory loss or decay, since the motivated forgetting is not necessarily permanent; ideas are shelved in the unconscious, not destroyed. Fifth, the repressed ideas and the process of repression are unconscious.

**Defense mechanisms.**    With his development of the structural hypothesis and ego psychology, Freud (1923, 1926) expanded his theory of repression. He described several mental operations, called "defense mechanisms," by means of which the ego warded off unconscious ideas, and he delineated other factors (that is, guilt and external reality) that affected the intrapsychic conflict. The mechanisms of defense can be viewed as variants of repression proper (Madison, 1961). This development is noteworthy because it signaled the beginning of a movement within psychoanalysis away from its troublesome emphasis on instinctual drives and toward the ego and the processes that regulate behavior.

The defense mechanisms of the ego that were formulated by Freud were classified, extended, and described by his daughter Anna (A. Freud, 1936/1946). Briefly, they are as follows.

*Repression* is a defense whereby ideas and emotions are forcefully kept from consciousness by means of selective, motivated forgetting. (This is the specific definition of *repression;* it should not be confused with the general definition, which describes the way all defense proceeds.) An example of repression cited earlier is the amnesia of Breuer's patient Anna O. for her traumatic experiences.

*Isolation* is the splitting off of ideas from feelings. It is, thus, a partial repression—a repression of emotions only. For example, a veteran might blandly tell stories of his traumatic war experiences without experiencing the guilt (or satisfaction) of observing and engaging in the killing.

*Reaction formation* is a defense in which repression is maintained by substituting for a threatening idea its opposite. A person might control sexual fantasies by becoming excessively moralistic and viewing sexual activity as dirty, animalistic behavior.

*Projection* is a defense wherein the drive-related fantasy is attributed to another person. For example, a husband with unconscious extra-marital sexual interest might jealously ascribe adulterous desires to his wife. Here the repression is maintained by disowning the impulses and attributing them to someone else.

*Undoing* is the taking back of or making amends for an impulse or guilt-ridden thought or action. A woman whose relationship with her mother was strained and who was prone to fleeting aggressive fantasies might, following such thoughts, "spontaneously" decide to send her a gift.

*Displacement* is a defense in which the unconscious fantasy is directed away from the original object toward a relatively neutral one.

*Turning against the self* is a variation of displacement in which the impulse, usually aggressive, is displaced from the external object toward the self in the form of self-denigration, self-blame, and so forth. The woman who unconsciously blames her husband for her unhappiness and lack of fulfillment might become depressed, guilt-ridden, and self-abasing.

*Rationalization* is the use of emotionally neutral, objective reasoning to explain a behavior or its avoidance when a drive-related idea is the motivating factor. For example, a literary critic might rationalize his reading a pornographic novel several times by citing its artistic merit, intriguing plot, and sophisticated style, when his interest really derives from its explicit sexual imagery.

*Denial* is a poorly defined defense with which the person blocks out obvious aspects of reality to avoid their painful consequences. Refusing to accept the death of a loved one and denying the seriousness of a terminal illness are examples of denial.

*Identification* is a defense in which the person, usually first as a child, adopts the characteristics (values, attitudes, behaviors, and so forth) of a significant other. (For the child, identification with the parents is an inevitable outcome of learning and maturation. Hence, identification is much more than a defense.) Identification is often used to defend against the trauma of separation or of loss of love. For example, while his father is out of town, a little boy might behave "just like dad," looking after his mother, carrying out the trash, insisting that his younger brother behave, and so on.

Repression and the mechanisms of defense operate to regulate the instinctual drives. However, anxiety is believed to be an intervening agent in the process. This intervention is generated by the instinctual drive and instigates the action of the defense. Anxiety "signals" the ego that some danger is posed by an instinctual drive (Freud, 1926). Anna Freud (1936/1946) distinguished four types of anxiety motivating repression and defense: (1) superego anxiety, aroused because of internalized inhibitions and prohibitions imposed by the conscience and the ego-ideal; (2) objective anxiety (in childhood), caused by the fear of direct, interpersonal conflict in which the parents exert control over the child's instinctual-drive expression; (3) anxiety about the strength of drives, induced by the fear of being excessively stimulated by one's instinctual drives and consequently being helpless to control them; and (4) anxiety stemming from conflicts between incompatible aims, in which incompatible instinctual tendencies—for example, sexual and aggressive impulses directed at the same loved object—create intrapsychic discord and anxiety. All these sources of anxiety are hypothesized to derive from the action of the instinctual drives. We shall consider subsequently whether anxiety must be drive-related for repression and defense to operate. One can argue that anxiety is the motivator and that it need not have an instinctual cause.

## Experimental research

We noted at the beginning of this chapter that Freud's concepts and methods of inquiry made the experimental investigation of psychoanalytic theory a difficult, if not fruitless, task. The difficulty, thoroughly debated by Mischel (1973) and Wachtel (1973), centers on Freud's extensive use of covert constructs—that is, those that can only be inferred from behavior and not directly measured or observed. This covert quality of psychoanalytic constructs seems to make it impossible to formulate operational definitions and testable hypotheses, both of which are necessary for experimentation. The psychoanalytic theory of motivation exemplifies this problem. The fundamental motivational constructs, instinctual drive and repression, are both theorized to be unconscious. Fortunately, repression is nevertheless observable by others. An unavoidably circular logic seems to arise from the concept of instinctual drive, just as in other theories of drive and instinct. Freud *inferred* motivational drive from multiple observations of his psychoanalytic patients as an explanation for their behavior. Once the concept was believed to be valid and given theoretical status, Freud and his successors interpreted subsequent clinical observations as *evidence* for the existence of instinctual drive—but its existence had originally been inferred from just such observations. Definitions of instinctual constructs are by nature circular, and attempted experimental verification of such constructs is consequently misdirected. Certain aspects of the theory of repression, however, are apparently definable, measurable, and testable. Since Freud emphasized that "the theory of repression is the cornerstone on which the whole structure of psychoanalysis rests" (1914b, p. 16), investigation of repression has compelled attention by researchers. We shall briefly review the experimental methods and the evidence.

Numerous studies before 1950 were generally supportive of the psychoanalytic theory of repression, but they were woefully inadequate in that they lacked sufficient methodological rigor to justify a final judgment of the validity of the concept of repression (Zeller, 1950a). Because of the inadequacy of these studies, Zeller (1950a, 1950b) proposed a research model that has become the standard for experimental investigation of repression. In putting forth his requirements, Zeller made two stipulations: first, the experimenter must induce repression in the laboratory so that there is control over its content and operation; second, the experimenter must be able to lift, or dissolve, the repression so that what was repressed can return, unmarred by the nonrepressive forces of memory decay and loss.

Zeller performed the first three experiments (1950b, 1951) using this paradigm. Table 3-2 lists the procedures in his first experiment (1950b). Since this study stands as a model for those performed later, we shall discuss it in some detail. All subjects were first required to learn a list of nonsense syllables to a criterion of one correct trial—that is, well enough to recall the whole list correctly in one run through it. Nonsense syllables were used because they were emotionally neutral. Three days later, the subjects returned to the laboratory and were asked to recall the list and then relearn it to the one-trial criterion. At this point all subjects had learned and relearned the neutral materials to the same level. They were then divided into an experimental group and a control group. All subjects were then given a seemingly innocuous block-tapping task in which they had to duplicate a pattern presented by the experimenter. The experimenter manipulated the task so that all the control subjects performed well and presumably had a pleasant experience, and all the experimental subjects failed and pre-

**TABLE 3-2.** Experimental design for research on repression

|  | Experimental group | Relative performance | Control group |
|---|---|---|---|
| Session 1 | Learning | = | Learning |
|  | Retention test | = | Retention test |
| Session 2 | Retention test | = | Retention test |
|  | Repression-inducing task |  | Neutral task |
|  | Retention test | < | Retention test |
| Session 3 | Retention test | < | Retention test |
|  | Repression-lifting task |  | Neutral task |
|  | Retention test | = | Retention test |
| Session 4 | Retention test | = | Retention test |

Adapted from "An Experimental Analogue of Repression: II. The Effect of Individual Failure and Success on Memory Measured by Relearning," by A. Zeller, *Journal of Experimental Psychology*, 1950, *40*, 411–422. Copyright 1950 by the American Psychological Association. Reprinted by permission.

sumably experienced unpleasantness in the form of ego threat. It was hypothesized that at this juncture the threatening experience would become associated with the neutral materials and that repression would be manifest in poorer recall and relearning of the nonsense syllables. This hypothesis was tested by having the subjects recall the list and then relearn it. As hypothesized, the experimental group performed significantly more poorly than the control group on both recall and relearning. (We can express this difference as "experimental < control.") During a third session, three days later, both groups were again asked to recall and relearn the list; the group difference (experimental < control) remained intact. Both groups then engaged in the block-tapping task, but this time, in order to "lift the repression," the experimenter manipulated the task so that *both* groups performed well and had a positive experience. They were again asked to recall and relearn the nonsense syllables. This time, there was no group difference. This result (experimental = control) was maintained in a fourth session, again involving recall and relearning. In conclusion, the results of the experiment clearly supported the theory of repression as it was operationally defined by Zeller.

Subsequent experiments by Zeller (1950b, 1951) and others (Aborn, 1953; D'Zurilla, 1965; Flavell, 1955; Holmes, 1972; Holmes & Schallow, 1969; Merrill, 1954; Penn, 1964; Truax, 1957), designed to refine the method used in Zeller's original study, all yielded results consistent with the theory of repression. Using Zeller's paradigm, these experiments revealed that ego threat was associated with poor recall compared with recall in the absence of such a source of anxiety and that this decline in recall could be removed.

Four of the experiments, however (Aborn, 1953; D'Zurilla, 1965; Holmes, 1972; Holmes & Schallow, 1969), offered an alternative explanation: their findings suggested that the decline in recall performance could be explained by cognitive interference (Holmes, 1974). The ego-threatening situation probably elicited thoughts regarding self-esteem, creativity, intelligence, emotional adjustment, and so forth that might have interfered with recall of the neutral material and would have lost their interfering tendencies when the threat was removed. Holmes's experiment (1972) serves as an illustration of this approach. Holmes expanded Zeller's research paradigm, using three groups of subjects. All subjects took a bogus personality test and received one of three types of feedback: ego-threat, in which they were told that they were poorly adjusted; ego-enhancement, in which they were told that they had leadership potential and were creative; and, as a control, neutral, in which they were given innocuous, average information. In accordance with the interference explanation, Holmes hypothesized that the neutral group would have the best recall and that *both* the ego-threat and ego-enhancement groups would have poorer recall, because

either negative or positive thoughts would induce cognitive interference. The results occurred as hypothesized. Moreover, Holmes was
able to demonstrate a "lifting" of the memory decline in both experimental groups, when the threatening or enhancing feedback was removed. These results, with the others cited above, suggest that a more
parsimonious explanation for the results of experiments using Zeller's
paradigm might involve cognitive interference, rather than repression.

In conclusion, these studies do not definitely support the psychoanalytic theory of repression; cognitive interference is a plausible alternative explanation of their results. Does this failure to experimentally
validate hypotheses derived from the theory of repression seriously call
into question the "cornerstone" of psychoanalytic theory, as Holmes
(1974) has suggested? Probably not. The reasons are complex and are
rooted in the argument regarding the philosophical and real-world
meanings of scientific experimentation. We shall mention two points
briefly.

The first problem pertains to what D. T. Campbell and Stanley
(1963) term the trade-off between internal and external validity in designing experiments. The fundamental goal of experimental inquiry is
to provide control over all conditions that determine the results except
those under study. The degree to which the methods and definitions
meet this standard is a reflection of the internal validity of the experiment. On the surface, repression experiments appear internally valid;
they control what is learned, specify the time of recall after learning,
manipulate experimental variables such as ego threat, and so on. Their
drawback relates to external validity—the meaning of the results outside the laboratory. Does the operational definition of *repression* used
in Zeller's paradigm truly reflect the psychoanalytic concept of repression? Experimentalists (such as Holmes, 1974) seem to think so, and
they suggest that the inconclusiveness of the experimental results calls
all of psychoanalytic theory into question. Psychoanalysts and psychoanalytic scholars (such as Madison, 1961) seem to think not. They
argue that the learning and recall of nonsense syllables, the vague, de-
ceptive manipulation of ego threat, and the failure to determine
whether the threat was related to the instinctual drives or whether the
decline in performance was unconscious make the experimental situations artificial analogs bearing little resemblance to the real-life situations in which Freud's detailed theory of repression and defense was
intended to apply. Hence, the answers depend on one's viewpoint.

A second problem of the repression research is related to the problem
of external validity and is epistemological—that is, it has to do with the
methods of obtaining knowledge. If the concept of repression has not
been adequately operationalized in the experimental research—and
close inspection would reveal that it has not—then a question arises
regarding the applicability of the usual modes of scientific inquiry to

psychoanalytic theory. Epistemologists are pessimistic on this issue (Peterfreund, 1971; Ricoeur, 1970). The challenge of studying concepts such as instinctual drive, primal repression, and the unconscious in the usual laboratory settings appears to be staggeringly difficult. This problem seems inherent in the structure of psychoanalytic theory. However, we must realize that untestability is not the same as invalidity. Scientific appraisal of psychoanalytic motivational constructs may have to await refinement of the theory by current scholars, to whom we shall now turn for a short examination of their contributions.

## Motivation and ego psychology

Psychoanalytic theory is primarily a "drive" psychology. That is, the instinctual drives give impetus and direction to behavior, and repression and defense have in the main only a reactive role. When Freud developed the structural viewpoint late in his writings (1923, 1926), he began to de-emphasize the role of the instinctual drives. Instead he shifted his attention toward an ego psychology, in which the ego and other nonmotivational sources (the superego and external reality) were seen as significant determinants of behavior. This change in theoretical emphasis was most apparent in the structural and adaptive hypotheses. Quite typically, Freud did not appreciably revise psychoanalytic theory to accommodate his new insights and incorporate them into its mainstream. This task was left to his successors, most notably Hartmann (1939/1958, 1950, 1952).

In a monograph, *Ego Psychology and the Problem of Adaptation,* Hartmann (1939/1958) put forth a thorough reworking of the psychoanalytic concepts of reality and ego, a reworking that had been begun by Freud (1926). Hartmann did not view the environment solely as a source of frustration and gratification of the instinctual drives. That view of reality would require that the individual undergo changes simply to have his or her instinctual needs satisfied, a process he termed *autoplasticity.* Rather, Hartmann conceived of psychological adaptation as also requiring a process of *alloplasticity,* an active shaping of the environment by the individual. These processes demand a reciprocal relationship between the individual and the environment. Hartmann's view of adaptation as involving autoplastic and alloplastic processes made it necessary to reformulate the concept of the ego. Freud had conceived of the ego as a structure for control and regulation. Hartmann expanded this concept to posit components of the ego that were independent of intrapsychic conflict and could be used powerfully for affecting the environment. Hartmann designated the functions of the ego that at birth were free of influence by the instinctual drives as the conflict-free sphere of the ego. He named this independence of the conflict-free sphere *primary autonomy.* Behaviors that were developed in the process of intrapsychic conflict could over time become part of the conflict-free sphere of the ego by attaining secondary autonomy. The basic notion here is that thoughts and actions that were originally motivated by the instinctual drives can become intrinsically motivated—that is, satisfying or rewarding in their own right, independently of reducing instinctual tension. For example, a man who becomes attracted to painting because it provides him with chances to view nude models might subsequently be motivated to continue not because of indirect sexual gratification but because of the intrinsic rewards of art. Or a young woman who enters law school to foil her mother's plans that she be a housewife and mother might subsequently be motivated to continue as an attorney not because of the diverted aggression against her mother but because the career holds intrinsic value for her feelings of self-esteem and competence. Hartmann used the term *change of function* for the process by which a behavior originally motivated by instinctual drives gains secondary autonomy.

The theory of ego autonomy, as developed by Hartmann and extended by others (for example, D. Rapaport, 1951), is a critical addition to the psychoanalytic theory of motivation; it provides a concept of derivative motivations, by means of which behavior is motivated directly by sources other than the "appetitive internal force" (D. Rapaport, 1960) of instinctual drives. Freud dealt with derivative motivation in an incomplete manner in his concept of sublimation (Fenichel, 1945). He viewed sublimation as an adaptive process by which the instinctual drives attained discharge in an appropriate, socially acceptable channel. For example, one might seek aggressive gratification by becoming a surgeon or sexual gratification by becoming a movie censor. Thus, through sublimation, sexual and aggressive satisfaction could be gotten safely without the usual negative consequences imposed by society for sexual and aggressive behavior.

Derivative motivations are explained more thoroughly by Hartmann's frequently misunderstood concept of neutralization (Hartmann, 1939/1958, 1952). In the course of ego development, the instinctual urges are constantly controlled and regulated, so that they lose much of their primacy, or demand in motivating behavior; that is, they are neutralized. These neutralized sources of motivation are less likely to cause conflict and hence can provide impetus to behavior directly, without requiring strict repression and defense. Sexuality and aggression are thus toned down, or "defused," in their impact on behavior.

The theory of ego autonomy thus eases the heavy reliance of psychoanalytic theory on the instinctual-drive construct to explain the motivation of behavior. By postulating an autonomous, conflict-free ego sphere, the theory allows many behaviors to be explained as being directly motivated or caused by factors unrelated to the instinctual drives.

Conceptually, this is immensely important. It means that a behavior is *not necessarily* a defense against the instinctual drives or a compromise between drive and defense. The theory of ego autonomy also appears to be a better subject for experimental investigation than psychoanalytic theory is, since it does not hold that unobservable instinctual drives are the only possible causes of behavior or that unconscious repression and defense are the only consequences. Developed within the adaptive framework, the emerging research on cognitive controls and cognitive styles as autonomous ego functions (Gardner, Holzman, Klein, Linton, & Spence, 1959; Holzman, 1970; G. S. Klein, 1970) might eventually yield the scientific support for these ego-psychological concepts that has been so difficult to gain for traditional psychoanalytic concepts such as repression.

Another development in ego psychology that is worthy of mention is the concept of ego motives. Hartmann (1950) turned his attention to this group of behavioral tendencies, which Freud had included in the self-preservative drives in his early version of motivation theory. These ego motives, such as egoism and self-assertion, consisted of "strivings for what is useful." Hartmann viewed ego motives as motivating behaviors independent of the instinctual drives. Since the ego is the source of such motives, no conflict occurs; motive and behavior are linked. For example, achievement arises from an ego motive to achieve.

An important notion that derives from Hartmann's theory of ego motives is R. W. White's concept of competence (1959, 1963). White theorizes that organisms are programmed "to have an effect." He hypothesizes an instinct-like force—*effectance motivation*—to account for competence, mastery, and related behaviors. Like the ego motives, competence is an intrinsic source of motivation independent of the instinctual drives of sex and aggression.

Erikson's well-known model of psychosocial development (1950), although loosely put together, offers an important revision of Freud's genetic component of motivation. Erikson emphasizes the interplay between the individual's biological endowment and development, his or her ego, and the environment in which he or she lives. For Erikson, fixation arises not only from psychosexual conflict but also from psychosocial "crises"—that is, from problematic interactions between the individual's instinctual expression and the social environment in which it occurs. Thus, one's instinctual heritage *and* one's social heritage affect the motivation of subsequent behavior.

Erikson depicted his theory of ego development in terms of a stage model of the life cycle (see Table 3-3), and his psychosocial model parallels Freud's psychosexual model. Note that Erikson's major contributions pertain to the emphasis on psychosocial crises, rather than psychosexual conflicts. As in Freud's model, crises at each of the stages in Erikson's model may go unresolved, creating psychosocial fixations,

**TABLE 3-3.** Erikson's psychosocial model of development

| Period | Psychosexual stage | Psychosocial crises | Positive outcome |
|--------|--------------------|--------------------|------------------|
| Early infancy | Oral | Trust versus mistrust | Trust, hope |
| Late infancy | Anal | Autonomy versus shame and doubt | Independence, volition |
| Preschool | Phallic | Initiative versus guilt | Purpose, direction |
| School age | Latency | Industry versus inferiority | Competence, effectiveness |
| Adolescence | Genital | Identity versus role confusion | Conviction, fidelity |
| Adulthood |  |  |  |
| Early |  | Intimacy versus isolation | Love |
| Middle |  | Generativity versus stagnation | Caring |
| Late |  | Ego identity versus despair | Satisfaction, wisdom |

or be resolved positively. Positive outcomes result in ego strengths such as purpose, competence, and wisdom.

In recent years, a number of efforts have been made to maintain and expand the clinical aspects of the psychoanalytic theory of motivation while revising or discarding the cumbersome metapsychological language, which is so heavily laden with physicalist concepts (Breger, 1969; G. S. Klein, 1967, 1969; Loevinger, 1969; Peterfreund, 1971). The details of the theories concerned are considerably beyond the scope of the present discussion, but all the theories are aimed at updating the psychoanalytic theory of motivation in light of current thought and research, especially that generated in cognitive psychology and information-processing technology. These revisions, although still in their infancy, show promise for strengthening the psychoanalytic theory of motivation by sifting and winnowing its concepts and supplementing them with new knowledge.

## Conclusions and critique

We shall not attempt a summary of the psychoanalytic theory of motivation; the lengthy foregoing discussion was itself merely a scant summary of the far-reaching concepts and principles in the theory. Rather, we shall present a general evaluation of this most complex motivational theory. In following the evaluation, the reader should keep in mind the same issues that provided an undercurrent in the presentation of the theory itself: Are we considering Freud's early or late concepts? Part of the theory or the whole of it? The clinical or the metapsychological theory?

Fortunately, although psychoanalytic theory attempts to comprehensively explain behavior, it has a consistent motivational core which was altered little throughout its development and which pervades its many viewpoints: the conflict between instinctual drive and defense. The psychoanalytic theory of motivation has pros and cons that derive from the same sources—its concepts and methods—so its assets are also its liabilities.

Perhaps the major advantage of the psychoanalytic theory of motivation is its scope. No other motivation theory comes close to providing causal explanations for so many behaviors with such complexity. By elaborating on its basic principle of drive versus regulation, psychoanalytic theory offers explanations for many motivated activities, ranging from dreams, fantasies, and slips of the tongue to vocational choice, interpersonal attraction, and psychological health and adjustment. Explanations are provided not only for overt behaviors but also for covert processes, such as memory and cognition. This extensive scope yields a holistic view of human motivation: all behavior, down to the smallest detail, is integrated with the basic motivational principles. Behavior is ultimately purposive and motivated; to use Freud's terminology, it is "psychically determined." A common misunderstanding of psychoanalytic explanation in this regard is that it reduces the causes of all behavior to instinctual factors. This was true of the early theory, but, as the structural and adaptive viewpoints make clear, factors other than instinctual drives (namely, guilt and the environment) play instrumental roles in determining behavior. Influences on behavior include both the contemporary and the historical. From the structural viewpoint, the ego mediates many contemporary causal factors (id, impulses, demands of reality, and guilt) that are presently influencing the person, but the behavioral outcome is also determined by historical factors derived from psychosexual and psychosocial development. Hence, the explanatory breadth of psychoanalytic theory resides chiefly in its capacity to account for both the motivational and nonmotivational causes of behavior. Instinctual drives are the only motives, but not the only causes.

Another merit of the theory is that it accounts for differences in motivation among individuals and is therefore capable of providing unique explanations of a person's behavior. Such explanations take into account many motivational and developmental factors that vary from individual to individual—for example, the strengths of the instinctual drives and the defenses, psychosexual and psychosocial development, environmental interactions, and ego functions. Consequently, the strength of psychoanalysis lies in the intensive investigation and detailed explanation of the single case. It is this attention to individual differences that has made psychoanalytic theory the most influential theory of personality and psychopathology. It provides the constructs for classifying individuals, both normal and abnormal, and within its classifications provides unique explanations of motivated behavior. Since it is a clinical theory, it also specifies the means by which motivational factors can be altered: through a lengthy process of psychoanalytic psychotherapy, a complex method of behavior change rooted in the early work of Breuer and Freud, the contemporary and historical causes that affect ego functioning can be realigned.

A noteworthy aspect of the psychoanalytic theory of motivation is that—despite its encumbrance with physicalist concepts—cognitive processes (memory, thinking, and so forth) are significant in motivating behavior. In the definition of instinctual drive, Freud is careful to emphasize that drive-related thinking, not some physiological process, is what provides impetus to behavior. However, in contrast with cognitive theories that we shall consider later, the psychoanalytic view always views emotion *and* cognition as working together as a source of motivation. Cognitions that motivate behaviors are thus appetitive and demanding; they constitute "peremptory ideation," a forceful train of motivated thought (G. S. Klein, 1967).

Criticisms of the psychoanalytic theory of motivation can be classed under two headings: the restrictiveness of the motivational constructs and the dubious scientific status of the theory.

Psychoanalytic theory is frequently characterized as having an intrapsychic bias; that is, its main emphasis in explaining the motivation of behavior is said to be on persistent activity of unconscious, biologically given instinctual drives. This characterization leads to criticisms of Freud's theory as too restrictive in three areas. First, conscious experience is given only tip-of-the-iceberg status; the unconscious is the fundamental source of motivation. The problems here are obvious. This near-exclusive reliance on the unconscious prevents conscious volition and choice from having any significant impact on behavior. Thus, the psychoanalytic view is distorted in that it virtually excludes conscious awareness from the motivational process. This problem has been addressed by contemporary theorists (for example, G. S. Klein, 1967; D. Rapaport, 1960) but remains unresolved. Second, even though Freud discussed the influence of motivations other than sex and aggression (for example, self-preservative devices), he saw the instinctual drives as insistent and as inevitable sources of conflict. Behaviors that might be motivated by direct, nonconflictful factors, such as the desires for achievement, love, self-esteem, and competence, are consequently reducible to offshoots of the drive/defense conflict. The explanation of behavior as mere tension reduction, never as a positive striving, is an obvious shortfall, which the ego psychologists have attempted to remedy by their emphasis on ego motives and adaptation. Third, the biological basis of motivation has left the theory without sufficient latitude to account for the effects of learning on behavior. Learned behaviors are implied throughout the theory, especially in the concepts of ego growth and development, but the mechanisms of learning are unspecified and are assumed to be linked with the instinctual drives (D. Rapaport, 1960). This omission, though perhaps inevitable given Freud's background and training, remains the most restrictive shortcoming of the theory.

The second general area of criticism pertains to the scientific status of the motivational constructs. Such criticism arises from the frequent failures and inconsistencies in experimental investigations of psychoanalytic hypotheses. The fundamental problem is not invalidation of psychoanalytic constructs in the laboratory but rather the inability of researchers to derive testable operational definitions. This inability arises jointly from the physicalistic language in which the motivational concepts are formulated and from the ever-present, nonmeasurable, covert processes that are assumed to underlie these concepts. The result is that, in the main, psychoanalytic concepts cannot be investigated in a scientific laboratory. However, they are not necessarily invalid or untrue, since the experiments that might prove them so cannot be performed. Ultimately, the validity of the psychoanalytic theory of motivation depends on the validity of the less scientific clinical methods used by Freud and his successors in its formulation, expansion, and verification.

Recently, renewed attempts have been made to conceptualize and investigate psychoanalytic hypotheses. These studies appear well-controlled, replicated, and responsive to earlier criticisms, such as those of Holmes (1974). Although they have not been performed within the strict format of the repression paradigm, they nonetheless have implications for the psychoanalytic theory of motivation. Two solid findings have emerged. First, it appears that the unconscious stimulation of instinctual drives (by means of subliminal stimulation) does produce predicted increases in psychological symptoms and decreases in the effectiveness of repression and other defenses (Silverman, 1976). Second, it appears that individuals use "perceptual defense" or "selective inattention" to unconsciously avoid anxiety-evoking stimuli (Blum & Barbour, 1979).

In the final analysis, the status of the psychoanalytic theory of motivation, as of any other, depends on the definition. If *motivation* is defined as an "appetitive internal force" (D. Rapaport, 1960), then psychoanalytic theory is compelling and provocative. If not, the theory is deficient. Whatever one's inclination, however, Freud's theory provides a unique and controversial analysis of human motivation. If Freud had lived today amidst the influence of experimental psychology, psychoanalysis would have been different. The question is "To what extent?"

# CHAPTER 4

# Motivation toward Self-Actualization: The Humanistic Theories of Rogers and Maslow

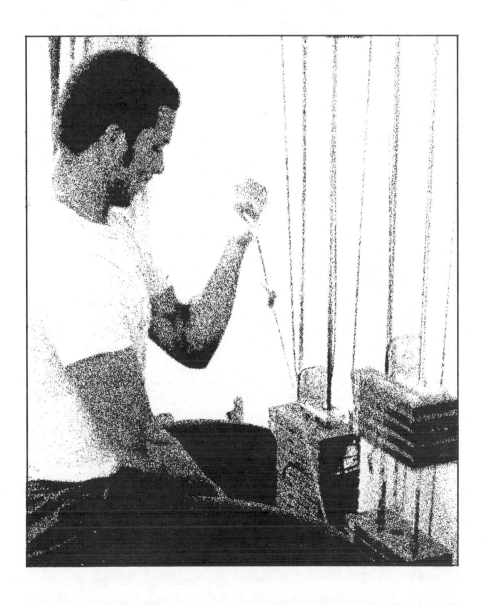

*An instinct is always and inevitably coupled
with something like philosophy of life.[1]*

C. G. Jung

Humanistic psychology is an emergent and highly influential area of
contemporary psychology with a rich heritage in psychology, existential philosophy, and the humanities. It has only recently become identi-
fiable as a unified psychological discipline. In founding the Association
of Humanistic Psychology in 1962, Abraham Maslow called humanistic psychology "the third force." In his view, it offered conceptions of
motivation and behavior that were distinct from those offered by the
other main currents of psychology—psychoanalysis and behaviorism.
These conceptions differed both in their content and in the methods by
which they were developed; they were seen as uniquely human, taking
into account the motivational capacity of and experience of such things
as love, self-esteem, and freedom, and they were aimed at studying in
detail the unique behavior of a single individual.

The term *humanistic psychology* has become an umbrella for a diverse group of theorists and perspectives. Among those who have become identified with the humanistic-psychology movement are such
divergent theorists as Rollo May, noted psychoanalyst and existential
psychologist, Fritz Perls, founder of Gestalt therapy, Arnold Lazarus, a
central figure in behavior therapy, Eric Berne, founder of transactional
analysis, Maharishi Mahesh Yogi, proponent of transcendental medi-
tation, and Albert Ellis, founder of rational-emotive therapy. At first
glance, such diversity appears staggering. It has led critics to view humanistic psychology as a mixture of viewpoints and models, rather
than as a coherent system for explaining behavior. To a certain extent,
this view is valid. Yet there exists in psychology a main current of humanistic thought that began with Jung's theory of personal growth and
fulfillment and has culminated in Maslow's theory of needs and self-
actualization. This theoretical core of humanistic psychology is
founded on a model of human motivation that—as is consistent with
the designation of "third force"—is conceptually different from models

---

[1]From *The Practice of Psychotherapy*, Vol. 16 of *The Collected Works of C. G. Jung*
[H. Read, M. Fordham, G. Adler, and W. McGuire (Eds.), R. F. C. Hull (trans.)], p.
81. © 1954 by the Bollingen Foundation. Reprinted by permission of Princeton University Press and of Routledge & Kegan Paul, Limited.

of motivation in the psychoanalytic and behaviorist traditions. We shall lend our attention to the theories in that main current of humanistic thought.

## Two issues in humanistic psychology

Humanistic psychology comprises many points of view, and recently several attempts have been made to isolate the principles and concepts common to all (Buhler & Allen, 1972; Maddi & Costa, 1972; Misiak & Sexton, 1973). We shall restrict ourselves to two general issues pertinent to our subsequent discussion: the humanistic conceptions of motivation and need and the humanistic perspective on research methodology.

### Motivation and need

The humanistic perspective is distinguished by motivational constructs that emphasize both psychological growth and the full realization of human potential. According to this viewpoint, human behavior is primarily motivated by a person's striving to become as fully human as possible—to be competent, effective, creative, and imaginative. Motivated behavior is hence a striving to find one's real self. Its goal is personal enhancement. The term *self-actualization* is generally applied to this broad motivation toward attaining one's potential. The general feature of humanistic theories of motivation is their emphasis on the "higher" needs and motives that are distinctively human and that constitute positive forces for human growth and fulfillment.

Two aspects of this view of motivation should be emphasized. First, this view assumes that the motive toward self-actualization and personal growth is unlearned. Hence, self-actualization and related motivational constructs are like instincts in that they are innate and they forcefully propel the organism toward action. As we shall see, however, the instinctlike nature of the humanistic motivational constructs is clearly different from that of the ethological and psychoanalytic constructs. Second, motivation is assumed to affect behavior in a straightforward manner. That is, behavior arises simply and directly from a single motive, such as a "need for security." Security needs lead to security-seeking behaviors. Behavior does not result from a compromise between a motive and a defense against it, as psychoanalytic theory would contend. The crucial point here is that humanistic theories suggest that behavior arises directly from an underlying source of motivation. They downplay the roles of intervening constructs (such as tension reduction) and complex processes (such as the interaction of instinctual drive, anxiety, defense, and so forth that yields a compromise formation).

### Research methods

Humanistic theorists are highly critical of the traditional scientific procedures that have guided the bulk of research on motivation. The experimental method requires that constructs be operationally defined and then investigated in controlled situations. Humanistic theorists maintain that this process artificially reduces the meaningfulness of the constructs and makes generalizations to real-life contexts difficult and frequently inappropriate. Moreover, they contend that the experimental analysis of motivation ignores determinants of behavior such as values, experiences, personality, and the social environment. These perceived shortcomings of the experimental approach arise from its apparent antagonism to two basic methodological principles implied in the humanistic view—holism and phenomenology. The holistic study of behavior emphasizes the totality of internal and environmental influences on an individual. It does not include the separate analysis of each influence. Phenomenology is the study of the individual's subjective experience of reality. Humanistic psychologists emphasize that an individual's experience cannot be averaged or grouped with the experience of anyone else; it is unique, and generalization from one person's experience to another's is inappropriate. Obviously such a stance is at odds with the rigors of the experimental method. Control and prediction, the cornerstones of science, appear to be unworkable in a domain of investigation in which it is imperative to preserve the totality and individuality of human experience, as the holistic and phenomenological approaches dictate.

This issue of method is not to be taken lightly. In both humanistic and nonhumanistic theories, investigative procedures influence motivational concepts. Humanistic theorists' methods—like Freud's—are clinical, not experimental. Evidence is gathered from the intensive observation of single cases. The behavior for which they seek motivational explanations occurs mainly in naturalistic settings, not in the laboratory. Since humanistic theories are essentially clinical, the motivational core of each theory is embedded in a larger theory of personality.

The debate over the relative merits of theories and their characteristic research methods—or paradigms, as Kuhn (1962) calls them—has had a vigorous past and will not subside in the near future. The clash between theories is ultimately a clash between paradigms. But the scientific current of belief in contemporary psychology clearly places the humanistic perspective in a minority position. Like the psychoanalytic construct of repression, most humanistic motivational constructs are vulnerable to the criticism that they cannot be operationally defined and adequately investigated in a scientific paradigm and so cannot be experimentally validated. Unlike psychoanalytic theory, which had scientific aspirations encumbered by 19th century methods, humanistic theories claim no allegiance to the contemporary scientific ethic. Rather, they claim the obvious but the overlooked—that knowledge can result from other methods than the experimental. The humanistic perspective on method is akin to Aristotle's persuasive analysis of reasoning and empiricism: science can minimize error but does not necessarily maximize truth. Humanistic theorists view their naturalistic methods and their emphasis on the individual as imperative for a broad understanding of the complexities of human motivation.

Ultimately, the credence one gives to humanistic theories of motivation depends on how far one accepts the humanistic perspective on method. One must be willing to grant that knowledge about motivation does not emanate exclusively from the scientific laboratory. This is essential, since the theories to be discussed here do not rely on experimental evidence. They stand instead upon the common observations and interpretations of divergent theorists and adherents.

## Introduction to the two theories

The plan of this chapter is to selectively survey two primary theories of motivation that can be interpreted as humanistic by the criteria that their constructs be related to self-actualization and fulfillment and their methods be based on a holistic and phenomenological view. Because the boundaries for delineating humanistic theories are not firmly established, our selection may not agree with those of others. We have selected, however, two theories that place heavy emphasis on motivation. There are many other humanistic theories, but all others are relatively incomplete in their models of motivation. Those have not been included.

The first theory we shall discuss is the actualization theory of Carl Rogers. Rogers's theory is phenomenological in that it emphasizes the effect of motivational influences on the subjective experience of the individual. Rogers has been, and remains, a mainstream figure in humanistic psychology.

The second theory is the need-hierarchy theory of Abraham Maslow. Maslow's theory is holistic in that it accounts for the many motivational forces that act upon the individual and attempts to order them in importance. Maslow's theory is identified today as the primary humanistic theory of motivation.

Rogers's theory is a single-construct theory; that is, it emphasizes one primary source of motivation as the basis of behavior. In Rogers's theory this master motive is the tendency to progress toward personal fulfillment and meaning. Maslow's theory is a multiple-construct theory, emphasizing many sources of motivation. It endeavors to generate a system in which several motives, ranging from "basic" needs, such as those for food and security, to "higher" needs, such as that for self-actualization, motivate behavior.

Since each is a major theory in itself, our discussion will of necessity be narrow and restricted to concepts that are significant with regard to motivation.

## The actualization theory of Carl Rogers

Carl Rogers has been a central figure in humanistic psychology for more than 30 years. In both content and method, his writings on personality and clinical psychology are definitive statements of humanistic principles. At the core of his comprehensive theory is a central assumption about the motivation of behavior: that an inherent tendency provides a consistent impetus toward psychological growth and fulfillment.

Rogerian theory can be viewed as a reaction against psychoanalytic concepts, which Rogers considers abstract encumbrances that do more to obscure than to explain the motivation of human behavior. Instead, Rogers relies on concepts and processes that he believes are rooted in human experience. The resulting theory is a significant break from the influence of intrapsychic models of motivation.

### Background and influences

Carl Rogers was born in 1902 in a suburb of Chicago. Two aspects of Rogers's childhood seem to have had a noteworthy impact on his personal development, career choice, and eventual theorizing (Rogers, 1967). The first was the religious atmosphere in his family. His parents were devout fundamentalists, and they imparted their religious beliefs and their related values to their children. Accordingly, they fostered independence and autonomy by placing upon each child a sense of responsibility for his or her decisions and actions. Instrumental in the process of fostering autonomy was the living of the Protestant ethic—that through hard work and individual achievement one becomes spiritually and psychologically strong. One result of these family dynamics was that Rogers, like Freud, was a conscientious, exceptional student. The second influence was the rural atmosphere of a farm near Chicago where Rogers lived during his adolescence. He thought highly of his experiences on the family farm for two reasons. First, the daily work that was required of him gave him a sense of connection with nature and provided a catalyst for his philosophizing about the relationship between man and environment. Second, he developed a personal interest in agriculture, which led him in his early college years to the investigation of agricultural problems by means of the scientific method.

His interest in science gave way to an interest in religion and the pursuit of a career in the ministry. In the process, he rejected the fundamentalist religious views of his parents and adopted a theology that was humanistic, rather than dogmatic. His humanistic philosophy and concern for human problems eventually led him to a Ph.D. in clinical psychology from Teachers College at Columbia University. During his training, he perceived the division between clinical work and experimental psychology, a division he saw as artificial and as destructive to the understanding of human behavior (Rogers, 1959).

From these beginnings, Rogers launched an immensely productive intellectual career. He began professionally as a clinical psychologist in a child-guidance clinic and has since held several prestigious positions at major universities. His name has become synonymous with client-centered therapy, which is based on a theory of human behavior and change that evolved through his many books (for example, Rogers, 1939, 1942, 1951, 1959, 1961, 1969). Throughout his theorizing, Rogers has relied mainly on his experiences in and observations of human relationships as sources of data. Hence, his observational method and his theory are intertwined.

## Motivational constructs

Rogers formulates his theory of motivation around a single motive that moves the organism progressively toward psychological growth and fulfillment. Rogers's central motivating force is thus teleological; that is, it provides an ultimate goal toward which behavior is directed.

Three other distinctive features of the Rogerian theory of motivation should be emphasized at the outset. First, unlike Freud, Rogers stresses the role of conscious experience as a determinant of behavior. Though acknowledging that forces outside one's awareness influence one's thoughts and actions, he minimizes their importance; his theory contains no intrapsychic mass of motivating forces that, like an iceberg, lurks mostly outside awareness. A person is aware of striving to grow and develop psychologically by behaving in appropriate ways.

Second, in combination with his emphasis on conscious factors in motivation, Rogers describes behavior as being phenomenologically motivated. By this he means that the factors existing in the person's present subjective experience (for example, desires and fears) are critical to the behavioral outcome. Consequently, although the overall goal of fulfillment exists all the time, the motivational force that directs the organism in quest of that lofty endpoint waxes and wanes as a result of its immediate motivational state in a given situation. Rogers therefore rejects the determinism that is explicit in Freud's model of psychosexual sources of motivation. Instead of such a deterministic view of motivation, Rogers emphasizes contemporaneous factors—those present in the "here and now" of a person's experience. These factors are both internal and external.

The third distinctive feature of Rogerian theory derives from the second. Rogers sees the conscious, phenomenological impact of one's basic motivational tendency as arising from interaction with the environment, especially its interpersonal aspects. Human relationships are therefore central in Rogers's theory of motivation. They produce conditions that promote psychological growth by enabling a person's motivational tendency to take its natural course, or they produce conditions that frustrate, channel, or block such progressive striving.

**The actualizing tendency.**    The fundamental construct in the Rogerian theory of motivation is what Rogers terms the "actualizing tendency." He defines this as "the inherent tendency of the organism to develop all its capacities in ways which serve to maintain or enhance the organism" (1959, p. 196). Although Rogers does not use the term, he is suggesting that the actualizing tendency is an instinct or is instinctlike; it is inherent and therefore part of a person's biological equipment. Remember, too, that the actualizing tendency is the only motive force in Rogers's system. All other motivations derive from this single source.

As Rogers's phrase "maintain or enhance" suggests, the actualizing tendency has a two-tiered function. The first function, maintenance, provides for the meeting of "basic" needs, such as hunger, sustenance, safety, and so forth. This tendency to maintain the organism is primary and necessary for survival (Rogers, 1959). Rogers did not postulate additional drives or motives to account for this general motivation toward maintenance (as did Maslow, who will be discussed later in this chapter). The second function of the actualizing tendency, enhancement, motivates the organism toward growth-related activities. This motivation is toward the attainment of the organism's potential, so the motivation varies from organism to organism. For a writer, the potential might be a significant, critically acclaimed novel; for a stutterer, it might be greater clarity in oral communication, and for a 10-month-old infant, the potential might be his or her first steps. Hence, the actualizing tendency has both a preservative *and* a growth function.

The motivational mechanisms underlying the maintenance and enhancement functions of the actualizing tendency are quite different. A maintenance function, such as avoiding danger, *reduces* tension by satisfying a basic need (for safety). However, an enhancement function, such as striving for personal growth by means of achievement and success, can *increase* tension by subjecting the individual to pressures and demands (Rogers, 1959). Thus, in being motivated by the actualizing tendency an organism sometimes seeks to avoid or lessen stimulation and sometimes seeks to increase it.

By postulating tension increase as a mechanism of motivation, Rogers's theory adds a dimension that was lacking in psychoanalytic theory. For Rogers, the enhancement function—motivation for personal growth, attainment of potential, and so forth—is explained by a tendency to increase stimulation, or tension. For Freud, such enhancement is explained only as a byproduct (defense, compromise formation, and so on) of a tendency to reduce the tension created by instinctual drives.

The actualizing tendency is hypothesized to be present in all living organisms, from amoeba to zebra (Rogers, 1959), and it gives impetus to changes in the organisms' behavior. However, the operation of the actualizing tendency is more complex and more prone to varying forms of expression among humans. People and their environments, obviously, are different from animals and animal environments, and the most important difference that influences the actualizing tendency is that of cognition. Rogers (1959) uses the term *symbolization* to describe the distinctively human propensity to represent experience symbolically—for example, to think about oneself and others and to impute meaning to one's social relationships and feelings. This cognitive processing of experience leads to variant forms of the actualizing tendency.[2] For example, the safety needs of animals are maintained largely by fighting and fleeing. Maintenance of safety is symbolized more broadly in humans. Besides fight or flight, people take preventative steps by subscribing to health and accident insurance, planning safe environments, and so on. Similarly, self-enhancement is symbolized broadly in humans by providing a panorama of options and choices for personal growth. For animals, enhancement is restricted to the attainment of species-specific potential. For example, a falcon is enhanced by the development of speed and agility in the air.

**The self and the tendency toward self-actualization.**    The most significant form of the actualizing tendency in humans is the tendency toward self-actualization (Rogers, 1959). This motivational tendency is a component of the actualizing tendency, and it refers to the motivation to maintain or enhance that portion of experience that is symbolized in the self. The self is Rogers's primary personality construct. He defines it as "the organized consistent conceptual gestalt composed of perceptions of the characteristics of the 'I' or 'me' and the perceptions of the relationships of the 'I' or 'me' to others and to various aspects of life, together with the values attached to these perceptions" (Rogers, 1959, p. 200). Consistent with his phenomenological perspective, Rogers conceives of the self not as a structure but as a process. It is the person's view, in the here and now, of his or her unique identity. The self is an experience. The tendency toward self-actualization is the person's motivation to behave consistently with his or her self-concept at the moment; it is a tendency to maintain or enhance the self.

---

[2]In a recent and thoroughgoing extension of Rogerian motivational theory, Wexler and Rice (1974) have elaborated the cognitive variables that were treated only lightly in its original formulation.

Rogers (1959) uses the concept of congruency to describe the relation between the actualizing tendency and the self-actualizing tendency (and other needs, to be discussed below). If one's symbolization of oneself and one's total experience are congruent (in agreement), then the actualizing and self-actualizing tendencies are similar and unified in purpose. If, however, the experience of self and the total experience are incongruent, the self-actualizing and actualizing tendencies might be in conflict, motivating the person toward incompatible goals. For example, if a man behaves assertively, thus experiencing power and strength, at the same time that he perceives himself as passive and meek, then general experience and the specific experience of self are in conflict. The actualizing tendency motivates one to interact with stimuli that maintain and enhance the self, whereas the self-actualizing tendency motivates one to behave consistently with one's self-concept. Antagonism, or incongruence, between the actualizing and self-actualizing tendencies can result in maladaptive symptoms.

The fact that the actualizing tendency and its derivative, the self-actualizing tendency, obtain satisfaction from an ever-changing series of stimuli and behaviors is accounted for by the organismic valuing process. This is the process by which satisfaction or value is derived from experience. It describes the fact that at one moment an infant values food; at a later moment, stimulation; still later, rest.

**The needs for positive regard and self-regard.**   Besides the actualizing and self-actualizing tendencies, Rogers (1959) postulates two additional sources of motivation: the need for positive regard and the need for self-regard. These needs are secondary sources of motivation; that is, they derive from the actualizing tendency and are *learned* early in infancy. The need for positive regard motivates the person to attain "satisfaction" from significant others (for example, mother, father, loved one, friend). The need for positive regard is satisfied by the approval of others and is frustrated by their disapproval. The need for positive regard and the actualizing tendency conflict when a behavior that would satisfy one of them would frustrate the other. For example, the comfort afforded a teenager at home by positive regard from his parents might conflict with his separation from them to actualize himself by pursuing a college education.

The need for self-regard is the need to be satisfied with oneself. Satisfaction is self-approval; frustration is self-disapproval. Self-regard can be experienced independently of positive regard from others. This need thus has an internalized, or intrapersonal, basis for fulfillment. The needs for positive regard and self-regard are motivations that channel part of the actualizing tendency and its resultant satisfaction into two aspects of experience—regard from others and regard from oneself. Since one's experience with others and experience of one's self are interrelated, so are the two needs.

The Rogerian concept of need stresses the importance of the social environment in satisfying needs. For example, the satisfaction of some needs requires particular behaviors from other people, such as approval. Furthermore, satisfaction of such needs may be congruent or incongruent with satisfaction of one's actualizing tendency. For example, satisfaction of one's need for approval may be incongruent with the autonomy and independence that would satisfy one's actualizing tendency. According to Rogers, congruency between needs and actualization can be optimally attained from those significant others who offer unconditional positive regard (Rogers, 1959). Unconditional positive regard is a consistent way of relating to a person such that he or she perceives total acceptance of his or her self; no aspect of the self is perceived as more or less worthy of positive regard. It is important to note that a person can be positively regarded (or totally accepted) without his or her behavior necessarily being approved of.

To feel unconditional positive regard is to feel "prized." The essence of the concept resides in the positive value attributed to the *whole* person irrespective of the values attributed to particular behaviors. For example, parents prize their child even though they are not especially fond of dirty diapers, temper tantrums, or cookie crumbs in the shag rug.

A group of social experiences opposite to those of unconditional positive regard will create a *condition of worth*. Rogers believes that such experiences lead to need/actualization incongruency. "A condition of worth arises when the positive regard of a significant other is conditional, when the individual feels that in some respects . . . he is prized and in others not" (1959, p. 204). The receiving of positive regard is contingent on behaving in certain ways. For example, a man might value his wife for her domestic skills but not for her professional interests. Her perceived worth is conditional, not total. Such conditional acceptance from others becomes "internalized"—made part of the self. A person then values a behavior positively or negatively because of the condition of worth that was derived from interactions with others, not necessarily because of the organismic valuing process. Such a derived value might conflict with those that maintain or enhance the self. Over time, unconditional positive regard produces a fully functioning person; conditions of worth produce psychological maladjustment.

**Summary.**   The distinctive features of the Rogerian theory of motivation are its emphases on conscious experience, the phenomenological perspective of the person, and the role of interpersonal relationships. The actualizing tendency is postulated as the single inherent source of motivation; its aim is the maintenance and enhancement of the organism. In humans, as the self-concept develops, part of this motive force becomes a tendency toward self-actualization. Although the ultimate goal of actualization—fulfillment—remains constant, the actualization tendency is ever-changing in that its source of satisfaction varies from moment to moment. Depending on the environmental context, it can either induce or reduce tension in the organism. The needs for positive regard and self-regard are learned through experiences with significant others and within oneself. Satisfaction of the needs for positive regard and self-regard can be either congruent or incongruent with satisfaction of the actualizing tendency.

## Constructs explaining individual differences

Rogers's constructs explaining individual differences are strikingly different from Freud's, both in number and in nature. Rogers contends that complex theories of personality which are laden with metaphors and ill-defined constructs do more to obscure the understanding of behavior than to aid it. Hence, he purposely limits his constructs to those that are fundamental for explanation. Moreover, he steers clear of troublesome constructs or unobservables, such as psychic energy and intrapsychic structures. Instead, Rogers describes his constructs as processes that are sensitive to changes in the person and the environment.

Rogers stresses uniqueness. He sees a motivated behavior as arising from the uniqueness of the person as he or she interacts with the environment. However, Rogers emphasizes the conscious phenomenology of the individual and does not care to speculate about the intrapsychic dynamics that might be operative.

On the question of classifications within which individuals might be grouped on the basis of their motivated behaviors, Rogers's viewpoint on individuality is also apparent. Rogers (1961) avoided the use of personality classifications because it would blur the most important message in his theoretical analysis: that the determinants of behavior are rooted uniquely in the here-and-now experience of a person in an interpersonal context. Although he was not friendly to such classifications, he did specify two divergent patterns of behavior that would arise over time as results of congruent and of incongruent experiences (1959); these were noted briefly above. The *fully functioning person* is an individual who has been able to actualize his or her potentialities because he or she experienced needs for regard that were congruent with the actualizing tendency; such experiences occurred as consequences of receiving unconditional positive regard. Although being fully functioning does not involve having any particular traits or abilities, it does include several distinctive characteristics. The main one is openness to experience. This openness is a state of flexibility in which the individual is fully conscious of experiences with others and the self. The concept of openness to experience is one of adaptive functioning and psychological health in which anxiety and conflict are minimized.

In stark contrast to openness to experience is a negative pattern of behavior that Rogers calls *psychological maladjustment.* A maladjusted behavior pattern arises from a series of incongruent experiences. Anxiety plays a central role. Psychological maladjustment is induced by conditional regard from others. Under these circumstances, an individual must appraise self-actualizing behaviors—those enacted for maintenance or enhancement of the self—as negative because the behaviors are not unconditionally valued, or prized. Initially, this incongruency and the accompanying anxiety it creates lead to the use of defenses, which occur in two primary forms: distortion of experience, in which experience is selective such that conditional regard and its negative consequence are minimized or transformed, and denial of experience, in which awareness of experience is blocked.

In both defensive processes, incongruence leads to a narrowing of conscious experience. The process Rogers describes in which anxiety arouses defense is similar to the psychoanalytic version: denial is akin to repression; distortion is like some form of partial repression. Yet there are central differences. Freud argued that defenses were necessary for adaptation to the instinctual drives, and therefore inevitable; Rogers argues that defenses are caused by social relationships that place conditions on the intrinsic value of the person. Thus, defensiveness is caused not by the pressures of negative motive forces, as Freud hypothesized, but rather by the negative impact of adverse social relationships on the natural course toward actualization. Freud was pessimistic about change because the instinctual drives were immutable; Rogers is optimistic because he believes in the possibility of change through intervention in the social, not the biological, sphere. Accordingly, his goal is the alleviation of conditions of worth in families, schools, organizations, and society. The inherent tendency of the organism toward maintenance and enhancement can then take its natural path of growth and fulfillment.

## An example of application: Client-centered therapy

From the preceding discussion, it is clear that Rogers hypothesizes that behavioral outcomes motivated by the actualizing tendency and related needs will vary as a function of a person's interaction with the social environment. Positive interactions enable the actualizing tendency to maintain and enhance the individual. Negative interactions interfere with this inherent tendency.

Since Rogers is a clinical psychologist, it is not surprising that much of his work focuses on ways to alleviate the ill effects of negative social experiences on self-actualization. His major vehicle in this regard is client-centered therapy, with which he has become a figurehead for a generation of counselors and therapists.

The essence of client-centered therapy resides in a therapeutic relationship between a therapist, or psychological helper, and a client, or person seeking help. From Rogers's perspective, it is assumed that psychological maladjustment, defensiveness, and so forth are brought about by an incongruence between self and experience. The goal of the therapeutic relationship is to reinstate congruence—that is, to enable the inherent tendency toward self-actualization to restore full functioning to the person.

Rogers (1957) hypothesized that for change toward self-actualization to occur in the client, he or she must perceive and accept three therapeutic conditions or "attitudinal characteristics" of the therapist:

1. *Genuineness.* Within the therapeutic relationship, the therapist must be congruent, genuine, and integrated. The therapist must be accurately aware of himself or herself and flexibly and deeply involved in self-experience. Rogers notes, however, that a therapist need not fully disclose thoughts and feelings nor be constantly genuine outside the therapeutic relationship.

2. *Unconditional positive regard.* The therapist must be able to prize and accept whatever the client is experiencing. The therapist's unconditional positive regard thus provides a counterpoint to the conditions of worth levied by significant others. This should increase client self-regard and congruence.

3. *Accurate empathy.* The therapist must accurately empathize with and understand the client's phenomenology. The goal is for the therapist to sense the client's experience as if it were his or her own and to communicate such perceptions to the client with clarity and insight.

Rogers states that these therapeutic conditions are "necessary and sufficient" to enable a person to become congruent and self-actualized. Rogers views the therapeutic relationship as unique, or atypical of relationships of everyday life. However, he contends that the attributes of the therapeutic relationship—genuineness, unconditional positive regard, and accurate empathy—are applicable to all relationships. Although amplifications of Rogers's theory have been made—for example, by Wexler (in Wexler & Rice, 1974) in his analysis of information-processing in the client/therapist relationship—Rogers's scheme for motivational change has remained largely unchanged since its inception.

A commendable aspect of this framework for motivational change is Rogers's prescription for research. Rogers (1957) put forth a very testable hypothesis: if one or more of the necessary and sufficient therapeutic conditions (genuineness, unconditional positive regard, and empathy) is absent in a therapeutic relationship, constructive change toward self-actualization will not occur. This and related hypotheses constituted a well-spring for an immense research literature. To evaluate the hypotheses, the design of a typical study requires that the presence of therapeutic conditions be related to measures of outcome, or change. Genuineness, unconditional positive regard, and empathy are generally measured by rating scales (for example, Truax & Carkhuff, 1967), with which samples of therapy sessions are coded and quantified by independent judges. Innumerable outcome measures can be used; typical measures involve changes in self-congruence, ratings of maladjustment, and so on.

A voluminous body of research on Rogers's hypotheses has yielded ambiguous results. Mitchell, Bozarth, and Krauft (1977) conclude, after an extensive review, that the links that Rogers hypothesized between the therapeutic attitudes of the therapist and the personal growth of the client are weaker and less generalizable than the theory specifies. These findings suggest, within Rogers's motivational framework, that the self-actualization tendency is not a strong motive force.

## Conclusion: Rogers

The distinctive aspects of Rogers's theory are apparent. First, Rogers has constructed a truly humanistic theory of motivation with none of the intrapsychic influences of psychoanalytic theory. His theory has explanatory simplicity yet potency. The constructs and processes are clear, understandable, and, to a certain extent, commonsensical. Moreover, they have application for remedying human problems. Second, his central motivational construct, the actualizing tendency, is flexible and responsive to the environment. Freud conceived of the instinctual drives as unceasingly pushing for gratification, creating tension and conflict in the process. In contrast, the actualizing tendency may or may not create tension and may or may not be immersed in conflict. Third, the issue of the applicability of experimental investigation looms critical over Rogers's theory, as over Freud's. Although Rogers has streamlined his constructs, they remain difficult to define operationally. This is the bane of instinctlike conceptions of motivation, and Rogerian theory is not immune. The constructs are hard to define, and Rogers is vague about the environmental conditions that are purported to cause changes in motivation. When the conditions are specified, as in the therapeutic relationship, research findings suggest that hypothesized changes in motivation and behavior are weak. Nevertheless, Rogers and his followers have been productive researchers. Rogers's legacy is obvious in a massive research literature (see, for example, Hart & Tomlinson, 1970; Wexler & Rice, 1974). Much of the research, however, bears only distantly on his theory of motivation.

## The need-hierarchy theory of Abraham Maslow

Maslow was the most eminent figure in humanistic psychology. He strove to maintain unity between the principles of humanistic psychology and his theory of motivation, and the concept of self-actualization is a central component of his system. However, unlike Rogers, Maslow attempted to map out the influences of other sources of motivation and their relations with one another and with self-actualization. His explanatory system uses many constructs, defined as needs, and a hierarchal arrangement of their motivational potencies. Consequently, his theory is more complex and detailed than Rogers's, and it offers a greater breadth of analysis. Moreover, there is a difference in emphasis. Rogers discusses motivational constructs in the context of his personality theory; Maslow discussed personality constructs in the context of his motivation theory. For Maslow, human motivation was the cornerstone of psychology. His writings since 1954 were exclusively about motivation and related concepts.

### Background and influences

Maslow was born in New York City in 1908. The son of a successful Jewish businessman, he grew up in a non-Jewish suburb of Brooklyn. As a consequence, he felt socially isolated and was almost friendless. He turned inward and channeled his energies and interests into reading and scholarship. In his school years, he was heavily influenced by philosophers and classicists. Balance to his intellectual pursuits was provided by regular, hard work in the family business, a large manufacturing concern (M. H. Hall, 1968).

Maslow viewed as the turning points in his life his marriage and his entry into the University of Wisconsin (M. H. Hall, 1968). At Wisconsin, he became a devotee of behaviorism and experimental psychology and in 1934, under the direction of Harlow, wrote his doctoral dissertation on primate sexuality and dominance. His early publications were based on experimental studies of animals. His disenchantment with behaviorism began with his readings in psychoanalysis and Gestalt psychology and reached its peak at the birth of his first child (Goble, 1970). His viewpoint gravitated during these years from a narrow and rigidly scientific conception of psychology to one that was broader in subject matter and method and, especially, in tune with the complexities and uniqueness of the human experience.

Maslow returned to New York early in his career to take a position at Brooklyn College. There his humanistic psychology began to emerge in conjunction with his continued intellectual and personal growth. The intellectual stimulation in his professional life was immense. He sought out the most influential psychologists and social scientists, many of whom had recently fled Europe in the wake of Hitler's rise to power. His contacts with them gave fertility to his ideas, and their personal lives and accomplishments provided material for his theory of human motivation. He focused on the positive elements of human psychology and endeavored to construct a theory aimed at the understanding of human potential and the motivation to achieve it.

In 1954 this early effort culminated in the first edition of *Motivation and Personality*, his far-reaching analysis of human motivation in terms of a hierarchy of inherent needs. From this foundation, Maslow extended his motivational concepts and delved into the implications of his scheme for optimum human functioning and well-being (for example, Maslow, 1965, 1968, 1971). As his theory emerged and his writings multiplied, so did his acceptance and influence. At Brandeis University, he founded the Association of Humanistic Psychology in 1962. In 1967 he was elected president of the American Psychological Association. Maslow died in La Jolla, California, in 1970.

In method and content, Maslow's theory of motivation is the epitome of humanistic psychology. His focus was exclusively on the positive and the potentially positive components of human experience. He disdained data from deviant or abnormal populations. Yet his approach was rooted in the tradition of clinical psychology—the intensive, holistic study of individuals. Accordingly, he designated his theory of motivation as "holistic-dynamic." Let us now turn to his legacy.

## Motivational constructs

Maslow's humanistic theory of motivation differs from Rogers's in one critical respect. Although it postulates that self-actualization is the highest source of motivation, Maslow's theory acknowledges other sources that take precedence over striving toward psychological growth and fulfillment. Hence, he proposes a system of multiple motives that are arranged in order of their strength, or potency, for influencing behavior. Self-actualization is placed atop a hierarchy of motives, all of which must be satisfied before it has an impact on behavior. These other motives are organismic needs. This hierarchal scheme depicts psychological growth as *a* motive but not *the* motive and explicitly specifies the other motivational goals that must be attained before behaviors motivated by self-actualization will occur. Maslow's theory thus does not explain self-actualization as a unique motivational tendency that steers the organism toward the ideal goal of enhancement and fulfillment. Rather, Maslow gives self-actualization the status of a determinant of behavior, in that it *causes* a specified domain of behaviors to occur when it becomes operative. It is not an ill-defined goal or tendency whose exact motivational impact is unspecified, as conceptualized by Rogers. Instead, it is a specific need that, like the others, motivates the organism to behave in such a way as to attain satisfaction.

**Basic needs.**    The fundamental constructs in Maslow's theory are the basic needs[3] (Maslow, 1970). They are arranged in a hierarchy, ranging from the physiological needs (lowest) to the self-actualization need (highest). All the basic needs are innate and therefore can be affected by genetic variation. Although the needs are biological in origin, only behaviors that satisfy the biological needs—eating, drinking, breathing, and so forth—are unlearned. Behaviors that satisfy other needs are learned; eating satisfies hunger, but what satisfies a higher basic need, such as the need for love? The answer is not absolute; it depends, of course, upon what one has learned is satisfying. The basic-need concept is thus midway between the instinctual and environmental interpretations of motivated behavior. Instinct theorists would contend that a specific behavior is predetermined in detail by the nature of the instinct—for example, that the sexual instinct leads to a particular sexual act. Environment theorists would contend that a behavior is determined not by a fixed internal state, such as instinct, but by the demands of the environment, such as cultural influences and learning. In contrast to these two extremes, Maslow designates the basic needs as *instinctoid;* they are universal in the human species and are biologically given, but their instinctual nature is weak, so that their effects on behavior can be modified or inhibited by the environment. The basic needs hence do not *drive* the person to behave in particular ways; rather, they *select* an *array* of behaviors that are need-satisfying.

Basic needs have five characteristics:

1. Failure to gratify a basic need results in a directly related form of dysfunction or disturbance, either physiological or psychological. For example, a lack of vitamins can produce malnutrition; a lack of love can produce depression.
2. Restoration of the gratification remedies the dysfunction or disturbance.
3. The continued presence of gratification for a basic need prevents dysfunction or disturbance and brings on a state of health and growth. Vitamins are necessary for physical health and growth; love makes the world go around.
4. In certain free-choice situations, the gratification of one basic need will be preferred over the gratification of others. A hungry child, if given food and toys, will prefer eating to playing.
5. The prolonged satisfaction of a basic need will reduce its demands to a low ebb or render it inactive. Eating a nutritious diet on a regular basis lessens pangs of hunger; being loved lessens strivings for affection and attention.

[3]Founding a theory on a set of needs is not unique to Maslow. For example, Murray (1938) listed 40 needs that purportedly motivated behavior. Murray, however, did not organize them hierarchically, as did Maslow.

Adopting these five defining characteristics, Maslow (1970) delineated five classes of basic needs: the physiological needs, the safety needs, the belongingness and love needs, the esteem needs, and the self-actualization need[4] (see Figure 4-1). They are placed in that order in a need hierarchy according to their motivational strength. The lowest needs (physiological) are the strongest, and the highest need (self-actualization) is the weakest. The lower needs are biological; the higher needs are psychological, and, as such, one tends to "value" the higher needs more than the lower needs—that is, to view their satisfaction as more "humanly" rewarding, more meaningful, more fulfilling, and so on. The basic needs become operative according to the principle of prepotency. This principle states that the lowest need, having the greatest strength, or prepotency, plays the foremost role in motivating behavior until it is "fairly well" gratified. Then the next need in the hierarchy, having the next-greatest prepotency, becomes the dominant source of motivation, and so on until self-actualization, the highest and weakest need, becomes prepotent. The ascent of the need hierarchy thus depends on the sufficient satisfaction of each prior need. A "chronically gratified" need ceases to be an active organizer of behavior, thereby allowing the next need in the hierarchy to predominate.

We shall discuss the basic needs, starting with the lowest and strongest and proceeding up the hierarchy.

The physiological needs are the strongest of the basic needs and therefore the lowest on the hierarchy. Maslow believed that these needs were numerous and hence did not attempt to compile a comprehensive list. However, he did put forth two criteria for their definition: they are relatively independent of one another and of other motivations, and they have some specifiable physical base. The classic examples are hunger, thirst, sex, and breathing. The physiological needs as sources of motivation bear a close resemblance to the instinct concept: they provoke specific consummatory behavior aimed at satisfaction. Periodic failure to gratify the physiological needs will prevent transition to the next stage of the hierarchy. Such failure would ultimately influence a person's attitudes toward future events and stifle the emergence of behaviors motivated by higher basic needs.

If the physiological needs are well satisfied, the safety needs become prepotent—the needs for security, stability, dependency, protection, structure and order, freedom from fear and anxiety, and so forth. These needs often manifest themselves in global world views and outlooks, such as those found in religion, philosophy, and even science—ideologies that make one feel safe. They become the active mobilizers of behavior in real emergencies—for example, accidents or natural disas-

---

[4]Maslow also discussed two additional classes but did not place them in his need hierarchy. These were the cognitive needs (desires to know and understand) and the esthetic needs.

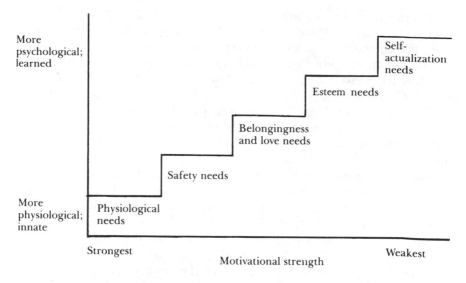

**Figure 4-1.** Maslow's need hierarchy.

ters. The needs for safety are especially pronounced in children and tend to become less influential in the course of development. Their prepotency in adulthood, resulting from insufficient gratification in childhood, is often associated with neurosis. The safety needs function exactly as the physiological needs do, but they are weaker.

If the physiological and safety needs are fairly well gratified, the needs for belongingness and love will emerge and dominate motivated behavior. These needs in general produce a striving for affectionate relationships with others—for a place in an intimate couple, family, or group. Maslow emphasizes that satisfaction of these needs requires both receiving and giving love. Frustration of these needs causes feelings of rejection, ostracism, loneliness, and friendlessness; continued deprivation might lead to severe psychopathology. Behaviors motivated by the need for love might serve the additional function of fulfilling a physiological need, sex. As this example shows, when higher needs emerge, the probability increases that behavior will be multiply satisfying. Again, these needs operate identically to those lower on the hierarchy, but their intensity is less.

The attainment of belongingness and love makes way for the motivational dominance of the esteem needs. These basic needs comprise two subsets: self-esteem and esteem of others. The former includes the needs for strength, achievement, competence, independence, and so forth. The latter includes such needs as status, prestige, recognition, attention, and appreciation. Lack of satisfaction of the esteem needs leads to feelings of inferiority and helplessness and might over time give rise to despondence, depression, and neurotic behaviors. Drawing from the Rogerian analysis of positive regard, Maslow reasons that satisfaction of esteem needs derives from *deserved* respect and esteem from self and others. By this standard, esteem would not be satisfying if it involved deception of self or others.

Satisfaction of all these prior basic needs sets the stage for the emergence of the uppermost need in the hierarchy—the self-actualization need. Maslow defines this need in much the same way as Rogers. "What a man *can* be, he *must* be. He must be true to his own nature. . . . [The self-actualization need is thus a] desire to become more and more what one idiosyncratically is, to become everything that one is capable of becoming" (Maslow, 1970, p. 46). At this level, need-satisfying behaviors show the greatest differences from individual to individual. Satisfaction might involve painting for one person, playing football for another, and child rearing for yet another. As the highest need, self-actualization is the weakest and the most modifiable by the environment. Yet it, too, can be unsatisfied and thus produce negative consequences for the individual.

The need-hierarchy concept implies that the sequence in which basic needs emerge is fixed and that a higher need emerges only after the preceding need has been satisfied. Maslow (1970) notes, however, that the sequence described is typical but not unchangeable. He points to many instances in which needs emerge in reverse order. For example, a person's love needs may occupy a superior place on the hierarchy to the esteem needs and emerge only after sufficient gratification of the latter through achievement, competence, recognition, and the like. However, such reversals are individual peculiarities and constitute rare departures from the norm. Maslow also makes it clear that one set of needs does not have to be fully satisfied for the next set to emerge. Rather than depicting a shift in prepotency as an on/off phenomenon in which the emergence of one set of needs signals the decline of the prior set, Maslow prefers to discuss the shift in terms of an increase in the *proportion* of satisfied needs among the needs in each set in the hierarchy. For example, as the proportion of satisfied physiological needs increases, the proportions of satisfied needs in the other sets also increase. The increases are greatest for the needs just one step above physiological needs in the hierarchy and least at the top. Maslow illustrates this gradual emergence by a hypothetical example in which an 85% satisfaction of the physiological needs results in satisfaction of 70% of the safety needs, 50% of the love needs, and 10% of the self-actualization need. Hence, the proportions of satisfaction decrease as the hierarchy is ascended. Increasing the proportions at the lower end to such an extent that the needs there are "fairly well" satisfied and consequently no longer prepotent should allow for increased proportions at the upper end.

Two issues we've brought up in discussing other theories are especially relevant to the need-hierarchy theory (Maslow, 1970). The first is whether motivational influences are conscious or unconscious. Maslow does not see this issue as critical for his concept of basic needs; the influences are not necessarily unconscious or conscious. However, a person typically is unaware of the influence of the needs in directing his or her behavior.

The second issue concerns the role of causal factors other than the basic needs. Maslow acknowledges that there are nonbasic needs and motivations. However, they are not as significant or powerful as the basic needs. He also emphasizes that *not* all behavior is motivated, even though all behavior is caused by something. Some behavior is determined exclusively by elements in the "external field"—environmental forces, demands, or contingencies. For example, if you want to see a movie, standing in line to buy a ticket is a behavior imposed upon you by the throng of others who want to see the movie. Further, some behaviors not caused by the environment are nevertheless unmotivated. One example is what Maslow calls *expressive behavior.* Such behavior is not purposive or motivated; it is merely a reflection of the personality. A person might dress in a zany fashion, crack jokes, and play tennis with relish because of the expressive functions of those behaviors, rather than because of their need-satisfying functions. Another important kind of behavior that is personally determined yet not motivated by the basic needs comes about by the principle of functional autonomy (Allport, 1961). The essence of this principle is that behaviors that initially were motivated by basic needs come to have value and satisfaction in themselves. Such behaviors are performed not only because they gratify the original motivating need but also, sometimes, because they are intrinsically satisfying or because of the satisfactions that have become associated with the behaviors. The behaviors have become autonomous—that is, need free. For example, eating can be rewarding for reasons other than satiating hunger. Functional autonomy is especially common among the higher needs, but it can occur in any behavior that is need motivated. Functionally autonomous behaviors, then, are those motivated by secondary or acquired satisfactions independent of those prompted directly by the basic needs. Maslow sees such autonomously motivated behaviors as instrumental in the formation of a person's character, as they can be maintained when the environment is not directly satisfying needs.

**Mechanisms of motivation.**   The mechanisms of motivation are a controversial element of the need-hierarchy theory. Maslow (1968) distinguishes between two motivational mechanisms: deficiency motivation (D-motivation) and growth motivation, or motivation through being (B-motivation). Deficiency motivation is operative when there is a deficiency in satisfaction, arising from an unfulfilled need. This state of deprivation motivates the organism to seek the goal that would alleviate the deficiency. Hunger leads to eating; lack of love leads to striving for affection. D-motivation implies a state of tension that motivates the organism to reduce it. The concept of D-motivation is an equilibrium notion, in which the imbalance caused by tension causes action to restore the balance. Hence, the mechanism is analogous to tension reduction in psychoanalytic theory. The deficiency-motivation mechanism, however, is operative only for the four lower basic needs in the hierarchy (physiological, safety, love, and esteem needs).

The growth-motivation mechanism, which is dramatically different, operates only for the self-actualization need. Self-actualization motivates the person to grow, not to overcome deprivation. At this highest stage of the need hierarchy, one is not deficient in satisfactions of lower needs. One is living *and* developing. In growth motivation, no sense of urgency drives the individual to attain a particular goal; rather, there is a steady progression toward the actualization of potential. Here, enhancement is viewed in much the same way as Rogers views it. At this stage people are not motivated but metamotivated—they are beyond need gratification. They are in a state of *being*, not a state of deprivation. If anything, the growth-motivation mechanism operates by tension induction, rather than tension reduction, since new experiences and stimulations are sought, not avoided. B-motivation alters behavior dramatically. Behaviors that were D-motivated in the past may become B-motivated. For example, a man who married to satisfy the basic need for love (D-love) might find his marital relationship to be enhancing and fulfilling (B-love), thus promoting self-actualization and growth. He would also have corresponding shifts in perception (D-perception to B-perception) and in thinking (D-cognition to B-cognition). The qualitative differences between deficiency motivation and growth motivation divide the need hierarchy into two distinctly different levels: the D-motivated needs (physiological, safety, love, and esteem) and the B-motivated need (self-actualization).

In his later writings, Maslow (1971) turned his theorizing exclusively to the issues of growth, metamotivation, and being. His quest led him to the concept of eupsychia, a utopialike prescription for living that might optimize the emergence and furtherance of B-motivation.

Maslow's presumed mechanisms of motivation are noteworthy with reference to Rogers and Freud. All three theorists assume that tension reduction is a primary mechanism of motivation. In contrast to Freud, Maslow and Rogers also suggest that tension induction may operate in growth-motivated behaviors. Maslow, however, is unique in hypothesizing that tension-reducing behaviors (those that are D-motivated) might become tension-inducing behaviors (B-motivated) once self-actualization has been achieved.

**Summary.**    Maslow's theory of motivation is depicted in his hierarchy of the five sets of basic needs. These needs are described as "instinctoid," and they take precedence over other needs and influences on behavior. Among the basic needs, the strongest (and therefore lowest in the hierarchy) requires satisfaction first, so that satisfaction proceeds from the lowest need (physiological) to the highest (self-actualization). The subsequent need in the hierarchy will become prepotent and dominate behavior only when the preceding one is sufficiently satisfied. The highest need elicits growth motivation; the others elicit deficiency motivation.

## Constructs explaining individual differences

We have mentioned that Maslow placed primary emphasis on his motivation constructs; his constructs for explaining individual differences in personality were relatively undeveloped. Although his theory, like Rogers's, aims ultimately at the holistic understanding of an individual's motivational dynamics, Maslow's use of personality classifications is sparse. Theoretically, Maslow might have developed five personality types, each corresponding to the predomination of a set of basic needs. However, he describes the characteristics of each stage of need satisfaction but does not systematically differentiate among groups of individuals by means of need-related personality constructs. Instead, Maslow speculated in detail about the characteristics of only one personality type—the *self-actualizing person.*

The self-actualizing person is Maslow's conception of the mature, psychologically healthy person. As implied in the discussion of basic needs, psychological well-being corresponds directly to the level of need satisfaction that a person has attained; the higher the need, the greater the psychological health. The self-actualizing person is one who has ascended the need hierarchy and, having gratified the D-motivated needs, is now B-motivated.

The self-actualizing person has a number of personal characteristics that distinguish him or her from the crowd (Maslow, 1970). Table 4-1 is a partial list of some of the attributes of such self-actualizing persons. It is apparent from this list that Maslow's self-actualizing person is much like Rogers's fully functioning person. Maslow's conception, however, is perhaps even more idealized than that of Rogers. The attributes Maslow specifies derive from his "impressions" of a few self-actualized persons whom he either interviewed or read about. His sample, obviously, was representative of only an infinitesimal fraction of the population.

Maslow attempted to temper his utopian conception of self-actualizers by pointing to their "imperfections." They were not gods, and by the standards of society they might not even be viewed as psychologically healthy. In his case studies of self-actualizers, he found some of them to be unsympathetic, egocentric, discourteous, antisocial, and

**TABLE 4-1.** Some characteristics of self-actualizing persons

More efficient perception of reality
Greater adaptation to the environment
Greater acceptance of self, others, and nature
Greater spontaneity
Greater attention to problems outside themselves
Greater comfort with solitude and privacy
Greater independence from culture and environment; self-containedness
Greater freshness of appreciation for a variety of experiences
Greater tendency to have mystical (peak) experiences
Greater sense of identification with humanity
More profound interpersonal relationships (B-love)
Greater creativity
More philosophical sense of humor

guilt-prone. Although they were growth motivated, they manifested some of the negative feelings and behaviors that make human beings complex. This observation led Maslow (1971) to conclude that human nature resides somewhere between good and evil.

With the self-actualizing person as the ideal, Maslow designates two other extreme types of personality functioning. A failure of personal growth because of lack of need satisfaction results in the disruption of psychological functioning and, over time, might lead to neurosis or to some other form of psychopathology (Maslow, 1970). Being deprived of need satisfaction leads to "threat," and threat seems to be a special form of anxiety that elicits neurotic behavior as a maladaptive attempt to reduce the deprivation. At the other extreme, Maslow (1970) made a distinction between transcendent and nontranscendent self-actualizers. A nontranscender is a "merely healthy" self-actualizer; a transcender is something special. The transcender's behavior is determined by factors that are beyond even the metamotivation of the self-actualizing need. Besides sharing with nontranscenders the characteristics of the self-actualizing person, transcenders have a catalog of distinctive characteristics, the essence of which seems to reside in the attainment of higher levels of consciousness, being, and mysticism. Like Buddhist masters, people in this subset of self-actualizers have risen even above the lofty upper bounds of growth motivation. "They are after all superior people" (Maslow, 1971, p. 289).

## An example of application: Work motivation

Unlike the theories of Freud and Rogers, Maslow's theory has not had its major application in the clinical areas of psychotherapy and counseling, although the theory does sketch general relationships between motivation and personality. Maslow (1965) hypothesized that work experience had a major impact on need satisfaction and personal growth, so he focused on the motivational problems encountered by employees in work organizations. Since the theory assumed that work motivation was explainable through the constructs and principles of the need-hierarchy theory, there were clear implications for organizational management. According to Maslow, a manager should create a "climate" for employees in which they might attain their fullest potential—that is, become self-actualized in their jobs. If this could be achieved, their work and other aspects of their lives would become B-motivated. Theoretically, employees would become less frustrated, more satisfied, and—most importantly from a management perspective—more productive. The optimum employee climate to be structured by management should involve increasing opportunities for higher-need satisfaction through greater job responsibility, independence, status, and the like.

The application of Maslow's need-hierarchy theory to work motivation has become widely accepted and is widely used by practicing managers (Steers & Porter, 1975). The theory also has greatly influenced theorists, researchers, and writers in the field of management and organizational behavior. Maslow's writings span diverse topics such as job performance, leadership and management, organizational systems and behavior, and employee needs and satisfactions (Mitchell & Moudgill, 1976).

The widespread application of Maslow's need-hierarchy model to organizational management has stimulated a large research literature, and the findings raise questions regarding the construct validity of the model (Wahba & Bridwell, 1976).

Most research has measured need and need gratification by means of a questionnaire. The most widely used instrument is the Porter (1962) Need Satisfaction Questionnaire (NSQ). The NSQ was designed to measure a modified version of Maslow's need hierarchy. The NSQ's version of the hierarchy omits physiological needs, presumably because it was assumed that these were generally satisfied among workers. Second, the NSQ included an autonomy need as a separate step in the hierarchy, placing it between the esteem needs and the self-actualization need. (In Maslow's formulation, autonomy is one of the esteem needs.) The modified hierarchy of needs—security (safety), social (love), esteem, autonomy, and self-fulfillment (self-actualization)—was operationalized by 13 items (see Table 4-2). For each item, subjects respond on a 7-point scale to three questions: (1) How much is there now? (2) How much should there be? and (3) How important is this to me? There are four scores for each need: (1) the how-much-is-there-now score, (2) the how-much-should-there-be score, (3) the how-important-is-this-to-me score, and (4) the need-deficiency score. The first three scores are obtained by separately totalling the three item-scores for each question. The fourth score, need deficiency, is calculated by subtracting the how-much-is-there-now score from the how-much-should-there-be score for each item and totalling across the items.

**TABLE 4-2.** Examples of items from the Need Satisfaction Questionnaire

| Item | Need category |
| --- | --- |
| The feeling of security associated with one's position | Security needs |
| The opportunity for developing close friendships | Social needs |
| Prestige inside the organization (i.e., regard received from others within the organization) | Esteem needs |
| The opportunity for independent thought and action | Autonomy needs |
| The opportunity for personal growth and development | Self-fulfillment needs |

The NSQ and related questionnaires have been used to investigate two hypotheses derived from Maslow's need-hierarchy theory. The first is the deprivation/domination hypothesis. This states that the greater the deprivation (deficiency, or lack of gratification) of a need, the greater its dominance (prepotency, or importance). In other words, the least-gratified need should be the most important. The results of ten studies using managers, executives, professionals, and factory workers did not strongly confirm the deprivation/domination hypothesis. Partial support was found for the hypothesis with reference to the autonomy and self-fulfillment needs, but no apparent support was uncovered for the security, social, and esteem needs (Wahba & Bridwell, 1976).

The second hypothesis derived from Maslow's theory, the gratification/activation hypothesis, can best be operationalized as follows: the greater the satisfaction of a need, (1) the lesser the importance of that specific need *and* (2) the greater the importance of the need at the next level of the hierarchy. Although many studies of this hypothesis have been done, the most pertinent ones have used longitudinal designs, collecting data on the same sample at different points in time (Wahba & Bridwell, 1976). D. T. Hall and Nougaim (1968), using interviews of managers over a five-year period, and Lawler and Suttle (1972), using NSQ scores of managers over a one-year period, both failed to find support for the gratification/activation hypothesis.

The apparent failure of the research data to offer support for the validity of Maslow's need hierarchy poses a curious paradox: the theory appears to have immense practical utility but very little scientific credibility. Several explanations might account for this incongruity. First, as Cofer and Appley (1964) noted, Maslow's concepts are vague and imprecise and thus hard to operationalize in doing research. Many questions still echo unanswered: What is a need? How does it motivate behavior? How is it gratified or deprived? Can people specify their needs and their need-gratifications? Is the need hierarchy the same for everyone? Second, the problem of measurement in testing Maslow's theory is staggering. How can researchers measure that which cannot be clearly specified? Moreover, the major effort at measurement, Porter's Need Satisfaction Questionnaire, is plagued by psychometric problems: its reliability and validity data are sparse; it is encumbered by response biases; and its factors do not correspond precisely to Maslow's classification of needs (Wahba & Bridwell, 1976).

Despite the practical appeal of Maslow's need-hierarchy theory and its value for generating research interest, it appears that work motivation is better understood by means of other models (J. P. Campbell & Pritchard, 1976). Need achievement theory (Chapter 8), equity theory (Chapter 9), and attribution theory (Chapter 10) offer viable alternatives.

### Conclusions: Maslow

Maslow's need-hierarchy theory is a comprehensive, humanistic theory of motivation. Unlike Rogers, Maslow emphasizes the impact of numerous human needs on behavior. Self-actualization, for Maslow, is not a goal-directed force that shapes human destiny. Rather, it appears in his theory as a developmental concept. Self-actualization becomes operative only after preexisting needs have been put to rest. It is the highest form of motivation, but it is not *always* guiding behavior, as the Rogerian version is; its influence emerges only if lower needs are adequately satisfied.

Although the need-hierarchy scheme has obvious appeal and explanatory power, the theory itself has two major shortcomings. First, it is unclear from Maslow's writings how the five basic needs were selected, why they are ranked as they are, and why others were not included. The best explanation for each seems to reside in Maslow's application of humanistic values and beliefs, rather than scholarly and scientific considerations. Second, this theory is unscientific in that it is based neither on systematic clinical observations nor on experimental data. However, Maslow does strive throughout his writings to state his assumptions and viewpoints about motivated behavior in terms of testable hypotheses. The problem for research is one of defining and measuring the basic needs. One such attempt with the self-actualization need (Shostrom, 1964) has yielded guardedly promising results (Tosi & Lindamood, 1975). Another attempt has been made to measure all five needs (J. Hall & Williams, 1973), but validity data are sparse.

## Conclusions and critique: Rogers and Maslow

There are a great many differences between the humanistic theory of Rogers and the humanistic theory of Maslow. The major difference is that Maslow incorporates several motive forces into his need-hierarchy model, whereas Rogers relies heavily on a single motive force toward growth. Despite the differences, however, there are two central points of similarity: a humanistic view of motive constructs and the clinical method of investigation. We shall turn to these briefly for evaluation, but as noted earlier in this chapter, evaluation of these theories depends directly on one's adherence to or dissension from the humanistic perspective.

The major contribution of humanistic theories of motivation resides in what they emphasize. In stark contrast to instinctual and psychoanalytic motivation theories, humanistic theories play down what they consider to be "lower" motivations, such as sex and aggression. They see these bases of motivation as present but not predominant. Rather, they are mere residuals of human evolution, whereas truly human motivation is vastly different and far more complex. The primary sources of motivation in humans are indeed inherent and instinctlike, but they vary considerably from instincts and from one another, both in their goals and in the ways they work. Humanistic theories stress motivations whose goals are the enhancement and fulfillment of the organism and which are therefore "higher" motivations. The particular behaviors enacted to attain these goals vary from person to person and from situation to situation. The critical point is that self-actualization is a higher goal. The motivation is to grow—not to defend and control, as postulated by Freud. The emphasis is not on any particular motivated behaviors but rather on the *course* of motivated behavior.

In humanistic models, the process of gratification does not consist exclusively in the reduction of tension created by an unfulfilled need. A need also may *create* tension as the person strives for new experiences and stimulations. This departure from the tension-reduction mechanism of motivation is most significant. Tension reduction is at the core of both the psychoanalytic theory of motivation and, as we shall see in the next chapter, Hull's theory of motivation. Rogers and Maslow explicitly emphasize that *both* tension induction and tension reduction can occur. The optimal level theories of motivation (Chapter 6) share this viewpoint but start from a very different theoretical base.

A related contribution of the humanistic theories is the role accorded the environment in influencing the motivation of behavior. Psychoanalytic theory—except for the adaptive viewpoint as elaborated in ego psychology—depicts the environment as a source of "objects" for the gratification of the instinctual drives. The humanistic view is strikingly different. First, because humanistic theories are clinical and human in their emphasis, the interpersonal sphere of the environment is crucial: other people are central in providing satisfaction for needs such as positive regard, love, and esteem, and even for elements of enhancement and actualization. Second, motivation is given a dynamic emphasis by the idea that the social environment can also frustrate one's basic motivational tendencies: other persons can levy conditions of worth upon the person, thwart the person's needs for love and esteem, and so forth. The interpersonal world is thus seen as a potent factor in motivated behavior. It satisfies or frustrates the motivational tendency toward actualization. In general, humanistic theories have a more complex view of the social environmen. than psychoanalytic theory; other persons can provide growth *and* help the individual to overcome deprivation, can increase *and* decrease tension resulting in the satisfaction of needs.

Over time, interaction with the environment produces individual differences that, according to these humanistic theories, result from satisfactions or frustrations of basic needs, including self-actualization. The self-actualizing person and the fully functioning person exhibit a set of consistent behaviors that have arisen from the unimpeded operation of the motive toward growth. Motivation thus has a temporal dimension. It not only operates from moment to moment—in the here and now— but also has long-term consequences in the form of personality characteristics caused by particular interactions between motive and environment.

The criticisms of humanistic theories of motivation pertain directly and indirectly to the humanistic perspective on theory construction and methodology. From a scientific perspective, the problem that permeates each of these theories derives from its adherence to a paradigm that emphasizes holism and generalizability at the expense of control and prediction. This paradigm has had an impact both on the constructs of the theories and on the theories' susceptibility to experimental validation. In evaluating the self-actualization perspective on motivation, two experimental psychologists, Cofer and Appley (1964), succinctly present the critics' position by stating that the shortcomings of humanistic psychology result "from the vagueness of its concepts, the looseness of its language, and the inadequacy of the evidence related to its major contentions" (p. 692). In other words, the deficiencies of humanistic theories are their imprecise constructs and principles and their dubious scientific status. Humanists, of course, explain this criticism as an example of the very view of people and science that they are combating. Hence, the clash between paradigms continues with no clear victor. Applications of the theories—client-centered therapy and utilization of the need-hierarchy model in management—paradoxically have generated little empirical support for the theoretical constructs yet have garnered considerable influence among practitioners.

The foregoing criticisms cannot be taken lightly. The experimental paradigm is gaining, rather than losing, prominence within psychology. If humanistic theories are to endure as important perspectives on motivation, it seems that they must sharpen their constructs so that they are investigable. Rogers and Maslow have made serious attempts at doing so, but further sophistication is needed.

These problems notwithstanding, the self-actualization theories have laid bare elements of motivation that are obscured or de-emphasized by others. Their contribution is unique and significant, especially as a framework for guiding research and describing applications to work, counseling, and so forth.

CHAPTER **5**

# Stimulus-Response Theories of Motivation: The Hull/Spence Tradition

*This is no science, it is only the hope of a science.*[1]

William James,
*referring to the
status of psychology
in 1892*

Clark L. Hull was not afraid to be wrong. On the basis of limited evidence, he and his colleague Kenneth Spence formulated a very comprehensive theory of learning and motivation. Because the theory was so broad, and because its predictions were testable, attempts to verify the Hull/Spence theory took 20 years and occupied hundreds of journal articles. No other theory has ever so dominated the areas of learning and motivation.

## Influences on Hull

There were three important influences on Hull: the research of Ivan Pavlov and E. L. Thorndike, the work of Walter Cannon and other physiologists, and the behaviorism of John Watson.

### Pavlov and Thorndike: Classical conditioning

One of the most famous early psychologists, Ivan Pavlov, won the Nobel Prize for his research on the digestive system of dogs, but he changed his field from physiology to psychology when he became intrigued by the anticipatory salivation his dogs would exhibit before any food was introduced into their mouths. Pavlov began his careful study of the process later named *classical conditioning* by pairing a neutral stimulus, such as a bell, with food. Normally, dogs would salivate when presented with food. After a few pairings in which a bell was sounded each time that food was presented, the dogs began to salivate at the sound of the bell even though no food was present. Pavlov termed the food an "unconditioned stimulus" (UCS), the bell a "conditioned stimulus" (CS), salivation to the food the "unconditioned response" (UCR), and salivation to the bell the "conditioned response" (CR). Pavlov showed that nearly any stimulus that immediately preceded the UCS for several pairings could soon elicit a CR. Hull would use this classical-conditioning model extensively throughout his theory.

[1]From *Text-book of Psychology: Briefer Course*, by W. James. New York: Holt, 1892.

Hull would not adopt Pavlov's view of motivation, however. Pavlov believed that the dog's motivation for salivating to the bell was contained within the stimulus itself, the bell. Pavlov was combining learning and motivation. Whereas one might say the animal had merely learned that the bell preceded the food, Pavlov would say the bell had acquired motivational properties as well.

A similar principle can be seen in the theorizing of E. L. Thorndike, an influential S-R (stimulus-response) learning theorist. Thorndike is best known for his contribution to education and for his law of effect: "Of several responses made to the same situation, those which are accompanied or closely followed by satisfaction to the animal will, other things being equal, be more firmly connected with the situation, so that, when it recurs, they will be more likely to recur" (1911, p. 244). Although the law of effect might appear to say that an animal does something *in order to* obtain a reward, closer inspection reveals that it does not. It says that, if an animal is presented with a stimulus (S) and performs a response (R), and R is followed by a reward, the reward strengthens the bond between S and R. (One can think of the hyphen in "S-R" as a bond growing stronger with every reward.) The more times Thorndike rewarded cats for escaping from an elaborate box, the more adept they became at escaping. The animals, however, were not performing certain movements *in order to* get out to obtain the reward. They were performing the responses, said Thorndike, because those responses had become strongly connected to the stimulus situation of being in the box. Thus, like Pavlov, Thorndike believed the motivation was contained within the stimulus itself. The responses had become "stamped in." When the stimulus was presented, the responses had to follow.

Thorndike and Pavlov were early learning theorists, and they thought motivation could be explained by their principles of learning. Pavlov thought the animal would learn that the bell was associated with food, and the bell would then acquire some of the motivational properties of food. Thorndike thought reward connected the S and R so strongly that, when the S was presented, the animal would have to perform the R. Neither man was explicitly concerned with what would happen if the animal was not hungry. Motivation resided in the stimulus, and with proper pairing of the bell and food, the animal would learn. Thus motivation was considered a topic secondary to and subsumed under learning. With the advent of Hullian theory, however, the topic of motivation would become a separate—and crucial—concept.

## Cannon: Homeostasis

A second important influence on Hull was the work of Cannon, Richter, and others who studied the relations between behavior and physiology. Hull believed that motivation was biologically induced. For that reason, the physiological theories of Walter Cannon (see Chapter 2) were particularly relevant. Cannon had described the body as a self-balancing system with a vast number of sensory receptors in strategic locations, such as the stomach, throat, and skin. The function of these receptors was to detect nonoptimal states—both internal and external—and signal the person to eat, drink, or do whatever was needed to restore optimal conditions. *Homeostasis* was the term Cannon used to denote the state in which all receptors detected equilibrium—that is, there were no conditions to be corrected. A homeostasislike principle would play an important role in Hull's theory.

## Watson: Behaviorism

The third important influence on Hull was behaviorism, a scientific viewpoint whose chief early spokesman in the United States was John B. Watson. Watson maintained that all evidence used in psychology must be scientifically obtained and therefore publicly observable. He did not consider introspection a valid way of obtaining evidence, since the target of introspection is by definition not publicly observable. Thus, concepts such as "ego" have no place in psychology, because they cannot be defined objectively in terms of observable events. What *can* be observed and measured is behavior. Those who insisted on behavior as the only evidence objective enough for psychologists to study were called "behaviorists," and the behavioristic viewpoint would greatly influence Hull.

Stimulus-response psychologists believe that every response of an organism to a stimulus is a result of either an innate reflex or learning. Since innate responses seemed to be beyond psychological manipulation, S-R psychologists soon identified themselves with the study of learning, investigating the ways in which stimuli and responses become associated. Both stimuli and responses are publicly observable physical events; hence, S-R psychologists are certainly within the mainstream of the behavioristic tradition. They measure responses—that is, behavior.

Although Hull's theory is behavioristic, it has features that distinguish it from other behavioristic theories, most notably that of B. F. Skinner, the most prominent behaviorist over the last 40 years. Hull focused on the relations between observable stimuli and responses, but he also hypothesized unobservable processes and states—such as "drive"—which are central to his theory of motivation. Such constructs are termed "intervening variables" because they are *assumed* (not observed) to exist *between* a stimulus and a response. The Hull/Spence theory of motivation rests heavily on the use of intervening variables. In using the concept "drive," Hull and Spence were in a neobehavioristic tradition with which Skinner's viewpoint was at first relatively consistent. However, the emergence of Skinner's operant theory left no room in his version of behaviorism for intervening variables such as motivation. The Skinnerian position is worth noting briefly before turning to a discussion of the Hull/Spence theory.

**Skinner.**    Skinner's early research and methodology were frequently cited in Hull's first major book (1943) on learning and motivation. In *The Behavior of Organisms* (1938), Skinner called the concept of drives such as hunger and thirst "useful" in explaining the variability of behavior. Since animals would work for food only occasionally, the hypothetical state "hungry" was used to describe the condition of an animal when striving for food did occur. Thus, Skinner maintained in 1938 that the concept of the "hunger drive" explained why eating behavior occurred at some times and not at others.

By the 1950s, however, the esteem in which Skinner held the term *drive* had decreased markedly. Drive was no longer useful or convenient but was instead entirely superfluous (Skinner, 1953, pp. 33–35, 144). Since deprivation is presumably the only way that drive can be created, the concept of drive is not needed. The statement "Water deprivation results in drinking" refers only to observable phenomena and is therefore a testable hypothesis. "Water deprivation causes thirst, which causes drinking" adds nothing to the prior statement except an internal drive, which cannot be observed. Skinner's disapproval of the use of intervening variables, such as thirst, has earned him a reputation as a "nonmotivational theorist." Intervening concepts such as motivation are absent from Skinnerian theory.

Skinner thinks it is counterproductive to posit intervening variables to help "explain" behavior. Attributing a behavior to an "expectancy" or the "id" retards scientific progress. Skinner says that an explanation should not appeal to

> events taking place somewhere else, at some other level of observation, described in different terms, and measured, if at all, in different dimensions. . . . When we attribute behavior to a neural or mental event, real or conceptual, we are likely to forget that we still have the task of accounting for the neural or mental event. When we assert that an animal acts in a given way because it expects to receive food, then what began as the task of accounting for learned behavior becomes the task of accounting for expectancy. The [latter] problem is at least equally complex and probably more difficult [1950, pp. 193–194].

Needless to say, Skinner's viewpoint is not shared by all psychologists. Consider the "ponderostat" proposed by Nisbett (1972). As described under "Hunger" in Chapter 2, the ponderostat is a hypothetical mechanism that detects whether an animal is at its proper weight. Since a ponderostat is not observable, Skinner would oppose using the concept to help explain behavior. However, Nisbett's ponderostat is entirely consistent with the physiology of the hypothalamus. Given this consistency, the existence of a weight-regulatory mechanism seems reasonable. Further, postulating this mechanism enables Nisbett to make *new* predictions about the sexual behavior, emotionality, and taste sensitivity of overweight people. Thus, the hypothesis of a ponderostat is suggested by prior physiological research and can yield testable predictions about phenomena not used to generate the hypothesis. In this way circularity is avoided. Nevertheless, Skinner holds the view that unobservables such as the ponderostat are not appropriate for a science of behavior.

The viewpoint that all nonobservable theoretical constructs should be discarded from science is termed *radical empiricism*. Bolles (1967) is one of the many theorists who believe that radical empiricism is far too great a price to pay in order to remove mysticism from psychology. He thinks that, as long as every term is securely anchored to data, it cannot contain surplus meaning. If "drive" is postulated to be the result of deprivation and the energizer of behavior, then the construct is carefully defined and can be used to make predictions. For example, Bolles would probably agree with Skinner that psychologists should not attribute behavior to a "pugnacious instinct" (James, 1890), which has no operational definition. However, Bolles and the present authors would disagree with Skinner's assertion that no such theoretical construct can be useful.

We shall next consider a few very important intervening variables that Hullian theory uses for explaining motivation.

## Hull and the Perin/Williams studies

Hullian theory itself was founded on some extremely simple studies. Two of the most important were done by Hull's students, Perin (1942) and Williams (1938). In these experiments, rats were trained to run down a straight wooden alleyway to a food reward. One group of rats had been deprived of food for 22 hours, a second group for 3 hours. Hull had postulated that longer food deprivation would cause higher motivation, or drive ($D$). He also had postulated that the more times an animal was rewarded for running down an alley, the more strongly the animal would acquire the habit ($H$) of running whenever it was placed in that alley. One could increase the $H$ of alley-running in rats by rewarding them over and over for doing just that. To no one's surprise, the Perin/Williams studies showed that increased $D$ (hunger) resulted in faster running speeds down the alleyway toward the food, and the more times an animal had previously been rewarded for alley-running (increased $H$), the faster was its running speed.[2] At first glance this appeared to be an obvious, uninteresting result. However, Hull's treatment of $D$ and $H$ had profound implications.[3]

---

[2]In the earliest studies, resistance to extinction was used instead of running speed as the dependent variable.

[3]The term *drive* was popularized by Woodworth (1918), who thought this term had the advantage of being devoid of the problems associated with the word *instinct* and

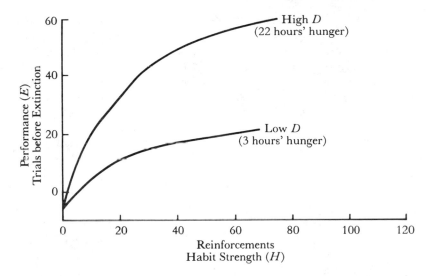

**Figure 5-1.** The Perin/Williams data show that, as the number of reinforcements increases, the curves diverge. Hull concluded that the relation between $D$ and $H$ must be multiplicative. If $H$ is zero, no amount of $D$ will cause performance of the behavior. *(Adapted from "Behavior Potentiality as a Joint Function of the Amount of Training and the Degrees of Hunger at the Time of Extinction," by C. T. Perin,* Journal of Experimental Psychology, *1942, 30, 93–113. Copyright 1942 by the American Psychological Association. Reprinted by permission.)*

Hull postulated that $D$ and $H$ contributed equally to the performance of any activity. More precisely, performance ($E$, which stands for "excitatory potential") was equal to drive ($D$) multiplied by habit ($H$). The formula $E = D \times H$ was based exclusively on the Perin/Williams data, which are presented in Figure 5-1. Having inferred a multiplicative relation, Hull predicted that performance would occur only if $D$ and $H$ were both greater than zero.

## Hull's motivational construct: Drive (D)

Hull (1943) considered biological needs the sole sources of motivation and considered reduction of those needs the definition of *reinforcement*. For example, as hunger increased, $D$ would increase. If an animal was fed, need and therefore $D$ would be reduced. Because Hull maintained that an organism was motivated to reduce biological needs, he is called a drive-reduction theorist. The principle of drive reduction bears some

---

the nonscientific notions associated with terms such as *desire* and *purpose*. Woodworth (1918, p. 36) had also first suggested the distinction between $D$ and $H$ (drive and mechanism). However, the distinction was developed much more fully by Hull (1943).

relation to Cannon's principle of homeostasis. Cannon believed that an organism "tried" to return to its optimum whenever certain physiological states became too extreme. For example, if body temperature rises much beyond 98.6° Fahrenheit or falls much below 98.6°, the body sweats or shivers, thus promoting a return to the optimal temperature. Hull believed that an organism always "tried" to return to a state of having no biological needs, or, in Hull's terminology, no drive ($D$). However, this return always occurred by means of drive *reduction*, whereas Cannon's principle of homeostasis implied that the optimal state would sometimes be achieved by reduction but at other times by an increase in some index, such as body temperature.

## Generalized drive

To the basic principle that biological need was the source of drive, Hull added an astounding corollary: an increase in a drive—say, hunger— would not just energize behaviors related to that drive, such as looking for food and chewing; an increase in $D$ would energize *all* behaviors. A somewhat hungry person would run faster, chew harder, throw farther, jump higher, and perform any other behavior with more motivation than a satiated person. Hull conceived of $D$ as a completely general energizer.

The idea of $D$ as a general energizer sounded so counterintuitive that it quickly generated a great deal of experimentation. A fruitful line of research was initiated by Spence and Taylor, who used the multiplicative relation and the idea of generalized $D$ to test one of the most famous hypotheses in psychology, the Yerkes/Dodson law (Yerkes & Dodson, 1908). This hypothesis states that on easy tasks optimal performance will occur under very high motivation. On difficult tasks, optimal performance occurs under lower motivation, high motivation being disruptive.

Here's an example to illustrate how Hull's theory was used by Spence and Taylor to demonstrate the Yerkes/Dodson law. Suppose someone asked your friend Marie, "Which planet is called the red planet?" She'd probably find that question fairly easy and answer "Mars." The reason the question is easy is that the dominant response, "Mars," is correct. Marie was probably reinforced in high school for learning that response, so its level of $H$ is high. We'll say that Marie's $H$ is 10 for the habit of associating "Mars" with "red planet." The response with the next highest association to "red planet" might be "Venus," but "Venus" has an $H$ of only 1 to "red planet." Its $H$ is so low because it has not received much reinforcement as a response to "red planet." Suppose also that Marie scored low on the Taylor Manifest Anxiety Scale, indicating that she's a low-anxiety person. Taylor thought that anxiety fit the Hullian definition of drive, and according to Hull a drive energizes *all* behaviors. Therefore, Marie's low $D$

(we'll say she scored a 1) should energize both her $H$ of saying "Mars" and her $H$ of saying "Venus" to the "red planet" question. What is Marie's total excitatory potential ($E$) for each behavior?

$$E = D \times H$$
$$E_{\text{MARS}} = 1 \times 10 = 10$$
$$E_{\text{VENUS}} = 1 \times 1 = 1$$

Since $E_{\text{MARS}}$ is 9 excitatory-potential units greater than $E_{\text{VENUS}}$, Marie will probably answer correctly.

Now let's look at how Mike would do on this question. Mike is an extremely anxious person; he scored 10 on the Taylor Manifest Anxiety Scale. This high $D$ would energize all his behaviors, according to Hull. What are his $E$ values for answering "Mars" and for answering "Venus"?

$$E = D \times H$$
$$E_{\text{MARS}} = 10 \times 10 = 100$$
$$E_{\text{VENUS}} = 10 \times 1 = 10$$

Since Mike's $E_{\text{MARS}}$ is a whopping 90 units greater than $E_{\text{VENUS}}$, he'll *certainly* answer "Mars." Marie's difference between $E_{\text{MARS}}$ and $E_{\text{VENUS}}$ was only a paltry 9 units, so she would probably get the question correct, but not with the speed or certainty with which Mike would. Thus, on easy tasks such as the "red planet" question, high $D$ is better than low $D$. This is the first half of the Yerkes/Dodson law.

Let us now examine the Hullian analysis of a difficult task. Suppose I ask Marie, "Who was Gerald Ford's running mate during the 1976 Presidential election?" The dominant association to this question might be "Nelson Rockefeller." This response has a high $H$ for Marie; we'll say $H = 10$. The correct answer, however, is "Robert Dole." This response has an $H$ of only 1. The reason this is a tough question is that the dominant response is incorrect. Let's calculate $E$ for these two behaviors for Marie, who has a low $D$ of only 1.

$$E = D \times H$$
$$E_{\text{ROCKY}} = 1 \times 10 = 10$$
$$E_{\text{DOLE}} = 1 \times 1 = 1$$

We can see that Marie is likely to answer incorrectly since $E_{\text{ROCKY}}$ is 9 units greater than $E_{\text{DOLE}}$.

Let's examine next the performance of Mike, whose $D = 10$.

$$E = D \times H$$
$$E_{\text{ROCKY}} = 10 \times 10 = 100$$
$$E_{\text{DOLE}} = 10 \times 1 = 10$$

Mike, the high-$D$ person, is *sure* to answer incorrectly. At least with a little extra concentration or contemplation, the low-$D$ person might have a chance at this question; the high-$D$ person is doomed. Thus for difficult tasks, high drive is a drawback. This is the second half of the Yerkes/Dodson law. Note that Hull's generalized-drive principle plays a role in this analysis: both the correct $H$ and the incorrect $H$ are multiplied by $D$. When the correct $H$ is dominant (easy task), high $D$ is best, because high $D$ makes the correct response more dominant. When the incorrect $H$ is dominant (difficult task), high $D$ is detrimental, because high $D$ makes the incorrect response more dominant.

The most powerful example of the Yerkes/Dodson law in the memory of one of the authors occurred during his first day of basic training in the army. At the least appropriately named place in the world—Fort Bliss, Texas—four columns of scared GIs were lined up to enter the mess hall. The sergeant gave a complicated command, "File from the right, column right, [pause] march!" This means that the file of men on the extreme right will do a "column right": they follow the first man as he turns to the right toward the mess hall. The next column will follow immediately behind the last man in the right-hand column, and so on. First, however, during the pause in the sergeant's command, the front man in the *left* file must turn around and shout to his file of men "Stand fast," which means "We're not going anywhere just yet." The leaders of the next two files in turn shout "Stand fast." The leader of the right-hand file then shouts "Column right." After these four men have given their orders to their individual files, the sergeant completes the order by shouting "March!"

The sergeant shouted "File from the right, column right." The file leaders chimed in "Stand fast, stand fast, stand fast, stand fast." As soon as the last file leader bungled by saying "Stand fast," he knew his health was in jeopardy. The author thought (and he's sure these are the exact words he used to himself), "It's understandable. He heard 'Stand fast' three times. It now has a higher $H$ than 'Column right.' He's got very high $D$, so $E$ for 'Stand fast' is much higher than $E$ for 'Column right.' This is a tough task for the kid. The sergeant should *lower* the $D$ level. Then the kid might not blurt out 'Stand fast.' He might be able to rehearse 'Column right' calmly a few times to build up its $H$." Instead, the sergeant threatened to break every bone in the file leader's body if he didn't get it right the second time. (When $D$ is raised, the dominant habit is even more likely to occur.) The platoon went through the command again. Sergeant: "File from the right, column right." File leaders: "Stand fast, stand fast, stand fast, stand fast." As soon as he did it again, he groaned. The helpful sergeant hit him over the head with his hat a dozen times, threatening great bodily harm if he didn't get it right the next time. The command was repeated; the file leader bungled again. The moral of the Yerkes/Dodson law is clear: easy tasks are done best under high $D$, tough tasks under low $D$.

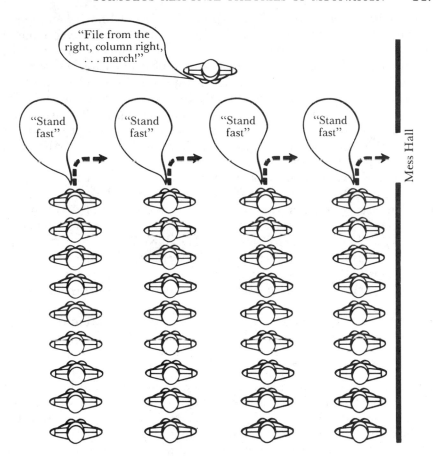

**Figure 5-2.** The army and the Yerkes/Dodson law.

Hull's notion of drive as a general energizer seemed to be adequate in explaining the Yerkes/Dodson law. (See, however, Hill, 1957, who is of the opinion that the generalized-drive principle does not explain the Yerkes/Dodson law adequately.) Still, the counterintuitive nature of this principle has prompted a great deal of research designed to test its validity in other areas. One group of studies, for example, dealt with drive summation. These studies were based on the hypothesis that if $D$ is completely general then a habitual behavior should be performed more vigorously when two drives are at high levels than when only one is. That is, if a drive energizes all behaviors, two drives together should produce higher $D$ and hence greater $E$. In 1952, Meryman found that the startle response is greater among hungry animals than among satiated animals. The hungry animals have two drives, hunger and conditioned fear; the satiated group has only the fear drive.

Another way to test the generalized-drive hypothesis is by the technique of drive substitution. In a study by Webb and Goodman (1958), animals that were trained to bar-press for food while hungry were later tested while satiated—that is, without the original drive. Some of them were tested while the apparatus was flooded with water. This condition activated an aversive drive that substituted for the original hunger drive. The satiated animals in the flooded apparatus did bar-press more than the satiated animals in a normal apparatus. Some drive-substitution studies, however, did not find support for drive as a general energizer. Dees and Furchtgott (1964), for example, could not support the substitution of an aversive drive for hunger, as Webb and Goodman had done.

There are several reasons for the occurrence of contradictory findings in drive-substitution and drive-summation studies. For example, the addition of a drive might not always increase the level of performance of a behavior, even if Hull was absolutely correct. By the Yerkes/Dodson law, addition of a drive may raise $D$ above the optimum and *decrease* performance, not increase it. Nevertheless, Hull came to the conclusion that several studies did pose serious problems for his statement that drive was a completely general energizer. In his final book (1952), Hull retreated somewhat and said that *sometimes* a drive would generalize to energize habits learned under different drive conditions.

## The drive stimulus ($S_D$)

From what we've seen of Hullian theory so far, we might believe that Hull's generalized-drive principle is illogical. For example, if someone becomes hungry while writing, wouldn't Hull have to predict that the increase in $D$ (hunger) would result in more vigorous writing? Yet we all know that when one becomes hungry while writing, one does not write more vigorously. Instead, one stops writing and raids the refrigerator. Hull had a solution to this problem. Biological need has two consequences in Hull's theory. The first, increased $D$, has been discussed. Hull also said that increased $D$ causes a drive stimulus ($S_D$), such as hunger pangs. This second consequence of biological need, $S_D$, played a very important role in Hullian theory.

Food is an unconditioned stimulus (UCS), and salivation is an unconditioned response (UCR). Pavlov showed that when a stimulus precedes or accompanies a UCS, the conditioned stimulus (CS) eventually acquires the power to elicit the UCR. Hull said that the $S_D$ could serve as a CS. From the first time a baby is fed when hungry, the $S_D$ of hunger pangs is present during presentation of the UCS (milk). Eventually, through Pavlovian conditioning, the $S_D$ by itself can bring about salivation, sucking, and other UCRs. Thus, through conditioning, an $S_D$ such as hunger pangs comes to "remind" people of food. $S_D$ directs behavior. Whereas $D$ is a *general* energizer, $S_D$, through its association with a particular goal, channels behavior toward the one goal appropriate for that $S_D$. For example, Hull would say that the $S_D$ of a dry mouth would cause water-seeking behavior through the association of that $S_D$ with drinking. However, the increase in $D$ (thirst) would energize whatever behavior was being undertaken.

The $S_D$ came to play an increasingly prominent role in Hullian theory. Recall that Hull had defined *reinforcement* as need reduction. Several researchers pointed out a serious difficulty of this definition: need reduction begins long after an animal ingests food. For example, Kohn (1951) showed that a hungry animal will lessen its rate of bar pressing for food as soon as food is loaded directly into its stomach. This lessening of the bar-press rate occurs long before the stomach loading can possibly have had any nutritive effect. Need reduction has not taken place, yet the animal is no longer motivated.

Sheffield and his colleagues performed a few crucial studies that have become famous for further discrediting the relation Hull proposed between need reduction and reinforcement. For example, Sheffield and Roby (1950) showed that animals will work for a reward of saccharin. Saccharin has no nutritive value and cannot reduce biological need. Yet it serves quite well as a reinforcer. Since studies such as this one weakened the postulated relation between reinforcement and *need* reduction, Hull decided (1952, p. 6) that $S_D$ reduction was the source of reinforcement. Although reduction of need might not take place for many minutes after eating, reduction of the $S_D$ (hunger pangs) would occur very rapidly. Thus the behavior of running down an alleyway for food would be reinforced very quickly.

## Hull's learning construct: Habit (H)

Hull postulated that a habit gained strength whenever a performance of the response was followed by reinforcement—and only then. Even if an animal was in a stimulus situation and performed the correct response, the animal would not increase the frequency of that response unless reinforcement was given. Reinforcement was absolutely necessary for the learning of a habit to occur. This rather strong statement by Hull was challenged by one of his contemporaries, Edward C. Tolman, an important theorist.

Tolman believed that Hull's brand of behaviorism was incorrect in analyzing all behavior down to the smallest, or most "molecular," S-R level. For example, Hull would say that learning the way to go downtown is accomplished by performing the correct response (left or right turn) to each environmental stimulus and then receiving reinforcement of each correct response. Since traversing the route requires many responses, many individual S-R bonds have to be learned. These individual S-R bonds (habits) are then linked together into the act of going downtown. Tolman believed that such molecular S-R analyses were inappropriate. Tolman maintained that the reason Hull could train rats to run down an alleyway to obtain food was not that reinforcement built up a chain of habits; the rats ran down the alleyway because they wanted to reach the goal. These animals were running for a purpose. The term *purposivist* was applied to Tolman because of his emphasis on the goal-directedness of behavior. His analysis is termed "molar" because its basic unit of analysis is larger than that in the molecular analysis of Hull.

Tolman insisted that learning consists in more than the formation of S-R connections. Indeed, by interacting with the surroundings, an animal could generate its own "cognitive map" of the environment. This information, stored in its memory, could enable the animal to do *new* things, for which it had received no training and no reinforcement.

This was blasphemy to Hull, of course. How could an animal do something it had never learned to do? Since $E = D \times H$, when $H = 0$, $E = 0$. Without $H$, there could be no learned performance.

### Goal anticipation

An experiment by Tolman and Honzik (1930a) demonstrates Tolman's point of view. Figure 5-3 shows the maze used. After a few trials, rats preferred Path 1, the shortest, when running to the goal box. Path 3 was least preferred, and Path 2 was intermediate. That is, $E_1 > E_2 > E_3$. When an obstruction was placed at A, the rats took Path 2. The crucial test occurred when an obstruction was placed at B. Since Path 2 has the second-highest excitatory potential, we might expect that when Path 1 was blocked, rats would try Path 2 next. Instead, they switched directly to Path 3. Tolman would say that during training the rats were not learning S-R units; instead, they were constructing a "cognitive map." While traversing the maze during training, they built up "expectancies." Consequently, they "knew" that a block at B meant paths 1 and 2 were both obstructed. Note that Tolman is ascribing higher-order cognition to the rats. These animals "expect" and "anticipate" as they strive toward the goal. This is surely a far cry from the strict, objective, S-R behaviorism of Hull.

Hull realized that people anticipate goals, but he did not want to introduce unobservable, cognitive concepts such as "anticipation" into his theory. Only behavior can be observed and measured, so Hull tried to explain foreknowledge of the goal by resorting to Pavlovian conditioning. To illustrate the Hullian explanation of goal anticipation, we shall look at a short segment of one man's day—the few minutes between waking up and eating breakfast.

**Proprioceptive stimuli.** Our subject lives next to a junior-high school. Every weekday the school band begins practice at 8:00 A.M. When the band begins playing (UCS$_1$), the subject immediately wakes

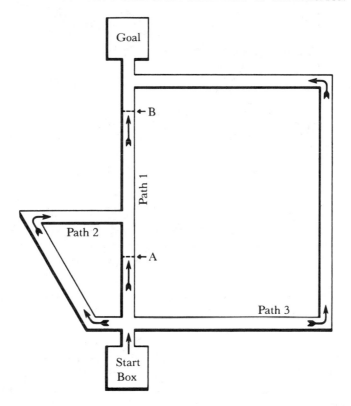

**Figure 5-3.** Rats preferred Path 1 to Path 2, and Path 2 to Path 3. Yet if point B was blocked, the animals switched immediately from Path 1 to Path 3. Tolman and Honzik (1930a) inferred that the rats had a "cognitive map" of the maze. *(Adapted from "Introduction and Removal of Reward, and Maze Performance in Rats," by E. C. Tolman and C. H. Honzik,* University of California Publications in Psychology, *Vol. IV, No. 17. Published in 1930 by the Regents of the University of California. Reprinted by permission of the University of California Press.)*

up and grits his teeth ($UCR_1$). Gritting his teeth is an unconditioned response: it happened automatically, without being learned, the first day he heard the band. The next stimulus he's aware of is the bathroom light going on. The bright light ($UCS_2$) causes the subject to squint ($UCR_2$). This response, too, was unlearned. Next, our subject feels the cold water in the shower running over his head. When he feels the cold water ($UCS_3$), he inhales sharply ($UCR_3$). Figure 5-4 diagrams the subject's morning so far.

Every response the subject makes (or anyone makes) creates stimuli—proprioceptive stimuli. When a pitcher reports that he doesn't feel he's "on" today, for example, he means the responses he's making are

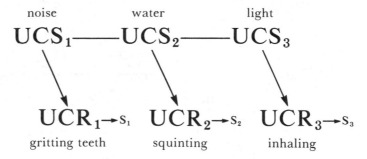

**Figure 5-4.**

creating stimuli in his muscles and tendons that he recognizes as different from the stimuli he feels when he's pitching well. Some people,
such as gymnasts, have to be very sensitive to the stimuli created by
their own movement. However, everyone's muscle movements create
stimuli to some extent. Gritting one's teeth ($UCR_1$), squinting
($UCR_2$), and inhaling ($UCR_3$) create stimuli of which one is aware. In
Figure 5-4, each small $s$ represents the proprioceptive stimuli created
by a UCR.

Look now only at the event $UCS_2 \rightarrow UCR_2$ and the proprioceptive
stimulus $s_1$, which occurs just before that event. Pavlov had already
shown that a stimulus that precedes or accompanies a UCS becomes
conditioned to the UCR. The proprioceptive stimuli caused by the subject's gritting his teeth are present when $UCS_2$ occurs. Consequently,
$UCR_2$ (squinting) becomes conditioned to those proprioceptive stimuli.
Similarly, inhaling becomes conditioned to the proprioceptive stimuli
from squinting. These conditioned associations are shown in Figure
5-5 by dashed arrows.

Look now at the following chain of stimuli and responses:
$UCS_1 \rightarrow UCR_1 \rightarrow s_1 \rightarrow UCR_2 \rightarrow s_2 \rightarrow UCR_3$. The noise of the band,
$UCS_1$, is the first stimulus the subject receives in the morning. Inhaling
sharply, $UCR_3$, is the last response in the behavior chain. Through
two conditioned associations they have become linked. Thus, the first
stimulus in the morning can provide foresight and anticipation of an
event in the future. This is one way in which Hull met Tolman's claim
that a future goal can influence present behavior. Hull recognized that
even a strict S-R theory like his had to take into account such cognitive
concepts as anticipation of goals and Tolman's cognitive maps of the
environment.

**Fractional anticipatory goal responses.**    Hull's theory had another feature, very similar to the one just described, that helped explain
how future events influenced present behavior.

Let's add one more link to the behavior chain. After showering, our
subject stumbles downstairs to the real goal, breakfast. Breakfast is the

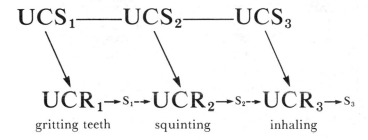

$$UCS_1 \longrightarrow UCS_2 \longrightarrow UCS_3$$

$$UCR_1 \xrightarrow{S_1} UCR_2 \xrightarrow{S_2} UCR_3 \xrightarrow{S_3}$$

gritting teeth  squinting  inhaling

**Figure 5-5.** Each UCR becomes conditioned to the preceding proprioceptive stimuli.

goal stimulus ($S_G$), more or less similar to the mash Hull placed at the end of the alleyway for his rats. Eating is the goal response ($R_G$). Figure 5-6 shows the lengthened behavior chain.

Figure 5-6 includes $S_D$, the drive stimulus. Recall that $S_D$, by initially being present when eating occurs, has become associated with eating—the goal response, $R_G$. $S_D$ is present all during the behavior chain, but eating cannot occur until food—the goal stimulus, $S_G$—appears. Before the subject reaches the breakfast table, $S_D$ cannot bring about all the eating behaviors that have become conditioned to it. The subject can't munch on the shower curtain. However, $S_D$ can bring about fractional parts of the goal response: the subject can begin to

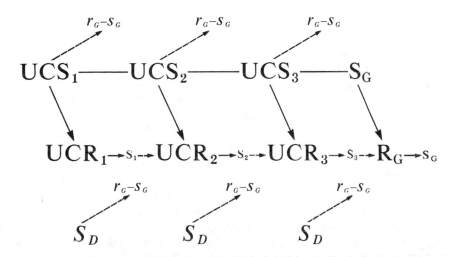

**Figure 5-6.** Fractional anticipatory goal responses ($r_G$-$s_G$) help guide the organism toward the goal in two ways. First, the environmental stimuli elicit $r_G$-$s_G$, which are fractional parts of the subsequent goal response. Second, $S_D$, which is present before the goal is reached, also brings about $r_G$-$s_G$.

salivate or to smack his lips. Such parts of the goal response are called *fractional anticipatory goal responses* and are symbolized as $r_G$. Like all movements, $r_G$ creates proprioceptive stimuli, $s_G$. In Figure 5-6, each $S_D$ notation is followed by $r_G$-$s_G$ to show that $S_D$ (because of its association with the goal response) elicits fractional anticipatory goal responses, which produce internal stimuli. Fractional responses are important in Hullian theory; they serve to guide the organism toward the goal, by causing a fractional part of the goal response to occur before the goal is reached. The $r_G$-$s_G$ "reminds" the subject of the appropriate goal.

The fractional goal responses also guide the subject to the goal in another way. Fractional goal responses are elicited not only by $S_D$ but also by each environmental stimulus (UCS) encountered en route to the goal. The goal itself brings about the goal response $(R_G)$. $UCS_3$ occurs just a moment before the goal and, through Pavlovian conditioning, comes to be associated with the goal. The environmental stimulus $(UCS_3)$ cannot bring about the full goal response because the subject is not yet at the goal; it can elicit a fractional anticipatory goal response $(r_G$-$s_G)$. $UCS_2$ isn't quite so closely associated with the goal; it elicits $r_G$-$s_G$ more weakly. By eliciting fractional goal responses, the environmental stimuli preceding the goal remind the person of the goal and energize his or her movement toward that goal. Thus, the two ways in which these fractional goal responses guide a person to a goal are (1) by $S_D$, which occurs before the goal is attained, eliciting $r_G$-$s_G$ and (2) by the environmental stimuli, which are encountered before the goal is reached, eliciting $r_G$-$s_G$. Both $S_D$ and the environmental stimuli can therefore remind the person of the goal.

Imagine, for example, a small child dragging her father to the annual circus at the local fairgrounds. When she has arrived at the circus—the goal $(S_G)$—she has the time of her life. Just outside the circus gate $(S_3)$ she was yanking her father's wrist to get him to walk faster; she had dilated pupils and cardiac acceleration $(r_G)$ in anticipation of all the cotton candy she was going to inhale. A little before that $(S_2)$, she was only in a mild frenzy, her heart rate $(r_G)$ somewhat above normal. Long before she got there $(S_1)$, she showed slight signs of arousal $(r_G)$. These fractional responses served as means of directing the child toward the $S_G$. Should she make a wrong turn, she would encounter stimuli that had never been associated with circuses of prior years. These environmental stimuli would elicit no fractional goal responses. Only those stimuli associated with the well-known route to the fairgrounds are able to elicit these fractional goal responses $(r_G$-$s_G)$. Therefore these environmental stimuli, by eliciting fractional goal responses, can guide the child to the goal. The fractional goal responses have become strongly conditioned to the $S_D$ or to environmental stimuli encountered en route to the goal. They become more strongly conditioned to the stimuli that are closer to, and therefore more closely associated with, the goal.[4]

## The learning/performance distinction

Tolman and his students performed several experiments that influenced Hull when he revised his theory in 1952.[5] The most important experiments were done by Blodgett (1929) and Tolman and Honzik (1930b). In the latter study, three groups of rats were used. Each rat was placed in the start box of one of Tolman's complex mazes. It had to find its way through the maze to the goal box. Each time that the rat entered a cul-de-sac counted as an error.

Rats in one group found a food reward every time they entered the goal box. This group quickly learned to zip through the maze without making more than a few errors.

Rats in a second group found nothing when they entered the goal box. The experimenter merely took them out of the goal box once they arrived there. Needless to say, the rats in this second group made a lot of "errors" as they ambled aimlessly through the maze. They showed only a small reduction in the number of errors from one trial to the next.

The third group was the crucial one. For the first 10 trials, these rats were like the second group: they received no reward. They made many errors. On Trial 11 and on every trial thereafter, however, these animals received a reward when they entered the goal box. The critical trial was the 12th. Hull would have to say that since there was no reward on trials 1 to 10, no $H$ could have been built up, no learning could have occurred, and Trial 11 would be the first learning trial. On Trial 12, Group 3 should therefore perform slightly better than on Trial 11, reflecting the small amount of learning that occurred on Trial 11. Hull was wrong. On Trial 12, Group 3 performed just as well as Group 1, which had been rewarded on every trial. Figure 5-7 shows the performance of the three groups.

How could one reinforcement (on Trial 11 for Group 3) be just as effective as eleven reinforcements (on trials 1 to 11 for Group 1)? Tolman said this experiment demonstrated latent learning. The Group-3 animals were learning plenty on the first 10 trials, even though they were getting no reward. They simply had no reason to exhibit their learning by racing efficiently through the maze to the goal box. On

---

[4]Although Hull did mention the association of $r_G$–$s_G$ with environmental stimuli, Spence (1956) emphasized their excitatory (incentive) properties more than Hull did.

[5]It is a matter of debate whether the changes Hull made in his theory between 1943 and 1952 were a result of the studies done by Tolman and his students. Atkinson (1964, p. 189) believes they were. Hilgard and Bower (1966, p. 174) are of the opposite opinion. Regardless, Hull's 1952 theory did accommodate the magnitude-of-reward studies better than his 1943 theory did.

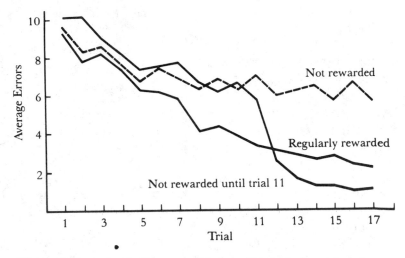

**Figure 5-7.** Animals first rewarded on Trial 11 showed an immediate improvement in performance, not the gradual improvement shown by the regularly rewarded group beginning with Trial 2. Tolman inferred that "latent learning" was occurring on trials 1 to 11 for the group not rewarded until Trial 11. *(From " 'Insight' in Rats," by E. C. Tolman and C. H. Honzik, University of California Publications in Psychology, Vol. IV, No. 14. Published in 1930 by the Regents of the University of California. Reprinted by permission of the University of California Press.)*

trials 1 to 11, their learning was not demonstrated; it was latent. The animals learned, but they had no reason to perform.

This experiment demonstrates the "learning/performance distinction." When a teacher gives a test, the test is directly measuring performance. If the questions are poor, the teacher may conclude from the low grades that learning has not occurred. However, low performance does not always imply little learning, as the latent-learning experiment shows. Unless certain conditions are met, performance will not accurately reflect learning.

The theoretical significance of the latent-learning experiment was that it showed that learning could occur without reward. Tolman had long maintained that learning does not consist in the acquisition of S-R habits stamped in by reinforcement. Instead, an animal acquires "expectancies." It learns what to expect as it moves through its environment. This can occur *without* reward.

More than a decade after the latent-learning study, Crespi (1942, 1944) performed research that provided more embarrassment for the Hullian position. Crespi ran three groups of rats down a long alleyway to a goal box. One group received 1 food pellet in the goal box; the other groups received 16 pellets and 256 pellets, respectively. After 19 trials the running speeds of the animals had stabilized. A direct relation between reward size and running speed resulted, as predicted by Hullian theory, which says that greater magnitude of reward causes $H$ to build up more quickly. On Trial 20, however, Crespi began feeding all groups 16 pellets in the goal box. Immediately the running speed of the 256-pellet group decreased and that of the 1-pellet group increased. The decreased speed among the 256-pellet group was a sign that Hull's 1943 theory was in need of repair. Why should the 256-pellet animals run slower when they get a smaller reward? They aren't unlearning the $H$ they have acquired. Their $D$ hasn't diminished (they are still hungry). Since $E = D \times H$, and $D$ and $H$ aren't dropping, how can $E$ drop? Hull eventually explained this situation by introducing a new factor into the equation.

### Introduction of incentive ($K$)

The final version of Hull's theory (1952) included a new term, $K$, incentive. (According to psychological lore, $K$ was named after Kenneth Spence, who worked with Hull for many years.) Hull removed quantity and quality of reward as determinants of $H$. Instead, these two factors would determine the magnitude of $K$. Hull's new equation was therefore $E = D \times H \times K$. Hull could now explain why the 256-pellet group decreased performance in Crespi's experiment. The incentive had been decreased; $K$, and therefore $E$, had diminished. Latent learning, however, was still a problem for Hull, since he continued to insist that reinforcement was necessary for learning to occur. K. W. Spence (1956), in his own elaboration of Hullian theory, disagreed with Hull and agreed with Tolman that reinforcement was not necessary. Merely pairing a stimulus with a response was adequate to engender learning. And Spence, more than Hull, emphasized the incentive ($K$) properties of fractional anticipatory goal responses. As an organism perceives stimuli closer and closer to the goal, the fractional responses become closer approximations to the final, full, goal response. The fractional responses help pull the organisms toward the goal. By including $K$, Hull and Spence added the "carrot" to their theory to complement the "stick," $D$.

Hull was a drive-reduction theorist: he believed that all reinforcement was drive reduction. (Hull and his followers have at times modified this statement, but the terms they have substituted, such as *need reduction* and *drive-stimulus reduction*, have the same import.) Organisms were motivated to reduce drive. However, the introduction of $K$ to the Hull/Spence theory greatly complicated the matter. A child who sees a circus sign one block before the circus turns toward that sign. Her behavior of turning toward that stimulus results in a fractional part of the goal response. Since the goal response reduces drive, so should the fractional goal response. However, the fractional response gets the child excited about the ultimate goal. Thus the fractional response has *drive-increasing* properties. How can something both reduce and increase drive? This mess that Hull got into is appropriately known as the "Hullian paradox." Introduction of $K$ may have solved some problems, but it created a few more. What would Hull say about an appetizer eaten before a meal? Does it reduce hunger (it is food), or does it increase hunger (after an appetizer, everyone seems more eager to eat)?

## Sheffield's drive-induction theory

Many solutions to the Hullian paradox have been proposed. Sheffield's is the most famous. Sheffield (1966), first of all, says that reinforcement has nothing to do with drive reduction. He maintains that only things that *increase* drive can be reinforcing. Sheffield points out that to a person deprived of food, water, or sex, the appropriate goal would cause immediate excitement, not quiescence. The fact that people sky-dive, ski, and race autos indicates that drive induction can be reinforcing.

Sheffield can explain learning without $D$ reduction. Assume you come to a fork in the road; should you go left or right? You have previously been rewarded for going right. Therefore all the environmental stimuli on the right cause energetic fractional goal responses that invigorate responses in that direction. Orienting toward stimuli on the left causes you to perceive stimuli not associated with any goal response, $R_G$. Therefore there are no fractional responses to excite movement in that direction. Because the stimuli on the right have drive-inducing (reinforcing) properties, you continue in that direction. You thus learn to turn right at the fork.

The theoretical controversy between drive reduction and drive induction will recur several times throughout this book, as it did in Chapters 3 and 4.

## Extensions of S-R theory

### Frustration

Frustration is a topic that has been treated by a wide variety of theorists with diverse viewpoints. Within the Hullian framework alone, several theorists have proposed analyses of frustration. We shall discuss the theories of Sheffield and Amsel, since both rely on the fractional-anticipatory-response mechanism already discussed.

Sheffield defines *frustration* as the response to a situation in which the goal is cued but the goal response cannot be made. Let us reexamine his drive-induction theory with this definition in mind. A person en route to the goal response ($R_G$) of devouring a thick, juicy steak passes environmental stimuli (restaurant signs) along the way. These stimuli elicit fractional responses: the person cannot perform the entire goal response, because he has not reached the goal yet. These fractional responses are exciting, being parts of the arousing $S_G$. They are also frustrating, since they remind the person of the impending feast, which he can't yet have. In other words, the goal is cued but, as yet, the goal response cannot be made. The frustration of this situation is manifested by an increased vigor of responding as the person approaches the restaurant. When the person is just about to receive his steak, the $S_G$ is *really* being cued by the environmental stimuli—for example, the sight and aroma of the steak. The frustration and therefore the excitement are at their greatest nearest the goal. That is why frustration would be worse if the waitress told the customer that the restaurant was out of steak only after he'd sat at a table for 20 minutes than it would be if she told him as soon as he entered the restaurant. Frustration results from nonattainment of the goal only after the goal has been cued (or as it's being cued). If the goal is not cued in some way, there is no frustration, according to this theory.

A related concept in social psychology is "the frustration of rising expectation" (Davies, 1967). According to this notion, social unrest occurs when the people expect a goal and are then disappointed. The urban riots of the 1960s occurred during President Johnson's "War on Poverty," not during President Nixon's subsequent administration. Yet voting records show that Johnson had been overwhelmingly more popular among minority groups than Nixon was. Johnson gave minorities unfulfilled expectations, resulting in frustration. Nixon never gave them expectations; therefore there was no frustration.

Another illustration of frustration resulting from the cuing of an absent goal may be familiar to everyone. Suppose you're waiting for an elevator on the fifth floor. You push the "down" button and glance at the numbers above the elevator door. As the elevator descends slowly from the 20th floor, it makes frequent stops. It's teasing you with expectation, but it never seems to arrive. You push the button again. As the elevator lingers for a long time on the sixth floor, you push the button just about through the wall. Pushing the button harder or more often doesn't make the elevator come sooner. However, the stimulus of the approaching elevator brings about fractional goal responses. Since the goal is not present, this is frustrating to you, and the frustration causes an increase in the vigor of responding.

The frustration theory that has produced the largest body of research is that of Amsel (1958). The theory, which bears some similarity to an earlier theory of frustration (Brown & Farber, 1951), has only a few major principles. *Frustration* is defined as the nonreinforcement of a previously reinforced response. Frustration is postulated to have both generalized-drive properties and cue properties (analogous to $D$ and $S_D$ in the Hullian system). Finally, frustration is aversive, and therefore responses that end frustration will be reinforced.

Several experiments have shown the energizing effects of frustration. Amsel and Roussel (1952), for example, constructed a runway with two goal boxes, one halfway down the runway and one at the end. Rats were run from the start box to the first goal box, where they received food on only half the trials—called reinforcement trials. (The other trials were called frustration trials.) All rats were then allowed to run to the second goal box, where they were always fed. Running speed in the second half of the runway was faster on frustration trials than on reinforcement trials. According to Amsel's theory, not being fed in the first goal box caused frustration, and the subsequent running response received extra drive.

A more diabolical experiment is one by Haner and Brown (1955). Children were required to put 36 marbles in the holes of a peg-boardlike apparatus in order to receive a prize. The experimenter, however, could surreptitiously cause the marbles to fall out of place by pushing a hidden button. Whenever that happened, the child had to push a lever that reset the whole apparatus so he or she could begin again. The experimenter recorded the pressure the child exerted on the lever and the number of marbles in place when the experimenter had sabotaged the pegboard. As predicted, the more marbles the child had in place when the experimenter pushed the button, the harder the child pushed the reset lever. To be denied the goal when you have one more marble to go causes more frustration than when you have 35 marbles to go.

Experimental support for the internal-cue properties of frustration $(S_F)$ is not as strong as the support for the drive properties of frustration. One reason that the presence of these internal cues is difficult to prove is that a frustration situation has many external as well as internal cues that can serve as stimuli for the learning of new responses. However, Brown and Farber (1951) suggest that the internal $S_F$ common to frustration situations may help explain why many responses to frustration are inappropriate or even counterproductive. For example, as $S_F$ occurs because of frustration in a situation, aggression may be learned as an appropriate response to the $S_F$. This response may be appropriate because it restores access to the goal and ends the aversive condition of frustration. If frustration and the accompanying $S_F$ later occur in a totally different situation, $S_F$ may elicit the aggression that has become conditioned to $S_F$, even though aggression may be wholly inappropriate in the new situation.

Despite the many differences among the analyses of frustration, most S-R theories do maintain that frustration has energizing properties. The increase in motivation following frustration, however, may not always have good consequences. As the Yerkes/Dodson law points out, extremely high drive may detract from the performance of a difficult task. An increase in drive may be helpful if failure to attain the goal has been due to a lack of effort, but it may not help if nonattainment has been due to a lack of thought.

## Acquired drives

In the late 1940s, Neal Miller began a series of experiments showing that previously neutral stimuli could acquire drive properties. To this point in the chapter, we have been discussing mainly primary drives, with which the organism is born. Miller was interested in acquired drives, which are learned. In his initial demonstration, Miller (1948) constructed a two-compartment box. One compartment was black and the other white. A door separated the two compartments. A rat was initially shocked in the white compartment for a few sessions. Later the rat was placed in the white side and not shocked. Despite the absence of shock, the rat quickly learned to turn a wheel that opened the door, allowing it to jump over to the other side. Miller showed that rats would learn any of a variety of responses that would allow access to the black compartment. What was motivating this wheel-turning behavior? Miller said it was fear. By Pavlovian, or classical, conditioning, the white side had acquired some of the fear-inducing properties of shock. The animal then worked to open the door in order to escape the white compartment; the reward for this work was a decrease in fear. Thus, escape from the white side can be divided into two factors. First, the white side acquired fear-inducing properties through classical conditioning. Miller labeled this process "fear as an acquired drive." Second, the animal learned to escape this fear by instrumental conditioning. Turning the wheel to open the door was rewarded by drive reduction, following a typical instrumental-conditioning paradigm. Miller and O. H. Mowrer called this explanation of escape from fear the "two-factor theory," the two factors being classical and instrumental conditioning.[6]

[6]Most theorists no longer consider the two-factor theory an adequate explanation of avoidance behavior. Research has shown that previously neutral stimuli can acquire drive properties, just as Miller stated. However, innovations in avoidance-behavior methodology (for example, Sidman, 1953) and theory (for example, Herrnstein, 1969) have shown that the two-factor theory is inadequate. (See also Herrnstein & Hineline, 1966; Hineline, 1970.) Discussion of the evolution of avoidance-behavior theory is both outside the domain of and beyond the scope of this chapter.

Hull recognized the importance of secondary, or "acquired," drives in his theory. He believed that primary drives and especially secondary drives were responsible for the motivation of all human behavior.

## Avoidance behavior

Miller's research was extended by some important work by Richard Solomon and his colleagues in the 1950s. Solomon used an apparatus similar to Miller's except that the two compartments of the "shuttle box" were identical and that the animals (dogs) could always freely jump over a short partition into the next compartment. The most important new feature of Solomon's apparatus was a warning signal (a light), which preceded the shock by 10 seconds. The dog was placed in one compartment. The signal came on; 10 seconds later the shock was delivered through the floor of that compartment. The animal scurried over the partition to the other side. Shortly thereafter the signal recurred. A shock in the second compartment followed in 10 seconds, and so on. By jumping to the other side after the signal, the animal could avoid the shock entirely. Needless to say, all animals very quickly learned to do so. Solomon and Wynne (1954) noted that after learning this avoidance behavior, the animals seemed unperturbed when the warning signal came on. They calmly proceeded to the other side in less than 10 seconds. One might think that, if the dogs avoided the shock for a long time, they would forget all about it and tarry too long; then they would get reminded. That didn't happen. After the first avoidance trials, dogs went as long as *two years* without receiving another shock. Why didn't this avoidance behavior extinguish?

Solomon and Wynne (1954) offered two new principles to account for this extreme resistance to extinction. First, after only a small number of trials, the dogs moved to the other side a second or two after the onset of the warning signal. In one or two seconds, no fear response to the signal could develop. Since the avoidance response took place before fear could develop, fear would never occur in the presence of the warning light. The way to extinguish a fear response to the light is to allow the fear to occur, prevent the dog from jumping to the other side, and then withhold any shock. However, if the dog jumps before the light can generate fear, there will never be any fear to extinguish. Hence extinction will be very difficult to achieve. Solomon and Wynne call this the principle of "anxiety conservation."

The second principle is that of "partial irreversibility." Infrequently a dog would tarry for several seconds before jumping, although never so long that it received a shock. On the trial after such tarrying, the animal's reaction to the light was very rapid, indicating that the delay on the prior trial had been long enough to allow some fear motivation to again develop. However, didn't the "tarrying" trials constitute rare opportunities for fear to extinguish, since the light was followed by fear and—owing to the avoidance response—fear was followed by no shock? Not so, said Solomon and Wynne. Avoidance responses established on the basis of traumatic shock will not completely extinguish in this way. Thus, Solomon and Wynne deemed the fear reactions "irreversible." Consider the following example, which is based on a situation somewhat similar to Solomon and Wynne's.

Every Tuesday morning around 10:30, the city of Chicago sounds an air-raid alarm so that anyone who wants to practice avoiding air raids can do so. Suppose you work in the building next to the city's huge siren. Every Tuesday morning when it's 10:15 (this stimulus is your warning signal), you go into the basement, where you can't hear that infernal siren. You emerge at 10:45. You've avoided the siren. Suppose one Tuesday you have to stay in your office because the boss is talking to you. Ten-thirty comes and goes with no siren: the city has stopped the air-raid drills. Your avoidance behavior extinguishes, so you stay in your office next Tuesday. The removal of the unconditioned stimulus (siren) has caused extinction.

Suppose instead that on the Tuesday when Chicago ended its air-raid drills you had fled to the basement. "I've avoided the siren," you would have thought. "Success!" (Reinforcement.) You would have had no way of knowing there was no siren. Solomon and Wynne's dogs did the same thing. They avoided the shock after seeing the warning. Because they jumped to the other side, they had no way of knowing whether Solomon and Wynne had even plugged in the shock generator. The way to extinguish the avoidance behavior would be to force the animals to stay in their side of the compartment *long* after the warning came on. Then they would detect the absence of shock, and the warning signal would lose its fear-arousing properties. The avoidance behavior kept the animals from determining whether there still was shock, so the signal maintained its fear-arousing properties. For this reason, *avoidance behavior is extremely resistant to extinction.* In Freud's terms, an animal performing an avoidance response is not "reality testing." It is not staying around long enough to see whether shock is still part of the environment. A way to extinguish a classically conditioned response (fear) is to remove the unconditioned stimulus (shock). However, if the animal has left, it can't detect whether the unconditioned stimulus has been removed.

## Approach/avoidance conflicts

Some stimuli have both positive and negative outcomes associated with them. Persons trying to decide whether to interact with such ambivalent stimuli are in an "approach/avoidance" conflict. For example, perhaps you want to tell your boss off, but you're afraid to do so. What do you do? N. E. Miller (1944) extended his research on aversive conditioning to the area of approach/avoidance conflict.

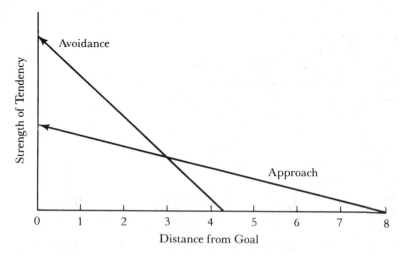

**Figure 5-8.** The steepness of the avoidance gradient allows approach only to distance 3. Thereafter the superiority of the avoidance gradient prevents further approach and encourages displacement to an object other than the goal. *(From "Experimental Studies of Conflict," by Neal E. Miller. In J. McV. Hunt (Ed.), Personality and the Behavior Disorders. Copyright 1944. Renewed © 1972. The Ronald Press Company, New York.)*

Figure 5-8 depicts Miller's model of an approach/avoidance conflict. As one approaches the ambivalent object, both the approach and the avoidance tendencies grow stronger; however, the avoidance tendency grows more quickly. Suppose a goal you have long hungered for is that of telling your boss he's incompetent. However, you also wish to remain employed. One day you get a memo from the boss saying he doesn't like the way you treat customers. That's the last straw. You jump up from your desk (which your boss has moved into the boiler room) and start toward his office. You are thus moving up the approach gradient toward your goal of insulting the boss. As you get close to his office, you get less bold. You have moved confidently from distance 8 (in Figure 5-8) to distance 3, but suddenly you stop. Beyond distance 3 the avoidance gradient is higher than the approach one. (At any point, the net tendency to approach is equal to the height of the approach gradient at that point minus the height of the avoidance gradient at that point.) To move closer is therefore prohibited. As you retreat to distance 4, however, your boldness returns, since the approach gradient is higher. You return to 3 only to pause again. Since you can't get any closer to the boss (the avoidance gradient being superior), you yell at the boss's secretary, who is at distance 3, the closest point to the boss where the avoidance gradient isn't superior. Taking out anger on a third party is a typical example of the process that Freud called "displacement."

Suppose the boss had just announced he was in a horrible mood. Your fear of him would be greater. The avoidance gradient would be displaced upward and to the right. Figure 5-9 illustrates this situation. Now the gradients cross at distance 5, so you kick the dog. This activity is far removed from kicking the boss, but with the avoidance gradient so high, it's as close as you can get.

## Punishment

Closely related to the topic of avoidance is the topic of punishment. Avoidance behavior is the performance of an instrumental response in order to prevent or delay the onset of an aversive stimulus. Punishment is the application of an aversive stimulus contingent on a particular response. In the former, one performs in order to avoid something bad. In the latter, one gets something bad because of the way one has performed.

An explanation of the effect of punishment on learning was advanced in 1911, when Thorndike postulated the law of effect, half of

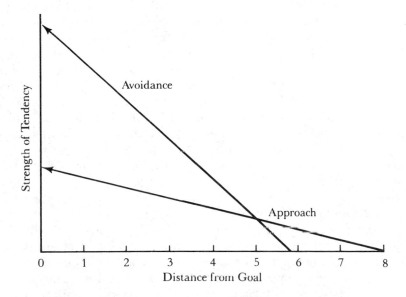

**Figure 5-9.** Because the avoidance gradient is farther to the right than in Figure 5-8, the person will not approach as closely to the goal, and displacement will be to a rather remote object. (*From "Experimental Studies of Conflict," by Neal E. Miller. In J. McV. Hunt (Ed.),* Personality and the Behavior Disorders. *Copyright 1944. Renewed © 1972. The Ronald Press Company, New York.*)

which dealt with reward and half with punishment. The first part of the law of effect stated that, when a stimulus is followed by a response and that response is followed by a "satisfying state of affairs," the animal will tend to repeat the response the next time the stimulus occurs. In other words, rewards "stamp in" S-R bonds. Hull endorsed this part of the law of effect.

The second half of the law stated that, when a stimulus is followed by a response and that response is followed by an "annoying state of affairs," the animal will tend not to repeat the response the next time the stimulus occurs. In other words, punishments weaken S-R bonds. However, Thorndike eventually discarded this second half of the law of effect. He found that sometimes a punishment would discourage the response it followed, but sometimes a punishment would actually strengthen the response it followed. Thorndike never could explain when punishments worked and when they didn't.

The most important research done on punishment was a series of studies by Estes in 1944. He showed that, following acquisition of the bar-press response, animals who are mildly punished for bar pressing and then have their bar-pressing responses extinguished emit just as many bar presses during extinction as those animals who are extinguished without prior punishment. The punishment, although stifling responses while the punishment was in progress, did nothing about reducing responses once the punishment was turned off. *Punishment merely suppresses a response. It does not extinguish a response.*

Suppose a mother wants to keep her son's hands out of the cookie jar. She first rigs up a photoelectric beam just above the jar. Whenever the child reaches for the lid, he interrupts the beam and gets shocked. He quickly stops trying to steal cookies. If the photoelectric system breaks down, however, he goes back to the cookie jar. The shocks haven't changed his knowledge concerning the rewards in the jar.

If Mom now removes all the cookies from the jar, however, the behavior will stop the next time the photoelectric system breaks down: the child will go to the cookie jar to steal cookies, discover that the jar is empty, and consequently stop his attempts to steal cookies from the jar. He will realize he's wasting his time. If Mom hadn't bothered with the photoelectric beam in the first place, however, her son would have found out about the empty cookie jar even sooner. Without shock he would have learned immediately not to reach toward the jar: his response would have extinguished. Punishment suppressed his response and thereby *postponed* extinction. The crucial point is that in order for extinction to occur the son would have to realize his responses would not be rewarded. Punishment postponed this realization, because punishment suppressed his responding. (To be fair to Estes, we must point out that he would not have used such cognitive terms as *realize* in his discussion of punishment.) As long as the child was not responding, he could not learn that his responses would go unrewarded. One might note that our prisons work mainly on a punishment system.

The second important principle of punishment concerns response compatibility. Punishment is usually effective in suppressing a response when the response to the punishing stimulus is incompatible with the punished response. The reason shock suppresses a bar-press response, for example, is that the responses to shock are fear, cowering, freezing, and so on. These responses are incompatible with bar pressing. It is impossible to cower in the corner and bar-press simultaneously.

Gwinn (1949) performed an experiment that illustrates this principle. Animals were placed in a compartment at the beginning of a circular runway. The grid in this start box was electrified. When the current was turned on, the animals raced out of the start box and around the circle. Gwinn then introduced an electrified grid in the runway, about halfway around the circle. One might predict that the shock in the runway would punish the animals for running all the way around the circle. Perhaps they would leave the electrified start box and stop before they got to the second grid. Instead, the animals ran around the circle *faster* when the second grid was added. The response to the punishing stimulus was running. This response was perfectly compatible—in fact, identical—with the response that was being performed when the punishing stimulus occurred.

In the supermarket, note how many parents punish their children for crying by slapping them. Needless to say, the response to the punishing stimulus is very compatible with the response that the parent is trying to eliminate. Therefore, that stimulus is ineffective as a punishment.

In the following situation, both these principles of punishment—nonextinction of responses and response compatibility—played an important role. In 1966 one of the authors worked in a hospital for retarded children. One child was a 12-year-old girl who was big, strong, and affectionate. The hospital was badly understaffed, so one nurse had to wheel around a cart containing the medication for several dozen children. Often, when the nurse got to the girl's ward room, the girl would impose an affectionate bear hug on the nurse. This behavior kept the nurse from dispensing the medication on time. Furthermore, since the girl outweighed the nurse, the behavior was somewhat dangerous. One option the nurse might have tried was to punish the behavior by shouting at the child. The staff members believed that this would have the extremely unsatisfactory side effect of causing the child to fear the nurse. Furthermore, the behavior would return if the punishment were ever removed. (They suspected the punishment would have been effective, however, since the response to the punishing stimulus probably would have been withdrawal, which was incompatible with hugging.) They decided on an alternate plan. The girl would help the nurse push the cart. The child would shove the cart, and the nurse's hands would rest on the child's waist, shoulders, or head. This contact was just what the child wanted. Since the child could not push the cart and hug the nurse simultaneously, the problem was solved. Such a technique is called counterconditioning. Counterconditioning consists in teaching a new response that is incompatible with the undesirable response. It is frequently an excellent alternative to punishment.

Occasionally punishment and counterconditioning can be used together. In the same hospital were children who performed self-mutilating behavior. The staff would have liked to teach them behavior incompatible with self-mutilation. However, every time they began such instruction, the children would panic and revert to self-mutilation. New learning was impossible while self-mutilation was going on. Punishment might have been effective in this situation. Punishment only suppresses, not extinguishes, a response, but counterconditioning would be possible while the self-mutilation was suppressed by punishment. Had the new, counterconditioned response been reinforced a great deal, its $H$ would have been so high that, even when the punishment was removed, the self-mutilation would not return. The new response incompatible with self-mutilation, if it had a higher $H$, would be performed instead of the self-mutilation.

## Applications and extensions

A number of studies have shown that the Hull/Spence formulations can provide valuable insight in areas not directly investigated by Hull or Spence. For example, Cottrell and others (Cottrell, Rittle, & Wack, 1967; Zajonc & Sales, 1966) have shown that the presence of an audience raises a person's generalized-drive level. To test this hypothesis, Cottrell et al. performed a learning experiment using pairs of words used by Spence decades earlier. One list contained stimulus words, each of which had a closely associated word as the response (for example, adept . . . skillful). Subjects being watched by an audience learned this easy list faster than subjects working alone. However, on a second list, which was much more difficult, the subjects working alone performed better. These are precisely the results one would expect if the presence of an audience causes an increase in generalized drive.

Another topic that provides a modern application of Hull's generalized-drive principle has been systematically investigated by Perlmuter and Monty (1977). These authors suggest that, when one has a high level of perceived control in a situation, a generalized increase in motivation will result. To test this hypothesis the experimenters had two different groups of subjects learn to associate several pairs of words for a subsequent memory test. Both groups were given the left-hand member of each pair. One group, the *forced group,* was also assigned a right-hand member of each pair to learn to associate with each left-hand member. The subjects in the *choice group* were allowed to choose which of five possible right-hand words would be associated with each left-hand one. When memory for these associations was tested later, the choice group performed much better. Some might believe that this result occurred not because the choice group had higher drive but because the subjects in the choice group chose words that were somehow easy to associate with the left-hand words. We can reject this explanation for two reasons. First, when subjects are allowed to choose the right-hand members of only the first three pairs, their performance is superior to that of the forced group on those pairs *and* the nine other pairs on that list. Second, Perlmuter, Scharff, Karsh, and Monty (1980) have shown that subjects in the choice group compared to subjects in the forced group show superior performance on a nonmemory task that is occurring simultaneously with the memory task. These results seem to indicate that, when one perceives that one has control in a situation, *generalized* drive is increased.

Another valuable extension of Hullian theory is the Easterbrook hypothesis. Easterbrook (1959) suggested that under high drive a person restricts his or her examination of environmental cues. On an easy task, missing some minor cues might not hurt at all. In fact, ignoring such cues might save time and promote more efficient performance of the task. Thus, high drive is best for such easy tasks. On tough tasks, however, ignoring part of the complicated stimulus situation could be very detrimental to performance. Therefore, tough tasks are done best under low drive, when cue utilization is broad. The Easterbrook hypothesis thereby provides a new analysis of the Yerkes/Dodson law.

A recent study by Matthews and Brunson (1979) provides an interesting test of this hypothesis. Two groups of subjects were used. One was comprised of people whose behavior pattern has come to be called "Type A." These are hard-driving people who have been found to be susceptible to heart disease and other cardiovascular ailments (Jenkins, Rosenman, & Zyzanski, 1974). The other group contained people who were not Type A. All subjects had to perform two tasks simultaneously. The primary task involved naming the color of ink in which various words were written. This was a very tricky task. The word *red,* for example, might be written in blue ink, thus increasing the temptation to say "red" as the correct answer. This task therefore demanded close attention. The second task required the subject to press a telegraph key whenever a light was illuminated. The light was located in the periphery of the subject's vision. The results of the study were that Type-A people were superior to non-Type-A people on the primary task but were inferior on the peripheral task. This is precisely what the Easterbrook hypothesis would predict if we assume that Type-A people have narrow cue utilization because of their high drive. It seems very likely that Type-A people do have high drive, since other work has shown, for example, that Type-A people work at or near their maximal rate even when there is no pressing deadline (Burnam, Pennebaker, & Glass, 1975).

## Conclusions and critique

Both proponents and opponents of Hullian theory agree that Clark Hull had an enormous impact on the study of motivation.

One of his most important contributions was the clear separation of $D$ and $H$. Whereas Thorndike thought that conditioning (learning) gave the stimulus motivational properties, Hull was able to show that $D$ and $H$ were independent. Reinforcement does not give the stimulus the power to compel the response; an $H$ has to be energized by $D$ in order for behavior to occur. If either is zero, there will be no behavior.

The main contribution of Hullian theory was that, more than earlier theories, it made reasonably testable predictions. Researchers quickly got down to the business of determining whether its predictions were accurate. Unfortunately, much of the evidence was inconclusive. For example, although some studies supported Hull's generalized-drive principle, many others did not. After an extensive review of generalized-drive experiments, Bolles (1967) concluded, "Generalized drive has turned out to be a puny fellow compared with the big $D$ we had expected to find; he cannot carry much explanatory weight" (p. 303).

A study typical of those challenging some portion of the Hullian conception of drive is one by Birch, Burnstein, and Clark (1958), which showed that motivation does not necessarily increase with length of deprivation. Birch et al. found that the vigor of food-approach behavior in rats increased dramatically around the normal feeding time but decreased after the feeding time even if the rats were not fed. If $D$ increases with hours of deprivation, then rats not fed for 37 hours should run faster to food than rats not fed for 25 hours. But the fastest running speeds occurred at approximately the normal feeding time, not during the subsequent hours. Evidently, other conditions than hours of deprivation influence $D$.

Although hundreds of studies have been done in order to support or refute the Hull/Spence model, some psychologists were less concerned with the empirical predictions of the theory than with its philosophical stance—in particular, its view of Man. The theory reduced humans to animals and reduced both humans and animals to machines that, when stimulated, emitted predictable responses. The use of instincts to explain both nonhuman and human behavior, earlier in the century, had reflected the Darwinian idea of continuity between species. Hull rejected the broad use of instincts, but he agreed with instinct theorists that the principles governing nonhuman and human behavior were identical. Animals, from pigeons to humans, fell within the domain of the principles he identified (Hull, 1943, 1952).

Hull, as an S-R psychologist, emphasized the powerful influence that environmental stimuli have on observable responses. (Hull included internal stimuli in his theory, although he thought they could be externally detected and measured.) Because of the importance of environmental stimuli, very little attention was paid in Hull's theory to individual differences. Because theorists in the behaviorist tradition maintain that the same principles govern the behavior of pigeons, rats, dogs, and humans, their concern with individual differences is minimal. Hull never considered the organism to be a significant determinant of the observed behavior. Since Hull's goal was "given the stimulus, to predict the response," the organism was relegated to the role of perceiver and responder. This very mechanistic role of the human organism repelled many psychologists, especially since Hull's theory claimed to provide the basis for explanations of moral values, religious practices, politics (Hull, 1943, p. 399), and other areas not easy to research in white rats. Does moral, cultural, and religious man do no more than respond mechanically to stimuli? Hull appeared to say that S-R principles were enough to explain all human behavior.

# CHAPTER 6

# Optimal Level Theories

*For in everything it is no easy task to find the middle.*

*Aristotle*

Several experiments appeared in the 1950s whose results were difficult to explain within a Hullian, drive-reduction framework. These experiments showed that animals would expend effort in order to obtain rewards that did not reduce drive or that even increased it.

## Early studies

Butler (1954) showed that monkeys would bar-press to open a window that would allow them a brief glance at an electric train set! How could watching an electric train reduce drive? Harlow, Harlow, and Meyer (1950) showed that monkeys would work for hours on a complicated lock mechanism. When a monkey finally succeeded in opening the lock, no reward was offered. The animal would just relock the mechanism and start over. What could possibly be rewarding this activity? For that matter, why does a jigsaw-puzzle fanatic work feverishly on a puzzle for a dozen hours?

An easy answer is available to explain all these behaviors: merely posit a curiosity drive, which is reduced when one investigates locks or peers at electric trains. In other words, to explain behavior X, merely posit a behavior-X drive, which is satisfied when behavior X is performed. Such an "explanation," however, is not very helpful. To say that someone is curious because of a curiosity drive explains nothing. For this reason, psychologists were not eager to posit a "curiosity drive" to explain behaviors such as those just mentioned.

About 1960, three areas of research converged to suggest a better explanation for curiosity behavior. The first area included an unusual study by Haber (1958). Subjects were asked to rate the pleasantness of various water temperatures, which they sampled by dipping their hands in pails of water. Haber found that, after subjects were adapted to 68°, slightly warmer and cooler temperatures were rated pleasant and much warmer or cooler temperatures were rated unpleasant. The butterfly-shaped curve in Figure 6-1 shows that moderate discrepancies from the temperature to which a person had been adapted were rated the most pleasant.

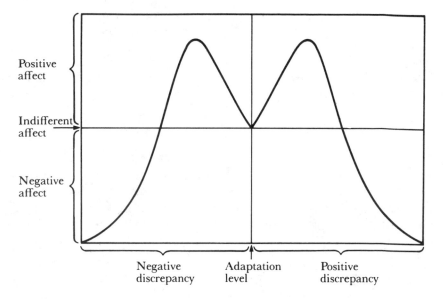

Positive affect

Indifferent affect

Negative affect

Negative discrepancy　　Adaptation level　　Positive discrepancy

**Figure 6-1.** As discrepancy from the adaptation level increases in either direction, affect first increases and then decreases. *(From "Discrepancy from Adaptation Level as a Source of Affect," by R. N. Haber,* Journal of Experimental Psychology, *1958, 56, 370–375. Copyright 1958 by the American Psychological Association. Reprinted by permission.)*

The second line of research included several studies of exploratory behavior. The intensity of such behavior was surprising. For example, Butler and Harlow (1954) gave monkeys the opportunity to open a window to get 30-second glimpses of laboratory equipment. Some animals showed no decrease in responding after 20 hours of continuous testing! In 1925, Dashiell had found that rats would cross an electrified grid in order to explore a maze that contained no obvious reward. These and other studies showed how highly motivated animals are to explore their environment.

Perhaps the most influential line of research in the area of exploratory behavior, however, was that of Dember and Earl, whose two influential articles (Dember & Earl, 1957; Dember, Earl, & Paradise, 1957) described a very simple experiment. A figure-eight apparatus was constructed with vertical black and white stripes in one loop of the 8 and horizontal black and white stripes in the other. Dember and Earl hypothesized that the loop with the horizontal stripes would provide a constant stimulus as a rat moved through that half of the runway. The vertical stripes would provide a far more complex stimulus, the black and white stripes alternating as the animal moved. One rat at a time was placed in the apparatus, and the amount of time the animal chose to remain in each loop was noted. Dember and Earl found that all the animals that initially preferred the horizontal stripes eventually moved into the loop containing the vertical stripes, the more complex stimulus. Of the animals that initially preferred the vertical stripes, only one of the rats showed any subsequent preference for the horizontal stripes.

To explain these results, Dember and Earl hypothesized that for each individual there is a level of environmental complexity to which it has become accustomed. Further commerce with stimuli of this complexity level is rather boring, since the individual has already learned about stimulation at this level of complexity. However, stimuli somewhat more complex than the usual fare are quite interesting. Such stimuli are new and different, and they arouse curiosity. Stimuli that are *extremely* discrepant from the usual level in being much more complex are not interesting to the individual. They are confusing and may also be frightening, causing the individual to withdraw from the stimuli. Hence, any individual will show maximal preference for stimuli moderately discrepant from the level to which it has become accustomed. Dember and Earl used the term *pacer* to describe the preferred level of stimulation—one somewhat more complex than the usual fare. In their experiment, rats that initially chose to interact with the vertical stripes did so because such stimulation represented their pacer. These rats rarely entered the horizontally striped area, because it was too simple. Animals that initially chose the horizontally striped side did so because this low-complexity stimulus represented the pacer for them. The vertical stripes were far too complex. However, as the animals continued to interact with the horizontal stripes, this pattern became less and less complex. It became boring. They then shifted to a new, more complex pacer by moving to the side with vertical stripes.

The animals that shifted from the horizontal to the vertical stripes demonstrated an important aspect of optimal level theory: the simplification principle. This principle states that through exposure a stimulus becomes more simple. The horizontal stripes may initially have represented the pacer for some animals, but as the animals interacted with those stripes for an extended period of time, the stripes became too simple. A new, more complex stimulus was sought. The vertical stripes were then chosen because they were closer to the pacer than were the simplified horizontal stripes.

One of the authors applies Dember and Earl's "pacer principle" when he teaches introductory psychology. About the third week of the term, he asks the students to fill out a questionnaire about their opinion of the course. One of the questions is the following:

Rate the difficulty of this course by circling the appropriate number:

| 1 | 2 | 3 | 4 | 5 | 6 | 7 |
|---|---|---|---|---|---|---|
| far too easy | too easy | slightly too easy | about right | slightly too hard | too hard | far too hard |

If the average response is less than four, the author concludes that he's boring the students. If it's greater than five, he's confusing them. If it falls between four and five, he must be approximating the students' pacer. After perusing the ratings, he can make any necessary adjustments. Since he wants the students to be maximally motivated, he tries to teach right at their pacer.

The pacer principle and the simplification principle can be reapplied continually to the same individual. Suppose a woman is teaching her young son something about astronomy. Since he initially knows nothing about astronomy, she begins at a simple level. The child is soon eager to learn about more advanced topics, topics at his pacer. So the mother takes him to the planetarium or buys a few books. Interaction with this stimulation results in its simplification. Now that the child understands this new material, it is no longer slightly too complex; it is no longer a pacer. It is now the level to which the child has become adapted. A new, higher pacer is needed, and the child is eager to interact with more complex material. Dember and Earl would predict that, with judicious presentation of new pacers, the child will continually chase the pacer up the complexity continuum. In summary, interaction with the pacer causes it to become boring, this event necessitates a more complex pacer, and so on.

There are important and interesting relations between Haber's study and Dember and Earl's. Haber showed that subjects preferred moderate discrepancies in either direction from the temperature to which they had become accustomed. Dember and Earl showed that a moderate discrepancy from the accustomed complexity level was preferred. Thus, it appears that Haber's research pertained to discrepancies in either direction, whereas Dember and Earl's pertained to discrepancies in one direction. However, if it can be assumed that temperatures deviating in either direction from the adaptation level are equally complex, then the two halves of Haber's graph each represent the application of Dember and Earl's pacer principle: an individual prefers stimuli that are moderately complex, ones slightly more complex than the level to which the individual has become adapted.

A difference between the two areas of research is that Haber dealt with habituation to an adaptation level, moderate deviations from which are preferred. Dember and Earl did not deal with mere habituation, which is a temporary phenomenon, since a person may habituate now to one and later to another temperature. Dember and Earl were concerned with something more permanent—actual learning that occurs as an organism comes to prefer more complex stimulation than before. As was shown in the astronomy example, more complex stimulation is preferred as the organism learns about the stimuli present at the lower levels of stimulus complexity.

A third line of research that began in the 1950s, research on sensory deprivation, was concerned with the level of stimulation a person prefers to maintain. For example, Bexton, Heron, and Scott (1954) offered to pay subjects $20 for each day they remained in a stimulus-deficient room. An air conditioner and an electric fan masked noise. Subjects were blindfolded and wore long cardboard cuffs over their arms and hands to prevent their touching anything. They could move only in order to eat or go to the washroom. In other words, subjects were being paid to do and perceive nothing. The experimenters found that two days was the longest that most people could tolerate this sensory deprivation. Some subjects even reported bizarre and frightening hallucinations. Apparently the lack of stimulation was extremely aversive.

## Principles of optimal level theory

Several theorists considered research done by Haber, Dember and Earl, Bexton et al., Butler, and others to be outside the domain of Hullian theory. Within a period of 15 years, these theorists had postulated that there is an optimal level of arousal or stimulation. Although the various theories proposed by Berlyne (1960), Duffy (1962), Hebb (1949), Leuba (1955), Malmo (1959), and Walker (1964) are all somewhat different, they have enough commonalities so that a single "modal model" can be presented.

### Preference for an optimal level of stimulation

First, all these theorists believe that an animal or person has an optimal level of external stimulation. (They disagree on the mechanism by which optimization proceeds—that is, on whether the individual is trying to optimize the amount of arousal, of psychological complexity, or of something else.) Individuals try to adjust the stimulation from their environments so that it closely approximates their own optimums. Figure 6-2 represents the relation between stimulation level and preference; this relation will be referred to as the "inverted-U curve."

Subjects in Bexton et al.'s sensory-deprivation experiment were far below their optimal level of stimulation. (In fact, S. Smith and Myers (1966) have shown that sensory-deprivation subjects are so desperate for stimulation that they will turn on a recorded stock market report over and over.) Their hallucinations, too, may be considered a way of creating their own stimulation when the environment provides none. The subjects are merely trying to move from point A to point B in Figure 6-2.

Point B is the pacer, in Dember and Earl's terminology. This level of stimulation is maximally motivating because it is slightly more complex than that at point A, the level to which the person is accustomed. People are motivated to interact with this level of stimulation, as evidenced by the millions of hours spent every year on jigsaw puzzles, crossword puzzles, mystery stories, and so forth.

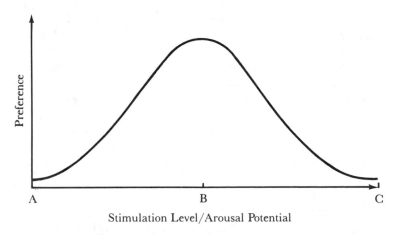

Stimulation Level/Arousal Potential

**Figure 6-2.** The inverted-U curve.

There are many examples, however, of persons' being at point C in Figure 6-2. When stimulation is excessive, a person will try to decrease it in order to return to the optimal level. Milgram (1970) believes that urban life may cause a person to be at point C most of the day. The urban-dweller may ignore stimuli and other people in order to reduce the high level of stimulation. Insensitivity may be adaptive in this instance, because it reduces stimulation from C to B.

The main difference among the various optimal level theorists concerns the labeling of the horizontal axis in Figure 6-2. Exactly what are people trying to optimize? Berlyne, the most prominent psychologist in this field, believes that certain stimulus properties have "arousal potential." These properties include novelty, incongruity, surprisingness, and complexity, all of which Berlyne calls "collative variables." His theory says that the degree to which a stimulus has these properties determines its arousal potential, and the overall level of arousal potential is what people try to optimize. A person will seek moderate amounts of novelty or complexity in order to approximate his or her optimal level of arousal potential. Although the optimal level differs from person to person, everyone has an optimal level.

Haber's study fits Berlyne's theory well. Water temperatures identical to the adaptation level are completely boring. After becoming adapted to 68°, a subject won't find another pail of 68° water very arousing. Nor will 67° or 69° cause much arousal. As the temperatures diverge from the adaptation level, however, their novelty and surprisingness both increase; their amounts of collative variation are closer to the person's optimum. These temperatures are rated more pleasurable, but, as the temperatures get too shocking, preference again decreases.

Several other studies also show that people prefer an optimal level of collative variation. Dorfman (1965) constructed six visual stimuli that varied in complexity, Berlyne's most heavily researched collative variable. Subjects indicated their preference for each stimulus. Some subjects preferred more complex stimuli; some preferred less complex stimuli. Regardless of which stimulus a subject found most pleasing, his or her preference ratings fell off as one moved away in either direction from the most preferred stimulus. The inverted-U curve was strongly confirmed.

Two groups of subjects, however, could not exhibit an inverted-U curve. One group preferred the least complex stimulus, so their preference curve looked like the first "curve" in Figure 6-3. Another group preferred the most complex stimulus, so their preference curve looked like the second curve in Figure 6-3. Optimal level theories predict one of these two curves, instead of the inverted U, only when the stimuli from which a subject must choose are too complex or too simple; the experimenter's stimuli in such cases do not represent the whole complexity spectrum for that subject. The first curve in Figure 6-3 represents the right half of the inverted U; the second curve, the left half. If Dorfman had included stimuli even more simple and more complex, the curves in Figure 6-3 would instead be inverted U's.

## Stimulus simplification

A second principle that all optimal level theorists share is the same as Dember and Earl's "simplification principle": with repeated exposure, stimuli become less arousing, less stimulating, less complex. In short, they become boring. Exposure moves a stimulus to the left along the complexity continuum in Figure 6-2. (A student has called this the

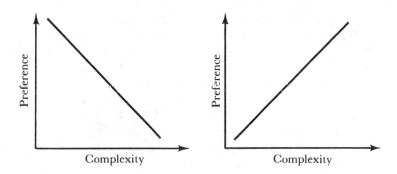

**Figure 6-3.** Preference curves for some subjects in Dorfman's study (1965). These curves represent the two halves of Figure 6-2. Optimal-level theorists would predict that, had a larger continuum of complexity been presented, each of these curves would have been extended to become an inverted-U curve.

"oldie but goodie" principle. When a new pop record is played, it sounds great—it is at point B in Figure 6-2. After 10,000 exposures to it, everyone is bored. The record has simplified to a tedious jingle—it is at point A. Then it goes off the air. After five years of incubation, the habituation has dissipated. The stimulus has moved back to point B. Now when one hears this "oldie but goodie" on the radio, it sounds stupendous again. Because it is reheard only once, it does not rehabituate and return to point A.)

Repeated exposure, however, does not always lead to boredom. If a stimulus at point C in Figure 6-2 is repeated a few times, habituation to that stimulus may cause it to move just as far as point B. Thus, repetition can increase preference. With unlimited repetition, however, the stimulus would eventually become boring. To predict the effect of repetition on preference, it is necessary to know both the initial location of the stimulus on the continuum and the amount of repetition.

The two main principles presented so far have been the inverted-U relation between preference and stimulus variation (especially complexity) and simplification with experience. G. F. Smith and Dorfman (1975) combined the two in an excellent test of optimal level theory. Visual stimuli of low, medium, and high complexity were shown to subjects either 20 times, 10 times, 5 times, or once. Subjects were then asked to indicate how much they liked each stimulus. Figure 6-4 contains the results.

Liking for the simplest stimuli generally decreased with repeated exposure, because such exposure will cause a stimulus to simplify. If the stimulus is initially at or below the optimum, simplification will move it farther from the optimum, and liking for the stimulus will decline.

The most complex stimuli were liked more as the number of exposures increased. In simplifying, those stimuli moved toward the optimum. Had the number of exposures been greater, the curve for the most complex stimuli would have resembled the inverted U.

Finally, liking for the stimuli of intermediate complexity showed first an increase, then a decrease. If those stimuli were slightly more complex than the optimum at the beginning of the experiment, with repeated exposure they would first approach, then pass the optimal level. That would result in the preference curve actually obtained. Many other studies (such as Berlyne, 1970; L. B. Cohen, 1969; Saegert & Jellison, 1970) have supported this same principle: the effect of repetition on preference depends on the amount of repetition and the initial complexity of the repeated stimulus.

## The effect of experience on preference for complexity

A third principle of optimal level theory is that persons experienced with a certain kind of stimulus will prefer more complexity than those

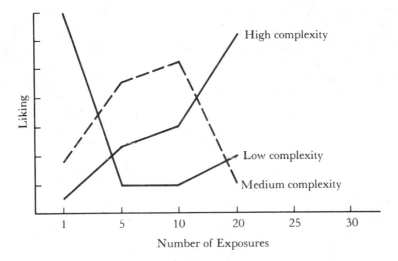

**Figure 6-4.** Liking of visual stimuli as a function of stimulus complexity and number of exposures. *(From "The Effect of Stimulus Uncertainty on the Relationship between Frequency of Exposure and Liking," by G. F. Smith and D. D. Dorfman,* Journal of Personality and Social Psychology, *1975, 31, 150–155. Copyright 1975 by the American Psychological Association. Reprinted by permission.)*

having less experience. A clever experiment by Vitz (1966a) illustrates this principle.

Vitz composed six tone sequences that varied in complexity. The simplest used only 2 pitches, 1 duration, and 1 volume level. The most complex used 18 pitches, 8 durations, and 4 volume levels. Subjects rated the tone sequences for pleasantness. The inverted-U relation between complexity and pleasantness was confirmed. Then, in a subsequent part of the study, Vitz looked at preference as a function of prior musical experience. He found that both the high- and low-musical-experience groups had inverted-U preference curves and that the high-musical-experience group's curve was farther to the right. As Figure 6-5 shows, the tone sequences optimally complex for the low-experience group were too simple for the high-experience group. That more experienced subjects prefer more complex stimuli is a common finding (see, for example, Munsinger & Kessen, 1964; Vitz, 1966b). There are at least two reasons that they do.

First, as stimuli are repeatedly experienced, they become more boring—that is, less arousing. New, more arousing stimuli must be sought as experienced subjects habituate to old stimuli. Dember and Earl would express this idea as the experienced subjects' need for a very complex pacer. Accordingly, Vitz's musically sophisticated subjects preferred more complex music.

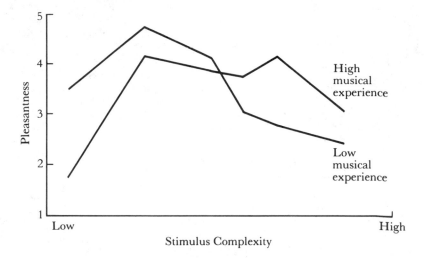

**Figure 6-5.** Pleasantness of auditory stimuli as a function of stimulus complexity and subjects' prior musical experience. (*Adapted from "Affect as a Function of Stimulus Variation," by P. Vitz,* Journal of Experimental Psychology, *1966, 71, 74–79. Copyright 1966 by the American Psychological Association. Reprinted by permission.*)

Second, people who repeatedly experience a stimulus not only habituate to it, they become able to organize it. Imagine a novice chess player trying to study a chessboard early in the game. He has 32 pieces to contemplate. The experienced player, in contrast, sees the same arrangement of pieces as constituting the Sicilian defense. With this one concept, the experienced player has grouped 32 items into one. The simplification is enormously economical.

An experiment by Munsinger and Kessen (1964) illustrates this principle. Children and adults both preferred irregular polygons of intermediate complexity, substantiating the inverted-U curve. However, the complexity preferences of children and adults differed when the stimuli were strings of letters of the alphabet. Whereas the irregular polygons were unfamiliar to both age groups, adults were much more familiar with letter combinations, such as diphthongs and syllables, than children were. Adults possessed what Munsinger and Kessen called "coding schemes," which grouped disparate items into a unified chunk. Coding schemes simplified for adults what was complex for children. Where a child sees three letters, an adult sees one syllable. In order to perceive three units, the adult needs to see three syllables—perhaps nine letters. The adult's optimal complexity level appears to be higher than the child's, because the units with which the adult works are bigger.

## Summary

Optimal level theories are based on a very few principles: (1) Individuals will attempt to maintain an optimal amount of what Berlyne calls "collative variation." Stimuli that are too complex, too arousing, or too incongruous will be shunned, as will stimuli that are insufficiently complex, arousing, or incongruous. (2) An individual will be motivated to interact with stimuli closest to that individual's optimal level. Interaction with a stimulus causes it to simplify. (3) Coding schemes, or organizational principles, can reduce the perceived complexity of a stimulus by joining separate units into a unified whole.

# Applications of optimal level theory

The most noteworthy feature of optimal level theory is its extremely wide application. The theory has been applied to topics far beyond its original domain and is today one of the most important theories in environmental psychology, the area of psychology dealing with the interaction between the physical environment and man's behavior.

## Child development

Perhaps the most prominent application of optimal level theory has occurred in the area of child development. In 1966, Brennan, Ames, and Moore showed that as children mature from 4 to 14 weeks of age, their preferred stimulus-complexity level rises. Karmel (1969) found the same for infants up to 20 weeks of age. It is impossible to tell from these experiments, however, whether the older infants preferred higher complexity because of their greater age or because of their greater experience. In a study, Fantz and Nevis (1967) compared the stimulus preferences of children raised in an institution and children raised in private homes. In general, children raised at home preferred more complex stimuli. Since the two groups were of the same age, the difference between their preferences must have been a result of their differential experience. Many investigators (for example, Dennis, 1960; Spitz, 1945) have noted the developmental retardation that is characteristic of institutionalized children raised in a stimulation-deficient environment. One possible reason for this retardation is that the meager stimulation available to each child in the typical understaffed institution causes the child's optimal complexity level to be set very low. Therefore, a child reared in an institution will exhibit a preference curve similar to the left-hand curve in Figure 6-3. He or she will not wish to interact with stimuli whose higher complexity is attractive to noninstitutionalized children; that is, the child will not be motivated to seek new experiences and to learn.

Sackett (1965) demonstrated this principle in a carefully controlled study using rhesus monkeys. Because the subjects were monkeys rather than human infants, Sackett could totally control their early environment. In the most pertinent part of his study, five groups of animals were used. These groups differed markedly in the amount of stimulation they had received during the first 2½ years of life. The most deprived animals had been raised in total isolation during their first year and near-total isolation for the succeeding 1½ years. At the other extreme were monkeys that had been born in the jungle. Sackett measured the amount of time each monkey spent exploring a stimulus presented on a screen. The stimuli differed in complexity. Figure 6-6 contains the results of the exploration tests for three of Sackett's five groups. The results clearly show that the monkeys raised in the most enriched environment preferred the most complex stimuli. The most deprived monkeys showed minimal exploratory behavior and no clear preference for any level of stimulus complexity.

Burton White (1967, 1969) has used human infants in a research program analogous to that of Sackett. One group of institutionalized infants experienced the regular regimen of hospital care. An enrichment group differed from this control group in three ways: (1) extra handling of the infant was performed during the first 36 days of life; (2) during the second month of life, objects were placed nearby for the infant to explore; and (3) during the third month, new explorable objects were introduced, and the infant was frequently placed in the prone position (lying face downward). White assumed that infants at this age, when placed face downward, would frequently raise their heads and look around. In their usual supine position, the infants would be more likely to remain passive in the body-shaped depression in the soft mattress.

At first glance, these three modifications seem very minor. Yet each of them is designed to increase the child's stimulation. White found that the enrichment group accomplished several visual and motor milestones, such as the ability to reach for an object, far earlier than the control group. One can hypothesize that the extra stimulation given to the enrichment group moved their pacer up and promoted cognitive growth.

The studies we've discussed thus far have examined complexity of stimulation as an influence on cognitive growth. However, the amount of complexity a child prefers can also serve as a measure of cognitive growth.

Many investigators have found that children participating in Head Start programs showed no improvement on standardized tests. Arkes and Boykin (1971) speculated that a test of complexity preference might be a more general measure of cognitive growth. Thus, children participating in a Head Start program and children attending a sum-

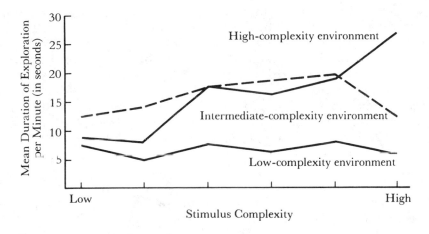

**Figure 6-6.** Exploration of visual stimuli by rhesus monkeys raised in high-, low-, and intermediate-complexity environments. *(Adapted from "Effects of Rearing Conditions upon the Behavior of Rhesus Monkeys (Macaca Mulatta)," by G. P. Sackett, Child Development, 1965, 36, 855–868. Copyright 1965 by The Society for Research in Child Development, Inc. Reprinted by permission.)*

mer nursery school were shown geometric patterns varying in complexity. These stimuli were somewhat similar to blocks and puzzles used during the Head Start program. At the beginning of the summer, the nursery-school children preferred significantly more complexity than the Head Start children did. By the end of the summer, however, the complexity preferred by the Head Start children had increased significantly: the two groups' preferences were the same. The Head Start children definitely came to prefer more complex stimulation because of their participation in the program. That may have been a cognitive milestone that no standardized test could have detected.

Optimal level theory, however, does *not* imply that more environmental stimulation is always better. Excessive stimulation may slow sensorimotor development. Wachs, Uzgiris, and Hunt (1971) found a large number of significant *negative* correlations between infant development and intense, inescapable stimulus bombardment in the home. One reason for this may be that large excesses of stimulation distract the child during learning experiences.

The complexity of environmental stimulation, in fact, is the key in the controversial explanation of childhood autism offered by Moore and Shick (1971). They believe that autistic children have their optimal complexity levels set at extremely low levels of stimulation. Moore and Shiek hypothesize that children experience a critical period during which the level of environmental stimulation influences the level at which the child's own optimum will be set. If there is a great deal of stimulation during this critical period, then the child will prefer a high level of stimulation. Moore and Shiek believe further that autistic children are neurologically advanced as fetuses; they are so advanced that they experience their critical period while still in the uterus. Since there is minimal stimulation during the critical period of such children, their optimal complexity level is near zero. Hence they will always withdraw from any stimulation. This theory helps to explain two puzzling observations that have been made of autistic children. First, many of these children spend a large portion of the day performing some repetitive motion. This "stereotyped behavior" often includes rocking or hand motions. One reason that this behavior goes on for so many hours may be that it is extremely boring: it approaches the very low level of stimulation that is an autistic child's optimum. Second, Hutt and Hutt (1968) have noted that such stereotyped behavior seems to increase whenever the child is approached by someone or is otherwise aroused. Any increase in stimulation would, of course, move such a child away from the established optimal complexity level. Performance of stereotyped behavior is therefore an effort to restore the optimum. It should be emphasized, however, that Moore and Shiek's formulation is a hypothesis, not a fact.

We have emphasized the importance of *amount* of stimulation in determining the child's optimal complexity level. A study by Yarrow, Rubenstein, Pedersen, & Jankowski (1972) also points to the importance of *type* of stimulation. Yarrow and his associates looked at the home environment of 41 infants 5 months of age. The environments were rated with regard to the variety, complexity, and responsiveness of the inanimate objects with which the child could come into contact. (*Responsiveness* refers to the feedback potential of an object—that is, whether a change in the object occurs as a result of interaction with it. The mobile hung above a baby's crib would be responsive, since batting it would produce a noise and a change in its appearance.) Yarrow also measured each child's functioning on a wide variety of cognitive, motor, and language tasks. He found strikingly high correlations between infants' functioning and the responsiveness, complexity, and variety of the inanimate sources of stimulation. Many of Yarrow's correlations are reproduced in Table 6-1.

These data provide another indication that children who have a stimulating environment are cognitively advanced over those with a less stimulating environment. Note, however, that responsiveness of the environment is a measure of *type* of stimulation, not amount. The study by Wachs et al. showed that both excessive and deficient amounts of stimulation may be detrimental to cognitive growth; this study by Yarrow et al. shows that the responsiveness of the stimulation may also be critical.

**TABLE 6-1.** Relations between dimensions of inanimate stimulation and infant functioning

| Infant functioning | Inanimate stimulation | | |
| --- | --- | --- | --- |
| | Responsiveness | Complexity | Variety |
| General status | | | |
| Mental developmental index | .27* | | .36* |
| Psychomotor developmental index | .28* | | .51** |
| Motor development | | | |
| Gross | .27* | | .42** |
| Fine | .33ᴬ | | .37* |
| Goal behaviors | | | |
| Goal orientation | .30* | | .41** |
| Reaching and grasping | .46** | .32* | .38* |
| Secondary circular reaction | .51** | .46** | .33* |
| Cognitive function | | | |
| Problem solving | | | .50** |
| Object permanence | | | .30* |
| Exploration | | | |
| Looking at novel stimulus | .28* | .30* | .35* |
| Manipulating novel stimulus | | .35* | .48** |

*Significant at the .05 level of confidence.
**Significant at the .01 level of confidence.

Adapted from "Dimensions of Early Stimulation and Their Differential Effects," by L. J. Yarrow, J. L. Rubenstein, F. A. Pedersen, and J. J. Jankowski, *Merrill-Palmer Quarterly,* 1972, *18*, 205–218. Reprinted by permission of the Merrill-Palmer Institute.

Robert White stressed this topic in 1959 when he wrote one of the most influential papers on motivation ever published. White believes that the primary motivation is neither the need for sex, as Freud thought, nor that for food and water, as Hull thought, but that for "competence," or "effectance." Any parent or babysitter knows how young children can become completely engrossed in some activity that does nothing more than effect some result. Children (and adults) take great joy in making things happen. A parent who becomes exasperated at picking up an object that a child has thrown out of the crib 517 times knows that the child is having a great time (at the parent's expense). Even psychologists have noted the obvious pleasure children experience in repeating some interesting occurrence. White believes that the most prevalent drive in human behavior is this motivation to have an effect on the environment. For it, White coined the term *effectance motivation.* Most important, the result of this interaction with the environment is that the child achieves competence in dealing with his or her surroundings. During the motivated interaction, learning and cognitive growth occur. As greater competence in dealing with the environment is achieved, the child seeks and masters new and more complex stimulation.

It can be seen from Yarrow's study and White's theory that stimulation occurring in response to a child's interaction might be the kind the child would be most highly motivated to seek. Such interaction could result in a child's feeling of mastery, of being competent and having an effect on the environment. This effectance motivation is one of the ego motives that neo-Freudians believe are important sources of motivation, independent of sex and aggression (see Chapter 3).

## Environmental applications

Environmental psychology is concerned with the interaction between human behavior and the physical environment. Since optimal level theory deals with precisely that interaction, many optimal level theorists have participated prominently in the area of environmental research.

The most obvious prediction such theorists would make is that there is an optimal level of environmental complexity that people prefer. Sensory-deprivation research has shown that *minimal* levels of environmental stimulation are extremely aversive. Milgram (1970) hypothesizes that urban-dwellers resort to unlisted phone numbers, curt interpersonal communication, and general indifference in order to reduce stimulation, since their environment provides a *maximal* level of stimulation, which also is aversive. Hypo- and hyperstimulation are aversive to everyone, but there may be large differences among persons' optimal amounts of stimulation, depending on the complexity of the environments to which they have become adapted. Figure 6-7 shows a hypothesized relation between complexity and preference as a function of habitat. The authors suggest that, although both rural- and urban-dwellers exhibit the typical inverted-U curve, rural-dwellers' optimal complexity level may be set lower than urban-dwellers'. An interesting experiment by Haggard, As, and Borgen (1970) supports this hypothesis. Men living alone in the tundra of northern Norway showed less severe reactions to a sensory-deprivation experiment than did men living in the city of Oslo. This difference would be expected if it is assumed that total sensory deprivation is further from the optimal level of the Oslo subjects than it is from that of the men who have become habituated to the isolated conditions of life in the tundra.

The importance of optimal level theory in environmental preference has recently been recognized by architects and city planners. An important article by Rapoport (1971) demonstrates the close relation between architecture and psychology. Rapoport suggests that the reason very low and very high levels of stimulation are not preferred is that they contain a minimum of usable information. Environmental stimuli of low complexity provide a meager amount of information. Such stimuli are therefore boring. The phenomenon of highway hypnosis, for example, attests to the dearth of stimulation in a long drive on a straight, barren highway. But environmental stimuli of very high complexity are so chaotic and confusing that a person cannot extract much information from them, either. Rapoport's point is simply that stimuli

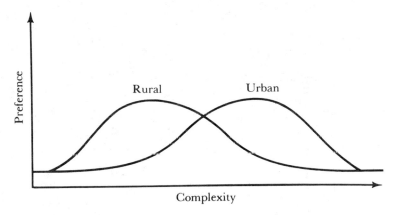

**Figure 6-7.** Hypothesized relation between type of environment and location of the inverted U on the complexity continuum.

with an optimal amount of complexity are able to elicit interest from the observer. This is, of course, the central tenet of optimal level theory.

Arkes and Clark (1975) have used the optimal level theory to predict the amount of environmental complexity that people will prefer on the basis of the complexity of a task they have just performed. College students viewed four slides showing environmental scenes of varying complexity. Most scenes were of forests, mountains, or other natural settings. The subjects rated the slides on a 10-point preference scale. One-third of the subjects then worked on ten easy anagrams, one-third on moderately difficult anagrams, and one-third on extremely difficult anagrams. Lastly, subjects viewed and rated new environmental scenes, which had been matched with the originals for complexity. The changes in preference from the first to the second rating session were calculated. The results are shown in Figure 6-8.

Subjects who had fractured their skulls trying to solve difficult anagrams increased their preference for simpler slides. The difficult task had exceeded the optimal level of complexity. Subjects performing this task, therefore, preferred low-complexity environmental scenes in order to return to the optimum. Conversely, subjects who were bored unscrambling easy anagrams (such as *HGO*) showed increased preference for more complex slides and decreased preference for simpler ones. The group attempting intermediate-difficulty anagrams showed its only increase in preference for slides of low-intermediate complexity. The conclusion is clear: preference for environmental complexity is influenced by the complexity of *prior* stimulation. After a dull day behind a desk, a jazz concert would be great. After a hectic day supervising 300 kids, a little peace and quiet would be fine. Optimal level theory is an interactionist theory; both the characteristics of the en-

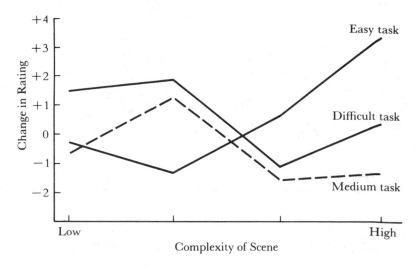

**Figure 6-8.** Difference between successive ratings of environment as a function of complexity of scene and difficulty of intervening task. *(Adapted from "Effects of Task Difficulty on Subsequent Preference for Visual Complexity," by H. R. Arkes and P. Clark,* Perceptual and Motor Skills, *1975, 41, 395–399. Reprinted by permission of the publisher.)*

vironment and the characteristics of the organism must be taken into account.

### Individual differences

Because optimal level theory states that each person has his or her own optimal level of stimulation, psychologists have investigated variables related to the selection of a person's optimum.

Burt (1937) and Eysenck (1947), for example, agree that introverts tend to prefer simpler stimuli, extroverts more complex ones. Referring back to Figure 6-7, the inverted U on the left would represent the preference of introverts, the one on the right that of extroverts. This hypothesis, however, has not received unanimous experimental support (Bryson & Driver, 1972).

Quay (1965) has advanced an interesting hypothesis about psychopaths that can easily be interpreted in terms of optimal level theory. He suggests that psychopaths are continuously in a state of stimulus deprivation and that they are therefore constantly motivated to seek stimulation. Note that if psychopaths have a very high optimal complexity level, the condition described by Quay would occur: such people would always be struggling to find stimulation so that their optimal level could be attained. Skrzypek (1969) tested Quay's hypothesis by assessing the stimulus-complexity preferences of psychopathic and neurotic delinquents. Skrzypek predicted that neurotics, who are chronically anxious, would constantly be stimulated from within and would therefore be unlikely to seek extra stimulation. In contrast, psychopaths would always want more stimulation. Indeed, psychopaths did prefer more complex stimuli than neurotics on a preference test. After the preference test, both neurotics and psychopaths were subjected to 40 minutes of sensory deprivation and then tested again. Psychopaths increased their preference for complex stimuli more than neurotics did. Evidently the period of sensory deprivation provided a stimulation level far below the optimal level of psychopaths but only somewhat below that of neurotics. Both groups, as expected, sought complexity following the deprivation, but the psychopaths apparently were particularly desperate for complex stimulation. In another part of the same experiment, following assessment of complexity preference, neurotics and psychopaths were asked to perform very difficult auditory discriminations, a task that was designed to arouse anxiety. The subjects then took another preference test. The neurotics' preference for complexity decreased—apparently their natural and induced anxiety level provided quite enough arousal—whereas the psychopaths' preference did not change. The amount of anxiety induced by the task was trivial to the psychopaths. All these results would follow from the supposition that neurotics are usually above their optimal complexity level and psychopaths are usually below theirs.

Fromm (1972) suggests that level of stimulation may also be a factor in aggression. According to Fromm, some of the aggression seen in recent years may result from the fact that some people cannot attain an adequate amount of stimulation through everyday interaction with their surroundings. Violence is therefore needed to create a sensation intense enough to reach the person's high optimal level of stimulation.

## Esthetics

Art and science have rarely enjoyed a close relationship, and the psychology of esthetics has remained a rather isolated area of study. However, recent work by several optimal level theorists has begun to rejuvenate the scientific study of artistic experience.

An experiment by Konecni, Crozier, and Doob (1976) provides a good example of how optimal level theorists would analyze esthetic preference. This experiment, however, is unique in that it also uses optimal level theory to test a principle of Freudian theory! Recall that Freud supported the cathartic theory of aggression, and research to be reviewed in Chapter 7 supports the notion that an angered subject will experience heightened arousal, which then can be dissipated through an aggressive act. A person with heightened arousal would be at point C in Figure 6-2. This person would not want to interact with complex stimulation. However, a person who had already vented his or her anger by retaliation would be at point A or point B. This person would prefer more complex stimulation. The Konecni et al. study tested these predictions by annoying two groups of subjects. One group of subjects (annoy–shock) had the opportunity to shock the person who had annoyed them. The other group just sat and waited after having been annoyed (annoy–wait). A control group was neither annoyed nor given the opportunity to shock anyone. The experimenters found that the annoy–wait subjects—that is, those who were given no opportunity to work off their anger—subsequently chose to listen to complex music less often than the other two groups did. This is precisely what we would expect from subjects who are already above their optimal level of arousal.

L. B. Meyer (1967), speaking from an artistic point of view, says that "what creates or increases the information contained in a piece of music increases its value. Of course in either linguistic or musical communication a completely random series of stimuli will in all likelihood communicate nothing" (pp. 27–28). What Meyer is saying is the first principle of optimal level theory: humans prefer an optimal level of stimulus variation. The variable that Meyer emphasizes, uncertainty, is the one most easily manipulated. *Uncertainty* in this instance refers to the predictability of a stimulus event. After "do-re-mi-fa-so-la-ti," most listeners expect "do." "Do" has low uncertainty. Its occurrence would be predictable and boring. Suppose, instead, "fa" occurred. This unexpected event would have high uncertainty. It would be novel, surprising, and therefore more arousing. If "fa" were *too* surprising, however, then neither "do" nor "fa" would be particularly pleasing. Optimal levels of uncertainty are most pleasing.

Meyer also restates the second principle of optimal level theory, mentioned earlier in this chapter: "Assuming that two works are generally of the same quality of excellence, it is, I think, clear that the more complex can be reheard with enjoyment more often than the simpler" (1967, p. 51). In other words, with repeated exposure, a stimulus above the optimal complexity level will approach the optimum; a stimulus at or below the optimum will move away from it. This is what the G. F. Smith and Dorfman (1975) study found.

Meyer also mentions the importance of a "schema," or pattern, within a musical work: "The capacity of the human mind to perceive and relate patterns to one another and to remember them appears to limit complexity" (1967, p. 36). Just as the master chess player uses one concept to encode several stimuli, thereby reducing their complexity, the trained ear can detect structures within music. This ability was advanced as a possible explanation of Vitz's finding (1966a) that musically experienced subjects preferred complex tone sequences.

A final topic mentioned by Meyer that nicely fits into optimal level theory is the increasing complexity of musical styles as they mature:

"As the musical community (composers, performers, and listeners) becomes familiar with the typical processes, procedures, and schemata of a style, syntax and structure tend to become more involved and complex. Less probable progressions are used with greater frequency, schemata become more intricate and less obvious, and hierarchic structures become more extended" (1967, pp. 116–117). The musical community gets used to a style, thus reducing its perceived psychological complexity. Then, in order for a new musical work to be pleasurable, it must violate the style, so that listeners cannot apply their learned coding schemes (Munsinger & Kessen, 1964) so easily. When this means of reducing complexity is eliminated, the piece is perceived as more complex and thus closer to the optimal level.

Other theorists have also noted the very close connection between optimal level theory and artistic experience (see, for example, Berlyne, 1971; Walker, 1980). The application of this theory to visual and auditory art forms represents one of the few scientific investigations of esthetics.

## Economics

An economist, Tibor Scitovsky, has suggested that traditional economic theories have not been based on the principles of human motivation. Traditional economists have assumed, for example, that people are willing to spend money to maintain such comforts as shelter or convenient transportation. Scitovsky (1976) uses optimal level theory to show why this fundamental economic assumption may be in error.

Scitovsky claims, first, that one's comfort or discomfort is determined by the *level* of arousal, the optimal level being the most comfortable level, of course. Second, feelings of pleasure are caused by *changes* in the level of arousal up toward the optimum from a point that is too low or down toward the optimum from a point that is too high.

These two simple principles have an important implication: discomfort must precede pleasure! If one stays at the optimal level at all times, one never will experience a change toward the optimum. Therefore, one will never experience pleasure. In order to experience pleasure, one must at least temporarily move from the optimum to a less comfortable position. Only then will a pleasurable change toward the optimum level be possible.

This has several consequences for economic theory, which assumes that people are willing to pay to satisfy their *most pressing* needs. Presumably, when this need has been met to a greater extent than has some other need, people should shift their expenditures to try to satisfy that other need. However, this shift may not occur, because the process of satisfying the first need is pleasurable. The movement toward the optimum causes pleasure, and therefore the activity may be continued long after the need is partially satisfied. The second need will not be satisfied until satisfaction of the first need no longer produces pleasure. Such behavior may seem irrational to economists, but it is the inevitable result of Scitovsky's two principles.

Scitovsky's analysis also helps shed some light on the behavior of the "idle rich." Able to afford all the comforts, such people are firmly resting at the optimal level. Because this means that they will experience no pleasure, however, it is necessary for such people to take up, for example, dangerous pastimes to remove themselves from the optimal level. Only then will the pleasure of returning to the optimal level be possible. Scitovsky suggests, like Fromm (1972), that the increase in violence in our society may be the result of being too comfortable; to achieve pleasure we have to do something that will temporarily yank us away from the optimum level of stimulation.

## Conclusions and critique

A major problem of optimal level theories is that verification of the inverted-U relation is difficult. As Figure 6-9 shows, three relations between complexity and preference are permissible according to optimal level theory. The problem is that an inverted-U relation allows so many possible curves that the theory is difficult to refute, and any theory not susceptible to disproof is worthless.

There are ways, however, to constrain the number of permissible complexity/preference relations. If the optimal level of a subject is known and complexities of the various stimuli presented to the subject span a range above and below the optimum, then an inverted U must be found in order to support the theory. However, most optimal level research does not specify an individual's optimal level before testing the subject. Therefore, any of the three curves in Figure 6-9 is entirely acceptable. With so many acceptable results available, it is difficult to put the theory to a stringent test.

Optimal level theory began as an attempt to explain many phenomena that appeared to be outside the jurisdiction of Hullian theory. Yet the theory can also comment on some aspects of Hullian theory itself. For example, Hull maintained that drive reduction defined reinforcement. For the state Hull usually induced in his experimental animals, hunger, that may have been true. If hunger pangs and other such highly aversive stimuli lie at point C in Figure 6-2, then an animal will prefer drive (hunger) reduction. However, if an animal is kept in a sensory-deprivation chamber, such as an animal cage, then it will prefer drive (arousal) increase. If an animal is at point A in Figure 6-2, then Sheffield will appear to be correct as the animal seeks stimulation by solving puzzles and bar-pressing for visual stimulation. In other

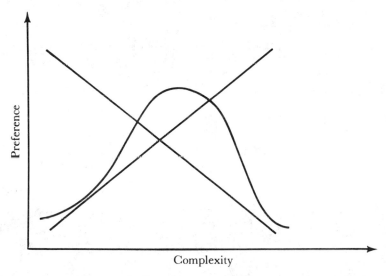

**Figure 6-9.** Three relations between preference and complexity, all of which are permitted by optimal level theory.

words, the first half of Figure 6-3 is a Hullian curve and the second half is a Sheffield curve. Perhaps they both are correct, because each theorist is describing an animal that has different needs than the animal described by the other theorist.

There are two other differences between Hullian theory and optimal level theory. First, optimal level theory has matured to encompass a wide variety of topics: environmental psychology, child psychology, architecture, music, and even industrial relations. Second, in optimal level theory the individual plays a more active role, constantly seeking the activity with the right amount of psychological complexity (Walker, 1964) or collative variation (Berlyne, 1960). Thus, the individual's life is not spent in 100-meter dashes separated by periods of quiescence, as Hullian theory would imply. Instead, the individual is constantly trying to match his, her, or its optimal level.

# CHAPTER 7

# Social Learning Theories: The Cognitive Perspectives of Rotter and Bandura

*You can observe a lot by just watching.*

*Yogi Berra*

Social learning theories seek to explain the complex effects of the social environment upon the behavior of the individual. Although they employ many of the motivational principles of traditional learning theories such as Hull's and Tolman's, they are unique in several ways.

Social learning theories avoid such concepts as drive and drive reduction, which they believe imply an automatic, fixed way of behaving: certain stimuli will produce certain responses—food reduces hunger and produces eating; avoidance reduces fear. In place of drive constructs, social learning theorists postulate cognitive mediating variables. They assume that reinforcement by itself does not automatically motivate behavior. Instead, the active processing of information regarding motivational variables is critical in determining behavior. Thus, hungry persons will not simply eat. They will think about the time and the situation, whether they can wait, whether the available food is of sufficient quality, and so forth. Behavioral decisions are thus largely under the control of the person. The person is not viewed as a pawn of powerful environmental incentives. Person variables such as expectancy, attention, and appraisal are therefore fundamental to social learning theories.

This emphasis on cognition requires that some of the traditional assumptions regarding reinforcement be recast. The expectancy or anticipation of reinforcement is sufficient for a behavior to be motivated; it is not imperative that a reinforcement be attained. For example, observing another person being reinforced for solving a puzzle may prompt an observer to give the puzzle a try. Thus, reinforcement can be vicarious. Recent theoretical developments have even placed emphasis on self-reinforcement, the individual's own control of rewards and punishments.

Social learning theory, with its emphasis on cognition, has proven to be enormously applicable to a number of motivational topics of current concern, such as pornography and aggression. For example, consider a child who sees a film of someone achieving a desired goal by aggression. Since the child does not receive any reinforcement, a Hullian might predict that no learning would take place. But a social learning theorist, as we shall see, would rely on *observational learning* and *vicarious reinforcement*, contending that a child can learn to use aggression even if the child receives no tangible reinforcement for doing so.

Two theorists, Julian Rotter and Albert Bandura, have greatly influenced social learning theory. Like Freud, Rogers, and Maslow, both Rotter and Bandura are clinical psychologists. However, unlike their predecessors, their theories did not arise solely from naturalistic observation. Rather, they were developed from findings in the psychological laboratory. Consequently, the constructs of their theories are relatively crisp and precise and have been the objects of many research projects.

We shall discuss first the theories of Rotter and Bandura, then the research on aggression and pornography.

## *Rotter: Expectancy-value theory*

Julian Rotter has been an active theorist and researcher in social learning theory for almost three decades. His book *Social Learning and Clinical Psychology* (1954) and his subsequent theoretical contributions (for example, Rotter, 1966, 1967) have stimulated hundreds of publications and influenced many current social learning conceptions.

At the core of Rotter's social learning theory, as in other learning theories, is a model of motivation (Rotter & Hochreich, 1975). Rotter assumes that human behavior is motivated by the attainment of goals. However, he rejects drive reduction as a motivational mechanism. Rather, he relies heavily on the empirical law of effect: reinforcement is any event that affects a person's movement toward a goal. Positive reinforcers facilitate movement toward a goal (for example, good grades motivate a student to continue to study). Negative reinforcers inhibit movement toward a goal (for example, painful falls may reduce a toddler's motivation to walk).[1] This scheme is not unlike other learning theories. The major twist comes about in a concept which Rotter terms the *meaningful environment*. For Rotter, events do not necessarily affect behavior; only *meaningful* events will do so. For example, a child will keep her room clean in return for a weekly allowance only if she needs the money and can be certain that she will indeed get it. Only then will the allowance be part of her meaningful environment. From this example we can see that Rotter places strong emphasis on the cognitions of the individual. The person must process information from the environment and match it with memories of past experiences. For a behavior to be motivated, there must be a strong reinforcer and a high probability that it will be attained. In other words, in Rotter's theory both value and expectancy play a role in motivation.

---

[1]Most learning theorists, unlike Rotter, would use the term *punishment* to describe the inhibition of movement toward a goal. In traditional learning terms, reinforcement—positive and negative—always facilitates and never inhibits goal attainment (Brown & Herrnstein, 1975, p. 567).

For Rotter, social learning is not simply the acquisition of behavior by reinforcement or drive reduction. Social learning is a complex process involving the interaction of the individual with his or her meaningful environment (Rotter, Chance, & Phares, 1972). We shall discuss briefly the critical variables, constructs, and principles in Rotter's expectancy-value form of social learning theory.

## Basic constructs and predictive variables

Complex human behavior can be explained and predicted by means of four variables (Rotter, Chance, & Phares, 1972; Rotter & Hochreich, 1975).

1. A *psychological situation* (Ps) is any situation or part of a situation to which a person is responding. Two aspects of this variable are important. First, it places emphasis on the changing, dynamic nature of the environment and assumes that an individual's responses also are variable. For example, in a brief time period a student's situation and behavior may both vary. The student may be pushy and assertive on the bus, smiling and ingratiating when talking to a professor, and quiet and contemplative in the library. Second, the concept of Ps emphasizes that any situation is interpreted subjectively: an exam may be an opportunity for pride and achievement for one person and a frightful horror for another.

2. The second variable, *behavior potential* (Bp), refers to the likelihood that a certain behavior will occur in a given situation. Behaviors are defined broadly (motor acts, thoughts, feelings, and so forth) and each has a different potential. For example, waiting in a long line for a concert ticket may evoke an array of behaviors—yawning, daydreaming, anger, mumbling, and so on. For a given individual, the potential for each of these behaviors to occur will vary. Descartes is likely to daydream; Machiavelli is likely to be angered.

3. The third variable, *expectancy* (E), refers to the individual's assumption about the probability that a specific reinforcement will occur for a specific behavior in a specific situation. For example, a "scratch" golfer (a very good one) will have a high expectancy of a low score (reinforcement) for good play (behavior) on an easy golf course (situation). This variable sets Rotter's theory apart from conventional learning theories such as Hull's, because it assumes that expectancy is determined by previous experience and that it is measurable. This concept implies that knowing that a person is motivated, or goal-directed, is insufficient to predict his or her behavior; one must also know whether the person expects to attain the goal. One runner attempting to go 10,000 meters may give up simply because she thinks she cannot make it. Another runner, for whom the run is just as important, might continue because of a more positive expectancy of success. As can be seen from this example, however, subjective expectancies for reinforce-

ment may or may not correspond to real probability. The runner who stopped might have been able to finish; the runner who continued might not have been able to finish.

Expectancies also may vary in generality. Some expectancies may be specific for single situations—for example, a person's expectancy of success on the tennis court. But an individual may have *generalized expectancies* (GE) as well in which he expects that reinforcement received in one situation will occur in other situations. For example, a good tennis player may expect to be good at Ping-Pong or racquetball without having played either. Such generalized expectancies may or may not be accurate.

4. The fourth predictive variable, *reinforcement value* (RV), refers to the strength of a reinforcement. The RV is defined by the degree of preference for a given reinforcement relative to others if the probability of each reinforcement occurring is equal. For example, a father tells his daughter that he will buy her an ice-cream cone if she practices her guitar for an hour. She asks "Where?" When he answers "Baskin-Robbins," she practices diligently, not just because she is an ice-cream freak but also because among the 31 equally probable flavor selections (reinforcements) is her favorite, Jamoca Almond Fudge.

Although individuals differ in the degree to which they value a given reinforcement, cultures, groups, and families do produce consistent reinforcement values. Money, for example, has reinforcement value for almost all individuals in our society.

Rotter contends, however, that reinforcements do not occur as isolated events. Instead, people come to expect reinforcement–reinforcement sequences. For example, one reinforcement (good grades) may lead to an expectation of future reinforcements (graduation–good job–high salary–early retirement in Hawaii). The value of one reinforcement is thus enhanced by expectancy of future reinforcements.

On the basis of these four constructs—Ps, Bp, E, and RV—behavior can be predicted. For any given psychological situation (Ps), the behavior potential can be expressed by the equation $BP = f(E + RV)$, which is interpreted as "behavior potential is a function of expectancy for reinforcement and the value of the reinforcement." Since the relationship between E and RV is additive, the magnitude of BP can depend on E and RV either independently or jointly. In theory, either E or RV could be zero, and BP could still be substantial.

To illustrate, consider the following situation. Mario Driver sits in the cockpit of a Formula One Ferrari in the pole position on the grid of the U. S. Grand Prix (Ps). He is considering two driving strategies, $BP_1$ and $BP_2$. $BP_1$ would be an aggressive, fast-paced race aimed at winning the race. $BP_2$ would be a more cautious, somewhat slower race aimed at placing among the top five finishers. For $BP_1$, Mario's $RV_1$ is moderately strong, since winning the American Grand Prix brings honor, fame, and money. For $BP_2$, however, Mario's $RV_2$ is even stronger, because finishing in the top five would give him enough total points on the racing circuit this year to make him the annual Grand Prix champion, an honor perhaps at the pinnacle of the racing world. In five previous Grand Prix races, Mario has won once, finished in third place twice, finished near the end once, and failed to finish once because of an accident. His expectancy $(E_1)$ for winning this race is therefore less than his expectancy $(E_2)$ for placing in the top five. Mario's behavior can be predicted by considering the following equations for Ps.

$$BP_1 = f(E_1 + RV_1)$$

aggressive 1/5 winner
race of race

$$BP_2 = f(E_2 + RV_2)$$

cautious 2/5 annual
race champion

$BP_2$ is more likely to occur than $BP_1$, because both expectancy and reinforcement value of $BP_2$ are greater.

### Generalization constructs: Need and its components

Rotter and Hochreich (1975) note that the use of the $BP = f(E + RV)$ formula is limited to the prediction of a specific behavior from specific expectancies and reinforcers. This focus on specifics is laudable for hypothesis testing in research settings. However, the formula is too narrow for application in naturalistic settings where it is necessary to explain and predict general classes and patterns of behaviors, such as achievement, aggression, and so forth.

To provide generalization beyond the psychological laboratory, Rotter relies on the concept of need and its components. A need is defined as a class of behaviors that are similar in that they attain the same or similar reinforcements. A need thus gives common direction to many related responses. Needs are determined by experience; they are elicited by environmental cues, not by shifts in physiological states, by the demand for tension reduction, or the like.

Rotter and Hochreich (1975) list six broad need categories. The needs and specific forms appear in Table 7-1. Note that, although these needs bear some resemblance to those identified by Maslow and Rogers, they are conceptualized in a social learning framework. Thus, they are neither instinctual nor hierarchically arranged.

Recall that the formula $BP = f(E + RV)$ can be used only to predict the behavior potential for a *specific* behavior. Since a need is manifested in a *class* of behaviors, one must examine the behavior potential

**TABLE 7-1.** Socially learned needs

| Need category | Specific form of need |
|---|---|
| 1. Recognition/status | Need to excel, need to be competent, need to be better than others in school, profession, and so on, need to attain social status |
| 2. Dominance | Need to control others, need to be powerful, need to be a leader |
| 3. Independence | Need to make one's own decisions, need to be self-reliant, need to achieve without aid of others, need to be self-rewarding |
| 4. Protection/dependency | Need to be helped, need to be secure and protected |
| 5. Love and affection | Need for acceptance and liking by others, need to be loved and regarded, need to be respected |
| 6. Physical comfort | Need for bodily pleasures, need to avoid pain and discomfort, need for physical satisfactions associated with security |

Based on Rotter and Hochreich, 1975, pp. 101–102.

(BP) for each of those behaviors that might satisfy the need. In this way, one can determine whether need satisfaction will take place. For this multibehavior analysis, Rotter presents another formula, very similar to the previous one: $NP = f(FM + NV)$. The three need components involved in this formula are need potential, freedom of movement, and need value.

1. *Need potential* (NP) refers to a set of behaviors directed toward the same goal. A person who wants to help others—to be altruistic— may have a need potential made up of a class of altruistic behaviors such as donating money to charities, volunteering to assist a needy group, and training to be a social worker.

2. The second need component, *freedom of movement* (FM), refers to expectancies that a set of behaviors will satisfy the needs that a person values. Thus, freedom of movement is really need-satisfaction expectancy. The person who wants to be altruistic, for example, may strongly expect that doing volunteer work and becoming a social worker would be helpful behaviors but that donating money would probably not be particularly helpful because the amount of money available for donation is too small to be significant. The various need-satisfaction expectancies are averaged to determine FM.

$$\text{FM}^{\text{altruism}} = \frac{\overset{\text{volunteer work}}{E_1} + \overset{\text{social work}}{E_2} + \overset{\text{donations}}{E_3}}{3}$$

High freedom of movement is thus directly related to a high expectancy that a particular need will be satisfied.

3. The third need component, *need value* (NV), refers to the value of one set of reinforcements as compared to others. For example, in a

social situation, the greater value of one set of reinforcements may motivate a person to gain acceptance and liking from others (love and affection need), rather than achieve status and aggrandizement (recognition/status need).

The values of the three need components are assumed to be averages of the specific predictive variables of which they are composed. Therefore, the need components are defined as:

$$NP = \frac{(BP_1 + BP_2 \ldots + BP_n)}{n}$$

$$FM = \frac{(E_1 + E_2 \ldots + E_n)}{n}$$

$$NV = \frac{(RV_1 + RV_2 \ldots + RV_n)}{n}$$

The formula for the general prediction of behavior thus becomes NP $= f(\text{FM} + \text{NV})$.

Let us now examine an application of the need-potential analysis. Rotter and Hochreich (1975) present a specific hypothesis regarding the behavior of one who has high NV and low FM. Rotter hypothesizes that a person who has a high need value for competence (craves recognition and status) but low freedom of movement (does not expect to be competent) is likely to avoid the expected failure by fulfilling the need in fantasy. Such avoidance of failure may involve actual physical separation from situations that demand competence, or it may involve cognitive distortion and defense (such as repression) to mask the failure to be competent. Satisfaction in such cases is likely to be obtained symbolically. Thus, this high-NV/low-FM individual may avoid situations in which competence is evaluated—by not trying to get into college, for example, or by not applying for challenging jobs. He is incompetent. His highly-valued need can then never be rewarded through appropriate behaviors, and he is left, like Walter Mitty, to daydreams and fantasies of greatness. For Rotter, such *avoidance* and *irreal behaviors* commonly include psychological defenses and symptoms of maladjustment.

## Conclusions: Rotter

Rotter's expectancy-value form of social learning theory has three important strengths. First, it is a learning theory geared exclusively to complex human behavior in a social environment. As a consequence it has considerable heuristic value and numerous applications in personality development and measurement, social psychology, psychopathology, and psychotherapy (see Rotter, Chance & Phares, 1972). Second, it places emphasis on individual variation in learning and motivation. All people are goal-directed, but their goals, expectancies, and reward values are individually defined. Cognitive processes are paramount in this scheme. Third, Rotter has placed a premium on research and consequently generated many testable hypotheses. The immense psychological literature on internal versus external control of reinforcement which will be discussed in Chapter 11, arose in great part from Rotter's initial theoretical contribution (that is, Rotter, 1966).

The straightforward specificity of the theory, however, also has an element of weakness. The theory's brevity leads to incompleteness. The implied cognitive processes, especially those regarding the expectancy and freedom of movement constructs, are in need of expansion and precision. Also, the theory becomes predictably less specific and precise when it is extended to broad applications in naturalistic settings.

## Bandura: Modeling theory and self-regulation

The foundation of another social learning theory was put forth by Albert Bandura and his former student Richard Walters in *Social Learning and Personality Development* (1963). This book, like few others in psychology, spawned many rich ideas and an immense research literature, which today are at the forefront of the learning approaches to abnormal behavior. Since Walters's untimely death in 1968, Bandura (for example, 1969, 1971a, 1971b, 1977b) has become the central theorist for what is now known as cognitive social learning theory.

The distinguishing feature of Bandura's social learning theory revolves around his analysis of how people learn by observing others. This general type of learning, which involves such processes as imitation, identification, copying, matching, and the like, is called *modeling*. For Bandura, modeling is the primary way in which all human behavior is learned (Bandura, 1977b, p. 22). Through Bandura's careful theorizing and innovative experimentation, it has become clear that modeling is not merely a monkey-see/monkey-do phenomenon. Rather, modeling is a complex process made up of several mediating variables hypothesized to occur between the observation of a behavior and the modeling of a response.

The fundamental characteristics of the modeling process can be described as follows. A person first anticipates that he or she will be reinforced (rewarded or punished) for behaving as another person has done. This anticipation leads the observer to carefully attend to the behavior of a model (the modeling stimuli). While observing the behavior of the model, the observer processes and symbolizes relevant information about the model (symbolic coding), organizes and structures the

$$\text{Anticipated} \rightarrow \text{Attention} \rightarrow \text{Modeling} \rightarrow \left\{ \begin{array}{l} \text{Symbolic coding} \\ \text{Cognitive organization} \\ \text{Rehearsal} \end{array} \right\} \rightarrow \text{Modeled}$$

Anticipated → Attention → Modeling → { Symbolic coding / Cognitive organization / Rehearsal } → Modeled
reinforcement                stimuli                                                                response

**Figure 7-1.** Fundamental characteristics of the modeling process. *(Adapted from* Social Learning Theory, *by A. Bandura. Copyright © 1977 by Prentice-Hall. Reprinted by permission.)*

information (cognitive organization), and mentally rehearses the model's behavior (rehearsal). The observer finally responds by matching the behavior of the model. This process is depicted in Figure 7-1.

Two aspects of Bandura's modeling paradigm are critical. The first pertains to the concept of reinforcement. According to Bandura, one does not have to be *directly* reinforced for modeling to take place; people learn without getting instrumental rewards. Reinforcement is therefore indirect, or vicarious. The impact of the reinforcement resides in *anticipation* of reward or punishment for the modeled behavior. Hence, in stark contrast to other analyses of modeling (for example, Miller & Dollard, 1941), Bandura does not conceptualize reinforcement as a response consequence that reduces drive.

A second important feature of the modeling paradigm pertains to the strong role it attributes to cognitive processes. As noted in the preceding paragraph, the perception of anticipated reinforcement focuses the person's attention on the model. As long as attention is maintained, information regarding the behavior to be modeled is gathered. As the model is observed, cognitive processing produces a verbal or imaginal concept of the model, and this coded information can then be used in enacting the modeled behavior. Whether the behavior is performed or not, however, it can be coded in memory for subsequent use.

## Modeling effects

Modeling can produce four primary effects, or types of social learning responses (Bandura, 1971a).

1. The observation of a model may lead to *novel responses*—that is, behaviors in which the learner has not previously engaged. Bandura refers to this as the *observational learning effect*. A teenager, for example, may begin smoking after watching his football idol smoke on a television talk show.

2. Modeling may lead to an increase of a previously learned inhibition. This is referred to as an *inhibitory effect*. For example, suppose a 9-year-old has learned to regulate her aggression quite well. This learning might be further enhanced—that is, her aggression might be even more inhibited—by watching her father successfully regulate his aggressive responses when he is angered.

3. Response inhibitions may also be decreased. This is referred to as a *disinhibitory effect*. In this case, the 9-year-old would become more

aggressive—her inhibitions regarding aggression would be weakened—by observing her father *fail* to regulate his aggression.

4. Existing behaviors also may be facilitated, or prompted. This phenomenon is referred to as a *response facilitation effect*. For example, a man might become more talkative after observing an outgoing, affable friend in a social situation. His increased talkativeness has been facilitated, or prompted, by watching the model.

Recently, Bandura (1977b) expanded the domain of modeling effects to include *abstract modeling* and *creative modeling*. Abstract modeling consists of observers deriving principles underlying a modeled performance and using such principles to generate behavior that transcends that which they have observed. Language learning and the acquisition of moral knowledge are two examples of such abstract modeling. In each case, rules and principles are learned in addition to the specific modeled behavior. Creative modeling is similar, but innovation in this instance comes from the learner's exposure to different models who provide information that can be combined by the learner in unique ways. For example, a painter may create a new abstract form after modeling several accomplished painters in cubism, Fauvism, and abstract expressionism.

Hence, the potential effects of modeling are indeed broad. They range from the modification of existing behaviors to the acquisition and generation of new ones.

## Modeling processes

The various effects of modeling—novel responses, inhibitory and disinhibitory effects, facilitative responses, abstraction, and creative responses—are mediated by the following four component processes (Bandura, 1977a).

*Attentional processes* are those that determine which models are selected from the array of modeling influences and which aspects of the modeled behaviors are attended to. Only information that is attended to can produce a modeling effect.

Attentional processes are affected by characteristics of the modeling stimuli and by characteristics of the observer. One important characteristic of modeling stimuli is their functional value. When observing an instructor, for example, a prospective commando might attend to the techniques of guerilla warfare that are being taught but not to the instructor's manner of speaking. Another important characteristic of modeling stimuli is their affective value. You are much more likely, for example, to model the behavior of someone you like than that of someone you have little feeling about. The instructiveness and complexity of the model's behavior also are influential aspects of the attentional process.

The observer characteristics that can influence the attentional process are such things as previous experience, sensory capacity, arousal level, perceptual set, and motivational level of the observer. For example, the commando will attend to modeled techniques of guerilla warfare if in the past he has been reinforced for doing so.

*Retention processes* make up the second component of modeling. These processes are necessary to enable a modeled behavior to occur in the absence of the model. The observer, by converting the brief modeling experience into mental symbols, can store the experience in memory for future reference. This symbolic coding may be verbal (using words) or imaginal (using images). Once coded and organized in the observer's mind, the modeling experience can then be symbolically rehearsed to increase retention of the memory.

Consider this example of retention processes. A dance student closely watches a solo routine performed by an experienced dancer in the Merce Cunningham troupe. She carries away a mental picture, or image, of an intricate set of movements that were modeled. The next week during dance practice, the student often conjures up the memory of the routine and mentally rehearses it.

Once the model's behaviors are symbolically coded, the symbolized memories can be used by the observer to guide his or her behavior. The response guidance function, composed of motor reproduction processes, converts the symbolic representations into pertinent behaviors. Such behavioral reproduction involves temporal and spatial organization of the observer's responses to match the model's.

Reproduction is determined by several variables. The observer must have the physical capabilities and the necessary skills involved to match the model's performance. Watching Abdul-Jabbar stuff a basketball down into the basket, for example, is unlikely to produce a modeling effect in an observer who is only five-feet-two. An observer also must carefully watch his or her reproductions and receive accurate feedback about the performance. The reproductions are then corrected to more closely approximate the modeled behavior. Many trials and adjustments usually are necessary before the mental image can be transformed into the desired behavior. The more complex the behavior being modeled, the more trials the observer will need to make.

An observer may, in fact, learn a great deal about a model's behavior and be capable of performing the behavior but still not exhibit the modeled behavior. Acquisition does not necessarily lead to performance. The fourth component of modeling, *motivational processes*, determines whether the outcome of a modeling experience is performance or nonperformance. Quite simply, modeling is likely to take place if the behavior has positive effects, rather than negative, or punishing, ones.

The positive value of the matched behavior can be determined in three ways. First, direct reinforcement can motivate a modeling effect. For example, a child may clean up the classroom the way the teacher does because the teacher praises him for doing so. Second, and more commonly, the source of motivation can be vicarious reinforcement, in which the learner's observation of the rewards or punishments the model receives acts as an incentive for the observer to model the behavior without direct reinforcement. For example, Arlo Guthrie may have patterned his singing after his father, Woody, because of the accolades he saw Woody receive for his artistry. A girl may become a voracious reader because of the apparent enjoyment she observes her mother receiving from books. Third, self-reinforcement, or evaluative reactions by the observer regarding his own behavior, may also affect modeling.

The four components of the modeling process form an interlocking system; all are necessary for modeling to take place. Thus, failure of an observer to match a model's behavior may result from one or more of the following: insufficient attention to the modeled events, inadequate processing and retention of the modeling stimuli, difficulties in reproducing the model's behavior, or weak motivation to enact the modeled behavior.

The four component processes are summarized in Figure 7-2. (Note that this scheme subsumes that presented in Figure 7-1.)

Bandura (1977b) contends that this modeling process is essentially the same for all observers and models. Children and adults, men and women, Democrats and Republicans—all will model behavior using the same processes. However, the particular contents of each component will vary. (For example, young children rely primarily on imaginal coding in retention, whereas adults rely primarily on verbal coding.) Moreover, the modeling process remains unaltered for a wide variety of modeling modalities. Live modeling, verbal modeling (written descriptions of behaviors, instructions, rules, and so on), and symbolic modeling (television, films), although they might vary in effectiveness, all produce modeling effects by means of the same processes. All require attention to and retention of the modeled event; all require reproducing the model's behavior; all require adequate motivation.

## Self constructs

The hallmark of Bandura's social learning theory is the emphasis on the cognitive activity of the learner. The modeling processes are imbued with concepts such as attention, symbolic coding, retention, self-observation, and self-reinforcement. The learner is an active processor of information and not a passive recipient of reinforcers.

Recently, Bandura (1977a, 1978) expanded his theory to include concepts of a self-system. The self-system has a unique relationship with the environment that Bandura terms *reciprocal determinism*. The self and the environment are interdependent, each influencing and regulating the other.

Two self-system concepts are critical for understanding the role of motivation in Bandura's theory: self-reinforcement and self-efficacy.

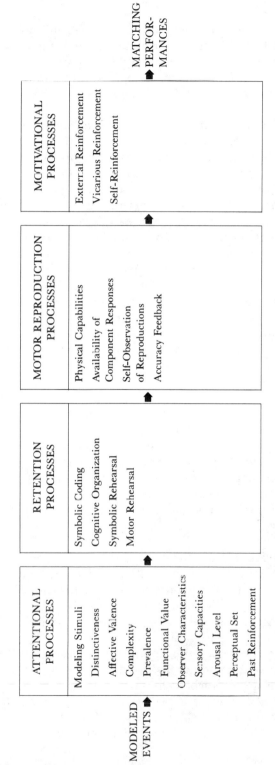

**Figure 7-2.** The four component processes of modeling. *(From Social Learning Theory, by A. Bandura. Copyright © 1977 by Prentice-Hall. Reprinted by permission.)*

**Self-reinforcement.** The concept of reciprocal determinism implies that an individual is not bound to the environment for reinforcement. Instead, a person can allocate his or her own rewards and punishments. A student, for example, can berate herself for not attaining a high grade on a term paper; a laborer can praise himself for a hard day's work.

The notion that one can self-reinforce indicates that one can motivate oneself as well. Behavior can be regulated, or managed, by the individual. The self-regulation processes are made up of three components: self-observation, judgmental processes, and self-response.

Self-observation is the process by which a person monitors and evaluates his or her own performance. Awareness of performance characteristics such as quality and quantity enables the learner to perceive standards and then create incentives to maintain or alter the behavior. For example, a musician may observe that he is playing a piece of music particularly well. The standard of performance is discerned through self-observation.

Judgmental processes constitute a logical next component of the self system, because these are the processes by which some standard for performance is selected and applied. Thus, the musician's observation of his performance may lead him to select a new standard based on his own experience, on the modeled behavior of a former teacher, or on some other criterion, but the quality of the performance in question is judged by the musician himself.

Self-response is the last self-regulatory process. In the self-response process, an observed performance is rewarded or punished by the person based on the person's judgment of whether the performance matched a selected standard. A near-perfect musical performance will lead the musician to feel good about himself, to feel competent and accomplished; a poor performance might lead to self-derogation.

These three components of the self-regulation process are summarized in Figure 7-3.

**Self-efficacy.** Bandura suggests that the motivation of behavior arises from the self-regulatory processes of observation, judgment, and response. However, the self-reinforcement concept does not provide a reason for why these processes are important. Bandura's (1977a) answer to this question is his concept of self-efficacy, or personal expectations of competence in a performance situation.

Bandura describes two classes of expectations: outcome expectations and efficacy expectations. Outcome expectations are defined as a person's probability estimate that a certain behavior will lead to certain outcomes (or reinforcements). An efficacy expectation is the person's estimate that he or she can perform the behavior required for the outcomes. The former is a knowledge of what to do; the latter is a judg-

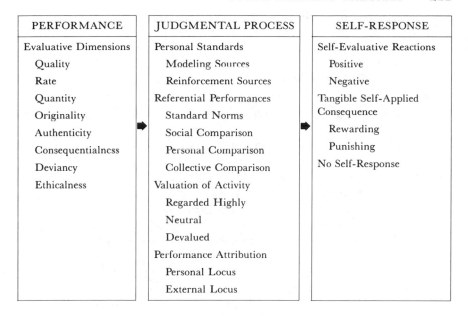

| PERFORMANCE | JUDGMENTAL PROCESS | SELF-RESPONSE |
|---|---|---|
| Evaluative Dimensions | Personal Standards | Self-Evaluative Reactions |
|   Quality |   Modeling Sources |   Positive |
|   Rate |   Reinforcement Sources |   Negative |
|   Quantity |   Referential Performances | Tangible Self-Applied |
|   Originality |     Standard Norms | Consequence |
|   Authenticity |     Social Comparison |   Rewarding |
|   Consequentialness |     Personal Comparison |   Punishing |
|   Deviancy |     Collective Comparison | No Self-Response |
|   Ethicalness |   Valuation of Activity | |
| |     Regarded Highly | |
| |     Neutral | |
| |     Devalued | |
| |   Performance Attribution | |
| |     Personal Locus | |
| |     External Locus | |

**Figure 7-3.** Component processes in self-regulation. *(From* Social Learning Theory, *by A. Bandura. Copyright © 1977 by Prentice-Hall. Reprinted by permission.)*

ment of whether it can be done. Efficacy expectations, in other words,
are an individual's beliefs regarding his or her mastery, competence,
and ability in any given situation. The individual's expectation of self-
efficacy, then, determines the person's level of motivation for performing a particular task.

Expectations of self-efficacy are based on four sources of information. *Performance accomplishments* affect efficacy expectations through
the retention in memory of personal successes and failures. A good musician expects to be able to master a new piece with practice. *Vicarious
experiences* affect expectations by the symbolic coding of previously
modeled activities. By observing a gymnastics teacher, for example, a
student might expect to be able to master a routine. *Verbal persuasion*
involves prompting, coaxing, praising, and so forth by others. It tends
to influence efficacy expectations only temporarily. An experienced
diver can persuade a novice to dive once off a 3-meter board by talking
about the excitement of the dive and by allaying the novice's fears, but
those persuasions probably would not convince the novice to use the 3-
meter board for the remainder of the summer. *Emotional arousal* can
be influential in determining expectations of self-efficacy, especially in
threatening situations in which fear and anxiety decrease the efficacy
expectations. Someone who is fearful of snakes would be able to approach a snake only if relaxed and free of anxiety. Of these four influ-

ences, performance accomplishments appear to be most effective in strengthening efficacy expectations (Bandura, Adams, & Meyer, 1977).

### Conclusions: Bandura

Bandura's social learning theory has made several significant contributions. First, like Rotter's theory, it is geared exclusively to understanding human learning and motivation in complex social environments. Second, the theory of reinforcement involves symbolic rewards. The anticipation of reinforcement and the vicarious experience of seeing a model reinforced are sufficient motivators for learning; a person need not be rewarded or punished as traditional theories of learning require. Third, Bandura strongly emphasizes cognitive processes. The modeling process is saturated with cognitive mediators such as attention and retention, and the theory clearly depicts the learner as an active processor of information from both present learning contexts and past experience. Fourth, Bandura's recent development of concepts and principles pertaining to the self is a logical extension of the theory's cognitive emphasis. Bandura conceptualizes the behavior of an individual as being largely self-regulated and determined by complex processes of observation, judgment, and response. Thus, people can reinforce themselves and therefore motivate their own behavior, their behavioral choices being determined chiefly by the individual's appraisal of self-efficacy.

At least two criticisms, however, can be directed at Bandura's social learning theory. First, although the theory is complex and persuasive, it appears to be largely descriptive, rather than explanatory. The principles and processes by which perceived information is coded and translated into behavior are not precisely explained, although they are thoroughly described. If not exactly forgivable, this is an understandable weak point given the relative newness of the theory. Bandura remains furthermore an active theorist (see, for example, 1977a, 1978a), and his theory is formulated to permit scientific investigation. Second, like other broad theories (such as Freud's), Bandura's theory can be faulted, ironically, for explaining too much. Almost any behavior in any situation can be explained after the fact, and the covert nature of the cognitive mediating variables gives them a plasticity that invites careless application. The concepts must be honed and the processes specified.

## *Research on aggression*

The analysis of aggression may well be the most important topic in motivational psychology. Four main approaches to this analysis have received substantial attention, some of which we have briefly mentioned in earlier chapters. We will briefly review the four approaches and then discuss the available evidence.

In the ethological approach (see Chapter 2), Lorenz and others point out that aggression plays an essential role in the lives of lower animals: it results in more even distribution of the species over the food source, more advantageous mating opportunities for the stronger members of the species, and higher survival probabilities for the species as a whole. Since humans are descended from these lower animals, we have inherited their aggressive tendencies. Aggression, then, is viewed as an instinct, inherent in every human. The need to perform instinctual acts is strong, and, if the act is postponed too long, vacuum behavior (behavior unrelated to the immediate situation) will occur.

In the psychoanalytic approach (see Chapter 3), Freud postulates a death instinct (Thanatos) that is manifested in aggression, including aggression toward oneself. Freud believed that the pressure of this instinct could be relieved by performing an aggressive act. Thus, aggression in this approach is the way in which the death instinct manifests itself in behavior.

The frustration-aggression approach represents an interesting hybrid of Freudian theory and learning theory and was formulated in 1939 by John Dollard and several of his colleagues. The core of this theory is straightforward: "aggression is always a consequence of frustration . . . and, contrariwise, the existence of frustration always leads to some form of aggression" (Dollard, Doob, Miller, Mowrer, & Sears, 1939, p. 1).

N. E. Miller's (1944) analysis of an approach/avoidance conflict (see Chapter 5) was an offshoot of this frustration-aggression hypothesis. Thus, the urge to aggress is represented by the approach gradient in Figure 5-8; the fear of punishment or retaliation for doing so is represented by the avoidance gradient. The target actually receiving aggression would be the person present at the point where the two gradients intersect.

The social learning approach leads one to predict that committing an aggressive act or even observing such an act would lead to an increase in aggression, particularly if the initial aggression was not punished. This is so because the initial aggression may disinhibit subsequent aggression or teach the person aggressive means of achieving desired ends.

### Catharsis versus social learning theory: The evidence

The ethological, Freudian, and frustration-aggression viewpoints all subscribe to the notion of catharsis; that is, they all assert that the tendency toward aggression can be relieved through an aggressive act. According to these viewpoints, commission or even observation of an act of aggression temporarily leads to a decrease in subsequent aggression.

Social learning theory, however, predicts that observing or committing an act of aggression would increase a person's subsequent aggressions. This would be particularly true, as mentioned earlier, if the original aggressive act went unpunished. A number of studies have been conducted that shed light on these conflicting viewpoints.

In this section, we will review their evidence. We begin with several pieces of evidence that have been cited in support of the frustration-aggression hypothesis and of Miller's related approach/avoidance analysis.

Perhaps the most famous piece of evidence is the high negative correlation between the price of cotton in 14 Southern states from 1882 to 1930 and the number of lynchings in those states during those years. The number of lynchings increased as the price of cotton dipped frustratingly low. Needless to say, those lynched were not responsible for the low price of cotton.

Fitz (1976) provided support for Miller's analysis of aggression by showing that angered subjects who were not afraid of their frustrator (low avoidance gradient) aggressed against the person who angered them more intensely than they aggressed against other targets. However, subjects who feared their frustrator (high avoidance gradient) aggressed most intensely against a displaced target.

Several other studies also have shown that frustration can lead to displaced aggression. For example, N. E. Miller and Bugelski (1948) denied campers an eagerly awaited trip to a local carnival. The campers then gave low ratings to two nationalities included on a questionnaire the campers filled out. The two nationalities had played no part in the cancellation of the trip to the carnival.

Although the frustration-aggression hypothesis has a great deal of support, the absolute nature of the main postulate ("frustration *always* leads to some form of aggression") quickly came under fire. Many theorists believed that there would be circumstances in which frustration would lead to a nonaggressive response. Typical of the early studies dealing with this point was an important one by Davitz (1952). Some groups of children were praised for competitive and aggressive behaviors; other groups were rewarded for constructive and cooperative behavior. Subsequently all children were frustrated by stopping a movie at the critical point in the story and by taking away the candy the children were devouring. Then all children participated in a free-play situation. In this situation, those previously praised for aggression acted aggressively, whereas those praised for cooperative behavior behaved constructively. The point of the Davitz study is that frustration does not *necessarily* lead to aggression. As we mentioned in Chapter 5, frustration energizes behavior; which behavior is energized, however, is largely determined by learning. This finding is, of course, entirely consistent with social learning theory.

A generation of more sophisticated tests of catharsis versus social learning theory began in the 1960s with experiments such as that of Hokanson and Shetler (1961). Subjects in this study were harassed and frustrated by an experimenter who posed either as an undergraduate or as a professor. Some of the harassed subjects subsequently had an opportunity to shock this pest. Hokanson and Shetler found that following harassment, the subjects showed an increase in blood pressure compared to the nonharassed control group. Those who were given an opportunity to aggress against (shock) their undergraduate-assailant then showed a pronounced drop in blood pressure; those who were not given the opportunity to aggress showed only a small decrease in blood pressure. However, those who aggressed against the professor-assailant showed only a slight increase in blood pressure compared to nonaggressing subjects. Since blood pressure is considered a measure of arousal, we may conclude from these facts that harassed subjects attacking the undergraduate-assailant experienced a decrease in arousal—that is, catharsis occurred. The finding that attacking a low-status person results in decreased arousal provided support for the catharsis hypothesis. Catharsis, however, did not occur for those subjects who attacked the higher status professor. This result is not consistent with catharsis theory.

Another result of this study not supportive of the catharsis viewpoint is that the arousal decreases following aggression occurred only in males (Hokanson & Edelman, 1966). According to the catharsis hypothesis, angered subjects who aggress should show a reduction in physiological arousal regardless of their sex. A crucial study by Hokanson, Willers, and Koropsak (1968) helps to explain why this did not occur. First, these experimenters showed that males exhibited a greater decrease in physiological arousal after they aggressed against a provocateur than after they made a prosocial response toward the provocateur. Conversely, females showed greater decreases in arousal following prosocial responses than following aggression. The experimenters then rewarded males for making prosocial responses and females for making aggressive responses. It should surprise no one that males and females later performed the behaviors for which they previously had been rewarded. What was very surprising, however, was that the reward resulted in females' showing arousal decreases following *aggression* and males' showing arousal decreases following *prosocial responses.* The reward caused each sex to reverse not only its mode of behavior but also *its pattern of physiological catharsis.*

In perhaps the most astounding study on this subject, Stone and Hokanson (1969) showed that, if subjects are rewarded for shocking themselves, they will eventually show *decreases* in physiological arousal following these self-administered shocks. Normally, shocking oneself does not lead to arousal decreases. The significance of this study lies in its demonstration of the power of anticipated reward over the occurrence of catharsis. The power of anticipated reward, of course, is a central tenet of social learning theory (see Figure 7-1).

Consider how social learning theory would explain the sex difference observed in catharsis. In general, males are more likely than females to have been rewarded for aggression. Males exhibit catharsis following aggression. Females, however, are generally socialized to be "nice." They exhibit catharsis following prosocial acts. These sex differences can be reversed merely by giving rewards for exhibiting the opposite behavior. The lack of catharsis following aggression toward a high-status person may be analyzed in the same way: rewards are unlikely to occur if you shock your professor. (Please remember that.)

A study that neatly depicts the application of both catharsis and social learning principles is one by Geen, Stonner, and Shope (1975). The study had several groups and several stages. First, some subjects were actually shocked by a confederate of the experimenter. Others were not shocked. Second, some subjects subsequently had the opportunity to shock the confederate, some saw the confederate shocked by the experimenter, and some merely waited while the confederate was not shocked. Finally, all subjects got to shock the confederate. Note that for some subjects this represented a second opportunity to shock the confederate. Catharsis theories would predict that those who have already shocked the confederate once would be the least likely group to give intense shocks during the second opportunity. In fact, the opposite occurred. Those who had given a shock earlier were the most punitive during their second chance. This contradicts catharsis theories, but it supports the disinhibition notion predicted by social learning theory: aggression facilitates further aggression. On the other hand, a blood-pressure index showed that those angered subjects who had a chance to shock the confederate on the first opportunity showed at that time a decrease in arousal greater than that shown by any other group. In other words, the physiological index supported the catharsis theories. The conclusion to be drawn from this complex study is a simple one: Aggression may make one temporarily more calm. It may make one feel better. It will not, however, lead to less aggression. Aggression leads to more aggression. The physiological data support the catharsis theories, but the behavioral data support social learning theory.

## Aggression and sports

The ethologist Konrad Lorenz once suggested that the risk of war between nations could be lessened if mankind's aggressive tendencies could be vented through less destructive activities. He suggested international sports competition to replace international military competition. The idea was simple: sports would provide a safe outlet for catharsis. Although Lorenz subsequently disavowed this idea, the issue lingers. Related to this is the notion that sports spectators vicariously undergo catharsis by watching others compete. What does the evidence show about sports participants and sports spectators undergoing catharsis during sports events?

First, we'll look at the data on the participants. Patterson (1974) gave high school football players a hostility test one week before and one week after the football season. Catharsis theories would predict that after smashing into people for a full season, the players should exhibit much less hostility after the season than before it. The opposite was true. Apparently, smashing into people disinhibits hostility.

Zillman, Katcher, and Milavsky (1972) had an experimenter anger subjects, some of whom then rode an exercise bicycle. Bicycle riding was presumed to be a tension-reducing activity that would provide a safe outlet for pent-up anger. All subjects then had the chance to shock the experimenter. The subjects who had performed the strenuous bicycle riding were most punitive, exactly the opposite of the catharsis theories' predictions. Several other studies support this result.

The findings of both the Patterson and the Zillman et al. studies are consistent with social learning theory. Other data pertaining to sports participants and observers also are supportive of social learning theory's principle that observing aggression can lead to aggression. M. D. Smith (1978) interviewed Canadian amateur hockey players and hockey spectators. Both groups were asked whether they had learned how to hit another player illegally from watching professional hockey. Table 7-2 presents the results. Observational learning apparently took place both in the participants and in the observers.

Goldstein and Arms (1971) attempted to assess whether football fans experienced any vicarious catharsis during the game. The researchers found that spectators were more hostile after the Army-Navy game

**TABLE 7-2.** Have you ever learned how to hit another player illegally in any way from watching professional hockey?

| Respondents | Learned how to hit illegally (%) | | |
| | Yes | No | Not sure |
| --- | --- | --- | --- |
| Players | 56.9 | 42.1 | 1.0 |
| Nonplayers | 55.3 | 44.1 | 0.7 |
| Total | | | |
| Percentage | 56.6 | 42.5 | 0.9 |
| Number | 426 | 320 | 7 |

From "Social Learning of Violence in Hockey," by M. D. Smith. In F. L. Smoll and R. E. Smith (Eds.), *Psychological Perspectives in Youth Sports*. Copyright © 1978 by Hemisphere Publishing Corporation, Washington, D.C. Reprinted by permission.

than before it, whether the spectator was for the winning team or the losing one. (Disinhibition of hostility does not depend on the final score.) However, there was no difference in hostility among the spectators before and after a gymnastics meet.

Participating in and watching aggressive sports may have benefits, but reducing aggression doesn't appear to be one of them.

## Television and aggression

Bandura is of the opinion that watching televised violence can lead to aggression. Thus, through observational learning effects and disinhibitory effects, a child may learn new aggressive behaviors from TV and can be disinhibited from performing aggressive behaviors already learned. We will present two categories of evidence relevant to Bandura's opinion. The first contains evidence on the short-term effects of televised violence. The second category deals with long-term effects.

**Short-term effects.**    Research in this category examines the influence of an aggressive film on immediately subsequent behavior. The results of a very large number of studies are fairly consistent: televised violence leads to increases in aggressive behaviors (Geen, 1976).

Drabman and Thomas (1974) performed a prototypic study. One group of third and fourth graders watched a violent cowboy film. A matched group did not. Then each subject was individually taken to a nearby area for further testing. Before the testing began, however, the experimenter said he'd have to do a few chores. The youngster was asked to monitor the behavior of two very young children playing in the next room while the experimenter was busy. All third and fourth graders were happy to accept this responsibility, which involved watching a closed circuit TV supposedly depicting the two children playing in the next room. There were in fact no children in the next room; a film was displayed on the TV monitor. During the film, a fight broke out between the two children with occasional catastrophes taking place as they continued to quarrel. The purpose of the experiment was to determine how long the third and fourth graders would wait before alerting the experimenter to the calamity next door. Those who saw the violent cowboy film waited much longer before seeking aid compared to those who had not seen the film.

Many other studies have given similar results. Liebert and Baron (1972), for example, showed some youngsters a 3.5-minute film of a track meet; another group saw a 3.5-minute violent sequence from a TV crime show. (To make the experimental films especially realistic, the experimenters sandwiched the films between some commercials.) Subjects who saw the violent film, compared to those who saw the nonviolent film, were more willing to hurt another child in a subsequent play session.

**Long-term effects.**    Bandura (1973) suggested that anxiety is conditioned to aggression through normal learning principles. If you see a great deal of aggression then while safely sitting in front of your TV, aggression may cease to cause you much anxiety. You may then be able to aggress more freely, because your inhibiting anxiety will be much lower.

Cline, Croft, and Courrier (1973) and Thomas, Horton, Lippincott, and Drabman (1977) examined physiological responses to televised violence of people who normally watched a lot of TV violence and those who did not. The Thomas et al. study began with the usual two groups employed in short-term studies; one saw a violent film and one saw a nonviolent film. The subjects, 8- to 10-year-old children, then were asked to keep an eye on the young children next door by watching the TV monitor, just as was done in the Drabman and Thomas (1974) study described earlier. The subjects' physiological responses were monitored during the experiment. Those who first watched the violent film showed less arousal at the (simulated) bloodshed among the two youngsters than did those who first saw the nonviolent film. In addition, those children who had reported watching a lot of violent TV shows were in general less aroused during the violent episodes in the experiment. Thus it was concluded that habitual watching of TV violence has the long-term effect of lowering one's arousal to aggression. Bandura's (1973) analysis of aggression would lead us to suggest that those who have less anxiety about aggression will be more likely to engage in it.

Other long-term studies have looked at actual aggressive behavior, rather than physiological indices. Friedrich and Stein (1973) and Parke, Berkowitz, Leyens, West, and Sebastian (1977) used similar procedures. Children of various ages were exposed to aggressive or nonaggressive films for several days or weeks. Behavior was assessed during a subsequent period. In general, those who saw the aggressive films behaved more aggressively during these subsequent periods. Some studies (for example, Milgram & Shotland, 1973), however, have failed to replicate this result.

All of the aggression studies mentioned so far have been experimental studies in which the experimenter does one thing to one group (shows a violent film) and something else to another group (shows a nonviolent film). If the groups differ on some score or behavior, we may confidently attribute their different behavior to the fact that the experimenter treated the two groups differently; that is, we attribute the differences in their behavior to the differences in the films they saw.

In studies investigating long-term effects, however, this experimental design is difficult to use. It is unethical, for example, to ask one group of parents to raise children on a steady diet of violent TV shows and another group to raise their children on a diet of nonviolent shows.

Therefore, most long-term studies do not manipulate the amount of violence viewing in the subjects but instead recruit subjects, some of whom already watch a great deal of TV violence and some of whom do not. However, children who differ in the amount of TV violence they watch may also differ on other factors as well. For example, the high-violence viewers could be of higher or lower intelligence than the low-violence viewers. If these two groups then differ in the amount of violence they engage in, can we attribute this difference to their differential TV-violence viewing? Of course not. Intelligence may be the key factor. We can't be sure. Therefore, we must interpret the following long-term studies with some caution.

Both of the following studies were cited in the 1972 Surgeon General's Report dealing with television and violence. We recommend this report to anyone seriously interested in the subject.

Lefkowitz, Eron, Walder, and Huesmann (1972) found that the violence level of TV programs preferred by third graders was significantly related to the amount of aggression these children were exhibiting up to ten years later. Dominick and Greenberg (1972) found that the amount of TV violence viewed was related to how willing young boys and girls were to use violence and how effective they thought it would be in getting what they wanted. The findings of these two studies are cause for particular concern; as Gerbner (1969) has reported, one week of prime-time TV can contain 400 murders.

**Summary.**   In recent years social learning theory has dominated the research on aggression and violence. The research findings show that exposure to real violence or filmed violence appears to facilitate the expression of violence. Both the expression of newly witnessed means of violence and the expression of violent acts already in one's repertoire are more likely to occur following the observation of violence by others. There are qualifications to this conclusion, however. As Bandura predicts, if the aggressive model is punished, the facilitative effect is less likely to take place. Furthermore, the evidence on long-term effects is not quite as conclusive as the evidence on short-term effects. This is a result mainly of the methodological difficulties inherent in long-term studies.

## Pornography and aggression

In Chapter 2 we presented evidence that pornography causes increases in physiological arousal and results in temporary increases in customary sexual behavior. In recent years there has been concern that pornography may bear a causal relation to violence, particularly violence against women. In this section we present the most recent evidence.

We begin by noting that there is a difference between scientific evidence and what is called evidence in the popular press. If a sex offender is found to have a great deal of pornography in his home, this fact is occasionally cited as evidence that pornography causes aggression. An equally plausible explanation is that some other factor—perhaps the attitude of the offender's father toward women—may have precipitated both the interest in pornography and the violence. The pornography, like the violence, may be an effect, not a cause. The mere correlation between pornography and aggression is therefore not in itself conclusive scientific evidence that pornography *causes* aggression.

One difficulty encountered in examining the evidence on the effects of pornography is that so much of the evidence appears contradictory. Sometimes exposure to explicit erotic stimuli appears to inhibit subsequent aggression (for example, Baron, 1974a, 1974b; Baron & Bell, 1977; Frodi, 1977). At other times it appears to facilitate later aggression (for example, Baron, 1977; Donnerstein & Barrett, 1978; Donnerstein, Donnerstein, & Evans, 1975). Some researchers (see Mosher, 1971a, 1971b) have even found that exposure to sexually explicit material doesn't appear to have any effect on subsequent behavior in terms of exploitative behavior, verbal aggressiveness, or exploitative attitudes toward women.

Out of this mass of conflicting data have evolved a few theories to explain the discrepancies. Donnerstein et al. (1975) suggest that pornography has two influences. First, it causes increases in arousal, which may facilitate later aggression (Bandura, 1973). Second, pornography may cause attentional shifts: because of its high attention-getting properties, pornography may postpone or eliminate any thinking about aggression or retaliation. Donnerstein et al. (1975) suggest that mild pornography has more "attentional shift" value than arousal value and therefore would inhibit aggression. Stronger pornography would have relatively more arousal value than "attentional shift" value and therefore would facilitate aggression. Baron and Bell (1977) provided lukewarm support for this theory. In their study, mild pornography did indeed inhibit aggression, but more explicit pornography had no real effect. Baron and Bell (1977) suggested that, had their erotic material been more arousing, it might have produced the facilitation in aggression predicted by Donnerstein et al. (1975).

A related theory by L. A. White (1979) also has received some support. White hypothesized that pornography leading to positive affect causes subsequent decreases in aggression, whereas pornography leading to negative affect causes subsequent increases in aggression. If mild pornography causes positive affect and "hard core" pornography causes negative affect, then the Donnerstein et al. (1975) theory would make the same predictions as White's (1979) theory would. Also consistent with White's theory is a report by Baron (1979) that females *increased* their aggressiveness after viewing erotic scenes that had caused a *decrease* in aggressiveness in males (Baron & Bell, 1977).

The females rated the scenes as unpleasant, whereas the males rated them as pleasant, just as White would predict. White's theory may be the best guess to date as to why pornography sometimes facilitates and sometimes inhibits later aggression.

One relatively recent finding (Donnerstein & Barrett, 1978) is that, when pornography causes an increase in aggression, the increased aggression is directed equally against victims of either sex. This result is consistent with a few different theories, one of which hypothesizes that pornography increases the strength of any behavior, because it boosts general drive, à la Hull. An angered subject who is shown pornographic material and who remains angry may, when given a chance to retaliate against his annoyer, be more aggressive than before because of his increased drive, regardless of the sex of the annoyer.

One interesting feature of the Donnerstein and Barrett (1978) study was that physiological arousal among males aggressing against a female annoyer was quite high and that this arousal persisted after the aggression. Yet, the males were not more aggressive toward the female target than toward male targets. Donnerstein and Barrett hypothesized that general societal disapproval of aggression against females may have prevented the males from manifesting the higher level of aggression against females consistent with the males' high level of arousal. (Recall Bandura's (1973) maxim that anticipated punishment would decrease the likelihood of a response.)

Donnerstein and Hallam (1978) used two shock situations to overcome this factor. They assumed that following the first opportunity to aggress, males would have fewer inhibitions against administering electric shock to a female. After all, following the original aggression, nobody was going to express disapproval of the males. Given a second opportunity to aggress, the effect of prior pornography on aggression would be freer from the prohibition against hurting females. The exact procedure was as follows: Half the subjects were paired with a male confederate, half with a female confederate. The male subjects received shocks from the confederate, purportedly for the poor job the subject did in writing an essay. Subjects then spent 3.5 minutes watching an aggressive film, a pornographic film, or no film. Then the subjects were given an opportunity to administer shocks to the confederate who had shocked them. Ten minutes later a second opportunity to retaliate occurred. Figure 7-4 depicts the intensity of shock during the immediate-retaliation and delayed-retaliation sessions.

During the immediate retaliation session, those who saw either film gave more shocks than those who saw no film. The sex of the target made no significant difference. During the second session, during which the men presumably would have fewer inhibitions against hurting a woman (since they'd already done it once), both film-watching

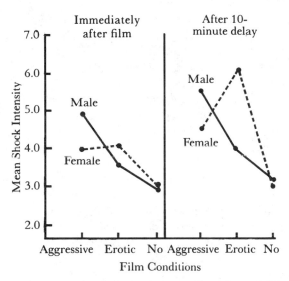

**Figure 7-4.** Average shock intensity as a function of film conditions, sex of target, and time of aggression opportunity. *(From "Facilitating Effects of Erotica on Aggression against Women," by E. Donnerstein and J. Hallam. In* Journal of Personality and Social Psychology, *1978, 36, 1270–1277. Copyright 1978 by the American Psychological Association. Reprinted by permission.)*

groups again showed aggression increases, but the pornographic-film group showed particularly large aggression increases when the target was a woman.

There was another interesting result of this study. The male subjects rated the pornographic film near the midpoint on a 5-point scale of aggressiveness. Since the pornographic film was chosen by the experimenters to be free of aggressive cues, there exists the possibility that the sexual behaviors by the men in the film were perceived by the experimental subjects as inherently somewhat aggressive. If such is the case—that is, if sexual behavior in pornographic films is seen as a form of aggression—then the research on the effects of viewing aggression on subsequent aggressive behavior becomes relevant to the research on the effects of viewing pornography on subsequent aggressive behavior.

The relation between aggression and pornography was rather directly investigated in another study by Donnerstein (1980). Since there is some evidence that recent pornography contains a great deal of violence toward women, Donnerstein contrasted this violent type of pornography with less aggressive pornography. The experiment was otherwise similar to prior ones. Male subjects were first either angered or treated in a neutral manner. After then being shown either an aggressive-erotic, erotic, or neutral film, they were given the chance to deliver shocks to either a male or a female. The aggressive-erotic film resulted in increased shocks, particularly when the victim was a female. This study also had an interesting additional finding: even non-angered subjects showed increased hostility toward females after viewing the aggressive-erotic film. In prior research, the effect of erotic films was often limited to subjects who had been angered. The increased aggression toward females following the viewing of the aggressive-erotic film is entirely consistent with what we might expect from observational learning effects.

**Summary.**   Our conclusions about the relationship between pornography and aggression must be tentative since the evidence is not complete. Pornography has been shown to have inconsistent effects on subsequent aggression. Factors determining the nature of the effect may include whether the viewer's affective reaction is positive or negative and whether the pornography is mild or hard core. However, the facilitative effect of pornography on subsequent aggression appears to be more likely if (1) the subject is angered, (2) the subject has lessened inhibitions against hurting the target, and (3) the pornography has aggressive content.

Note that, in both the pornography research and the general aggression research, the principles of social learning theory are prevalent. Observational learning effects and disinhibition effects are measured, and the anticipated punishment of the aggressor is manipulated. In these important areas of research, social learning theory provides the tools of the trade.

## Conclusions and critique: Rotter and Bandura

The social learning theories of Rotter and Bandura show several strong points. Both theorists have applied reasonable scientific standards to theory development and validation. Consequently, each is afforded stature from a behavioral-science perspective. Research has been persistent and vigorous, resulting in successful extensions of the theories in new areas. Applications have also been numerous, especially in clinical areas pertaining to behavior change and psychotherapy.

Common sense tells us that motivational variables are covert and internal. Both Rotter and Bandura, however, have derived mediating variables that are uniquely human without the encumbrances of drive and instinct constructs. Variables such as attention and expectancy have advantages for explaining motivation in that they are neither biological nor unconscious. Motivation can therefore be conceptualized as involving *choice and awareness*. Bandura's concepts of self-reinforcement and self-efficacy epitomize these assumptions regarding human motivation. Curiously, these social learning theorists appear to have summoned back to the field of motivation those issues pertaining to free will and the like.

The major pitfall of social learning theories appears to be an unavoidable one. The emphasis on cognitive mediating variables carries with it a predictable dilemma: that which cannot be observed cannot be precisely defined and measured. Concepts such as expectancy have been roundly criticized (see, for example, Wilkins, 1977) for this reason. Still, the problem appears to be one of degree. Bandura's concept of symbolic coding clearly has more meaning and expectancy power than Freud's concept of primary-process thinking. Since hypothetical constructs and intervening variables constitute the fiber of motivation constructs, the goal of theory development should be to approximate the greatest clarity and precision possible. The theories of Rotter and Bandura are commendable representatives of this viewpoint. "Empty-organism" or "black-box" theories such as Skinner's, devoid of covert concepts and processes, lack viable concepts of motivation.

Although social learning theories certainly differ sharply from the radical behaviorism of Skinner, they also are far more cognitive than even the neobehaviorism of Hull. In social learning theory, reinforcement may be symbolic or vicarious, and a person's expectations concerning reward are important. Social learning theory assumes that the organism does not play as passive a role as Hullian theory would lead us to believe. Since the social learning organism is not pushed and pulled merely by biologically derived drives and incentives, social learning theory has a far broader range of application than Hullian theory. As a result, it has become very influential in such diverse areas as child-rearing techniques, the influences of television, and therapy.

# CHAPTER 8

# Field Theory: The Contributions of Kurt Lewin

*S-R theories do well in predicting stupid be-havior, but are much less convincing in predicting intelligent behavior.*[1]

*Neal Miller*

Kurt Lewin greatly influenced psychology in several ways. First, his theorizing spanned a wide range of topics, including social conflicts, personality theory, child development, group dynamics, learning, and cross-cultural research. Far more than any other psychologist of his generation, Lewin sought to apply psychology to the pressing needs of society, such as conflict resolution and the understanding of prejudice. Because this text deals solely with issues in motivation, however, only those portions of Lewin's theorizing relevant to motivation will be discussed in this chapter.

Second, Lewin is important in that his ideas profoundly influenced the motivational theorists who followed him. Theorists such as Atkinson, Festinger, and Heider, who are discussed in later chapters, all were influenced by Lewinian theory.

Finally, Lewin is important because he was one of the most prominent advocates of Gestalt psychology. Because his theory stressed motivational topics, however, he was unique among Gestalt theorists. Nevertheless, his basic viewpoint was heavily influenced by the traditional Gestalt psychologists with whom he was associated early in his career. For that reason, we shall briefly introduce some principles of Gestalt psychology in order to give the reader an idea of the philosophy that influenced Lewin.

## Background: Principles of Gestalt theory

Max Wertheimer founded Gestalt theory in 1912, and the publication of books by Köhler (1929) and Koffka (1924) more than a decade later introduced the theory to American psychologists. Both books challenged the trial-and-error theory of Thorndike (1911) as the true description of learning. Thorndike's puzzle-box experiments were ridiculed as being artificial and (pardon the expression) stupid. The

[1]From "Some Reflections on the Law of Effect Produce a New Alternative to Drive Reduction," by Neal Miller. In M. R. Jones (Ed.), *Nebraska Symposium on Motivation, 1963.* Copyright 1963 by the University of Nebraska Press. Reprinted by permission.

reason the cat inside the puzzle box took so many trials and errors to escape is that Thorndike set up the situation so that the solution was impossible to perceive. There is no logical connection between pulling a wire loop and being released from a box, yet pulling the loop was the only "solution" to Thorndike's puzzle box. Thus, argued the Gestaltists, the cat had to "learn" the solution in a stupid, trial-and-error manner.

Gestalt theorists emphasized insight, rather than trial-and-error learning. They believed that in a normal learning situation the entire problem and solution are accessible to the subject's perception. Solution occurs when the subject can perceptually and cognitively organize the situation properly. Insight is this organizing of the field in order to solve the problem. Only in artificial situations such as Thorndike's, when the subject cannot possibly perceive all relevant aspects, does trial-and-error learning occur. This attack on Thorndike and behaviorism by the Gestalt psychologists began a vigorous theoretical feud in the United States.

One of the central tenets of Gestalt psychology is that the whole is greater than the sum of its parts. This principle reveals the Gestalt emphasis on looking at the whole field, rather than at individual elements. For example, in Figure 8-1, the same element is seen as "13" or as "B," depending on its surroundings. Analysis of the individual element, taken out of context, would not reveal its identity. Only consideration of the entire field would reveal whether the element was a letter or a number.

## Principles of Lewin's field theory

### Interaction of person and environment

Behaviorists such as Watson and Hull emphasized environmental stimuli and de-emphasized the individual in the determination of human behavior. Lewin, however, proposed that behavior is a function of both the person and the environment. His famous equation $B = f(P,E)$ reflects this belief. Lewin maintained that different people exposed to

$$\text{ABC}$$

$$\text{12B14}$$

**Figure 8-1.** The same stimulus is perceived differently, depending on its relation to the entire field.

identical environmental situations might act differently. Although Lewin would agree with behaviorists that a person is a function of his or her environment, $P = f(E)$, he would also say that the environment is a function of the person, $E = f(P)$. For example, one of the authors perceives his grandfather's homemade horseradish as a chemical to be used for unclogging drainpipes. The author's father sees the same stuff as one of the most delicious foods he's ever tasted. Thus, the same environmental stimulus can be perceived differently by different people.

Lewin used the term *lifespace* to denote all the contemporaneous factors, both internal and external, that can influence a person's behavior. All irrelevant factors—those that do not influence behavior—lie outside what Lewin termed "the foreign hull" (a slam at Clark Hull). Lewin represented the lifespace as a closed geometric figure, as in Figure 8-2.

Within the lifespace are the person (P) and various regions toward or away from which the person might move. For example, as you sit at home studying, you might consider leaving the region of lifespace in which you are located (S). You might choose to take a nap, thereby moving toward region N of your lifespace. Or, you might choose to raid the refrigerator (R), go to the library (L), or enter some other region in your lifespace.

Psychological space, however, is different from physical space. You can remain right where you are, yet choose to perform any of several activities. As you sit studying, you are in region S of your lifespace. You can stop studying and begin daydreaming, thereby entering region D of your lifespace, even though physically you haven't moved. Physical space and psychological space ("hodological space" in Lewin's terminology) do not perfectly coincide. A primary reason they do not is that a person is unaware of many aspects of the surrounding physical space. Therefore, those aspects cannot influence the choice of behavior; they are not included in the person's lifespace.

In defining *lifespace,* Lewin mentions only *contemporaneous* factors,

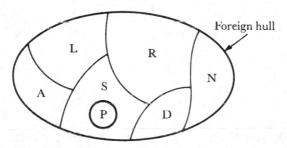

**Figure 8-2.** Lewin's representation of a lifespace. *(Adapted from* Principles of Topological Psychology, *by K. Lewin. Copyright 1936 by McGraw-Hill, Inc. Reprinted by permission.)*

aspects of the person's internal and external environment that are present now. Lewin, like most Gestalt theorists, is ahistorical. Whereas theorists such as Freud or Thorndike were extremely interested in knowing past behavior in order to predict present behavior, Lewin believed that the past was reflected in the present. If a psychologist can determine what a person's feelings are toward all regions in the lifespace right now, it will be of no further use to determine what occurred in the past to engender those feelings. Knowledge of childhood experiences, or reinforcement history, is not necessary if current motivational influences can be accurately assessed. Furthermore, the current lifespace will undergo modification as a person interacts with his or her environment in a continuous stream of behavior.

## The directedness of behavior

According to Lewin, behavior within a lifespace is directed. Several classes of behavior are available to an individual, and all have the property of directedness.

The first class of behavior is behavior directed toward some other region of the lifespace. If a person is presently doing the dishes (D), for example, and then goes back to watch TV, we can describe the behavior as having the direction from D to TV. Lewin would represent this direction as $d_{D,TV}$.

Another class of behavior is behavior directed toward that region of the lifespace in which one is already located. The behavior of a person engrossed in a jigsaw puzzle (J) is directed from J to J. This is represented as $d_{J,J}$.

A third class of behavior is behavior directed away from the region in which one is presently located but not toward any specific other region. If a private is assigned to KP duty by his sergeant, he is interested in moving from the region of his lifespace in which he is located (KP) to any other region ($-$KP). This is represented as $d_{KP,-KP}$.

A fourth class of behavior is behavior directed away from some remote portion of the lifespace. If the private is now standing on the highway (H) with his thumb out, having gone AWOL to escape KP, the direction of his behavior is $d_{H,-KP}$, or away from KP, which is a portion of his lifespace that the private is no longer occupying.

These four classes exhaust all types of behavior a person may exhibit.

## Force

Because Lewin conceived of all behavior as being directed, the forces that cause a person to actually *move* in the four directions described above play a paramount role in his theory. These forces are Lewin's motivational constructs.

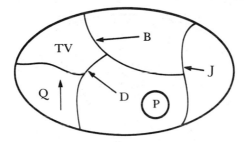

**Figure 8-3.** Watching TV is the goal for a person presently doing the dishes.

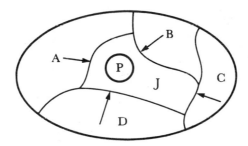

**Figure 8-4.** A person engrossed in a jigsaw puzzle does not want to leave that region of the lifespace.

Since all behavior is directed, force in Lewinian theory is represented by a vector—an arrow in Lewin's lifespace diagrams. A force from region A to region B is represented by an arrow pointing in the appropriate direction, the length of the arrow representing the magnitude of the force. Figure 8-3 represents the lifespace of a person who wants to watch TV. Figures 8-4, 8-5, and 8-6 represent the three other general types of directed behavior.

A force can be calculated for each region of the lifespace. However, the force actually influencing a person is the force in the region of the lifespace in which the person is presently located. In order to calculate force, three variables must be taken into account: valence, distance, and tension.

**Valence (V).**    Any region in the lifespace toward which a person is attracted has positive valence. Any region in the lifespace from which the person is repelled has negative valence. Lewin made no statement about any universal cause of positive valence, such as drive reduction. He did say, however, that factors such as the quantity or quality of the goal certainly influence its valence. We shall let G stand for quantity and quality of the goal.

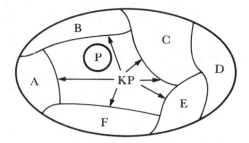

**Figure 8-5.** A person doing KP wants to leave that region of the lifespace.

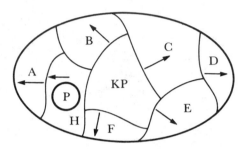

**Figure 8-6.** A person in region H fleeing from KP duty.

**Distance (e).**[2]    The magnitude of a force is directly related to the magnitude of the valence, but it is inversely related to the distance between the person and the valented object. For example, if the distance between a child and the ice-cream cone she wants is small, the force toward the cone is huge; if the distance is immense, the force is small. Even if the real distance is great, a person might—because of overconfidence or optimism—perceive the distance as small. Remember, too, that Lewin always refers to psychological, not physical, distance.

**Tension (t).**    Before presenting Lewin's concept of tension, we must briefly touch on some of his ideas concerning personality. Lewin believed that, like the environment, the person (P) contained a large number of regions. Even though P appears as a circle in Figures 8-3 through 8-7, when Lewin was discussing inner-personal topics, P was always drawn in the same subdivided fashion in which the lifespace was drawn. Each region within P thus corresponds to one aspect of P's personality.
    Whenever a person has a need, desire, or intention, some area of the

---

[2]The "e" stands for the German word for "distance," *Entfernung*.

personality is in a state of tension. If you are hungry, one region is in a state of tension; if you want to find the book you misplaced, another region is in a state of tension. As soon as the goal is attained, the tension is dissipated.

Tension has several important properties. First, *it induces valence in the environment*. The fruit in the refrigerator, for example, has no valence until an appropriate area of the personality is in a state of tension. Second, tension is nondirectional. Force—which combines tension, valence, and distance—is directional, but tension is not. Tension is the motor of the motivational apparatus, not the steering wheel. Third, tension occurs as the result of needs, either biological or nonbiological. The nonbiological needs, called "quasi-needs," make Lewin's use of the concept "tension" much broader than Hull's use of "drive." For example, the intent to finish a task creates tension, as does the desire to solve a problem.

**The calculation of force.**     Now that we have enumerated the three determinants of force, we can present Lewin's formal equation. *Force is defined as follows:*

$$\text{force} = f\left(\frac{\text{valence}}{\text{distance}}\right) - f\left(\frac{\text{goal properties, tension}}{\text{distance}}\right) = f\left(\frac{G,t}{e}\right)$$

This equation says that force is directly proportional to the valence of the goal and inversely proportional to the distance from the goal. Furthermore, since valence is determined both by tension and by properties of the goal (such as its quality), force can also be said to be directly proportional to tension and goal properties.

Since valence can be negative, force can be negative. For example, if a dangerous animal is in the lifespace, force toward that region of the lifespace will be negative; there will be a force vector pushing the person away from that valented object. For both positive and negative valences, as the distance from the valented object decreases, the force (either attraction or repulsion) increases.

The numerator of the equation, force $= f\left(\frac{G,t}{e}\right)$, serves as a good illustration of how Lewin's system combines organismic and environmental variables. Tension is a nondirected organismic variable. Valence is a property of an object located in the environment. Valence draws its value (its sign and some of its magnitude) from the person's tension. Unlike tension, force is directed; specifically, it is directed from the organism to the valented object. However the connection between the organism and the object is not rigid, as is the connection between the stimulus and the response in the "habit" of the Hullian system. For example, Figure 8-7 represents the lifespace of a child en route from his home (A) to a candy store (G). If an obstruction (snarling dog)

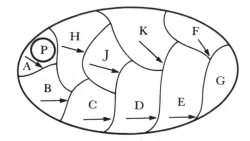

**Figure 8-7.** An unexpected obstruction in C would cause the person to choose an alternate route.

occurs in region C, the child may take any of several detours around the obstruction. Thus, force causes directed behavior; it does not cause the execution of an S-R habit, which can be altered only by further learning. The inflexibility of learned S-R bonds is avoided in Lewin's system. Consequently, Lewin's lifespace bears more resemblance to Tolman's "cognitive maps" than to Hull's chain of S-R bonds.

In summary, force is directly related to valence and inversely related to psychological distance. Tension induces valence, and it is valence that guides behavior (Heider, 1960).

## *Lewinian analysis of traditional motivational topics*

### The goal gradient

Hull had hypothesized (1932, p. 26) that the goal reaction ($R_G$) becomes most strongly conditioned to those stimuli closest to the goal and progressively less strongly conditioned to stimuli farther from the goal. This differential conditioning, Hull said, was the chief cause of the goal gradient, which is manifested in more rapid locomotion as the animal approaches the goal.

Lewin had an extremely simple explanation for the goal gradient. His force formula states that force increases as distance from the goal decreases. As the goal is neared, therefore, force increases. Consequently, vigor of responding and speed of response also increase.[3]

### The Yerkes/Dodson law

The Yerkes/Dodson law states that difficult tasks are done best under low drive and easy tasks are done best under high drive. Chapter 5 detailed the Hull/Spence explanation of this law.

---

[3]Lewin (1938, pp. 165–167) qualified this statement. Variables other than force influence speed. Lewin mentioned the physical details of the situation: friction, inertia, work. For example, is a person running in sand or running on concrete? Such variables certainly influence the force/speed relation, and Lewin believed they were not trivial.

The Yerkes and Dodson results (1908) can also be explained by field-theory principles. According to Lewin or any of the other Gestalt theorists, problem solving occurs by a restructuring of the total situation. If the person can view the total field, insight into the solution will occur. If force is too great, however, the person will not survey the situation carefully. Hence, the insight needed to solve the problem will not be achieved, and learning will be retarded. For very easy problems, surveying only part of the field may be adequate to yield insight. Strong force will be helpful. On difficult tasks, where a careful survey is needed, strong force will be detrimental. For example, Lewin (1935, p. 83) cites the *umweg*, or "detour," problem. A barrier is placed between a young child (P) and some attractive goal (G), such as a toy. Figure 8-8 illustrates this situation. The force is directed toward the toy, so the child approaches the barrier. In order to obtain the toy, however, the child has to turn *away* from the toy and proceed around the barrier. The more attractive the toy is, the higher is the valence. The higher the valence, the higher the force *toward* the barrier. Thus Lewin correctly predicts that this difficult problem (for a young child) is made more difficult by a greater positive valence, which causes a more than optimal level of motivation.

### Increased locomotion under deprivation

Hull was influenced by the research of Richter (1927), who found that, when stomach contractions occurred in a rat, the rat would become quite restless. Hull believed that this result lent support to his belief that drive was a general energizer. Lewin interpreted the result differently.

According to Lewin, as hunger increases, tension increases. Tension normally induces valence in some appropriate goal object in the lifespace. If—as in Richter's study—there is no appropriate goal object, the animal has no force *toward* any goal object. As the animal becomes increasingly uncomfortable in its present lifespace region, however, it

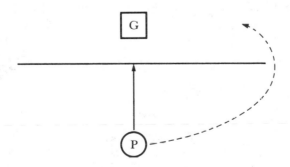

**Figure 8-8.** The *umweg*, or detour, problem.

develops force to leave that region; that is, $f_{A, -A}$ increases, rather than $f_{A,X}$ toward some particular region X in which there is a positively valented object. This force to leave A is manifested in increased restlessness as the animal tries to escape from its present lifespace region.

## Displacement

Freud documented the defense mechanism of displacement, which consists in the substitution of one goal object for another. The teacher, for example, who cannot physically punish her cantankerous pupils may vent her anger on her own children instead. Lewin treated displacement at great length, but he called the phenomenon "substitution."

Assume that a man wishes to play golf. The appropriate inner-personal region will have tension, and the appropriate goal object in the environment will have positive valence. If, owing to an unseasonable monsoon, the man cannot play golf, the goal is not achieved and the tension persists. However, the tension can seep out of the inner-personal region where it originated and enter adjacent regions. (The inner-personal regions are arranged in Lewin's scheme so that regions corresponding to similar activities are always adjacent and are separated by permeable boundaries.) An inner-personal region corresponding to practice-putting on the living-room rug may then receive some tension, and the new appropriate goal object will therefore acquire substitute valence. Putting on the rug will therefore dissipate some of the tension generated by the desire to play golf.

Lewin distinguishes between substitute valence and substitute value. Putting on the rug has substitute valence. Now, if the rain suddenly stops and the man is able to golf, will he do so? If he no longer wishes to golf, putting on the rug can be said to have substantial substitute value. Not only did our golfer choose that substitute activity, but its performance dissipated so much of the original tension that he does not attempt the original activity when it becomes possible to do so. Substitute value is typically assessed by just such a resumption test; to the extent that the alternate activity has substitute value, the original activity will not be resumed. It can be seen that Freud's "displacement" and Lewin's "substitution" are very similar.

## New motivational phenomena investigated within the Lewinian framework

### The Zeigarnik effect

Before you read on any further, get a pencil and paper and take the ten-item test on page 237. You ought to be able to do pretty well on it. Time yourself; allow only 20 seconds for each of the ten tasks. If you finish one task early, you cannot go back and work on previous tasks.

1. English cities. Name any three cities in England.
   a.
   b.
   c.
2. Continents. Name any five of the seven continents of the world.
   a.
   b.
   c.
   d.
   e.
3. Constellations. Name any four constellations.
   a.
   b.
   c.
   d.
4. Books of the Bible. Name any three of the first five books of the Bible.
   a.
   b.
   c.
5. Diseases. Name any three diseases beginning with S.
   a.
   b.
   c.
6. Vegetables. Name any four vegetables beginning with C.
   a.
   b.
   c.
   d.
7. South American capitals. Name any four capitals of South American countries.
   a.
   b.
   c.
   d.
8. Campus buildings. Name any four buildings on your campus.
   a.
   b.
   c.
   d.
9. European countries. Name any five countries in Europe.
   a.
   b.
   c.
   d.
   e.
10. Governors. Name the last three governors of your state.
   a.
   b.
   c.

Now turn the page for further instructions.

Your task now is to recall the ten tasks you've just been asked to do. Write on a separate sheet. Take no more than 30 seconds. Jot down the names of the tasks, not the correct answers. You need not get the name exactly right. If you recall having been asked to name ten friends, just write "friends." After you've recalled the tasks that come to mind, stop. Don't bother trying to dredge up the tasks that are difficult to recall. Just write down the ones that are easiest to recall.

Now go back and score your ten tasks. Mark each task either "completed" or "incomplete," depending on whether you were able to finish the task in the time allowed.

Now calculate two ratios: (1) number of incomplete tasks you were able to recall divided by the total number of incomplete tasks; (2) number of completed tasks you were able to recall divided by the total number of completed tasks.

Lewin predicts that ratio 1 is bigger than ratio 2. How did his prediction turn out in your case? (If it didn't work, there are several explanations, which we will offer later.)

Greater recall of unfinished than of finished tasks is called "the Zeigarnik effect." Lewin's student Bluma Zeigarnik (1927) tested this hypothesis of greater recall in a series of several experiments. The prediction is based on Lewin's concept of tension. Lewin (1951) lists the assumptions underlying the Zeigarnik effect: (1) The intention to reach a certain goal (such as listing English cities) corresponds to tension in some region of the personality. (2) The tension is released when the goal is reached. (3) Tension leads not only to actual movement toward the goal but also to thinking about the goal. Therefore, if a goal is reached, the tension dissipates, and the person thinks about it no longer. If the goal is not reached, the tension persists, and the thought of the goal remains. Now, if asked to recall the tasks, the subject has uppermost in mind those goals he or she did not reach, because tension persists only for unfinished tasks. Consequently, there is greater recall for unfinished tasks; this is the Zeigarnik effect.

The magnitude of the Zeigarnik effect is extremely sensitive to several variables. A few are obvious. One is effort: A subject who is very involved in the ten tasks—who is trying hard to generate English cities, continents, and so on—will naturally have greater tension. The unfinished tasks will therefore be nagging the subject vividly. Recall for them will be high, and the Zeigarnik effect will be larger. If the subject is not trying very hard to complete the ten tasks, the effect will be smaller.

Another important variable is the amount of pressure to recall. (This "induced pressure" is most difficult to control when the ten tasks are administered without personal contact, as was done here.) If the subject is threatened with great bodily harm should all ten tasks not be recalled, then there is great pressure to recall *both* finished and unfinished tasks. Let RU equal the normal recall rate for the unfinished tasks (50%). Let RF equal the normal recall rate for the finished tasks (25%). The Zeigarnik effect will be 50%/25% = 2.00. Now, assume that the experimenter applies great pressure for the subject to recall everything. If RU rises to 100% and RF to 75%, then the Zeigarnik effect sinks to 100%/75% = 1.33. Thus, the Zeigarnik effect is greatest when the induced pressure to recall is minimal. Under too much pressure, the difference between the residual tension of finished and unfinished tasks becomes an insignificant fraction of the total tension, and the Zeigarnik effect is negligible.

Marrow (1938) performed an important variation of the typical Zeigarnik experiment. Subjects were given ten tasks, as usual, but unusual instructions. The subjects were told they would be interrupted during their work on a task if it was apparent to the experimenter that the subject was demonstrating ability to do the task. Consequently, the subjects believed that not finishing a task meant successful performance in the eyes of the proctor. If the proctor allowed a subject to work all the way through the task, the subject would believe he or she had demonstrated inadequate performance. Thus, finished tasks would signal poor performance. Marrow actually interrupted subjects on randomly chosen tasks. Marrow then asked for recall of the tasks. A greater proportion of finished than of unfinished tasks was recalled. Even though this result is the opposite of what Zeigarnik initially found, it confirms the principle that tasks associated with persisting tension are better recalled. The subjects perceived the finished tasks as incomplete, since the proctor had apparently seen no evidence of adequate performance. Clearly, *subjective* perception of the event is critical. Once again, Lewin shows how important it is to consider the person's *interaction* with the environment, rather than just the environment itself; B = $f$(P,E).

## Conflict

One of Lewin's most important contributions was his analysis of conflict. Since Lewin's concerns included prejudice and group dynamics in general, conflict was a natural topic for him to treat in some detail. We shall present Lewin's analysis of three general types of conflict.

**Approach/approach conflict.** Figure 8-9 represents an approach/approach conflict. A person is torn between two attractive goals. The person is at a location in the lifespace where the forces toward the two goals are equal.

An example of an approach/approach conflict is a dilemma experienced by a friend of one of the authors. An insurance salesman, he sold

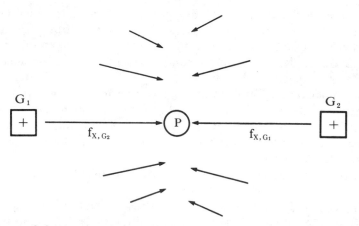

**Figure 8-9.** Approach/approach conflict; the person is at point P. *(From* The Conceptual Representation and the Measurement of Psychological Forces, *by K. Lewin. Copyright 1938 by Duke University Press. Reprinted by permission.)*

more policies than anyone else in his district. His prize was either $1000 or a 10-day, all-expense-paid trip to London for him and his wife. The company asked him to choose between the two rather attractive options—a classical approach/approach conflict. Lewin calls this type of conflict "unstable." Suppose our friend does something that moves him *slightly* closer to one of the goals. According to Lewin's formula for force, this decrease in distance toward one goal ($G_1$) will increase the force toward that goal. (Whenever the denominator, distance, decreases, force increases.) And as the distance from $G_1$ decreases, the distance from $G_2$ increases, resulting in a decrease in the force toward $G_2$. The person will be pulled by the greater force of $G_1$. Lewin's formula dictates the rule that whenever—for whatever reason—the distance from one goal is lessened, the conflict is ended by movement toward that goal. Therefore, an approach/approach conflict is unstable and will not persist long. The salesman's fleeting thought of sending his young daughter to college in 15 years made him opt for the cash. Any small movement toward one goal tips the scales.

**Avoidance/avoidance conflict.**    The second type of conflict, avoidance/avoidance, is diagrammed in Figure 8-10. In this type of conflict, the person must choose between two unattractive alternatives. An avoidance/avoidance conflict is particularly agonizing because it is stable. As the person moves toward one of the negative goals, the distance to that goal diminishes, and the negative force of the goal increases. The person is therefore repelled back toward the other goal. However, as the person approaches that other goal, *its* negative force increases, and the person is repelled from *that* goal. As either goal is approached,

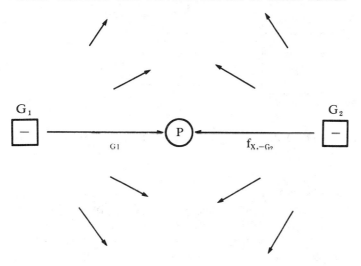

**Figure 8-10.** Avoidance/avoidance conflict. *(From* An Introduction to Motivation, *by J. Atkinson.* © *1964 by Litton Educational Publishing, Inc. Reprinted by permission of Van Nostrand Reinhold Co.)*

then, the goal becomes more repellent. Thus, the person vacillates between the two valented objects.

The most satisfying way to resolve an avoidance/avoidance conflict is to leave the situation. In a Lewinian lifespace diagram, this solution would be represented as motion on a line perpendicular to a line connecting the two valented objects.

In 1974, the Supreme Court ordered President Nixon to surrender tapes of conversations to the special prosecutor. Nixon had two options. He could obey the order—and some very incriminating evidence would be revealed. He could disobey the order—and even his strongest supporters in Congress would vote for his immediate impeachment and conviction. These were two very unattractive options, indeed. In 1973, Nixon had been able to resolve a similar avoidance/avoidance conflict by leaving the situation—that is, firing the special prosecutor, Archibald Cox. In 1974, Nixon could not dissolve the conflict in this way. In Lewin's terminology, there was a strong *barrier* to leaving the situation. Therefore, one of two negatively valented objects had to be chosen.

If one cannot leave the situation, the only way to resolve an avoidance/avoidance conflict is to restructure the situation; one or both of the two valented objects must be reevaluated up or down. Then the person is able to choose the lesser of the two evils, because the greater negative force from one object overwhelms the lesser negative force of the other.

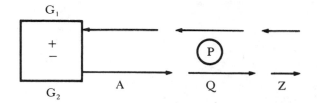

**Figure 8-11.** Approach/avoidance conflict. At point Q, the forces are equal and opposite.

**Approach/avoidance conflict.** The final type of conflict is approach/avoidance. In this stable conflict, a region of the lifespace has both positive and negative valence. A child may want a cookie from the cookie jar (positive valence) but knows Mom will punish him for eating cookies before dinner (negative valence). The child is both attracted and repelled by the same object. Figure 8-11 illustrates this situation. Point Q represents the equilibrium point, where the positive and negative forces are equal and opposite. It is at this point that the child will vacillate. Lewin states (1951, p. 263) that the negative forces are stronger close to the goal than the positive forces are. Figure 8-12 represents this principle, which is nearly identical to Miller's approach/avoidance concept (see Figure 5-8). As the child approaches the cookie jar, the dominant negative force repels him. As he begins to leave the kitchen, the dominant positive force attracts him. He will waver at Q until he resolves the stable conflict by restructuring the situation. For example, the child may decide that the cookies are probably stale, thus eliminating most of the positive valence. (Lewin never provided a satisfactory explanation for postulating dominance of a negative force close to the goal.)

## Level of aspiration

Lewin and his students, particularly Festinger, Dembo, and Escalona, applied Lewin's concept of force in predicting the difficulty levels with which people would choose to interact. The study of a person's level of aspiration proved important for several reasons. First, its subject matter includes issues in such interesting areas as vocational choice—for example, whether a person aspires toward a prestigious occupation or one that does not pose even a small challenge. Second, the level-of-aspiration studies were influential in formulation of the theory of "need for achievement," one of the most important motivational theories in the history of psychology. Finally, Lewin's analysis of level of aspiration was a psychological application of expectancy-value theory, a theory that has dominated the psychological study of decision making for many years. Lewin's application of expectancy-value theory will be discussed at the end of this chapter, and "need-achievement" theory will be elaborated in Chapter 9.

We'll use the following situation to illustrate how Lewin's concept of force can be used to predict the difficulty level with which a person will choose to interact. Assume that a college freshman has to choose among three tasks in his lifespace. He can register for Differential Equations, Trigonometry, or Addition, any of which will satisfy his college's mathematics requirement. These three courses vary greatly in difficulty. Toward which level of difficulty will the student aspire?

Lewin, of course, would answer this question by estimating the force toward each of the valented objects. Recall that the first component of force is valence. What are the positive valences, the valences associated with success, in each of these three lifespace regions? Success in a very difficult course would be most gratifying; thus, the positive valence associated with success in Differential Equations would be quite high— say, +10. Success in Addition would be unexciting; its positive valence would be only +1. Success in Trig might have a valence of +5.

The next component of force is distance from the person to the valented object. In level-of-aspiration studies, however, instead of distance Lewin uses a very similar construct that also gauges how far a person is from a goal. Lewin uses probability, which he terms "potency." For example, success in Differential Equations is only a remote possibility; its potency is .1, because success at this task is perceived as quite distant. Probability of success in Addition is quite high; potency equals .9 there, because the goal is seen as not very distant at all. Potency is .5 for

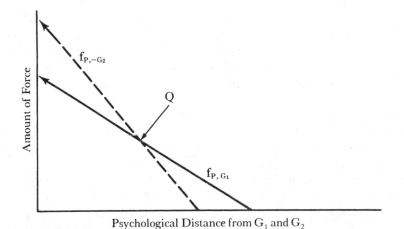

**Figure 8-12.** The gradients of an approach/avoidance conflict. *(Adapted from* An Introduction to Motivation, *by J. Atkinson.* © *1964 by Litton Educational Publishing, Inc. Reprinted by permission of Van Nostrand Reinhold Co.)*

**TABLE 8-1.** Calculation of force toward three goals of varying difficulty

| Goal | $V_{succ}$ | $Po_{succ}$ | $Force_{succ}$ | $V_{fail}$ | $Po_{fail}$ | $Force_{fail}$ | Total force |
|---|---|---|---|---|---|---|---|
| Differential equations | 10 | .1 | 1.0 | $-$ 0.5 | .9 | $-0.45$ | $+0.55$ |
| Trigonometry | 5 | .5 | 2.5 | $-$ 5 | .5 | $-2.5$ | 0 |
| Addition | 1 | .9 | 0.9 | $-20$ | .1 | $-2.0$ | $-1.1$ |

Trig. Table 8-1 summarizes the calculations of force toward each course. The positive force toward each goal ("$Force_{succ}$") is calculated by multiplying its valence by its potency: $F_{succ} = V_{succ} \times Po_{succ}$.

Toward each goal there is also some negative force, because failing any of these tasks would have negative valence. Failing the toughest course would not be devastating; no one could severely blame the student for doing poorly on a task of great difficulty. Therefore, failing Differential Equations has a valence of only $-0.5$. Failing Addition would be humiliating; it has a valence of $-20$. Failure in Trig might have a valence of $-5$.

For each task, the potency of failure equals 1.0 minus the potency of success. Multiplying the negative valence by the potency of failure yields the negative force associated with each task. The positive and negative forces are then algebraically summed to obtain the final resultant force toward each task. In this example, the force toward the most difficult course is highest; therefore, Lewin would predict that the student will attempt that course. The formula for calculating resultant force toward any level of difficulty is $F_{total} = (V_{succ} \times Po_{succ}) + (V_{fail} \times Po_{fail})$. (The second addend is never positive, because $V_{fail}$ is never positive.) Check Table 8-1 to be sure you understand the formula.

When we have predicted what difficulty level a person will choose, we can find what Lewin termed the *goal discrepancy*, which is simply the difference between the level to which the person aspires and the level last mastered. Suppose another college offers nine math courses, ranging from Addition (difficulty level 1) to Differential Equations (difficulty level 9). A student has just conquered Algebra (level 3). Among the remaining courses, Trigonometry (level 5) has the highest resultant force for the student, so she will attempt it next. Her goal discrepancy is $+2$ (see Table 8-2).

Fear of failing promotes large goal discrepancies. For a student who is very afraid of failing, the negative valences of the easy and intermediate tasks are extremely large. $V_{fail}$ might be a traumatizing $-30$ for Addition. These huge negative valences produce large negative forces for all but the highest difficulty levels. The really difficult courses don't have very negative valences and forces, because no one can blame you for failing such difficult tasks. Therefore, the fear-of-failure student whose record is depicted in Table 8-3 will opt for Differential Equations! Since she mastered level 5 (Trig) last time, her

**TABLE 8-2.** A student who attempted level 3 (Algebra) last time will now aspire toward level 5 (Trigonometry), showing a goal discrepancy of +2.

| Difficulty level | Task | $V_{succ}$ | $Po_{succ}$ | $Force_{succ}$ | $V_{fail}$ | $Po_{fail}$ | $Force_{fail}$ | Total force |
|---|---|---|---|---|---|---|---|---|
| 9 | Differential equations | 10 | 0 | 0 | − 0.5 | 1.0 | −0.5 | −0.5 |
| 8 | Analytic geometry | 9 | 0 | 0 | − 1.0 | 1.0 | −1.0 | −1.0 |
| 7 | Calculus | 8 | 0.1 | 0.8 | − 2.0 | 0.9 | −1.8 | −1.0 |
| 6 | Solid geometry | 7 | 0.2 | 1.4 | − 2.0 | 0.8 | −1.6 | −0.2 |
| 5 | Trigonometry | 6 | 0.5 | 3.0 | − 4.0 | 0.5 | −2.0 | +1.0 |
| 4 | Geometry | 5 | 0.6 | 3.0 | − 6.0 | 0.4 | −2.4 | +0.6 |
| 3 | Algebra | 3 | 0.7 | 2.1 | −10.0 | 0.3 | −3.0 | −0.9 |
| 2 | Multiplication-division | 2 | 0.8 | 1.6 | 15.0 | 0.2 | −3.0 | −1.4 |
| 1 | Addition | 1 | 0.9 | 0.9 | −20.0 | 0.1 | −2.0 | −2.1 |

goal discrepancy is a huge +4. From this analysis we would expect that those who have high fear of failure will exhibit more unrealistically high vocational aspirations than those who have low fear of failure (Lewin, Dembo, Festinger, & Sears, 1944; Mahone, 1960).

Level-of-aspiration studies provide a good example of how Lewin uses his motivational principle, force, to make nonobvious predictions.

## Decision making

**Maximizing expected value.** As mentioned earlier, level-of-aspiration studies are an application of what has come to be known as expectancy-value theory. In order to calculate resultant force toward

**TABLE 8-3.** A student who is afraid of failure aspires toward a very difficult task in order to escape from much of the large negative valence associated with failure. Because she chose level 5 last time, her choice of level 9 results in a goal discrepancy of 4.

| Difficulty level | Task | $V_{succ}$ | $Po_{succ}$ | $Force_{succ}$ | $V_{fail}$ | $Po_{fail}$ | $Force_{fail}$ | Total force |
|---|---|---|---|---|---|---|---|---|
| 9 | Differential equations | 10 | .1 | 1.0 | − 1 | .9 | −0.9 | +0.1 |
| 8 | Analytic geometry | 9 | .1 | 0.9 | − 2 | .9 | −1.8 | −0.9 |
| 7 | Calculus | 8 | .2 | 1.6 | − 6 | .8 | −4.8 | −3.2 |
| 6 | Solid geometry | 7 | .2 | 1.4 | − 8 | .8 | −6.4 | −5.0 |
| 5 | Trigonometry | 6 | .5 | 3.0 | −10 | .5 | −5.0 | −2.0 |
| 4 | Geometry | 5 | .6 | 3.0 | −15 | .4 | −6.0 | −3.0 |
| 3 | Algebra | 3 | .7 | 2.1 | −20 | .3 | −6.0 | −3.9 |
| 2 | Multiplication-division | 2 | .8 | 1.6 | −25 | .2 | −5.0 | −3.4 |
| 1 | Addition | 1 | .9 | 0.9 | −30 | .1 | −3.0 | −2.1 |

any difficulty level, the value (valence) of that goal is multiplied by its expectancy (potency). The product represents amount of motivation. Expectancy-value theory has long dominated psychological investigation of how people make decisions.

Easily the most influential book ever written on the topic of economic decision making is *Theory of Games and Economic Behavior,* by Von Neumann and Morgenstern (1944). Kurt Lewin attended a series of lectures given by Von Neumann. Perhaps as a result of that event, Gestalt psychologists have been most prominent among psychologists in the study of economic behavior.

The orthodox method of making sound economic decisions is based on the rule that one should always adopt the course of action that maximizes expected value. The expected value for a course of action is determined by multiplying each possible outcome by the probability that that outcome will occur and then summing the products. Here's an example.

In 1971, one of the authors was driving his beat-up car from Ann Arbor to Minneapolis to attend a convention. In Gary, Indiana, the red light on the dashboard came on, indicating that the car was overheating. The author coaxed the car to a dealership in Gary to assess the problem. The dealer said that if our hero drove very slowly and stopped frequently, he had a 75% chance of getting the car the 30 miles or so to Chicago, where his parents lived. There he could borrow his parents' car and continue to Minneapolis. However, he had a 25% chance of completely destroying the motor, thereby losing the $450 value of the car. The dealer said he'd be glad to do the repairs for $200, but it would take a day. Under the disbelieving stare of the dealer, the author pulled out a pencil and paper and drew the chart reproduced in Figure 8-13.

The author had to decide whether to try to drive to Chicago. He knew that he should maximize expected value. The act of trying to drive to Chicago had a .75 probability of succeeding, in which case he would have to pay $200 to have the car repaired in Chicago while he was in Minneapolis. The act had a .25 probability of failing, in which case the author would lose the whole value of the car ($450) and would have to call his parents in Chicago to ask them to drive out and pick up their beleaguered son somewhere on the Indiana toll road (at least a $25 inconvenience to his parents). To calculate the expected value (Ev) of driving to Chicago, one multiplies the value (v) of each outcome by its probability (p) of occurring. Then sum the products.

$$Ev = (v_1)(p_1) + (v_2)(p_2)$$
$$Ev = (-\$200)(.75) + (-\$475)(.25) = -\$268.75$$

Therefore, the expected value of driving to Chicago is $-\$268.75$.

The act of not trying to drive to Chicago entailed asking the author's

|  | Arrive Safely in Chicago<br>p=.75 | Destroy Car en Route to Chicago<br>p=.25 |
|---|---|---|
| Drive to Chicago | $200 for Repairs | $450 Car Destroyed and $25 Inconvenience to Parents |
| Leave Car in Gary | $200 for Repairs and $100 Inconvenience to Parents | $200 for Repairs and $100 Inconvenience to Parents |

**Figure 8-13.** Calculation of expected value for two courses of action. The expected value of driving to Chicago was $(-\$200)(.75) + (-\$475)(.25) = -\$268.75$. The expected value of leaving the car in Gary was $(-\$300)(.75) + (-\$300)(.25) = -\$300$.

parents to pick him up in Gary, drive him to Chicago, give him their car, get a neighbor to drive them out to Gary to get his car the next day, and drive the car back to Chicago to await his return from Minneapolis with their car—assuming he could talk them into it. Whether the author's car would have made it to Chicago or not, the decision of not trying for Chicago would cost $200 in repairs and at least $100 worth of inconvenience to the parents. Therefore, the expected value of not trying to get to Chicago was $Ev = (-\$300)(.75) + (-\$300)(.25) = -\$300$.

The author now knew the following things: (1) The expected value of any course of action is the cost of each possible outcome multiplied by the probability that that outcome will occur. (2) It is sensible to choose the course of action with the highest expected value. (3) Trying to get to Chicago has a smaller negative expected value than not trying to get to Chicago.

The author quickly explained this reasoning to the incredulous dealer. Then he headed for Chicago, convinced he was the most rational human alive. (He made it.)

Lewin's level-of-aspiration analysis is based on the same principles as the decision rule predicting that people will maximize expected value. Both analyses multiply probability by value (or valence). Both predict choice of the option with the highest expected value. Many authors have noted the very close relation between Lewin's use of expectancy-value theory and decision theory (for example, Edwards, 1954; Siegel, 1957).

The rule that predicts choice of the option with the highest expected value, however, is far too rational to be correct. Humans are not that rational. For example, Las Vegas casinos are not charitable organizations. Placing a bet at a Las Vegas casino has much lower expected value than not placing a bet. Yet people by the thousands continue to go to Las Vegas. The prediction that people always choose options that maximize expected value is obviously mistaken. Perhaps people should do that, but they don't.

In order to take into account human irrationality, psychologists, mathematicians, and economists have modified expectancy-value theory. We will not, however, explain their modifications. Delving into those modifications would take us far from the central point of our discussion, which is that level of aspiration and decision making can be analyzed by expectancy-value theory. Lewin used the expectancy-value analysis ingeniously to examine behavior in conflict situations. Should I drive to Chicago? Should I choose a tough course? Should I opt for the cash or for the trip to London? Lewin's exploration of such topics derived entirely from his simple force formula based on valence and distance.

## Conclusions and critique

A large number of theorists (including Atkinson, 1964; Bolles, 1967; Estes, 1954) have criticized Lewinian theory for its rather casual definitions, which appeal more to intuition than to data. An example from Atkinson (1964, p. 105) illustrates this point. Lewin stated that "tension" is caused by need, and needs are "those acts or behaviors which generally are recognized as a syndrome indicating a need" (Lewin, 1938, p. 99). This definition is wholly inadequate. Most of Lewin's terms are not operationally defined. As Estes (1954) pointed out, Lewin uses no truly objective terms that could serve as a basis for the definition of or communication about his concepts. *Behavior* is defined as "any change in the lifespace." But how is one supposed to know when a change in a subject's lifespace occurs? What behavior can we use as a measure showing that the lifespace has changed? Lewin's lack of operational definitions creates impossible measurement problems. Since some areas of Lewinian theory, such as level of aspiration, require rather subtle mathematical manipulations, measurement problems make predictions from those areas very tenuous. For example, if the valence of failing trigonometry were $-5$ rather than $-4$ in Table 8-2, the predicted class would be geometry, not trigonometry. How are we to know whether $-5$ or $-4$ is the more appropriate valence value?

Estes's most severe criticism is that Lewinian theory is unable to make *any* firm predictions. Lewin was adept at constructing plausible accounts that explain a behavior by describing the lifespace, forces, and so forth that must have been present for the behavior to occur. But such conjectures can be used only in hindsight. The theory is so vague, and therefore so flexible, that *any* behavior can easily be "predicted" after the event has already occurred. Where the theory fails miserably is in its ability to predict behavior before it occurs. For example, on the basis of an organism's movement, one can assume that the resultant force was in that direction. However, one can deduce the magnitude and direction of the force only *after* one has observed the locomotion. Prediction is not possible; therefore, refutation of the theory is not possible. In short, Lewin does not seem to present a well-defined, empirically based theory. Instead, he seems to present a new and interesting way of looking at behavior.

Another deficiency of Lewinian theory is its inadequate treatment of individual differences. Since the idea that behavior is a function of both the person and the environment is basic to Lewinian theory, one would think that individual differences would play a large role in the determination of behavior and, therefore, in the theory. However, Lewin very rarely mentioned such differences and, instead, assumed that his experimental manipulations would affect everyone similarly. Perhaps Lewin's inadequate treatment of individual differences is the result of his emphasis on ahistorical analysis, which stresses contemporaneous influences on behavior. Persisting personality traits are inherent properties of the person, but only because prior experience has made them so. For this reason, taking enduring personality traits into account may have seemed to Lewin to be incompatible with his principle that influences in the here and now could completely explain behavior.

A feature that did not endear Lewin to experimentalists was the very casual manner in which much of his research was executed. Many of his most important studies lacked important control groups. Other studies were run with rather haphazard procedures. Stimuli were introduced when the experimenter thought they "might be effective." Reliability among observers was not always reported; this is an unfortunate omission, since observers were often asked to estimate such things as frustration and degree of interdependence among subjects.

Despite these weaknesses, Lewinian theory has played a prominent role in the study of motivation. First, and perhaps its most important contribution, field theory added a wide range of new topics to the jurisdiction of motivational theory. Lewin's studies on recall of interrupted tasks and on level of aspiration were new and important.

Second, Lewin introduced a theory far more cognitive than the then-dominant theory of Clark Hull. Hull saw no reason to include anything other than stimuli and responses in his theory. Human beings, in Lewin's view, however, evaluated probabilities and assessed the relative strengths of valences. Lewin was inserting the thinking individual between the $S$ and the $R$. Thus, Lewinian theory is an important ancestor of cognitively oriented contemporary motivational theories.

Finally, Lewinian theory strongly influenced achievement-motivation theory, the very important theory we shall elaborate next.

# CHAPTER 9

# The Theory of Achievement Motivation

*Seest thou a man diligent in his business? He shall stand before kings.*

*Proverbs 22:29*

The theory of achievement motivation, unlike Freudian, Hullian, or Lewinian theory, is concerned exclusively with motivation. It has been an exceptionally influential theory and has been applied to areas as diverse as the prediction of a student's academic performance and the prediction of a country's economic growth. It has also been used in the study of sexual and racial differences in motivation. Both its practical nature and its controversial nature have made it one of the most heavily researched theories in recent years.

The theory of achievement motivation was formulated by McClelland and Atkinson, who, along with Clark and Lowell, wrote *The Achievement Motive* in 1953. This book documented the first five years of work on the theory. Since then, several books and hundreds of articles have been written, many by the same people who originated the theory.

## Measurement of achievement motivation by the TAT

McClelland and his colleagues hypothesized that an achievement situation arouses positive feelings in some people and negative feelings in others. He chose to use the Thematic Apperception Test (TAT) developed by Henry A. Murray to measure such individual differences in the motive to enter an achievement situation. Murray called this motive the "need to achieve"; the name has come to be abbreviated "n Ach."

Murray had constructed the TAT to measure "psychogenic" needs of the personality. Subjects were asked to write stories about pictures shown to them. Each picture was so ambiguous that it did not suggest one dominant theme. Instead, the theme of the story was generated by the subject's personality. In other words, the TAT was a projective test: the subject projected his or her own needs into the story. Murray believed that the subject's needs could be accurately assessed by careful examination of the story told in response to a TAT picture.

Several experiments were designed to determine the validity of the TAT.

## Validation of the TAT as a measure of a biological need

Atkinson and McClelland began by testing the validity of the TAT in measuring a biological need. For this it was necessary to use a need that could be made stronger—in an objectively defined way—among one group of subjects than among another in order to test the TAT's validity. If the TAT, when given to both groups, could detect the difference in intensity of that need, the test could be considered a valid measure of a need. Hunger was chosen as the need that would be objectively manipulated.

Atkinson and McClelland (1948) tested three groups of men who had not eaten for 1, 4, or 16 hours. The men were asked to write stories to a set of TAT pictures. Having devised an elaborate, objective means of scoring the stories for content related to the need for food, Atkinson and McClelland found that the content did vary among the three groups of men. As hunger increased, the stories dealt more and more frequently with needing food and overcoming food deprivation. The authors concluded that the TAT could be used to assess the magnitude of a need.

## Validation of the TAT as a measure of n Ach

The next important step was to use the TAT on what Lewin had called "quasi-needs," or nonbiological needs. To this end, McClelland and his colleagues devised a scoring system to assess achievement need. They then used this scoring system to see whether the TAT could reliably distinguish people in an obvious achievement situation from those not in an achievement situation. This was analogous to the study in which the TAT did discriminate among hungry and nonhungry men. Could the TAT do as well with a quasi-need such as achievement?

**Procedure.**    Six groups of males were used in this experiment (McClelland et al., 1953, Chapter 3). The experiment consisted of two parts: subjects were given first a paper-and-pencil test and then a TAT.

Subjects in the achievement-oriented group were told that the initial paper-and-pencil test was a measure of their ability and were asked to put their names on their papers. The test was said to be the same one used by the government to choose leaders to work in Washington. The experimenter conducted himself formally, and no feedback was given concerning how well the subjects did on this test. The TAT was then given.

The success group was treated identically to the achievement-oriented group, except that the subjects were led to believe they had done extremely well on the test.

The failure group was also treated identically to the achievement-oriented group, except that the subjects were led to believe they had done poorly on the test.

The success/failure group resembled the achievement-oriented group, except that the subjects were told they had done well on the initial tasks in the test and later (but before taking the TAT) were told they had done poorly on the later tasks.

In the relaxed group, a graduate student told the subjects that he needed some normative data on some paper-and-pencil tasks he was developing. He asked subjects to take the paper-and-pencil test and not to put their names on it. He conducted himself informally.

The last group of subjects was the neutral group. The neutral condition resembled the relaxed condition in that the experimenter identified himself as a graduate student and conducted himself informally, but the experimenter made no effort to minimize the importance of the initial tasks. The neutral condition was included to assess the achievement imagery that would be present in TAT stories when the experimenter tried not to influence the achievement motive in any way other than by his mere presence.

**Results.** Table 9-1 contains the mean n-Ach score for each group. Just as in the food-deprivation study, the TAT stories reflected the intensity of a subject's motive. Subjects in the relaxed group had not been

**TABLE 9-1.** Mean n Ach (measured by the TAT) as a function of experimental condition

| Condition | n Ach |
|---|---|
| Relaxed | 1.95 |
| Neutral | 7.33 |
| Achievement-oriented | 8.77 |
| Success | 7.92 |
| Failure | 10.10 |
| Success/failure | 10.36 |

From *The Achievement Motive*, by D. C. McClelland, J. W. Atkinson, R. W. Clark, and E. L. Lowell. Copyright 1953 by Irvington Publishers, Inc. Reprinted by permission.

placed in an achievement situation, and their TAT responses contained negligible achievement imagery. The neutral group's n-Ach score reflects the achievement motivation that is aroused in a typical classroom situation. The remaining four groups have higher n-Ach scores, since in those groups the need to achieve was more forcefully aroused. Note that of these four groups the lowest score was produced by the success group. This result is what Lewin would predict: since those subjects actually believed that they had achieved the goal (success), they had no "persisting tendency" that would have been revealed in their TAT stories. Another important finding is that the achievement-oriented group scored below the two failure groups. McClelland (1961) states that three conditions are necessary to arouse the motive to succeed. The subject must consider himself or herself personally responsible for the outcome, must have knowledge of the outcome, and must perceive some risk concerning the chances for success. Since subjects in the achievement-oriented group received no feedback about the results of their performance, their need to achieve was not maximally aroused. Therefore, their achievement imagery was lower than that of either failure group.

**Further evidence.**    The results of the experiments on hunger and n Ach were very encouraging to McClelland and his colleagues. The two studies had shown that the TAT was able to detect motivational differences among subjects in whom a need was aroused to varying degrees by prior manipulation. However, the studies had validated the TAT only by showing its sensitivity to differences in a need aroused by different *environmental* influences. McClelland and his colleagues were even more interested in individual differences in the need to achieve. This concern was guided by the idea behind the Lewinian formula B = $f$(P,E) that behavior—in particular, achievement behavior—could be influenced by characteristics of both the person and the environment.

Several experiments have investigated differences between people who score high in n Ach on the TAT and those who score low. Among the earliest were those by Lowell (1952), who showed that high-n-Ach people scored better than low-n-Ach people on both verbal and mathematical tests. Yet high-n-Ach people are no more intelligent than low-n-Ach people (Heckhausen, 1967). Thus, n Ach, though not correlated with IQ, does predict performance. This conclusion gave McClelland confidence that the TAT n-Ach score was a valid indicator of achievement motivation.

Since the early studies by Lowell, many other studies have investigated the relation between n Ach and performance measures. N Ach has been found to be correlated with school grades (as by Cox, 1962), worker productivity (Block, 1962), performance in clerical tasks (as by Atkinson & Raphelson, 1956), and even success of United States presidents (Donley & Winter, 1970). Findings such as these indicate that the TAT can provide a valid measure of achievement motivation.

## Abbreviations

It is customary to use several abbreviations when discussing the theory of achievement motivation. So that the reader will be prepared for these abbreviations when they occur, and so that a handy reference will be available, we present them here.

n Ach—need to achieve, typically measured by the TAT (Thematic Apperception Test)

$T_s$—tendency to achieve success

$M_s$—motive to achieve success; the n-Ach score on the TAT is a measure of $M_s$

$P_s$—probability of success

$I_s$—incentive value of success

$T_{af}$—tendency to avoid failure

$M_{af}$—motive to avoid failure, typically measured by the TAQ (Test Anxiety Questionnaire)

$P_f$—probability of failure

$I_f$—incentive value of failure

$T_r$—resultant achievement motivation

$T_{ext}$—motivation based on extrinsic factors

PI—perceived instrumentality

$T_g$—inertial tendency

$M_{-s}$—motive to avoid success

## Motivational constructs

### The tendency to achieve success ($T_s$)

An achievement situation is any situation in which a person "knows that his performance will be evaluated (by himself or by others) in terms of some standard of excellence and that the consequences of his actions will be either a favorable evaluation (success) or an unfavorable evaluation (failure)" (Atkinson, 1964, pp. 240–241). "The tendency to achieve success" is the motivation to enter a particular achievement situation. This motivation is determined by three factors: (1) the strength of a person's motive to achieve success ($M_s$), which is assessed by the TAT n-Ach score; (2) the probability of success the person believes he or she has on a particular task, which is called "probability of success" ($P_s$); and (3) the incentive value of success ($I_s$) on that particular task. These three factors combine multiplicatively to determine the tendency to achieve success ($T_s$); that is, the tendency to achieve success is equal to motive to achieve success multiplied by the probability of success multiplied by the incentive value of success: $T_s = M_s \times P_s \times I_s$. Let us review these three factors in more detail.

To calculate $T_s$, the motivation to enter a particular achievement situation, we must first know something about the person's personality—namely, the strength of the person's motive to achieve success, $M_s$. Because this motive is a personality characteristic, it is transsituational: a person carries it from one situation to another. $T_s$ is motivation in a *particular* achievement situation. $M_s$ is a motive that, as a personality characteristic, is relevant to *all* of the achievement situations a person enters. $T_s$, motivation, has three determinants, one of which is $M_s$, motive.

Second, we must know the person's *subjective* probability of success $(P_s)$ in the given situation. How likely does the person believe his or her success is? Unlike $M_s$, $P_s$ is different for every situation. It must be assessed anew each time someone faces an achievement situation.

Finally, how much incentive value does success have? If the person succeeds, will it be cause for joy (high $I_s$) or merely for a shrug of the shoulders (low $I_s$)?

We have now defined the three determinants of $T_s$ (the tendency to achieve success). However, it is necessary to know only two determinants, $M_s$ and $P_s$, in order to calculate $T_s$, because $I_s$ (incentive) is assumed to be $1 - P_s$.

This assumption that $I_s = 1 - P_s$ is quite logical, because it merely assumes that the more difficult a task is, the higher will be the incentive value of succeeding. Getting an A in a ridiculously easy course ($P_s = .9$) won't elicit much admiration; $I_s$ is a paltry .1. Getting an A in an extremely difficult course ($P_s = .1$) will send the student into ecstasy; $I_s = .9$. The assumption that $I_s = 1 - P_s$ has been researched by Litwin (1958, reported in Atkinson & Feather, 1966). Litwin found that subjects would assign greater monetary values (high $I_s$) to tasks of greater difficulty (low $P_s$). In a ring-toss game, the amount of money that subjects felt a "ringer" was worth was directly related to the distance the player stood from the peg while trying to toss the ring over it. Lewin and his students had made the same assumption in their level-of-aspiration research: the higher the difficulty level, the greater the valence of success (Lewin et al., 1944).

Most experimenters investigating $T_s$ first assess the $M_s$ of each subject and then place him or her in a situation whose $P_s$ is presumed to be known. This is usually done by announcing some norm to the subject: "We've found that about 50% of undergraduates can perform this task successfully" ($P_s = .5$). Different groups of subjects are given different bogus norms ($P_s$ is set at a different value for each group), and $T_s$ is then calculated for each group. Table 9-2 shows $T_s$ at five $P_s$ levels for a subject high in $M_s$ and for a subject low in $M_s$. These $T_s$ values were generated by the equation $T_s$ (tendency, or motivation, to approach an achievement situation) $= M_s$ (motive to achieve success) $\times P_s$ (subjective probability of success) $\times I_s$ (incentive value of success), using the assumption that $I_s = 1 - P_s$.

Two extremely important conclusions can be drawn from the data in Table 9-2. First, people who have the motive to achieve success will tend to prefer intermediate-difficulty tasks ($P_s = .5$). Second, the

**TABLE 9-2.** Calculation of $T_s$ at five $P_s$ levels for subjects high ($M_s = 5$) and low ($M_s = 1$) in the motive to achieve success: $T_s = M_s \times P_s \times I_s$ where $I_s = 1 - P_s$

| $P_s$ | $M_s = 5$ | $M_s = 1$ |
|-------|-----------|-----------|
| .1 | $5 \times .1 \times .9 = 0.45$ | $1 \times .1 \times .9 = .09$ |
| .3 | $5 \times .3 \times .7 = 1.05$ | $1 \times .3 \times .7 = .21$ |
| .5 | $5 \times .5 \times .5 = 1.25$ | $1 \times .5 \times .5 = .25$ |
| .7 | $5 \times .7 \times .3 = 1.05$ | $1 \times .7 \times .3 = .21$ |
| .9 | $5 \times .9 \times .1 = 0.45$ | $1 \times .9 \times .1 = .09$ |

greater the $M_s$, the greater one's preference for intermediate-difficulty tasks. Several interesting studies substantiate these conclusions. Mahone (1960) and Morris (1966) have found that young adults who are high in n Ach (that is, high in $M_s$) aspire toward vocations of intermediate difficulty. Other experimenters (such as Veroff & Peele, 1969) have taken advantage of this principle in their use of the ring-toss game to measure n Ach: subjects may choose the distance from which to toss the rings over the peg. Those with high n Ach stand at an intermediate distance from the ring. Those with low n Ach do not show a preference for intermediate distances.

The formula $T_s = M_s \times P_s \times I_s$ has another interesting characteristic. Atkinson (1964) points out that those with high $M_s$ take great pride in their achievements. In other words, they really enjoy success. Accordingly, the total incentive in an achievement situation may be thought of as ($M_s \times I_s$), where the magnitude of $M_s$—the person's capacity for enjoying success generally—is multiplied by the incentive value that success in that situation would represent. Then the formula becomes $T_s = P_s \times (M_s \times I_s)$. The $P_s$ is "expectancy." The ($M_s \times I_s$) is "value." Thus, the $T_s$ formula is yet another representative of expectancy-value theory. The influence of Lewin in the theory of achievement motivation is quite strong.

## The tendency to avoid failure ($T_{af}$)

When people with high $M_s$ perceive an achievement situation, they perceive the possibility of attaining a success. They have motivation to approach such a situation, since it holds out the possibility of successful accomplishment. But people may also view an achievement situation quite differently. The situation may hold out the possibility of failure, shame, and humiliation. Thus, entering an achievement situation elicits anxiety and fear of failure in some people. They are said to be high in the motive to avoid failure ($M_{af}$), and since an achievement situation can be failed, they have a motive to *avoid* achievement situations.

One of the most widespread devices used to assess $M_{af}$ (the motive to avoid failure) is the Test Anxiety Questionnaire (TAQ), developed by Sarason and Mandler. This questionnaire has been employed to assess $M_{af}$, because it asks questions about the subject's anxiety in an achievement situation—namely, the situation of facing a test. One item on the questionnaire, for example, asks, "How often do you think of ways of avoiding a test?"

Just as $M_s$ (motive to achieve success) produces $T_s$ (tendency to approach success), so $M_{af}$ (motive to avoid failure) produces $T_{af}$ (tendency to avoid failure). $T_s$, being motivation toward achievement situations, is always expressed as a positive number; $T_{af}$, being motivation away from achievement situations, is always negative. $T_{af}$ inhibits $T_s$—that is, it inhibits a person's entrance into an achievement situation. $T_{af}$ also acts to inhibit performance once a person has entered an achievement situation (Atkinson, 1964, p. 246).[1]

$T_{af}$ (like $T_s$) has three determinants. The first is the person's $M_{af}$, which is often assessed with the TAQ. The second is the person's estimate of the probability of failing ($P_f$). The third is the incentive value of failure ($I_f$). $I_f$ is always a negative number, because failure is a negatively valued event. The formula for $T_{af}$ should look familiar: $T_{af} = M_{af} \times P_f \times I_f$. Since $I_f$ is negative, $T_{af}$ will be negative.

It is assumed that $I_f = -(1 - P_f)$. This assumption is analogous to the assumption for $I_s$. Failing a very difficult task ($P_f = .9$) causes little shame ($I_f = -.1$); failing an easy task ($P_f = .1$) is humiliating ($I_f = -.9$).

Table 9-3 shows $T_{af}$ at five $P_f$ levels for a subject high in $M_{af}$ and

**TABLE 9-3.** Calculation of $T_{af}$ at five $P_f$ levels for subjects high ($M_{af} = 5$) and low ($M_{af} = 1$) in the motive to avoid failure: $T_{af} = M_{af} \times P_f \times I_f$ where $I_f = -(1 - P_f)$

| $P_f$ | $M_{af} = 5$ | $M_{af} = 1$ |
|---|---|---|
| .1 | $5 \times .1 \times -.9 = -0.45$ | $1 \times .1 \times -.9 = -.09$ |
| .3 | $5 \times .3 \times -.7 = -1.05$ | $1 \times .3 \times -.7 = -.21$ |
| .5 | $5 \times .5 \times -.5 = -1.25$ | $1 \times .5 \times -.5 = -.25$ |
| .7 | $5 \times .7 \times -.3 = -1.05$ | $1 \times .7 \times -.3 - -.21$ |
| .9 | $5 \times .9 \times -.1 = -0.45$ | $1 \times .9 \times -.1 = -.09$ |

one low in $M_{af}$. These $T_{af}$ values were generated by the equation $T_{af}$ (tendency to avoid failure) $= M_{af}$ (motive to avoid failure) $\times P_f$ (probability of failure) $\times I_f$ (incentive value of failure).

$M_{af}$ produces *some* tendency to avoid any achievement situation, re-

[1]Atkinson has modified this statement somewhat (Atkinson & Birch, 1974). He now believes that the major impact of $T_{af}$ is to *delay entrance* into achievement situations.

gardless of its $P_f$. However, a situation in which $P_f$ (or $P_s$) $= .5$ is the most anxiety provoking. Furthermore, the higher a person's $M_{af}$, the more that person's dislike for situations in which $P_f = .5$ will surpass his or her dislike for situations in which $P_f$ is some other number. Mahone (1960) and Morris (1966) report that many high-$M_{af}$ persons have unrealistically high vocational aspirations. As Table 9-3 indicates, extremely difficult tasks aren't very aversive, because their $I_f$ is low. (Who can be disappointed in you for failing in your effort to swim the Arctic Ocean?) On very easy tasks, the chance of failing is slim. Consequently, high-$M_{af}$ people can escape some of their anxiety by choosing very difficult or very easy tasks.

$T_{af}$, like $T_s$, can be expressed using concepts from expectancy-value theory. Atkinson (1964, p. 244) describes $M_{af}$ as the "capacity for reacting with shame and embarrassment when the outcome of performance is failure." We can consider the negative incentive value of failure in a particular situation to be $(M_{af} \times I_f)$, where $M_{af}$ represents the individual's capacity to feel ashamed of failure and $I_f$ represents the extent to which this particular failure would elicit shame. Then $T_{af} = P_f \times (M_{af} \times I_f)$. Once again, motivation equals expectancy multiplied by value.

### Resultant achievement motivation ($T_r$)

So far, we have discussed $M_s$ and $M_{af}$ separately. In reality, all people have both motives to some extent. The majority of studies indicate that $M_{af}$ and $M_s$ are independent personality characteristics (for example, Brody, 1963; Litwin, 1958; Mahone, 1960; C. P. Smith, 1961); a person who is high in $M_s$ may or may not be low in $M_{af}$.

Since every person has both $M_s$ and $M_{af}$, each achievement situation will elicit some $T_s$ and some $T_{af}$. Will the person approach the situation or avoid it? The answer depends entirely on which tendency is greater, $T_s$ or $T_{af}$. Further, the strength of the person's total motivation toward or away from the situation depends on the extent to which the greater tendency exceeds the lesser one. In order to calculate total motivation, we need to know both $T_s$ and $T_{af}$.

The resultant achievement motivation ($T_r$)—the net tendency to approach an achievement situation—is equal to the magnitude of the tendency to approach the situation minus the magnitude of the tendency to avoid it. Since $T_{af}$ is always negative, $T_r = T_s + T_{af}$.[2]

To find $T_r$, we can calculate $T_s$ and $T_{af}$ separately and then add them. The formula for $T_r$ is then $T_r = (M_s \times P_s \times I_s) + (M_{af} \times P_f \times I_f)$. But there is a shorter way. Using algebraic substitution, we can derive the equivalent formula $T_r = (M_s - M_{af})(P_s \times I_s)$. This

---

[2]Some texts present the equation as $T_r = T_s - T_{af}$. When $T_{af}$ is defined as a negative quantity—as we defined it above—that presentation would be mathematically incorrect.

last equation allows us to find resultant motivation more simply. The first factor, $M_s - M_{af}$, is the key. It tells us whether $T_r$ will be positive or negative—that is, whether the person will approach or will avoid an achievement situation. If the motive to achieve success is greater than the motive to avoid failure ($M_s > M_{af}$), then the ($M_s - M_{af}$) factor will be positive and therefore resultant achievement motivation will be positive. The person will want to enter an achievement situation. What if the motive to avoid failure is greater than the motive to achieve success ($M_{af} > M_s$)? Then the ($M_s - M_{af}$) factor will be negative, and resultant achievement motivation will be negative. The person will not want to enter an achievement situation.

Table 9-4 contains calculations of $T_r$ for four hypothetical persons with different relations between $M_s$ and $M_{af}$. Note that the more $M_s$ exceeds $M_{af}$, the more a person prefers intermediate-difficulty tasks ($P_s = .5$). Conversely, the more $M_{af}$ exceeds $M_s$, the more a person dislikes intermediate-difficulty tasks. This prediction is similar to Lewin's prediction that those for whom failure had a strong negative value would prefer very difficult tasks. Where Atkinson and Lewin differ is that Lewin did not predict that such people might also prefer very easy tasks.

Regardless of task difficulty, people in whom $M_{af}$ exceeds $M_s$ always have negative intrinsic motivation toward an achievement situation. Therefore, they will not enter such a situation unless there is enough positive *extrinsic* motivation (such as desire for money) to overcome their negative intrinsic motivation.[3] The equation $T_r = T_s + T_{af}$ predicts only the intrinsic motivation—the tendency to approach or avoid an achievement situation as determined by preference for the situation in itself, independent of any "extra added incentives." Therefore, the total resultant motivation is $T_r = T_s + T_{af} + T_{ext}$, where $T_{ext}$ is motivation based on extrinsic factors, without which people in whom $M_{af}$ exceeds $M_s$ would never enter an achievement situation.

## Experimental tests of the theory of achievement motivation

Some early experiments were performed by Atkinson and his students to test the predictions that people for whom $M_s > M_{af}$ would prefer intermediate-difficulty tasks and that $M_{af} > M_s$ people would prefer very easy or very difficult tasks.

Atkinson and Litwin (1960) asked college men to participate in a ring-toss game. Subjects were allowed to stand anywhere between 1

---

[3]Atkinson and Birch have softened this statement. They have speculated that an $M_{af} > M_s$ person may enter an achievement situation without extrinsic rewards if certain other conditions are met. (See Atkinson & Birch, 1974, p. 299 for details.)

**TABLE 9-4.** Calculation of $T_r$ at five $P_s$ levels for subjects differing in $M_s$ and $M_{af}$: $T_r = (M_s - M_{af})(P_s \times I_s)$

| | $M_s = 5, M_{af} = 1$ |
|---|---|
| $P_s = .1$ | $4 \times .1 \times .9 = 0.36$ |
| .3 | $4 \times .3 \times .7 = 0.84$ |
| .5 | $4 \times .5 \times .5 = 1.00$ |
| .7 | $4 \times .7 \times .3 = 0.84$ |
| .9 | $4 \times .9 \times .1 = 0.36$ |

| | $M_s = 2, M_{af} = 1$ |
|---|---|
| $P_s = .1$ | $1 \times .1 \times .9 = .09$ |
| .3 | $1 \times .3 \times .7 = .21$ |
| .5 | $1 \times .5 \times .5 = .25$ |
| .7 | $1 \times .7 \times .3 = .21$ |
| .9 | $1 \times .9 \times .1 = .09$ |

| | $M_s = 1, M_{af} = 2$ |
|---|---|
| $P_s = .1$ | $-1 \times .1 \times .9 = -.09$ |
| .3 | $-1 \times .3 \times .7 = -.21$ |
| .5 | $-1 \times .5 \times .5 = -.25$ |
| .7 | $-1 \times .7 \times .3 = -.21$ |
| .9 | $-1 \times .9 \times .1 = -.09$ |

| | $M_s = 1, M_{af} = 5$ |
|---|---|
| $P_s = .1$ | $-4 \times .1 \times .9 = -0.36$ |
| .3 | $-4 \times .3 \times .7 = -0.84$ |
| .5 | $-4 \times .5 \times .5 = -1.00$ |
| .7 | $-4 \times .7 \times .3 = -0.84$ |
| .9 | $-4 \times .9 \times .1 = -0.36$ |

and 15 feet from the peg. All men were assessed for $M_s$ and $M_{af}$. Figure 9-1 shows the locations chosen as a function of the subjects' achievement motives. As predicted, $M_s > M_{af}$ men preferred an intermediate-difficulty task more than $M_{af} > M_s$ men did. However, contrary to prediction, $M_{af} > M_s$ men did not show maximal preference for the extreme tasks.

Several more recent studies designed to test this same principle have used academic settings. For example, Isaacson (1964) has shown that $M_s > M_{af}$ men choose college majors of intermediate difficulty more often than $M_{af} > M_s$ men do. Similarly, deCharms and Carpenter (1968) showed that $M_s > M_{af}$ children chose arithmetic problems of intermediate difficulty and $M_{af} > M_s$ children chose problems of extreme difficulty or ease.

One of the more provocative studies on this topic was done by Veroff and Peele (1969), who were interested in the effect busing would have on the achievement motivation of Black children. Veroff and Peele found that Black males who were bused showed a significant increase

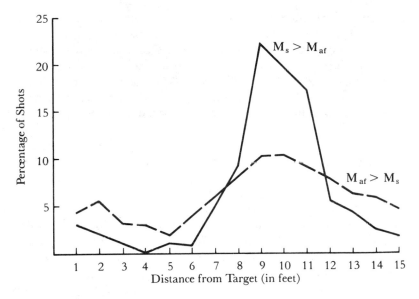

**Figure 9-1.** Percentage of shots at each distance from target as a function of achievement motives. *(Adapted from "Achievement Motive and Test Anxiety Conceived as Motive to Approach Success and Motive to Avoid Failure," by J. W. Atkinson and G. H. Litwin, Journal of Abnormal and Social Psychology, 1960, 60, 52–63. Copyright 1960 by the American Psychological Association. Reprinted by permission.)*

in "autonomous achievement motivation." This increase was accompanied by a *decrease* in level of vocational aspiration. If it is assumed that low-n-Ach males have unrealistically high aspirations, the drop in aspiration to a realistic level was a beneficial result of the busing program.

Another educational implication of the achievement theory was tested by Atkinson and O'Connor (1963, discussed in Atkinson & Feather, 1966). If $M_s > M_{af}$ children are in a classroom situation in which their $P_s$ is very high—that is, far above .5—they will not be maximally motivated. If they are placed in a class in which all children have about the same ability, their $P_s$ will be approximately .5, and they will be highly motivated. $M_{af} > M_s$ children, however, would be maximally inhibited in a class of their own ability level. Atkinson and O'Connor tested these predictions. In general, $M_s > M_{af}$ children did conform to the predictions by performing better in the ability-grouped classes; results for the $M_{af} > M_s$ children were not conclusive. There are influences that may have moderated the results for those children, and some of these will be discussed later in the chapter.

Probably the most important study done to test the theory of achievement motivation was that by Feather (1961). Feather's measure was the number of trials for which subjects would persist on an impossible task. The task was to trace an Euler diagram, using a pencil, without retracing a line or lifting the pencil from the paper. Each subject was given a stack of identical cards, each containing a copy of a diagram, as shown in Figure 9-2.

The subject could work on each card until it was defaced by an un-successful attempt. Then the next card was tried, and the next, and the next, until the subject gave up.

Feather tested $M_s > M_{af}$ men and $M_{af} > M_s$ men. Half the sub-jects in each group were told that the $P_s$ on the task was .7, the other half that it was .05. Feather counted the cards each man went through before quitting. Table 9-5 contains the results.

The $M_s > M_{af}$ men persisted longer when $P_s$ was .7 than when it was .05. Failure of the first few attempts caused the subject to lower his $P_s$ estimate. After a few failures, the subject began thinking that the $P_s$ might be .7 for Einstein but only .6 for him. After a few more failures, .5 might seem more reasonable. Thus, as the subject begins to fail, the $P_s$ estimate approaches .5, the level at which the subject shows maxi-mal motivation. Consequently, he persists. When the initial $P_s$ is .05, however, failure causes the $P_s$ estimate to move farther from the region of maximal motivation. Failure at $P_s = .05$, then .04, then .03 causes the subject to have very little interest. The result is minimal per-sistence.

The results for the $M_{af} > M_s$ man should be entirely different. As he fails a task on which $P_s$ is .7 and begins to lower his $P_s$ estimate, the

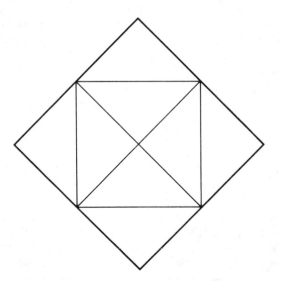

**Figure 9-2.** Euler diagram.

**TABLE 9-5.** Number of subjects showing high persistence and low persistence as a function of achievement motives and stated difficulty of task

| Motive type | Stated task difficulty | Persistence High | Low |
|---|---|---|---|
| $M_s > M_{af}$ | $P_s = .7$ | 6 | 2 |
| | $P_s = .05$ | 2 | 7 |
| $M_{af} > M_s$ | $P_s = .7$ | 3 | 6 |
| | $P_s = .05$ | 6 | 2 |

Adapted from "The Relationship of Persistence at a Task to Expectation of Success and Achievement-Related Motives," by N. T. Feather, *Journal of Abnormal and Social Psychology*, 1961, *63*, 552–561. Copyright 1961 by the American Psychological Association. Reprinted by permission.

$P_s$ will move toward the region he hates the most—intermediate difficulty. He will show little persistence on such a task. When the initial $P_s$ is .05, however, failing the task causes the $P_s$ estimate to become even more extreme. Since this subject finds extreme $P_s$ values not very aversive, he will persist longer. Table 9-5 supports all these predictions.

## Three elaborations of the theory

The theory of achievement motivation has been elaborated somewhat during the last decade. Most of the elaborations have consisted in altering the original equation so that it will remain applicable when certain situations occur. Because the alterations are subject to further alteration themselves, their inclusion in a text is something of a gamble. Although textbook authors usually limit themselves to discussion of the better-established topics, new and controversial ideas make up the vanguard of psychology. Here, then, are three elaborations of the theory of achievement motivation.

### Perceived instrumentality (PI)

What would your own motivation be toward a course in inorganic chemistry? If you were planning to become a chemist, the course would be a vital link in a long chain of professional training. But if this were the first and last chemistry course you ever planned to take, your motivation would probably be substantially less. Yet $M_s$, $M_{af}$, and $P_s$ would be identical in the two situations. Achievement-motivation theory predicts that motivation should therefore be identical.

Raynor (1969, 1970) recognized this weakness in the theory. He proposed an elaboration of the original theory to take into account the importance of an achievement activity in one's long-range plans. Suppose that you are a budding chemist taking this first course. If you are an $M_s > M_{af}$ person, the amount by which $M_s$ exceeds $M_{af}$ will multiply the probability and incentive of success, producing your total motivation toward the course; that is, $T_r = (M_s - M_{af})(P_s \times I_s)$. As you evaluate the $P_s$ and $I_s$ of this first course, however, you'll also be aware of all the subsequent chemistry courses you'll have to take as a chemistry major, as well as all those graduate courses and all those evenings in the laboratory. Each of these activities is one step on the long road to becoming a chemist. Each new step is contingent on successful completion of the prior step; that is, this is a multistep contingent path. Each step is *instrumental* in achieving your final goal. Therefore, as you ponder the $P_s$ and $I_s$ for this first step, the $P_s$ and $I_s$ of all the subsequent steps are also significant. Their $P_s$ and $I_s$ also multiply your $M_s - M_{af}$. If becoming a chemist takes four steps, the formula for total resultant tendency is

$$T_r = (M_s - M_{af})([P_{s1} \times I_{s1}] + [P_{s2} \times I_{s2}] + [P_{s3} \times I_{s3}] + [P_{s4} \times I_{s4}]).$$

For the $M_s > M_{af}$ person, $T_r$ will always be greater in a multistep contingent path than in a one-step path: a prospective chemistry major who is $M_s > M_{af}$ will be more motivated in a first chemistry course than a prospective poet will be.

The prediction for the $M_{af} > M_s$ person is just the opposite. When this person perceives a task as being instrumental in attaining access to several other achievement tasks, his or her negative ($M_s - M_{af}$) is multiplied by more probabilities and incentives than if the person perceived a one-link "chain." Consequently, a contingent path is more threatening to the $M_{af} > M_s$ person than a noncontingent path. Therefore, this person should prefer the noncontingent path, because it is less negatively motivating.[4]

Even though a contingent path is more threatening to an $M_{af} > M_s$ person than a noncontingent path is, a contingent path frequently has some extrinsic reward associated with its successful completion. The extrinsic reward may be so great as to overcome the person's negative intrinsic motivation. This fact may falsify the prediction that $M_{af} > M_s$ people will prefer a noncontingent path. In situations without large extrinsic reward, however, the prediction should be confirmed.

Raynor (1970) tested his predictions in an introductory psychology class. The students were asked two questions designed to assess how important they believed the psychology course would be for their future career plans. Those who responded that the course was important were

---

[4]Raynor distinguishes three types of paths: contingent, noncontingent, and one-step. The first is a multistep path in which success on one step is necessary in order to attempt the next one. A noncontingent path is a multistep path in which success on one step is not necessary in order to attempt the next one. Raynor treats the noncontingent path and the one-step path similarly in that he does not apply the expanded $T_r$ formula to them. That formula applies only to contingent paths.

**TABLE 9-6.** Mean grade in psychology as a function of achievement motives and perceived instrumentality

| | Perceived instrumentality | |
|---|---|---|
| Motive type | Low | High |
| $M_s > M_{af}$ | 2.93 | 3.37 |
| $M_{af} > M_s$ | 3.00 | 2.59 |

Adapted from "Relationship Between Achievement-Related Motives, Future Orientation, and Academic Performance," by J. O. Raynor, *Journal of Personality and Social Psychology,* 1970, *15,* 28–33. Copyright 1970 by the American Psychological Association. Reprinted by permission.

termed the high-PI (perceived instrumentality) group. They were assumed to consider the course part of a contingent path. The low-PI subjects were assumed to consider the course the sole link of a one-step (in effect, a noncontingent) path. All subjects were classified by dominance of $M_s$ or of $M_{af}$. Table 9-6 contains the average final grades for the four groups. As predicted, $M_s > M_{af}$ students performed better when they perceived the course to be instrumental to future plans, and $M_{af} > M_s$ students performed worse in that circumstance. Entin and Raynor (1973) have shown that this predicted interaction occurs even when the contingent path is the shortest possible length—two steps. That is sufficient to create added motivation for $M_s > M_{af}$ people and added inhibition for $M_{af} > M_s$ people.

Raynor believes that this elaboration of achievement theory is very important because it allows the analysis of real-life situations not treated adequately by the original McClelland/Atkinson model. Most of the tasks that subjects perform in laboratory experiments have zero PI: the subject perceives the task not to be instrumental in any way to his or her future plans. The original theory predicts well in those instances. But the theory should also be applicable to real-life situations in which the subject occasionally undertakes tasks crucial to future goals. For those situations, the theory must take PI into account to make accurate predictions.

## Inertial tendency ($T_g$)

The persistence of an unfulfilled wish is a phenomenon discussed by both Freud and Lewin. Perhaps the most careful analysis of it was done by Lewin's students investigating the Zeigarnik effect. More recently Weiner (1965) has extended the analysis to the theory of achievement motivation.

Weiner proposes that success consummates the tendency to attain an achievement-related goal. Failure allows the tendency to continue undiminished. Consequently, if someone fails a task, the resultant ten-

**TABLE 9-7.** Resultant tendency, including inertial tendency, as a function of motive type and number of consecutive failures

|  | $M_s = 2, M_{af} = 1, P_s = .5$ on Trial 1 |
|---|---|
| Trial 1 | $1 \times .5 \times .5 = .25$ |
| Trial 2 | $1 \times .4 \times .6 = .24; .24 + .25 = .49$ |
| Trial 3 | $1 \times .3 \times .7 = .21; .21 + .49 = .70$ |
| Trial 4 | $1 \times .2 \times .8 = .16; .16 + .70 = .86$ |

|  | $M_s = 1, M_{af} = 2, P_s = .5$ on Trial 1 |
|---|---|
| Trial 1 | $-1 \times .5 \times .5 = -.25$ |
| Trial 2 | $-1 \times .4 \times .6 = -.24; -.24 + -.25 = -.49$ |
| Trial 3 | $-1 \times .3 \times .7 = -.21; -.21 + -.49 = -.70$ |
| Trial 4 | $-1 \times .2 \times .8 = -.16; -.16 + -.70 = -.86$ |

dency for that task will persist following the failure and will augment the motivation for the task when it is attempted again. Table 9-7 presents some hypothetical data. Note that, every time a task is failed, two adjustments to the resultant-tendency formula must be made. First, $P_s$ is lowered as the subject realizes that the task is tougher than he or she thought. Second, all the motivation of the previous unsuccessful trial is added to the resultant tendency calculated for the present trial. This second adjustment is analogous to the persistence of tension following nonattainment of the goal. The motivation remaining from a trial and augmenting motivation on the next trial is called "inertial tendency" $(T_g)$. The formula for resultant tendency, modified to take $T_g$ into account, is $T_r = (M_s - M_{af})(P_s \times I_s) + T_g$.

Inspection of Table 9-7 reveals that $M_s > M_{af}$ people should always show an increase in motivation following failure. The reason is that failure causes the inertial tendencies from all prior trials to build up, creating a larger and larger resultant tendency on subsequent trials.

Another important prediction of Weiner's inertial-tendency elaboration of achievement theory is that $M_{af} > M_s$ people do more poorly as the number of failures increases. Their resultant tendency is always negative, and this negative tendency is consummated following success but persists following failure. Therefore, the person faces the negative inertial tendency of the prior unsuccessful trial *and* the negative tendency of the present trial. As the number of failures increases, the negative tendency grows larger and larger. Whereas $M_s > M_{af}$ people seem to thrive on failure, $M_{af} > M_s$ people are buried by it.

The concept of inertial tendency helps the theory of achievement explain a few findings that it could not otherwise explain. Figure 9-3, for example, shows the results of an experiment by Lucas (1952). These results illustrate the different effects failure has on individuals of different anxiety levels. The inertial-tendency predictions are confirmed.

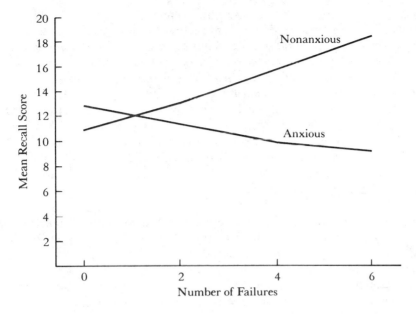

**Figure 9-3.** Recall performance as a function of number of failures and level of anxiety. *(From "The Interactive Effects of Anxiety Failure and Interserial Duplication," by J. D. Lucas,* American Journal of Psychology, *1952, 65, 59–66. Reprinted by permission of The University of Illinois Press.)*

People high in anxiety ($M_{af} > M_s$) do more poorly after failure; people low in anxiety ($M_s > M_{af}$) do better after failure (Weiner & Schneider, 1971).

## Motive to avoid success ($M_{-s}$)

Consider any of the studies on achievement-related behavior that you have read about in this chapter. If the subjects had varied on some relevant characteristic, the results would probably have been different. For example, for a study in which the experimental task was intellectual, suppose the subjects had varied markedly in intelligence. The effects of individual differences in resultant achievement motivation would likely not have been so pronounced, since ability obviously contributes to success or failure. What about an individual difference that is more easily defined and less obvious in its effects on achievement? In particular, might the study have yielded different results as a function of the sex of the subjects?

The answer is yes. Males and females experience achievement differently. Their expectations and analyses of the achievement situation are different. Their values of success and failure differ. Their performance in achievement situations and attributions about their performance are dissimilar. Although sex differences are apparent, however, knowledge of the contributing factors involved is sparse. The reason for this appears to be the masculine orientation of the achievement concept. The development and validation of achievement measures were carried out on primarily male samples, and the experimental manipulations of achievement arousal have primarily involved tasks that are characteristically masculine, such as mathematics problems (Denmark, Tangri, & McCandless, 1978). The few achievement studies that have used female subjects have generated results that are both inconsistent and dissimilar to those for males (Sarason & Smith, 1971). Evidently, the central constructs of achievement-motivation theory, $M_s$ and $M_{af}$, are insufficient to explain achievement-related behavior in women.

**Horner's formulation.**    This deficiency in achievement-motivation theory prompted Horner (1968) to postulate a "motive to avoid success" ($M_{-s}$) as a critical determinant of females' achievement behavior. It was conceptualized as a latent, stable personality characteristic that is established early in development, during acquisition of the female's sex-role identity. $M_{-s}$ consists of a predisposition to become anxious in achievement-oriented situations that are inherently competitive and therefore not "feminine." If it is true that women, more than men, are socialized to value social relationships and affiliation, a competitive achievement situation creates a conflict that threatens sex-role identity and self-concept or arouses a fear of social rejection. Hence, the anticipation of success evokes anxiety that inhibits otherwise positive achievement-oriented motivation and performance. According to the expectancy-value model of motivation within which the construct was devised, the strength of $M_{-s}$ should be the function of the probability of success (expectancy) and the consequences of success (value). By implication, the prospect of success on a masculine task with a male competitor should maximally arouse inhibitory anxiety and produce the greatest decrease in performance.

Although Horner did not place $M_{-s}$ in a resultant-tendency equation, it can be assumed to have an additive effect. Hence, a woman might have high $M_s$ and low $M_{af}$ but still have a low $T_r$ because of the avoidance tendency arising from $M_{-s}$. Presumably, the resultant-tendency equation for women would be altered as follows to accommodate the motive to avoid success: $T_r = (M_s - M_{af} - M_{-s})(P_s \times I_s)$. This revised equation has considerable significance for female achievement. It suggests that females have a conflict between their motivation to succeed and their socialized sex-role attributes such that the maintenance of their sex-role identities may inhibit otherwise achievement-oriented strivings.

To test her theoretical formulation, Horner devised a projective measure in which subjects wrote stories (similar to TAT stories) to a verbal cue that described what was clearly an experience of success by a female: "After first-term finals, Anne finds herself at the top of her medical school class." Among female subjects, 66% wrote stories containing $M_{-s}$ imagery (conflicts regarding success, expected negative results of success, and so on). Only 9% of male subjects given the same cue with a male character ("John") did so. $M_{-s}$ therefore appeared to be a pervasive female attribute that was uncharacteristic of men.

Subsequently, Horner divided women into groups according to whether their stories had high or low $M_{-s}$ imagery. She then placed subjects in a noncompetitive situation (in which they worked alone) and in a mixed-sex competitive situation (in which they performed against males and other females). The results supported her hypotheses: high-$M_{-s}$ women performed better alone than in competition, and low-$M_{-s}$ women performed better when competing. In high-$M_{-s}$ women, presumably, the competitive situation aroused an inhibitory anxiety associated with their fears that success would be incongruent with their femininity or would cause social rejection, especially from the males.

**Research.**    The $M_{-s}$ construct has had considerable value in stimulating research of females' motivation and performance in achievement-oriented situations. In the main, two areas of investigation have emerged: (1) studies of so-called moderator variables, or subject characteristics, that affect the amount and type of $M_{-s}$ imagery, and (2) studies of the effects of $M_{-s}$ on performance in achievement settings.

Samples of female college students commonly voice $M_{-s}$ imagery to the original Anne cues used by Horner (1968). The proportion of women projecting $M_{-s}$ imagery appears to be substantial, in the range of ⅔ to ¾ (Horner, 1968, 1972; Garske, 1975a; Makosky, 1976), and these proportions seem to have remained stable over the past decade (Denmark et al., 1978). Although $M_{-s}$ imagery appears to be generally characteristic of college women, it is clearly moderated by many factors. The presence of female motive-to-avoid-success fantasies varies as a function of age (Horner, 1972; Monahan, Kuhn, & Shaver, 1974), race and social class (Weston & Mednick, 1970), national origin and background (Feather & Raphelson, 1974), and sex-role orientation (Cabellero, Giles, & Shaver, 1975; O'Leary & Hammack, 1975). Despite the apparent variations in $M_{-s}$ imagery among females, however, the findings are generally supportive of Horner's hypothesis that $M_{-s}$ is a relatively common characteristic among females.

With male subjects, however, unpredictable results have been obtained that raise questions regarding the female-specific nature of motive-to-avoid-success ideation. In striking contrast to Horner's (1968) finding that only 9% of the males projected $M_{-s}$ imagery, L. W. Hoffman (1974) found that the proportion of the $M_{-s}$ imagery in males (77%) surpassed that in females (65%). Obviously, this suggests that $M_{-s}$ is not a uniquely feminine trait. Themes accompanying the imagery nevertheless were different for males and females; females tended to express affiliative loss (as Horner predicted), and males tended to express conflict regarding the value of achievement. Thus, although both males and females voiced fearfulness and avoidance regarding success, their reasons for the conflict were related to their respective sex-role attributes of masculinity and femininity.

The considerable variability in $M_{-s}$ imagery has raised questions regarding the construct validity of Horner's projective measures. Are responses to the cues eliciting an inhibitory personality trait as Horner hypothesized? Or, can $M_{-s}$ imagery be explained in some other way? One rival explanation is that $M_{-s}$ imagery may reflect the operation of sex-role stereotypes regarding the different outcomes of success for males and females.

For example, in studies where males and females received *both* the John and Anne cues, both sexes projected greater $M_{-s}$ imagery to the Anne cue (Feather & Raphelson, 1974; Monahan et al., 1974). These results suggest that both males and females *perceive* that there are greater negative consequences for outstanding achievement in medical school for a woman than for a man. A recent study by Juran (1979), however, suggests that even these negative sex-role stereotypes for female achievement may be waning. The Juran results showed that both male and female subjects viewed Anne in a medical setting in a positive, socially desirable way. She was perceived as competent but not unfeminine. Contrary to the $M_{-s}$ hypothesis, Anne was rated as significantly more positive in a medical setting than in a neutral setting. Clearly, outstanding female achievement did not generate negative consequences relative to comparable male achievement and was actually viewed more positively than less-achieving female behavior.

The validity problems with Horner's original measures have spurred attempts to modify and extend the original measure (for example, Horner, Tresemer, Berens, & Watson, 1973; J. T. Spence, 1974) and develop new measures with questionnaire formats within Horner's framework (Zuckerman & Allison, in press) and within the psychoanalytic perspective (Cohen, 1974). These alternative measures also appear to have difficulties, chief of which are a lack of validity data and an apparent relationship with measures of fear of failure (Shaver, 1976).

Since Horner's $M_{-s}$ projective measure appears to be affected by many factors and has questionable construct validity, it is not surprising that the few studies of the effects of $M_{-s}$ on performance have yielded inconsistent results. Makosky (1976) found that high $M_{-s}$ women performed best on a feminine task when competing against a woman and low $M_{-s}$ women performed best on a masculine task when competing against a man. However, acknowledging that Horner's Anne cue was more likely measuring personal sex-role orientation than $M_{-s}$, Makosky concluded that women do indeed compete when the competition is appropriate and compatible with sex-role preferences for achievement. S. W. Morgan and Mausner (1973) found that high school girls were more likely than boys to show performance decrements when working in mixed-sex pairs. However, this sex difference was independent of $M_{-s}$ imagery. Karabenick and Marshall (1974) found partial support for Horner's hypothesis that $M_{-s}$ imagery would show the greatest relation to inhibition of performance when a female was competing with a male, but this finding occurred only for those women who were low in affiliation needs and high in $M_{-s}$.

Two studies have reported findings opposite to those Horner's theory predicts. Sorrentino and Short (1974) found that women performed better on "masculine" tasks than on "feminine" tasks and, further, that this difference was greatest for those high in $M_{-s}$ imagery. Garske (1975a) found that females performed better when they were competing against a male on a task typically considered "masculine" than when they were performing alone. Moreover, the hypothesized effects on performance of fear of social rejection and negative feedback from the male were not revealed, even though the female sample produced a high proportion of $M_{-s}$ imagery. Thus, creating optimal conditions for $M_{-s}$ in women as specified by Horner's theory—performance on a "masculine" task with negative feedback from a male competitor by high-$M_{-s}$ women who fear social rejection—failed to produce the predicted performance decrement.

**Critique and reformulations.** Despite the popular appeal of the $M_{-s}$ construct and the flurry of research that it has stimulated, $M_{-s}$ has received at best only partial empirical support (Zuckerman & Wheeler, 1975; Tresemer, 1976). The problem of measurement that pervades achievement-motivation research is no less pronounced with regard to $M_{-s}$. Projective measures, including Horner's, are laden with psychometric problems. It appears remarkable in hindsight that a single item—the Anne cue—could ever have been presumed to be a reliable index of a complex personality construct. Because of this central measurement problem, it is not surprising that validity studies have yielded contradictory results. As yet, attempts to remedy the shortcomings in the measurement of $M_{-s}$ have not been successful (Shaver, 1976). Thus, $M_{-s}$ has not significantly disentangled the complexities of female achievement behavior and motivation.

However, two outgrowths of the $M_{-s}$ literature are noteworthy and promising. First, there appears to be renewed interest in focusing on $M_{-s}$ not as a negative consequence of success in itself but as a consequence of the perceived social rejection that results from success. Conceptualized in this manner, $M_{-s}$ becomes a specific form of the motive to avoid failure ($M_{af}$). Shaver (1976) hypothesized that $M_{-s}$ and $M_{af}$ are conceptually similar and that the two constructs are confounded in the original Horner measure and subsequent revisions. Solid empirical support for this hypothesis has been provided by Jackaway and Teevan (1976). They found significant correlations between $M_{-s}$ and $M_{af}$ under neutral and achievement-arousal conditions in both males and females. Jackaway and Teevan conclude that for those (especially women) whose affiliative and achievement needs are linked, $M_{-s}$ and $M_{af}$ may be equivalent. For such individuals, a fear of social rejection associated with $M_{-s}$ is equal to a fear of failure.

Another perspective in the $M_{-s}$ literature views female achievement conflict as a result of situational determinants in the achievement setting, rather than as an underlying personality construct. From this viewpoint, avoidance of success is not a motive at all; it is a direct result of the expectancies of positive versus negative consequences for achievement in a given situation. In situations in which women avoid success, then, such avoidant behavior would not arise from a fear of success but from a fear of the punishments (disapproval, rejection, and so forth) associated with success. Several studies strongly document the impact of situational factors on avoidant behavior in achievement situations (for example, Jellison, Jackson-White, Bruder, & Martyna, 1975; Argote, Fisher, McDonald, & O'Neal, 1976; Bremer & Wittig, 1980).

## The development of achievement motivation

We have examined the ways in which $M_s > M_{af}$ people differ from $M_{af} > M_s$ people in motivation toward achievement-related activity, but how do $M_s$ and $M_{af}$ develop? We shall discuss first the development of achievement motivation in children and then its development in adults.

### In children

There are two classic studies dealing with the question of how achievement motivation develops in children. The first was done by Winterbottom (1953). In one part of her study, she asked mothers at what age they expected their sons to be able to perform certain tasks by themselves. Winterbottom found that mothers of high-n-Ach boys placed earlier independence demands on their sons than mothers of low-n-Ach boys did. For example, the mean number of tasks (among those on Winterbottom's list) expected of a 7-year-old was about twice as great for high-n-Ach boys as for low-n-Ach boys.

Although this is the most widely cited finding of Winterbottom's study, it has not gone unchallenged. Krebs (1958) has found no relation between age of independence training and n Ach in college males. Moss and Kagan (1961) have suggested that early or late parental demands may result in low n Ach and that intermediate demands produce the highest achievement motivation. Furthermore, C. P. Smith (1969) points out that Winterbottom did not clearly distinguish between independence demands (to do it by oneself) and achievement demands (to do it well). Her questionnaire items confounded the two. Consequently, since some theorists (such as Rosen, 1959) believe that achievement training is more important for achievement motivation than independence training is, Winterbottom's finding cannot be a definitive statement on the importance of independence training for achievement motivation. C. P. Smith (1969) and Torgoff (1958, cited in C. P. Smith, 1969) both suggest that independence training and achievement training may be unrelated. Hence, it is necessary to distinguish carefully between the two when assessing parental behavior toward children.

Several investigators have found that *timing* of independence or achievement training is not as critical as parental *reinforcement* of independence or achievement behavior. Teevan and McGhee (1972) have provided evidence that the parents of high-n-Ach males reward independence behavior, whereas the parents of low-n-Ach males do not. V. J. Crandall, Preston, and Rabson (1960) have found that nursery-school-age children whose mothers reinforced their achievement behavior exhibited strong achievement behaviors outside the home. Katz (1967) has shown that the scores of young Black boys on the Test Anxiety Scale for Children (TASC) are related to general level and type of parental reinforcement. The TASC score, which can be considered a measure of $M_{af}$, correlates positively with the amount of punishment used by either parent and correlates negatively with the amount of positive reinforcement used by either parent.

The second classic study investigating differences between high- and low-n-Ach children was done by Rosen and D'Andrade (1959). The subjects were boys aged 9 to 11. The experimenters tested each boy in his home on a series of tasks in which the parents could also participate. Both the child's performance on the various tasks and—more important—the parents' interactions with the child during the tasks were recorded. There were several differences between parents of high- and low-n-Ach boys. The largest difference occurred in the warmth of the mothers toward their sons: the mothers of high-n-Ach boys were far warmer. Another difference was that both the mothers and the fathers of high-n-Ach boys tended to make higher estimates of their sons' subsequent performance than the parents of low-n-Ach boys; they simply expected more of their sons. In addition, fathers of high-n-Ach boys did not tell their sons how to perform a task. When a father "coached" his high-n-Ach son, he tended to give nonspecific hints. The father of a low-n-Ach boy would take over the task by dictating exactly how it was to be performed.

Since parents of high-n-Ach boys have a higher opinion of their sons' competence than parents of low-n-Ach boys do (C. P. Smith, 1969), it seems reasonable that a low-n-Ach boy's father would feel that his help was surely needed. His taking over the task, however, would undermine the child's feeling of competence, thus fulfilling the father's low expectations. This kind of reciprocal influence between parent and child poses an important research problem. Smith points out that the researcher must somehow decide whether a child-rearing practice causes the child's personality characteristics or whether the child's personality elicits certain child-rearing practices. Because of numerous methodological difficulties such as this, the development of achievement motivation in children, though an important topic, has received little conclusive research. Moreover, there are almost no studies of the development of achievement motivation in female children.

## In adults

In the early 1960s, McClelland and his associates embarked on a research program designed to determine whether $M_s$ could be instilled in adults. In particular, McClelland wanted to train businessmen to become successful by altering their personalities.

The program McClelland began had four aspects. Early in the program, people were taught to write TAT stories with high achievement imagery. A similar technique was tried successfully by Burris (1958, reported in McClelland & Winter, 1969), who found that merely by reinforcing achievement fantasies he was able to effect an increase in college students' grades. The subjects in McClelland's program were also taught the TAT scoring system and were encouraged to use its labels and categories in describing their own real-life situations.

The second major thrust of the program was to convince the participants that their life situations required the development of an achievement motive.

The third part of the program was designed to get participants to set goals for themselves. They also were encouraged to keep a record of their progress toward those goals so that they would have a constant reminder of their commitment.

Finally, McClelland stressed "interpersonal supports" as necessary to create a warm, encouraging atmosphere for the program. Since the participants were in a program designed to change their personalities, the program director was really a therapist. For this reason, McClelland believed that the same techniques that improve therapist/client interaction should be used in his program.

McClelland's program has been tried several times in locations throughout the world. McClelland and Winter (1969) present several tables that document its success. Reviewing the results of the programs in India, McClelland and Winter (1969) conclude:

> Analysis of several measures of individual behavior and economic effects demonstrated that the participants in achievement motivation

courses showed significant improvement in many aspects of entrepreneurial performance, both as compared with themselves and as compared with three matched groups of controls. Course participants show more active business behavior. Specifically, they work longer hours. They make more definite attempts to start new business ventures, and they actually start more such ventures. They make more specific investments in new, fixed, productive capital. They employ more workers. Finally, they tend to have . . . larger percentage increases in the gross income of their firms [p. 230].

## *Societies and their achievement motivation*

Thus far we have been looking at the relation between an individual's achievement motivation and his or her performance on various tasks. If n Ach can successfully predict the behavior of individuals, however, perhaps it can do just as well for groups of individuals. Accordingly, in the 1950s McClelland began a research program to examine the achievement motivation of entire societies and the performance of those societies as gauged by various economic indexes.

In his most famous application of this technique, McClelland (1961) hypothesized that high levels of n Ach among Greek citizens preceded the golden age of Greek civilization and that low levels of n Ach preceded the decline. McClelland based this hypothesis on his belief that n Ach, particularly among entrepreneurs, influences the economic growth of a society and that economic growth is responsible for the growth and decay of a civilization.

In order to determine whether n Ach and the course of Greek civilization were actually correlated, however, it is necessary to ascertain the n-Ach scores of Greek citizens during the Greek periods of growth (900 B.C. to 475 B.C.), climax (475 B.C. to 362 B.C.), and decline (362 B.C. to 100 B.C.). How is it possible to give the TAT to Greek citizens who have been dead 2500 years? To circumvent this problem, McClelland analyzed a wide variety of writings preserved from the Greek periods of growth, climax, and decline. He was careful to choose, from each period, writings that dealt with the same general topics. These writings were then analyzed by the usual TAT scoring system, and an average n-Ach score for each period of Greek civilization was obtained. Exactly as McClelland had predicted, a rise in n Ach preceded the height of Greek civilization, and a drop in n Ach preceded its decline. The implication, of course, is that a society will flourish only to the extent that it is concerned with achievement.

This intriguing analysis has also postdicted trends in the British economy over a 350-year period, and the analysis has been used to predict economic differences between countries (McClelland, 1961). Thus, there appears to be evidence that n Ach can be used to predict societal as well as individual achievement.

## *Alternate analyses of achievement motivation*

### The HP analysis

During the 1960s and 1970s, alternate analyses of achievement motivation were proposed by those dissatisfied with the McClelland/Atkinson model. Some critics suggested relatively minor corrections to the model; a few suggested a substantial overhaul. Birney, Burdick, and Teevan (1969) belong to the latter group of theorists. Their alternative analysis was prompted by dissatisfaction with several of the Atkinson group's theoretical assumptions and conclusions from research.

First, Birney et al. point out that, although the results obtained by Atkinson and Litwin (1960) and shown in Figure 9-1 are usually cited to support Atkinson's theory, they actually provide strong evidence against the theory. Contrary to the theory's predictions, $M_{af} > M_s$ subjects showed the greatest preference for a task with an intermediate probability of success, although less preference for it than $M_s > M_{af}$ subjects showed. Atkinson would predict that $M_{af} > M_s$ people should show maximal preference for tasks with extreme probability; that was clearly not so. Moulton (1965) also found that $M_{af} > M_s$ people did not prefer tasks with extreme $P_s$.

Second, Birney et al. object to Atkinson's assumption that $I_s = 1 - P_s$. They point out that the importance of the task may affect incentive, as may an extrinsic reward contingent on successful performance. Finally, $M_s > M_{af}$ subjects may be indifferent to $P_s$ estimates given by others and instead may respond only to their own personal standards. In contrast, $M_{af} > M_s$ people may be extremely sensitive to $P_s$ estimates given by others. These and other considerations led Birney et al. to conclude that the relation between $I_s$ and $P_s$ is an unanswered empirical question. $I_s$ is simply not always equal to $1 - P_s$.

Third, Birney et al. strongly disagree with Atkinson's 1964 statement that performance by an $M_{af} > M_s$ person is inhibited both before entering an achievement situation (not wanting to enter) and while in the situation (doing poorly during the task). Birney et al. believe that the $M_{af} > M_s$ person certainly has great fear of failure but that this fear does not necessarily inhibit performance once the person is in an achievement situation. Fear may initiate any of several behaviors, including inhibition of effort, leaving the situation, or even *increasing* achievement behavior.

The alternative formulation proposed by Birney et al. includes categories of personality types somewhat different from those used by Atkinson. Unlike the Atkinson group, Birney et al. measure fear of failure by using the TAT and scoring the TAT stories for "Hostile Press" (HP). HP themes are ones "in which the central figures strive to escape, adjust, or overcome. There is no sense that these figures are trying to accomplish something of their own" (Birney et al., 1969, pp. 87–88). The figures are reacting to hostile, threatening aspects of the environment. The core of the theory is straightforward: "Our guiding assumption is that [subjects] who display HP imagery to pictures of tasklike situations where evaluation is possible will display avoidance behavior in achievement-task situations" (Birney et al., 1969, p. 93).

Use of the TAT to measure HP is a marked departure from the practice typical among the Atkinson group—use of the Test Anxiety Questionnaire (TAQ) to measure fear of failure. The TAQ has been criticized by several theorists, including Heckhausen (1968), who believes that the TAQ contains too many items inquiring about physiological arousal. Signs of arousal are likely to occur in approach situations as well as avoidance situations; for this reason, the TAQ may not be accurately measuring avoidance tendencies only.

Birney et al. present substantial evidence that the HP measure is valid. For example, Teevan, Smith, and Loomis (1964, reported in Birney et al., 1969) asked high-HP and low-HP subjects to predict how they would do in a shooting-gallery task. Subjects were also asked to state the highest and lowest scores they could get without being surprised. The difference between these high and low scores was called the "confirming interval." High-HP subjects proved to have wider confirming intervals than low-HP subjects. Teevan et al. believed that a wide interval would be characteristic of persons who feared failure, because, by giving themselves such a wide range of acceptable scores, they made it very unlikely that they would experience failure.

Recent evidence favoring the HP analysis over the traditional achievement analysis ($T_r$) comes from a study by Ceranski, Teevan, and Kalle (1979). These authors assessed the preference subjects had for tasks of low, intermediate, or high difficulty. Those with high-HP scores preferred the extremes, just as predicted; resultant achievement motivation ($T_r = T_s + T_{af}$) was not related to task preference, contrary to what the Atkinson group would predict. Thus, the HP measure proved to have superior predictability in this study.

Since the HP score is uncorrelated with the TAQ score, it is not surprising that the HP measure is related to variables that are likewise unrelated to the TAQ. For example, Birney et al. summarize a large number of studies showing that high HP scores are related to higher grades in elementary school, high school, and college. This finding is, of course, completely opposite to what Atkinson would predict, since subjects high in fear of failure ($M_{af} > M_s$) are supposed to be inhibited in academic situations; they are supposed to perform poorly. However, Birney et al. point out that when a high-HP subject cannot avoid an achievement situation—when he or she is forced to participate—one way to avoid failure is to work extremely hard. Nothing prevents failure better than success.

Although the Birney et al. analysis has not attained the popularity of the McClelland/Atkinson model, it may have helped foster some of the modifications made in Atkinson's theory. For example, Raynor's addition of perceived instrumentality accommodates the criticism by Birney et al. that the importance of a task should influence resultant motivation.

## A new model: Self-esteem/confidence

In this section we present a new alternative analysis of achievement motivation based partially on some earlier work by Korman (1970), Kukla (1972), and R. A. Jones (1977).

The main premise of our new model is quite simple: self-esteem and confidence are the factors that differentiate people with high achievement motivation from people with low achievement motivation. High achievers have higher self-esteem and confidence than low achievers, although these differences in confidence aren't always reflective of true differences in ability. In other words, people with high self-esteem and confidence don't necessarily have the ability to warrant that level of confidence.

The notion that self-esteem determines achievement motivation is not altogether foreign to the McClelland/Atkinson model. Recall that according to their model a $M_s > M_{af}$ person wants to approach every achievement situation, whereas a $M_{af} > M_s$ person wants to avoid every achievement situation. These are the same predictions we would derive from a model based on self-esteem/confidence. The fact that high self-esteem people are low in anxiety (R. Crandall, 1973) is analogous to being low in $M_{af}$ and therefore motivated toward evaluative situations. The fact that low self-esteem people are high in anxiety (Brockner, 1979) is analogous to high $M_{af}$; such people would be motivated away from evaluative situations.

An achievement-motivation theory based on self-esteem/confidence has an important feature that the traditional model does not. High self-esteem people have performance expectations higher than those of low self-esteem people (Atkinson, Bastian, Earl, & Litwin, 1960; Brockner, 1979; Covington & Omelich, 1979). When faced with the same task, the $P_s$ estimates of high-self-esteem people will therefore be higher than those of low-self-esteem people. The warping of $P_s$ by self-esteem is not taken into account in the traditional achievement model, which assumes that the two factors are completely independent.[5]

The optimistic probability estimates of the high achievers help the new model recover the most obvious prediction from the traditional model: those high in achievement motivation will always do better in

---

[5]A relation between motivation and expectancy was suggested very early by Atkinson (1957) but then ignored in later work.

an achievement situation than those low in achievement motivation. The self-esteem/confidence model makes almost the same prediction. Those who are highly motivated have higher $P_s$ estimates. There is a great deal of evidence (summarized in R. A. Jones, 1977) that high expectation and high confidence lead to high performance. For example, Battle (1965) showed that students who were more confident of attaining the grades to which they aspired persisted longer on a task. Needless to say, dogged persistence on a task will enhance the chance of succeeding at it. Thus, high confidence becomes a self-fulfilling prophecy; it leads to good performance that justifies the initial confidence.

There is a difference between the McClelland/Atkinson model and the self-esteem/confidence model with regard to the superior performance of high-self-esteem individuals. When the task is very easy, the original model predicts better performance by $M_s > M_{af}$ individuals compared to $M_{af} > M_s$ individuals. On very easy tasks the new model makes a different prediction. On very easy tasks the expectations of the low-self-esteem group are so high that they cannot be exceeded by those of the high-self-esteem group. However, because of their optimistic view of their own ability, the high-self-esteem persons will not believe that much effort is needed to succeed on this easy task. They therefore expend little effort. The low self-esteem persons, because of their pessimistic attitude toward their own ability, will believe that some effort is required. Therefore, on these very easy tasks, the low-self-esteem group may do better than the high-self-esteem group. This prediction, which differs from that of the traditional theory, has been verified both in the experimental laboratory (Kukla, 1974) and in classroom research. Covington and Beery (1976) point out that highly anxious students (whom we equate with low-self-esteem individuals) may actually do better than minimally anxious (high-self-esteem) students when the task is easy or very highly structured. For example, Grimes and Allinsmith (1961) found that, using a highly structured reading program, the high-anxiety group outperformed the low-anxiety group. In a less structured program, the usual reverse pattern of results occurred.

The self-esteem/confidence model can explain some of the traditional experiments often cited to support the Atkinson/McClelland model; indeed, the predictions may even be more easily made using the new model. The Feather (1961) experiment, often mentioned as an experiment critical to the original theory, found that high achievers persisted longer while failing an easy task. Low achievers persisted longer while failing a difficult task. According to the self-esteem viewpoint, these results would simply be due to the fact that low self-esteem people would be highly motivated to protect their fragile self-esteem. Failure on an easy task ($P_s = .7$) would be devastating to low self-esteem subjects. As Feather (1961) showed, they did not persist as they confronted such a situation. However, they wouldn't be threatened by failing a truly difficult task ($P_s$ = .05). Low self-esteem subjects (whom we equate with $M_{af} > M_s$ subjects) did, in fact, persist longer on the difficult puzzles.

The self-esteem/confidence model is also supported by a number of articles showing that self-esteem correlates positively with educational and occupational accomplishment (Coopersmith, 1967; Rosenberg, 1965). Bachman & O'Malley (1977) have recently replicated these findings, although they have also shown that self-esteem during the high school years has little causal impact on subsequent educational and occupational attainment. The reason for the high correlation between high school self-esteem and educational and occupational accomplishment is that all three factors are caused by the same prior variables, such as family background or prior educational performance.

Perhaps the new model's most helpful contribution is that it clarifies the confused situation with regard to achievement in females. A large number of studies have shown that females have lower expectations of success than do males (V. C. Crandall, 1969; Frieze, 1975; Montanelli & Hill, 1969). This sex difference in confidence appears as early as age 7 (V. C. Crandall, 1969). The lower expectations of women would thus account for their lack of motivation in some achievement settings (for example, Makosky, 1976). Given the disarray into which the "fear of success" concept has fallen, the self-esteem/confidence outlook may provide some welcome insight.

The new model also easily explains the perceived-instrumentality modification of the McClelland/Atkinson model. The more steps a person sees on a contingent path, the harder that path becomes. If each step has probability of failure, a multistep path is obviously harder to complete than a one-step path. As we have seen, the new model states and evidence shows that high-self-esteem people prefer harder tasks (multistep paths), whereas low-self-esteem people prefer easier tasks (a one-step path). This is precisely the data obtained by Raynor.

The final modification of the McClelland/Atkinson model, inertial tendency, is also easily accommodated by the self-esteem model. Recall the Lucas (1952) data presented in Figure 9-3, and recall that R. Crandall (1973) has shown that those with high self-esteem have low anxiety. The top line in Figure 9-3 can therefore be relabeled "High SE." Brockner (1979) has shown that those with low self-esteem are high in anxiety, so the bottom line in Figure 9-3 can be relabeled "Low SE." The new, relabeled graph can be supported with studies showing that, following failure, those with high self-esteem compared to those with low self-esteem expect to perform better, have more positive thoughts (Brockner, 1979), evaluate the task more favorably (Stotland, Thorley, Thomas, Cohen, & Zander, 1957), and show much less decrement in performance (Shrauger & Rosenberg, 1970; Solley & Stagner, 1956). In other words, predictions based on self-esteem provide much the same data as the inertial tendency formula based on $M_s$ and $M_{af}$.

An advantage of the self-esteem/confidence model is that it can explain a number of new findings that pose problems for the original model. For example, Trope (1975) introduced the concept of diagnosticity to the area of achievement motivation. Assume that high-ability people will have a 90% chance of succeeding at task A whereas low-ability people will have only an 80% chance. On task B, high-ability people will succeed 90% of the time but low-ability people only 10% of the time. Trope would say that task B is more diagnostic of ability than task A. On task A, the success rates of the two groups are so similar that a successful person cannot be confidently said to be a high-ability person. On task B, the disparity between the success rates is so great that based on a participant's performance we can "diagnose" his or her ability level rather confidently. Trope showed that $M_s > M_{af}$ people prefer high diagnosticity tasks more than $M_{af} > M_s$ people do.[6] This result is not predicted by the original model, but it can easily be explained in terms of self-esteem. This may also be said of the findings of Buckert, Meyer, and Schmalt (1979), who found that among tasks of equal diagnosticity, $M_s > M_{af}$ people prefer difficult tasks and $M_{af} > M_s$ people prefer easier ones. Merely change "$M_s > M_{af}$" to "high self-esteem" and "$M_{af} > M_s$" to "low self-esteem," and the results become easier to interpret.

Another major research area interpretable within the self-esteem framework includes studies by deCharms (1976) and Miller, Brickman, and Bolen (1975). The deCharms program (which will be discussed in more detail in Chapter 11) involved enhancing the opinions school children had of their own competence. This effort at boosting self-esteem resulted in significant academic improvement. The experiment by Miller et al. improved children's performance in mathematics by telling the children either that they had good mathematical ability or that they had high motivation in mathematics. Miller et al. measured self-esteem as well as mathematical performance and found that groups that improved the most in one of these areas also improved the most in the other area. Note that neither the deCharms program nor the Miller program involved teaching the skill that would be assessed. Both programs sought merely to raise self-esteem, which in turn led to higher achievement in the skill area.

In summary, we suggest that high self-esteem and confidence will result in high motivation in achievement situations, depending, of course, on such factors as diagnosticity and difficulty.

---

[6]This result was not replicated in a study by Buckert, Meyer, and Schmalt (1979).

## *The dynamics-of-action theory*

In 1970, Atkinson and his colleague, David Birch, put forth a new motivational theory they termed *the dynamics of action*. Since that time, the original theory of achievement motivation has been largely incorporated into the new dynamics-of-action theory. We therefore will very briefly present the new theory here, highlighting those features most pertinent to achievement motivation.

Consider first the important experiment by Feather (1961) discussed earlier. Feather found that persistence on an achievement task depended on the motives of the subject and the difficulty of the task. Suppose, however, that subjects were told that, when they no longer wanted to work on the achievement task, they could switch to some physical exercise, such as jogging. For some people, jogging is a favorite pastime; for these people, persistence on the achievement task would have been very low. For others who consider jogging to be a painful waste of perspiration, persistence on the achievement task would have been very great. The point is that motivation toward any task is influenced by the alternative behaviors available. This point sounds obvious, but its implications are rather profound.

Figure 9-4 depicts a situation that will help us examine the implications of the Atkinson/Birch viewpoint. Behaviors A, B, and C are available. The person begins doing A, but because of the rapid increase

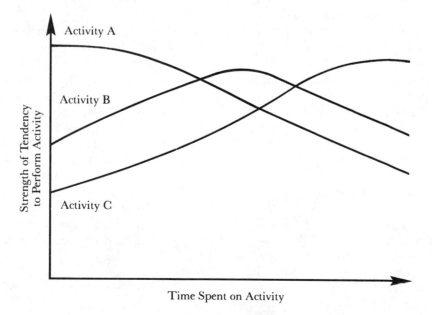

**Figure 9-4.** Changes in behavior occur as tendencies rise or fall in strength.

in the tendency to do B, behavior A is quickly abandoned. An observer of our subject would see the performance of whatever behavior had the greatest tendency at that time, because each behavior can occur at a given time only if the other behaviors' tendencies are lower. Thus, the characteristics of the other tasks are absolutely critical.

Note an important difference in viewpoint between this theory and a theory such as that of Clark Hull. Hull's theory has been characterized as having organisms participate in 100-yard sprints with periods of total quiescence between the sprints. If Clark Hull were to sponsor a TV game show, it would be called "Go for the Goal," and contestants would sleep in cages between trials. In contrast to this view, Atkinson and Birch insist that people are *always* active. Unless in a coma, people are performing some behavior. This stream of activity consists of changes from one behavior to another, much as we have depicted it in Figure 9-4. By examining the forces that move behavior A up or down on the graph, we can predict when A will be done and for how long it will be done.

Two of the most important factors determining the level of any behavior tendency are called *instigating forces* and *consummatory forces*. If behavior A were eating a steak, the smell of a steak over a charcoal grill would constitute a powerful instigating force, moving up my tendency to perform behavior A. Devouring the steak would constitute a consummatory force, moving downward my tendency to continue to perform behavior A. By exposure to instigating or consummatory forces, my tendencies toward various behaviors rise or fall. Note that performing any behavior X results in a consummatory force on that behavior. This in turn causes that behavior's tendency to drop, ensuring that some new behavior will eventually emerge as the one with the greatest tendency.

The application of this theory to achievement motivation is moderately complex. However, one principle accounts for several important findings: $M_s > M_{af}$ people have greater instigating forces toward achievement behaviors than do those with less achievement motivation. This principle results in several obvious predictions. Those with high achievement motivation will spend a lot of time doing achievement activities, they will enter such activities quickly, and they will leave such activities, in general, after longer periods of time than those with less achievement motivation. The dynamics-of-action theory does differ from the original theory on a few achievement predictions, but the majority of the old theory's predictions have not been modified.

Dynamics-of-action theory is so new that only a few experimental tests of it have been done, some confirming it (for example, Kuhl & Blankenship, 1979) and some not (for example, Yates & Revelle, 1979). The theory is so complex in its entirety that computer simulations are sometimes necessary to test its implications, so a full evaluation of the theory will have to await further research. The theory's approach, however, has already proven provocative and refreshing.

## Conclusions and critique

The theory of achievement motivation has had its critics—some of them very severe—and much of the criticism has been aimed at the instrument used to assess the need to achieve. Entwisle (1972), for example, cites several studies indicating that the internal consistency of the TAT is abysmally low. This means that the amount of achievement imagery in a story told to one TAT picture correlates poorly with the amount of achievement imagery in a story told to a different TAT picture. How can n Ach be said to be a stable personality motive if it varies greatly from one picture to another? Entwisle also presents evidence that the TAT's test/retest reliability is unacceptably low, as are correlations between the various measures of achievement motivation.

There has also been disenchantment with the validity of the n-Ach score. In an important review of the literature, Klinger (1966) concluded that n-Ach scores do not constitute an adequate measure of motivation. This conclusion was based on the fact that only about half the published studies reported a significant relation between n Ach and some measure of performance. If n Ach has no predictive validity, it is a worthless statistic.[7]

Atkinson and his colleagues are certainly aware of these criticisms, all of which they have vigorously attempted to refute. Atkinson's defense of the TAT's reliability has two parts. First, Atkinson points out that, in achievement research, the subject population is usually divided rather grossly into high- and low-n-Ach groups. Hence, a subject who is above the median on the first test need only be above the median on the retest in order to exhibit an n-Ach score stable enough for research purposes. Since 72.5% of subjects did exhibit such stability (Lowell, reported in McClelland et al., 1953, Chapter 7), low test/retest reliability based on the *exact* n-Ach score does not trouble Atkinson; the exact score is rarely used in achievement research.

Second, Atkinson, Bongort, and Price (1977) have shown that, even if the TAT had atrociously low reliability, the test could still have highly accurate predictive ability. And isn't the ability to predict behavior the crucial feature of any psychological test?

Atkinson supports the validity of the TAT with a diverse (and rather indignant) defense. The key to this defense is the Yerkes/Dodson law,

---

[7]Ceranski, Teevan, and Kalle (1979) have recently shown that using the TAT to measure fear of failure results in superior predictive power compared to $T_r$. This is an interesting development since the TAT has typically been used previously to measure only $M_s$, not $M_{af}$.

which is used to explain why a consistently positive relation between n Ach and performance is not always obtained.

As previously mentioned, the Yerkes/Dodson law states that the relation between intensity of motivation and efficiency of performance is curvilinear, easy tasks being done best under high drive and difficult tasks being done best under low drive (see Figure 9-5). Assume that a person with low n Ach and one with high n Ach attempt the same easy task. As Figure 9-5 indicates, the high-n-Ach person would perform better. The TAT, then, would appear to have predictive validity for performance on that task. However, if the two persons attempted a difficult task, the high-n-Ach person would perform more poorly than the low-n-Ach person, owing to the greater than optimal level of motivation of the high-n-Ach person. In this instance, the TAT would appear to have poor predictive validity. Atkinson summarizes his defense succinctly:

> If the relationship between intensity of motivation and efficiency of performance is curvilinear, . . . then the relationships of individual differences in n Achievement and Anxiety to performance can be positive, negative, or zero, depending upon the conditions and requirements of the task. . . . This possibility now seems one of the most plausible explanations of the now-you-see-it-now-you-don't character of the relationship between n Achievement and level of performance [Atkinson, 1974, pp. 200–201].

However, even this defense of the theory of achievement motivation is subject to criticism. A theory that allows a positive, negative, or zero relation between motivation and performance *must* specify which is

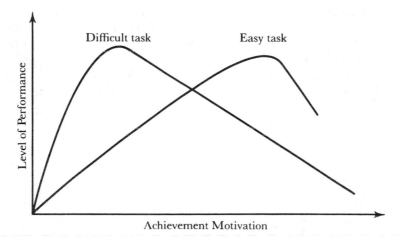

**Figure 9-5.** As task difficulty increases, the drive level at which optimal performance occurs decreases.

expected *before* the performance measure is obtained. Since nearly any relation is permitted by the theory, disconfirmation of the theory is impossible unless the type of relation is specified in advance. Any theory that is not susceptible to disproof is, of course, scientifically worthless.

"Now-you-see-it-now-you-don't" relations between n Ach and performance have been the source of substantial criticism of the theory of achievement motivation. D. Solomon (1968, cited in Entwisle, 1972) thinks that one general achievement motive cannot possibly explain all behavior occurring in the diverse situations in which a person's performance can be evaluated against some standard of excellence. Discussing the lack of transsituational stability of n Ach, Klinger (1966) states: "It seems clear that whatever n Ach scores measure is quite ephemeral, capable of registering differently in different fantasy instruments, differently in fantasy as contrasted with cognitive task instruments, and differently at different times in the same experimental session with the same or similar instruments" (p. 300).

Despite the criticisms of the theory of achievement motivation, however, it must be said that the theory has generated a large amount of research during the last 20 years. Much of the research has dealt with important practical issues, such as vocational aspiration, ability grouping in the classroom, and achievement motivation among women. The broad scope of the theory has been responsible for some criticism (such as that by Klinger quoted above), but this breadth also contributed to its great importance in the evolution of motivational theory.

Weiner (1972) terms the theory of achievement motivation "quasicognitive." Although it is less mechanistic than Hullian theory, it does not provide a large role for cognition. The subject brings $M_s$ and $M_{af}$ to each achievement situation; then the subject need determine only the $P_s$ and the perceived instrumentality. Thus, a person needs to make only two cognitive evaluations in an achievement situation.

The next group of theories we shall consider, consistency theories, will place far greater stress on the role of cognition in determining motivation.

# CHAPTER 10

# Cognitive-Consistency
# Theories

*Nobody goes there anymore. It's too crowded.*

*Yogi Berra*

As Singer (1966) wrote, "In recent years the development and extension of theories of cognitive consistency has been the largest single category of productive social-psychological research" (p. 47). In the years
since that statement appeared, theories of cognitive consistency have
undergone even further elaboration in some of the most intriguing research done in all of psychology.

The central tenet of consistency theories is that when a person's cognitions are in a conflicting or inconsistent relation with one another,
the person is motivated to reduce that conflict. For example, despite the
fact that I often drive 80 miles per hour, I tell my young daughter that
one should always obey the law. Since my statement is inconsistent
with my behavior, I am motivated to do something, such as eliminate
my tendency to speed. This act will remove the inconsistency and return me to a homeostatic cognitive state. Homeostasis here has much
the same meaning as it had for Cannon (see Chapter 5)—a neutral,
quiescent state. All consistency theories are homeostatic theories in that
they postulate that a person always wants to return to a state in which
all his or her thoughts and actions are consistent with one another.

We shall discuss five of the cognitive-consistency theories: balance
theory, Osgood and Tannenbaum's congruity theory, equity theory,
cognitive-dissonance theory, and self-perception theory.

## Balance theory

Two theorists, Heider and Newcomb, have formulated similar balance
theories.

Heider, like Lewin, was a Gestalt theorist, and the Gestalt principles
used initially to describe perceptual phenomena came to influence
Heider's description of interpersonal relations. According to Gestalt
psychologists, certain figures, or *Gestalten,* are more stable than others
and tend to be remembered more accurately. Other figures containing
deviations from the stable figures tend to be transformed into the *Gestalten* at the time of recall. There appears to be a pressure to perceive
symmetrical, balanced, orderly figures. Heider's balance theory is
based on the application of this principle to interpersonal situations.

## Motivational constructs

Heider's balance theory is often called "the $p$-$o$-$x$ theory"; $p$ is a person, $o$ is some other person, and $x$ is an impersonal entity that $p$ and $o$ have opinions about. In the part of the theory most relevant to this discussion (Heider, 1946), Heider dealt with the relations between only these three elements.

Figure 10-1 illustrates balanced relations between $p$, $o$, and $x$. A plus sign means liking or approval; a minus sign means the opposite. These relations are called "balanced" because there is no pressure to change them. The status quo is acceptable to $p$. In the first example diagrammed, you and your roommate, whom you like, both support the Republican party. This is a perfectly happy arrangement. In the second, you and your roommate, whom you like, both hate modern art—another satisfactory arrangement. In the third, your obnoxious neighbor says your new car is ugly. It's no wonder you dislike him; he obviously has poor taste.

Figure 10-2 contains imbalanced relations. In the first example, your friend, whom you like, dislikes the way you dress. Heider says (1946, pp. 107–108) that "if no balanced state exists, then forces toward this state will arise." This motivational principle predicts that you will start disliking your friend, you will start disliking your wardrobe, or you will try to get your friend to like your wardrobe. If one of these three changes occurs, the system will be in a state of balance.

In the second example, your roommate, whom you like, announces she strongly supports capital punishment. You are repulsed by capital punishment. Something must change. You must revise either your

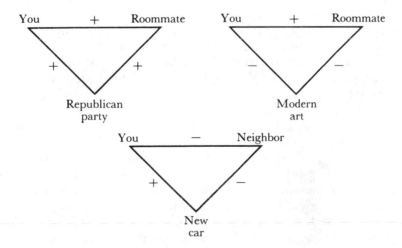

**Figure 10-1.** Three examples of balanced relations.

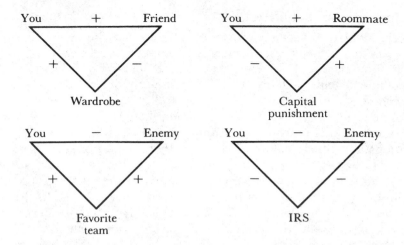

**Figure 10-2.** Four examples of imbalanced relations. However, Heider has termed the fourth configuration "ambiguous."

opinion of your roommate or your opinion of capital punishment or your roommate must change her opinion.

In the third example, you see someone you dislike supporting your favorite team. Again, something is amiss.

The last example pictured is a special case; Heider terms such configurations "ambiguous." Someone whom you dislike hates the IRS, which you also dislike. By analogy with the maxim "The enemy of my enemy is my friend," you should like the IRS, but you don't. With no positive bond anywhere in the three relations, attitude change simply cannot be predicted by Heider's system.

Note that all balanced triads have zero or two minus signs. A quick way to determine whether a triad is balanced is to multiply its three signs. A positive product signifies balance, a negative product imbalance. Remember that the triple-minus configuration, however, is not necessarily imbalanced.

Closely related to Heider's balance theory is that of Newcomb (1956). Newcomb's theory, called "the $ABX$ theory," emphasizes influences on interpersonal attraction and communication. Hence, Newcomb is most concerned with the bond between the two subjects ($A$-$B$ bond) and how this bond is affected by their sentiment toward some object $X$. Newcomb believes that the most important variable influencing attraction between two persons is the similarity of their attitudes (for example, in the first example in Figure 10-1, to the extent that $A$ and $B$ feel positively toward $X$, $A$ and $B$ will like each other).

Interpersonal attraction always and necessarily varies with perceived similarity regarding important and relevant objects (including the persons themselves). While I regard similarity of attitudes as a necessary rather than a sufficient condition, I believe that it accounts for more of the variance in interpersonal attraction than does any other single variable [Newcomb, 1956, p. 579].

Newcomb's motivational principle is the same as Heider's. If a situation such as that depicted in the first example in Figure 10-1 exists and *A* receives new information revealing that *B* feels negatively about *X*, then the attraction of *A* to *B* will likely decrease. The positive sign between *A* and *B* will be replaced by a negative sign, which will restore balance. Similarly, if *A* begins to dislike *B*, *A* may distort *B*'s true, positive opinion of *X*. This distortion will change the *B-X* bond to negative, thereby restoring balance.

There are a small number of differences between Heider's and Newcomb's versions of balance theory. Whereas Heider's theory has only balanced and imbalanced configurations, Newcomb's also has "nonbalanced" ones. A nonbalanced triad has a negative *A-B* (or, in Heider's terminology, a negative *p-o*) bond. Both the third and fourth examples in Figure 10-2 are nonbalanced configurations according to Newcomb. Newcomb (1968) reasons that, if the two persons have a negative bond, there will be no pressure to change the other person's opinion about anything. "Imbalance" would not be an appropriate description for a situation in which *A* could say "I don't care what that jerk (*B*) thinks about the United Nations (*X*)" because there would be no motivation toward balance. Carroll (1977) has presented evidence that, when a negative *A-B* bond is present, no motivation toward restoring balance is present; however, when a positive *A-B* bond exists, motivation toward balance is present. This supports Newcomb's distinction between nonbalanced and imbalanced configurations.

## Experimental evidence

A large number of research findings support Heider's and Newcomb's balance theories. One of the first was that by Jordan (1953), who had subjects rate hypothetical balanced and imbalanced situations for pleasantness. The higher ratings given the balanced situations indicated to Jordan that those were the situations toward which his subjects would normally strive. Other studies adopted the methodology of Morrissette (1958), who asked subjects to predict the nature of the missing bond in a triad. For example, a subject would be given: "I like Joe. He likes modern art. How do you think I would feel about modern art?" Studies involving the rating of hypothetical situations give general support to the balance-theory predictions.

Numerous studies also strongly support Newcomb's contention that similarity of attitudes fosters attraction (for example, Byrne, 1961; Izard, 1960; Newcomb, 1956). Byrne (1961) asked subjects to fill out an opinion questionnaire and two weeks later asked the same subjects to examine the questionnaire answers of another person. The subjects were asked to estimate how much they would like that person. Subjects examining questionnaires filled out identically to their own rated the other person extremely high (6.5 on a 7-point scale). Similarly, Izard (1960) found that female college students tend to choose best friends who are significantly similar to themselves according to the Edwards Preference Scale.

Perhaps even more supportive of the balance theories are studies that actually change the attraction between two persons during the course of an experiment and then test for any resulting attitude change. The theories predict that, if a triad initially contains three positive bonds and the $p$-$o$ bond is then changed to negative, the attitude of one of the persons toward $x$ must change in order to preserve balance. Exactly this design was used in a study by Burdick and Burnes (1958). First, a faculty member gave an informal talk to some undergraduates. Those students whose ratings of the speaker indicated that they liked him changed their attitude toward the position he advocated. Then, in a second talk, the same speaker proceeded to berate the students. Following this lecture, the students' opinion moved away from the position that the speaker had advocated in the original talk. Burdick and Burnes also found that students who had expressed strong affiliation needs on the TAT were significantly less stable in their opinions; that is, they were more likely to change their opinions toward or away from that of the speaker as he appeared first pleasant, then obnoxious. Perhaps people with high affiliation needs would be more sensitive to the $p$-$o$ bond and hence would more easily experience a state of imbalance. Therefore, they would be more likely to change their opinions in order to restore balance.

A rather sophisticated experiment by Steiner and Peters (1958) clearly illustrates some of the intricacies of balance theories. The real subject and a confederate of the experimenters were asked to give the right answer to a simple problem. At the beginning of the experiment, the experimenters allowed several minutes for the subject and the confederate to interact; the confederate established himself as a likable person, thus creating rapport and a positive $p$-$o$ bond. During the question-and-answer session, the confederate always gave his answer first, and frequently he gave an obviously incorrect answer. Assume you are the real subject. Will you go along with this likable person by conforming with his incorrect answers? Figure 10-3 diagrams the situation. The other person has just said he favors option $A$. You can achieve balance by agreeing. This conformity will produce a configuration with three positive bonds—a balanced state. If you disagree, the negative $p$-$x$ bond will produce imbalance.

Steiner and Peters looked at the difference between subjects who generally conformed with the confederate's incorrect answers over a long series of trials and those who did not conform. The nonconformers

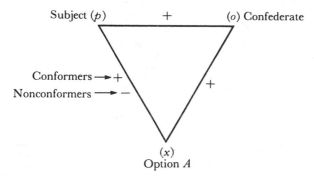

**Figure 10-3.** The situation in the experiment by Steiner and Peters (1958).

were more rejecting of the confederate, as measured by postexperimental ratings. Since the nonconformers had a negative $p$-$x$ bond, rejecting the confederate would create a negative $p$-$o$ bond, restoring balance. Further, nonconformers, more than conformers, tended to underestimate the number of times they had disagreed with the confederate. Thus, nonconformers were trying to minimize the negativity of the $p$-$x$ bond, as would be expected of those nonconformers who wanted to maintain a positive $p$-$o$ bond.

Balance theory also provides a helpful analysis of our attitudes toward communicators and their communications. Suppose you're a strong law-and-order advocate. While watching the evening news, you see a film of a police/student confrontation. How will you feel about the objectivity and trustworthiness of the newscaster if she states that the police were at fault for the disturbance? Would your opinion of the newscaster improve if she claimed the students were the instigators? Precisely this study was done by Zanna, Klosson, and Darley (1976). Using a real film of a police/student riot, the experimenters dubbed in either an announcer who blamed the students or one who blamed the police. Based on their responses on a questionnaire, subjects who watched the TV film were divided into propolice and prostudent groups. Table 10-1 contains the ratings of the newscast and newscaster made by each group. As balance theory would predict, if the subject liked the students and the newscaster liked the students, the subject liked the newscaster. Otherwise, the subject believed that the newscaster was biased.

## Criticisms

Although balance theory is supported to some extent by a large variety of studies, the theory has a few serious flaws. One problem—shared with another consistency theory to be discussed later—is the multiple-mode problem: there is more than one way for $p$ to correct an imbalance. This problem can be illustrated by reexamining Steiner and

**TABLE 10-1.** Ratings of the newscast and the newscaster in the Zanna et al. (1976) experiment.

|  | Prostudent subjects | | Propolice subjects | |
| --- | --- | --- | --- | --- |
|  | Students blamed | Police blamed | Students blamed | Police blamed |
| Accuracy/objectivity of newscast | 5.7 | 6.2 | 7.3 | 4.2 |
| Credibility/objectivity/ trustworthiness of newscaster | 5.8 | 6.3 | 7.0 | 5.8 |

From "How Television News Viewers Deal with Facts that Contradict Their Beliefs: A Consistency and Attribution Analysis," by M. P. Zanna, E. C. Klosson, and J. M. Darley. In *Journal of Applied Psychology*, 1976, *6*, 159–176. Copyright 1976 by V. H. Winson & Sons. Reprinted by permission.

Peters's study. A subject who hears the confederate choose option 1 has several ways of achieving balance. He can change his opinion about option 1. ("Maybe 1 isn't such a bad answer after all.") He can lower his opinion of the confederate. ("Anybody who chooses 1 has got to be nuts.") He can incorrectly perceive the confederate's opinion. ("He said '1,' but I know he meant to say '2.') He can try to change the confederate's opinion. ("Let's consider the other option.") He can minimize the importance of the issue so that the imbalance can be tolerated. ("So what if we disagree? Who cares about this problem anyhow?") Abelson and Rosenberg (1958) point out that the subject can also stop thinking, thereby ignoring the fact that an imbalance exists. (See the *Congressional Record* for examples!) Balance theory cannot predict which of these many possible activities will occur. For example, an experimenter who creates an imbalance may find no attitude change toward the other person. This finding does not disconfirm balance theory: the subject may have chosen another means of restoring balance. Consequently, to test the theory, the experimenter must meter every single possible means. This is impractical, if not impossible.

A second problem of balance theory is that all bonds are treated as if they were equally important and therefore equally susceptible to change in order to restore balance. In most triads, however, the bonds are not equally strong. For example, if a husband and wife disagreed over what wine to order with dinner, a divorce would probably not ensue. Their feelings about the wine are less strong than their feelings about each other. Yet balance theory makes no statement concerning the relative durability, importance, or magnitude of the bonds.

A third problem is that it is difficult to know exactly what constitutes balance. Frequently one's opinion of another person or an object has both positive and negative aspects. If the *p-o* bond is ambivalent, is there balance? The lack of a clear definition of the homeostatic state is a most serious problem in cognitive-dissonance theory, which will be discussed later in the chapter. Further discussion of this topic therefore will be deferred until then.

## *Osgood and Tannenbaum's congruity theory*

The consistency theory proposed by Osgood and Tannenbaum (1955) is more limited in scope than balance theory. It deals with attitude change caused by communication. The theory is more precise than balance theory and for this reason is easier to test.

### Motivational constructs

Osgood and Tannenbaum propose that it is cognitively more parsimonious to evaluate related concepts in a similar manner. If person $B$ advocates policy $X$, it is easier for me to have the same opinion of $B$ and $X$ than to have different opinions of them. Therefore, my evaluations of $B$ and $X$ will tend to migrate toward each other. This is the motivational principle of congruity theory.

Osgood and Tannenbaum measure attitude by using the semantic differential, a psychometric device created by Osgood. The semantic differential includes a 7-point evaluative scale, as shown in Figure 10-4. The subject is given a list of people and topics and is asked to rate each one separately on the evaluative scale. For example, a liberal subject might rate a liberal politician $+3$, modern art $+1$, gun control 0, capital punishment $-1$, and a conservative politician $-3$.

Suppose the subject is then shown a press release indicating that the liberal politician $(+3)$ supports capital punishment $(-1)$. Whereas balance theorists would call the situation "imbalanced," Osgood and Tannenbaum would call it "incongruous." Congruity is achieved by movement of the subject's evaluations of the politician and capital punishment toward each other. This theory is called a "compromise theory," because the final evaluations of the items are at points between their original locations.

The most important principle summarizing Osgood and Tannenbaum's equations is that *the less polar item moves more.* (On the semantic-differential scale, $+3$ and $-3$ are the poles.) The item closer to the neutral point moves farther toward the polar item than the polar item moves toward the more neutral item. Our liberal subject, then, would evaluate the liberal politician somewhat less favorably and capital punishment much more favorably. Similarly, if the conservative politician came out for modern art, the subject would feel slightly less negative about the conservative and substantially more negative about modern art.

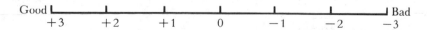

Good $\qquad$ Bad
$+3 \qquad +2 \qquad +1 \qquad 0 \qquad -1 \qquad -2 \qquad -3$

**Figure 10-4.** The evaluative dimension of the semantic differential, a measurement technique developed by Osgood, Suci, and Tannenbaum (1957).

A rather counterintuitive prediction is made when a highly polar source supports a less polar item of the same sign. For example, if your best friend ($+3$) says she likes classical music ($+1$), congruity theory would predict that you would like classical music much more and your friend a little less!

Osgood and Tannenbaum have added to congruity theory several correction factors designed to increase the accuracy of the predictions. One is a correction for incredulity. Suppose you were to read that the president ($+3$) is in favor of quadrupling the income tax ($-3$). You might be skeptical that the president ever said that, since no politician interested in reelection and self-preservation would dare propose such a thing. Consequently, you would not lower your opinion of the president or raise your opinion of taxes by the usual amount. The wider the disparity between the source and the opinion attributed to that source, the greater the chance for incredulity. Therefore, the wider the disparity, the greater the "incredulity correction," which lowers the amount of opinion change predicted by the original equation.

A second correction factor is quite straightforward. Osgood and Tannenbaum propose that one's attitude toward the source of a statement is not as movable as one's attitude toward the object of a statement. For example, if a Soviet leader ($-1$) says he favors disarmament ($+2$), disarmament moves slightly more downward and the Soviet leader slightly less upward than the original equation would predict.

## Proposed modifications

Congruity theory has received experimental support from studies done by Osgood and his associates. However, Rokeach and Rothman (1965) have pointed out that, well as the theory predicts attitude change following a communication, some important modifications make the predictions even better. Rokeach and Rothman's major criticism is one of the principle that, when two unequally valued objects are juxtaposed, the final evaluations must lie between the two original ones. Consider the following example.

Suppose that "golfer" is rated $+1$ and "president" is rated $+3$. If the president reveals that he is a golfer, we would rate him slightly above $+2$, according to congruity theory. However, being a president is so much more important a fact about a person than his choice of hobbies that most people would ignore the $+1$ entirely and rate "president who golfs" $+3$. A final rating need not lie *between* the two related terms. One term may be so overwhelmed by the other that the final evaluation is identical with one of the two original evaluations. Whereas Osgood and Tannenbaum say the less *polar* item moves more, Rokeach and Rothman say the less *important* item moves more.

Consider a second example. Suppose that "brain surgeon" is rated $+2$ and "sloppy" is rated $-1$. Congruity theory would predict that a brain surgeon accused of being sloppy would be rated slightly less than +1. However, most people would actually rate "sloppy brain surgeon" as even more negative than the −1 given "sloppy." Once again, the composite rating need not lie between the two original ones.

Even though congruity theory, with the modifications proposed by Rokeach and Rothman, makes accurate prediction possible, the theory has not received a great deal of attention.

## Equity theory

The consistency theory that has been most influential in the analysis of work behavior is equity theory. Almost every modern textbook on management or industrial relations treats this important psychological theory.

### Motivational constructs

Adams (1963, 1965) proposed that, when people evaluate their own transactions with others, inputs and outcomes are carefully weighed. Inputs are those factors that may earn some return for one's personal investment—factors such as effort, education, or talent. Outcomes are returns or rewards, such as salary or fringe benefits. As I weigh my own inputs and outcomes, I compare them to the inputs and outcomes of other people. Equity occurs when the ratio of my outcomes to inputs is equal to the ratio of the other person. This may be represented mathematically by the following equation.[1]

$$\frac{O_{self}}{I_{self}} = \frac{O_{other}}{I_{other}}$$

An example of an equitable situation would be one in which my friend and I work just as hard (equal input) and receive equal pay (equal outcome).

Inequity occurs when the ratio of my outcomes to inputs is different from the other person's ratio. If the other person has qualifications equal to mine, if we work equally hard, and if she earns more than I do, inequity exists. Inequity exists also if the other person earns less than I do. In either case, the inequity creates tension, and this tension has motivating properties that impel the person to eliminate the inequity.

There are several ways of accomplishing the inequity reduction. (1) If I feel inequitably underpaid, I can change my own inputs by not

[1]A refinement of this formula has been offered (Walster, Berscheid, & Walster, 1973). For the purposes of this introduction to equity theory, however, the original formula will suffice.

$$\frac{O_{self}}{I_{self}} \neq \frac{O_{other}}{I_{other}} \; ; \; \frac{O_{self}}{I_{self}} = \frac{O_{other}}{I_{other}}$$

**Figure 10-5.** Inequity based on my low outcome can be reduced if I reduce my input.

$$\frac{O_{self}}{I_{self}} \neq \frac{O_{other}}{I_{other}} \; ; \; \frac{O_{self}}{I_{self}} = \frac{O_{other}}{I_{other}}$$

**Figure 10-6.** Inequity based on my low outcome can be reduced by increasing my outcome.

working so hard. Figure 10-5 depicts this situation. (2) I can increase my outcomes by convincing the boss that I deserve a raise, as shown in Figure 10-6. (3) I can cause the other person to increase her input by asking her to do extra work. (4) I can ask the other person to reduce her outcomes by asking her not to accept some fringe benefits.

Reduction of inequity may occur in other ways as well. I may decide that the other person is not really a fair person with whom I should compare myself; equity may then be restored by comparing myself to a different person who is in a position identical to mine. Finally, I may restore equity by cognitively distorting the situation: "Being paid so little is really good for me. This adversity helps to build my character."

## Experimental evidence

Dozens of experiments have been performed to test equity theory in work situations. In a study dealing with the effects of underpayment, Lawler and O'Gara (1967) hired undergraduates to do some interviews. Some people were paid 10¢ for each interview (underpaid), whereas others were paid 25¢ for each interview (equitably paid). It was found that, compared to the equitably-paid students, the underpaid students spent less time on each interview, thereby decreasing their input. Also, the underpaid students performed more interviews in a given time period, thereby increasing their outcome (pay). The situation is diagrammed in Figure 10-7. By decreasing input and increasing outcome, the underpaid interviewers reestablished equity.

Several studies have examined the influence of inequity caused by overpayment. Adams and Jacobsen (1964) hired three groups of students to perform a proofreading task. One group of subjects was told

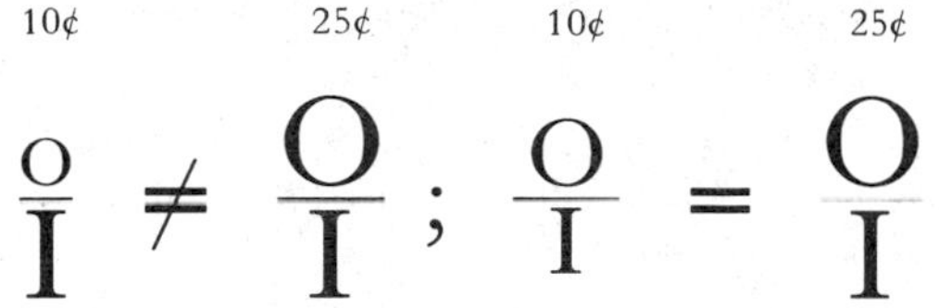

$$10¢ \qquad 25¢ \qquad 10¢ \qquad 25¢$$

$$\frac{O}{I} \neq \frac{O}{I} \; ; \; \frac{O}{I} = \frac{O}{I}$$

**Figure 10-7.** The 10¢ group decreases input and increases outcome, thereby restoring equity.

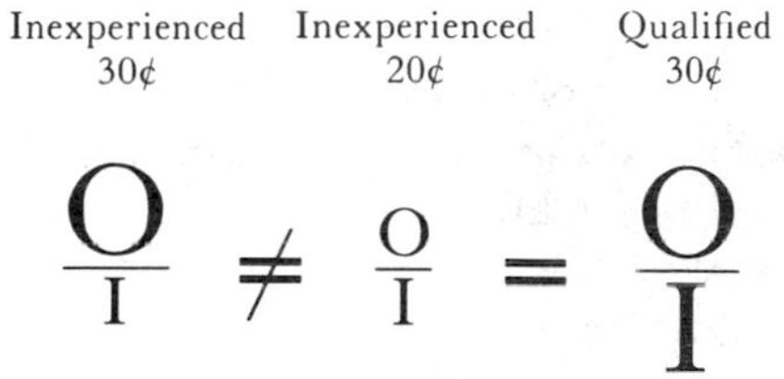

$$\text{Inexperienced} \quad \text{Inexperienced} \quad \text{Qualified}$$
$$30¢ \qquad\qquad 20¢ \qquad\qquad 30¢$$

$$\frac{O}{I} \neq \frac{O}{I} = \frac{O}{I}$$

**Figure 10-8.** Of the three groups in the Adams and Jacobsen (1964) study, only the inexperienced group paid 30¢ a page experienced inequity.

that despite their inexperience, the subjects would be paid the same rate (30¢ a page) as regular proofreaders. This group is thus the overpaid group, since they are getting an outcome usually reserved for people with a greater input (more experience). A second group was told that, because of their inexperience, the subjects would be paid only 20¢ a page. A third group was told that they were well-qualified and that the subjects would therefore receive 30¢ a page. Figure 10-8 depicts the situation. Note that the first group is the only group that experienced inequity. Adams and Jacobsen found that the overpaid group spent more time on each page (increased input). As a result they completed fewer pages and received less pay (reduced outcome). This restored equity.[2]

One of the most realistic tests of equity in an industrial situation was done by Pritchard, Dunnette, and Jorgenson (1972). When hiring 253 men to work as clerks for one week, the experimenters promised a wage of about $2 an hour. Soon after they began working, subgroups of men were told that they would be underpaid, overpaid, or paid an equitable amount. On job-satisfaction questionnaires filled out during the work week, both underpaid *and overpaid* workers expressed less

---

[2]The methodology of some of the overpayment studies has been criticized by Pritchard (1969). Other authors (for example, Goodman & Friedman, 1971) do not believe that these criticisms seriously undermine equity theory.

satisfaction than equitably paid workers. Apparently, inequity of either type is somewhat aversive.[3]

The lengths to which people will go to restore equity are illustrated in a fascinating study by D. R. Schmitt and Marwell (1972). Two workers could choose to work cooperatively and make a lot of money, or they could choose to work separately and make only a little money. However, the cooperative condition varied. In the equity/cooperation conditions, the two subjects evenly split the large reward if they chose to cooperate. In the inequity/cooperation condition, the subjects unevenly split the large reward if they choose to cooperate. The results were striking. Of course, when faced with the option of cooperating for a large reward evenly split or working alone for a small reward, cooperation was the overwhelming choice. However, when the lucrative cooperation option became inequitable (but still very profitable), 40% of the pairs stopped cooperating and chose to work separately for a lower but equal reward. This result may be economically irrational, but it certainly dramatizes the strong motivation to restore equity.

Occasionally a dramatic event provides a valuable real-world opportunity to test a psychological theory. Such was the case in December of 1975 when major league baseball abolished the "reserve clause" that had bound players to a specific team. First, stars tried to negotiate huge salary increases with the team on which they were already playing. If these negotiations proved unsuccessful, the player would "play out his option." This meant that he had to play with his present team for one year, usually at a much reduced salary, before he was allowed to become a "free agent," offering his services to the highest bidder. Playing out one's option must have been particularly galling for the stars who could read in the newspapers how other stars were signing multi-million-dollar contracts. Those playing out their option at a reduced salary would have felt grossly underpaid. One way to restore equity would be to decrease performance. Lord and Hohenfeld (1979) showed that such players exhibited a drastic decrease in performance while playing out their option, just as equity theory would predict.

Although most of the early research testing equity theory involved work situations, much of the recent research has examined the theory's predictions in social situations, even in intimate social situations. For example, Murstein (1972) had subjects rate the physical attractiveness of a large number of couples who were engaged or dating regularly. Since the people were rated individually, raters did not know who was dating whom. The results showed that the members of each dating pair were surprisingly close to each other on the physical-attractiveness dimension. If physical attractiveness is considered an "input" in the

---

[3]A study by Rivera and Tedeschi (1976) suggests that, although subjects publicly express dislike for inequitable situations in which they are overpaid, they might privately express preference for such an arrangement.

equity equation and if it is assumed that each member of the couple is receiving equivalent output, then equity theory requires that physical attractiveness also be equivalent for the two participants. Berscheid, Walster, and Bohrnstedt (1973) also found that couple members who rated their desirability equal to that of their partners were more satisfied with the relationship than were members who rated their desirability as unequal.

Occasionally, for one reason or another, a couple consists of two persons who are not equally attractive. Equity theory would allow for this situation only if the less attractive member can provide inputs other than beauty, thereby restoring equity to the relationship. Berscheid et al. tested this prediction in a survey study. It was found that, if a person claimed to be more attractive than the partner, the partner was said to be the richer, the more loving, and the more self-sacrificing. Obviously, the multimillionaires aren't using their "good looks" to attract the beauty queens; other assets can enter the equity equation.

Perhaps it strikes the reader as rather crass that equity theory treats the topic of romance in such a mercantile fashion. Yet, it is this wide applicability of the theory that makes it so valuable.

Equity theory has been used to analyze the famous Zimbardo (1973) study in which students were assigned the roles of jailers and prisoners in a mock prison. The brutal derogation of the prisoners by the guards caused the outcomes of the prisoners to plummet drastically. To restore equity, the guards attributed to the prisoners a large number of very undesirable characteristics, thereby reducing the prisoners' inputs. In a related study, Lerner and Simmons (1966) found that, when a student was shocked for making errors on a task and the observers knew the student would continue to be shocked for such mistakes, the observers devalued the student. When lower outputs are accompanied by lower inputs, equity is maintained.

As a final example, consider the anger and bewilderment Americans feel when a country that has received billions of U.S. dollars in foreign aid suddenly demonstrates anti-American sentiment. Such aid, however, throws the equity equation completely out of balance for the receiving nation, and, as we've seen already, inequitable relations are less preferred. Gergen (1969) and Gergen and Gergen (1971) have shown that benefactors are liked more when the beneficiary feels that the favor can be exactly repaid. If country X cannot possibly repay country Y, country Y may find its altruism resented.

## Cognitive-dissonance theory

Almost as famous as cognitive-dissonance theory is Zajonc's remark that "no theory in social psychology has stimulated more research than the theory of cognitive dissonance" (1968, p. 359). Since the formulation of dissonance theory by Leon Festinger in 1957, hundreds of articles and books have tested the theory's predictions in an extremely wide variety of situations. Because its domain is wider than the social configurations studied by balance theory or the changing attitudes studied by congruity theory, cognitive-dissonance theory has both more applicability and more ambiguity.

## Motivational constructs

The basic principles of dissonance theory are simple. Cognitive dissonance results when a person maintains two inconsistent cognitions. Cognitive dissonance is an aversive state, and—like hunger or thirst—it must be reduced. When a person experiences cognitive dissonance, he or she is motivated to reduce it, thereby returning to a state of cognitive consonance. This motivational principle is the core of the theory of cognitive dissonance. Festinger explicitly states that dissonance has the same energizing properties as other motives, such as hunger or frustration.

Several examples may help clarify what Festinger means by *dissonance*. Suppose you realize that you are a heavy smoker, and you are also aware that smoking has been shown to cause cancer. These thoughts are dissonant. The theory says dissonance must be reduced. You can accomplish this by changing your behavior: you can stop smoking. Or you can change your opinion: you can decide that the relation between smoking and cancer has not been proved. Either way, dissonance is reduced and consonance is restored.

Take another example. Despite your friend's advice, you buy a 1958 Edsel. The car proves to be chronically in need of repair. You have two inconsistent thoughts: "I paid $1000" and "This car is worth $0." How do you reduce dissonance? "Oh, having an old car is fun, even if it doesn't run well." "Old cars increase in value far beyond what it costs to repair them." "Taking this car into the shop all the time has taught me a lot about how engines work." "Pushing my car to the nearest service station has given me a lot of good exercise."

## Four areas of early cognitive-dissonance research

Festinger's book *A Theory of Cognitive Dissonance* (1957), the first complete statement of cognitive-dissonance theory, contained four main sections, each of which lent support to the theory.

**Postdecisional dissonance.**   Whenever a decision is made, the negative aspects of the chosen alternative and the positive aspects of the rejected alternative are sources of dissonance: if I opt for a big car, its huge gas consumption produces a dissonant cognition, as does the economy of the small car I spurned. Dissonance can be reduced by increasing the attractiveness of the chosen alternative and decreasing the attractiveness of the rejected one. The decision will then seem eminently sensible.

Illustrative of this point is an experiment by Brehm (1956). Female undergraduates were allowed to choose a gift for themselves from a set of items that they had previously rated for desirability. Half the subjects were offered a choice between two items that they had rated as about equally desirable. The other half were offered a choice between two items that they had rated rather differently. The first group represents the high-dissonance condition. Since the two items were so close in attractiveness, the rejected alternative would have many attractive features. Awareness of those features would be dissonant with the choice actually made. The dissonance could be reduced by reevaluating the chosen alternative upward and the rejected alternative downward in a postdecisional evaluation. That is precisely what occurred. The other group represents the low-dissonance condition. Since the rejected item had fewer attractive features than the chosen one, not much dissonance was present. Consequently, the postdecisional evaluation showed less change in the low-dissonance group.

Aronson and Mills (1959) tested postdecisional dissonances in a different way. They told subjects—female undergraduates—that they were seeking students to participate in a discussion group whose topic was sex. Subjects who decided to join underwent either severe, mild, or no "initiation" to the "group." In the severe condition, the subject had to read aloud to a male experimenter a list of erotic words and two passages describing sexual activity—supposedly to demonstrate that she was mature enough for the discussion group. In the mild initiation, the subject merely had to read aloud a list of sex-related words. Subjects in all groups then listened to a tape recording purportedly typical of the group discussions and were asked to rate it for interest. The tape turned out to contain a tedious discussion of reproduction in lower animals.

As expected, subjects in the severe-initiation condition rated the discussion as more interesting than the other subjects did. They had undergone an embarrassing experience in order to join a dull discussion—surely a dissonant pair of events. They could reduce dissonance by reevaluating the discussion upward. For the other subjects, the decision to join the group had not been costly, and therefore the dull discussion produced no dissonance. They had no need to inflate the rating of the discussion.

Festinger has succinctly summarized this area of research with a homily: we come to love that for which we have suffered. That is true, of course, only if we have more or less chosen to endure the suffering. Only then is there any dissonance to be dissipated by distorting one's attitude toward the suffering: "Deciding to join this fraternity was a good move. The initiation wasn't so bad. Besides, it was worthwhile because this is such a great group—lots better than those others I decided not to join."

**Forced compliance.**   One of the most controversial areas of cognitive-dissonance research is forced compliance. The controversy over forced compliance has centered on (but has not been confined to) an experiment by Festinger and Carlsmith (1959). Subjects were asked to perform a colossally boring manual task. On finishing the task, a subject was told that the experimenter who would normally tell the next subject about the task was absent. The subject was asked whether he would kindly do it. Half the subjects were offered $1 to tell the next subject that the task was fun; half were offered $20. Once again, put yourself in the subject's position. You have just been bored to death, and now you are telling a fellow student the task is loads of fun. Surely these are dissonant cognitions. If offered $20, however, you should experience little dissonance, since you have adequate justification—$20— for telling this obvious lie. Festinger called the $20 subjects the "forced-compliance group"; the cash "forces" the subject to comply with the experimenter's request. Now put yourself in the place of the $1 subject. You have agreed to lie, and there is no compelling reason to do so. (You are a member of the "insufficient-justification group.") You can reduce the dissonance between cognitions by revising your opinion of the task upward.

In cognitive-dissonance theory, attitude change is predicted for the insufficient-justification group and not for the forced-compliance group. Indeed, Festinger and Carlsmith found that the $1 subjects rated the manual task as much more interesting than the $20 subjects did.

Festinger summarizes this area of research with another homily: use kid gloves to get attitude change. If you force compliance by paying someone $5000 to vote for your candidate, the person will vote for your candidate but still feel the guy is a bum. If you can get someone to perform an act that favors your candidate without providing sufficient justification for the act, the person will be in a state of dissonance. To reduce this dissonance, he may improve his opinion of your candidate.

Forced-compliance studies immediately came under attack. The study by Festinger and Carlsmith just described was the main target of critics, who offered several explanations of the greater attitude change among the $1 subjects. Some of the alternative explanations were refuted. The most serious problem for dissonance theorists, however, was that the results of the study were not consistently replicable. Indeed, many studies showed that greater monetary incentive caused more attitude change—not less change, as dissonance theorists would predict. (Greater attitude change resulting from greater monetary incentive has been termed "the incentive effect.") Elms (1967) and Janis and

Gilmore (1965) have reasoned that advocating a position contrary to one's attitude induces one to dredge up from memory experiences that might support the new position and to invent supportive arguments. A result of these efforts might be a belief that perhaps the new position isn't so implausible after all. Of course, if one is paid more to advocate the new position, more enthusiastic scanning of past experiences and invention of arguments will take place. For this reason, convincing oneself that the new position is plausible will occur more under high-reward conditions—the exact opposite of what dissonance theory predicts.

Both those who favor the incentive position and those who favor the dissonance position have available several supportive studies. A study by Carlsmith, Collins, and Helmreich (1966) attempted to resolve the conflict. In the study done by Janis and Gilmore (1965), subjects had been paid to write an essay advocating a viewpoint the opposite of their own. Carlsmith et al. (1966) reasoned that the Janis and Gilmore (1965) essay-writing procedure did not really commit the subjects to the counterattitudinal position they were describing. Hence, writing such an essay produced little dissonance: "The experimenter knows I really didn't believe what I was writing." Carlsmith et al. put one group of subjects in such an essay-writing situation and found an in-centive effect: attitude change varied with amount of reward. Carl-smith et al. put another group in a situation similar to that in Festinger and Carlsmith's study. The subjects had to tell another subject (really a confederate of the experimenters) that the experiment was fun. In this second situation, the real subject would assume that his listener would believe what he was saying. Here there would be dissonance. Carl-smith et al. found that in this second group the prediction of dissonance theory was confirmed: attitude change was inversely related to amount of reward. In short, what may be critical is commitment to the untruth. In the essay-writing condition, there is little commitment and therefore little dissonance. Lying to a fellow student in a face-to-face situation requires more commitment; therefore, more dissonance is created.[4]

The study by Carlsmith et al. has by no means erased all doubts concerning dissonance theory. It does, however, illustrate the impor-tance of subtle methodological variations.

**Exposure to information.**    A third area of research discussed in Festinger's book concerns exposure to information. If one is in a state of dissonance because one has been told something discrepant with one's own opinion, one can reduce the dissonance by seeking out new consonant information and avoiding new dissonant information. An exception occurs only when one is experiencing a very large amount of

[4]See Linder, Cooper, & Jones (1967), which represents a similar attempt to recon-cile the incentive and dissonance positions.

dissonance. Should the dissonant information become overwhelming, a person might find it easier to seek out the small amount of additional dissonant information needed to change his or her mind than to accumulate the large amount of consonant information needed to offset the substantial dissonance.

In support of his theory, Festinger (1957) cites a study by Wallen (1942). Each subject indicated which adjectives in a list of 40 described himself or herself and which did not. A week later, the subject was shown another copy of the same list, made out by someone who was supposedly evaluating the subject. This person agreed with the subject on half the adjectives. Two days later, the subject attempted to recall the ratings made by the other person. Recall was significantly better for the adjectives on which the two ratings agreed. Dissonant information was recalled more poorly.

Another study investigating the effects of exposure to dissonant information was done by Allyn and Festinger (1961). Before hearing a talk recommending that the minimum age for driving a car be raised, one group of teenagers was warned what the message would be. The other group was not warned but was told instead to study the personality of the speaker. Presumably, the message was dissonant with the views of both groups. Attitude change toward the position recommended by the speaker was much greater for the latter group. Allyn and Festinger reasoned that the teenagers with prior knowledge of the topic could more easily reduce dissonance by rejecting the speaker than by changing their opinion.

The total amount of support for the prediction of dissonance theory concerning exposure to new information is not impressive. Brehm and Cohen (1962, p. 93), two strong adherents of dissonance theory, and others (Freedman & Sears, 1965) have stated that this area of the theory has not been well supported by experimental research. In particular, there is little evidence that subjects avoid information that would increase dissonance.

**Social support.**   The final area treated by Festinger (1957) concerned the efforts a person would make to bolster his or her consonant cognitions and reduce dissonant ones by seeking social support. If other persons holding the same opinion can be cited, one's own opinion seems more sensible; if persons holding the opposing opinion can be discredited, their dissonant ideas can be disregarded.

As examples of this process, there exist two very unusual automobile clubs in the United States. One consists of owners of Edsels; the other consists of owners of Corvairs. These two car models have been subjected to more ridicule through the years than any other cars. Edsel owners must have felt substantial dissonance when people laughed on hearing what car they owned. Corvair owners must have experienced dissonance when they learned how unsafe Ralph Nader claimed their car was. One way to reduce such dissonance is to gather all the Edsel owners together and all the Corvair owners together so that they can tell one another what a fine car they all purchased. This social support bolsters one's confidence in owning the car and minimizes the barbs of the critics.

Festinger (1957) cited a field study by Festinger, Riecken, and Schachter (1956) illustrating how people seek social support to reduce dissonance. A West Coast group of about 30 people believed that a vast flood would sweep across North America on a certain day and that they would be rescued by flying saucers before the catastrophic flood took place. Needless to say, neither the flood nor the saucers arrived according to schedule. Here, then, were people with two extremely dissonant cognitions: "I predicted floods and flying saucers" and "There were no floods or flying saucers." Following disconfirmation of the cult's predictions, the members immediately began feverish proselytizing. What they needed was more people who would accept their beliefs, thus reducing the dissonance engendered by the inaccuracy of those beliefs.

In summary, the four traditional areas of research—postdecisional dissonance, forced compliance, exposure to information, and social support—all have the same basic principles in common. When two cognitions or a cognition and an action are incompatible, the person is in a state of dissonance. This dissonance can be reduced by changing one's attitude, changing one's action, seeking support for one's cognitions, or rejecting as unimportant or immaterial any dissonant cognitions.

## Expansions of the theory

Since Festinger's publication of *A Theory of Cognitive Dissonance,* the theory has been expanded into areas somewhat removed from its original domain.

**Modification of traditional drives through cognitive dissonance.**    Some of the most dramatic experiments done to test dissonance theory have used dissonance to negate traditional sources of motivation, such as hunger and thirst. An experiment by Mansson (1969) illustrates this area of research.

Subjects first ate saltines covered with a sauce composed of horseradish, tabasco, and catsup. After incinerating the subjects' palates with this concoction, the experimenter asked each subject whether he or she would consent to drink absolutely no water for 24 hours. Some subjects were given insufficient justification for complying with this request; other subjects were told how crucial the second part of the experiment was. Needless to say, any subject who devoured the crackers and sauce and then agreed to the request would surely be in a state of dissonance. One way for the subject to reduce this dissonance would be to deny being thirsty. Subjects in the high-dissonance group—those who were given insufficient justification for going without water for 24 hours—dramatically decreased their ratings of their thirst after the dissonance was aroused. Furthermore, when given an opportunity to take a final drink of water before beginning their voluntary dehydration, they drank less than any other experimental group. Apparently they were very successful in denying their thirst in order to reduce their dissonance.

Denial of pain also has been studied in a few experiments, one of the most thought-provoking being that by Brock and Buss (1962). Both male and female subjects opposed to using shock in research were asked to do just that. Some of the subjects were given little opportunity to decline (low choice); other subjects were given ample opportunity (high choice). Each subject then faced a 10-button panel that ostensibly controlled shocks delivered to a nearby student, who was really a confederate of the experimenter. The subject (not the confederate) was first given shocks labeled 1, 2, and 5, and was asked to rate the painfulness of each. Higher numbers meant more severe shocks, and shock number 5 was quite noxious. The subjects then delivered shocks to the "victim," half of each group delivering only shock levels 1 through 5, the other half delivering only levels 6 through 10. Subsequently, subjects again rated the painfulness of shock 5. For high-choice subjects, shocking someone must have created substantial dissonance. Those subjects reduced their dissonance by lowering their estimates of the painfulness of shock 5 ("Oh, I'm not such a bad person. This hardly hurts at all"). Low-choice subjects did not lower their ratings. They had less dissonance because they had the cognition that they had been more or less forced to participate. Brock and Buss also asked each subject how much he or she had felt obligated to deliver the shocks. Those who had delivered stronger shocks and those who had shocked females reported more obligation, even though the experimenters had exerted no more pressure in these circumstances. These subjects decreased dissonance by claiming they had been forced to participate.

**Partial-reinforcement effect.**   One of the basic principles of learning is that organisms emit more responses during extinction after partial reinforcement than during extinction after continuous reinforcement. This phenomenon is called the "partial-reinforcement effect." Several explanations have been proposed to explain this effect, and one of the most unusual relies on the theory of cognitive dissonance.

Imagine an animal running down a runway in order to obtain food. The effort exerted in the runway is not wasted; food justifies the exertion. However, an animal that is only infrequently fed experiences dissonance on a large number of the trials. It has hustled down the runway for nothing. There is insufficient justification for the running, so the animal has to develop some "extra preference" to justify its behavior: "Even though there was no food, I didn't mind running down here. I needed the exercise anyway."

When extinction begins, the animal under partial reinforcement, like the animal under continuous reinforcement, has to realize that food is no longer present. However, the animal under partial reinforcement also has to extinguish all the extra preference it has generated before it will stop running. Consequently, extinction will take longer for a partially reinforced response.

This explanation at first seems unlikely. The work reported by Festinger (1961) concerning the partial-reinforcement effect was done only with rats. Can rats reduce dissonance or develop extra preference? Doesn't cognitive-dissonance reduction demand sophisticated cognition? Nevertheless, there is evidence that tends to support Festinger's explanation.

First, studies show that an effortful response takes longer to extinguish than a less effortful response (Aiken, 1957). Festinger claims that animals performing an effortful response to gain a morsel of food have to develop extra preference to justify that behavior. The presence of the extra preference retards extinction.

Second, Festinger has shown that an empty compartment in which animals were delayed en route to food also seems to acquire extra preference. Such a compartment, because it has no obvious reward, insufficiently justifies any exertion toward it. Therefore, extra preference for it is acquired.

It must be said that the cognitive-dissonance explanation of the partial-reinforcement effect has not generated a great deal of research. The reason may be that psychologists are unsure whether to take it seriously. Can a rat reduce dissonance?

**Dissonance as a drive.**    Festinger and his colleagues have repeatedly stated that dissonance should act much as any other drive does. One of the more interesting tests of this notion was a study by Cottrell, Rajecki, and Smith (1974). This study was designed to test whether "cognitive dissonance produced by making a decision has the energizing effects upon the performance of an irrelevant task that are ascribed to D in Hull-Spence theory" (p. 81). Recall from Chapter 5 that the theory predicts that, as D increases, the dominant response becomes more likely to occur.

Cottrell et al. induced dissonance in one group of subjects by having them choose between two gifts that they had rated only slightly different in desirability. Subjects in another group were merely given a gift without having to make a choice. Subjects subsequently were asked to read very briefly presented words, some of which were shown frequently, some infrequently. Some of the recognition trials, however, were really pseudorecognition trials; the exposure time was so brief that no word could be adequately seen. The experimenters found that on these trials the subjects experiencing dissonance were more likely than the other subjects to respond with the higher-frequency words. Dissonance acted like a drive in the Hull/Spence model; as D increased, the dominant response became more likely.

**Individual differences in dissonance reduction.**    A small amount of research has investigated individual differences in the amount and mode of dissonance reduction.

Janis (1954) and A. R. Cohen (1959) have found that people with low self-esteem are more easily persuaded than those with high self-esteem. People with high self-esteem apparently find it fairly easy to reject information dissonant with their own opinions: people with low self-esteem, who have less faith in their own opinions, are influenced by dissonant information.

Glass (1968) says that research on the relations between dissonance reduction and personality variables other than self-esteem has been "generally unrewarding" (p. 618). Only a few studies have found relations worthy of note. One is the investigation by Burdick and Burnes (1958) that is mentioned under "Balance Theory" above. Burdick and Burnes found that persons with a high need for affiliation seemed to be more persuadable. Another is a study by Kleck and Wheaton (1967), who found that highly dogmatic people are less likely to recall dissonant information than less dogmatic people are.

Glass (1968) also suggests that Byrne's (1961) repression/sensitization scale might be used to predict individual differences in mode of dissonance reduction. A person who is assessed as a "repressor" may be more likely to deny or repress dissonant information; "sensitizers," who cogitate about such things as dissonant information, may be more likely to discredit the information instead.

**Dissonance reduction and memory.**    One of the most common ways of creating dissonance is to persuade people to say something publicly that they genuinely do not believe. The public statement and the true belief are in conflict, thereby creating dissonance. Bem and McConnell (1970) asked students who believed in increased student control over their university's curriculum to write an essay advocating precisely the opposite. The typical result occurred: students shifted their opinion toward the attitude expressed in the essay. So far, this experiment merely replicates dozens of others showing that people reduce dissonance by shifting their beliefs toward what they have stated. However, Bem and McConnell then asked the subjects to recall what their initial opinion was before they had written the essay. Since the students had written their names on the initial attitude questionnaire, it was clear to the students that their accuracy in recalling their initial opinion could be easily checked. Nevertheless, students falsely recalled that they had initially been much more in favor of decreased student control than they really were! Students misremembered their initial opinion by claiming that they had really remained consistent with their present opinion all along. This warping of memory has been replicated by Goethals and Reckman (1973), who found that people misremembered their initial opinion on the issue of busing school children to achieve racial balance. One would think that people wouldn't "forget" their attitudes on such issues. However, forgetting dissonant cognitions is a good way to produce consonance.

## Critique

The theory of cognitive dissonance has been not only heavily researched but also heartily criticized. The two major types of criticism have been theoretical and methodological.

The major theoretical criticism is that no one can be sure when two cognitions are dissonant with each other. Aronson (1968) suggests that the situation is so ambiguous that a guideline has developed: "If you want to be sure, ask Leon [Festinger]" (p. 8). Aronson correctly points out that not only logical inconsistencies but also psychological inconsistencies cause dissonance. The parents of a prospective student surprised one of the authors in his office one vacation afternoon while that author was wearing some ragged shorts and a T-shirt. The author isn't inconsistent, but he very well may have caused dissonance. (Certainly some of their cognitions changed.) How can we predict whether a situation will cause dissonance? Aronson suggests that when expectancies are violated, dissonance results. This rule seems broader than Festinger's original definition: "Two elements are in a dissonant relation if . . . the obverse of one element would follow from the other" (1957, p. 13). Yet the domain of dissonance research has dramatically broadened since Festinger's early work. As the definition of *dissonance* broadens to encompass the research, the definition becomes less precise. It is simply not clear what constitutes a dissonant relation between two cognitions.

The second theoretical problem is the multiple-mode problem, discussed earlier as a flaw in balance theory. It is extremely difficult to predict which method a person will adopt in order to reduce dissonance. The problem, however, is even more severe in dissonance research than in balance-theory research. In balance-theory research, the situation usually contains a small number of items and bonds; thus, the configuration is of manageable size. As the reader has probably noted, dissonance research usually demands a great deal of theatrics in a rather complex social situation. The number of ways in which a subject can reduce dissonance is greatly magnified. An experimenter who tests for a particular attitude change may find none—not because the theory is wrong, not because dissonance wasn't aroused, but because the subject has used another mode of dissonance reduction. As motivational research has moved from rats in runways to humans in social situations, the number of possible responses by the subject has increased. An experimenter may not be able to anticipate or measure all of them, especially if the theory cannot reliably predict which one will take place.

The multiple-mode problem is related to another difficulty. Because dissonance research is so complex, experimental results are frequently open to several interpretations. The various interpretations of the experiment by Festinger and Carlsmith (1959), in which subjects were paid $1 or $20 to lie, illustrate this problem. Because subjects in dissonance experiments are exposed to such intricate deceptions, bribes, and evaluations, why the subject arrives at his or her final opinion or rating is often not clear.

Several methodological problems have also plagued dissonance research. Chapanis and Chapanis (1964), in a blistering review, note that some researchers adopt such questionable procedures as discarding large numbers of subjects and reassigning subjects from the experimental group to the control group *after* the analysis of the dependent variable. Given the difficulty of agreeing on the interpretation of dissonance experiments that were rigorously conducted, it is understandable that interpretation is particularly dangerous when 80% of the subjects have been rejected. Zajonc (1968) summarizes some of the methodological problems in the following manner:

> The conceptual bravado of dissonance psychologists has been accompanied by an appropriately cavalier approach to experimentation. Experiments on dissonance have almost without exception been extremely imaginative and engaging; so much so, in fact, that one simply finds it difficult to resist their implications or ignore their results. But researchers on dissonance have not exactly been compulsive about following standard procedures. Experiments in the area of counterattitudinal behavior, for example, are all extremely complicated, and their replications and extensions are never faithful in reproducing previous conditions. Each experiment uses different attitude issues, different attitude measures, and different means to induce subjects to make counterattitudinal statements. Many of these experimental manipulations involve the resources of a minor theatrical production [pp. 390–391].

In summary, the complexity of dissonance experiments, their susceptibility to alternative interpretations, their methodological shortcomings, and even ambiguity in the theory itself have all provided targets for opponents of the theory of cognitive dissonance.

## Self-perception theory: An alternative to dissonance theory

In 1967 Daryl Bem proposed an alternative explanation for many of the phenomena treated by the theory of cognitive dissonance. The alternative, self-perception theory, was important in its own right, and it also bore a close relation to another important theory maturing around the same time, attribution theory. Our discussion of Bem's self-perception theory will therefore also serve as an introduction to attribution theory, full coverage of which will be deferred until the next chapter.

The guiding principle of self-perception theory is that one can infer one's own beliefs from one's behavior. If there are no strong internal cues providing a person with information about his own beliefs, that person can only take the role of an observer. He observes his own behavior, and on the basis of that behavior, he infers his beliefs. Suppose someone asks you whether you like pistachio nuts. After thinking, you say that you really don't care much one way or the other. Then you notice that for the past hour you've been eating only the pistachios from a bowl of mixed nuts. Now, having realized this, you infer: "I must like pistachio nuts; I've been eating them." Had another person been watching you fish them out, she would have surmised that you did like them. When you were asked whether you liked them, you observed your behavior, as she could have, and inferred from it your taste for pistachio nuts. Bem calls his theory "self-perception theory" because beliefs are inferred from perception of one's own behavior.

This theory has been applied to many cognitive-dissonance phenomena, including the effect of insufficient justification as studied by Festinger and Carlsmith (1959). Had you observed a subject being paid $20 and then telling someone the task was fun, you probably would attribute that statement to the fact that the subject was being paid so much. Self-perception theory says the subject does the same thing. She also perceives herself being paid and telling a lie; as an external observer would do, the subject attributes her false statement to the large bribe. An observer of a subject who was paid $1 would infer that the subject must really like the task; $1 wouldn't be enough to elicit the false testimony. The subject himself makes the same observation, arrives at the same conclusion (that he must really like the task), and consequently raises his opinion of the task. This process would produce the results Festinger and Carlsmith obtained: higher ratings of the task by the $1 subjects than by the $20 subjects. Note that Bem's explanation seems to involve no motivational principles. There is no dissonance that must be reduced. This is the most important difference between cognitive-dissonance and self-perception theories.

Many studies done under the auspices of cognitive-dissonance theory have been reinterpreted by self-perception theory. There are studies, however, whose results seem explicable by only one of the two theories.

For example, self-perception theory cannot explain studies that show dissonance to be a drive with properties similar to those of other drives. The study by Cottrell, Rajecki, and Smith (1974), discussed earlier, is an example, as are several others showing how dissonance resembles D in Hull/Spence theory (Cottrell & Wack, 1967; Pallak & Pittman, 1972; Waterman, 1969). Since self-perception theory is basically non-motivational, any study showing that dissonance has motivational properties does not support Bem's theory.

Other studies can be explained by self-perception theory and not by cognitive-dissonance theory. Kiesler, Nisbett, and Zanna (1969) asked each of their subjects to deliver a persuasive argument advocating something that the subject already supported—the fight against air pollution. No dissonance was created. After agreeing to give the speech, the subject heard a confederate of the experimenters say that he would also give a speech on the topic assigned to him (auto safety). The confederate gave one of two reasons: (1) auto safety was something he strongly supported, or (2) the experiment they were participating in seemed worthwhile. Note that the confederate who gives reason 1 is saying that his belief in the cause supports his action. He is termed a "belief-relevant" confederate, since his beliefs about auto safety are relevant to his actions. The confederate who gives reason 2 is not saying that his actions have anything to do with his beliefs about auto safety; he just thinks the experiment is good. He is termed a "belief-irrelevant" confederate. The real subjects were then asked to evaluate their feelings about air pollution. Subjects who had overheard belief-relevant confederates opposed air pollution more strongly than those who had heard belief-irrelevant confederates.

Kiesler et al. maintain that subjects hearing belief-relevant confederates assume that they, like the confederates, must be agreeing to give the speech because they support the cause. They infer their beliefs from their antipollution behavior and rate pollution very negatively. Subjects hearing belief-irrelevant confederates see that behavior and belief need not be closely related in this instance, so they do not infer beliefs from their antipollution behavior. They therefore do not rate pollution so negatively. Note that, since no dissonance is aroused, cognitive-dissonance theory can make no prediction here. Self-perception theory, however, predicts that people infer their beliefs from their own behavior unless belief and behavior are experimentally disconnected, as they were for the belief-irrelevant subjects. For the belief-relevant subjects, the realization that they were to make a speech against air pollution moved their original belief even further in that direction.

Since cognitive-dissonance theory and self-perception theory so often make identical predictions, it is difficult to say which theory is generally more useful in predicting human behavior. Some theorists see little difference between the theories (Tedeschi, Schlenker, & Bonoma, 1971) or believe that no crucial test between them may be possible (Greenwald, 1975). Taylor (1975) has pointed out that only on very inconsequential issues are the internal cues so poor that people need to observe their own behavior to decide what their beliefs must be. Taylor also shows that self-perception theory makes successful predictions when subjects perform proattitudinal behavior, as in the study by Kiesler et al., but does not often make successful predictions when subjects perform counterattitudinal behavior. Accordingly, dissonance theory may be more successful than self-perception theory in predicting behavior when dissonance is likely to be aroused. When consonant behavior is performed, dissonance theory makes no prediction and self-perception theory can then provide insight.

Although self-perception theory uses no explicit motivational principle, as do consistency theories, it is not irrelevant to the study of motivation. Assume that Bem is right: dissonance is not needed to explain the results of Festinger and Carlsmith's study. The $1 subjects improve their opinion of the task because they perceive themselves saying the task is fun for no sufficient reason and therefore conclude that they like the task. Would these subjects choose to do the task again if given the opportunity? Because they have attributed their positive statements about the task to their own feelings, not to the cash, they would be more likely to do the task again than the $20 subjects would. The way a subject explains his or her statement ("I said it for the money" or "I said it because the task really was fun") surely influences any subsequent motivation toward the task.

This is the kernel of attribution theory: individuals' attributions of their own behavior to a particular cause influence their evaluation of that behavior and their motivation to perform that behavior again. Bem's self-perception theory is closely related to attribution theory, and it is this important theory that will be discussed in the next chapter.

CHAPTER **11**

# Theories
# of Causal Attribution

*I used to enjoy baseball until I started getting paid for it.*

*Major League outfielder*

Attribution theories are at present the most prominent influences on the study of human motivation. Unlike the theories that we have discussed thus far, they do not address themselves to internal forces that give rise to motivated behavior—forces such as instinctual drive and need for achievement. Attribution theories are concerned with how a person *perceives* the causes of his or her own behavior and the behavior of others, not with the ultimate causes themselves. Since people ascribe causation not only to the actor but also to the environment, theorists studying the attribution process consider internal motivation as a significant, but not the only, cause of behavior.

Attribution theories place weighty emphasis on the role of cognition. They assume that people strive to explain, understand, and predict events. This effort entails a constant processing of information about the behavior of oneself and others and the attribution of it to the actor, the environment, or both. If a person concludes that the actor was instrumental in causing a particular behavior, he or she is making an attribution to an internal cause such as motivation or intention. Attribution theories, then, focus on the cognitive attribution of causation, including motivation. Moreover, according to these theories, the causal attributions one makes guide one's decisions. (For example, a student who believes that academic success is a result mainly of luck will probably not study very hard.) Therefore, attribution theories emphasize cognition not only as central to the attribution process but also as influential in behavior.

There is no one, unified, comprehensive attribution theory. Rather, there is a network of perspectives and models that offer guideposts for discerning the "why" of behavior. As such, attribution theories are enormously useful in postdictively analyzing the causes of behavior but less so in prediction.

Attribution theories are unique in that they are composed of concepts and principles that people commonly use in explaining behavior, not ones that exist only in the psychologist's lexicon. They can be viewed as the layman's theories of perceived motivation. They view understanding the process of attributing causes to behavior as ultimately the most meaningful task.

## Major theories of causal attribution

There are three major theories of causal attribution. The first is Heider's analysis of the attribution process. This was the first attribution theory, and it remains the most significant statement on causal attributions. It is basic to the other theories. The second is Jones and Davis's theory of correspondent inferences. It extends and revises Heider's theory and concentrates on the attribution of behavior to causes within the actor. The third is Kelley's theory of multiple causal attributions, which represents the most current advances in attribution theory.

### Heider: Naive analysis of attribution processes

Fritz Heider is the acknowledged founder of attribution theory. He provided a philosophical analysis of the problems of attribution in his paper on phenomenal causality (1944) and presented a formal theory of attribution processes in social behavior in his book *The Psychology of Interpersonal Relations* (1958). The method and content of his theory derived from field theory, pioneered by Lewin and his colleagues. Heider's theory, however, is unique in that it appealed to what he called "common-sense psychology" as a source of insight and knowledge about interpersonal behavior. He reasoned that a thorough understanding of motivation required an understanding of the "theories" that people use in their everyday relations with others. He viewed scientific theories formulated by psychologists and other scholars as cumbersome abstractions that bemuddled the concepts and processes used by laymen in assessing the motivations and causes of behavior. Consequently, Heider referred to his approach as "naive" and relied exclusively on simple, meaningful terms such as *can, try,* and *pleasure* to explain attribution processes, rather than complex, ambiguous terms such as *instinctual drive, self-actualization,* and *quasi-needs.* Using this commonsense vernacular, Heider assembled a comprehensive theory of interpersonal behavior that included the perception of the other person, the analysis of action, the influence of environmental variables on attribution processes, and many other topics. The discussion here will of necessity be restricted to his central notions regarding the attribution process.

**Attributions to dispositional properties.** Heider's attribution theory had two fundamental assumptions. First, people use similar principles in the perception of other persons and in the perception of physical objects. Second, people strive for prediction and understanding of their world. Using these two assumptions, Heider observed that a person imposes stability and predictability on both the interpersonal and the physical environments by attributing transient events to invariant underlying conditions.

Suppose your neighbor contributes a large sum of money to a local charity. You might attribute to that neighbor a generous disposition. By making this attribution, you are endowing your neighbor with a stable personality trait on the basis of a single generous act. Or, suppose the elevator in your apartment building fails to stop at your floor. You might attribute to the elevator a touchy wiring system. Again, you are endowing something with a stable trait on the basis of one transient event. To repeat: Heider reasoned that a person imposes stability and predictability on both the interpersonal and the physical environments by attributing transient events to invariant underlying conditions. These underlying conditions are called *dispositional properties.*

These properties "dispose," or cause, persons and objects to act in certain ways under certain circumstances. The quality of dispositional properties varies between objects and persons. A ball rolls because it has the physical property "roundness." A woman laughs not because of her physical characteristics but because of her personal characteristics; she is "happy" or "good-humored" or "giddy." Hence, the processes of attributing dispositions to an object and to a person are similar, but the content of the attributions is qualitatively different.

The distinguishing feature of the attribution process is, therefore, the propensity to seek causal explanations of events in one's physical and social environments by ascribing to objects and persons impersonal and personal dispositions, respectively.

**Explanations of behavior and its outcome.** The distinguishing feature just cited applies, of course, to explanations of human behavior. People tend to explain any behavior by attributing particular dispositional properties to the person, to the environment, or to both. Heider's model of the way we explain behavior thus closely resembles Lewin's model of behavior as a function of the person and the environment.

Moreover, people also explain the *outcome* of a behavior by making attributions to the person, the environment, or both. We attribute an outcome—for example, success or failure at a task—to a joint function of factors within the person and factors within the environment. Heider says outcomes are attributed to *effective personal force* and *effective environmental force.*

Effective personal force has two components: power and motivation. Power is determined mainly by ability, because ability is necessary for motivated behavior to produce a successful outcome. A person who has a poor background in mathematics cannot solve a complex differential equation, no matter how motivated he or she might be. The motivational component of effective personal force is called *trying,* and it in turn has two components: intention and exertion. Intention, the qualitative component, represents "what" the person is trying to do. Exertion, the quantitative component, represents "how hard" a person is trying—how much effort is being expended. Once a person has the intention to act, the strength of the motivation is reflected in the amount of exertion. To sum up: personal force requires both ability and trying, and trying is composed of intention and exertion.

The main component of impersonal, or environmental, force is what Heider calls *task difficulty*. Assume that you succeed on a very difficult task. You therefore must have substantial ability. It might be said, then, that your success was due to great personal force, because only a great personal force could have overcome a great environmental force—task difficulty. It can be seen that environmental force and outcome combine to determine the estimate of personal force. If environmental resistance is high but you succeed anyway, the outcome is attributed to ability. ("She must have a lot of ability to have done that job.") Heider often refers to such an attribution as an attribution to "can," since the person with ability "can" do the task. If a person fails a very difficult task, the failure is most likely attributed to task difficulty: one says that in this instance environmental force was too great to be overcome by personal force. Generally, when someone succeeds at a very easy task or fails a very difficult one, task-difficulty attributions are typical. ("He succeeded because the task was a cinch." "He failed because the task was impossible.") On tasks of moderate difficulty, attributions to personal factors—trying and ability—are more likely to occur. ("She succeeded because she tried hard." "She failed because she isn't very talented.")

Besides the stable, dispositional property of task difficulty, Heider assumed that the environment also included less stable, variable factors that could affect behavioral outcomes. He subsumed these unpredictable, yet significant, environmental influences under *luck*. Luck can favorably or unfavorably change the course of any action in unsystematic fashion.

The outcome of any behavior is therefore attributable to some combination of personal characteristics (ability, trying) and environmental contingencies (task difficulty, luck). Heider reasoned that the relation between the personal and impersonal components of causation was additive. That is, an outcome is due to some personal force *plus* some environmental force. Even if one of the forces is zero, there will be an outcome. He also reasoned that the personal component was a multiplicative function of ability and trying (actually exertion). These two relations are depicted in the following equation: outcome = $f$(personal force + impersonal force), where personal force = ability × trying. Either a personal *or* an impersonal force can by itself produce an outcome, but personal force requires *both* ability and motivation. This is true in theory but probably not in real life. It is difficult to imagine a behavioral outcome in which both personal *and* impersonal force are not influential, even though one of the forces might be very small.

Heider's model of the attribution process is summarized in Figure 11-1. To trace the process that this model describes, assume that one is

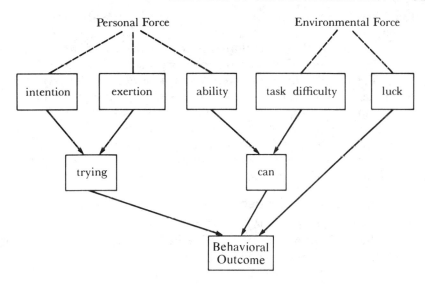

**Figure 11-1.** Heider's attribution scheme. *(Adapted from* The Psychology of Interpersonal Relations, *by F. Heider. Copyright 1958 by John Wiley & Sons, Inc. Reprinted by permission.)*

attempting to explain why a *B* student got an *A* in a course. An attribution to "trying" is obvious; it must be assumed that the student intended to perform well and put forth effort by studying. However, the attribution to trying is not sufficient to explain the outcome. One must also consider "can," which is a joint function of ability and task difficulty. If the course was easy, one might expect that many students got an *A* and that they did not have to possess outstanding ability or even try hard. But if the course was difficult, one might expect that only a few students got an *A* and that both ability and trying were likely causes of scholastic success. Moreover, if the exams were essay, luck would probably be seen as having only minimal influence. But if the exams were true-and-false, "lucky guessing" might be viewed as contributing to the course grade.

In general, Heider hypothesizes that people are "biased" toward causal attributions; they search for a "sufficient reason" to account for every occurrence. Moreover, Heider believes that causal attributions are tilted toward personal, rather than impersonal, explanations. This tendency to accentuate personal causation at the expense of environmental causation often leads to misattribution, especially when environmental causation was in fact quite significant. Heider never attempts to fully account for this propensity, but deCharms (1968) has suggested that the basic principle of human motivation is to strive to be effectual in producing an impact on one's environment—in being a causal agent. This motive results in an inflated view of one's effective personal force, a view that accounts for the bias toward internal at-tributions.

Heider's analysis of the attribution process is the cornerstone of mod-ern attribution theory; the other major theories can be viewed as refine-ments and embellishments of Heider's attribution model. Although some of the concepts and processes proposed in Heider's theory have received empirical support (see, for example, Thibaut and Riecken, 1955), the major shortcoming of the theory is its neglect of specific, operationally defined hypotheses that can be investigated in the experi-mental laboratory. A proposed remediation was attempted by E. E. Jones and Davis (1965) in their theory of correspondent inferences.

## Jones and Davis: Correspondent inferences

E. E. Jones and Davis (1965) have developed an "act-to-disposition" model of the attribution process to refine Heider's theory by specifying more exactly how an observer infers the causes of behavior. Like Heider, they assume that behavior has intended effects and that an observer strives to explain behavior by attributing invariant disposi-tions either to the actor or to the environment. Unlike Heider, they analyze only attributions to personal causation; impersonal causation becomes important only by implication when personal attributions are weak or nonexistent. Jones and Davis further limit their model to sit-uations in which the actor is obviously cognizant of the outcome of his or her action (knowledge) and is capable of producing the desired ef-fects (ability). Hence, their analysis is pertinent only when a person chooses a course of action and is capable of carrying it out—that is, where a person is "trying" and "can."

Jones and Davis depict the attribution process—within the re-strictions specified above—as an act–intention–disposition sequence (see Figure 11-2). The behavior and its effects are first observed. ("He's going into the bank with a gun!") The observer then endeavors to infer the acting person's intentions. ("He plans to rob the bank!") Finally, the inference of intention results in the observer's attributing personal dispositions to the actor. The attributions can vary from strong to weak. Such dispositions might include personality traits. ("He's ruthless and dishonest.") The attribution process thus proceeds from act to intention to disposition.

**Correspondence.**    Jones and Davis formulated a "theory of corre-pondent inferences" to explain the attribution process in their act-to-disposition model. In order to better understand this theory, let's first see how it would apply to a hypothetical situation.

Suppose a professor is sitting in her office when a student strolls in and exclaims, "That lecture you gave this morning was the most

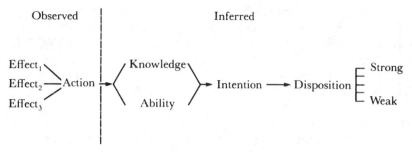

**Figure 11-2.** The act–intention–disposition model of attribution. *(Adapted from "From Acts to Dispositions: The Attribution Process in Person Perception," by E. E. Jones and K. E. Davis. In L. Berkowitz (Ed.), Advances in Experimental Social Psychology (Vol. 2), Copyright 1965 by Academic Press, Inc. Reprinted by permission.)*

glorious event in the history of human communication. You are the most fabulous teacher in the world." After she gives him an *A*, she stops to consider his motivation for saying that. His statement was very outspoken, of course. The professor might therefore attribute outspokenness to the student. "He said that because he's just an outspoken person; no matter how embarrassing it might have been to say that, he just had to." Her description of the statement and her description of the student then correspond. Both the person and the statement are labeled "outspoken."

However, the professor then notices that this student has a *D*− average. She might then decide that, although the statement is outspoken, the student is really a devious, ingratiating flatterer. Her description of his statement and her description of him no longer correspond. One is positive and one is negative. This noncorrespondence has arisen because she attributes his statement to a powerful environmental force: threat of a low grade. The power that the professor has over him induces him to emit a statement that he does not really believe.

Jones and Davis say that, when an observer attributes a disposition to another person, that disposition may or may not correspond with the face value of the person's behavior. If the attributed intention and the surface meaning of the behavior are parallel, then the disposition ascribed to the other person does correspond with the behavior. ("He intended to speak his mind. He's an outspoken person.") Correspondence is less when environmental force clouds the observer's confidence that the actor's intention matches the behavior. ("But maybe he just intends to improve his grade. He does have a *D*−. He's desperate.

That might be the only reason he said those things.") The descriptions of the behavior and the person no longer correspond. Whenever environmental force is high, the observer is in a quandary. Why is the actor doing that? He must really mean it (high correspondence). Or maybe he's just putting on an act because of the situation he's in (low correspondence).

**Influences on correspondence.**   The degree of correspondence between a behavior and an attribution is affected by two principal variables. The first is social desirability. Jones and Davis say that the effects that most people intend their behaviors to have are socially desirable ones. Observing that someone's behavior has desirable effects tells one very little about the person's true intentions—only that the observed behavior is normative. Behaviors that are socially desirable therefore do not elicit strong, confident attributions. For that reason, the theory of correspondent inferences predicts that highly correspondent attributions will arise from behaviors that are "out of role," or depart from the norm. For example, a nonnormative behavior such as reading in the lunch line is more likely to evoke strong dispositional inferences ("very studious," "highly achievement-oriented") than a normative behavior such as reading in the library. In general, atypical, out-of-role behaviors are assumed by observers to be less socially desirable because they are rare. Such behaviors should produce attributions more highly correspondent ("She's quiet at parties because she's introverted") than the attributions that typical, in-role behaviors produce ("He's quiet at work because he works at a library. I suspect he's really a loudmouth").

The second major variable that Jones and Davis say affects correspondence is the number of noncommon effects observed to accompany the action. Another example will help illustrate what Jones and Davis mean by noncommon effects.

Suppose that Natasia, a young married woman who plans to have children, is considering three career choices: homemaker, teacher, physician. The choice she makes will lead observers to attribute certain dispositions to her. How correspondent will these attributions be? Each of the three choices would produce a particular combination of effects from the following list:

1. Personal satisfaction and valuable contribution
2. Professional contacts
3. Career independent of husband
4. Activities consistent with traditional feminine role
5. Extensive experiences with children
6. High social status

The choice of homemaker would have effects 1, 4, 5; teacher, 1, 2, 3, 4, 5; physician, 1, 2, 3, 6. Effect 1 is a "common effect"—it is common to all the choices. Hence, it is uninformative; an observer could not infer anything about Natasia from the fact that she chose a career that was satisfying and valuable. It is not a basis for attributing any disposition to her. The remaining effects are "noncommon"—that is, none of them arises from *every* career choice. They are therefore bases for attribution. For example, if Natasia chooses to be a homemaker, an observer might infer that she is both traditionally feminine and child-oriented. Now, what determines the strength of such attributions? If Natasia becomes a physician, an observer might infer that she is moderately professionally directed, moderately independent, and strongly interested in social status. The first two attributions are only moderately correspondent because another choice (teacher) would also have had the effects that produce those attributions. The third is strongly correspondent because the effect that produces it results uniquely from that choice. In other words, the degree of correspondence, or the strength of the attribution, is inversely related to the number of alternative behaviors that would also have had the noncommon effect on which the attribution is based.

Jones and Davis hypothesize that a third variable, the personal involvement of the observer, has a direct impact on correspondence. They delineate two types of personal involvement: hedonic relevance and personalism, both of which are hypothesized to increase correspondence. Hedonic relevance is present whenever the effects of the actor's behavior are rewarding or punishing to the observer. If a professor volunteered to write a very complimentary letter of recommendation for you on the basis of your performance in his course, you would be quite pleased. His action would have much (positive) hedonic relevance for you. You would attribute the professor's kind offer to his positive personality traits. ("He's a fine person to do such a nice thing.") His behavior and the intention to which you attributed it would have high correspondence as a result of the hedonic relevance his action had.

Personalism, a special case of hedonic relevance, is present when the actor intends to benefit or harm the observer and when the observer is aware of this intention. Many acts have hedonic relevance but no personalism, as when a professor moves her class from the first floor to the ninth floor, not knowing that one student is petrified of heights. Because the professor did not intend to harm anyone and because the student knows the teacher is unaware of his fear, there is little likelihood that a diabolical disposition will be attributed to her. If the teacher had moved the class with the intention of frightening this student whose fear he had told her about, then both personalism and act-disposition correspondence would be high. Note that, for personalism to be high, the perceiver must decide that the actor knew that the act would harm or benefit the perceiver. If I secretly find out that you are severely allergic to beets, and I intend to harm you with a beet casserole at dinner, you will not think me a nasty fellow, despite my nasty deed. If you ever find out, however, that I did indeed know about your allergy, personalism and correspondence will increase.

**Critique.**    The theory of correspondent inferences is a significant extension of Heider's attribution theory. Jones and Davis amplify the cognitive component of the attribution process by enlarging the sources of information used for inference: to actual observed behaviors, they add potential behavior choices. Moreover, their systematic formulation of the attribution process as an act–intention–disposition sequence allows critical experimentation, which has resulted in empirical support for the model (for example, Garske, 1974, 1975b; E. E. Jones, Davis, & Gergen, 1961; E. E. Jones & Harris, 1967).

The major shortcoming of both Heider's and Jones and Davis's theories is their emphasis on causal attributions of others' behavior and their comparative neglect of attributions of one's own. These theorists imply that causes are discerned from the behavior of self and others, but they build their theories around only the latter. Kelley (1967) continues the refinement of attribution theory begun by Jones and Davis. He extends the analysis to take into account causal entities in the environment and the process of making attributions about oneself, both of which Jones and Davis de-emphasized.

## Kelley: Processes of multiple causal attribution

The most significant contributions to attribution theory in recent years have been made by Kelley in a series of essays (1967, 1971, 1972, 1973). Kelley's central theme is that causal attribution is generally a complex process that takes into account the *joint* influence of multiple causes to produce a given effect. Attribution therefore entails the selection from several causes of the one or ones that afford the observer the best explanation of a behavior. Kelley emphasizes that this attribution process pertains to the observed behaviors of others *and* of oneself. In constructing his theory, Kelley relies heavily on Heider's model, but he provides elaborations and analyses that generate new hypotheses and lay bare the critical issues in inferring the causes of behavior.

Kelley has developed two sets of concepts—actually "mini-theories"—to explain the process of causal attribution in two kinds of situations. The first model employs what Kelley calls "covariation" concepts. It applies to situations in which the attributor has information from multiple observations with which to make an inference. The second model employs "configuration" concepts. It applies to situations in which the attributor has information from only a single observation.

**The covariation model of attribution.** For situations in which an attributor has information from two or more observations of a behavior, Kelley's analysis relies on a pivotal notion, the covariation principle. He states it as follows: "An effect is attributed to one of its possible causes with which, over time, it covaries" (1973, p. 109). This principle says that the attribution of a behavioral effect to some cause (in the person or the environment) depends on the observation that the effect and the cause have always occurred together before. For example, a student who gets good grades but who has repeatedly performed poorly on standardized tests of achievement might attribute his or her poor performance on another such test to some difficulty arising from this type of test. Here, the effect (poor performance) and the cause (type of test) covary; that is, they have been associated over time.

Kelley uses a three-dimensional model to depict the multiple causes that can covary with any given effect. For any behavior, there exist three kinds of possible causes: (1) external stimuli, which are placed along an entities dimension; (2) the observer (another person or oneself), who is placed along a persons dimension; and (3) the situation, or context, in which the behavior occurs, which is placed along a time/modality dimension. These dimensions appear to exhaust the domain of possible causes. The first two dimensions are similar to Heider's categories "environmental" and "personal" causation; time/modality is an added category of sources. Kelley depicts these three source dimensions by means of a three-dimensional solid that he terms an "attributional data table" (see Figure 11-3).

In seeking a causal explanation for a behavior, an attributor applies the covariation principle to each of the source dimensions. That is, he or she tries to discover whether the behavior is systematically associated with some element on that dimension. For each dimension, the attributor's judgment is based on a different criterion. For an entity, or stimulus, to cause a behavior, it must be distinctive from other entities; that is, the behavior must covary with only one entity or stimulus and not with others. For a person to cause a behavior, the behavior must be unique to that person; that is, others should not behave similarly (Kelley calls such uniqueness "lack of consensus"). For a situation (time/modality) to cause a behavior, there must be a lack of consistency over time or in different situations; that is, other contexts should not elicit the same behavior. Hence, in discerning causes, one applies the covariation principle by cognitively scanning the dimensions of entities, persons, and time/modality and evaluating the possible causes in each by using the criteria of distinctiveness, consensus, and consistency, respectively. The covariation principle implies that this process can result in attributing the behavior to a cause on a single dimension (for example, the person) or to the interaction of elements on two or more dimensions. For example, a good student might perform poorly only on

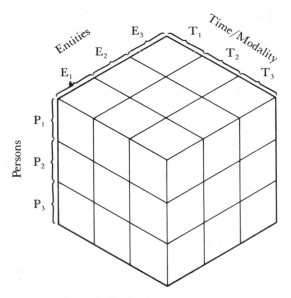

**Figure 11-3.** Kelley's three-dimensional model of causal attribution. *(Adapted from "The Processes of Causal Attribution," by H. H. Kelley, American Psychologist, 1973, 28, 107–128. Copyright 1973 by the American Psychological Association. Reprinted by permission.)*

standardized achievement tests that are given in the spring. The cause is an interaction of sources on two dimensions: entities (type of test) and time/modality (season of the year).

The use of the covariation principle in the attribution process can be illustrated by an example. A college student, Jeff, attempts to infer the causes of his occasional insomnia. Figure 11-4 depicts his attribution process. Jeff first examines the stimuli that might be influential. He sees that his insomnia occasionally occurs in each of three environments—the college dorm, his parents' home, and hotels. Hence, no distinctive entity is responsible. He then checks to see whether other persons experience the same occasional sleeplessness and finds that they do. Hence, there is consensus. His personal attributes are not causal; his insomnia is not caused by the fact that he is peculiar in some way. He then looks at several situations that precede his attempts to sleep. He discovers that he sleeps normally after an evening of studying or attending a basketball game. However, he finds that his insomnia follows his first date with a woman he has just met. There is therefore a lack of consistency among the situations, and so Jeff attributes his insomnia to a time/modality source: he has found that insomnia covaries with having a date with an unfamiliar woman.

**The configuration model of attribution.** Kelley also developed a model for the attribution process when one cannot make repeated ob-

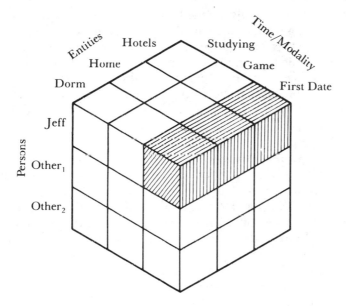

**Figure 11-4.** Attribution analysis of Jeff's insomnia.

servations of a behavior and must deduce a cause from a single obser-vation. The attributor is without a time/modality perspective and must decide among internal causes (persons), external causes (entities), and combinations thereof. This process does not take place blindly or igno-rantly. Rather, the attributor utilizes causal schemata—that is, "con-figurations," or patterns, of information about the plausible causes of a given behavior (Kelley, 1972). A causal schema is a cognition, or way of thinking, about particular behaviors and their alternative causes. It derives from one's prior experience. The schema permits causal at-tributions on the basis of minimal data that can be provided through a single observation. Consider an example. An amateur golfer would be likely to attribute a professional's shotmaking to skill after seeing *one* difficult, long-iron shot land softly within a few feet of the pin. This person-attribution would likely arise because of the low likelihood that some distinctive stimulus (such as the wind) was responsible and be-cause of a schema that such a shot by a professional could be made repeatedly over time.

This configuration, or schematic model, of the attribution process yields two principles: the discounting principle and the augmentation principle. Like the covariation principle, each can pertain to attribu-tions of one's own behavior or of another's. The discounting principle is that "the role of a given cause in producing a given effect is dis-counted if other plausible causes are also present" (Kelley, 1973, p. 113). This principle suggests that internal attributions will be weak-ened if possible external causes are also present, and, conversely, that external attributions will be weakened if possible internal causes are also present. The augmentation principle is a variant of the discounting principle. It predicts enhancement of a (positive) internal attribution when the behavior takes place in a context containing considerable external obstacles. For example, a person should see himself or herself as particularly capable after performing well on an extremely difficult task but not necessarily after performing well on a moderately difficult task.

**Implications of Kelley's theory.**    A central implication of Kelley's configuration concepts, and to a lesser extent of his covariation concepts, is the identification of sources of misattribution—that is, errors in attribution. Expanding on Heider's supposition that we are biased toward attributions to personal causation, Kelley delineates the types and processes of misattribution, many of which entail underrepresentation of environmental causes.

One of the most fruitful offshoots of Kelley's analysis of misattributions is the proposal by E. E. Jones and Nisbett (1971) of a discrepancy in inferential tendencies between actors and observers. Jones and Nisbett contend that there is a systematic tendency for actors to attribute their own behaviors to environmental causes and observers of the same behaviors to attribute them to internal causes (personality, dispositions, traits). They surmise that the discrepancy arises from differences between the actor and the observer in the availability and prominence of information. The actor, being immersed in the context of the behavior, is more aware of situational demands. Hence, she attributes her behavior to external causes. The observer is distanced and capable of comparing and contrasting the actor's behavior with that of others and so is more likely to make internal attributions.

Kelley's view of the attribution process is significant for its emphasis on multiple causes, especially those that reside in entities and situations. His model suggests that attribution is a highly cognitive activity that entails the processing of complex information about causes. His establishment of a clear continuity between causal attributions for self and other broadens the scope of attribution theory immensely. Kelley's analysis, while being pertinent to the understanding of motivation, emphasizes the multiplicity of causes for behavior and thereby supplements important motivational constructs—such as intention—that were central to the theories of Heider and of Jones and Davis.

## Conclusions: Heider, Jones/Davis, and Kelley

There are obvious differences among the three foregoing attribution theories, mainly in their points of emphasis and their scope of explanation. They all, however, have some characteristics in common. First, in all the theories, we ascribe to behaviors causal explanations that can reside in the person or in the environment. (Jones and Davis imply environmental causation when correspondent inferences are lacking.) We thereby distinguish motivation from environmental determinants of behavior and perceive it as one of several personal causes (such as ability). Second, in the process of causal attribution we interpret intentions and motivations as dispositions and traits. Attributions of personality thus result from observations of intended actions, and people have a propensity to view the transient motivations of themselves and others in stable, dispositional terms. Third, the number and complexity of causal factors present in any context makes misattribution possible. The causes of behavior can therefore be misinterpreted. Usually, misattribution overrates personal causation at the expense of environmental causation: a behavior can appear motivated when it is not. Finally, all attribution theories assume minimal determinism in behavior (Shaver, 1975); other theories of motivation take positions on the ultimate determinants of behavior. The psychoanalytic and instinctual theories, for example, assume biological bases for motivation, and the behavioral theories assume environmental bases for causation. Attribution theory, in contrast, implies that the *influence* of such determinants is less critical than the *attribution* to such determinants. The emphasis is not on the *cause* of action but on the *perceived cause*; the attribution of causation, not necessarily actual causation, is the focus for understanding motivation.

## *Research on attribution and motivation*

The results of diverse experiments bear directly on the processes of causal attribution, including research dealing with intrinsic and extrinsic motivation, achievement, biases in attribution, attitude change, and emotional arousal.

### Intrinsic and extrinsic motivation

A person is intrinsically motivated to perform an activity if he or she undertakes it for no reason other than to perform the activity itself. Thus, if a person is intrinsically motivated to do jigsaw puzzles, no money or other external reward is needed in order to entice the person to do them. Performance of the activity is itself rewarding. A person is extrinsically motivated to perform an activity if he or she undertakes it because of an expected, subsequent, external reward.

The conditions that lead a person to attribute his or her performance to intrinsic or extrinsic sources of motivation have become exceptionally important research topics during recent years. Consider the consequences of each type of attribution. A person who believes he or she is performing an activity because it's intrinsically enjoyable is likely to perform that activity again in a wide variety of situations. However, a person who believes he or she is performing an activity solely because of external rewards will probably return to that activity only when expecting to be rewarded for doing so. Whether someone makes an intrinsic or an extrinsic attribution has enormously important implications, particularly in such areas as education and industry (see, for example, Notz, 1975). If a worker decides she is performing an activity solely because of effective environmental forces—that is, if she is making an external attribution—then constant incentives, prodding, surveillance, and pressure will be needed to keep her performing. If a student decides he is performing because of effective personal force—that is, if he is making an internal attribution—then he will continue to perform with little or no external pressure.

**The effect of reward on intrinsic motivation.** Although the distinction between intrinsic and extrinsic motivation had been discussed earlier in the psychological literature (for example, Atkinson, 1964; Hunt, 1965; Koch, 1956; R. W. White, 1959; Woodworth, 1918), the recent surge of interest began with some simple, provocative studies by Deci (1971, 1972a, 1972b).

Deci's early experiments all had similar formats. Each subject was asked to work on several three-dimensional block puzzles. The puzzles were interesting, and Deci presumed that this challenging task would have substantial intrinsic motivation. One-third of the subjects were told before they began the task that they would be paid for each puzzle they completed (expected-money group). One-third of the subjects were told *after* they had worked the puzzles that they would be paid for each puzzle they had completed (unexpected-money group). One-third of the subjects were never offered money (no-money group). After the puzzle session, when the experiment was presumably over, the subjects were left alone to read magazines, work on some more puzzles, or do whatever they liked. The experimenter left the room for several minutes while another experimenter unobtrusively observed the subjects. To the extent that subjects returned to the puzzles, they were said to be intrinsically motivated. Since they would receive no money for performance during this period and since they believed their performance was not even being monitored, any work on the puzzles would seem to be the result of intrinsic motivation.

The subjects who had never been paid spent more time doing puzzles during this period than the expected-money group, and the unexpected-money group spent as much time doing puzzles during this final session as the no-money group. The attributional analysis of these results is straightforward. Subjects who expect payment attribute their performance to the cash. ("I'm doing this because I'm being paid to.") After the experimenter pays the subject and leaves the room, there is no reason to return to the puzzles, since further payment is not expected. Whatever intrinsic interest the puzzles may have possessed initially, the attribution of performance to the money decreases intrinsic interest in them. The very important point here is that extrinsic rewards may undermine intrinsic motivation.

Deci's finding is predicted by Kelley's discounting principle, mentioned earlier. This principle states that a person will discount the role of a particular cause in producing an effect if other possible causes are present. Deci's expected-money subjects have a very prominent cause to which they can attribute their behavior—the cash. Consequently, they discount the role of intrinsic motivation.

One might think that paying the unexpected-money subjects would decrease their intrinsic motivation to work on the puzzles the next time they had a chance. But they learned of the payment only after they had completed their internal attribution, and therefore the cash did not cause an external attribution. Because they had not been working *for* money, these subjects returned to the puzzles as much as the no-money subjects did.

Several studies with children as subjects show the paramount importance of motivational attribution (Greene & Lepper, 1974; Lepper & Greene, 1975; Lepper, Greene, & Nisbett, 1973). Lepper, Greene, and Nisbett recorded the amount of time that children used felt-tip drawing pens during a free-play period. Then one-third of the subjects did some drawings in order to receive a reward, one-third drew and received an unexpected reward, and one-third drew and received no reward. Time spent with the drawing pens was then assessed during a free-play period one to two weeks later. Children who had drawn for a reward drew significantly less than others. Once again, extrinsic reward diminished intrinsic motivation.

The decrease in intrinsic motivation sometimes caused by external rewards was termed the *overjustification effect* by Lepper et al. (1973). This term seems appropriate: if a person already has intrinsic motivation toward an activity, that would seem to be adequate justification for performing the activity. Being given a tangible reward for performing the activity would constitute overjustification.

Lepper and Greene (1975) also have shown that adult surveillance can reduce the intrinsic motivation of children toward an activity. The child apparently attributes his or her behavior to external sources: "I'm doing it because he's watching me" rather than "I'm doing it because I like to do it." When surveillance is removed, subjects who have made an external attribution are no longer motivated to perform the activity.

The view that extrinsic rewards can adversely affect total motivation is not shared by all theorists. Atkinson (1964, 1974) has assumed that extrinsic motivation is simply added to the level of achievement motivation in order to produce total motivation in a given situation. In fact, Atkinson has maintained that extrinsic motivation is needed to lure into an achievement situation any person whose motive to avoid failure is greater than the motive to succeed. Positive extrinsic motivation must be added to the person's negative intrinsic motivation in order to obtain any achievement-producing behavior. However, the work of Deci, Lepper and his colleagues, and deCharms (1968) indicates that the relation between the two types of motivation may not be additive. If the relation were additive, Deci's expected-money group would have spent more time working on the puzzles at the end of the experiment than the other groups did. Instead, that group spent less time.

The overjustification effect has profound implications. During the 1960s, behavior-modification programs were born, and their immense success in shaping human behavior with reinforcers was responsible for their growth during the subsequent decade. The overjustification effect suggests that bribing people with reinforcers will get them to perform the desired behavior as long as the reinforcers are being dispensed. However, as soon as the reinforcers stop, there may be a cessation of the desired behavior or, worse yet, even less of the desired behavior than was present before the reinforcement program was begun.

Two recent studies (Loveland & Olley, 1979; McLoyd, 1979) have shown that giving rewards for behaviors of high initial interest results in the typical overjustification effect, but that giving rewards for behaviors of low initial interest results in the increase in behavior sought in all behavior-modification programs. Since such programs usually have as their aim the increase of some infrequent behavior, these two studies are very encouraging in showing that the overjustification effect may not occur for such initially infrequent behaviors. Unfortunately, the Loveland and Olley (1979) investigation showed that the beneficial effect of reward on such behaviors evaporated after only seven weeks. Indeed, several behavior modification experts have lamented the fact that the benefits of the reinforcement program rarely endure beyond the last reinforcement and that modification of behavior in one environment rarely generalizes to any other environment (Ayllon & Azrin, 1968; Baumeister, 1969; Kazdin & Bootzin, 1972; Keeley, Shemberg, & Carbonell, 1976). There also are a few instances of postreinforcement performance decreasing below prereinforcement levels (Greene, Sternberg, & Lepper, 1976; Johnson, Bolstad, & Lobitz, 1976; Meichenbaum, Bowers, & Ross, 1968).

Despite these clear demonstrations of the overjustification effect, however, the attribution-theory explanation of the effect has not received unanimous support. First, a number of studies have not found the effect in situations in which attribution theory would predict it (for example, Farr, 1976; Farr, Vance, & McIntyre, 1977; Hamner & Foster, 1975; J. S. Phillips & Lord, 1980). Second, a number of studies have found that—although tangible rewards, such as cash, produce the overjustification effect—verbal rewards typically do not (for example, Anderson, Manoogian, & Resznick, 1976; Deci, 1971, 1972; Dollinger & Thelen, 1978). It is not apparent from consideration of the discounting principle why *type* of reward should make a difference. Third, much recent evidence indicates that young children do not use the discounting principle (Karniol & Ross, 1976; Shultz, Butkowsky, Pearce, & Shanfield, 1975; M. C. Smith, 1975). Yet, it is young children who have been used in a very large number of studies demonstrating the overjustification effect.

To reconcile these difficulties, alternatives to the attribution-theory explanation have been proposed to explain the overjustification effect. One alternative emphasizes the role of perceived competence (Arkes, 1978, 1979; Deci, 1975; Lepper & Greene, 1978; Karniol & Ross, 1976). Consideration of the study by Anderson et al. (1976) may prove instructive. Children in a positive-verbal-reinforcement group drew pictures in the presence of an experimenter for 8 minutes. After each 2-minute interval, the experimenter said such things as "You're pretty good at this" and "You really did a good job." Children in the money group were told after each 2-minute period that they had earned another 5¢ as the experimenter pushed a stack of pennies toward the child. Clearly, the verbal reinforcement contains a message about the child's high level of competence; the monetary reward does not. The overjustification effect occurred only for the money group. The verbal reward showed no postreinforcement performance decrease.

The main thesis of the explanation based on competence is that feelings of competence and mastery insulate the behavior from the overjustification effect. Some behavior-modification programs have purposely included verbal reinforcement following removal of the tangible reward. This strategy often results in maintenance of the target behavior (for example, Chadwick & Day, 1971; Reisinger, 1972) or even in an increase in the desired behavior over the level that occurred during tangible reward (Hewett, Taylor, & Artuso, 1969).

The fact that children cannot use the discounting principle poses no problem for the competence explanation. Children are able to judge when they have performed competently (J. Masters, 1971, 1972; Nelson & Dweck, 1977). When youngsters make this judgment, they are less susceptible to the overjustification effect.

Another finding explained by the competence analysis is one by Karniol and Ross (1977). These investigators found that subjects rewarded for a high level of performance show much less overjustification effect than those rewarded for mere participation in the task. Those rewarded explicitly for good performance would be expected to feel competent and therefore should continue to show interest in the task long after reinforcement has been withdrawn (Arkes, 1979; Arnold, 1976; Boggiano & Ruble, 1979; Rosenfield, Folger, & Adelman, 1980).

The importance of competence and mastery in human motivation was stressed by Robert White as early as 1959. In an influential article, White noted that ego psychologists had abandoned the Freudian notion that id impulses were the main motivations for behavior (see Chapter 3). Instead, ego motives such as mastery of one's environment were seen as critical to human behavior. White also noted that neo-Hullians, whom we now call optimal-level theorists, had discovered the intense motivational properties of exploration and curiosity (see Chapter 6). White concluded that humans have a motive to competently interact with and achieve mastery of their environment; White (1959) called this "effectance motivation." Since such positive feelings of mastery will not end when a tangible reinforcer is terminated, such feelings may reduce the postreinforcement decrement that is the hallmark of the overjustification effect.

**The Yerkes/Dodson law and the Easterbrook hypothesis revisited.** Recently McGraw (1978) suggested that reward facilitates performance when tasks are straightforward, simple, and obvious. When tasks demand ingenuity, discovery, or creativity, reward may prove detrimental to performance.

This generalization would seem compatible with the Hull/Spence explanation of the Yerkes/Dodson law (see Chapter 5). When the dominant response is correct, as is the case with simple tasks, increasing either drive ($D$) or incentive ($K$) will make the dominant response even more dominant. When the dominant response is incorrect, as is the case when the nonobvious solution must be "discovered," increasing $D$ or $K$ will make the task even more difficult.

Closely related to the Yerkes/Dodson law is the Easterbrook hypothesis, mentioned earlier in Chapter 5. The Easterbrook hypothesis states that increased motivation may result in the perception of fewer environmental cues. An experiment by Bahrick, Fitts, and Rankin (1952) will illustrate the relation of the Easterbrook hypothesis to the detrimental effects of reward. Subjects were asked to do two simultaneous tasks. The primary task involved keeping a pointer over a moving target. The secondary task required the subject to push a button whenever lights came on at the edge of one's visual field. Some subjects were rewarded for good performance on the two tasks; some subjects were not rewarded. Bahrick et al. found that the rewarded subjects did more poorly on the secondary task than did the nonrewarded subjects. This study shows that increased motivation can restrict perusal of environmental cues, just as the Easterbrook hypothesis would predict. Thus, even *during* performance, reward can have detrimental effects if the task requires broad sampling of environmental stimuli. This is in addition to the results of many overjustification-effect studies that often demonstrate detrimental effects of reward after the reinforcement.

**Other factors.**    Condry and Chambers (1978) and Lepper and Greene (1978) point out that reward may change the way in which the subject interacts with the task. As a tourist, I will take the leisurely scenic route between Cleveland and Detroit; as a truckdriver, I will fight the frantic traffic on the interstate between Cleveland and Detroit. Reward (salary) will cause a decrease in my enjoyment of the task, because under the reward condition I perform the task much differently. This analysis may help explain the results of a study by Amabile (1979), who found that, when subjects were told that their artwork would later be evaluated, the artwork was less creative than when no evaluation was anticipated. Similarly, the baseball player who was quoted at the beginning of this chapter may have found to his displeasure that being paid to play also means one has to play with injuries, on extremely hot days, until 1 A.M., and so on.

**Equity theory and overjustification.**    In the previous chapter, we presented motivational evidence based on equity theory. One important conclusion we drew was that increased pay would result in *increased* performance (Lawler & O'Gara, 1967). The overjustification research, however, would lead one to believe that increased rewards (without competence information) would result in *decreased* performance. How can these two results be reconciled?

An interesting study by Folger, Rosenfield, and Hays (1978) helps clarify the issue. Half of the subjects in this study were given high pay for playing a crossword game; half were given low pay. Each of these groups was then subdivided, half of each group being *told* to do the task (low choice) and half being *asked* to do it (high choice). The experimenters then measured the amount of time the subjects interacted with the task after the experiment was supposedly over. The results are displayed in Figure 11-5. The overjustification effect occurred for the high-choice subjects, whereas the equity-theory effect occurred for the low-choice subjects. If a worker *must* do a task, high pay improves intrinsic motivation. If the worker can choose whether to do the task, high pay may decrease intrinsic motivation.

Perhaps the influence of reward on intrinsic motivation may best be summarized this way: the connotation and context of the reward are important. Does the reward convey a message of competence? Does it change the nature of the task interaction? Does it result in too much motivation? Is the task required? All these factors seem to be relevant.

## Achievement

During the last few years, attribution theory has been used to clarify some research on achievement motivation. The two theories have proved to be remarkably complementary: where explanation by the theory of achievement motivation stops, explanation by attribution the-

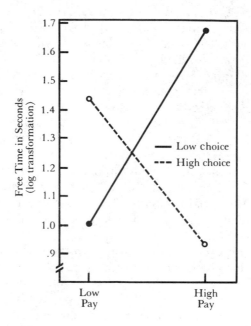

**Figure 11-5.** Effects of choice and pay on interaction time. *(From "Equity and Intrinsic Motivation: The Role of Choice," by R. Folger, D. Rosenfield, and R. Hays. In* Journal of Personality and Social Psychology, 1978, 36, 557–564. Copyright 1978 by the American Psychological Association. Reprinted by permission.)

ory begins. We shall see that $M_s > M_{af}$ people differ from $M_{af} > M_s$ people (see Chapter 9) in the way they attribute success and failure. Because of their different attributions, people having the two personality types respond quite differently to the same task outcome.

Recall that Heider postulated that an outcome could be attributed to effective personal force (internal attribution) or effective environmental force (external attribution). Heider also divided personal force into two components: power ("can") and motivation ("trying"). *Power* means ability. It is the relatively unchanging capability of a person as he or she enters any task situation. *Motivation,* of course, refers to a person's willingness to exert himself or herself. Unlike power, motivation is under the voluntary control of the subject and therefore does vary situationally. Thus, an outcome can be influenced by power, motivation, and effective environmental force.

Whether a person is able to perform a task depends on the interaction of these three components. The equation "exertion = difficulty/power" describes their relation. People with little power must exert themselves more to succeed at a given task than must people with great power.

**Predicting attributions of success and failure.** The covariation principle can often predict whether a person will attribute an outcome to an internal cause (power or motivation) or an external cause (effective environmental force). Weiner and Kukla (1970) showed that, when a majority of others succeed at a task, a subject is likely to attribute his or her own success to an external cause ("It was an easy task."). When the majority succeed, a failure is attributed to an internal cause. ("I must be stupid.") Similarly, when the majority of others fail, a failure is attributed externally ("It was a tough task."), and success is attributed internally ("I must be brilliant."). In other words, covariance leads to external attribution; that is, when one's own outcome and everyone else's covary, one attributes one's own outcome externally. Lack of covariance between outcomes leads to internal attribution.

Weiner and Kukla's study did not attempt to distinguish between the two types of internal attribution, ability and motivation. Later work by Weiner did make this distinction, as well as a parallel distinction between two types of external attribution. Recall that power (or ability) is a stable internal attribution and motivation (or effort) is an unstable internal attribution. Effort is called "unstable" and ability "stable" because effort, but not ability, can vary as one continues to work on a task. If you have no mathematical ability, you have no mathematical ability. During the course of an algebra problem, then, your ability won't change, but your effort may. Similarly, Heider (elaborated by Weiner, 1972) hypothesized that there exist a stable external attribution (task difficulty) and an unstable external one (luck). A task won't miraculously get easier as you look at it, but you might believe that fickle luck will shift. Hence, the four possible attributions can vary on two dimensions, the internal/external dimension and the stable/unstable dimension. Figure 11-6 summarizes the attributions.

|  | Internal | External |
|---|---|---|
| Stable | Ability | Task difficulty |
| Unstable | Effort | Luck |

**Figure 11-6.** Attribution classification scheme. *(From* Theories of Motivation: From Mechanism to Cognition, *by Bernard Weiner. Copyright © 1972 by Rand-McNally College Publishing Company, Chicago, Table 6.1, p. 356. Reprinted by permission.)*

Frieze and Weiner (1971) tested the logic of these attributions in a rather complex investigation. In the part most relevant to this discussion, Frieze and Weiner asked subjects to ascribe hypothetical successes and failures to ability, effort, task difficulty, or luck, as a function of past performance on the same task. For example, subjects were asked "You have just succeeded at a task you've succeeded at 50% of the time in the past. How much do you think your recent success was due to your high ability, ease of the task, great effort, and good luck?" Subjects estimated the influence of each of these four causes on a scale from 0 to 3. Figure 11-7 contains the results.

When past successes have been infrequent, present success is at-

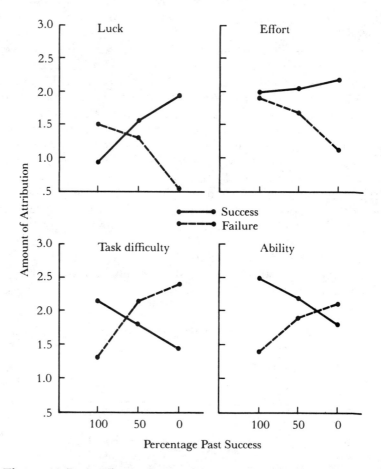

**Figure 11-7.** Attributions as a function of present outcome and past performance. *(From "Cue Utilization and Attributional Judgments for Success and Failure," by I. Frieze and B. Weiner. Journal of Personality, 1971, 39, 591–606. Reprinted by permission of Duke University Press.)*

tributed predominantly to the unstable causes—luck and effort. When past successes have been more frequent, present success is attributed to the stable causes—task difficulty and ability. Attributions of failure are mirror images of success attributions. Frieze and Weiner's study compels an important conclusion: To the extent that a new outcome differs from old ones, the attribution is made to unstable causes. To the extent that a new outcome is the same as old ones, the attribution is made to stable causes.

**The influence of attribution on affect.**    Which attribution one makes (among the four possible) for one's own success or failure greatly influences the emotion one experiences. As an example, imagine your professor is handing back the graded exams. You cautiously peer into your examination book. It's an *A*! You feel like a genius. At last merit has triumphed! The internal attribution you are making leads to enormous positive feelings. But wait! Everyone else around you got an *A*. Even what's-his-name, who *never* studies, got an *A*. Obviously it was a very easy test. You no longer can attribute your success internally—to ability. You must attribute it externally—to the ease of the test. You don't feel as elated following this external attribution as you did following the internal one. In general, internal attributions result in a greater affect (positive or negative feelings) than external attributions.

Riemer (1975) performed a clever study that demonstrated this point. Subjects were led to believe that their fine piano playing was a result of one of the four causes. A subsequent questionnaire probed how each subject felt about his or her performance. Those whose good performance was attributed internally felt better about it than those whose good performance was attributed externally.

In a similar study, Feather (1967) found the same result. Subjects rated the difficulty of various tasks. Half the tasks were measures of skill; in half, the outcome depended on chance. Subjects also rated how good or bad they would feel after succeeding or failing at each of the tasks. Feather found that on difficult tasks, success made subjects feel more positive if the outcome was a result of skill, rather than chance. Similarly, on easy tasks, failure made the subjects feel more negative if the outcome was based on skill. Figure 11-8 contains a summary of the results. Feather suggested that the axiom $I_s = 1 - P_s$ (see Chapter 9) be modified to $I_s = C(1 - P_s)$, where C represents the degree of perceived internal control. When the subject believes skill is being tapped, affect ($I_s$ or $I_f$) is greater regardless of task outcome. This difference is revealed in the steeper slopes for skill tasks in Figure 11-8.

An ambiguity in Feather's study is that internality/externality is confounded with stability/instability. Skill is synonymous with ability, the stable internal attribution. Chance is synonymous with luck, the

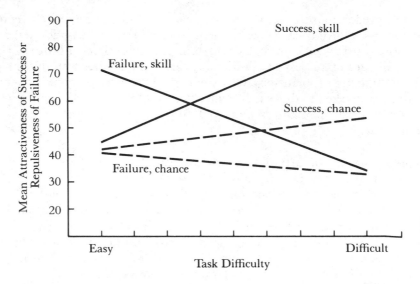

**Figure 11-8.** Mean attractiveness of success and repulsiveness of failure as a function of task difficulty and attribution of task outcome to skill or chance. *(Adapted from "Valence of Outcome and Expectation of Success in Relation to Task Difficulty and Perceived Locus of Control," by N. T. Feather,* Journal of Personality and Social Psychology, *1967, 7, 372–386. Copyright 1967 by the American Psychological Association. Reprinted by permission.)*

unstable external attribution. Therefore, skill and chance differ on both dimensions, and the difference in affect cannot be unequivocally attributed only to the internal/external dimension. Nevertheless, when Feather's study is considered along with Riemer's, it appears compatible with the notion that internal attribution causes greater affect than external attribution. (See also Karabenick, 1972.)

**The influence of achievement motives on attribution.** This idea that achievement motives influence attribution became even more important when it was found that $M_s > M_{af}$ subjects tend to attribute success to internal causes more than $M_{af} > M_s$ people do. This finding has very important implications. Following a success, $M_s > M_{af}$ people will experience substantial positive affect, because such people typically attribute success to their ability. It's no wonder their resultant achievement motivation is positive. Their experiences of high positive affect make them eager to enter further achievement situations. Following a success, $M_{af} > M_s$ people, however, do not experience much positive affect, because they make an external attribution—usually to luck. Consequently, they are generally not interested in entering achievement situations.

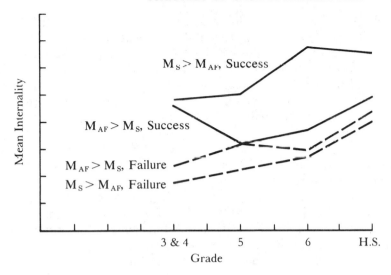

**Figure 11-9.** Mean tendency to make internal attributions as a function of grade level, motive type, and task outcome. *(Adapted from "An Attributional Analysis of Achievement Motivation," by B. Weiner and A. Kukla,* Journal of Personality and Social Psychology, *1970, 15, 1–20. Copyright 1970 by the American Psychological Association. Reprinted by permission.)*

Weiner and Kukla (1970) studied the relation of internality/externality to achievement motives in youngsters ranging from third grade to high school. The results for the male subjects are presented in Figure 11-9.

As can be seen, $M_s > M_{af}$ boys attribute success internally more than $M_{af} > M_s$ boys do. (The difference is statistically significant beyond grade four.) Consequently, $M_s > M_{af}$ subjects will experience substantial positive affect following success, whereas $M_{af} > M_s$ subjects will not. Note also that $M_s > M_{af}$ boys are less likely to attribute failure internally, although this difference is not statistically significant. They might not feel as bad as $M_{af} > M_s$ boys after failure, since they are somewhat less likely to make an internal attribution. We shall return to this point shortly.

A study by Weiner and Potepan (1970) also supports this analysis. Subjects high or low in achievement motivation were asked to ascribe their success or failure on a midterm to the four possible causes. Weiner and Potepan found that n Ach was correlated .36 with the tendency to attribute success to internal factors and −.26 with the tendency to attribute failure to internal factors.

In short, $M_s > M_{af}$ people attribute success internally and feel pride in their accomplishment. $M_{af} > M_s$ people attribute success externally, thereby *not* experiencing much personal pride. It's understandable that they don't approach achievement situations.

The failure attributions of $M_{af} > M_s$ persons were investigated in a study by W.-U. Meyer (1970, reported in Weiner et al., 1971). Subjects failed five consecutive digit/symbol–substitution tasks. After each trial, subjects rated the extent to which luck, ability, effort, and task difficulty had influenced the outcome. Figure 11-10 shows one of the main results.

$M_s > M_{af}$ subjects were much more likely to attribute failure to effort than were $M_{af} > M_s$ subjects. This difference has important consequences. Since the effort attribution is internal, $M_s > M_{af}$ subjects experience substantial negative affect when they fail. However, effort is unstable: it can be changed. So an $M_s > M_{af}$ subject who fails Trial 1 tries extra hard on Trial 2. This extra exertion following failure may be just what is needed to achieve success. Thus, the unstable attribution is a real benefit: it promotes high motivation on subsequent trials.

Figure 11-11 contains another important result from the same study. This figure shows that, as the number of failures increases, $M_{af} > M_s$ subjects are more likely than $M_s > M_{af}$ subjects to attribute failure to low ability. This is a particularly devastating attribution. First, because it is internal, it results in substantial negative affect. Second, and

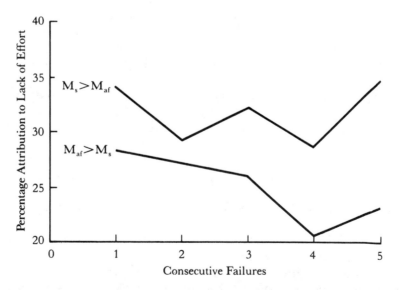

**Figure 11-10.** Percentage of attribution to lack of effort as a function of achievement motivation and number of failures. *(From Leistungsmotiv und Ursachenerklärung von Erfolg und Misserfolg, by W.-U. Meyer. Klett Verlag, Stuttgart, 1973. Reprinted by permission.)*

more important, ability is a stable attribution. Therefore, it's no use trying harder on the next trial; one's ability won't magically increase between trials. Accordingly, $M_{af} > M_s$ people will not persist in the face of failure, whereas $M_s > M_{af}$ people will. This is exactly the finding obtained by Lucas (1952), shown in Figure 9-3—the finding that Weiner's inertial-tendency formulation was designed to explain. Understanding that people having different motive types attribute both their successes and their failures differently helps to clarify the earlier findings.

**Sex differences.**   In another application of attribution theory to achievement motivation, recent research has shown that males and females attribute task outcomes differently. Ickes and Layden (1978) asked male and female undergraduates to attribute success and failure experiences to various causes. The males were far more likely than females to attribute their successes to internal causes. The males were less likely than females to attribute their failures to any cause whatsoever! The males apparently see failures as being rather improbable.

Similar results have also been found using much younger subjects. Nicholls (1975) and Dweck and Reppucci (1973) found that young girls attributed their failures to low ability, whereas young boys attributed their failures either to bad luck or to low effort. These differ-

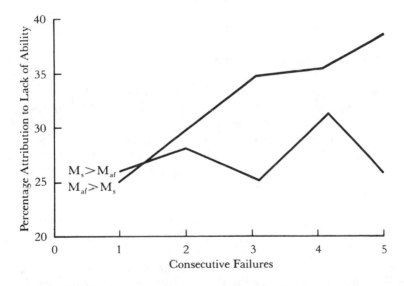

**Figure 11-11.** Percentage of attribution to lack of ability as a function of achievement motivation and number of failures. *(From* Leistungsmotiv und Ursachenerklärung von Erfolg und Misserfolg, *by W.-U. Meyer. Klett Verlag, Stuttgart, 1973. Reprinted by permission.)*

ential attributions are likely to have enormous consequences. Girls who attribute failure to ability should lower their $P_s$ estimates after a failure. Ability is stable. Once ineptitude is blamed as the cause of failure, therefore, one might as well give up. In contrast, boys should not become helpless following a failure. Neither luck nor effort is stable. Thus, there is no reason to decrease their $P_s$; there is still the possibility that increased effort will result in success. These differential attributions following failure may explain the very general finding that girls have lower expectancies of success than boys do (V. C. Crandall, 1969; Deaux & Emswiller, 1974; Feather, 1969).

The fact that girls have lower $P_s$ estimates in academic areas is particularly ironic, since they receive consistently higher grades than boys do during the elementary-school years (McCandless, Roberts, & Starnes, 1972). Dweck and Goetz (1978) support the suggestion that it is the girls' attribution of failure to ability which is responsible for their low $P_s$ estimates. In a number of laboratory experiments, Dweck and Goetz showed that boys bounce back from failure, whereas girls are buried by it. In an effort to explain how this state of affairs is engendered, the authors carefully observed teacher/student interactions in classrooms. It was found that boys received much more negative feedback from teachers than girls did, but most of this negative feedback had nothing to do with the boys' intellectual adequacy. On the other hand, 88% of the negative feedback girls received did pertain to intellectual aspects of their work. Dweck and Goetz suggest that this state of affairs may lead girls to make internal attributions for failure much more often than boys do.

In conclusion, it should be pointed out that sex differences in attribution closely resemble self-esteem differences in attribution. Males make attributions following successes and failures much as high-self-esteem people do; females make attributions as low-self-esteem people do. This relation is further strengthened by significant correlations that have been obtained between self-esteem and masculine sex-role identification (Ickes & Layden, 1978). All of these data on sex differences in attribution are highly consistent with the self-esteem model of achievement motivation presented in Chapter 9.

**Summary.**   The original version of the theory of achievement motivation related achievement to differences in personality. Attribution theory adds an intervening step: the causal attribution. Research has shown that people of the two motive types tend to attribute task outcomes differently. A reason that $M_s > M_{af}$ people are more willing than $M_{af} > M_s$ people to participate in an achievement activity is that the former enjoy great positive affect following a success and the latter do not. A reason that $M_s > M_{af}$ people persist after failure is that they attribute failure to unstable causes. $M_{af} > M_s$ people attribute their failures to ability. This stable attribution apparently promotes discouragement, $P_s$ deflation, and generally poor performance. The findings of the theory of achievement motivation therefore have not been displaced by attribution theory; they have been supplemented by it.

**Criticisms of the attribution/achievement model.**     Although the attribution-theory elaboration of the achievement model initially appeared to have great promise, recent researchers have been highly critical of it. First, the four-cell classification scheme proposed by Weiner (see Figure 11-6) has proved inadequate. For example, Falbo and Beck (1979) asked 226 undergraduates to provide explanations for successes and failures at various activities. Only 23% of the explanations fit into any of the four cells of Weiner's scheme. Thus, it appears that attribution theorists may be the only people making much use of that particular attributional model of achievement.

Because of the inadequacy of that scheme, a few alternative ones have been suggested (for example, Elig & Frieze, 1975). However, any rating form containing questions on the importance of certain attributions has the unfortunate tendency to bias the respondent's thinking toward those particular attributions. Open-ended questions have a different set of disadvantages (Elig & Frieze, 1979). Thus, the fair measurement of attributions is immensely problematic.

A second difficulty with the attributional model of achievement pertains more to theory than to measurement. Figure 11-12 (a) contains a summary of Weiner's attributional elaboration of achievement theory. People with high achievement motivation are hypothesized to make different attributions following a success or following a failure. These different attributions are postulated to lead to differences in performance. Patten and White (1977) tested this theory with several experiments, most of the results of which posed problems for Weiner's theory. First, the relation between achievement motivation and performance was independent of attributions made by the subjects. In other words, high achievers did better than low achievers in the absence of attribution differences between the groups. Second, a relation did exist between attribution to unstable causes and effort actually expended, but this relation was independent of achievement motivation. Since achievement motivation and attribution to unstable causes both influence performance independently (contrary to Weiner's model), Patten and White (1977) suggest consideration of the model in Figure 11-12 (b).

A related experiment by Covington and Omelich (1979) also proved embarrassing for the Weiner model. This study showed that level of achievement motivation was related only to ability attributions. Recall that Weiner and his colleagues suggested that, following failure, high achievers more than low achievers blamed their performance on low effort. Yet, no differences in effort attributions were found by

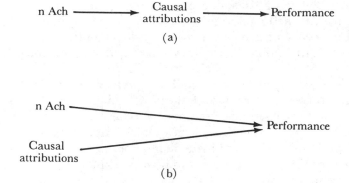

Figure 11-12. (a) Weiner's model; (b) Patten and White's model.

Covington and Omelich. The very complex results of the Covington and Omelich (1979) study are summarized in Figure 11-13, in which the relations between the significant variables are indicated. Note that the results are consistent with the self-esteem/confidence model discussed in Chapter 9. Achievement motivation is related to one's perception of one's own ability (self-esteem) and to one's expectancy on future trials (confidence). These, in turn, help determine future performance.

## Biases in attribution

Attribution theory appears to assume that a person logically evaluates the causes of his or her behavior. Sensible principles such as the covariation principle dictate the cause to which we attribute our behavior. However, there is a great deal of evidence that people are not entirely logical in attributing the causes of their behavior. Instead of making accurate attributions, people sometimes make blatantly self-serving attributions. In particular, people have a tendency to attribute successes to internal factors ("I'm brilliant!") and failures to external causes ("I was unlucky"). The former bias is called "ego-enhancing"; the latter is called "ego-protecting." Politicians mastered these two attributions long ago.

An experiment by D. T. Miller (1976) provides evidence for both of these biases. Two groups of subjects took a social perceptiveness test. One group was told that the test was valid and accurate; the other group was told that the test was new and not yet validated. The first group was the high-involvement group, because one would want to do well on a test that measured something as fundamental as one's social skills. The other group was the low-involvement group, since the results from an unvalidated test would not be very informative. Half of the subjects in each group were led to believe they had scored high, and half were led to believe they had scored low. All subjects then at-

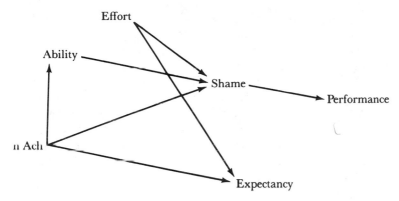

**Figure 11-13.** Significant relations between variables in the Covington and Omelich (1979) study.

tributed their performance to various possible causes. The results showed substantial attribution bias. Those who scored high tended to attribute their performance to internal causes, whereas those who scored low attributed their performance to external causes. Furthermore, the biases were more pronounced in the high-involvement subjects: with high involvement, the benefits of enhancing and protecting self-esteem are greater than with low involvement. Several other studies have found similar attributional biases (for example, Stevens & Jones, 1976).

## Attitude change

We touched on the relation between attribution and attitude change when discussing Bem's self-perception theory (Chapter 10). Recall that Bem stated that people infer their beliefs from their behavior. If their behavior of making a statement seems forced by external pressure, they do not come to believe the statement. If the behavior seems not to be caused by external pressure, they conclude that they must believe what they are saying and change their attitude accordingly.

Although there are minor differences between self-perception theory and attribution theory, the former can be comfortably subsumed under the latter. Bem's theory is a self-attribution theory: it predicts how a person will attribute his or her own behavior. As an attribution theory, self-perception theory can be restated in terms of internal and external attributions. For example, the forced-compliance group in cognitive-dissonance research can be considered an external-attribution group. If a subject is paid $20 to lie, he attributes his behavior externally and therefore does not change his attitude toward the statement he is making. The insufficient-justification group can be considered an internal-attribution group. The $1 given the subject does not justify her telling a lie. She therefore attributes this behavior internally ("I really must like this task, I guess") and changes her opinion accordingly.

The results of a few studies of attitude change can be explained by attribution theory but not by cognitive-dissonance theory. One, by Kiesler, Nisbett, and Zanna (1969), was mentioned in Chapter 10. Another, by Kiesler and Sakamura (1966), provides a purer example. A subject was paid either $1 or $5 to read a speech consistent with his or her own beliefs. (Because the speech was consistent with belief, no dissonance was aroused.) Then the subject was exposed to communication advocating the opposite viewpoint. It was found that the $5 subjects were more influenced by the subsequent countercommunication than were the $1 subjects. The attribution-theory explanation is straightforward. If a subject says something he believes in and he is paid little to say it, he makes an internal attribution. ("I believe this. That's why I said it.") Such opinions are resistant to countercommunications. But if he is paid quite a bit to say something he believes in, he will make an external attribution. ("I'll say anything for $5.") Such opinions are not resistant to countercommunications. Attribution theory can explain attitude change when dissonant *or* consonant acts are performed; cognitive-dissonance theory can explain attitude change only in the former situation.

An important study by Zanna and Cooper (1974) shows that cognitive-dissonance theory cannot *entirely* be subsumed under attribution theory. First, all subjects were given a placebo. One-third of the subjects were told the pill promoted relaxation, one-third were told it caused nervousness, and one-third were told it had no effect. Subjects were then either forced or asked to write a counterattitudinal essay. They formed the low- and the high-dissonance groups, respectively. (Writing something one disagrees with is not dissonant if one was forced to do so but is dissonant if one agreed to do so.) Zanna and Cooper found attitude change greatest in high-dissonance subjects who took the "tranquilizer." Dissonance should seem particularly intense if it is felt even under the influence of a tranquilizer; therefore, the "tranquilized" subjects in the high-dissonance group should experience the most dissonance and hence show the most attitude change.

The reason this experiment is important is that it substantiates the notion of dissonance as an aversive-drive state, the reduction of which is reinforcing. Attribution theory *alone* could not have predicted that the greatest attitude change would have occurred where it did. The manipulation by means of the placebo depended on the subjects' perception of some aversive state whose persistence through the "tranquilizer" gave them a reason to overestimate their dissonance. If there had been no aversive dissonant state to be magnified by the manipulation, the manipulation would not have worked. Maximal attitude change would not have been found in the tranquilizer group. This study lends support to the reality of dissonance as an aversive state while supporting the predictions that attribution theory makes concerning the effect of the placebos upon perceived magnitude of dissonance. The study indicates that, although many of the studies interpretable by cognitive-dissonance theory can be explained by attribution theory, not all can.

## Emotional arousal

**The James/Lange theory of emotion.**    One of the oldest theories of emotion was proposed almost simultaneously by William James and by a Danish psychologist, Carl Lange. The James/Lange theory is quite counterintuitive. It states that when a person perceives an emotion-producing stimulus, the body reacts with characteristic skeletal and visceral responses. It is these responses that are labeled "emotion." For example, if you turned around and saw a rattlesnake, would you be immediately afraid? No, says the James/Lange theory. First, you would begin pumping adrenaline into your bloodstream. You would inhale sharply. You would move quickly. These responses would in turn produce fear, according to the James/Lange theory. We label as "fear" the group of bodily responses we make to certain stimuli. If those responses did not occur, there would be no fear. The common-sense view of emotion can be expressed this way: "I see a bear. I am afraid. So I run." The James/Lange theory states: "I see a bear. I run. So I am afraid." Emotion is the consequence of responses, according to the James/Lange theory.

The James/Lange theory has not fared well. Cannon (1927) has correctly pointed out that it is very difficult to distinguish among emotions on the basis of differences among physiological responses. According to the James/Lange theory, each emotion should have its own characteristic group of responses. That is the only way emotions could be distinguished, since the responses alone determine emotion. Such differences have proved hard to find.

**Studies on misattribution.**    Schachter (1964) has proposed an interesting theory of emotion whose implications contradict the James/Lange theory. Schachter suggests that emotion is caused by physiological arousal plus a cognition that labels, or "steers," the arousal. For example, if injection of a chemical causes a person to become physiologically aroused, he might believe that he is sexually attracted to the nurse who gave him the injection, that he is petrified by the sight of the syringe, or that he is frightened by the weird-looking doctor who is approaching him with a scalpel. The cognition the person uses to label his arousal will determine which emotion he believes he has.

The importance of cognition in the experience of emotion is well illustrated by a quote from Bertrand Russell:

> On one occasion my dentist injected a considerable amount of adrenalin into my blood, in the course of administering a local anaesthetic. I turned pale and trembled, and my heart beat violently; the bodily symptoms of fear were present, as the books said they should be, but it was obvious to me that I was not actually feeling fear. . . . What was different was the cognitive part: I did not feel fear because I knew there was nothing to be afraid of. In normal life, the adrenal glands are stimulated by the perception of an object which is frightful or enraging; . . . when adrenalin is artificially administered, this cognitive element is absent, and the emotion in its entirety fails to arise [1927, p. 226].

In summary, emotion requires both arousal and the appropriate cognition.

Schachter and his colleagues (Schachter & Singer, 1962; Schachter & Wheeler, 1962) tested this two-factor theory of emotion using an experimental design that produced a situation similar to the one just described. Schachter and Singer administered epinephrine to several groups of subjects. This drug causes physiological arousal. Some subjects were informed that arousal would occur, some were not informed of the effects of the drug, and some were misinformed about the effects ("It will cause numbness and itching"). Finally, each subject spent time in a waiting room either in the presence of an angry fellow subject (a confederate of the experimenters) or with a euphoric, fun-loving confederate. The experimenters found that the informed subjects were least affected by the behavior of the confederate. The uninformed and misinformed subjects, however, acted either angry or euphoric, mimicking the confederate. An observer would surmise that the subjects felt angry or euphoric. More important, the subjects also would label their own emotion in these terms (as Schachter and Singer ascertained from self-reports). Yet physiologically there was no difference between the angry subjects and the euphoric subjects. Therefore, the emotions cannot be distinguished on the basis of differences in arousal. They *can* be distinguished by the different cognitions the two groups of subjects have.

An analysis of the same experiment in attribution-theory terms will prove instructive. The informed subjects experienced autonomic arousal and correctly attributed it to the injection they had received; the arousal was correctly attributed externally to the drug. The uninformed subjects were also aroused, but they incorrectly attributed their arousal to the offensive questionnaire they and the angry confederates were answering or to the frivolous situation they and the euphoric confederates found themselves in. These are misattributions, since we know from the control groups that these angry or euphoric confederates cannot by themselves genuinely cause much anger or euphoria. The uninformed subjects, by attributing their arousal to anything but the drug, are making a mistake. Therefore, we term this a misattribution.

This experiment by Schachter and Singer (1962)[1] casts very serious doubt on the James/Lange theory. The uninformed euphoric and angry subjects presumably would have the same physiological responses to the epinephrine. Yet these two groups exhibited radically different emotions. The James/Lange theory would lead us to believe that people having the same responses to a stimulus should also have the same emotion.

Another study demonstrating the powerful effects of misattribution is one by Nisbett and Schachter (1966). Subjects were administered a series of shocks that steadily increased in intensity. They reported when the shock became at all painful and when it became too painful to tolerate further. Before the shock session, all subjects were given placebos. Half were told the pill would cause tremors, butterflies in the stomach, and other symptoms that are identical to those associated with genuine arousal. The other half were told it would cause completely different symptoms. These two groups were further subdivided: half of each group was told the shocks would be painful (high-fear group); the other half was told the shocks would not be severe (low-fear group).

Among the low-fear subjects, those who were told the pill would cause arousal symptoms were able to tolerate far more shock than those told the pill would cause irrelevant symptoms. When the former subjects experienced true fear and arousal, they should have attributed it internally. ("I'm afraid of these shocks. They hurt!") Instead, these subjects misattributed their symptoms externally. ("Why am I shaking? Why am I petrified? It's that pill I took. He said the pill would make me feel this way.") These subjects believed that the shocks were not the source of their internal stimuli. Therefore, they were willing to tolerate more shock.

This rather devious technique of inducing misattribution has been used in the treatment of various emotional disorders (Ross, Rodin, & Zimbardo, 1969; Strong, 1970; Valins & Nisbett, 1972). Storms and Nisbett (1970) gave placebos to insomniacs. The insomniacs were told that the pill would cause alertness, an increase in heart rate, and other symptoms typically associated with insomnia. On nights when the insomniacs took this placebo, they fell asleep more quickly. (At least, they reported that they fell asleep more quickly. Actual onset of sleep was not measured.) Once again, misattribution occurred. Subjects falsely attributed their bedtime arousal to an external cause. Their symptoms on those nights were presumably caused by a pill, not by any inadequacy or abnormality of their own. This very comforting cognition—the external attribution—allowed the subjects to fall asleep

---

[1] The Schachter and Singer (1962) study has been heartily criticized by Maslach (1979) and by Marshall and Zimbardo (1979).

earlier. Storms and Nisbett also included another experimental group, in which the subjects were told that the drug would make them relax. These subjects took longer than usual to fall asleep! They expected less arousal after taking the pill. Since the pill actually was a placebo, true arousal did not change. These subjects were presumably quite concerned when their bedtime arousal persisted in the face of this tranquilizing drug. ("I really must be nervous.") This concern kept them awake even longer than usual.[2]

Valins and Nisbett (1972, p. 145) point out that this external-attribution ploy may be particularly helpful to a patient if worrying about a problem tends to exacerbate the problem. For example, assume someone is extremely nervous about speaking in front of an audience. Worrying about that fear before the speech takes place will ensure anxiety when the speech does occur. If the person is given a placebo and told it makes one feel anxious, she can attribute her arousal to this external source, thereby lessening the anxiety.

Valins and Nisbett point out, however, that external attribution is not always helpful in alleviating an emotional problem. First, if a person attributes her improvement to a drug, she may become psychologically dependent on that drug, even if it is a placebo. She may feel that it is absolutely necessary for her well-being. Second, the patient may not apply herself very strenuously to the treatment, since she believes that an external factor (the drug), not an internal factor (her own effort), is critical. Third, she will feel she is particularly ill if the drug does not work. This will exacerbate the problem. The subjects in Storms and Nisbett's study who were told the placebo was a tranquilizer illustrate this situation. When they felt nervous even under the influence of a "tranquilizer," they worried quite a bit and consequently took even longer to fall asleep. Thus, for a true cure to be completed, the subject cannot rely entirely on external factors.

**Misattribution and love.**    Some theorists believe that romantic love can be manipulated by misattribution. Now, you may think that psychologists have gone too far this time. Is nothing sacred? Let's look at the evidence.

The most famous experiment on this topic is one by Dutton and Aron (1974). Male subjects were approached either by a male or by a female experimenter, purportedly to interview the subject about the influence of scenery on creative expression. For half the subjects, the interview took place on a sturdy bridge 10 feet above a small rivulet. For the other half of the subjects, the interview took place on a long, wobbly, suspension bridge 230 feet above rocks and shallow rapids.

---

[2]Kellogg and Baron (1975) and Bootzin, Herman, and Nicassio (1976) failed to replicate this part of Storms and Nisbett's study.

The experimenters made the safe assumption that those interviewed in the latter situation would feel more aroused. During the course of the interview, the subjects were offered the phone number of the inter-viewer in case they wanted to find out more about the experiment at a later time. The female interviewers were called more often when the interview had taken place in the more arousing situation. The authors hypothesized that these subjects may have been misattributing their arousal to the attractiveness of the female interviewer. Being labeled as romantic interest, the arousal resulted in increased attraction toward the interviewer. (Calls to male interviewers were not influenced by bridge location.)

Many other studies on romantic love have been interpreted in this same way. For example, Driscoll, Davis, and Lipetz (1972) found a positive correlation between the amount of love a couple reported feel-ing for each other and the amount of parental interference in the rela-tionship. The experimenters suggested that the arousal caused by the meddling of the parents was misattributed to the attractiveness of the other member of the couple.

Rubin (1973) mentioned the advice of a helpful Roman who sug-gested that men take their female friends to watch the gladiators. As the woman watched the carnage on the battlefield, she would become physiologically aroused. According to this Roman advisor, if everything went well, the woman might attribute her arousal to her feelings to-ward the suitor, rather than the battle.

Although support for the misattribution explanation of these roman-tic love studies is not unanimous (Kenrick & Cialdini, 1977), an analo-gous explanation has proven useful in other areas, such as the enhancement of humor. Cantor, Bryant, and Zillmann (1974) found that previously aroused subjects rated material as funnier than did less aroused subjects. The experimenters claim that the arousal they in-duced in the first part of the experiment was carried over into the sec-ond part of the experiment, in which the subjects rated humorous material. Because the subjects misattributed their lingering arousal to the humorous material, they rated the material as more humorous. All of these studies make the same point: arousal can be steered by a cogni-tion, thereby producing the emotion appropriate for that cognition.

**Conditioned helplessness.**    Another example of the relation be-tween attribution and emotion is illustrated in the work of Seligman and his colleagues. Seligman's research is based on a phenomenon called "conditioned helplessness" (S. F. Maier, Seligman, & Solomon, 1969). When animals are given a series of unavoidable shocks and then a series of avoidable shocks, most of them will not learn the avoidance response. During the unavoidable shocks, the animals learn that they have no control over them. The animals maintain this "stoicism" when the experimental situation is changed so that they do have control over the shocks. It is as if the animals are making an external attribution when they should be making an internal one.

Seligman believes that conditioned helplessness is a true model of depression. He suggests that depressives chronically feel that what they do simply does not matter; they are helpless recipients of whatever their fate brings. Like the animals in the conditioned-helplessness studies, depressives constantly make external attributions ("I'm at the mercy of powerful others") when they should be making internal ones ("I can do something to change my situation"). Like the animals, depressives view what happens to them as independent of any response they might make.

W. R. Miller and Seligman (1973) tested this theory in a rather elaborate experiment. The subjects were people who had scored very high on a test of chronic depressiveness and people who had scored very low on the test. One of the two tasks both groups attempted was supposedly a manual-dexterity task, the outcome of which was determined by the subject's skill. The task was to raise a disk-shaped object carefully so that a ball bearing resting on the disk would not roll off. The subject succeeded if the disk was raised to the top of the apparatus with the ball still on the disk. An electromagnet surreptitiously controlled by the experimenter, however, was buried within the disk. The experimenter kept the magnet "on" during the first trial, so that everyone succeeded. The second task both groups attempted was to predict whether an X or an O would appear on the next frame of a slide projector. The results of this task were supposedly determined only by chance. Again, the experimenter arranged the results so that everyone succeeded at this task on the first trial.

Before each trial, the experimenter asked each subject what he or she thought the chances of success were on that trial. Figure 11-14 shows the change in subjects' estimates of the probability of success from Trial 1 to Trial 2 as a function of the subjects' personality type and the task description. As can be seen, nondepressed subjects acted quite rationally. If the task was described as a measure of skill, they radically raised their estimates after succeeding on Trial 1. ("I guess I'm pretty skilled at this.") If the task outcome was said to be determined by chance, these subjects barely changed their estimates from Trial 1 to Trial 2. ("So I got lucky this time. I might not next time.") Contrast these results with those for depressives, who changed their estimates only slightly more after success at a skill task than after success at a chance task. Since depressives feel that nothing they can do makes a difference, they hardly distinguish between skill and chance tasks. For depressives, there really is no such thing as a skill task—that is, a task on which what one does influences the result.

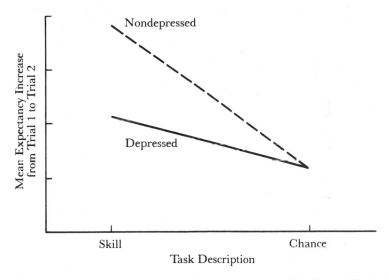

**Figure 11-14.** Mean expectancy increase from Trial 1 to Trial 2 as a function of personality type and task description. *(From "Depression and the Perception of Reinforcement," by W. R. Miller and M. E. Seligman,* Journal of Abnormal Psychology, *1973, 82, 62–73. Copyright 1973 by the American Psychological Association. Reprinted by permission.)*

Seligman's learned-helplessness analysis has had an immense impact on the study of depression, because the analysis helps reduce a complicated and common emotional malady to a model that can easily be investigated in the laboratory. However, this advantage of the learned-helplessness analysis is also its most controversial feature. Can the many types of depression in all their complexity be truly analogous to the failure of dogs to avoid shocks?

Buchwald, Coyne, and Cole (1978) and Depue and Monroe (1978) think the relation between true depression and Seligman's learned-helplessness model is very weak indeed. To make matters worse, Costello (1978), among others, has blasted the studies that Seligman uses to support his theory. And, finally, there are a number of studies whose results do not support Seligman's formulation (Kilpatrick-Tabak & Roth, 1978; Willis & Blaney, 1978). In 1978, Seligman and his colleagues presented a reformulation of the theory designed to eliminate many of the weaknesses in the original theory (Abramson, Seligman, & Teasdale, 1978). Let us first examine one of the studies that may have prompted the reformulation.

D. C. Klein, Fencil-Morse, and Seligman (1976) performed a study using a method that has become very common in the study of depression. Depressed and nondepressed subjects first worked on problems in

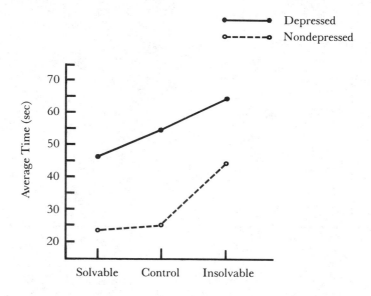

**Figure 11-15.** Average time to solve each anagram as a function of depression level and type of problems. *(Adapted from "Learned Helplessness, Depression, and the Attribution of Failure," by D. Klein, E. Fencil-Morse, and M. Seligman. In* Journal of Personality and Social Psychology, *1976, 33, 508–516. Copyright 1976 by the American Psychological Association. Reprinted by permission.)*

which they had to determine which of eight potential solutions was the correct one. Some subjects were given unsolvable problems, some were given solvable ones; a control group omitted this first phase of the study. In the second phase, subjects in all three groups tried to unscramble the letters in anagrams. Figure 11-15 depicts the average time it took to solve each anagram. The first important result was that being given unsolvable problems drastically impaired the later performance of the nondepressed subjects. The unsolvable problems presumably taught them to be helpless. This attitude of helplessness then hurt their performance on the subsequent anagrams. Note that the performance of these nondepressed, helpless subjects is on a par with that of some of the genuinely depressed subjects. The depressed subjects, according to Seligman, had learned to be helpless long before the experiment began.

There was a second crucial result in this study. The subjects working on unsolvable problems had been divided into thirds. One-third of the unsolvable-task subjects were led to believe that most people could solve all of the problems. As Weiner and Kukla (1970) had shown, this information would cause these failing subjects to attribute their failure

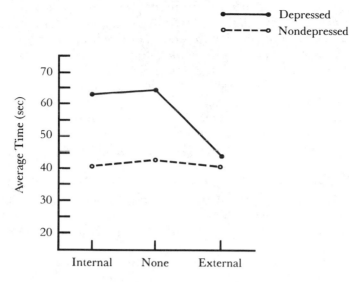

**Figure 11-16.** Average time to solve each anagram as a function of depression level and attribution instructions. *(Adapted from "Learned Helplessness, Depression, and the Attribution of Failure," by D. Klein, E. Fencil-Morse, and M. Seligman. In* Journal of Personality and Social Psychology, *1976, 33, 508–516. Copyright 1976 by the American Psychological Association. Reprinted by permission.)*

internally—that is, to low ability. Another third of the subjects were led to believe that hardly anyone could solve the problems, thus leading these subjects to attribute their failure externally, to the difficulty of the task. One-third of the subjects were given no information. Figure 11-16 contains the data for these unsolvable-problem subjects. The fact that the external attribution completely eliminated the debilitating effects of learned helplessness for the depressed subjects shows how critical one's attributions are in determining performance.

Because of studies such as this, emphasizing the important role of attributions, the revised learned-helplessness model was formulated (Abramson, Seligman, & Teasdale, 1978). The new model contains three dimensions along which learned helplessness may vary. The first dimension is anchored at the poles by personal helplessness and universal helplessness. For example, a father of a child dying of leukemia feels helpless, but so would anyone else in his position. He is therefore experiencing universal helplessness and would attribute his plight to external factors. However, a student who tried very hard to obtain good grades but nevertheless failed all her courses would experience personal helplessness. Others who might be more intelligent would get fantastic grades with that much studying; therefore, this person would attribute her helplessness to internal factors. As the Klein et al. study showed, the type of attribution for one's failures is extremely important in determining the effects of helplessness on future behaviors. We might expect the father of the dying child not to give up if a second child fell ill; we would expect the failing student, however, to give up quickly on subsequent courses.

The second dimension of helplessness is related to the generality of the emotion. If I learn to be helpless in competitive athletics, will this attitude generalize to my behavior in the business world? If so, my helplessness is "global." If not, it is "specific."

The final dimension of helplessness is stability. If my helplessness is short-lived, it is unstable; if it is long-lived, it is stable. For example, a global, personal, *stable* attribution for my failure on a test would be "I'm dumb." A global, personal, *unstable* attribution would be "I was tired."

This new formulation of the learned-helplessness model explains several findings that would have proven troublesome for the original model. For example, Douglas and Anisman (1975) found that failure on tasks advertised to be simple resulted in poor performance on subsequent tasks. Initial failure on tasks said to be difficult did not cause this subsequent decrement. According to the revised learned-helplessness model, failure at the easy tasks should lead to a global, internal attribution, whereas failure at the difficult ones should lead to a specific, external attribution. Only the global, internal attribution should cause the helplessness to generalize to the later tasks; if you believe you are stupid, that is reason to give up on nearly everything. If you believe that the task you just performed was too difficult for you, there's no reason to give up on later tasks that might be easier. (See also Tennen & Eller, 1977.)

The new analysis also helps clarify "helplessness-therapy" studies such as that of D. C. Klein and Seligman (1976), who found that solvable problems given after unsolvable ones helped eliminate the helplessness caused by the unsolvable problems. Presumably, the solvable problems change the global attribution to a more specific one when the subject realizes that he or she is not helpless on all tasks.

Although Klein et al. and other related studies were important in demonstrating the importance of attributions, all of the studies of this type *forced* certain attributions by giving people, for example, information about how many other people succeeded on the task. Just because an artificially created internal attribution makes one more helpless, however, does not necessarily mean that depressed people naturally make such self-defeating attributions. Independent evidence, though, does indicate that depressives make these attributions. Kuiper (1978) using adults and Diener and Dweck (1978) using children found that depressives made internal attributions for failure but nondepressives did not. This is exactly what the new model would predict.

Note that a subtle but important change has occurred between the original learned-helplessness model and the reformulation. Initially, it was postulated that depressed people felt helpless and therefore attributed the cause of various events to *external* factors. The new model emphasizes damaging *internal* attributions. The intents of the models appear to be similar in that both posit a debilitated victim surrounded by uncontrollable events. The prior model focused on perception of the external, controllable events, whereas the new model emphasizes the perceived internal weakness of the individual. Both models rely heavily on attribution theory.

## Competence revisited: Rotter, deCharms, and reactance theory

**Rotter.**    Closely related to the internal/external dichotomy of attribution theory is the central concept of Julian Rotter's (1966) theory. Rotter hypothesizes that some people believe that their behavior does have consequences: what they do makes a difference. In Rotter's terminology, such people have an internal locus of control. At the opposite end of the spectrum are those people who believe that they have no control over events: their behavior has no influence over either positive or negative occurrences. These people are said to have an external locus of control. Rotter (1966) has developed a personality scale that purports to measure the extent to which one is an "internal" or an "external."

Several studies have been done to test the validity of this scale. Seeman and Evans (1962) tested patients in a tuberculosis hospital. Subjects with an internal locus of control, as compared to the "externals," knew more about their own physical condition, asked their doctors and nurses more questions, and expressed less satisfaction about the amount of information they were being given concerning their health. The internals, then, certainly weren't passive. Similarly, Gore and Rotter (1963) found that, compared to "externals," Blacks scoring toward the "internal" end of the scale were more willing to perform ambitious activities on behalf of the civil rights movement. In both of these studies, the "internals" think they can control the positive and negative events in their lives; they therefore want to do something. The "externals" resemble people who have undergone extensive learned-helplessness training. Why bother to do anything if it won't make any difference?

The issue of control over one's life has been investigated in some extremely important studies involving nursing-home residents. Langer and Rodin (1976) and Schulz (1976) both gave elderly nursing-home residents control over certain important events in their lives, such as the schedules of visitors or the care of plants. Other elderly residents were not given these responsibilities. The spectacular findings were that, 3 weeks later (Langer & Rodin, 1976) and 2 months later (Schulz, 1976), the elderly people who controlled a portion of their own destinies showed superior health, attitudes, and activity levels. Rodin and Langer (1977) found that these beneficial effects persisted 18 months later. However, Schulz and Hanusa (1978) found that the people who had been given control over some aspects of their lives deteriorated more quickly than the comparison group once the experiment had ended. In the vocabulary of the reformulated learned-helplessness model (Abramson, Seligman, & Teasdale, 1978), we hypothesize that the subjects in the Langer and Rodin (1976) study may have made a *global* attribution of competence when they were given control of their lives, because this experiment included several features designed to foster the perception of control. The subjects in the original Schulz (1976) study may have made a *specific* attribution, since the only real change in their lives was the setting up of a visitor's schedule. This single feature may have caused the subjects to think that they could control this specific event, rather than that they could control their lives. When the event in the Schulz (1976) study ended, so did this specific attribution of control.

This group of studies dramatically illustrates the impact of helplessness and its opposite, competence. As we have seen earlier (Chapters 3 and 7), R. W. White (1959) and many others have stressed how important it is that people believe that their behavior has consequence. Bruno Bettelheim (1943) described how death soon followed hopelessness in the concentration camps; survival demanded the belief—sometimes the illusion—that one could still control some aspect of one's life.

**DeCharms.**    Richard deCharms (1968, 1976) has invented the Origin/Pawn concept to describe the feelings of competence versus helplessness. Closely related to attribution theory, deCharms's theory of personal causation contains a dimension running from Origin to Pawn. A person who feels like an Origin believes that she can originate her own behavior, can seek her own goals. In other words, this person is internally motivated. A person who feels like a Pawn believes that he is pushed around by others; his own motivations are immaterial. He feels that the cause of his behavior is external. Whether one feels like an Origin or a Pawn is central to deCharms's theory: "Man's primary motivational propensity is to be effective in producing changes in his environment. Man strives to be a causal agent, to be the primary locus of causation for, or the Origin of, his behavior; he strives for personal causation" (deCharms, 1968, p. 269). A person who feels like an Origin will be positively motivated, optimistic, and confident. A Pawn will feel powerless.

DeCharms (1976) put his theory to the test in an immensely ambitious program involving an urban school district. In an effort to
change the students in this school district toward an Origin orientation,
teachers participated in a week-long workshop emphasizing the development of intrinsic motivation in their students. In addition, skits,
demonstrations, and discussions were used to explore the teachers' use
of power in the classroom, and the teachers were given a rather substantial introduction to the theory of achievement motivation (see
Chapter 9).

After the training of the teachers was completed, the teachers in turn
introduced their students to the Origin/Pawn concept. Also, the students participated in activities stressing achievement motivation, realistic goal setting,[3] and positive self-concept. The goal of this whole
training program was to foster the belief in the students that they were
Origins capable of controlling their own personal development.

The test of this program is, of course, in the academic progress
shown by the participants. Children in this school district are usually
more than a half year behind on national norms by the fifth grade and
fall further behind as they go on to higher grades. Figure 11-17 depicts
standardized-test scores for the Origin-trained group and for the untrained comparison group at the end of two years. Note that the training has resulted in the students' beginning to move closer to the
national norms.

A second piece of evidence for the Origin/Pawn theory comes from a
consideration of the children's scores on an Origin/Pawn personality
test taken both before training had begun and after it had been completed. The subjects who had been in the training program were divided into "changers" (subjects below the median on the first
administration of the test but above the median on the second) and
"resistors" (subjects below the median on both administrations of the
test). Also tested were those in the untrained comparison groups who
fell naturally toward the Origin end or the Pawn end of the scale.
Figure 11-18 contains the results in terms of months below the national norms on a standardized test. The benefits of the program are
obvious. Note that the program in question does not teach skills such as
reading, writing, or arithmetic. The training program deals with *motivation,* and it has as its *result* the improvement in skills performance.

Note that the Rotter and deCharms theories discussed in this section
and many of the theories discussed in prior sections (see Chapter 7)
have the same thrust: feelings of competence have critical psychological
and even physical benefits. Feelings of helplessness have been implicated in depression, disease, and psychological as well as physical deterioration.

---

[3]Astute readers will note the relation between this factor and high n Ach. For a
more detailed description of this project, see deCharms (1976).

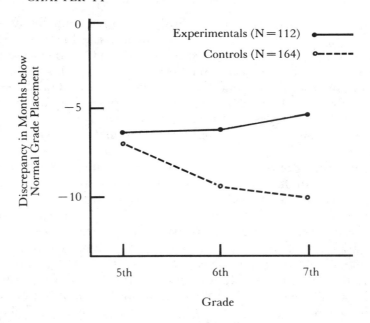

**Figure 11-17.** Average discrepancy in months from normal grade placement on the Composite Iowa Test of Basic Skills. *(From Enhancing Motivation, by R. deCharms. Copyright 1976 by Irvington Publishers, Inc., New York. Reprinted by permission.)*

**Reactance theory.** A person who feels competent believes that he or she is free to have an effect on the environment. What happens to the motivation of this person, though, when this freedom is threatened or eliminated? The answer to this question is the domain of reactance theory (Brehm, 1966).

The main premise of reactance theory is that, if a person's behavioral freedom is threatened, that person will be motivated to reestablish the freedom. This motivational force, because it is a reaction to a limitation on one's freedom to act, is called "psychological reactance."

Let's examine an incident from the experience of one of the authors in order to illustrate reactance theory. In 1963, I (H.A.) worked in my uncle's pharmacy during the summer. For the first two weeks or so I would eat lunch at a local restaurant. Every day I'd perform exactly the same ritual: sit at the counter, peruse the menu for 10 seconds, order a bacon, lettuce, and tomato sandwich from Shirley, the waitress. One day during the third week I mindlessly began my ritual again: sit at the counter, peruse the menu for 10 seconds, and . . . what's this!? Shirley slaps down a BLT sandwich in front of me before I've even ordered one. "Shirley, how do you know I'd have ordered a BLT today?" "You'd have ordered one, all right." Suddenly the BLT sandwich didn't look so appealing. Had a psychologist been there with a

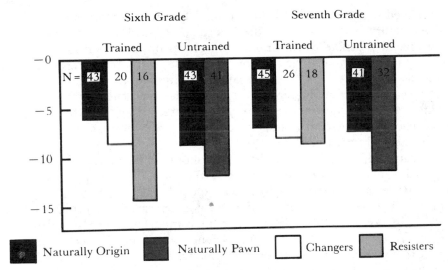

**Figure 11-18.** Average discrepancy from grade placement for naturally Origin and naturally Pawn subjects and for changers and resisters in training. *(Adapted from* Enhancing Motivation, *by R. deCharms. Copyright 1976 by Irvington Publishers, Inc., New York. Reprinted by permission.)*

handy rating form, I'd have rated the BLT sandwich far below other items on the menu. According to reactance theory, well-meaning Shirley had largely eliminated my freedom to order whatever I liked. By forcing the BLT on me, she had aroused my psychological reactance to reestablish my freedom. "Shirley," I said, "I really want a corned-beef sandwich instead."

A large number of experiments have been done to test reactance theory. One of the earliest was by Brehm, Stires, Sensenig, and Shaban (1966).[4] Subjects listened to four records and rated them for preference. The subjects were told that they would be able to select one of the records to take home the following day. The following day, however, the experimenter informed one group that the shipment of records had arrived but, alas, each subject's third-ranked record had not been included. All subjects then rerated all the records. The group that still had the third-ranked record available to them rated it the second time very much as they had rated it the first time, as mediocre. The group that no longer had the opportunity to choose the third-ranked record rated it much higher the second time, after they had learned of its unavailability. This is precisely what reactance theory would predict. The subjects were no longer free to choose the third-ranked record, so they reacted by reasserting their freedom: they wanted that record!

[4]This study involved three groups, but the results for one of the groups are not crucial to this discussion and so will not be discussed.

A related event occurred in the authors' Faculty Senate. One group had no faculty senator, because they were not entitled to one according to the Faculty Senate constitution. The group protested strongly, apparently resentful that their freedom was being restricted. The Senate changed the constitution, thus guaranteeing this group a faculty senator. Once appointed, however, this senator was almost never present at Senate meetings. Once the freedom was no longer restricted, there was no psychological reactance and therefore no more motivation toward the Senate and its activities.

Reactance theory also is useful in explaining the seemingly masochistic behavior of spite (Wicklund, 1970). For example, suppose I try to influence my friend's deliberation on whether to buy a huge Blatzmobile or a thrifty compact. Since I am concerned about the price of gas, I incessantly tell my friend that the compact is the only sensible choice. By doing this, I restrict my friend's freedom of decision. To regain this freedom, he buys the Blatzmobile. He must pay quite a bit of money to assert his freedom of choice. (Haven't you engaged in a less-preferred behavior in a manner consistent with reactance theory? Confess.)

Reactance to a threat to freedom often is the downfall of the high-pressure sale. By permitting no alternative other than compliance with the request to buy right now, the high-pressure sales technique drastically curtails the customer's freedom. To regain freedom, the customer refuses to buy.

Wicklund and Brehm (1968) investigated this phenomenon in order to discover when a subject would comply with high pressure and when the subject would show reactance. In the first part of the experiment, half of the subjects were led to believe that their social-judgment ability was quite high; half were led to believe it was low. In the second part, subjects first rated two job applicants and then were asked to judge which applicant would be best for the job. While the subject was in the midst of making this judgment, a note arrived, purportedly from another subject. For one group of subjects, the note said that one of the job applicants was better. For another group of subjects, the note said, "There is no question about it. Paul is the best . . . ." Control subjects received no note. The experimenters then asked the subjects to rate the applicants again. Table 11-1 contains the data indicating how the note caused the subjects to change their opinions between the two ratings. When subjects perceived themselves as competent, a strong note that posed a high level of threat to their decision freedom caused a "boomerang effect": the subjects changed their opinion away from that expressed in the note. When subjects perceived themselves as incompetent, no boomerang effect occurred.

Pallak and Heller (1971) have found that the boomerang effect is

**TABLE 11-1.** Average attitude change in the Wicklund and Brehm (1968) study. Positive numbers signify a change in attitude toward the opinion expressed in the note. Negative numbers signify a change in the opposite direction.

| Competence | Control | High threat | Low threat |
|---|---|---|---|
| High competence | −0.21 | −2.37 | 0.07 |
| Low competence | — | 0.76 | 2.14 |

From *Freedom and Reactance*, by R. A. Wicklund. Copyright 1974 by Lawrence Erlbaum Associates, Inc., Publishers, Potomac, Maryland. Reprinted by permission.

much more likely to occur when the person whose decision freedom is being threatened expects no subsequent interaction with the person attempting to influence the decision. When the person whose decision freedom is being threatened does expect later interaction, then greater threat leads to more compliance, not to a boomerang effect.

Reactance theory is applicable in a large number of everyday situations. Only half jokingly, Wicklund (1974) suggests that potential Saturday-night dates who "play hard to get" may have an intuitive understanding of reactance theory. If you deny the other person some freedom to act (to go out with you on Saturday night), reactance theory predicts that you will appear more attractive to that person (Berscheid & Walster, 1969).

## Conclusions and critique

We shall highlight some central aspects of attribution theory—both merits and shortcomings—that are especially relevant to the study of motivation.

Perhaps the outstanding merit of attribution theory is the breadth and flexibility it allows in the explanations of behavior that form its subject matter. For any given behavior, attribution theory holds that a variety of perceived causes are possible—some in the actor, some in the environment, and some (as Kelley suggests) in the situation. Occasionally a single cause, such as the actor's motivation, is sufficient to explain a behavior, but usually an attribution is to the interaction of multiple causes. This notion of multiple causation is an important contribution of the theory. Motivation alone would not explain, for example, why a student solved a math problem. The student must also have had a certain amount of mathematical ability, and the problem must not have been impossibly difficult.

The notion of multiple causation does not detract from the importance allotted to motivation as a perceived cause of behavior. Rather, an analysis of attributions specifies the conditions in which an observer will construe a behavior as motivated and, within those, the further conditions that determine whether the behavior will be attributed to motivation alone or to motivation interacting with other causes.

Another appealing aspect of attribution theory, especially advantageous for experimental psychologists who investigate hypotheses derived from the theory, is its emphasis on the role of cognitive processes in motivation. The process of causal attribution consists in information processing. A person observes an action, weighs information about the actor, the environment, and the situation, and derives cognitively an attribution to its cause or causes. The attribution process is thus a highly rational enterprise in which behavioral observations are made, processed, and causally interpreted. As noted earlier, there is therefore minimal determinism in behavior; it is not caused uniformly by some one omnipresent determinant, such as instinctual drive, optimal level, or need for achievement. Rather, causation is in the eye of the attributor. Moreover, the attributor is assumed to be functioning in a rational manner, drawing conclusions from thoughtful consideration of the alternatives. There is little room for irrationality and no room for unconscious processes in attribution theory.

This highly cognitive emphasis has some apparent benefits. The most noteworthy is a methodological one. The constructs and processes of causal attribution can be operationally defined and hence investigated in the experimental laboratory. The language of the theory is clear and understandable—"naive," in Heider's view—and meaningful for explaining causation. As the research cited illustrates, this terminology makes the theory accessible to experimentation. Hence, unlike theories (such as psychoanalytic theory) with vaguely defined terms and complicated principles, which are difficult to test scientifically, attribution theory has a potential to grow as theorists such as Kelley and Weiner formulate testable hypotheses. The sifting and winnowing that scientific inquiry imposes, which is necessary for the eventual betterment of attribution theory, can be accomplished.

However, the advantages of attribution theory—breadth of explanation and cognitive emphasis—also create shortcomings. The first criticism pertains to scope. Attribution theory, especially Kelley's model of multiple causation, provides a framework that appears to exhaust the possible causes of a given behavior. An action can be attributed to persons, entities, or situations or to the interactions of these factors. The problem is that the breadth of this theory might limit its application to one of mere description. With the wisdom of hindsight, one might look back on a behavior and apply an attributional analysis. There can be neither a correct nor an incorrect solution, because the theory accommodates the gamut of explanations. Thus, paradoxically, the advantage of globalness can also be a bane. Other massive theories, such as psychoanalytic theory, also have the ironic distinction of being too explanatory. This feature, of course, is not at all problematic if a theory is as adept at predictive explanation as it is at postdictive description. But attribution theory is not. Its prospects of becoming increasingly predictive are, however, promising. Kelley's work on causal schemata and Jones and Davis's theory of correspondent inferences do help predict the outcomes of causal attributions.

A second and more significant criticism of attribution theory derives from its cognitive emphasis. The question is straightforward and was eloquently raised by Guthrie (1952): Does thought lead to action? In particular, does cognitive analysis of causes necessarily lead to behavior? The question dwarfs any answer that can be attempted here. However, the assumption implicit in attribution theory that actions are related to attributions continues to be debated (see Bem, 1974). Thoughts about causation do not necessarily give rise to action (or inaction), and a person can act without thinking about the causes. The latter argument—that action can occur without cognition—is especially prevalent among adherents of theories whose motivational construct is an energizing or appetitive force. A cognitive theory that excludes noncognitive sources of motivation is restricted in much the same way as a noncognitive theory (such as Hull's) that minimizes cognitive sources. Explaining the many behaviors of an actor requires both sources of motivation.

A third criticism pertains to an assumption inherent in most attribution-theory experiments. A behavior occurs, and a person is asked what caused his or her behavior. The crucial assumption made in this situation is that the person is *aware* of what caused the behavior. However, recent research (Nisbett & Wilson, 1977) suggests that people have very limited awareness of the causes of their own behavior. Instead, when asked to identify the causes of their own behaviors, people generate likely causes, rather than actual causes. Much of the time we operate in a relatively mindless fashion, giving little thought to the causes of each behavior. When an attribution theorist thrusts a questionnaire into our hands, we are forced to locate a cause. We seek an obvious candidate, and mark the questionnaire accordingly. Unfortunately, Taylor and Fiske (1978) have summarized a good deal of evidence that we will very likely choose the most noticeable factor as the cause, whether that factor was the *real* cause or not. For example, if the chairs are arranged so that I face person A during a conference, I perceive her as causing the group's decision. If my chair faces person B, I perceive him as the prime cause. Since such trivial factors as chair orientation can determine our attributions of causality, there is good reason to believe that we choose the obvious cause, rather than the actual cause, when attempting to attribute our behavior. Perhaps attribution theory, like expectancy-value theory, is too logical to be an accurate description of human behavior.

Despite the important methodological and conceptual problems, however, attribution theory—with its highly cognitive orientation—provides a unique and insightful analysis of human motivation. The theory has become immensely popular in the last 15 years, and its value will become even greater as data are accumulated and the theory is refined.

CHAPTER **12**

# Retrospect
# and Discussion

Now that the major theories of motivation have been presented, it is time for some concluding remarks. We shall neither give capsule summaries of theories nor reiterate the many evaluative and concluding statements that we have already made. Rather, we shall review the previous chapters in three ways. First, we shall analyze a single example using each theoretical perspective. Second, we shall discuss some relations between a few selected theories—relations we have *not* discussed previously. Third, examples of the significance of motivation for analyzing and explaining behaviors will be discussed. Then, we shall examine where each of the theories stands on several basic issues in motivation.

## *An example of motivated behavior: Theoretical interpretations*

Suppose a professor gives her students the opportunity to do a project for extra credit. She informs the class that each student may choose to do any type of project—term paper, class demonstration, field work. The amount of extra credit awarded will depend on both the difficulty of the project and its quality. Easy projects done well will earn less than difficult projects done well. One of her students, Bob, opts to do a rather lengthy term paper—surely a challenging task. He triumphantly hands it in on time, confident that he has done a project worthy of an *A*. A few days later the paper is returned marked with a *C*. Bob becomes irate and argues vehemently with the professor. Unable to change her mind, he reluctantly accepts his poor grade. His self-esteem is dented, and he does not take advantage of the next extra-credit opportunity.

Several questions about Bob's motivation present themselves. What motivated him to choose to do such a difficult task in the first place? Why did he argue with the professor so angrily? Surely such an outburst wouldn't be effective in raising his grade. Why did Bob change his attitude about his own ability? Why didn't he change his attitude about the professor's ability instead? Finally, why did he give up?

Some people really buckle down and work hard after a setback. What happened to Bob's motivation?

Two important points are to be kept in mind before proceeding with the analyses of the term-paper example. First, although any theory is capable of explaining this example (or perhaps any other example), the focus and breadth of the explanations differ. One might expect the theory of achievement motivation, for example, to explain specifically achievement-related behavior more precisely and more completely than more general theories, such as psychoanalytic or consistency theory. The theoretical analyses of this example, therefore, will necessarily vary in validity and in the assumptions that they must make about the person and about the situation in which the behavior occurred.

A second and related point is crucial. Interpretations of real-life examples have occurred from chapter to chapter as devices for illustrating the constructs and principles of the theories. However, one should be cautious of judging the validity of any theory solely on the basis of such interpretations. Even though the interpretations may sound good, they are not necessarily correct. Let us emphasize that the validity of the theories can be assessed only by a careful reading of research findings, such as those presented in the chapters.

With these cautions, we proceed to the theoretical interpretations of the term-paper example.

## Psychoanalytic theory

Psychoanalytic theory would focus on two aspects of the example: the selection of a difficult, rather than an easy, project and the consequences of receiving a disappointing grade.

The theory would offer two alternative analyses of the selection of a difficult project. The first would derive from the orthodox form of the theory and would of course incorporate the instinctual drives as the motivating forces. In this analysis, the aggressive instinctual drive would probably be assumed to be influential. By choosing a difficult project, Bob gave himself an opportunity to perform a behavior related to aggression—a behavior that has elements of achievement, accomplishment, and competition. For instance, success on the term paper might have permitted "gratification" of Bob's aggressive instinctual drive by giving him a sense of power and allowing him to "defeat" the professor by doing well on the task that she had presented.

The second interpretation would derive from the adaptive viewpoint in psychoanalytic theory and ego psychology. This analysis would focus not on the role of instinctual drive but rather on the more positive motives Bob had for selecting the term paper as a project. From this perspective, the difficult project afforded a potential satisfaction for ego motives; success would be a way for Bob to feel competent and to attain a sense of mastery.

Psychoanalytic theory would also offer an explanation of the motivated behavior following receipt of a *C* on the paper, based on the theory of repression and defense. It would be assumed that the mediocre grade would constitute an "ego threat" and would produce anxiety and some defensive attempt at reducing it. One way for Bob to reduce the anxiety would be through repression, in which the anxiety-arousing elements of the grade would be forced from his consciousness. Or, Bob might rely on some other defense mechanism instead; that would depend on his personality development. He might dwell on the grade and attempt to intellectualize and rationalize his performance to himself by stressing that the library had been missing an essential reference or that he had been sick while writing the paper. Or he might displace the blame onto the professor by telling himself that the requirements were unfair and impossible or that her grading was biased. The result of any defense, however, would be to minimize the ego threat and the accompanying anxiety.

## Humanistic theories

Humanistic theories also would focus on Bob's selection of a difficult project and the consequences of receiving a *C*.

For Rogers, Bob's selection of the term paper would be motivated by his tendency toward self-actualization. Rogers would assume that, at the moment when Bob had his choice of projects, the difficult project offered a potential for self-actualization. A good grade would have provided "enhancement" of the self in relation to the academic environment and provided satisfaction of the learned need for self-regard.

For Maslow, the selection might be motivated by different needs, depending on the level of the need hierarchy at which Bob was functioning. It would be assumed, however, that he was functioning at one of the higher levels, because a safety need, for example, would probably have directed Bob to select an easy task. Most likely, the term paper offered satisfaction of the student's esteem need, in which case he was "deficiency-motivated," or of his self-actualization need, in which case he was "growth-motivated."

Rogers would contend that Bob's mediocre grade represented a condition of worth in which positive regard from the professor was apparently lacking. The lack of regard would produce anxiety and defensiveness in the form of either distortion or denial. Hence, Rogers would hypothesize a defensive process much the same as that hypothesized in psychoanalytic theory. Maslow, however, would be less explicit than psychoanalytic theory about the consequences of receiving a *C*. He would see the *C* as thwarting satisfaction of the need that motivated the selection of the term paper. That would tend to keep Bob at the currently predominant level of the need hierarchy and to slow his motivation toward psychological growth.

## Hullian theory

The Hullian analysis would be relatively straightforward. The behavior of writing a difficult term paper was not reinforced. Therefore, its $H$ did not increase, and that behavior would presumably be on an extinction schedule. The behavior that would occur the next time an extra project was possible would be one whose $H$ had been in second place the first time. Because the behavior with the formerly dominant $H$ (term-paper writing) had not been reinforced, the second-place behavior would now move into first place. Bob's behavior on the next trial (extra-credit opportunity) would therefore differ from the behavior that resulted in the mediocre grade.

Another important consideration for the Hullian analysis is that receipt of a $C$ would be frustrating. If in the past a particular response to frustration had been reinforced, that behavior would be likely to occur again in this frustrating situation. Such behaviors might include, for example, aggression or withdrawal from the situation.

Finally, frustration results in a drive increase. Since Hull postulated that $D$ was a general energizer, the $D$ increase would help energize whatever behavior followed the frustration. Thus, Bob may have gone into the professor's office for the purpose of quietly discussing his grade, but the $D$ increase caused by frustration may have resulted in behavior much more vigorous than he had initially intended.

## Optimal level theories

Optimal level theorists would be most concerned with the choice of the term paper as an extra-credit project. Why would Bob choose the term paper, rather than an easier or an even more difficult task? Such theorists would assume that a simpler task would have been boring for Bob, whereas a more difficult one would have been above his optimal level of complexity. Following the poor grade on the paper, however, the situation could change in one of two ways. First, interaction with the task (writing the term paper) might cause the task to simplify, as Bob learned (the hard way) how to write such papers. This interaction might result either in substantial simplification of the task to a point far below the optimum, so that Bob would not reattempt it, or in slight simplification, in which case the task might still remain close to the optimum. Second, in attempting to write a term paper, Bob might come to realize that such an endeavor was much more complicated than he had originally thought. Thus, the task of writing a term paper would move to a point much higher on the complexity continuum than its original position. At its new position, voluntarily writing a term paper for extra credit would not be a task that Bob would try again in the near future. Since he performed at a mediocre level on the term paper, Bob probably learned that writing a good paper is a far more difficult task than he originally had thought.

## Social learning theories

Both Rotter and Bandura would assume that the task of writing a lengthy term paper would have been rewarding for Bob. Rotter would rely on the law of effect to explain the task's reinforcement value: Bob had probably highly valued such tasks in the past. Bandura might assume that modeling also played a role in the student's choice of an extra-credit assignment: Bob may have had a friend who took great satisfaction in such projects, or he may have observed others being rewarded for doing term papers.

Besides reinforcement value, both Rotter and Bandura would emphasize expectancy variables in analyzing Bob's choice of project. Each would assume that Bob expected some reward. Rotter would term this *expectancy* and assume that the expected reward, possibly an *A*, would be a consequence of the quality of the writing. Bandura would term this *outcome expectation* but assume that direct reinforcement (an *A*) was not necessary. Bob might have expected self-reinforcement, such as personal satisfaction or pride in a job well done. Bandura would also hypothesize that efficacy expectations were a critical factor in Bob's choice. The student had to assume that he could *do* the task; that is, he had to feel competent and effective. This efficacy expectation could have arisen from several sources of information, such as previous performance accomplishments and vicarious experiences.

Both theorists would be likely to predict that Bob's probability of choosing such a project from the same professor in the future would diminish because of reduced reward value and decreased expectations.

## Field theory

The Lewinian level-of-aspiration analysis would apply to Bob's situation. The force toward any task the student might have chosen would be given by the formula $F = (V_{succ} \times Po_{succ}) - (V_{fail} \times Po_{fail})$. Because Bob chose to do a term paper, the force toward that task must have been higher than the force toward any other. Following the disappointing grade on that task, the potencies (probabilities) of success and failure would change, altering the force toward each of the various options. Since no task was chosen the next time an extra-credit opportunity occurred, we must conclude that the *C* caused Bob's force toward every one of the tasks to become negative.

## Achievement theory

To apply the theory of achievement motivation to this example, we must make some assumptions about the personality of the student. Let us assume that Bob was an $M_{af} > M_s$ person who perceived the course as having high instrumentality for his career plans. Let us assume also that for the task of writing the term paper, $P_s$ was initially .05. Bob chose such a task because $M_{af} > M_s$ people are maximally inhibited at intermediate $P_s$ values. Following receipt of the disappointing grade, which would constitute a failure in Bob's opinion, the $P_s$ would drop and the inertial tendency of that trial would be carried over to the next trial. Because the course was highly instrumental, the negative aspects of future achievement situations would have made the resultant achievement motivation and the consequent inertial tendency both quite negative. Therefore, although the failure moved the $P_s$ slightly farther away from intermediate values, it is likely that Bob's motivation toward the task would become quite negative. Consequently, he would not choose to write a term paper again.

## Consistency theories

Consistency theories would offer an explanation based on Bob's attitudes and opinions. If Bob had a reasonably decent opinion of himself, receiving a *C* would constitute discrepant information. He would therefore have to reduce the discrepancy somehow. These theories, however, would not specify the means of reduction. If Bob's self-esteem were particularly high, he might deny the credibility of the discrepant information ("That professor wouldn't recognize a good term paper if she saw one"), or he might minimize the importance of the poor grade ("This was just an extra-credit project. It wasn't as important as a required assignment"). Cognitive-dissonance theorists would probably explain the fact that Bob stopped trying by saying that whatever cognition Bob adopted to reduce his dissonance ("She doesn't grade fairly.") was inconsistent with continued effort.

## Attribution theories

An attribution theory would be able to specify that Bob, an $M_{af} > M_s$ student, would most likely attribute his failure to low ability. This failure would therefore lead to strong, negative affect (because the attribution is internal) and a tendency not to attempt similar projects again (because the attribution is stable). Recall that $M_{af} > M_s$ persons tend to give up in the face of failure, because they tend to attribute their failures to low ability.

## *Relations between the theories*

Even though the theories differ so radically on a number of issues, there remain some interesting similarities between them. In earlier chapters, we have noted some of the more obvious similarities, particularly when a theory was based on an older one. Here we shall enumerate some less obvious commonalities in order to show again how the same phenomena can be analyzed from widely divergent viewpoints.

## Psychoanalytic / Hullian

Since the Freudian analysis of various motivational phenomena has proved difficult to put to empirical test, attempts have been made to recast some of psychoanalytic theory in a Hullian S-R framework. Dollard and Miller (1950) made such an attempt on a large scale, but we will refer only to their reanalysis of the Freudian explanation of conflict and displacement.

In Chapter 5, we presented Miller's analysis of an approach/avoidance conflict. Miller postulates that when there are both approach and avoidance tendencies toward a goal object, the avoidance gradient is steeper than the approach gradient (see Figure 5-8). The approach tendency is therefore greater than the avoidance tendency only at locations distant from the goal object. An approach toward objects at the distant locations, rather than toward the original, corresponds to the psychoanalytic principle of displacement.

Support for this S-R reanalysis of displacement is contained in a study by N. E. Miller and Kraeling (1952). Hungry rats were first trained to run down an alleyway for food and then on subsequent trials were shocked for approaching the food area. The shock trials caused the food-approach behavior to cease. The animals were then retested in the original alleyway, in one somewhat different, or in one greatly different. It was found that the rats were more likely to approach the food area the more the test alleyway differed from the original. Thus, this finding showed that, as distance from the original goal increased, the avoidance tendency fell more rapidly, resulting in the superiority of the approach tendency, just as Miller's model predicted. The rats were able to approach a goal that was quite a bit different from the original; they were exhibiting displacement.

It is not surprising that Miller, a neo-Hullian, could apply an S-R analysis to displacement. The theories of Hull and Freud have a few important characteristics in common. First, both theorists postulate innate sources of motivation—sexual and aggressive instincts in psychoanalytic theory, primary drives (such as hunger, sex, and thirst) in Hullian theory. Second, both theorists state that drive reduction is the goal of behavior. In psychoanalytic theory, the individual strives to reduce tension and anxiety caused by the instinctual drives of sex and aggression. In Hullian theory, the individual strives to reduce primary biological drives. Thus, both Freud and Hull are homeostatic theorists. Finally, both Freud and Hull (unlike Lewin) are historical theorists; that is, both theorists sought to explain present behavior by examining the individual's past history. For Freud this meant examining the way in which the person's psychosexual development might have occurred. For Hull it meant an emphasis on the subject's reinforcement history.

## Psychoanalytic / social learning

Behaviorists, including the social learning theorists, have traditionally been critical of the psychoanalytic paradigm. In a nutshell, their major objection derives from psychoanalytic theory's overabundance of covert constructs, such as the unconscious, instinctual drives, and the id—constructs that are unobservable, immeasurable, and inaccessible to experimental manipulation. Throughout his theorizing, Bandura (for example, Bandura & Walters, 1963; Bandura, 1977b) has maintained the behaviorist's penchant for the observable. However, he did have to depart from this orthodox behavioral viewpoint in order to make his own covert constructs—the cognitive mediating variables—more palatable. The important difference between the internal variables of social learning theory and those of psychoanalytic theory, however, is that the former are manipulable, measurable, and controlled by external events (Bandura, 1969).

Recent theoretical developments on self-efficacy (Bandura, 1977a) have clouded this critical distinction between social learning constructs and psychoanalytic constructs. Recall from Chapter 7 that Bandura hypothesizes that one of the major variables affecting a person's motivation to perform is an efficacy expectation: the person's belief that he or she *can* perform the task—is skilled, competent, or effective. An appraisal of competence is therefore necessary for effective behavior. Note that Bandura's description of self-efficacious behavior bears an apparent resemblance to R. W. White's (1959, 1963) concept of competence. White defined competence as a broad class of behaviors that produced effects on the environment, without being intensely pushed by an internal drive or an instinct. Competence then is producing an effect. Since White is an ego psychologist, he adopted the psychoanalytic strategy of ascribing motivation to a competent behavior by means of a covert, internal mechanism. He termed the motivation to have an effect on the environment *effectance motivation*.

Thus, both Bandura, from the social learning viewpoint, and White, from the psychoanalytic viewpoint, see effective behaviors such as mastery, competence, and success as being explainable in terms of specific motivational factors. For Bandura, the critical variable is efficacy expectation; for White the critical variable is effectance motivation.

What are the differences, then, between the social learning and psychoanalytic approaches to competence? The fundamental difference derives from a difference in paradigms. Bandura (1977a) postulates that competent behavior is determined by the cognitive appraisal of efficacy based on specific sources of information such as performance accomplishments and vicarious experiences. Such expectation influences the level of motivation. R. W. White (1963) postulates that the motivation to be competent derives from an independent ego energy and acts much like an instinct to produce a generalized tendency to have an effect. For Bandura, the feeling of efficacy occurs *prior to* an effective behavior; for White, the feeling of efficacy occurs *after* a competent behavior (R. W. White, 1963, p. 185) and is a type of satisfaction.

This fundamental difference is more than one of terminology. In the social learning model, specific environmental events have an impact on efficacy expectations. Expectations and behaviors both are seen as quite changeable. A person is likely to engage in a behavior only when an appraisal of the efficacy of that behavior is positive. In the ego psychoanalytic model, effectance motivation comes steadily from within the individual, independent of environmental changes. The person is seen as generally striving to have an effect; self-estimation of competence is not seen as a significant aspect of effectance motivation.

### Psychoanalytic / consistency

There are at least two ways in which Freudian theory is related to consistency theory. First, as Janis (1959) points out, postdecisional conflicts (a feature of consistency theory) may have unconscious determinants (a feature of psychoanalytic theory). Janis cites as an example Freud's analysis (1905b) of the neurosis of "Dora," a woman who at age 16 had ostensibly been sexually approached by one of her father's friends. After she rejected the man's advances, Dora developed serious symptoms of conversion hysteria. Janis interprets Dora's symptoms as manifestations of acute postdecisional conflict resulting from her desire to have an affair with the man. Such an affair would have been so improper, however, that Dora was forced to spurn the man, despite this desire. The rejected alternative—having the affair—should be devalued, according to cognitive-dissonance theory. And, indeed, Dora did maintain that she disliked the man—thereby confirming the postdiction that dissonance theory would make. However, her hysterical symptoms developed because of *unconscious* longing for the man despite her conscious dislike of him. In matters of the unconscious, it is not clear whether dissonance theory is applicable; the postdecisional conflict discussed in Festinger's original statement of the theory did not extend to unconscious cognitions. Because Dora could not apply the usual dissonance-reducing techniques of revaluing the chosen alternative upward and devaluing the rejected one, the resulting persistent anxiety (dissonance) caused the conversion hysteria.

A second relation between psychoanalytic theory and consistency theory is based on the fact that most of the reactions to dissonant cognitions can be described in psychoanalytic terms. For example, in the study by Brock and Buss (1962) mentioned in Chapter 10, subjects lowered their estimates of the painfulness of shock after they administered it to innocent victims. By denying that the shock was noxious, the subjects were reducing their anxiety. Denial is a classic ego defense mechanism. In fact, many of the rationalizations used to reduce cognitive dissonance can be considered defense mechanisms.

Some of the most instructive investigations in this area are those by Bramel (1962, 1963). Male students were presented with bogus physiological evidence that they had homosexual tendencies. The subjects then estimated such tendencies in another subject. Subjects with high self-esteem were more likely to attribute homosexual tendencies to others than were subjects with low self-esteem. And, if the other subject was a student, homosexual tendencies were more likely to be attributed to him than if he was an inmate of the state prison. The cognitive-dissonance explanation of these results is as follows: For heterosexual subjects with high self-esteem, the information that they had homosexual tendencies was probably dissonant. Since the physiological evidence appeared incontrovertible, denial was not possible. However, if the subject could claim that others had these same tendencies, then he could feel less negative about his own supposed tendencies, especially if the "others" resembled himself. Therefore, if the other subject was a student too, the first subject ascribed homosexual tendencies to him, thus reducing dissonance. (Theorists preferring psychoanalytic terminology would call this a simple case of projection.) For those subjects with low self-esteem, the bogus evidence would not be so dissonant. Therefore, they would have less need to attribute homosexual tendencies to others.

There also is an apparent difference between the dissonance explanation of projection and the psychoanalytically based scapegoating theory of prejudice, which is also based on projection (Adorno et al., 1950). Bramel's subjects could more readily reduce dissonance by ascribing homosexual tendencies to their own group than by ascribing them to an "out-group," such as criminals. According to the scapegoating theory of prejudice, projection of one's own faults is more likely to be directed at the out-group. Are these two theories therefore in conflict? Probably not, according to Eldow and Kiesler (1966). In Bramel's study, denial was nearly impossible. A trait one obviously has may be made less odious by claiming that other respectable people have it, too. In the scapegoating situation, it is easy to deny that one is, for example, lazy, greedy, or unclean. Then such traits are projected onto a convenient low-power group. The psychoanalytically based scapegoating theory and dissonance theory as tested by Bramel have discussed situations that differed in whether denial was possible. When this difference is taken into account, the two theories appear more compatible.

Psychoanalytic theory and dissonance theory sharply differ, however, with regard to the source of motivation. Freud stated that the id was the source of all energy. Projection, denial, and other defense mechanisms were needed as the ego tried to keep unacceptable impulses in the id from being manifested. These impulses were instinctual and part of every person's heredity.

The motivational source in dissonance theory has not been explicitly stated (see Tedeschi, Schlenker, and Bonoma, 1971). Festinger states that people try to maintain consonance by reducing dissonance, but he does not say why. The authors' interpretation is that the motive to maintain consonance is learned. As Tedeschi et al. point out, in order to interact competently in the world, one tries to act reasonably consistently and tries to make sure that others do, too. To act inconsistently destroys the ease of interpersonal commerce. Consistent, rational behavior is rewarded; inconsistent, unpredictable behavior generally is not. Hence, dissonance theory need not make an appeal to inner, instinctual drives, as psychoanalytic theory does.

## Optimal level/achievement

Two theories that bear remarkable similarity despite their divergent origins are optimal level theory and the theory of achievement motivation. The most important graphs relevant to each theory are shown in Figures 12-1 and 12-2. Figure 12-1 is, of course, the inverted-U curve, discussed in Chapter 6. Figure 12-2 represents the major finding of Atkinson and Litwin (1960), discussed in Chapter 9. Needless to say, the curves are quite similar. Figure 12-2 contains two curves, one for $M_s > M_{af}$ people and one for $M_{af} > M_s$ people. Each is an inverted U, even though the $M_{af} > M_s$ curve is much flatter. The theory of achievement motivation predicts that $M_{af} > M_s$ people should avoid tasks on which $P_s = .5$ and prefer tasks with extreme $P_s$ values. Yet the graph suggests that $M_{af} > M_s$ people merely show less preference for the intermediate-$P_s$ task than do $M_s > M_{af}$ people. Apparently, people of either motive type described by achievement theory may exhibit the inverted-U curve, just as optimal level theory would predict.

In accordance with the similarity of the curves in Figures 12-1 and 12-2, some of the two theories' basic predictions also are similar. For example, a task whose $P_s = .1$ is initially not preferred by an $M_s > M_{af}$ person, but, if the person continues to succeed on such a task, his or her preference first goes up as $P_s$ rises toward .5 and then goes down as $P_s$ rises beyond .5. Similarly, as a person interacts with a complex stimulus, simplification based on continued experience results in first an increase and then a decrease in preference. The major difference between the theories is that only achievement theory makes specific

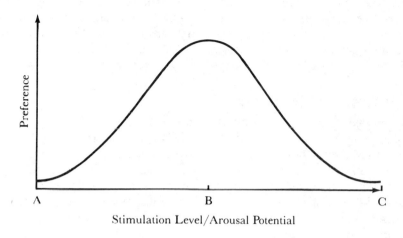

**Figure 12-1.** The typical inverted U of optimal level theory.

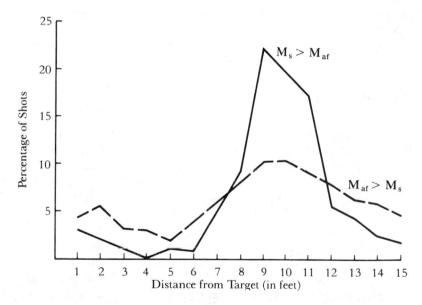

**Figure 12-2.** Percentage of shots at each distance from target as a function of achievement motives. *(Adapted from "Achievement Motive and Test Anxiety Conceived as Motive to Approach Success and Motive to Avoid Failure," by J. W. Atkinson and G. H. Litwin, Journal of Abnormal and Social Psychology, 1960, 60, 52–63. Copyright 1960 by the American Psychological Association. Reprinted by permission.)*

predictions about the effects of failure and its related $P_s$ decrease. Optimal level theory does not speak to the issue of what changes in complexity or arousal ensue as a result of failure. Also, only achievement theory varies its predictions as a function of personality (although, as Figure 11-2 shows, its predictions may not differ dramatically between $M_s > M_{af}$ and $M_{af} > M_s$ people).

## Optimal level / consistency

Many writers have noted that optimal level theory and dissonance theory appear blatantly contradictory. The former states that humans try to maintain some optimal level of complexity, whereas the latter claims that humans strive to eliminate all inconsistency in order to restore consonance. Singer (1966) and others have suggested, however, that humans may not try to reduce *all* dissonance. Instead, an optimal level of dissonance may be preferred. Mystery stories and magicians remain popular, for example, although they introduce dissonance. And no democracy could function if everyone demanded consonance; the majority and minority cannot both be satisfied. Some level of dissonance then is tolerated, even preferred, according to Singer. Dissonance reduction occurs only when the dissonance is relatively large, and then the person strives to reduce it only as far as the optimal level. If consonance is *too* complete, boredom will result. Under this analysis, consistency theory might be seen as a derivative of optimal level theory.

## Hullian / achievement

The verbal-learning studies that provided strong support for the Hull/Spence interpretation of the Yerkes/Dodson law have been reinterpreted in achievement-theory terms. Recall that Spence and his colleagues showed that an easy paired-associates list was learned best by high-drive (that is, anxious) people and that a difficult paired-associates list was learned best by low-drive people. However, Weiner (1966; see also Weiner and Schneider, 1971) showed that the Hull/Spence interpretation may not be complete.

In Chapter 9, evidence was presented that $M_s > M_{af}$ people typically increase their performance following failure and that $M_{af} > M_s$ people decrease theirs. Conversely, $M_s > M_{af}$ people decrease their performance following success, and $M_{af} > M_s$ people do the opposite. Weiner believes that these effects (caused primarily by inertial tendency) can explain Spence's results. Since easy tasks generally result in feelings of success, and since high-drive people perform better after success, high-drive people do well on easy tasks. Similarly, since difficult tasks are likely to cause failure, and since low-drive people do well after failure, low-drive people do well on difficult tasks. These are exactly the results Spence found. Which explanation is right—the Hull/

Spence formulation based on $D$ and $H$ or the achievement explanation based on personality traits and inertial tendency? Since they make identical predictions in the verbal-learning studies, it is impossible to use these studies as the basis for deciding which explanation is correct.

Weiner (1966), however, has performed a clever study that does allow a choice between the two explanations. The Hull/Spence theory would predict that high-anxiety people would do better on an easy task; achievement theory would predict that low-anxiety people would do better on any task following an initial failure. In Weiner's study, subjects performing an easy task were given false feedback indicating that they were doing poorly. The achievement-theory prediction was supported: the low-anxiety subjects did better than the high-anxiety subjects. Another group of subjects, performing a difficult task, received false feedback that they were doing well. Hull and Spence would predict that low-anxiety people would do better on a difficult task. Achievement theory would predict that high-anxiety people would do better, since such people do better after experiences of success. Again the achievement-theory prediction was supported. In light of these results, Weiner (1972) maintains that the Hull/Spence explanation of the verbal-learning studies is inferior to the achievement-theory explanation. When the normal relation between task difficulty and outcome (easy–success; difficult–failure) is maintained, the Hullian and achievement-theory predictions are identical, because Hull predicts that high-drive people do better on easy tasks and achievement theory predicts that high-drive people do better after success, and easy tasks are generally those that produce success. Only when the usual relations between task difficulty and outcome are broken (easy–failure; difficult–success) can the theories make divergent predictions.

### Physiological/optimal level/consistency

Recently, Richard Solomon (1980; Solomon & Corbit, 1974) formulated "opponent-process theory," which is able to encompass some of the data previously explained by consistency theory and optimal level theory and even some important physiological data from the imprinting and addiction literatures! The simple core of this versatile theory is presented in Figure 12-3, which represents a person's affective response to a new unconditioned stimulus (UCS). If the UCS is electric shock, the initial affective response is negative, of course. As the stimulus continues, a slight adaptation occurs during the duration of the shock. Following termination of the stimulus, a positive feeling—relief—replaces the negative affect. After numerous presentations of shock, a person's affective responses more closely resemble the pattern depicted in Figure 12-4: the initial negative affect is much smaller than when the shock was experienced the first time, and the positive affect after stimulus termination becomes much greater.

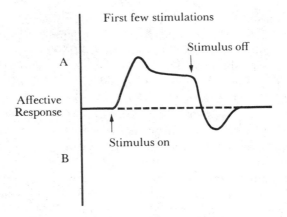

**Figure 12-3.** Affective response to a stimulus during its first few presentations. *(Adapted from "The Opponent-Process Theory of Acquired Motivation: The Costs of Pleasure and the Benefits of Pain,"* by R. L. Solomon. In American Psychologist, *1980, 35, 691–712. Copyright 1980 by the American Psychological Association. Reprinted by permission.)*

Exactly the same dynamics apply when the UCS is positive. Heroin addicts, for example, report a "rush"—a feeling of euphoria—when using heroin for the first few times. After each dosage wears off, the person feels negative affect. With habitual use, however, the initial euphoria disappears, and the negative affect afterward becomes agonizingly intense.

Solomon calls the initial affect the "*a* process"; the second affect is the "*b* process." These are always opposite affects. The *a* always diminishes, and the *b* always increases with repeated exposures. The stronger the *a* process is, the stronger the *b* process will be.

These few simple principles apply to a large number of situations. Consider the phenomenon of imprinting discussed in Chapter 2. When the very young bird is shown its mother (or substitute mother) for the first time, the animal becomes excited. Withdrawal of the mother results in distress calls from the young bird. After numerous exposures, presentation of the stimulus causes far less excitement, but its withdrawal causes far more distress. Since imprinting and many other phenomena appear to follow this opponent-process pattern, Solomon disagrees with Lorenz's claim that imprinting represents an unusual type of learning.

Although the application of the opponent-process model to various types of addictions (opiates, cigarettes, and so on) is obvious, its equally plausible application to recreation is not so obvious. Consider skydiving, which its adherents claim is a sport. (Some others consider it merely suicidal!) With the first few jumps, there is intense fear before

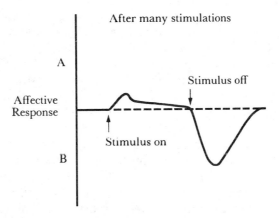

**Figure 12-4.** Affective response to a stimulus after many presentations. *(Adapted from "The Opponent-Process Theory of Acquired Motivation: The Costs of Pleasure and the Benefits of Pain," by R. L. Solomon. In* American Psychologist, *1980, 35, 691–712. Copyright 1980 by the American Psychological Association. Reprinted by permission.)*

and grateful relief after the jump. With continued experience, however, the fear beforehand diminishes and the positive affect afterward intensifies. Jogging and long-distance running also are analyzable in terms of opponent-process theory. Joggers and long-distance runners both often speak of the "high" they get from an experience that novices would find agonizing. The novices are staggering up Figure 12-3. The veterans are enjoying the glide down Figure 12-4.

Recall Scitovsky's corollary to optimal level theory: if one is at the optimal level, one cannot experience pleasure. One must move away from the optimum, thereby experiencing some discomfort. The return to the optimum will then be pleasurable. Thus, the attainment of pleasure demands prior discomfort, just as the opponent-process model predicts. Recall also a maxim of cognitive-dissonance theory: we come to love that for which we have suffered. If the *a* process is a 170° sauna, with experience we will come to love it—at least, we'll come to love the feeling that follows the sauna (the *b* process).

## Significance of motivation in behavioral analysis

Before concluding our discussion of motivation, it would seem appropriate to stress the importance of motivational considerations in the analysis of behavior.

As an example, let's consider the "track record" of compensatory education. Designed for underprivileged preschoolers, such educational programs attempt to eliminate the large scholastic differences between middle-class and lower-class children. In order to accomplish this goal, these programs provide training in various school-related skills. The success of such programs, in general, has been limited. Despite occasional silver linings (for example, Arkes & Boykin, 1971; Lazar, Hubbell, Murray, Rosche, & Royce, 1977), most evaluations of these programs have been of the dark-cloud variety (Westinghouse, 1969; M. Wolff & Stein, 1966).

In contrast to these lackluster results are the results of the compensatory-education program of deCharms, discussed in Chapter 11. A key difference between this program and many others is that deCharms's program stresses *motivational* change. The program is not geared toward developing new reading skills or new mathematics skills; instead, it is aimed at increasing motivation. The deCharms program is based partially upon the theory of achievement motivation. In fact, the training of the teachers in the deCharms program included having them participate in some of the experiments described in Chapter 9. Another very important component of the deCharms program is "Origin training," or training the children to feel responsible for their own behaviors. In short, the children are encouraged to make internal attributions for their behaviors. deCharms (1976, p. 174) reports correlations of +.45 and +.60 between the "Origin climate score" of each class and the learning rate in the classroom. These encouraging results suggest that motivation training may be a very effective technique for use in compensatory education (also see Deci, Nezlek, & Sheinman, 1981).

Another example illustrating the importance of motivational considerations in school performance comes from an informal experiment done by one of the authors. A few weeks before a class test, the students in the class were told that two articles in the library ought to be read. The subsequent test covered lecture material not in the articles, using a large number of multiple-choice items, and a request for the students' criticisms and comments on the two library articles.

Let's look first at the performance on the multiple-choice questions. For the purposes of the research, students were divided into those scoring above the median, at the median, and below the median. The middle group—the smallest—was then discarded. In Hullian terms, it is difficult to decide how much of the students' multiple-choice performance was based on $D$ and how much was based on $H$. Good performance on the multiple-choice items might have been caused by high motivation, by great learning, or by both. Thus, it is difficult to isolate the varying contributions to this performance of learning and motivation.

Now let's look at the students' performance on the articles question. A student who made any comment at all on the articles was deemed to have located the library and read the articles. A student who made no comment on the articles was deemed not to have read the articles.

| | Above median | Below median |
|---|---|---|
| Yes | 35 | 25 |
| No | 6 | 21 |

Did student read articles?

**Figure 12-5.** Number of multiple-choice questions answered correctly represents $D$ and $H$. Whether the student read the articles represents $D$. Thus, knowing the source of the motivation helps predict performance on the multiple-choice questions.

(Since there was no significant time pressure during the test, inadequate time would not be a possible reason for a student's failure to write any comment on the articles.) We contend that locating the articles in the library is a relatively pure measure of motivation—$D$, in Hullian terms. Negligible learning is involved in commenting on the articles, since credit was to be given for having read the articles, regardless of what was said about them. Figure 12-5 contains the relation between the scores on the two parts of the test. If a student was motivated (defined by reading the articles), the student was likely to do well on the multiple-choice questions. If the student was not motivated (defined by not reading the articles), he or she was very likely to do poorly on the multiple-choice questions. In other words, just knowing a student's $D$ would enable us to make reasonable predictions about how he or she would do on the test questions.[1] This suggests that motivation plays a major role in test performance.

Another example makes the same point. While teaching introductory psychology, one of the authors gave weekly quizzes whose results did not influence the students' grade in the course. Instead, the instructor examined each student's weekly quiz results and provided written advice on how to improve in the areas of weakness diagnosed by the quiz results. This written feedback was placed in a mailbox in a building all students entered at least once a week. The instructor noted how many weekly-quiz feedback sheets were picked up by each student. This number was correlated $+.40$ with the students' performance on the regular tests in the course (Arkes, 1980). In other words, merely knowing which students were motivated enough to pick up their feedback sheets provided the instructor with significant predictability for the students' total course performance.

---

[1] The statistical analysis of the data in Figure 12-5 is as follows: $\chi^2$ (1) = 8.35, $p < .01$.

The importance of motivation is emphasized in another context by McClelland (1978), who was involved with two projects in India in the 1950s and 1960s. In the first project, dedicated volunteers from the American Friends Service Committee (AFSC) spent 10 years and $1 million trying to improve the standard of living in a rural village. The volunteers provided health education, began village industries, administered medicines, and developed a corps of villagers to educate the village children. McClelland reports that, when the evaluation of the project was made nine years later, the results were extremely disappointing: "there were very few signs left in the village that the AFSC had ever been there" (p. 204).

The second project involved training small businessmen in India. The goal was to increase their achievement motivation. This project cost $25,000 and took 40 training days over a 6-month period. The result was a lasting increase in the standard of living for 4000 to 5000 people. The motivation training obviously was more effective than the practical training.

## Theories of motivation are everywhere

The theories covered in this text can provide insightful analyses of innumerable societal and interpersonal situations. We have selected three topics of current interest in order to demonstrate the ubiquity of motivational considerations.

### Sex differences in problem solving

Numerous investigators in the area of problem solving have noted that females perform worse than males on a rather wide variety of problem-solving tasks (for example, Carey, 1958; N. Maier, 1933). One possible explanation for this result is Horner's "motive to avoid success" (Chapter 9). However, given the difficulties this construct has encountered, we shall advance another explanation.

The Yerkes/Dodson law states that easy tasks are done better under high drive and difficult tasks better under moderate drive. Further, numerous studies done with people of various ages under various conditions have shown that females have a higher anxiety level than males (Levy, Gooch, & Kellmer-Pringle, 1969; Sarason, 1963; Stevenson & Odom, 1965; Walter, Denzler & Sarason, 1964). Therefore, if anxiety is considered a drive in the Hullian sense, then females would be at a disadvantage on difficult problem-solving tasks.

### Attributions and racial quotas

America's most famous Black psychologist, Kenneth B. Clark, recently wrote, "Probably the most disturbing manifestation of the persistence of racism is . . . that . . . Blacks are not held to the same standards . . .

[as Whites]" (1978, p. 25). This problem has made front-page news in recent years, largely because of the U.S. Supreme Court's *Bakke* and *Weber* decisions. (In the more famous of these two cases, Allan Bakke sued the Regents of the University of California because he had been denied admission to medical school, while less qualified minority students had been accepted under the school's quota system for minorities.) The practice of establishing racial quotas may indeed increase minority representation in various areas, but it can have important side effects for the minorities that are not so positive. Attribution theory can help us understand one of these side effects.

The application of attribution theory to racial quotas occurred to one of the authors when he heard the remark "I'd never go to a Black doctor. He probably became a doctor thanks to some affirmative-action program, not because he was a decent student." This remark obviously attributes a Black doctor's status to external causes—quotas. Usually, however, we attribute a doctor's status to internal causes—ability and hard work. Recall the discounting principle: if there are two sufficient causes for a behavior, we tend to discount one of the causes. This means that, if someone who is extremely talented appears to be the beneficiary of an affirmative-action program, we might discount any attributions to ability or effort as a cause for the success. Thomas Sowell, an economist, summarized this effect of the discounting principle in an article in the *New York Times Magazine* (Sowell, 1976): "Blacks achieved the economic advances of the 1960s once the worst forms of discrimination were outlawed, and the only additional effect of quotas was to undermine the legitimacy of Black achievements by making them look like gifts from the government" (p. 15). Quotas, then, represent something of a dilemma. They do increase minority representation, but they may cause people to attribute the minority's successes largely to external factors.

### Cognitive dissonance and therapy

Psychotherapy can be an effortful, painful procedure. Time, money, and emotional strain are the three major costs of the procedure. Cognitive-dissonance theory predicts that, when people engage in an effortful activity in order to attain a goal, that goal becomes more attractive. The Aronson and Mills (1959) study in which women suffered embarrassment in order to join what turned out to be a boring discussion group on sex is a good example of the principle. Cooper (1980) has hypothesized that therapy's rather effortful nature will cause people to desire strongly the goal of therapy, some change in one's behavior. However, Cooper then goes on to suggest that nearly *any* effortful behavior will cause people to want the goal of therapy; the therapy itself is not necessary!

One of Cooper's experiments will illustrate this point. People who

desired to decrease their fear of snakes presented themselves for therapy. Half of the subjects were given the opportunity to enter or not
enter the therapy, which the experimenter warned them would be
effortful and anxiety provoking. This was the high-choice group. The
other half of the subjects were given no choice. This latter group corresponds to the forced-compliance group in dissonance studies. In this
group we typically expect little attitude change. Half of the high-choice
and half of the low-choice subjects were given a 40-minute session of
implosion therapy, a typical but stressful therapeutic intervention for
snake phobias. The other half of the subjects in each group simply
exercised strenuously for 40 minutes. The experimenter then asked all
subjects to approach a snake. Many more of the high-choice subjects
approached the snake than did the low-choice subjects; the type of
"therapy" made no difference. This is precisely what cognitive-dissonance theory would predict: we come to love that for which we have
chosen to suffer. High effort causes an increase in liking only so long as
we are not forced into the effort. Cognitive-dissonance theory supports
the axiom of therapy; things must get worse before they can get better.

## Issues in motivation

There are four fundamental issues on which the theories we have discussed vary.

The first issue is that of the origin of motivation. Each theory tends
to align itself toward one side or the other of the perennial nature/
nurture controversy, holding motivation to be either primarily innate
or primarily learned.

The second issue pertains to the process of motivation: how does a
behavior become motivated? Here again, different theories offer different explanations. Some emphasize a quasiphysiological mechanism—
for example, the reduction of tension; others give a more prominent
role to thinking and cognition. In other words, people are thought to
behave in a particular way either because some internal mechanism is
operating or because they want to. Behavior is thus determined (or
caused), or it is chosen.

The third issue deals with individual differences in motivation. Some
theories are concerned about the differences in motivation that exist
from person to person. They seek to classify people by personality,
ability, and so forth as these groupings are related to motivation. Other
theories do not attempt to distinguish between differing patterns of motivated behavior.

The fourth issue is whether all behavior is motivated. Is all behavior
purposive? Is all behavior caused by the person? What role does the

environment play? Again, the theories differ in the extent to which they take such nonmotivational factors into account.

## Innate or learned origins?

The first issue on which the major motivational theories differ is that of the origin of motivation: is motivation innate or learned? The earliest theorists—James, Woodworth, McDougall, Freud, and Hull—thought that motivation was innate, that it was an inherited characteristic of the species. Both Freud and Hull postulated that all behavior was reducible to a few innate drives. How hunger or a sexual urge could account for the behavior of reading these very words, however, may leave the reader mystified. The appropriate Freudian or Hullian explanation might be quite circuitous, but these theories were parsimonious in one respect: they posited very few sources of motivation. Skiing, banjo picking, paper shuffling, trigger pulling—in fact, the whole range of human activity—could be reduced to a few primary drives. The domain of these theories—all of human behavior—made such parsimony attractive.

Later motivational theories were far more restrictive in the topics that their formulations were intended to explain. In addition, the domain of the later theories was further removed from the survival activities that had provided the data for some of the early theorists. For example, the majority of Hull's experiments had concerned the behavior of hungry rats toward food. A later theorist—Atkinson—looked at the behavior of people in an achievement situation. Although achievement may be important to a person, the immediate gratification of that motive is not necessary for survival. Because the more recent theories deal with motivation in very circumscribed situations in which the maintenance of life is not a factor, they posit only one source of motivation—a nonbiological one, such as a motive to achieve or a motive to be consistent. Such motives are learned.

Social learning theories also emphasize that the bases of motivation—the acquisition and processing of expectancies, reward values, vicarious experiences, and the like—are learned. However, they do not postulate learned motives.

## Mechanistic or cognitive processes?

Another important difference among the theories concerns the role of cognition in the choice of behavior. The first theory discussed, psychoanalytic theory, has a most interesting position on this issue. Freud did not believe that the human being was a mechanical, noncognitive responder to stimulation. Instead, he believed that a person must delicately resolve his or her innate urges (sexual and aggressive) with internalized controls (defenses). This conflict resolution was cognitive, involving ideation and thought. However, it was unconscious. Thus, the theory took the unusual position of affirming the role of thought in the selection of behavior while denying that such thought was readily accessible to the thinker. The role of cognition in psychoanalytic theory is thus highly idiosyncratic. Thoughts motivate behavior, but only those assumed to be associated with instinctual drives have motivating properties. Hence, the role of cognition in motivation is restricted to unconscious, drive-related processes. Conscious, drive-free thinking is not significant in motivation from the psychoanalytic viewpoint. Therefore, even though cognition and motivation are linked, the most salient process involves the reduction of tension created between drive-related thoughts and defenses. Although they are cognitive, the motivational processes are primarily mechanistic.

Behavioristic and humanistic psychologists were less willing to hypothesize the existence of unseen, unmeasurable processes. The humanistic theorists, especially Rogers and Maslow, implied a large role for conscious cognition in motivation but did not elaborate on the processes. In Hullian theory, the role of cognition in behavior selection and energization was minimized. Responses were bound to stimuli by sheer habit. When a subject perceived an incoming stimulus, the subject automatically emitted the response most frequently rewarded in the past. What energized this stimulus-response link was biological deprivation. Hull made very little mention of the subject's contemplation about the stimulus situation, but he was concerned with the applicability of his theory to the phenomena discussed by the more cognitively oriented theories. In his theory, as in Freud's, the main motivational process is tension reduction.

Optimal level, social learning, field, and achievement theories are all quasicognitive (Weiner, 1972, has already applied the term quasicognitive in describing the latter two theories). These theories postulate that the individual uses cognition in selecting behavior—for example, when evaluating his or her probability of succeeding on a particular task. Recent modifications and extensions of achievement theory make it somewhat more cognitive than its initial quasicognitive version. Similarly, Bandura's stipulation that the vicarious anticipation of reward is a sufficient incentive to behavior appears strongly cognitive.

Finally, consistency theory and attribution theory are the most cognitively oriented formulations. According to consistency theory, motivation arises whenever two thoughts (or a thought and an action) are inconsistent with each other. This process implies that, in order for motivation to occur, the person must perform genuine evaluation. Similarly, attribution theory emphasizes that causal attributions affect subsequent behavior. Such contemplation is far removed from the mechanistic stimulus-response psychology of Clark Hull.

The dichotomy between mechanistic and more cognitively oriented theories is revealed in a recent, interesting exchange between two prominent theorists. Bolles (1974) maintains that the recent surge of popularity enjoyed by cognitive theories is nothing new, since these theories are reminiscent of the cognitively oriented psychoanalytic theory of Freud, formulated three-quarters of a century earlier. Sears (1974), however, points out that human motivational theory has *always* been cognitively oriented and that only animal psychologists such as Bolles would say that mechanistic theories were *ever* in the mainstream of the study of motivation. The comments of these two theorists indicate the depth of the division between mechanistic and cognitive theories.

## The role of individual differences

The third issue differentiating motivational theories is the emphasis each gives to the role of individual differences. In some theories, the personality of the subject plays a most prominent role. In Freudian, humanistic, and achievement theories, the motivational consequences of various types of personalities are specified to some degree. In social learning theory and field theory, individual differences are purported to play a major role in the motivation of behavior, but the theories provide no means of measuring or assessing such differences. Similarly, Hull would occasionally recognize the role of individual differences, and some of his equations included a special factor to take into account individual variation. Yet Hull never systematically investigated this topic, nor was it ever prominent in his major books.

The original versions of optimal level theory included no mention of the role of individual differences in the motivation of behavior. Yet, as we saw in Chapter 6, subsequent work has suggested systematic differences in the level of stimulation maximally preferred as a function of personality type. Similarly, in attribution theory, recent work has indicated that people of various personality types attribute their successes and failures to different causes. These differing attributions have important implications for the motivation of subsequent behavior. In the highly cognitive theories of motivation—consistency and attribution theories—a small amount of research has indicated that personality variables, such as self-esteem, can influence the selection of behavior.

## The role of nonmotivational causes

The final issue pertains to the role given to causes other than motivation—such as the demands of the environment—in determining behavior. Just as with the other issues, there is again considerable divergence.

In general, the theorists whose motivational constructs are instinctual or instinctlike tend to minimize the role of other causes. These theorists see instinctual forces as so strong that other forces have only secondary effects on behavior. Freud is the best example of this viewpoint. For him, the instinctual drives of sex and aggression are the causes of behavior. Other causes—such as happenings in the environment—are "accidental." Hence, their causal role is down-played. The environment enters into the process of causation only when it provides an object for instinctual gratification or frustrates such gratification. Thus, the environment is merely *reactive* to the instinctual drives; it is not accorded a significant causal role. The humanistic theorists have a similar view. For Rogers, social relationships either facilitate or interfere with the actualizing tendency. For Maslow, the environment is merely a source of the satisfaction or thwarting of the basic needs.

At the other extreme, attribution theory is quite cognizant of the environment, which it views as instrumental in the causation of behavior. Consistently with Heider's analysis, the attributional viewpoint emphasizes the distinction between personal (internal) and impersonal (external, or environmental) causation. Whether an attribution is predominantly internal or predominantly external strongly affects subsequent behavior. If internal causation is greater than external causation, motivation is a critical variable and the person is seen as the "Origin" of behavior. If external causation is greater, motivation is less critical, and the person is seen as the "Pawn" of environmental forces.

For psychoanalytic theory, behavior is "overdetermined." If anything, that theory overemphasizes the role of motivation in the causation of behavior. For attribution theory, behavior is "minimally determined." This theory emphasizes the understanding of both internal and external causes in explaining behavior. Bandura's concept of reciprocal determinism, however, appears to strike some middle ground between these two extremes. He views the relationship between the person and the environment as mutually influential: the person observes and behaves in the environment and then receives feedback from it.

## A final word

In this book we have attempted to provide a very broad introduction to the most prominent psychological theories of motivation. We've enjoyed this endeavor. The "why" of human behavior has been a fascinating question for as long as there has been human behavior. In presenting the theories, historical trends among the many answers to the "why" question were often apparent: for example, optimal level theory was a reaction to the Hull/Spence model; achievement theory was strongly influenced by field theory. As we saw earlier in this chapter, many theories are related to each other in subtle, intricate ways. Uncovering these relations is intellectually satisfying for authors as well as (we hope) for students.

Also satisfying is the explanation of individual behaviors, particularly unusual behaviors. After spending ten hours pulling weeds out of his lawn, a former neighbor boasted that his (motley) lawn looked like a finely manicured golf course. We concluded that his extraordinarily poor vision was being warped by cognitive dissonance. Our dedicated editor told us that she stayed up until 4 A.M. to finish the last few pages of this manuscript. Hull pointed out that as the goal is approached, each $r_G\text{-}s_G$ draws one progressively more strongly toward the goal. The goal gradient is powerful, indeed, even if one's bedtime has long since passed. The car dealer in Gary and Shirley the waitress are probably still wondering about the unusual behavior of that fellow they met several years ago. If only they would read this text, they'd be able to explain his behavior. Now that you've read it, we hope you'll be able to understand human motivation more completely.

# References

Abelson, R. P., & Rosenberg, M. J. Symbolic psycho-logic: A model of attitudinal cognition. *Behavioral Science*, 1958, *3*, 1–13.

Aborn, M. The influence of experimentally induced failure on the retention of material acquired through set and incidental learning. *Journal of Experimental Psychology*, 1953, *45*, 225–231.

Abramson, L. Y., Seligman, M. E. P., & Teasdale, J. D. Learned helplessness in humans: Critique and reformulation. *Journal of Abnormal Psychology*, 1978, *87*, 49–74.

Adams, J. S. Toward an understanding of inequity. *Journal of Abnormal and Social Psychology*, 1963, *67*, 422–436.

Adams, J. S. Inequity in social exchange. In L. Berkowitz (Ed.), *Advances in experimental social psychology* (Vol. 2). New York: Academic Press, 1965.

Adams, J. S., & Jacobsen, P. R. Effects of wage inequities on work quality. *Journal of Abnormal and Social Psychology*, 1964, *69*, 19–25.

Adorno, T. W., Frenkel-Brunswick, E., Levinson, D. J., & Sanford, R. N. *The authoritarian personality.* New York: Harper & Row, 1950.

Aiken, E. G. The effort variable in the acquisition, extinction, and spontaneous recovery of an instrumental response. *Journal of Experimental Psychology*, 1957, *53*, 47–51.

Albert, I. B. REM sleep deprivation. *Biological Psychiatry*, 1975, *10*, 341–349.

Allport, G. W. *Pattern and growth in personality.* New York: Holt, Rinehart & Winston, 1961.

Allyn, J., & Festinger, L. The effectiveness of unanticipated persuasive communications. *Journal of Abnormal and Social Psychology*, 1961, *62*, 35–40.

Almli, C. R., & Weiss, C. S. Drinking behaviors: Effects of lateral preoptic and lateral hypothalamic destruction. *Physiology and Behavior*, 1974, *13*, 527–538.

Amabile, T. M. Effects of external evaluation on artistic creativity. *Journal of Personality and Social Psychology*, 1979, *37*, 221–233.

Amsel, A. The role of frustrative nonreward in noncontinuous reward situations. *Psychological Bulletin*, 1958, *55*, 102–119.

Amsel, A., & Roussel, J. Motivational properties of frustration: I. Effect on a running response of the addition of frustration to the motivational complex. *Journal of Experimental Psychology*, 1952, *43*, 363–368.

Anand, B., & Brobeck, J. R. Hypothalamic control of food intake in rats and cats. *Yale Journal of Biological Medicine*, 1951, *24*, 123–140.

Anand, B., Dua, S., & Singh, B. Electrical activity of the hypothalamic "feeding centres" under the effects of changes in blood chemistry. *Electroencephalography and Clinical Neurophysiology*, 1961, *13*, 54–59.

Anderson, R., Manoogian, S., & Resznick, J. The undermining and enhancing of intrinsic motivation in preschool children. *Journal of Personality and Social Psychology,* 1976, *34,* 915–922.

Andersson, B., Olsson, K., & Warner, R. G. Dissimilarity between the central control of thirst and the release of antidiuretic hormone (ADH). *Acta Physiologica Scandinavica,* 1967, *71,* 57–64.

Ardrey, R. *The territorial imperative.* New York: Atheneum, 1966.

Argote, L. M., Fisher, J. E., McDonald, P. J., & O'Neal, E. C. Competitiveness in males and females: Situational determinants of fear of success behavior. *Sex Roles,* 1976, *2,* 295–304.

Arkes, H. R. Competence and the maintenance of behavior. *Motivation and Emotion,* 1978, *2,* 201–211.

Arkes, H. R. Competence and the overjustification effect. *Motivation and Emotion,* 1979, *3,* 143–150.

Arkes, H. R. Teaching information processing system (TIPS): Evaluation in large introductory psychology class. *Teaching of Psychology,* 1980, *7,* 22–24.

Arkes, H. R., & Boykin, A. W. Analysis of complexity preference in Head Start and nursery school children. *Perceptual and Motor Skills,* 1971, *33,* 1131–1137.

Arkes, H. R., & Clark, P. Effects of task difficulty on subsequent preference for visual complexity. *Perceptual and Motor Skills,* 1975, *41,* 395–399.

Armstrong, E. A. The nature and function of displacement activities. In Society for Experimental Biology, *Physiological mechanisms of animal behavior (Symposium No. 4).* New York: Academic Press, 1950.

Arnold, H. J. Effects of performance feedback and extrinsic reward upon high intrinsic motivation. *Organizational Behavior and Human Performance,* 1976, *17,* 275–288.

Aronson, E. Dissonance theory: Progress and problems. In R. P. Abelson, E. Aronson, W. J. McGuire, T. M. Newcomb, M. J. Rosenberg, & P. H. Tannenbaum (Eds.), *Theories of cognitive consistency: A sourcebook.* Chicago: Rand McNally, 1968. Pp. 5–27.

Aronson, E., & Mills, J. The effect of severity of initiation on liking for a group. *Journal of Abnormal and Social Psychology,* 1959, *59,* 177–181.

Atkinson, J. W. Motivational determinants of risk-taking behavior. *Psychological Review,* 1957, *64,* 359–372.

Atkinson, J. W. *An introduction to motivation.* New York: Van Nostrand Reinhold, 1964.

Atkinson, J. W. Strength of motivation and efficiency of performance. In J. W. Atkinson & J. O. Raynor (Eds.), *Motivation and achievement.* Washington: V. H. Winston & Sons, 1974.

Atkinson, J. W., Bastian, J. R., Earl, R. W., & Litwin, G. H. The achievement motive, goal setting, and probability preferences. *Journal of Abnormal and Social Psychology,* 1960, *60,* 27–36.

Atkinson, J. W., & Birch, D. *The dynamics of action.* New York: Wiley, 1970.

Atkinson, J. W., & Birch, D. The dynamics of achievement-oriented activity. In J. W. Atkinson & J. O. Raynor (Eds.), *Motivation and achievement.* Washington: V. H. Winston & Sons, 1974.

Atkinson, J. W., Bongort, K., & Price, L. H. Explorations using computer simulation to comprehend thematic apperceptive measurement of motivation. *Motivation and Emotion,* 1977, *1,* 1–27.

Atkinson, J. W., & Feather, N. T. *A theory of achievement motivation.* New York: Wiley, 1966.

Atkinson, J. W., & Litwin, G. H. Achievement motive and test anxiety conceived as motive to approach success and motive to avoid failure. *Journal of Abnormal and Social Psychology,* 1960, *60,* 52–63.

Atkinson, J. W., & McClelland, D. C. The projective expression of needs: II. The effect of different intensities of the hunger drive on thematic apperception. *Journal of Experimental Psychology,* 1948, *38,* 643–658.

Atkinson, J. W., & O'Connor, P. *Effects of ability grouping in schools related to individual differences in achievement-related motivation* (Final Report, Office of Education Cooperative Research Program, Project 1283, 1963). Available in microfilm from Photoduplication Center, Library of Congress, Washington, D. C.

Atkinson, J. W., & Raphelson, A. C. Individual differences in motivation and behavior in particular situations. *Journal of Personality,* 1956, *24,* 349–363.

Atkinson, J. W., & Raynor, J. O. (Eds.) *Motivation and achievement.* Washington: V. H. Winston & Sons, 1974.

Ayllon, T., & Azrin, N. H. *The token economy: A motivational system for therapy and rehabilitation.* New York: Appleton-Century-Crofts, 1968.

Bachman, J. G., & O'Malley, P. M. Self-esteem in young men: A longitudinal analysis of the impact of educational and occupational attainment. *Journal of Personality and Social Psychology,* 1977, *35,* 365–380.

Bahrick, H. P., Fitts, P. M., & Rankin, R. E. Effects of incentive upon reactions to peripheral stimuli. *Journal of Experimental Psychology,* 1952, *44,* 400–406.

Bailey, P., & Bremer, F. Experimental diabetes insipidus. *Archives of Internal Medicine,* 1921, *28,* 773–803.

Bandler, R. J., & Flynn, J. P. Neural pathways from thalamus associated with regulation of aggressive behavior. *Science,* 1974, *183,* 96–99.

Bandura, A. *Principles of behavior modification.* New York: Holt, Rinehart & Winston, 1969.

Bandura, A. Analysis of modeling processes. In A. Bandura (Ed.), *Psychological modeling: Conflicting theories.* Chicago: Aldine-Atherton, 1971. (a)

Bandura, A. *Social learning theory.* Morristown, N. J.: General Learning Press, 1971. (b)

Bandura, A. *Aggression: A social learning analysis.* Englewood Cliffs, N. J.: Prentice-Hall, 1973.

Bandura, A. Self-efficacy: Toward a unifying theory of behavioral change. *Psychological Review,* 1977, *84,* 191–215. (a)

Bandura, A. *Social learning theory.* Englewood Cliffs, N. J.: Prentice-Hall, 1977. (b)

Bandura, A. The self-system in reciprocal determinism. *American Psychologist,* 1978, *33,* 344–358. (a)

Bandura, A. Self-reinforcement: Theoretical and methodological considerations. In C. M. Franks & G. T. Williams (Eds.), *Annual Review of Behavior Therapy* (Vol. 5). New York: Brunner/Mazel, 1978. (b)

Bandura, A., Adams, E., & Meyer, J. Cognitive processes mediating behavioral change. *Journal of Personality and Social Psychology,* 1977, *35,* 125–139.

Bandura, A., & Walters, R. H. *Social learning and personality development.* New York: Holt, Rinehart & Winston, 1963.

Barash, D. P. *Sociobiology and behavior.* New York: Elsevier, 1977.

Bargmann, W., & Scharrer, E. The site of origin of the hormones of the posterior pituitary. *American Scientist,* 1951, *39,* 255–259.

Baron, R. A. Aggression as a function of victim's pain cues, level of prior anger arousal, and exposure to an aggressive model. *Journal of Personality and Social Psychology*, 1974, *29*, 117–124. (a)

Baron, R. A. The aggression-inhibiting influence of heightened sexual arousal. *Journal of Personality and Social Psychology*, 1974, *30*, 318–322. (b)

Baron, R. A. *Human aggression*. New York: Plenum, 1977.

Baron, R. A. Heightened sexual arousal and physical aggression: An extension to females. *Journal of Research in Personality*, 1979, *13*, 91–102.

Baron, R. A., & Bell, P. Sexual arousal and aggression by males: Effects of type of erotic stimuli and prior provocation. *Journal of Personality and Social Psychology*, 1977, *35*, 79–87.

Bateson, P. P. G. The characteristics and context of imprinting. *Biological Reviews of the Cambridge Philosophical Society*, 1966, *41*, 177–220.

Bateson, P. P. G. Imprinting and the development of preferences. In A. Ambrose (Ed.), *Stimulation in early infancy*. New York: Academic Press, 1969.

Bateson, P. P. G. Imprinting. In H. Moltz (Ed.), *The ontogeny of vertebrate behavior*. New York: Academic Press, 1971.

Battle, E. S. Motivational determinants of academic task persistence. *Journal of Personality and Social Psychology*, 1965, *2*, 209–218.

Baumeister, A. A. More ado about operant conditioning—or nothing. *Mental Retardation*, 1969, *7*, 49–51.

Beach, F. A. The descent of instinct. *Psychological Review*, 1955, *62*, 401–410.

Beach, F. A. Characteristics of masculine "sex drive." In M. R. Jones (Ed.), *Nebraska Symposium on Motivation* (Vol. 4). Lincoln: University of Nebraska Press, 1956.

Beach, F. A. Neural and chemical regulation of behavior. In H. F. Harlow & C. N. Woolsey (Eds.), *Biological and biochemical bases of behavior*. Madison: University of Wisconsin Press, 1958.

Beaumont, W. *Experiments and observations on the gastric juice and the physiology of digestion*. New York: Dover, 1959. (Originally published, 1833.)

Bellows, R. T. Time factors in water drinking in dogs. *American Journal of Physiology*, 1939, *125*, 87–97.

Bellows, R. T., & Van Wagenen, W. P. The effect of resection of the olfactory, gustatory, and trigeminal nerves on water drinking in dogs without and with diabetes insipidus. *American Journal of Physiology*, 1939, *126*, 13–19.

Bem, D. Self perception: An alternative interpretation of cognitive dissonance phenomena. *Psychological Review*, 1967, *74*, 183–200.

Bem, D. Cognitive alteration of feeling states: A discussion. In H. London & R. Nisbett (Eds.), *Thought and feeling: Cognitive alteration of feeling states*. Chicago: Aldine, 1974.

Bem, D. J., & McConnell, H. K. Testing the self-perception explanation of dissonance phenomenon: On the salience of premanipulation attitudes. *Journal of Personality and Social Psychology*, 1970, *14*, 23–31.

Bergquist, E. Role of the hypothalamus in motivation: An examination of Valenstein's reexamination. *Psychological Review*, 1972, *79*, 542–546.

Berkowitz, L. Anti-Semitism and the displacement of aggression. *Journal of Abnormal and Social Psychology*, 1959, *59*, 182–187.

Berlyne, D. E. *Conflict, arousal and curiosity*. New York: McGraw-Hill, 1960.

Berlyne, D. E. Novelty, complexity and hedonic value. *Perception and Psychophysics*, 1970, *8*, 279–286.

Berlyne, D. E. *Aesthetics and psychobiology.* New York: Appleton-Century-Crofts, 1971.

Bernfeld, S. Freud's earliest theories and the school of Helmholtz. *Psychoanalytic Quarterly,* 1944, *13,* 341–362.

Berscheid, E., & Walster, E. *Interpersonal attraction.* Reading, Mass.: Addison-Wesley, 1969.

Berscheid, E., Walster, E., & Bohrnstedt, G. The body image report. *Psychology Today,* 1973, *7,* 119–131.

Bettelheim, B. Individual and mass behavior in extreme situations. *Journal of Abnormal and Social Psychology,* 1943, *38,* 417–452.

Bexton, W., Heron, W., & Scott, T. Effects of decreased variation in the sensory environment. *Canadian Journal of Psychology,* 1954, *8,* 70–76.

Birch, D., Burnstein, E., & Clark, R. A. Response strength as a function of hours of food deprivation under a controlled maintenance schedule. *Journal of Comparative and Physiological Psychology,* 1958, *51,* 350–354.

Birney, R. C., Burdick, H., & Teevan, R. C. *Fear of failure motivation.* New York: Wiley, 1969.

Blass, E. M., & Epstein, A. N. A lateral preoptic osmosensitive zone for thirst. *Journal of Comparative and Physiological Psychology,* 1971, *76,* 378–394.

Block, J. R. *Motivation, satisfaction and performance of handicapped workers.* Unpublished doctoral dissertation, New York University, 1962.

Blodgett, H. C. The effect of the introduction of reward upon the maze performance of rats. *University of California Publications in Psychology,* 1929, *4,* 113–134.

Blum, G. S., & Barbour, J. S. Selective attention to anxiety-linked stimuli. *Journal of Experimental Psychology: General,* 1979, *108,* 182–224.

Boggiano, A. K., & Ruble, D. N. Competence and the overjustification effect: A developmental study. *Journal of Personality and Social Psychology,* 1979, *37,* 1462–1468.

Bolles, R. C. *Theory of motivation.* New York: Harper & Row, 1967.

Bolles, R. C. Cognition and motivation: Some historical trends. In B. Weiner (Ed.), *Cognitive views of human motivation.* New York: Academic Press, 1974. Pp. 1–20.

Bootzin, R., Herman, C., & Nicassio, P. The power of suggestion: Another examination of misattribution and insomnia. *Journal of Personality and Social Psychology,* 1976, *34,* 673–679.

Boring, E. *A history of experimental psychology.* New York: Appleton-Century-Crofts, 1950.

Bowlby, J. *Attachment and loss* (Vol. 1). New York: Basic Books, 1969.

Brady, J. V., Boren, J. J., Conrad, D., & Sidman, M. The effect of food and water deprivation upon intracranial self-stimulation. *Journal of Comparative and Physiological Psychology,* 1957, *50,* 134–137.

Bramel, D. A dissonance theory approach to defensive projection. *Journal of Abnormal and Social Psychology,* 1962, *64,* 121–129.

Bramel, D. Selection of a target for defensive projection. *Journal of Abnormal and Social Psychology,* 1963, *66,* 318–332.

Breger, L. Dream function: An information processing model. In L. Breger (Ed.), *Clinical-cognitive psychology: Models and integrations.* Englewood Cliffs, N. J.: Prentice-Hall, 1969.

Brehm, J. W. Post-decision changes in the desirability of alternatives. *Journal of Abnormal and Social Psychology,* 1956, *52,* 384–389.

Brehm, J. W. *A theory of psychological reactance.* New York: Academic Press, 1966.

Brehm, J. W., & Cohen, A. R. *Explorations in cognitive dissonance.* New York: Wiley, 1962.

Brehm, J. W., Stires, L. K., Sensenig, J., & Shaban, J. The attractiveness of an eliminated choice alternative. *Journal of Experimental Social Psychology,* 1966, *2,* 301–313.

Bremer, T. A., & Wittig, M. A. Fear of success: A personality trait or a response to occupational deviance and role overload. *Sex Roles,* 1980, *6,* 27–46.

Brennan, W. M., Ames, E. W., & Moore, R. W. Age differences in infants' attention to patterns of different complexities. *Science,* 1966, *151,* 354–356.

Brenner, C. *An elementary textbook of psychoanalysis.* New York: International Universities Press, 1955.

Breuer, J., & Freud, S. (1895.) Studies on hysteria. In *The standard edition of the complete psychological works of Sigmund Freud* (Vol. 2). London: Hogarth, 1955.

Brock, T. C., & Buss, A. H. Dissonance, aggression, and evaluation of pain. *Journal of Abnormal and Social Psychology,* 1962, *65,* 197–202.

Brockner, J. The effects of self-esteem, success–failure, and self-consciousness on task performance. *Journal of Personality and Social Psychology,* 1979, *37,* 1732–1741.

Brody, N. N achievement, test anxiety and subjective probability of success in risk-taking behavior. *Journal of Abnormal and Social Psychology,* 1963, *66,* 413–418.

Brown, J. S., & Farber, I. E. Emotions conceptualized as intervening variables—with suggestions toward a theory of frustration. *Psychological Bulletin,* 1951, *48,* 465–495.

Brown, R., & Herrnstein, R. J. *Psychology.* Boston: Little, Brown, 1975.

Bryson, J. B., & Driver, M. J. Cognitive complexity, introversion, and preference for complexity. *Journal of Personality and Social Psychology,* 1972, *23,* 320–327.

Buchwald, A. M., Coyne, J. C., & Cole, C. S. A critical evaluation of the learned helplessness model of depression. *Journal of Abnormal Psychology,* 1978, *87,* 180–193.

Buckert, U., Meyer, W.-V., & Schmalt, H.-D. Effects of difficulty and diagnosticity on choice among tasks in relation to achievement motivation and perceived ability. *Journal of Personality and Social Psychology,* 1979, *37,* 1172–1178.

Buhler, C., & Allen, M. *Introduction to humanistic psychology.* Monterey, Calif.: Brooks/Cole, 1972.

Burdick, H. A., & Burnes, A. J. A test of "strain toward symmetry" theories. *Journal of Abnormal and Social Psychology,* 1958, *57,* 367–369.

Burnam, M. A., Pennebaker, J. W., & Glass, D. C. Time consciousness, achievement striving and the Type A coronary-prone behavior pattern. *Journal of Abnormal Psychology,* 1975, *84,* 76–79.

Burris, R. W. *The effect of counseling on achievement motivation.* Unpublished doctoral dissertation, Indiana University, 1958.

Burt, C. The analysis of temperament. *British Journal of Medical Psychology,* 1937, *17,* 158–188.

Butler, R. A. Incentive conditions which influence visual exploration. *Journal of Experimental Psychology,* 1954, *48,* 19–23.

Butler, R. A., & Harlow, H. F. Persistence of visual exploration in monkeys. *Journal of Comparative and Physiological Psychology,* 1954, *47,* 258–263.

Byrne, D. Interpersonal attraction and attitude similarity. *Journal of Abnormal and Social Psychology,* 1961, *62,* 713–715.

Cabellero, C. M., Giles, P., & Shaver, P. Sex-role traditionalism and fear of success. *Sex Roles,* 1975, *1,* 319–327.

Campbell, D. T., & Stanley, J. C. *Experimental and quasi-experimental designs for research.* Chicago: Rand McNally, 1963.

Campbell, J. P., & Pritchard, R. O. Motivation theory in organizational and industrial psychology. In M. D. Dunnette (Ed.), *Handbook of industrial and organizational psychology.* Chicago: Rand McNally, 1976. Pp. 63–130.

Cannon, W. B. The physiological basis of thirst. *Proceedings of the Royal Society,* 1918, *B 90,* 283–301.

Cannon, W. B. The James-Lange theory of emotions: A critical examination and an alternative theory. *American Journal of Psychology,* 1927, *39,* 106–124.

Cannon, W. B. "Voodoo" death. *American Anthropologist,* 1942, *49,* 169–181.

Cannon, W. B., & Washburn, A. L. An explanation of hunger. *American Journal of Physiology,* 1912, *29,* 441–454.

Cantor, J. R., Bryant, J., & Zillmann, D. Enhancement of humor appreciation by transferred excitation. *Journal of Personality and Social Psychology,* 1974, *30,* 812–821.

Carey, G. L. Sex-differences in problem-solving performance as a function of attitude differences. *Journal of Abnormal and Social Psychology,* 1958, *56,* 256–260.

Carlsmith, J. M., Collins, B. E., & Helmreich, R. L. Studies in forced compliance: I. The effect of pressure for compliance on attitude change produced by face-to-face role playing and anonymous essay writing. *Journal of Personality and Social Psychology,* 1966, *4,* 1–13.

Carpenter, C. R. Territoriality. In A. Roe & G. G. Simpson (Eds.), *Behavior and evolution.* New Haven, Conn.: Yale University Press, 1958.

Carroll, M. P. A test of Newcomb's modification of balance theory. *The Journal of Social Psychology,* 1977, *101,* 155–156.

Ceranski, D. S., Teevan, R., & Kalle, R. J. A comparison of three measures of the motive to avoid failure: Hostile press, test anxiety, and resultant achievement motivation. *Motivation and Emotion,* 1979, *3,* 395–404.

Chadwick, B. A., & Day, R. C. Systematic reinforcement: Academic performance of underachieving students. *Journal of Applied Behavior Analysis,* 1971, *4,* 311–319.

Chapanis, N. P., & Chapanis, A. Cognitive dissonance: Five years later. *Psychological Bulletin,* 1964, *61,* 1–22.

Clark, K. B. No. No. Race, not class is still at the wheel. *New York Times,* March 22, 1978, p. 25.

Cline, V. H., Croft, R. G., & Courrier, S. Desensitization of children to television violence. *Journal of Personality and Social Psychology,* 1973, *27,* 360–365.

Cofer, C. N., & Appley, M. H. *Motivation: Theory and research.* New York: Wiley, 1964.

Cohen, A. R. Some implications of self-esteem for social influence. In C. I. Hovland & I. L. Janis (Eds.), *Personality and persuasibility.* New Haven, Conn.: Yale University Press, 1959.

Cohen, L. B. Observing responses, visual preferences, and habituation to visual stimuli in infants. *Journal of Experimental Child Psychology,* 1969, *7,* 419–433.

Cohen, N. E. *Explorations in the fear of success.* Unpublished doctoral dissertation, Columbia University, 1974.

Cohen, S., Glass, D. C., & Singer, J. E. Apartment noise, auditory discrimination, and reading ability in children. *Journal of Experimental Social Psychology,* 1973, *9,* 407–422.

Commission on Obscenity and Pornography. *The report of the Commission on Obscenity and Pornography.* Washington, D. C.: U. S. Government Printing Office, 1970. *New York Times* edition published by Bantam Books.

Condry, J., & Chambers, J. Intrinsic motivation and the process of learning. In M. R. Lepper & D. Greene (Eds.), *The hidden costs of reward.* Hillsdale, N. J.: Erlbaum, 1978.

Cooper, J. Reducing fears and increasing assertiveness: The role of dissonance reduction. *Journal of Experimental Social Psychology,* 1980, *16,* 199–213.

Coopersmith, S. *The antecedents of self-esteem.* San Francisco: W. H. Freeman, 1967.

Costanzo, P. R., & Woody, E. Z. Externality as a function of obesity in children: Pervasive style or eating-specific attitude? *Journal of Personality and Social Psychology,* 1979, *37,* 2286–2296.

Costello, C. G. A critical review of Seligman's laboratory experiments on learned helplessness and depression in humans. *Journal of Abnormal Psychology,* 1978, *87,* 21–31.

Cottrell, N. B., Rajecki, D. W., & Smith, D. V. The energizing effects of postdecision dissonance upon performance of an irrelevant task. *Journal of Social Psychology,* 1974, *93,* 81–92.

Cottrell, N. B., Rittle, R. H., & Wack, D. L. The presence of an audience and list type (competitional or non-competitional) as joint determinants of performance in paired-associates learning. *Journal of Personality,* 1967, *35,* 425–434.

Cottrell, N. B., & Wack, D. Energizing effects of cognitive dissonance upon dominant and subordinate responses. *Journal of Personality and Social Psychology,* 1967, *6,* 132–138.

Covington, M. V., & Beery, R. G. *Self-worth and school learning.* New York: Holt, Rinehart & Winston, 1976.

Covington, M. V., & Omelich, C. L. Are causal attributions causal? A path analysis of the cognitive model of achievement motivation. *Journal of Personality and Social Psychology,* 1979, *37,* 1487–1504.

Cox, F. N. An assessment of the achievement behavior system in children. *Child Development,* 1962, *33,* 907–916.

Crandall, R. The measurement of self-esteem and related constructs. In J. R. Robinson & P. R. Shaver (Eds.), *Measures of social psychological attitudes.* Ann Arbor: Institute for Social Research, 1973.

Crandall, V. C. Sex differences in expectancy of intellectual and academic reinforcement. In C. P. Smith (Ed.), *Achievement-related motives in children.* New York: Russell Sage Foundation, 1969.

Crandall, V. J., Preston, A., & Rabson, A. Maternal reactions and the development of independence and achievement behavior in young children. *Child Development,* 1960, *31,* 243–251.

Crespi, L. P. Quantitative variation of incentive and performance in the white rat. *American Journal of Psychology,* 1942, *55,* 467–517.

Crespi, L. P. Amount of reinforcement and level of performance. *Psychological Review,* 1944, *51,* 341–357.

Dashiell, J. F. A quantitative demonstration of animal drive. *Journal of Comparative Psychology,* 1925, *5,* 205–208.

Davies, J. Toward a theory of revolution. *American Sociological Review,* 1967, *27,* 5–19.

Davis, C. M. Self-selection of diet by newly weaned infants. *American Journal of Disease of Children,* 1928, *36,* 651–679.

Davitz, J. R. The effects of previous training on postfrustrative behavior. *Journal of Abnormal and Social Psychology,* 1952, *47,* 309–315.

Deaux, K., & Emswiller, T. Explanations of successful performance on sex-linked tasks: What is skill for the male is luck for the female. *Journal of Personality and Social Psychology,* 1974, *29,* 80–85.

deCharms, R. *Personal causation: The internal affective determinants of behavior.* New York: Academic Press, 1968.

deCharms, R. *Enhancing motivation.* New York: Irvington, 1976.

deCharms, R., & Carpenter, V. Measuring motivation in culturally disadvantaged school children. *Journal of Experimental Education,* 1968, *37,* 31–41.

Deci, E. L. Effects of externally mediated rewards on intrinsic motivation. *Journal of Personality and Social Psychology,* 1971, *18,* 105–115.

Deci, E. L. Effects of contingent and non-contingent rewards and controls on intrinsic motivation. *Organizational Behavior and Human Performance,* 1972, *8,* 217–229. (a)

Deci, E. L. Intrinsic motivation, extrinsic reinforcement and inequity. *Journal of Personality and Social Psychology,* 1972, *22,* 113–120. (b)

Deci, E. L. *Intrinsic motivation.* New York: Plenum, 1975.

Deci, E. L., Nezlek, J., & Sheinman, L. Characteristics of the rewarder and intrinsic motivation of the rewardee. *Journal of Personality and Social Psychology,* 1981, *40,* 1–10.

Dees, J. W., & Furchtgott, E. Drive generalization. *Psychological Reports,* 1964, *15,* 807–810.

Delgado, J. Cerebral structures involved in transmission and elaboration of noxious stimulation. *Journal of Neurophysiology,* 1955, 261–275.

Delgado, J., Roberts, W., & Miller, N. Learning motivated by electrical stimulation of the brain. *American Journal of Physiology,* 1954, *179,* 587–593.

Dember, W. N., & Earl, R. W. Analysis of exploratory, manipulatory, and curiosity behaviors. *Psychological Review,* 1957, *64,* 91–96.

Dember, W. N., Earl, R. W., & Paradise, N. Response by rats to differential stimulus complexity. *Journal of Comparative and Physiological Psychology,* 1957, *50,* 514–518.

Denmark, F. L., Tangri, S. S., & McCandless, S. Affiliation, achievement, and power: A new look. In J. A. Sherman & F. L. Denmark (Eds.), *The psychology of women: Future directions in research.* New York: Psychological Dimensions, 1978.

Dennis, W. Causes of retardation among institutionalized children: Iran. *Journal of Genetic Psychology,* 1960, *96,* 47–59.

Depue, R. A., & Monroe, S. M. Learned helplessness in the perspective of the depressive disorders: Conceptual and definitional issues. *Journal of Abnormal Psychology,* 1978, *87,* 3–20.

Diener, C. I., & Dweck, C. S. An analysis of learned helplessness: Continuous changes in performance, strategy, and achievement cognitions following failure. *Journal of Personality and Social Psychology,* 1978, *36,* 451–462.

DiGuisto, E. L., Cairncross, K., & King, M. G. Hormonal influences on fear-motivated responses. *Psychological Bulletin,* 1971, *75,* 432–444.

Dilger, W. The behavior of lovebirds. *Scientific American,* 1962, *206,* 88–98.

Dimond, S. J. Visual experience and early social behavior in chicks. In J. H. Crook (Ed.), *Social behavior in birds and mammals: Essays on the social ethology of animals and man.* New York: Academic Press, 1970.

Dollard, J., Doob, L., Miller, N. E., Mowrer, O. H., & Sears, R. R. *Frustration and aggression.* New Haven, Conn.: Yale University Press, 1939.

Dollard, J., & Miller, N. E. *Personality and psychotherapy.* New York: McGraw-Hill, 1950.

Dollinger, S. J., & Thelen, M. H. Overjustification and children's intrinsic motivation: Comparative effects of four rewards. *Journal of Personality and Social Psychology,* 1978, *36,* 1259–1269.

Dominick, J. R., & Greenberg, B. S. Attitudes toward violence: The interaction of television exposure, family attitudes, and social class. In *Technical Report to the Surgeon General's Scientific Advisory Commission* (Vol. 3). 1972.

Donley, R. E., & Winter, D. G. Measuring the motives of public officials at a distance: An exploratory study of American presidents. *Behavioral Science,* 1970, *15,* 227–235.

Donnerstein, E. Aggressive erotica and violence against women. *Journal of Personality and Social Psychology,* 1980, *39,* 269–277.

Donnerstein, E., & Barrett, G. Effects of erotic stimuli on male aggression toward females. *Journal of Personality and Social Psychology,* 1978, *36,* 180–188.

Donnerstein, E., Donnerstein, M., & Evans, R. Erotic stimuli and aggression: Facilitation or inhibition. *Journal of Personality and Social Psychology,* 1975, *32,* 237–244.

Donnerstein, E., & Hallam, J. Facilitating effects of erotica on aggression against women. *Journal of Personality and Social Psychology,* 1978, *36,* 1270–1277.

Dorfman, D. D. Esthetic preference as a function of pattern information. *Psychonomic Science,* 1965, *3,* 85–86.

Douglas, D., & Anisman, H. Helplessness or expectation incongruency: Effects of aversive stimulation on subsequent performance. *Journal of Experimental Psychology: Human Perception and Performance,* 1975, *1,* 411–417.

Drabman, R. S., & Thomas, M. H. Does media violence increase children's tolerance of real-life aggression? *Developmental Psychology,* 1974, *10,* 418–421.

Driscoll, R., Davis, K., & Lipetz, M. Parental interference and romantic love: The Romeo and Juliet effect. *Journal of Personality and Social Psychology,* 1972, *24,* 1–10.

Duffy, E. *Activation and behavior.* New York: Wiley, 1962.

Dumas, C. L. *Principes de physiologie* (Vol. 4). Paris: Deterville, 1803.

Dutton, D. G., & Aron, A. P. Some evidence for heightened sexual attraction under conditions of high anxiety. *Journal of Personality and Social Psychology,* 1974, *30,* 510–517.

Dweck, C. S., & Goetz, T. E. Attributions and learned helplessness. In J. H. Harvey, W. Ickes, & R. F. Kidd (Eds.), *New directions in attribution research* (Vol. 2). Hillsdale, N.J.: Erlbaum, 1978.

Dweck, C. S., & Reppucci, N. Learned helplessness and reinforcement responsibility in children. *Journal of Personality and Social Psychology,* 1973, *25,* 109–116.

D'Zurilla, T. Recall efficiency and mediating cognitive events in "experimental repression." *Journal of Personality and Social Psychology,* 1965, *3,* 253–256.

Easterbrook, J. A. The effect of emotion on cue utilization and the organization of behavior. *Psychological Review,* 1959, *66,* 183–201.

Edney, J. J. Human territoriality. *Psychological Bulletin,* 1974, *81,* 959–975.

Edwards, W. The theory of decision making. *Psychological Bulletin,* 1954, *51,* 380–417.

Ehrenzweig, A. *The psychoanalysis of artistic vision and learning.* New York: George Braziller, 1965.

Ehrenzweig, A. *The hidden order of art.* Berkeley and Los Angeles: University of California Press, 1967.

Eibl-Eibesfeldt, I. *Ethology: The biology of behavior.* New York: Holt, Rinehart & Winston, 1970.

Eldow, D. W., & Kiesler, C. A. Ease of denial and defensive projection. *Journal of Experimental Social Psychology,* 1966, *2,* 56–69.

Elig, T. W., & Frieze, I. H. A multi-dimensional scheme for coding and interpreting perceived causality for success and failure events. *JSAS Catalogue of Selected Documents in Psychology,* 1975, *5,* 313.

Elig, T. W., & Frieze, I. H. Measuring causal attributions for success and failure. *Journal of Personality and Social Psychology,* 1979, *37,* 621–634.

Elms, A. C. Role playing, incentive, and dissonance. *Psychological Review,* 1967, *68,* 132–148.

Elms, A. C., & Janis, I. L. Counter-norm attitudes induced by consonant versus dissonant conditions of role-playing. *Journal of Experimental Research in Personality,* 1965, *1,* 50–60.

Entin, E. E., & Raynor, J. O. Effects of contingent future orientation and achievement motivation on performance in two kinds of tasks. *Journal of Experimental Research in Personality,* 1973, *6,* 314–320.

Entwisle, D. R. To dispel fantasies about fantasy-based measures of achievement motivation. *Psychological Bulletin,* 1972, *77,* 377–391.

Erikson, E. H. *Childhood and society.* New York: Norton, 1950.

Estes, W. K. An experimental study of punishment. *Psychological Monographs,* 1944, *57* (Whole No. 263).

Estes, W. K. Kurt Lewin. In W. K. Estes, S. Koch, K. MacCorquodale, P. E. Meehl, G. G. Mueller Jr., W. N. Schoenfeld, & W. S. Verplanck. *Modern learning theory.* New York: Appleton-Century-Crofts, 1954.

Estes, W. K., & Skinner, B. F. Some quantitative properties of anxiety. *Journal of Experimental Psychology,* 1941, *29,* 390–400.

Evvard, J. M. Is the appetite of the swine a reliable indicator of physiological needs? *Proceedings of the Iowa Academy of Science,* 1916, *22,* 375–414.

Eysenck, H. J. *Dimensions of personality.* London: Routledge & Kegan Paul, 1947.

Falbo, T., & Beck, R. C. Naive psychology and the attributional model of achievement. *Journal of Personality,* 1979, *47,* 185–195.

Fantz, R. L., & Nevis, S. Pattern preferences and perceptual cognitive development in early infancy. *Merrill-Palmer Quarterly,* 1967, *13,* 77–108.

Farr, J. L. Task characteristics, reward contingency, and intrinsic motivation. *Organizational Behavior and Human Performance,* 1976, *16,* 294–307.

Farr, J. L., Vance, R. J., & McIntyre, R. M. Further examinations of the relationship between reward contingency and intrinsic motivation. *Organizational Behavior and Human Performance,* 1977, *20,* 31–53.

Feather, N. T. The relationship of persistence at a task to expectation of success and achievement-related motives. *Journal of Abnormal and Social Psychology,* 1961, *63,* 552–561.

Feather, N. T. Valence of outcome and expectation of success in relation to task difficulty and perceived locus of control. *Journal of Personality and Social Psychology*, 1967, *7*, 372–386.

Feather, N. T. Attribution of responsibility and valence of success and failure in relation to initial confidence and perceived locus of control. *Journal of Personality and Social Psychology*, 1969, *13*, 129–144.

Feather, N. T., & Raphelson, A. C. Fear of success in Australian and American student groups: Motive or sex-role stereotype? *Journal of Personality*, 1974, *42*, 190–201.

Feather, N. T., & Simon, J. G. Attribution of responsibility and valence of outcome in relation to initial confidence and success and failure of self and other. *Journal of Personality and Social Psychology*, 1971, *18*, 173–188.

Feldman, S. M., & Waller, H. J. Dissociation of electrocortical activation and behavioral arousal. *Nature*, 1962, *196*, 1320–1322.

Fenichel, O. *The psychoanalytic theory of neurosis.* New York: Norton, 1945.

Festinger, L. *A theory of cognitive dissonance.* Evanston, Ill.: Row, Peterson, 1957.

Festinger, L. The psychological effects of insufficient rewards. *American Psychologist*, 1961, *16*, 1–11.

Festinger, L., & Carlsmith, J. M. Cognitive consequences of forced compliance. *Journal of Abnormal and Social Psychology*, 1959, *58*, 203–210.

Festinger, L., Riecken, H., & Schachter, S. *When prophesy fails.* Minneapolis: University of Minnesota Press, 1956.

Fishbein, W., & Gutwein, B. M. Paradoxical sleep and memory storage processes. *Behavioral Biology*, 1977, *19*, 425–464.

Fisher, A. E. Maternal and sexual behavior induced by intracranial chemical stimulation. *Science*, 1956, *124*, 228–229.

Fisher, W. A., & Byrne, D. Sex differences in response to erotica? Love versus lust. *Journal of Personality and Social Psychology*, 1978, *36*, 117–125.

Fitz, D. A renewed look at Miller's conflict theory of aggression displacement. *Journal of Personality and Social Psychology*, 1976, *33*, 725–732.

Fitzsimons, J. T., & Simons, B. J. The effect of angiotensin on drinking in the rat. *Journal of Physiology*, 1968, *198*, 39P–41P.

Flavell, J. Repression and the "return of the repressed." *Journal of Consulting Psychology*, 1955, *19*, 441–443.

Folger, R., Rosenfield, D., & Hays, R. P. Equity and intrinsic motivation: The role of choice. *Journal of Personality and Social Psychology*, 1978, *36*, 557–564.

Ford, C. S., & Beach, F. A. *Patterns of sexual behavior.* New York: Harper & Row, 1951.

Freedman, J. L., & Sears, D. O. Selective exposure. In L. Berkowitz (Ed.), *Advances in experimental social psychology* (Vol. 2). New York: Academic Press, 1965. Pp. 58–98.

Freud, A. *The ego and the mechanisms of defense.* New York: International Universities Press, 1946. (Originally published, 1936.)

Freud, S. (1894.) The neuropsychoses of defense. In *The standard edition of the complete psychological works of Sigmund Freud* (Vol. 3). London: Hogarth, 1962.

Freud, S. (1896.) Further remarks on the neuropsychoses of defense. In *Standard edition* (Vol. 3). 1962. Pp. 157–185.

Freud, S. (1900.) The interpretation of dreams. In *Standard edition* (Vols. 4 & 5). 1953.

Freud, S. (1905a.) Three essays on the theory of sexuality. In *Standard edition* (Vol. 7). 1953. Pp. 123–245.

Freud, S. (1905b.) Fragment of an analysis of a case of hysteria (A. Strachey & J. Strachey, trans.). In S. Freud, *Collected papers* (Vol. 3). London: Hogarth, 1933.

Freud, S. (1911.) Psychoanalytic notes on an autobiographical account of a case of paranoia (dementia paranoides). In *Standard edition* (Vol. 12). 1958. Pp. 3–82.

Freud, S. (1914a.) On narcissism: An introduction. In *Standard edition* (Vol. 14). 1957.

Freud, S. (1914b.) On the history of the psychoanalytic movement. In *Standard edition* (Vol. 14). 1957.

Freud, S. (1915a.) Instincts and their vicissitudes. In *Standard edition* (Vol. 14). 1957. Pp. 117–140.

Freud, S. (1915b.) Repression. In *Standard edition* (Vol. 14). 1957. Pp. 145–158.

Freud, S. (1917.) Mourning and melancholia. In *Standard edition* (Vol. 14). 1957. Pp. 237–258.

Freud, S. (1920.) *Beyond the pleasure principle.* London: Hogarth, 1948.

Freud, S. (1923.) *The ego and the id.* London: Hogarth, 1947.

Freud, S. (1926.) Inhibitions, symptoms and anxiety. In *Standard edition* (Vol. 20). 1959. Pp. 77–175.

Freud, S. (1933.) New introductory lectures on psychoanalysis. In *Standard edition* (Vol. 22). 1964. Pp. 3–182.

Freud, S. (1940.) An outline of psychoanalysis. In *Standard edition* (Vol. 23). 1964. Pp. 141–207.

Friedman, M. I., & Stricker, E. M. The physiological psychology of hunger: A physiological perspective. *Psychological Review,* 1976, *83,* 409–431.

Friedman, M., Byers, S. O., Diamant, J., & Rosenman, R. H. Plasma catecholamine response of coronary-prone subjects (Type A) to a specific challenge. *Metabolism,* 1975, *24,* 205–210.

Friedrich, L. K., & Stein, A. H. Aggressive and prosocial television programs and the natural behavior of preschool children. *Monographs of the Society for Research in Child Development,* 1973, *38* (4, Whole No. 151).

Frieze, I. H. Women's expectations for and causal attributions of success and failure. In M. Mednick, S. Tangri, & L. Hoffman (Eds.), *Women and achievement.* Washington: Hemisphere, 1975.

Frieze, I. H., & Weiner, B. Cue utilization and attributional judgments for success and failure. *Journal of Personality,* 1971, *39,* 591–606.

Frodi, A. Sexual arousal, situational restrictiveness, and aggressive behavior. *Journal of Research in Personality,* 1977, *11,* 48–58.

Fromm, E. The Erich Fromm theory of aggression. *New York Times Magazine,* Feb. 27, 1972, p. 14.

Fuller, J. L., & Thompson, W. R. *Behavior genetics.* New York: Wiley, 1960.

Garcia, J., Ervin, F. R., Yorke, C. H., & Koelling, R. A. Conditioning with delayed vitamin injections. *Science,* 1967, *155,* 716–718.

Garcia, J., Hawkins, W. G., & Rusiniak, K. W. Behavioral regulation of the *milieu interne* in man and rat. *Science,* 1974, *185,* 824–831.

Gardner, R. W., Holzman, P. S., Klein, G. S., Linton, H., & Spence, D. P. Cognitive control. *Psychological Issues,* 1959, Monograph 4.

Garske, J. P. *The effects of in-role and out-of-role sex-typed behavior upon the attribution of personality traits.* Paper presented at the annual meeting of the Midwestern Psychological Association, Chicago, May 1974.

Garske, J. P. *Female performance as a function of sensitivity to rejection and male feedback.* Paper presented at the annual meeting of the Midwestern Psychological Association, Chicago, May 1975. (a)

Garske, J. P. Role variation as a determinant of attributed masculinity and femininity. *Journal of Psychology*, 1975, *91*, 31–37. (b)

Geen, R. G. Observing violence in the mass media: Implications of basic research. In R. G. Geen & E. O'Neal (Eds.), *Perspectives on aggression.* New York: Academic Press, 1976.

Geen, R. G., Stonner, D., & Shope, G. L. The facilitation of aggression by aggression: A study in response inhibition and disinhibition. *Journal of Personality and Social Psychology*, 1975, *31*, 721–726.

Gerbner, G. The television world. In R. K. Baker & S. J. Ball (Eds.), *Mass media and violence.* Staff report to the National Commission on the Causes and Prevention of Violence. Washington, D. C.: U. S. Government Printing Office, 1969.

Gergen, K. J. *The psychology of behavior exchange.* Reading, Mass.: Addison-Wesley, 1969.

Gergen, K. J., & Gergen, M. K. International assistance from a psychological perspective. *The Yearbook of International Affairs*, 1971, *25*, 87–103.

Gibson, W. E., Reid, L. D., Sakai, M., & Porter, P. B. Intracranial reinforcement compared with sugar-water reinforcement. *Science*, 1965, *148*, 1357–1359.

Gill, M. Topography and systems in psychoanalysis. *Psychological Issues* (No. 10). New York: International Universities Press, 1963.

Glass, D. G. Individual differences and the resolution of cognitive inconsistencies. In R. P. Abelson, E. Aronson, W. J. McGuire, T. M. Newcomb, M. J. Rosenberg, & P. H. Tannenbaum (Eds.), *Theories of cognitive consistency: A sourcebook.* Chicago: Rand McNally, 1968.

Goble, F. G. *The third force: The psychology of Abraham Maslow.* New York: Grossman, 1970.

Goethals, G. R., & Reckman, R. F. The perception of consistency in attitudes. *Journal of Experimental Social Psychology*, 1973, *9*, 491–501.

Goldstein, J. H., & Arms, R. L. Effects of observing athletic contests on hostility. *Sociometry*, 1971, *34*, 83–90.

Goodman, P. S., & Friedman, A. An examination of Adams' theory of inequity. *Administrative Science Quarterly*, 1971, *16*, 271–288.

Gore, P. M., & Rotter, J. B. A personality correlate of social action. *Journal of Personality*, 1963, *31*, 58–64.

Green, K. F., & Garcia, J. Recuperation from illness: Flavor enhancement for rats. *Science*, 1971, *173*, 749–751.

Greenberg, S. G. Changes in total amount of stage four sleep as a function of partial sleep deprivation. *Electroencephalography and Clinical Neurophysiology*, 1966, *20*, 523–526.

Greene, D., & Lepper, M. R. Effects of extrinsic rewards on children's subsequent intrinsic interest. *Child Development*, 1974, *45*, 1141–1145.

Greene, D., Sternberg, B., & Lepper, M. Overjustification in a token economy. *Journal of Personality and Social Psychology*, 1976, *34*, 1219–1234.

Greenwald, A. G. On the inconclusiveness of "crucial" cognitive tests of dissonance versus self-perception theories. *Journal of Experimental Social Psychology*, 1975, *11*, 490–499.

Grimes, J. W., & Allinsmith, W. Compulsivity, anxiety, and school achievement. *Merrill-Palmer Quarterly*, 1961, *7*, 247–272.

Grossman, M. I., Cummins, G. M., & Ivy, A. C. The effect of insulin on food intake after vagotomy and sympathectomy. *American Journal of Physiology*, 1947, *149*, 100–102.

Grossman, M. I., & Stein, I. F. Jr. Vagotomy and the hunger-producing action of insulin in man. *Journal of Applied Physiology*, 1948, *1*, 263–269.

Grossman, S. P. Direct adrenergic and cholinergic stimulation of hypothalamic mechanisms. *American Journal of Physiology,* 1962, *202,* 872–882.

Grossman, S. P. The VMH: A center for affective reaction, satiety, or both? *Physiology and Behavior,* 1966, *1,* 1–10.

Grossman, S. P. *A textbook of physiological psychology.* New York: Wiley, 1967.

Grossman, S. P., & Grossman, L. Food and water intake following lesions or electrical stimulation of the amygdala. *American Journal of Physiology,* 1963, *205,* 761–765.

Grossman, S. P., & Grossman, L. Persisting deficits in rats "recovered" from transections of the fibers which enter or leave the hypothalamus laterally. *Journal of Comparative and Physiological Psychology,* 1973, *85,* 515–527.

Guthrie, E. R. *The psychology of learning* (Rev. ed.). New York: Harper & Row, 1952.

Gwinn, G. T. Effect of punishment on acts motivated by fear. *Journal of Comparative and Physiological Psychology,* 1949, *39,* 260–269.

Haber, R. N. Discrepancy from adaptation level as a source of affect. *Journal of Experimental Psychology,* 1958, *56,* 370–375.

Haggard, E. A., As, A., & Borgen, C. M. Social isolates and urbanites in perceptual isolation. *Journal of Abnormal Psychology,* 1970, *76,* 1–9.

Hall, D. T., & Nougaim, K. E. An examination of Maslow's need hierarchy in an organizational setting. *Organizational Behavior and Human Performance,* 1968, *3,* 12–35.

Hall, J., & Williams, M. *Work motivation inventory.* Conroe, Texas: Teleometric, 1973.

Hall, M. H. A conversation with Abraham H. Maslow. *Psychology Today,* July 1968.

Hamner, W. C., & Foster, L. W. Are intrinsic and extrinsic rewards additive? A test of Deci's cognitive evaluation theory of task motivation. *Organizational Behavior and Human Performance,* 1975, *14,* 398–415.

Haner, C. F., & Brown, J. S. Clarification of the instigation to action concept in the frustration-aggression hypothesis. *Journal of Abnormal and Social Psychology,* 1955, *51,* 204–206.

Harackiewicz, J. M. The effects of reward contingency and performance feedback on intrinsic motivation. *Journal of Personality and Social Psychology,* 1979, *37,* 1352–1363.

Harlow, H. F. Sexual behavior in the rhesus monkey. In F. A. Beach (Ed.), *Sex and behavior.* New York: Wiley, 1965.

Harlow, H. F., Gluck, J. P., & Suomi, S. P. Generalization of behavioral data between nonhuman and human animals. *American Psychologist,* 1972, *27,* 709–716.

Harlow, H. F., Harlow, M. K., & Meyer, D. R. Learning motivated by a manipulation drive. *Journal of Experimental Psychology,* 1950, *40,* 228–234.

Harnly, M. H. Flight capacity in relation to phenotypic and genotypic variations in the wings of *Drosophila melanogaster. Journal of Experimental Zoology,* 1941, *88,* 263–273.

Harris, G. W., & Michael, R. P. The activation of sexual behaviour by hypothalamic implants of aestrogen. *Journal of Physiology,* 1964, *171,* 275–301.

Harris, L. J., Clay, J., Hargreaves, F. J., & Ward, A. Appetite and choice of diet: The ability of the vitamin B-deficient rat to discriminate between diets containing and lacking the vitamin. *Proceedings of the Royal Society, Series B,* 1933, *13,* 161–190.

Hart, J. T., & Tomlinson, T. M. *New directions in client-centered therapy.* Boston: Houghton Mifflin, 1970.

Hartmann, H. Comments on the psychoanalytic theory of the ego. *Psychoanalytic Study of the Child,* 1950, *5,* 74–96.

Hartmann, H. The mutual influences in the development of the ego and id. *Psychoanalytic Study of the Child,* 1952, *7,* 9–30.

Hartmann, H. *Ego psychology and the problem of adaptation.* New York: International Universities Press, 1958. Pp. 362–396. (Originally published, 1939.)

Hebb, D. O. *The organization of behavior.* New York: Wiley, 1949.

Heckhausen, H. *The anatomy of achievement motivation.* New York: Academic Press, 1967.

Heckhausen, H. Achievement motive research: Current problems and some contributions toward a general theory of motivation. In W. J. Arnold (Ed.), *Nebraska Symposium on Motivation* (Vol. 16). Lincoln: University of Nebraska Press, 1968.

Heider, F. Social perception and phenomenal causality. *Psychological Review,* 1944, *51,* 358–374.

Heider, F. Attitudes and cognitive organization. *Journal of Psychology,* 1946, *21,* 107–112.

Heider, F. *The psychology of interpersonal relations.* New York: Wiley, 1958.

Heider, F. The Gestalt theory of motivation. In M. R. Jones (Ed.), *Nebraska Symposium on Motivation* (Vol. 8). Lincoln: University of Nebraska Press, 1960.

Heller, C. G., & Maddock, W. O. The clinical uses of testosterone in the male. *Vitamins and Hormones,* 1947, *5,* 393–423.

Henry, J. P., & Pearce, J. W. The possible role of cardiac atrial stretch receptors in the induction of changes in urine flow. *Journal of Physiology,* 1956, *131,* 572–585.

Herman, C. P. External and internal cues as determinants of the smoking behavior of light and heavy smokers. *Journal of Personality and Social Psychology,* 1974, *30,* 664–672.

Herrnstein, R. J. Method and theory in the study of avoidance. *Psychological Review,* 1969, *76,* 49–69.

Herrnstein, R. J., & Hineline, P. N. Negative reinforcement as shock-frequency reduction. *Journal of the Experimental Analysis of Behavior,* 1966, *9,* 421–430.

Hess, E. H. The relationship between imprinting and motivation. In M. R. Jones (Ed.), *Nebraska Symposium on Motivation* (Vol. 7). Lincoln: University of Nebraska Press, 1959.

Hetherington, A. W., & Ranson, S. W. Hypothalamic lesions and adiposity in the rat. *Anatomical Record,* 1940, *78,* 149–172.

Hewett, F. M., Taylor, F. D., & Artuso, A. A. The Santa Monica project: Evaluation of an engineered classroom design with emotionally disturbed children. *Exceptional Children,* 1969, *35,* 523–529.

Hilgard, E. R., & Bower, G. H. *Theories of learning.* New York: Appleton-Century-Crofts, 1966.

Hill, W. F. Comments on Taylor's "Drive theory and manifest anxiety." *Psychological Bulletin,* 1957, *54,* 490–493.

Hineline, P. N. Negative reinforcement without shock reduction. *Journal of the Experimental Analysis of Behavior,* 1970, *14,* 259–268.

Hoffman, H., & Ratner, A. A reinforcement model of imprinting: Implications for socialization in monkeys and men. *Psychological Review,* 1973, *80,* 527–544.

Hoffman, L. W. Fear of success in males and females: 1965 and 1972. *Journal of Consulting and Clinical Psychology*, 1974, *42*, 353–358.

Hokanson, J. E., & Edelman, R. Effects of three social responses on vascular processes. *Journal of Personality and Social Psychology*, 1966, *3*, 442–447.

Hokanson, J. E., & Shetler, S. The effect of overt aggression on physiological arousal. *Journal of Abnormal and Social Psychology*, 1961, *63*, 446–448.

Hokanson, J. E., Willers, K. R., & Koropsak, E. The modification of autonomic responses during aggressive interchanges. *Journal of Personality*, 1968, *36*, 386–404.

Holmes, D. S. Repression or interference: A further investigation. *Journal of Personality and Social Psychology*, 1972, *22*, 163–170.

Holmes, D. S. Investigations of repression: Differential recall of material experimentally or naturally associated with ego threat. *Psychological Bulletin*, 1974, *81*, 632–653.

Holmes, D. S., & Schallow, J. R. Reduced recall after ego threat: Repression or response competition? *Journal of Personality and Social Psychology*, 1969, *13*, 145–152.

Holt, R. R. Two influences upon Freud's scientific thought: A fragment of intellectual biography. In R. W. White (Ed.), *The study of lives: Essays on personality in honor of Henry A. Murray.* New York: Atherton, 1963. Pp. 364–387.

Holt, R. R. A review of some of Freud's biological assumptions and their influence on his theories. In N. S. Greenfield & W. C. Lewis (Eds.), *Psychoanalysis and current biological thought.* Madison: University of Wisconsin Press, 1965. Pp. 93–124.

Holt, R. R. Beyond vitalism and mechanism: Freud's concept of psychic energy. In B. Wolman (Ed.), *Historical roots of contemporary psychology.* New York: Harper & Row, 1966.

Holt, R. R. The development of primary process, a structural view. In R. R. Holt (Ed.), Motives and thought: Psychoanalytic essays in memory of David Rapaport. *Psychological Issues*, 1967, *5*, No. 2–3 (Monograph No. 18–19), 345–383.

Holzman, P. S. *Psychoanalysis and psychopathology.* New York: McGraw-Hill, 1970.

Horne, J. A. Recovery sleep following different visual conditions during total sleep deprivation in man. *Biological Psychology*, 1976, *4*, 107–118.

Horne, J. A. Restitution and human sleep: A critical review. *Physiological Psychology*, 1979, *7*, 115–125.

Horne, J. A., & Porter, J. M. Time of day effects with standardized exercise upon subsequent sleep. *Electroencephalography and Clinical Neurophysiology*, 1976, *40*, 178–184.

Horner, M. S. *Sex differences in achievement motivation and performance in competitive and noncompetitive situations.* Unpublished doctoral dissertation, University of Michigan, 1968.

Horner, M. S. Toward an understanding of achievement-related conflicts in women. *Journal of Social Issues*, 1972, *28*, 157–175.

Horner, M. S., Tresemer, D. W., Berens, A. E., & Watson, R. I. Jr. Scoring manual for an empirically derived scoring system for motive to avoid success. Unpublished manuscript, Harvard University, 1973.

Hull, C. L. The goal gradient hypothesis and maze learning. *Psychological Review*, 1932, *39*, 25–43.

Hull, C. L. *Principles of behavior.* New York: Appleton-Century-Crofts, 1943.

Hull, C. L. *A behavior system.* New Haven, Conn.: Yale University Press, 1952.

Hunt, J. McV. Intrinsic motivation and its role in psychological development. In D. Levine (Ed.), *Nebraska Symposium on Motivation* (Vol. 13). Lincoln: University of Nebraska Press, 1965.

Hutt, S., & Hutt, C. Stereotypy, arousal, and autism. *Human Development,* 1968, *11,* 277–284.

Ickes, W. J., & Layden, M. A. Attributional styles. In J. H. Harvey, W. J. Ickes, & R. F. Kidd (Eds.), *New directions in attribution research* (Vol. 2). Hillsdale, N. J.: Erlbaum, 1978.

Isaacson, R. L. Relation between n achievement, test anxiety, and curricular choices. *Journal of Abnormal and Social Psychology,* 1964, *68,* 447–452.

Ishikawa, T., Koizumi, K., & Brooks, C. M. Activity of the supraoptic neurons of the hypothalamus. *Neurology,* 1966, *16,* 101–106.

Izard, C. E. Personality similarity, positive affect, and interpersonal attraction. *Journal of Abnormal and Social Psychology,* 1960, *61,* 484–485.

Jackaway, R., & Teevan, R. Fear of failure and fear of success: Two dimensions of the same motive. *Sex Roles,* 1976, *2,* 283–294.

James, W. *Principles of psychology.* New York: Henry Holt, 1890.

Janis, I. L. Personality correlates of susceptibility to persuasion. *Journal of Personality,* 1954, *22,* 504–518.

Janis, I. L. Motivational factors in the resolution of decisional conflicts. In M. R. Jones (Ed.), *Nebraska Symposium on Motivation* (Vol. 7). Lincoln: University of Nebraska Press, 1959.

Janis, I. L., & Gilmore, J. B. The influence of incentive conditions on the success of role-playing in modifying attitudes. *Journal of Personality and Social Psychology,* 1965, *1,* 17–27.

Jellison, J. M., Jackson-White, R., Bruder, R. A., & Martyna, W. Achievement behavior: A situational interpretation. *Sex Roles,* 1975, *1,* 369–384.

Jenkins, C. D., Rosenman, R. H., & Zyzanski, S. J. Prediction of clinical coronary heart disease by a test for the coronary-prone behavior pattern. *New England Journal of Medicine,* 1974, *290,* 1271–1275.

Jensen, A. R. How much can we boost IQ and scholastic achievement? *Harvard Educational Review,* 1969, *39,* 1–123.

Johnson, S. M., Bolstad, O. D., & Lobitz, G. K. Generalization and contrast phenomena in behavior modification with children. In E. J. Marsh, L. C. Handy, & L. A. Hamerlynck (Eds.), *Behavior modification and families.* New York: Brunner/Mazel, 1976.

Jones, E. *The life and work of Sigmund Freud* (Vol. 1). New York: Basic Books, 1953.

Jones, E. E., & Davis, K. E. From acts to dispositions: The attribution process in person perception. In L. Berkowitz (Ed.), *Advances in experimental social psychology* (Vol. 2). New York: Academic Press, 1965.

Jones, E. E., Davis, K. E., & Gergen, K. J. Role playing variations and their informational value for person perception. *Journal of Abnormal and Social Psychology,* 1961, *63,* 302–310.

Jones, E. E., & Harris, V. A. The attribution of attitudes. *Journal of Experimental Social Psychology,* 1967, *3,* 1–24.

Jones, E. E., & Nisbett, R. E. *The actor and the observer: Divergent perceptions of the causes of behavior.* Morristown, N. J.: General Learning Press, 1971.

Jones, R. A. *Self-fulfilling prophecies.* Hillsdale, N. J.: Erlbaum, 1977.

Jordan, N. Behavioral forces that are a function of attitudes and of cognitive organization. *Human Relations,* 1953, *6,* 273–287.

Jouvet, M. Neurophysiology of the states of sleep. *Psychological Review,* 1967, *47,* 117–177.

Jung, C. G. *Memories, dreams, reflections.* New York: Pantheon, 1963.

Juran, S. A measure of stereotyping in fear-of-success cues. *Sex Roles,* 1979, *5,* 287–298.

Kalat, J. W., & Rozin, P. Specific hungers and poison avoidance as adaptive specializations of learning. *Psychological Review,* 1971, *78,* 459–486.

Karabenick, S. A. Valence of success and failure as a function of achievement motives and locus of control. *Journal of Personality and Social Psychology,* 1972, *21,* 101–110.

Karabenick, S. A., & Marshall, J. M. Performances of females as a function of fear of success, fear of failure, type of opponent, and performance-contingent feedback. *Journal of Personality,* 1974, *42,* 220–237.

Karli, P., Vergnes, M., & Didiergeorges, F. Rat-mouse interspecific aggressive behavior and its manipulation by brain ablation and by brain stimulation. In S. Garattini & E. Sigg (Eds.), *Aggressive behavior.* New York: Wiley, 1969.

Karmel, B. Z. The effect of age, complexity, and amount of contour on pattern preference in human infants. *Journal of Experimental Child Psychology,* 1969, *7,* 339–354.

Karniol, R., & Ross, M. The development of causal attributions in social perception. *Journal of Personality and Social Psychology,* 1976, *34,* 455–464.

Karniol, R., & Ross, M. The effect of performance relevant and performance irrelevant rewards on children's intrinsic motivation. *Child Development,* 1977, *48,* 482–487.

Katz, I. The socialization of academic motivation in minority group children. In D. Levine (Ed.), *Nebraska Symposium on Motivation* (Vol. 15). Lincoln: University of Nebraska Press, 1967.

Kazdin, A. E., & Bootzin, R. R. The token economy: An evaluative review. *Journal of Applied Behavior Analysis,* 1972, *5,* 343–372.

Keating, C. H., Jr. Minority report. In *Technical Report of the Commission on Obscenity and Pornography.* Washington, D. C.: U. S. Government Printing Office, 1970. *New York Times* edition published by Bantam Books.

Keeley, S. M., Shemberg, K. M., & Carbonell, S. Operant clinical intervention: Behavior management or beyond. Where are the data? *Behavior Therapy,* 1976, *7,* 292–305.

Kelley, H. H. Attribution theory in social psychology. In D. Levine (Ed.), *Nebraska Symposium on Motivation* (Vol. 15). Lincoln: University of Nebraska Press, 1967.

Kelley, H. H. *Attribution in social interaction.* Morristown, N. J.: General Learning Press, 1971.

Kelley, H. H. *Causal schemata and the attribution process.* Morristown, N. J.: General Learning Press, 1972.

Kelley, H. H. The processes of causal attribution. *American Psychologist,* 1973, *28,* 107–128.

Kellogg, R., & Baron, R. S. Attribution theory, insomnia, and the reverse placebo effect: A reversal of Storms and Nisbett's findings. *Journal of Personality and Social Psychology,* 1975, *32,* 231–236.

Kennedy, G. C. The role of depot fat in the hypothalamic control of food intake in the rat. *Proceedings of the Royal Society,* 1952–1953, *B 140,* 578–592.

Kenrick, D. T., & Cialdini, R. B. Romantic attraction: Misattribution versus reinforcement explanations. *Journal of Personality and Social Psychol-*

*ogy,* 1977, *35,* 381–391.

Kiesler, C. A., Nisbett, R. E., & Zanna, M. P. On inferring one's beliefs from one's behavior. *Journal of Personality and Social Psychology,* 1969, *11,* 321–327.

Kiesler, C. A., & Sakamura, J. A test of a model for commitment. *Journal of Personality and Social Psychology,* 1966, *3,* 349–353.

Kilpatrick-Tabak, B., & Roth, S. An attempt to reverse performance deficits associated with depression and experimentally induced helplessness. *Journal of Abnormal Psychology,* 1978, *87,* 21–31.

Kim, Y. K., & Umbach, W. Combined stereotaxic lesions for treatment of behavior disorders and severe pain. Paper presented at Third World Congress of Psychosurgery, Cambridge, England, August 1972. Cited in E. Valenstein, *Brain control.* New York: Wiley, 1973.

King, M. G. Stimulus generalizations of conditioned fear in rats over time: Olfactory cues and adrenal activity. *Journal of Comparative and Physiological Psychology,* 1969, *69,* 590–600.

Kleck, R. E., & Wheaton, J. Dogmatism and responses to opinion consistent and opinion inconsistent information. *Journal of Personality and Social Psychology,* 1967, *5,* 249–253.

Klein, D. C., Fencil-Morse, E., & Seligman, M. E. P. Learned helplessness, depression, and the attribution of failure. *Journal of Personality and Social Psychology,* 1976, *33,* 508–516.

Klein, D. C., & Seligman, M. E. P. Reversal of performance deficits in learned helplessness and depression. *Journal of Abnormal Psychology,* 1976, *85,* 11–26.

Klein, G. S. Peremptory ideation: Structure and force in motivated ideas. In R. R. Holt (Ed.), Motives and thought: Psychoanalytic essays in memory of David Rapaport. *Psychological Issues,* 1967, *5,* No. 2–3 (Monograph No. 18–19), 80–130.

Klein, G. S. Freud's two theories of sexuality. In L. Breger (Ed.), *Clinical cognitive psychology: Models and integrations.* Englewood Cliffs, N. J.: Prentice-Hall, 1969. Pp. 136–181.

Klein, G. S. *Perception, motives, and personality.* New York: Knopf, 1970.

Klinger, E. Fantasy need achievement as a motivational construct. *Psychological Bulletin,* 1966, *66,* 291–308.

Koch, S. Behavior as "intrinsically" regulated: Work notes toward a pretheory of phenomena called "motivational." In M. R. Jones (Ed.), *Nebraska Symposium on Motivation* (Vol. 4). Lincoln: University of Nebraska Press, 1956.

Koffka, K. *The growth of the mind* [R. M. Ogden, trans.]. London: Kegan Paul, Trench, Trubner & Co., 1924.

Köhler, W. *Gestalt psychology.* New York: Liveright, 1929.

Kohn, M. Satiation of hunger from food injected directly into the stomach versus food ingested by mouth. *Journal of Comparative and Physiological Psychology,* 1951, *44,* 412–422.

Konecni, V. J., Crozier, J. B., & Doob, A. N. Anger and expression of aggression: Effects on aesthetic preference. *Scientific Aesthetics,* 1976, *1,* 47–55.

Korman, A. K. Toward an hypothesis of work behavior. *Journal of Applied Psychology,* 1970, *54,* 31–41.

Krebs, A. M. Two determinants of conformity: Age of independence training and n achievement. *Journal of Abnormal and Social Psychology,* 1958, *56,* 130–131.

Krieckhaus, E. E. Innate recognition aids rats in sodium regulation. *Journal of Comparative and Physiological Psychology,* 1970, *73,* 117–122.

Kris, E. *Psychoanalytic explorations in art.* New York: International Universities Press, 1952.

Kuhl, J., & Blankenship, V. Behavioral change in a constant environment: Shift to more difficult tasks with constant probability of success. *Journal of Personality and Social Psychology,* 1979, *37,* 549–561.

Kuhn, T. S. *The structure of scientific revolutions.* Chicago: University of Chicago Press, 1962.

Kuiper, N. A. Depression and causal attributions for success and failure. *Journal of Personality and Social Psychology,* 1978, *36,* 236–246.

Kukla, A. Foundations of an attributional theory of performance. *Psychological Review,* 1972, *79,* 454–470.

Kukla, A. Performance as a function of resultant achievement motivation (perceived ability) and perceived difficulty. *Journal of Research in Personality,* 1974, *7,* 374–383.

Kuo, Z. Y. How are instincts acquired? *Psychological Review,* 1922, *29,* 344–365.

Kuo, Z. Y. Genesis of the cat's responses toward the rat. *Journal of Comparative Physiology,* 1930, *11,* 1–36.

Laborit, H. Correlations between protein and serotonin synthesis during various activities of the central nervous system. *Research Communications in Chemical Pathology and Pharmacology,* 1972, *3,* 51–81.

Langer, E. J., & Rodin, J. The effects of choice and enhanced personal responsibility for the aged: A field experiment in an institutional setting. *Journal of Personality and Social Psychology,* 1976, *34,* 191–198.

Lawler, E. E., & O'Gara, P. W. Effects of inequity produced by underpayment on work output, work quality, and attitudes toward work. *Journal of Applied Psychology,* 1967, *51,* 39–45.

Lawler, E. E., & Suttle, J. L. A causal correlation test of the need hierarchy concept. *Organizational Behavior and Human Performance,* 1972, *7,* 265–287.

Lazar, I., Hubbell, V., Murray, H., Rosche, M., & Royce, J. *The persistence of preschool effects: A long-term follow-up of fourteen infant and preschool experiments.* (Summary report of the Consortium on Developmental Continuity, Education Commission of the States, Grant 18-76-07843). Washington, D. C.: U. S. Department of Health, Education and Welfare, 1977.

Lefkowitz, M. M., Eron, L. D., Walder, L. O., & Huesmann, L. R. Television violence and child aggression: A followup study. In *Technical Report to the Surgeon General's Scientific Advisory Commission* (Vol. 3). 1972.

Lehrman, D. S. A critique of Konrad Lorenz's theory of instinctive behavior. *Quarterly Review of Biology,* 1953, *28,* 337–363.

Lehrman, D. S. Comparative physiology (behavior). *Annual Review of Physiology,* 1956, *18,* 527–542.

Leibowitz, S. F. Reciprocal hunger-regulating circuits involving alpha- and beta-adrenergic receptors located, respectively, in the ventromedial and lateral hypothalamus. *Proceedings of the National Academy of Science,* 1970, *67,* 1063–1070.

Lepper, M. R., & Greene, D. Turning work into play: Effects of adult surveillance and extrinsic rewards on children's intrinsic motivation. *Journal of Personality and Social Psychology,* 1975, *31,* 479–486.

Lepper, M. R., & Greene, D. Divergent approaches to the study of rewards. In M. R. Lepper & D. Greene (Eds.), *The hidden costs of reward.* Hillsdale, N. J.: Erlbaum, 1978.

Lepper, M. R., Greene, D., & Nisbett, R. E. Undermining children's intrinsic interest with extrinsic rewards: A test of the "overjustification" hypothesis. *Journal of Personality and Social Psychology,* 1973, *28,* 129–137.

Lerner, M. J., & Simmons, C. H. Observer's reaction to the "innocent victim": Compassion or rejection? *Journal of Personality and Social Psychology,* 1966, *4,* 203–210.

Leuba, C. Toward some integration of learning theories: The concept of optimal stimulation. *Psychological Reports,* 1955, *1,* 27–33.

Levine, S., & Brush, F. R. Adrenocortical activity and avoidance learning as a function of time after avoidance training. *Physiology and Behavior,* 1967, *2,* 385–388.

Levy, P., Gooch, S., & Kellmer-Pringle, M. L. A longitudinal study of the relationship between anxiety and streaming in a progressive and a traditional junior school. *British Journal of Educational Psychology,* 1969, *39,* 166–173.

Lewin, K. *A dynamic theory of personality.* New York: McGraw-Hill, 1935.

Lewin, K. *The conceptual representation and the measurement of psychological forces.* Durham, N. C.: Duke University Press, 1938.

Lewin, K. *Field theory in social science.* New York: Harper & Row, 1951.

Lewin, K., Dembo, T., Festinger, L., & Sears, P. Level of aspiration. In J. McV. Hunt (Ed.), *Personality and the behavioral disorders* (Vol. 1). New York: Ronald Press, 1944. Pp. 333–378.

Liebert, R. M., & Baron, R. A. Some immediate effects of televised violence on children's behavior. *Developmental Psychology,* 1972. *6,* 469–475.

Linder, D., Cooper, J., & Jones, E. Decision freedom as a determinant of the role of incentive magnitude in attitude change. *Journal of Personality and Social Psychology,* 1967, *6,* 245–254.

Littman, R. A. Motives, history, and causes. In M. R. Jones (Ed.), *Nebraska Symposium on Motivation* (Vol. 6). Lincoln: University of Nebraska Press, 1958.

Litwin, G. H. *Motives and expectancies as determinants of preference for degrees of risk.* Unpublished honors thesis, University of Michigan, 1958.

Loevinger, J. The meaning and measurement of ego development. *American Psychologist,* 1966, *21,* 195–206.

Loevinger, J. Theories of ego development. In L. Breger (Ed.), *Clinical-cognitive psychology: Models and integrations.* Englewood Cliffs, N. J.: Prentice-Hall, 1969. Pp. 83–135.

Lord, R. G., & Hohenfeld, J. A. Longitudinal field assessment of equity effects on the performance of major league baseball players. *Journal of Applied Psychology,* 1979, *64,* 19–26.

Lorenz, K. *King Solomon's ring.* New York: T. Y. Crowell, 1952.

Lorenz, K. *On aggression* [M. K. Wilson, trans.]. New York: Harbrace, 1966.

Loveland, K. K., & Olley, J. G. The effect of external reward on interest and quality of task performance in children of high and low intrinsic motivation. *Child Development,* 1979, *50,* 1207–1210.

Lowell, E. L. The effect of need for achievement on the learning and speed of performance. *Journal of Psychology,* 1952, *33,* 31–40.

Lucas, J. D. The interactive effects of anxiety failure and interserial duplication. *American Journal of Psychology,* 1952, *65,* 59–66.

Maddi, S. R., & Costa, P. T. *Humanism in personology.* Chicago: Aldine-Atherton, 1972.

Madison, P. *Freud's concept of repression and defense*. Minneapolis: University of Minnesota Press, 1961.

Mahone, C. H. Fear of failure and unrealistic vocational aspiration. *Journal of Abnormal and Social Psychology*, 1960, *60*, 253–261.

Maier, N. R. F. An aspect of human reasoning. *British Journal of Psychology*, 1933, *24*, 144–155.

Maier, S. F., Seligman, M. E. P., & Solomon, R. L. Pavlovian fear conditioning and learned helplessness. In B. A. Campbell & R. M. Church (Eds.), *Punishment*. New York: Appleton-Century-Crofts, 1969.

Makosky, V. P. Sex-role compatibility of task and of competitor, and fear of success as variables affecting women's performance. *Sex Roles*, 1976, *2*, 237–248.

Malmo, R. B. Activation: A neuropsychological dimension. *Psychological Review*, 1959, *66*, 367–386.

Mann, J., Sidman, J., & Starr, S. Effects of erotic films on sexual behaviors of married couples. In *Technical Report of the Commission on Obscenity and Pornography* (Vol. 8). Washington, D. C.: U. S. Government Printing Office, 1970.

Mansson, H. H. The relation of dissonance reduction to cognitive, perceptual, consummatory, and learning measures of thirst. In P. Zimbardo (Ed.), *The cognitive control of motivation*. Glenview, Ill.: Scott, Foresman, 1969. Pp. 78–97.

Marrow, A. J. Goal tension and recall: II. *Journal of General Psychology*, 1938, *19*, 37–64.

Marshall, G. D., & Zimbardo, P. G. Affective consequences of inadequately explained physiological arousal. *Journal of Personality and Social Psychology*, 1979, *37*, 970–988.

Maslach, C. Negative emotional biasing of unexplained arousal. *Journal of Personality and Social Psychology*, 1979, *37*, 953–969.

Maslow, A. H. *Motivation and personality*. New York: Harper & Row, 1954.

Maslow, A. H. *Eupsychian management*. Homewood, Ill.: Richard D. Irwin, 1965.

Maslow, A. H. *Toward a psychology of being* (2nd ed.). New York: Van Nostrand Reinhold, 1968.

Maslow, A. H. *Motivation and personality* (2nd ed.). New York: Harper & Row, 1970.

Maslow, A. H. *The farther reaches of human nature*. New York: Viking, 1971.

Mason, J. W., Maher, J. T., Hartley, L. H., Mougey, E., Perlow, M. J., & Jones, L. G. Selectivity of corticosteroid and catecholamine responses to various natural stimuli. In G. Serban (Ed.), *Psychopathology of human adaptation*. New York: Plenum, 1976.

Mason, W. A. The effects of social restriction on the behavior of rhesus monkeys: I. Free social behavior. *Journal of Comparative and Physiological Psychology*, 1960, *53*, 582–589.

Masters, J. Social comparison by young children. *Young Children*, 1971, *27*, 37–60.

Masters, J. Effects of success, failure, and reward outcome upon contingent and non-contingent self-reinforcement. *Developmental Psychology*, 1972, *7*, 110–117.

Masters, W. H., & Johnson, V. E. *Human sexual response*. Boston: Little, Brown, 1966.

Matthews, K. A., & Brunson, B. I. Allocation of attention and the type A coronary-prone behavior pattern. *Journal of Personality and Social Psychology*, 1979, *37*, 2081–2090.

Mayer, A. *Essai sur la soif: Les causes et son mecanisme.* Paris: Jouve et Boyer, 1900.

Mayer, J. Regulation of energy intake and the body weight: The glucostatic theory and the lipostatic hypothesis. *Annals of the New York Academy of Science*, 1955, *63*, 15–43.

McCandless, B., Roberts, A., & Starnes, T. Teachers' marks, achievement test scores, and aptitude relations with respect to social class, race, and sex. *Journal of Educational Psychology*, 1972, *63*, 153–159.

McClelland, D. C. *The achieving society.* Princeton: D. Van Nostrand, 1961.

McClelland, D. C. Managing motivation to expand human freedom. *American Psychologist*, 1978, *33*, 201–210.

McClelland, D. C., Atkinson, J. W., Clark, R. W., & Lowell, E. L. *The achievement motive.* New York: Appleton-Century-Crofts, 1953.

McClelland, D. C., & Winter, D. G. *Motivating economic achievement.* New York: Free Press, 1969.

McDougall, W. *An introduction to social psychology.* London: Methuen, 1908.

McGraw, K. O. The detrimental effects of reward on performance: A literature review and a prediction model. In M. R. Lepper & D. Greene (Eds.), *The hidden costs of reward.* Hillsdale, N. J.: Erlbaum, 1978.

McLoyd, V. C. The effects of extrinsic rewards of differential value on high and low intrinsic interest. *Child Development*, 1979, *50*, 1010–1019.

Meddis, R. *The sleep instinct.* London: Routledge & Kegan Paul, 1977.

Meichenbaum, D. H., Bowers, K. S., & Ross, R. R. Modification of classroom behavior of institutionalized female adolescent offenders. *Behaviour Research and Therapy*, 1968, *6*, 343–353.

Merrill, R. The effect of pre-experimental and experimental anxiety on recall efficiency. *Journal of Experimental Psychology*, 1954, *48*, 167–172.

Meryman, J. J. *Magnitude of startle response as a function of hunger and fear.* Unpublished master's thesis, State University of Iowa, 1952. Cited by Bolles (1967, p. 184).

Meyer, L. B. *Music, the arts, and ideas.* Chicago: University of Chicago Press, 1967.

Meyer, W.-U. *Selbstverantworklichkeit und Leistungsmotiv.* Unpublished doctoral dissertation, Ruhr Universität, Bochum, Germany, 1970.

Meyer, W.-U. *Leistungsmotiv und Ursachenerklärung von Erfolg und Misserfolg.* Stuttgart: Klett Verlag, 1973.

Milgram, S. The experience of living in cities. *Science*, 1970, *167*, 1461–1468.

Milgram, S., & Shotland, R. L. *Television and antisocial behavior.* New York: Academic Press, 1973.

Miller, D. T. Ego involvement and attributions for success and failure. *Journal of Personality and Social Psychology*, 1976, *34*, 901–906.

Miller, N. E. Experimental studies of conflict. In J. McV. Hunt (Ed.), *Personality and the behavioral disorders* (Vol. 1). New York: Ronald Press, 1944. Pp. 431–465.

Miller, N. E. Studies of fear as an acquirable drive: I. Fear as motivation and fear-reduction as reinforcement in the learning of new responses. *Journal of Experimental Psychology*, 1948, *38*, 89–101.

Miller, N. E., & Bugelski, R. Minor studies in aggression: The influence of frustrations imposed by the in-group on attitudes expressed toward out-groups. *Journal of Psychology,* 1948, *25,* 439–442.

Miller, N. E., & Dollard, J. *Social learning and imitation.* New Haven, Conn.: Yale University Press, 1941.

Miller, N. E., & Kraeling, D. Displacement: Greater generalization of approach than avoidance in a generalized approach-avoidance conflict. *Journal of Experimental Psychology,* 1952, *43,* 217–221.

Miller, R. L., Brickman, P., & Bolen, D. Attribution versus persuasion as a means of modifying behavior. *Journal of Personality and Social Psychology,* 1975, *31,* 430–441.

Miller, W. R., & Seligman, M. E. P. Depression and the perception of reinforcement. *Journal of Abnormal Psychology,* 1973, *82,* 62–73.

Milner, P. M. *Physiological psychology.* New York: Holt, Rinehart & Winston, 1970.

Mischel, W. On the empirical dilemmas of psychodynamic approaches: Issues and alternatives. *Journal of Abnormal Psychology,* 1973, *82,* 335–344.

Misiak, H., & Sexton, V. S. *Phenomenological, existential, and humanistic psychologies: A historical survey.* New York: Grune & Stratton, 1973.

Mitchell, K. M., Bozarth, J. D., & Krauft, C. C. A reappraisal of the therapeutic effectiveness of accurate empathy, nonpossessive warmth, and genuineness. In A. S. Gurman & A. M. Razin, *Effective psychotherapy: A handbook of research.* Oxford: Pergamon Press, 1979. Pp. 482–502.

Mitchell, V. F., & Moudgill, P. Measurement of Maslow's need hierarchy. *Organizational Behavior and Human Performance,* 1976, *16,* 334–349.

Mogenson, G. An attempt to establish secondary reinforcement with rewarding brain stimulation. *Psychological Reports,* 1965, *16,* 163–167.

Monahan, L., Kuhn, D., & Shaver, P. Intrapsychic versus cultural explanations of the "fear of success" motive. *Journal of Personality and Social Psychology,* 1974, *29,* 60–64.

Money, J. Components of eroticism in man: I. The hormones in relation to sexual morphology and sexual desire. *Journal of Nervous and Mental Disease,* 1961, *132,* 239–248.

Money, J. Prenatal and pubertal influence of androgen on behavior: Human clinical syndromes. In M. Sandler & G. L. Gessa (Eds.), *Sexual behavior: Pharmacology and biochemistry.* New York: Raven Press, 1975.

Montanelli, D. S., & Hill, K. T. Children's achievement expectations and performance as a function of two consecutive reinforcement experiences, sex of subject, and sex of experimenter. *Journal of Personality and Social Psychology,* 1969, *13,* 115–128.

Moore, D. J., & Shiek, D. A. Toward a theory of early infantile autism. *Psychological Review,* 1971, *78,* 451–456.

Morgan, C. T., & Morgan, J. T. Studies in hunger: II. The relation of gastric denervation and dietary sugar to the effect of insulin upon food intake in the rat. *Journal of Genetic Psychology,* 1940, *57,* 153–163.

Morgan, S. W., & Mausner, B. Behavioral and fantasied successes in men and women. *Journal of Personality,* 1973, *41,* 457–470.

Morris, J. L. Propensity for risk taking as a determinant of vocational choice: An extension of the theory of achievement motivation. *Journal of Personality and Social Psychology,* 1966, *3,* 328–335.

Morrissette, J. O. An experimental study of the theory of structural balance. *Human Relations,* 1958, *11,* 239–254.

Moruzzi, G., & Magoun, H. W. Brain stem reticular formation and activation of the EEG. *Electroencephalography and Clinical Neurophysiology,* 1949, *1,* 455–473.

Mosher, D. L. Psychological reactions to pornographic films. In *Technical Report of the Commission on Obscenity and Pornography* (Vol. 8). Washington, D. C.: U. S. Government Printing Office, 1970.

Mosher, D. L. Pornographic films, male verbal aggression against women, and guilt. In *Technical Report of the Commission on Obscenity and Pornography* (Vol. 8). Washington, D. C.: U. S. Government Printing Office, 1971. (a)

Mosher, D. L. Psychological reactions to pornographic films. In *Technical Report of the Presidential Commission on Obscenity and Pornography* (Vol. 8). Washington, D. C.: U. S. Government Printing Office, 1971. (b)

Moss, H. A., & Kagan, J. Stability of achievement and recognition-seeking behaviors from early childhood through adulthood. *Journal of Abnormal and Social Psychology,* 1961, *62,* 504–513.

Moulton, R. W. Effects of success and failure on level of aspiration as related to achievement motives. *Journal of Personality and Social Psychology,* 1965, *1,* 399–406.

Munsinger, H., & Kessen, W. Uncertainty, structure and preference. *Psychological Monographs,* 1964, *78* (9, Whole No. 586).

Murray, H. A. *Explorations in personality.* New York: Oxford University Press, 1938.

Murstein, B. I. Physical attractiveness and mental choice. *Journal of Personality and Social Psychology,* 1972, *22,* 8–12.

Myer, J. S. *Life and letters of Doctor William Beaumont.* St. Louis: C. V. Mosby, 1912.

Nelson, S. A., & Dweck, C. S. Motivation and competence as determinants of young children's reward allocation. *Developmental Psychology,* 1977, *13,* 192–197.

Newcomb, T. M. The prediction of interpersonal attraction. *American Psychologist,* 1956, *11,* 575–586.

Newcomb, T. M. Interpersonal balance. In R. P. Abelson, E. Aronson, W. J. McGuire, T. M. Newcomb, M. J. Rosenberg, & P. H. Tannenbaum (Eds.), *Theories of cognitive consistency: A sourcebook.* Chicago: Rand McNally, 1968. Pp. 28–51.

Nicholls, J. G. Causal attributions and other achievement-related cognitions: Effects of task outcome, attainment value, and sex. *Journal of Personality and Social Psychology,* 1975, *31,* 379–389.

Nisbett, R. E. Hunger, obesity, and the ventromedial hypothalamus. *Psychological Review,* 1972, *79,* 433–453.

Nisbett, R. E., & Schachter, S. Cognitive manipulation of pain. *Journal of Experimental Social Psychology,* 1966, *2,* 227–236.

Nisbett, R. E., & Wilson, T. D. Telling more than we can know: Verbal reports on mental processes. *Psychological Review,* 1977, *84,* 231–259.

Nissen, H. W. The effects of gonadectomy, vasotomy, and injections of placental and orchic extracts on the sex behavior of the white rat. *Genetic Psychology Monographs,* 1929, *5,* 451–549.

Nissen, H. W. *Development of sexual behavior in chimpanzees.* Paper presented at symposium on genetic, psychological, and hormonal factors in the establishment and maintenance of patterns of sexual behavior in mammals, Amherst University, 1954.

Notz, W. W. Work motivation and the negative effects of extrinsic rewards: A review with implications for theory and practice. *American Psychologist,* 1975, *30,* 884–891.

Novin, D. Visceral mechanisms in the control of food intake. In D. Novin, W. Wyrwicka, & G. A. Bray (Eds.), *Hunger: Basic mechanisms and clini-*

*cal implications.* New York: Raven Press, 1976.

Novin, D., Wyrwicka, W., & Bray, G. A. (Eds.). *Hunger: Basic mechanisms and clinical implications.* New York: Raven Press, 1976.

Olds, J. Effects of hunger and male sex hormone on self-stimulation of the brain. *Journal of Comparative and Physiological Psychology,* 1958, *51,* 320–324.

Olds, J., & Milner, P. Positive reinforcement produced by electrical stimulation of septal area and other regions of rat brain. *Journal of Comparative and Physiological Psychology,* 1954, *47,* 419–427.

O'Leary, V. E., & Hammack, B. Sex-role orientation and achievement context as determinants of motive to avoid success. *Sex Roles,* 1975, *1,* 225–234.

Osgood, C. E., Suci, G. J., & Tannenbaum, P. H. *The measurement of meaning.* Urbana: University of Illinois Press, 1957.

Osgood, C. E., & Tannenbaum, P. H. The principle of congruity in the prediction of attitude change. *Psychological Review,* 1955, *62,* 42–55.

Pallak, M. S., & Heller, J. F. Interactive effects of commitment to future interaction and threat to attitudinal freedom. *Journal of Personality and Social Psychology,* 1971, *17,* 325–331.

Pallak, M. S., & Pittman, T. The general motivational effects of dissonance arousal. *Journal of Personality and Social Psychology,* 1972, *21,* 349–358.

Panksepp, J., & Nance, D. M. Insulin, glucose, and hypothalamic regulation of feeding. *Physiology and Behavior,* 1972, *9,* 447–451.

Papez, J. A proposed mechanism of emotion. *Archives of Neurology and Psychiatry,* 1937, *38,* 725–743.

Parke, R. D., Berkowitz, L., Leyens, J. P., West, S. G., & Sebastian, R. J. Some effects of violent and nonviolent movies on the behavior of juvenile delinquents. In L. Berkowitz (Ed.), *Advances in experimental social psychology* (Vol. 10). New York: Academic Press, 1977.

Patten, R. L., & White, L. A. Independent effects of achievement motivation and overt attribution on achievement behavior. *Motivation and Emotion,* 1977, *1,* 39–59.

Patterson, A. H. *Hostility catharsis: A naturalistic quasi-experiment.* Paper presented at the annual convention of the American Psychological Association, New Orleans, September 1974.

Pelkwijk, J., & Tinbergen, N. Eine reizbiologische Analyse einiger Verhaltensweisen von *Gasterosteus aculeatus* L. *Zeitschrift für Tierpsychologie,* 1937, *1,* 193–204.

Penn, N. Experimental improvements on an analogue of repression paradigm. *Psychological Record,* 1964, *14,* 185–196.

Perin, C. T. Behavior potentiality as a joint function of the amount of training and the degree of hunger at the time of extinction. *Journal of Experimental Psychology,* 1942, *30,* 93–113.

Perlmuter, L. C., & Monty, R. A. The importance of perceived control: Fact or fantasy? *American Scientist,* 1977, *65,* 759–765.

Perlmuter, L. C., Scharff, K., Karsh, R., & Monty, R. A. Perceived control: A generalized state of motivation. *Motivation and Emotion,* 1980, *4,* 35–46.

Peterfreund, E. *Information, systems, and psychoanalysis.* New York: International Universities Press, 1971.

Phillips, A., Cox, V., Kakolewski, J., & Valenstein, E. Object-carrying by rats: An approach to the behavior elicited by brain stimulation. *Science,* 1969, *166,* 903–905.

Phillips, J. S., & Lord, R. G. Determinants of intrinsic motivation: Locus of control and competence information as components of Deci's cognitive evaluation theory. *Journal of Applied Psychology,* 1980, *65,* 211–218.

Phoenix, C. H., Goy, R. W., Gerall, A. A., & Young, W. C. Organizing action of prenatally administered testosterone propionate on the tissues mediating mating behavior in the female guinea pig. *Endocrinology,* 1959, *65,* 369–382.

Pliskoff, S. S., Wright, J. E., & Hawkins, D. T. Brain stimulation as a reinforcer: Intermittent schedules. *Journal of the Experimental Analysis of Behavior,* 1965, *8,* 75–88.

Porter, L. W. Jobs in management: I. Perceived deficiencies in need fulfillment as a function of job level. *Journal of Applied Psychology,* 1962, *46,* 375–384.

Powley, T. L. The ventromedial hypothalamic syndrome, satiety, and a cephalic phase hypothesis. *Psychological Review,* 1977, *84,* 89–126.

Pritchard, R. D. Equity theory: A review and critique. *Organizational Behavior and Human Performance,* 1969, *4,* 176–211.

Pritchard, R. D., Dunnette, M. D., & Jorgenson, D. O. Effects of perceptions of equity and inequity on worker performance and satisfaction. *Journal of Applied Psychology Monograph,* 1972, *56,* 75–94.

Quabbe, H. Chronobiology of growth hormone secretion. *Chronobiologia,* 1977, *4,* 217–246.

Quay, H. C. Psychopathic personality as pathological stimulus seeking. *American Journal of Psychiatry,* 1965, *122,* 180–183.

Rapaport, D. The autonomy of the ego. *Bulletin of the Menninger Foundation,* 1951, *15,* 113–123.

Rapaport, D. On the psychoanalytic theory of motivation. In M. Jones (Ed.), *Nebraska Symposium on Motivation* (Vol. 8). Lincoln: University of Nebraska Press, 1960. Pp. 173–247.

Rapaport, D. The autonomy of the ego. In M. Gill (Ed.), *The collected papers of David Rapaport.* New York: Basic Books, 1967. Pp. 357–367.

Rapaport, D., & Gill, M. The points of view and assumptions of metapsychology. In M. Gill (Ed.), *The collected papers of David Rapaport.* New York: Basic Books, 1967. Pp. 795–811.

Rapoport, A. Designing for complexity. *Architectural Association Quarterly,* 1971, *3,* 29–33.

Ratner, A. M., & Hoffman, H. S. Evidence for a critical period for imprinting in Khaki Campbell ducklings *(Anas platyrhynchos domesticus). Animal Behavior,* 1974, *22,* 249–255.

Raynor, J. O. Future orientation and motivation of immediate activity: An elaboration of the theory of achievement motivation. *Psychological Review,* 1969, *76,* 606–610.

Raynor, J. O. Relationship between achievement-related motives, future orientation, and academic performance. *Journal of Personality and Social Psychology,* 1970, *15,* 28–33.

Reisinger, J. J. The treatment of "anxiety-depression" via positive reinforcement and response cost. *Journal of Applied Behavior Analysis,* 1972, *5,* 125–130.

Richter, C. P. Animal behavior and internal drives. *Quarterly Review of Biology,* 1927, *2,* 307–343.

Richter, C. P. Total self-regulatory functions in animals and human beings. *Harvey Lectures,* 1942, *38,* 63–103.

Richter, C. P. On the phenomenon of sudden death in animals and man. *Psychosomatic Medicine,* 1957, *19,* 191–198.

Ricoeur, P. *Freud and philosophy.* New Haven, Conn.: Yale University Press, 1970.

Riemer, B. Influence of causal beliefs on affect and expectancy. *Journal of Personality and Social Psychology,* 1975, *31,* 1163–1167.

Rivera, A. N., & Tedeschi, J. T. Public versus private reactions to positive inequity. *Journal of Personality and Social Psychology,* 1976, *34,* 895–900.

Roberts, W. W. Both rewarding and punishing effects from stimulation of posterior hypothalamus of cat with same electrode at same intensity. *Journal of Comparative and Physiological Psychology,* 1958, *51,* 400–407.

Roberts, W. W., Steinberg, M. L., & Means, L. W. Hypothalamic mechanisms for sexual, aggressive, and other motivational behaviors in the opossum, *Didelphis virginiana. Journal of Comparative and Physiological Psychology,* 1967, *64,* 1–15.

Rodin, J. *Effects of distraction on performance of obese and normal subjects.* Unpublished doctoral dissertation, Columbia University, 1970. Cited in S. Schachter, Some extraordinary facts about obese humans and rats. *American Psychologist,* 1971, *26,* 129–144.

Rodin, J., & Langer, E. J. Long-term effects of a control-relevant intervention with the institutionalized aged. *Journal of Personality and Social Psychology,* 1977, *35,* 897–902.

Rogers, C. R. *The clinical treatment of the problem child.* Boston: Houghton Mifflin, 1939.

Rogers, C. R. *Counseling and psychotherapy.* Boston: Houghton Mifflin, 1942.

Rogers, C. R. *Client-centered therapy.* Boston: Houghton Mifflin, 1951.

Rogers, C. R. The necessary and sufficient conditions of therapeutic personality change. *Journal of Consulting Psychology,* 1957, *21,* 95–103.

Rogers, C. R. A theory of therapy, personality, and interpersonal relationships, as developed in the client-centered framework. In S. Koch (Ed.), *Psychology: A study of a science: Study 1. Conceptual and systematic* (Vol. 3: *Formulations of the person and the social context).* New York: McGraw-Hill, 1959.

Rogers, C. R. *On becoming a person.* Boston: Houghton Mifflin, 1961.

Rogers, C. R. Autobiography. In E. G. Boring and G. Lindzey (Eds.), *A history of psychology in autobiography* (Vol. 5). New York: Appleton-Century-Crofts, 1967. Pp. 343–384.

Rogers, C. R. *Freedom to learn.* Columbus, Ohio: Merrill, 1969.

Rokeach, M., & Rothman, G. The principle of belief congruence and the congruity principle as models of cognitive interaction. *Psychological Review,* 1965, *72,* 128–142.

Rosen, B. C. Race, ethnicity, and the achievement syndrome. *American Sociological Review,* 1959, *24,* 47–60.

Rosen, B. C., & D'Andrade, R. The psychosocial origins of achievement motivation. *Sociometry,* 1959, *22,* 185–218.

Rosenberg, M. *Society and the adolescent self-image.* Princeton, N. J.: Princeton University Press, 1965.

Rosenfield, D., Folger, R., & Adelman, H. F. When rewards reflect competence: A qualification of the overjustification effect. *Journal of Personality and Social Psychology,* 1980, *39,* 368–376.

Rosenzweig, M. R. The mechanisms of hunger and thirst. In L. Postman (Ed.), *Psychology in the making.* New York: Knopf, 1962. Pp. 73–143.

Ross, L., Rodin, J., & Zimbardo, P. G. Toward an attribution therapy: The reduction of fear through cognitive-emotional misattribution. *Journal of Personality and Social Psychology,* 1969, *12,* 279–288.

Rotter, J. B. *Social learning and clinical psychology.* Englewood Cliffs, N. J.: Prentice-Hall, 1954.

Rotter, J. B. Generalized expectancies for internal versus external control of reinforcement. *Psychological Monographs,* 1966, *80* (Whole No. 609).

Rotter, J. B. A new scale for the measurement of interpersonal trust. *Journal of Personality,* 1967, *35,* 651–665.

Rotter, J. B., Chance, J. E., & Phares, E. J. *Application of a social learning theory of personality.* New York: Holt, Rinehart & Winston, 1972.

Rotter, J. B., & Hochreich, D. J. *Personality.* Glenview, Ill.: Scott, Foresman, 1975.

Roux, J. La faim, étude physio-psychologique. *Bulletin de la Société d'Anthropologie de Lyon,* 1897, *16,* 409–455.

Rubin, Z. *Liking and loving: An invitation to social psychology.* New York: Holt, Rinehart & Winston, 1973.

Russek, M. Hepatic receptors and the neurophysiological mechanisms controlling feeding behavior. In S. Ehrenpreis & O. C. Solnitzky (Eds.), *Neurosciences research* (Vol. 4). New York: Academic Press, 1971.

Russell, B. *An outline of philosophy.* London: George Allen and Unwin, 1927.

Sackett, G. Effects of rearing conditions upon the behavior of rhesus monkeys *(Macaca mulatta). Child Development,* 1965, *36,* 855–868.

Saegert, S. C., & Jellison, J. M. Effects of initial level of response competition and frequency of exposure on liking and exploratory behavior. *Journal of Personality and Social Psychology,* 1970, *16,* 553–558.

Salzen, E. A. Imprinting and environmental learning. In L. R. Aronson, E. Tobach, D. S. Lehrman, & J. S. Rosenblatt (Eds.), *Development and evolution of behavior.* San Francisco: W. H. Freeman, 1970.

Sarason, I. G. Test anxiety and intellectual performance. *Journal of Abnormal and Social Psychology,* 1963, *66,* 73–75.

Sarason, I. G., & Smith, R. E. Personality. *Annual Review of Psychology,* 1971, *22,* 393–446.

Schachter, S. The interaction of cognitive and physiological determinants of emotional state. In L. Berkowitz (Ed.), *Advances in experimental social psychology* (Vol. 1). New York: Academic Press, 1964. Pp. 49–80.

Schachter, S. Some extraordinary facts about obese humans and rats. *American Psychologist,* 1971, *26,* 129–144.

Schachter, S. Nicotine regulation in heavy and light smokers. *Journal of Experimental Psychology: General,* 1977, *106,* 5–12.

Schachter, S., Goldman, R., & Gordon, A. Effects of fear, food deprivation, and obesity on eating. *Journal of Personality and Social Psychology,* 1968, *10,* 91–97.

Schachter, S., & Singer, J. E. Cognitive, social, and physiological determinants of emotional state. *Psychological Review,* 1962, *69,* 379–399.

Schachter, S., & Wheeler, L. Epinephrine, chlorpromazine, and amusement. *Journal of Abnormal and Social Psychology,* 1962, *65,* 121–128.

Schafer, R. *Aspects of internalization.* New York: International Universities Press, 1968.

Schiff, M. *Leçons sur la physiologie de la digestion* (Vol. 1). Florence: Loescher, 1867.

Schmitt, D. R., & Marwell, G. Withdrawal and reward allocation as responses to inequity. *Journal of Experimental Social Psychology,* 1972, *8,* 207–221.

Schmitt, M. Influences of hepatic portal receptors on hypothalamic feeding and satiety centers. *American Journal of Physiology,* 1973, *225,* 1089–1095.

Schneirla, T. The concept of development in comparative psychology. In

D. B. Harris (Ed.), *The concept of development: An issue in the study of human behavior.* Minneapolis: University of Minnesota Press, 1957. Pp. 78–108.

Schneirla, T. An evolutionary and developmental theory of biphasic processes underlying approach and withdrawal. In M. R. Jones (Ed.), *Nebraska Symposium on Motivation* (Vol. 7). Lincoln: University of Nebraska Press, 1959.

Schulz, R. Effects of control and predictability on the physical and psychological well-being of the institutionalized aged. *Journal of Personality and Social Psychology,* 1976, *33,* 563–573.

Schulz, R., & Hanusa, B. H. Long-term effects of control and predictability-enhancing interventions: Findings and ethical issues. *Journal of Personality and Social Psychology,* 1978, *36,* 1194–1201.

Scitovsky, T. *The joyless economy.* New York: Oxford University Press, 1976.

Sears, R. R. Discussion. In B. Weiner (Ed.), *Cognitive views of human motivation.* New York: Academic Press, 1974.

Seeman, M., & Evans, J. W. Alienation and learning in a hospital setting. *American Sociological Review,* 1962, *27,* 772–783.

Selye, H. *The stress of life.* New York: McGraw-Hill, 1956.

Shaver, K. G. *An introduction to attribution processes.* Cambridge, Mass.: Winthrop, 1975.

Shaver, P. Questions concerning fear of success and its conceptual relatives. *Sex Roles,* 1976, *2,* 305–320.

Sheffield, F. D. A drive-induction theory of reinforcement. In R. N. Haber (Ed.), *Current research in motivation.* New York: Holt, Rinehart & Winston, 1966.

Sheffield, F. D., & Roby, T. B. Reward value of a non-nutritive sweet taste. *Journal of Comparative and Physiological Psychology,* 1950, *43,* 471–481.

Shostrom, E. An inventory for the measurement of self-actualization. *Educational and Psychological Measurements,* 1964, *24,* 207–218.

Shrauger, J. S., & Rosenberg, S. E. Self-esteem and the effect of success and failure feedback on performance. *Journal of Personality,* 1970, *38,* 404–417.

Shultz, T. R., Butkowsky, I., Pearce, J. W., & Shanfield, H. Development of schemes for the attribution of multiple psychological causes. *Developmental Psychology,* 1975, *11,* 502–510.

Sidman, M. Two temporal parameters of the maintenance of avoidance behavior by the white rat. *Journal of Comparative and Physiological Psychology,* 1953, *46,* 253–261.

Sidman, M., Brady, J., Boren, J., Conrad, D., & Schulman, A. Reward schedules and behavior maintained by intracranial self-stimulation. *Science,* 1955, *122,* 830–831.

Siegel, S. Level of aspiration and decision making. *Psychological Review,* 1957, *64,* 253–262.

Silverman, L. H. Psychoanalytic theory: "The reports of my death are greatly exaggerated." *American Psychologist,* 1976, *31,* 621–637.

Simpson, J. B., & Routtenberg, A. Subfornical organ: Site of drinking elicitation by angiotensin II. *Science,* 1973, *181,* 1172–1174.

Singer, J. E. Motivation for consistency. In S. Feldman (Ed.), *Cognitive consistency.* New York: Academic Press, 1966. Pp. 47–73.

Skinner, B. F. *The behavior of organisms.* New York: Appleton-Century-Crofts, 1938.

Skinner, B. F. Are theories of learning necessary? *Psychological Review,* 1950, *57,* 193–216.

Skinner, B. F. *Science and human behavior.* New York: Macmillan, 1953.

Skinner, B. F. The phylogeny and ontogeny of behavior. *Science,* 1966, *153,* 1205–1213.

Skrzypek, G. J. Effect of perceptual isolation and arousal on anxiety, complexity preference, and novelty preference in psychopathic and neurotic delinquents. *Journal of Abnormal Psychology,* 1969, *74,* 321–329.

Smith, C. P. *Situational determinants of the expression of achievement motivation in thematic apperception.* Unpublished doctoral dissertation, University of Michigan, 1961.

Smith, C. P. (Ed.). *Achievement related motives in children.* New York: Russell Sage Foundation, 1969.

Smith, G. F., & Dorfman, D. D. The effect of stimulus uncertainty on the relationship between frequency of exposure and liking. *Journal of Personality and Social Psychology,* 1975, *31,* 150–155.

Smith, M. C. Children's use of multiple sufficient cause schema in social perception. *Journal of Personality and Social Psychology,* 1975, *32,* 737–747.

Smith, M. D. Social learning of violence in minor hockey. In F. L. Smoll & R. E. Smith (Eds.), *Psychological perspectives in youth sports.* Washington, D. C.: Hemisphere, 1978.

Smith, S., & Myers, T. I. Stimulation seeking during sensory deprivation. *Perceptual and Motor Skills,* 1966, *23,* 1151–1163.

Snyder, F., & Washburn, S. Toward an evolutionary theory of dreaming. *American Journal of Psychiatry,* 1966, *123,* 121–142.

Solley, C. M., & Stagner, R. Effect of magnitude of temporal barriers, type of goal and perception of self. *Journal of Experimental Psychology,* 1956, *51,* 62–70.

Solomon, D. Psychosocial deprivation and achievement. In National Institute of Child Health and Human Development, *Perspective on human deprivation.* Bethesda, Md.: Author, 1968.

Solomon, R. L. The opponent process theory of motivation: The costs of pleasure and the benefits of pain. *American Psychologist,* 1980, *35,* 691–712.

Solomon, R. L., & Corbit, J. D. An opponent-process theory of motivation: I. Temporal dynamics of affect. *Psychological Review,* 1974, *81,* 119–145.

Solomon, R. L., & Wynne, L. C. Traumatic avoidance learning: The principles of anxiety conservation and partial irreversibility. *Psychological Review,* 1954, *61,* 353–385.

Sorrentino, R. M., & Short, J. A. Effects of fear of success on women's performance on masculine versus feminine tasks. *Journal of Research in Personality,* 1974, *8,* 277–290.

Sowell, T. A black "conservative" dissents. *New York Times Magazine,* August 8, 1976, p. 14.

Speisman, J. C., Lazarus, R. S., Mordkoff, A. M., & Davison, L. A. The experimental reduction of stress based on ego-defense theory. *Journal of Abnormal and Social Psychology,* 1964, *68,* 367–380.

Spence, J. T. The Thematic Apperception Test and attitudes toward achievement in women: A new look at the motive to avoid success and a new method of measurement. *Journal of Consulting and Clinical Psychology,* 1974, *42,* 427–437.

Spence, K. W. *Behavior theory and conditioning.* New Haven, Conn.: Yale

University Press, 1956.

Spence, K. W. A theory of emotionally based drive (*D*) and its relation to performance in simple learning situations. *American Psychologist,* 1958, *13,* 131–141.

Spence, K. W., Farber, I. E., & McFann, H. H. The relation of anxiety (drive) level to performance in competitional and noncompetitional paired-associates. *Journal of Experimental Psychology,* 1956, *52,* 296–305.

Spitz, R. A. Hospitalism: An inquiry into the genesis of psychiatric conditions in early childhood. *Psychoanalytic Study of the Child,* 1945, *1,* 53–74.

Steers, R. M., & Porter, L. W. *Motivation and work behavior.* New York: McGraw-Hill, 1975.

Steiner, I. D., & Peters, S. C. Conformity and the A-B-X model. *Journal of Personality,* 1958, *26,* 229–242.

Stellar, E. The physiology of motivation. *Psychological Review,* 1954, *61,* 5–22.

Stevens, L., & Jones, E. E. Defensive attribution and the Kelley cube. *Journal of Personality and Social Psychology,* 1976, *34,* 809–820.

Stevenson, H. W., & Odom, R. D. The relation of anxiety to children's performance on learning and problem-solving tasks. *Child Development,* 1965, *36,* 1003–1112.

Stewart, W. A. *Psychoanalysis: The first ten years, 1888–1898.* New York: Macmillan, 1967.

Stone, L. J., & Hokanson, J. E. Arousal reduction via self-punitive behavior. *Journal of Personality and Social Psychology,* 1969, *12,* 72–79.

Storms, M. D., & Nisbett, R. E. Insomnia and the attribution process. *Journal of Personality and Social Psychology,* 1970, *16,* 319–328.

Stotland, E., Thorley, S., Thomas, E., Cohen, A. R., & Zander, A. The effects of group expectations and self-esteem upon self-evaluation. *Journal of Abnormal and Social Psychology,* 1957, *54,* 55–63.

Stricker, E. M. Thirst, sodium appetite, and complementary physiological contributions to the regulation of intravascular fluid volume. In A. N. Epstein, H. R. Kissileff, & E. Stellar (Eds.), *The neuropsychology of thirst: New findings and advances in concepts.* Washington, D. C.: V. H. Winston & Sons, 1973.

Stricker, E. M., & Zigmond, M. S. Brain catecholamines and the lateral hypothalamic syndrome. In D. Novin, W. Wyrwicka, & G. A. Bray (Eds.), *Hunger: Basic mechanisms and clinical implications.* New York: Raven Press, 1976.

Strong, S. R. Causal attributions in counseling and psychotherapy. *Journal of Counseling Psychology,* 1970, *17,* 388–399.

Tarchanoff, J. R. Zur Physiologie des Geschlechtsapparatus des Frosches. *Pflugers Archiv für die Gesamte Physiologie des Menschen und der Tiere,* 1887, *40,* 330–351.

Taylor, S. E. On inferring one's attitudes from one's behavior: Some delimiting conditions. *Journal of Personality and Social Psychology,* 1975, *31,* 126–131.

Taylor, S. E., & Fiske, S. T. Salience, attention, and attribution: Top of the head phenomena. In L. Berkowitz (Ed.), *Advances in experimental social psychology* (Vol. 11). New York: Academic Press, 1978.

Tedeschi, J. T., Schlenker, B. R., & Bonoma, T. V. Cognitive dissonance: Private ratiocination or public spectacle. *American Psychologist,* 1971, *26,* 685–695.

Teevan, R. C., & McGhee, P. E. Childhood development of fear of failure motivation. *Journal of Personality and Social Psychology,* 1972, *21,* 345–348.

Tennen, H., & Eller, S. J. Attributional components of learned helplessness and facilitation. *Journal of Personality and Social Psychology,* 1977, *35,* 265–271.

Thibaut, J. W., & Riecken, H. W. Some determinants and consequences of the perception of social causality. *Journal of Personality,* 1955, *24,* 113–133.

Thomas, M. H., Horton, R. W., Lippincott, E. C., & Drabman, R. S. Desensitization to portrayals of real-life aggression as a function of exposure to television violence. *Journal of Personality and Social Psychology,* 1977, *35,* 450 458.

Thorndike, E. L. *Animal intelligence.* New York: Macmillan, 1911.

Thorpe, W. H. The modern concept of instinctive behavior. *Bulletin of Animal Behavior,* 1948, *1,* 1–12.

Tinbergen, N. Social releasers and the experimental method required for their study. *Wilson Bulletin,* 1948, *60,* 6–52.

Tinbergen, N. *The study of instinct.* Oxford: Oxford University Press, 1951.

Tinbergen, N. "Derived" activities: Their causation, biological significance, origin, and emancipation during evolution. *Quarterly Review of Biology,* 1952, *27,* 1–32.

Tolman, E. C., & Honzik, C. H. "Insight" in rats. *University of California Publications in Psychology,* 1930, *4,* 215–232. (a)

Tolman, E. C., & Honzik, C. H. Introduction and removal of reward, and maze performance in rats. *University of California Publications in Psychology,* 1930, *4,* 257–275. (b)

Tosi, D. J., & Lindamood, C. A. The measurement of self-actualization: A critical review of the Personal Orientation Inventory. *Journal of Personality Assessment,* 1975, *39,* 215–224.

Tresemer, D. The cumulative record of research on "fear of success." *Sex Roles,* 1976, *2,* 217–236.

Trope, Y. Seeking information about one's own ability as a determinant of choice among tasks. *Journal of Personality and Social Psychology,* 1975, *32,* 1004–1013.

Truax, C. B. The repression response to implied failure as a function of the hysteria-psychasthenia index. *Journal of Abnormal and Social Psychology,* 1957, *55,* 188–193.

Truax, C. B., & Carkhuff, R. R. *Toward effective counseling and psychotherapy.* Chicago: Aldine, 1967.

Udry, J. R., & Morris, N. M. Distribution of coitus in the menstrual cycle. *Nature,* 1968, *220,* 593–596.

Valenstein, E. *Brain control.* New York: Wiley, 1973.

Valenstein, E., Cox, J., & Kakolewski, V. Reexamination of the role of the hypothalamus in motivation. *Psychological Review,* 1970, *77,* 16–31.

Valenstein, E., Kakolewski, V., & Cox, J. A comparison of stimulus-bound drinking and drinking induced by water deprivation. *Communications in Behavioral Biology,* 1968, *2,* 227–233.

Valins, S., & Nisbett, R. E. Attribution processes in the development and treatment of emotional disorder. In E. Jones, D. Kanouse, H. Kelley, R. Nisbett, S. Valins, & B. Weiner (Eds.), *Attribution: Perceiving the causes of behavior.* New York: General Learning Press, 1972. Pp. 137–150.

Verney, E. B. The antidiuretic hormone and the factors which determine its release. *Proceedings of the Royal Society,* 1947, *B 135,* 25 106.

Veroff, J., & Peele, S. Initial effects of desegregation on the achievement motivation of Negro elementary school children. *Journal of Social Issues,* 1969, *25,* 71–92.

Vitz, P. Affect as a function of stimulus variation. *Journal of Experimental Psychology*, 1966, *71*, 74–79. (a)

Vitz, P. Preference for different amounts of stimulus complexity. *Behavioral Science*, 1966, *11*, 105–114. (b)

von Haller, A. [trans. from 1747 original] *First lines of physiology.* Troy, N. Y.: Penniman, 1803.

Von Neumann, J., & Morgenstern, O. *Theory of games and economic behavior.* Princeton, N. J.: Princeton University Press, 1944.

Wachs, T. D., Uzgiris, I., & Hunt, J. McV. Cognitive development in infants of different age levels and from different environmental backgrounds: An exploratory investigation. *Merrill-Palmer Quarterly*, 1971, *17*, 283–317.

Wachtel, P. L. Psychodynamics, behavior therapy, and the implacable researcher: An inquiry into the consistency of personality. *Journal of Abnormal Psychology*, 1973, *82*, 324–334.

Wahba, M. A., & Bridwell, L. G. Maslow reconsidered: A review of research on the need hierarchy. *Organizational Behavior and Human Performance*, 1976, *15*, 212–240.

Walker, E. L. Psychological complexity as a basis for a theory of motivation and choice. In D. Levine (Ed.), *Nebraska Symposium on Motivation* (Vol. 12). Lincoln: University of Nebraska Press, 1964.

Walker, E. L. *Psychological complexity theory and aesthetics, or the hedgehog as aesthetic mediator (HAM).* Invited address to American Psychological Association convention, New Orleans, September 1974.

Walker, E. L. *Psychological complexity and preference: A hedgehog theory of behavior.* Monterey: Brooks/Cole, 1980.

Wallen, R. Ego-involvement as a determinant of selective forgetting. *Journal of Abnormal and Social Psychology*, 1942, *37*, 20–39.

Walster, E., Berscheid, E., & Walster, G. W. New directions in equity research. *Journal of Personality and Social Psychology*, 1973, *25*, 151–176.

Walter, D., Denzler, L. S., & Sarason, I. G. Anxiety and intellectual performance of high school students. *Child Development*, 1964, *35*, 917–926.

Wangensteen, O. H., & Carlson, H. A. Hunger sensations in a patient after total gastrectomy. *Proceedings of the Society of Experimental Biological Medicine*, 1931, *28*, 545–547.

Waterman, C. K. The facilitating and interfering effects of cognitive dissonance on simple and complex paired associates learning tasks. *Journal of Experimental Social Psychology*, 1969, *5*, 31–42.

Waxenberg, S. E., Drellich, M. G., & Sutherland, A. M. The role of hormones in human behavior: I. Changes in female sexuality after adrenalectomy. *Journal of Clinical Endocrinology*, 1959, *19*, 193–202.

Weary, G. Examination of affect and egotism as mediators of bias in causal attributions. *Journal of Personality and Social Psychology*, 1980, *38*, 348–357.

Webb, W. B. Sleep behavior as a biorhythm. In P. Coloquohon (Ed.), *Biological rhythms and human performance.* London: Academic Press, 1971.

Webb, W. B., & Goodman, I. J. Activating role of an irrelevant drive in absence of the relevant drive. *Psychological Reports*, 1958, *4*, 235–238.

Weiner, B. Need achievement and the resumption of incompleted tasks. *Journal of Personality and Social Psychology*, 1965, *1*, 165–168.

Weiner, B. The role of success and failure in the learning of easy and complex tasks. *Journal of Personality and Social Psychology*, 1966, *3*, 339–344.

Weiner, B. *Theories of motivation: From mechanism to cognition.* Chicago: Rand McNally, 1972.

Weiner, B., Frieze, I., Kukla, A., Reed, L., Rest, S., & Rosenbaum, R. Perceiving the causes of success and failure. In E. Jones, D. Kanouse, H. Kelley, R. Nisbett, S. Valins, & B. Weiner (Eds.), *Attribution: Perceiving the causes of behavior.* New York: General Learning Press, 1971.

Weiner, B., & Kukla, A. An attributional analysis of achievement motivation. *Journal of Personality and Social Psychology,* 1970, *15,* 1–20.

Weiner, B., & Potepan, P. A. Personality correlates and affective reactions toward exams of succeeding and failing college students. *Journal of Educational Psychology,* 1970, *61,* 144–151.

Weiner, B., & Schneider, K. Drive versus cognitive theory: A reply to Boor and Harmon. *Journal of Personality and Social Psychology,* 1971, *18,* 258–262.

Weiss, J. Psychosomatic disorders. In J. D. Maser & M. E. P. Seligman (Eds.). *Psychopathology: Experimental models.* San Francisco: W. H. Freeman, 1977.

Westinghouse Learning Corporation, Ohio University. *The impact of Head Start: An evaluation of the effects of Head Start on children's cognitive and affective development.* Washington, D. C.: U. S. Office of Economic Opportunity, 1969.

Weston, P., & Mednick, M. T. S. Race, social class and motive to avoid success in women. *Journal of Cross-Cultural Psychology,* 1970, *1,* 284–291.

Wexler, D. A., & Rice, L. N. *Innovations in client-centered therapy.* New York: Wiley, 1974.

Whalen, R. E. The concept of instinct. In J. L. McGaugh (Ed.), *Psychobiology: Behavior from a biological perspective.* New York: Academic Press, 1971.

White, B. L. An experimental approach to the effects of experience on early human behavior. In J. P. Hill (Ed.), *Minnesota symposium on child psychology: I.* Minneapolis: University of Minnesota Press, 1967.

White, B. L. The initial coordination of sensorimotor schemas in human infants—Piaget's ideas and the role of experience. In D. Elkind & J. Flavell (Eds.), *Studies in cognitive development.* New York: Oxford University Press, 1969.

White, L. A. Erotica and aggression: The influence of sexual arousal, positive affect, and negative affect on aggressive behavior. *Journal of Personality and Social Psychology,* 1979, *37,* 591–601.

White, R. W. Motivation reconsidered: The concept of competence. *Psychological Review,* 1959, *66,* 297–333.

White, R. W. Ego and reality in psychoanalytic theory. *Psychological Issues,* 1963, Monograph 11.

Wicklund, R. A. Prechoice preference reversal as a result of threat to decision freedom. *Journal of Personality and Social Psychology,* 1970, *14,* 8–17.

Wicklund, R. A. *Freedom and reactance.* Potomac, Maryland: Erlbaum, 1974.

Wicklund, R. A., & Brehm, J. W. Attitude change as a function of felt competence and threat to attitudinal freedom. *Journal of Experimental Social Psychology,* 1968, *4,* 64–75.

Wilkins, L., Jones, H. W., Holman, G. H., & Stempfel, R. S. Masculinization of the female fetus associated with administration of oral and intramuscular progestins during gestation: Nonadrenal female pseudohermaphrodism. *Journal of Clinical Endocrinology,* 1958, *18,* 559–585.

Wilkins, W. Expectancies in applied settings. In A. S. Gurman & A. M. Razin (Eds.), *Effective psychotherapy: A handbook of research.* New York: Pergamon Press, 1977.

Williams, S. B. Resistance to extinction as a function of the number of reinforcements. *Journal of Experimental Psychology,* 1938, *23,* 506–521.

Willis, M. H., & Blaney, P. H. Three tests of the learned helplessness model of depression. *Journal of Abnormal Psychology,* 1978, *87,* 131–136.

Wilson, E. O. *Sociobiology, the new synthesis.* Cambridge: Harvard University Press, 1975.

Winterbottom, M. R. *The relation of childhood training in independence to achievement motivation.* Unpublished doctoral dissertation, University of Michigan, 1953.

Wolff, C. T., Friedman, S. B., Hofer, M. A., & Mason, J. W. Relationship between psychological defenses and mean urinary 17-hydroxycorticosteroid excretion rates: I & II. *Psychosomatic Medicine,* 1964, *26,* 576–609.

Wolff, M., & Stein, A. *Factors influencing the recruitment of children into the Head Start program, summer 1965: A case study of six centers in New York City (Study II).* New York: Yeshiva University, 1966.

Woodworth, R. S. *Dynamic psychology.* New York: Columbia University Press, 1918.

Wyatt, R. J. Serotonergic and adrenergic systems in human sleep. In M. H. Chase (Ed.), *The sleeping brain* (Vol. 1 of *Perspectives in the Brain Sciences*). Los Angeles, Calif.: Brain Information Service/Brain Research Institute, UCLA, 1972.

Yarrow, L. J., Rubenstein, J. L., Pedersen, F. A., & Jankowski, J. J. Dimensions of early stimulation and their differential effects. *Merrill-Palmer Quarterly,* 1972, *18,* 205–218.

Yates, J. F., & Revelle, G. L. Processes operative during delay of gratification. *Motivation and Emotion,* 1979, *3,* 103–115.

Yerkes, R. M., & Dodson, J. D. The relation of strength of stimulus to rapidity of habit-formation. *Journal of Comparative and Neurological Psychology,* 1908, *18,* 459–482.

Young, P. *Motivation and emotion.* New York: Wiley, 1961.

Zajonc, R. B. Cognitive theories in social psychology. In G. Lindzey & E. Aronson (Eds.), *The handbook of social psychology* (Vol. 1). Reading, Mass.: Addison-Wesley, 1968.

Zajonc, R. B., & Sales, S. M. Social facilitation of dominant and subordinate responses. *Journal of Experimental Social Psychology,* 1966, *2,* 160–168.

Zanna, M. P., & Cooper, J. Dissonance and the pill: An attributional approach to studying the arousal properties of dissonance. *Journal of Personality and Social Psychology,* 1974, *29,* 703–709.

Zanna, M. P., Klosson, E. C., & Darley, J. M. How television news viewers deal with facts that contradict their beliefs: A consistency and attribution analysis. *Journal of Applied Social Psychology,* 1976, *6,* 159–176.

Zeigarnik, B. Über das Behalten von erledigten und unerledigten Handlungen. *Psychologische Forschung,* 1927, *9,* 1–85.

Zeller, A. An experimental analogue of repression: I. Historical summary. *Psychological Bulletin,* 1950, *47,* 39–51. (a)

Zeller, A. An experimental analogue of repression: II. The effect of individual failure and success on memory measured by relearning. *Journal of Experimental Psychology,* 1950, *40,* 411–422. (b)

Zeller, A. An experimental analogue of repression: III. The effect of induced failure and success on memory measured by recall. *Journal of Experimental Psychology,* 1951, *42,* 32–38.

Zillman, D., Katcher, A. H., & Milavsky, B. Excitation transfer from physical exercise to subsequent aggressive behavior. *Journal of Experimental Social Psychology,* 1972, *8,* 247–259.

Zimbardo, P. G. A Pirandellian prison. *New York Times Magazine,* April 8, 1973, 38–60.

Zingg, R. M. Feral man and extreme cases of isolation. *American Journal of Psychology,* 1940, *53,* 487–517.

Zuckerman, M., & Allison, S. N. An objective measure of fear of success: Construction and validation. *Journal of Personality Assessment,* in press

Zuckerman, M., & Wheeler, L. To dispel fantasies about the fantasy-based measure of fear of success. *Psychological Bulletin,* 1975, *82,* 932–946.

# Name Index

# Subject Index